The Yale Edition of the Complete Works of St. Thomas More

VOLUME 10

THE DEBELLATION OF SALEM AND BIZANCE

Published by the St. Thomas More Project, Yale University,
under the auspices of Gerard L. Carroll and Joseph B. Murray,
Trustees of the Michael P. Grace, II, Trust,
and with the support of the Editing Program of the
National Endowment for the Humanities
and the Knights of Columbus

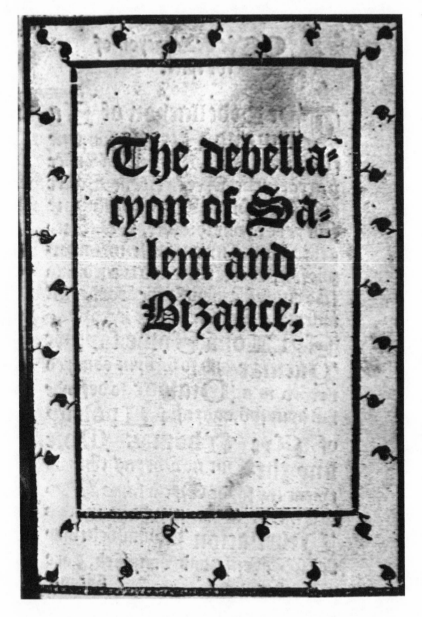

Title page, *The Debellation of Salem and Bizance*, 1533.

The Complete Works of
ST. THOMAS MORE

VOLUME 10

Edited by
JOHN GUY
RALPH KEEN
CLARENCE H. MILLER
and
RUTH MCGUGAN

Yale University Press, New Haven and London

Set in Baskerville type.
Printed in the United States of America by
Vail-Ballou Press, Binghamton, N.Y.

Library of Congress catalogue number: 63-7949
International standard book number: 0-300-03376-1

The paper in this book meets
the guidelines for permanence and durability
of the Committee on Production Guidelines
for Book Longevity of the Council on
Library Resources.

10 9 8 7 6 5 4 3 2 1

In Memory of
JOHN M. MURPHY
Deputy Supreme Knight
and Supreme Advocate
of the Knights of Columbus

Amicus verus Thomae Mori

ACKNOWLEDGMENTS

The editors of this volume, like those of all the others, are deeply indebted to the labors and the heritage of Richard Sylvester and to the unfailing support and encouragement of Louis Martz.

The introduction and commentary are the work of John Guy (with some contributions from Clarence Miller). Ralph Keen and Clarence Miller produced the text and textual introduction; Ruth McGugan provided a typescript of the 1533 edition and a preliminary collation of it with *The English Works* of 1557.

John Guy wishes to thank Rachel Guy for verifying and proofreading the entire volume, the Selden Society and *Moreana* for allowing him to revise biographical material on St. German from his earlier publications, and the British Academy's Small Grants Research Fund in the Humanities for providing travel and photocopying grants. Ralph Keen wishes to thank Clarence Miller, his master and mentor at Yale, now his senior colleague and friend, for the spirit of friendly collaboration, not just on this volume, that made his years at the More Project productive and happy ones.

We are grateful to Jay Williams of the Yale University Press for invaluable help in getting this volume (and its immediate predecessors) through the intricate process that led to a finished book. We especially thank Ann Hawthorne, who not only made the index but also, as copyeditor, brought our none too cleanly manuscript into order and consistency. As usual, we owe a large debt of gratitude to the assistants at the More Project: Kathleen Perry Buxton, Katherine Rodgers, Michele Margetts, and especially Raymond Lurie, who compiled the glossary. We also wish to thank Joseph Trapp, who read the entire manuscript and greatly lightened our labors by his edition of More's *Apology*.

Finally, we are grateful to the Knights of Columbus for their generous support of our edition.

J. G., R. K., and C. H. M.

Bristol, England;
Chicago, Ill.; St. Louis, Mo.

CONTENTS

ILLUSTRATIONS

xiii

INTRODUCTION

THE POLITICAL CONTEXT OF THE *DEBELLATION*

AT THREE O'CLOCK in the afternoon of Thursday, May 16, 1532, in the garden at York Place, Westminster, Thomas More handed back to Henry VIII the white leather bag containing the great seal of England and thereby resigned the office of lord chancellor. It was his inevitable reaction to the Submission of the Clergy, which had taken place some twenty-four hours before.[1] Yet, even on this bitter occasion for both the king and More, some of the warmth that had once characterized their relationship still remained. As More reminded Henry in March 1534, when that warmth had dissipated beyond recall, "Ye were so good and graciouse vn to me, as at my pore humble suit to discharge and disburden me, geving me licence with your graciouse favor to bestow the residew of my life in myn age now to come, abowt the provision for my soule in the service of God, and to be your Gracys bedisman and pray for you."[2] More had asked to withdraw entirely from public life in order to fortify his soul for the greater trials he knew must come and to pray for the king and his government—and Henry had replied kindly.

> It pleased your Highnes ferther to say vn to me, that for the service which I byfore had done you (which it than lyked your goodnes far aboue my deserving to commend) that in eny suit that I should after haue vn to your Highnes, which either should concerne myn honor (that word it lyked your Highnes to vse vn to me) or that should perteyne vn to my profit, I should fynd your Highnes good and graciouse lord vn to me.[3]

---

[1]J. A. Guy, *The Public Career of Sir Thomas More* (New Haven and Brighton, 1980), pp. 200–01 (hereafter cited as "Guy, *Public Career*"); G. R. Elton, *Studies in Tudor and Stuart Politics and Government*, 3 vols. (Cambridge, 1974–83), *1*, 169–72; hereafter cited as "Elton, *Studies*." Abbreviations and full titles of all works cited frequently in this Introduction will be found in the Bibliography preceding the Commentary. This section is a shortened version of my "Thomas More and Christopher St. German: the Battle of the Books," *Moreana*, 21 (1984), 5–25, revised and reprinted in Alistair Fox and John Guy, *Reassessing the Henrician Age: Humanism, Politics and Reform, 1500–1550* (Oxford, 1986), pp. 95–120.

[2]*The Correspondence of Sir Thomas More*, ed. Elizabeth F. Rogers (Princeton, 1947), pp. 488–89 (no. 198); hereafter cited as "Rogers."

[3]Rogers, p. 489.

More brought that suit to Henry VIII in the spring of 1534, when the king wished to include him, together with Bishop John Fisher, in an act of attainder as a misprisioner of the Nun of Kent's alleged treason. Pressure from his Council persuaded Henry to change his mind, for no evidence implicating More could be found. More's escape, however, owed nothing to Henry's earlier promises in the garden—quite the reverse—and More soon learned the terrible force of the king's wrath against a man who, as Henry believed, had betrayed his former trust and friendship.

What had Sir Thomas done to incur Henry's disapproval as a private citizen in Chelsea? In part, he had been writing books: at Eastertide 1533 his *Apology* was published by William Rastell, followed by *The Debellation of Salem and Bizance* about October of the same year.[1] In December 1533 More put the finishing touches to his *Answer to a Poisoned Book*, his confutation of George Joye's *Supper of the Lord*, which Rastell published some days before Christmas.[2]

Both the *Apology* and the *Debellation* were components of a public controversy which began toward the end of 1532 or at the beginning of 1533, when Christopher St. German wrote *A Treatise concerning the Division between the Spiritualty and Temporalty*, a tract printed at least five times between February 1533 and the end of 1537.[3] The book accused the clergy of undue harshness toward laymen and unfair partiality toward their fellow clergymen: the chief reason for St. German's discontent was the procedure used by the bishops and church courts in the detection, trial, and punishment of heretics. In *A Treatise concerning the Division*, St. German continued logically the attack on clerical privileges and alleged abuses he had already begun in his second dialogue of *Doctor and Student* (1530) and *A Little Treatise Called the New Additions* (1531), but he veered away from the theme of parliamentary power and statutory competence emphasized in *New Additions* in order to return to his principle, enshrined in both dialogues of *Doctor and Stu-*

---

[1]See More's *Apology*, ed. J. B. Trapp, The Yale Edition of the Complete Works of St. Thomas More, vol. 9 (New Haven and London, 1979), xviii, lxxxix–xci. The Yale edition of More is hereafter cited as *CW*, followed by the appropriate volume number. See also notes on 1/5–6 and 5/36, below.

[2]*CW 11*, 87; Rogers, p. 468 (no. 194).

[3]*A Short-Title Catalogue of Books Printed in England, Scotland, & Ireland and of English Books Printed Abroad 1475–1640*, comp. William A. Jackson, F. S. Ferguson, and Katharine F. Pantzer (London, 1976–1986), a revised and enlarged edition of the book by the same title compiled by A. W. Pollard and G. R. Redgrave (London, 1926); hereafter cited as *STC²* and *STC*, respectively. For the editions of *A Treatise concerning the Division*, see *STC²* 21586–21587.7 and *CW 9*, xcii–xciii.

dent, that neither greater nor less favor should be shown to the clergy than to the laity under English law.

A Treatise concerning the Division aimed to show, first, why grudges and division had arisen between clergy and laity over the years; and second, what reforms were needed to restore harmonious relations between them. St. German's purported stance was that of an impartial critic and arbitrator, but if we read between the lines, it becomes clear that his true purpose was to purchase peace between church and state at the expense of the clergy's jurisdictional independence. The law under which clergy and laity were to be equal was English common law and statute, except where the church could prove that an ecclesiastical law rested expressly on the law of God.[1] As in *New Additions,* St. German demanded the reform of greedy and slovenly clergymen and urged priests and laymen to stop defaming each other.[2] The clergy were to abandon the "olde course, pretendynge by confederacies and worldely policies, and streyte corrections to rule the people."[3] Detailed charges extracted from an anticlerical diatribe by Henry of Langenstein (attributed at that time to a much weightier author, Jean Gerson) were given a prominent place in St. German's argument.[4] But the principal themes of *A Treatise concerning the Division* were St. German's assaults on clerical immunity from disciplinary regulation in the royal courts and on *ex officio* procedure in church courts, together with his repudiation of the independent legislative powers of the two convocations of Canterbury and York.[5] Clerical immunity from royal justice, *ex officio* process in spiritual courts (especially in cases of alleged heresy), and provincial canons, in St. German's opinion, were vehicles of the church's shameless conviction that it could act in its own interests and conspire against the laity. In particular, the leniency of church courts in cases of clerical wrongdoing, the inquisitorial methods used against laymen by spiritual accusers, and the "oath of speaking the truth," under which accused persons could be forced to incriminate them-

---

[1]*A Treatise concerning the Division* (hereafter cited as *"Division"*) is reprinted as Appendix A in *CW* 9, 176–212. See pp. 194–95 and 197–203.

[2]*New Additions,* printed in *Doctor and Student,* ed. T. F. T. Plucknett and J. L. Barton, Selden Society Publications, vol. 91 (London, 1974), pp. 324–26, 328, 330–32 (hereafter cited as *"Doctor and Student"*). See also *Division, CW* 9, 178, 181–85, 187–88, 195–97, 204–07.

[3]*CW* 9, 180.

[4]*CW* 9, xlvi, lvi. The tract was *Declaratio defectuum virorum ecclesiasticorum,* printed in Gerson's *Opera omnia,* ed. Ellies du Pin, 5 vols. (Antwerp, 1706), 2, 314–18. St. German's extract is in chapter 2 of *Division (CW* 9, 181–83).

[5]*CW* 9, 185, 188–93, 197–203.

selves without any resort to jury trial, were denounced by St. German as unacceptable and divisive advantages enjoyed by the clergy.

St. German's *Treatise concerning the Division* was promptly challenged by More, whose *Apology*, published about Easter 1533, vigorously strove to defend the traditional privileges of church and clergy and to discredit both St. German's actual case and his personal motives for making it.[1] In addition, More included in the work a defense of his own conduct in the repression of heresy undertaken while he was lord chancellor.[2] The *Apology* was, in turn, answered by St. German's *Salem and Bizance*, published in September 1533.[3] The work was subtitled "A dialogue betwixte two englyshe men, wherof one was called Salem, and the other Bizance." Just why St. German invented such characters is far from plain, but two explanations are possible. Bizance may be a punning reference to a famous patriarch of Constantinople, St. Germanus (c. 674–733), or (more probably) the title *Salem and Bizance* may deplore the fact that Christendom was rent by internal quarrels like that between More and St. German, while the two greatest Christian shrines, Jerusalem and Constantinople, languished in the power of the Turk.[4] Either way, *Salem and Bizance* attacked More's *Apology* and renewed St. German's assault on what he still maintained were the biased and unjust procedures of the heresy laws and church courts. By way of rebuttal, More wrote *The Debellation of Salem and Bizance*. As he himself said, when *Salem and Bizance* came off the press at Michaelmas 1533, "I sodaynly went in hande therwyth, and made it in a breyde" (4/1–2). He also remarked that he composed *The Debellation* "in few days" (7/6).

St. German seemed to answer *The Debellation of Salem and Bizance* with *The Additions of Salem and Bizance*, published in mid-1534.[5] Yet the

---

[1]*CW 9*, lxvii–lxxxv.

[2]*CW 9*, 117–28.

[3]Reprinted as Appendix B, below. See also note on 5/36.

[4]These are J. B. Trapp's explanations, upon which I cannot improve (*CW 9*, lii, n. 1). Professor Trapp prefers the second explanation because *Salem and Bizance* expressly considers a crusade (see pp. 383–87, below). The validity of the second explanation is reinforced by St. German's appeal to English apocalyptic feeling in *Salem and Bizance* (Appendix B, pp. 384–87). When he calculated the number of the beast and prophesied the destruction of Islam, he was not engaging in a merely academic exercise in exegesis. The current of apocalypticism in St. German's thought has never been noticed and deserves study. A regular feature of criticism of the clergy was that they neglected their duty to rescue Jerusalem and Constantinople from infidel hands in favor of self advancement. See P. A. Throop, *Criticism of the Crusade* (Amsterdam, 1940); Professor J. B. Trapp kindly supplied this reference.

[5]*STC²* 21585.

title of *The Additions* was something of a misnomer, for it never mentioned More's *Debellation* at all and its first five chapters sidestepped the main theme of More's book, which had been the justification of inquisitorial procedures in church courts in cases of suspected heresy. St. German in *The Additions* instead continued his earlier attacks upon clerical greed and abuses, faults in liturgical observation, provincial canons, pilgrimages, the law of tithes, and so on (chapters 1 and 4). *The Additions* did introduce some new material: in chapter 2 St. German analyzed the technical limitations placed on ecclesiastical juridical process by the Act of Appeals of 1533 (24 Henry VIII, c. 12). In chapter 3 he fired an opening salvo in the campaign by which the history of St. Thomas Becket would be rewritten. However, St. German now had little to say about heresy and heretics beyond repeating his claim that "men wyll so lyghtly reporte as they do, that there be many heritikes" (sig. B₇v) and noting with satisfaction that the newly enacted heresy statute (25 Henry VIII, c. 14) had restored English law to the position reached immediately prior to Henry IV's statute *De heretico comburendo* of 1401 (sig. E₅v).

It was, in fact, Henry VIII's revised heresy law, which had received the royal assent on March 30, 1534, together with the First Act of Succession, that had vanquished More's defense of the status quo in his *Debellation*.[1] Legislation had overtaken the debate: there was little more to be said. The details of the new heresy law were not St. German's proposals in *Salem and Bizance,* but we have reason to suspect that St. German's writings and the Commons' campaign to change the law of heresy since 1532 had all along been connected.[2] Furthermore, this suspicion can be reinforced by hard evidence. St. German's entire literary output between *New Additions* (1531) and *The Additions of Salem and Bizance* was printed by Thomas Berthelet, the king's printer, and must thus be regarded as part of the propaganda campaign in support of Henry VIII's policy.[3] For scholars agree that the bulk of Berthelet's output as king's printer was material passed to his press by the government.[4] St. German's *New Additions, A Treatise concerning the Division, Salem and Bizance,* and its *Additions* were evidently components of the secondary line of royal propaganda justifying and exploring the

---

[1] See pp. lxv–lxvii, below.
[2] See pp. lxi–lxii, below.
[3] See *STC²* 21563–64, 21584–85, 21586–87.7.
[4] E. G. Duff, *A Century of the English Book Trade* (London, 1905), p. 11; G. R. Elton, *Policy and Police: The Enforcement of the Reformation in the Age of Thomas Cromwell* (Cambridge, 1972), pp. 173–74; hereafter cited as "Elton, *Policy and Police.*"

nature of the Henrician schism. Despite past assertions that none of St. German's books was published by Berthelet and that his writings have no relevance to a discussion of official propaganda,[1] Berthelet actually printed the three extant editions of *New Additions*, four of *A Treatise concerning the Division*, and one each of *Salem and Bizance* and its *Additions*.[2] The evidence of such wide patronage by the king's printer cannot be discounted. Yet, if *A Treatise concerning the Division* and *Salem and Bizance* were part of Henry VIII's campaign of propaganda, it follows that More, by answering St. German in his *Apology* and *Debellation*, was, in turn, rebutting that propaganda in the same manner in which Bishop Fisher, Thomas Abell, and others had confuted Henry's divorce propaganda.[3]

This political climate helps us to understand why More claimed in his *Apology* and *Debellation* not to know the identity of his opponent, devising an elaborate hoax by which St. German was characterized as an obscure country priest dubbed by More "the Pacifier" or "Sir John Some-say."[4] All of St. German's works were issued anonymously—a circumstance which has led modern scholars into difficulties. However, anonymity created few problems for St. German's contemporaries. It was common knowledge in Chancery Lane and at the Inns of Court that St. German had written *Doctor and Student*, as John Bale knew.[5] But *New Additions* was published by Berthelet as an appendix to *Doctor and Student*, as its title page made clear.[6] Next, *A Treatise concerning the Division* was manifestly from the same pen as *New Additions:* the ideas,

---

[1]Elton, *Policy and Police*, p. 173.

[2]See p. xxi, n. 3, above.

[3]J. K. McConica, *English Humanists and Reformation Politics under Henry VIII and Edward VI* (Oxford, 1965), pp. 125, 128; Michael Macklem, *God Have Mercy: The Life of John Fisher of Rochester* (Ottawa, 1967), pp. 154–55; Guy, *Public Career*, pp. 141–42, 180, 192–93; Elton, *Policy and Police*, pp. 175, 220–21. For Fisher's writings on the divorce see Edward Surtz, S. J., *The Works and Days of John Fisher* (Cambridge, Mass., 1967), pp. 19–24. One of them is mentioned in *Letters and Papers, Foreign and Domestic, of the Reign of Henry VIII*, ed. J. S. Brewer et al., 21 vols. (London, 1862–1932; reprint, Kraus, Vaduz, 1965), 5, 219 (no. 461); hereafter cited as *LP*. Thomas Abell's book against the divorce was *Invicta veritas*, published in May 1532 at "Luneberge" (Antwerp?). For Fisher's statement in 1535 on points concerning the divorce, see *LP 8*, 335–37 (no. 859.4). Henry VIII's divorce propaganda has recently been discussed by H. A. Kelly, *The Matrimonial Trials of Henry VIII* (Stanford, 1976), and by Virginia Murphy, "The Debate over Henry VIII's First Divorce: an Analysis of the Contemporary Treatises" (unpublished Ph. D. dissertation, University of Cambridge, 1984).

[4]*CW 9*, xl–xli and Commentary at 5/26–27, 42/4, 60/2, and 146/29. See note on 3/8, below.

[5]See pp. xxxiii–xxxiv, below.

[6]*Doctor and Student*, p. 315.

assumptions, definitions, and proposals, the list of clerical abuses and purported quotations from "John Gerson," the hypothetical cases and examples, even the prose style and sentence structure—all these are the same in the two books, for St. German was a repetitive man. Moreover, we know that *Salem and Bizance* and its *Additions* were by the same author as *A Treatise concerning the Division,* for all these books were on one side of a continuing controversy with More. Yet *New Additions* and *A Treatise concerning the Division* were also linked to St. German's 1531 program for parliamentary reform—his comprehensive draft scheme for the progress of Henrician Reformation. St. German's program included the preparation of an English New Testament, the reform of procedures for the investigation of heresy, the rigorous enforcement of liturgical worship, the abolition of clerical abuses and alleged profiteering, and the amelioration of poverty and social distress by secularized schemes of state roadworks, wage and price regulation, and local taxation. The parliamentary draft is extant in the Public Record Office; it was corrected by St. German after the fashion of an author in full charge of his text.[1] St. German's handwriting has been identified, in turn, by comparison with his holograph letter of 1539 to Thomas Cromwell and the original manuscript of his *Little Treatise concerning Writs of Subpoena.*[2] It is clear that the "St. German" who wrote these papers is our man, because his letter to Cromwell takes up family matters residual both to other legal documents concerning St. German and to his will, while *A Little Treatise concerning Writs of Subpoena* was another tract supplementary to *Doctor and Student.*[3]

If, however, St. German wrote the parliamentary draft and the related *New Additions* and *A Treatise concerning the Division,* we can no longer continue to suppose that More was ignorant of his opponent's true identity when he composed the *Apology* and *Debellation.* For More had been lord chancellor and chairman of Henry VIII's Council in Star Chamber when St. German published *New Additions* and prepared his parliamentary draft. The King's Council was responsible for managing government policy in parliament.[4] It stretches credulity too far to assume that anyone could seriously have drafted parliamentary legislation in 1531 without the knowledge, though not necessarily with the personal approval, of the lord chancellor. But the man who prepared

---

[1] See p. xl, below.

[2] J. A. Guy, *Christopher St. German on Chancery and Statute,* Selden Society Supplementary Series, vol. 6 (London, 1985), p. 149; hereafter cited as "Guy, *St. German.*"

[3] Guy, *St. German,* pp. 106–126.

[4] W. Notestein, "The Winning of the Initiative by the House of Commons," *Proceedings of the British Academy, 11* (1926), 126–28.

the parliamentary draft wrote *New Additions, A Treatise concerning the Division, Salem and Bizance,* and its *Additions.* More knew his opponent's identity. And there may be further evidence that he did. At the opening of the *Debellation,* More described one of his adversaries as by reputation "one greate cunnynge man" whose handwriting was "nere to gyther and with a smale hande" (4/29–31). It is not established from the passage in question that the "greate cunnynge man" was St. German—More mentioned "dyuerse" men who were his opponents (4/26). It may be that the "greate cunnynge man" confined himself to an attack on that passage of More's *Apology* that had confuted "certayne sermons" (4/36–5/7).[1] The fact remains, however, that More's account of the man's handwriting perfectly describes the compact lines and minute characters that were St. German's.[2]

More knew, then, that St. German was the author of *New Additions, A Treatise concerning the Division, Salem and Bizance,* and its *Additions,* and we must ask why he professed otherwise. Manifestly, More could not have refuted St. German while he remained lord chancellor. As a king's councillor and officer of state, he was bound by an oath not to subvert government policy, however much he might have disliked that policy personally.[3] In fact, none of St. German's proposals became translated into official government measures before May 1532—a fact that may even testify to More's activity behind the scenes before the Submission of the Clergy. Yet St. German's initial lack of impact cannot alter the fact that he had enjoyed Henry VIII's confidence when his parliamentary draft was conceived and when his books were passed to Berthelet for printing.[4] When More resigned the chancellorship in May 1532, his promise was not to meddle in affairs of state, but to

---

[1] *CW* 9, 12–18.

[2] See St. German's handwriting in the illustration facing this page.

[3] The oath of a king's councillor under Henry VI is printed by J. F. Baldwin, *The King's Council in England during the Middle Ages* (Oxford, 1913), pp. 353–54. A slightly shortened version in use by 1505 or 1506 is given in British Library, Lansdowne MS 160, fol. 282. The oath More took as lord chancellor is recorded in PRO, C 54/398: "Ye shall swere that well and trulye ye shall serve our soveraygn lord the kyng and hys peple in the office of the Chaunceller / And ye shall do right to all maner of peple pore and rych after the lawes and usagys of this realme / and trulie ye shall counsell the kyng and his counsell ye shall leyve and kepe / and ye shall not knowe nor suffer the hurte nor disherytyng of the kyng or that the rightes of the Croun be decreysed by any mean as ferforth as ye may lett yt / And yf ye may not lett yt ye shall make yt clerely and expressely to be knowen to the kyng with your advyse and counsell / And that ye shall doo and purchase the kyngis profite in all that ye resonablie may as God helpe you and the holye evangelyez." The word "leyve" seems to mean "leave alone" (*OED,* s.v. "leave" 5 and 13) or "believe, give credence to" (*OED,* s.v., "leve" *v.*2 2).

[4] Guy, *St. German,* pp. 21–23.

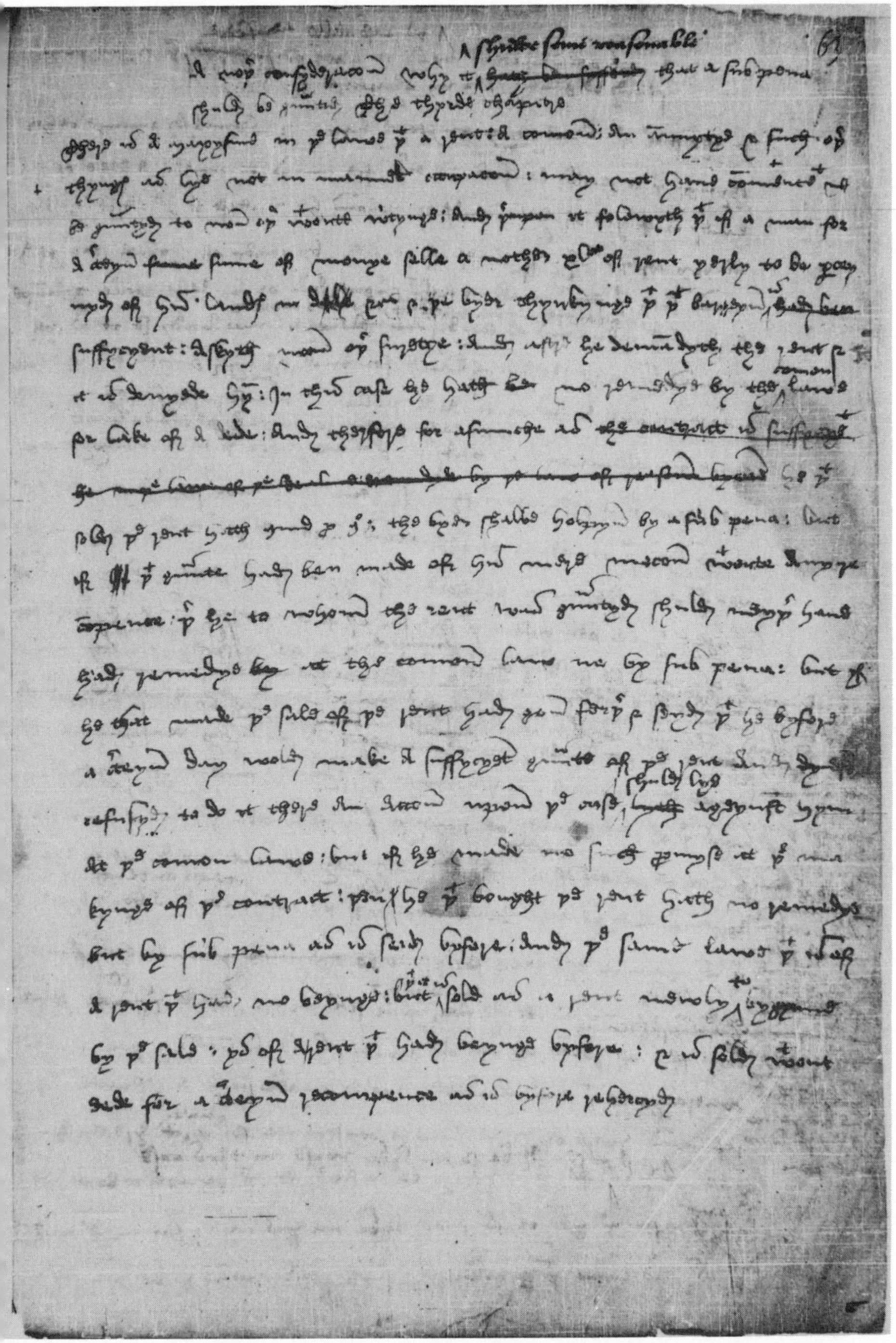

A Little Treatise concerning Writs of Supoena, British Library, MS Harley 829, fol. 63 (reduced).

fortify his soul and to pray for king and realm. His personal safety depended on that resolution. Nevertheless, when *A Treatise concerning the Division* was published some six months later, More dared to intervene. He thought that St. German was a dangerous man and he held it to be his catholic (and public) duty to refute the arguments of St. German's book. In political exile More apparently believed he might answer St. German provided he was circumspect. Thus discretion demanded that More profess ignorance of his "anonymous" adversary's identity in his *Apology* and *Debellation*. In this way he could also conscientiously maintain ignorance of the fact that *A Treatise concerning the Division* and *Salem and Bizance* were published with government approval. In short, More could defend himself from the charge of meddling in politics after his resignation, while his depiction of St. German as a misguided, rustic cleric in the *Apology* and *Debellation* added a note of irreverent humor that gave More a polemical advantage.

On its merits, More's device was indeed legally watertight; his professed ignorance of his enemy's identity was justified by the strict rules of English law. In law, a man could "know" only what had been certified to him directly, either verbally before witnesses or in writing. He "knew" no more nor less.[1] Because More had left the Council and withdrawn to Chelsea in May 1532, he could "know" thereafter only rumors or conjectures about St. German's role in government policy or about Berthelet's printings. London gossip was not legal "knowledge." Nevertheless, although More's technical position was strong in 1533, politics and coercion sometimes overtook law and morality in the turbulence of the 1530s. In particular, Henry VIII's fear of a catholic counteroffensive against his government's propaganda on divorce and schism in mid-1533 is well documented by his quest for intelligence.[2] Thomas Cromwell sent his servant Stephen Vaughan to Antwerp in early August 1533 to gain news of the underground press. Vaughan's report confirmed previous suspicions that at least one of Bishop Fisher's seven tracts against the divorce had reached Antwerp via Friars Peto and Elstow, "beyng the only men that have and do taken upon them to be conveyers of the same bookes into Englond, and conveyers of all other thinges into and out of Englond."[3] Vaughan urged that, "If

---

[1]On this point, see J. A. Guy, "The Origins of the Petition of Right Reconsidered," *Historical Journal*, 25 (1982), 294, 301.

[2]*LP 6*, nos. 116, 726, 899, 900, 902, 917, 934, 1324, 1369, 1370; *LP 7*, nos. 143.2, 440; R. B. Merriman, *The Life and Letters of Thomas Cromwell*, 2 vols. (Oxford, 1902), *1*, 360–62 (no. 52), 370–72 (no. 65).

[3]*State Papers during the Reign of Henry VIII*, Record Commission, 5 parts in 11 vols. (London, 1831–52), part 5, no. 372 (p. 490); hereafter cited as "*State Papers Henry VIII*."

pryvey serche be made and shortly, peradventure in the howse of the same Busshop shalbe founde his first copie." With reference to More, he continued: "Maister More hathe sent often tymes, and lately, bookes unto Peto in Andwerp, as his book of the confutacion of Tyndale, and Frythe his opynyon of the sacrament, with dyvers other bookes. I can no further lern of More his practises, but if yow consider this well, yow may perchance espye his crafte."[1] Although More had committed no legal offense in his literary defense of the catholic cause, he was suddenly under investigation.

Cromwell knew well enough that Vaughan had axes to grind. Nevertheless, he edited Vaughan's report only marginally when it arrived in England. The editor of the *State Papers* thought that a copy was prepared for Henry's eyes—it certainly looks from Cromwell's amendments to Vaughan's original as if such a copy was made for the king or Council.[2] If so, a misleading impression was given. For Vaughan's principal informant was none other than George Joye, the Zwinglian author of *The Supper of the Lord*—hardly an impartial observer of the catholic underground. Joye's name was deleted by Cromwell throughout the report in favor of the words "oon whoo."[3] Otherwise, Vaughan's "intelligence" was communicated virtually intact.

Since Vaughan had so exaggerated the danger in mid-1533, it was hardly surprising that fears were aroused of active catholic conspiracy. In January 1534, Cromwell personally interviewed William Rastell, More's printer, to investigate a rumor that More had written a reply to the *Articles Devised by the Whole Consent of the King's Most Honourable Council*, published by Berthelet in late December 1533 and distributed at court two days after Christmas.[4] The *Articles* were a piece of frontline official propaganda, probably devised at a Council meeting on December 2.[5] They defended the divorce, denounced Clement VII's excommunication of Henry VIII, asserted that the pope had no more authority than any other bishop *extra provinciam*, and accused him of heresy for denying the decree *Sacrosancta* of the Council of Constance (1415).[6] Copies were quickly nailed up in London and throughout the realm: it was the most extensive exercise in public persuasion since Henry's marriage to Catherine of Aragon had been annulled by

---

[1] *State Papers Henry VIII*, part 5, p. 490.

[2] *State Papers Henry VIII*, part 5, p. 489, n. 2; p. 490, nn. 2–4; p. 491, n. 1.

[3] *State Papers Henry VIII*, part 5, p. 489, n. 2; p. 490, n. 4.

[4] Rogers, pp. 467–68 (no. 194); *LP 6*, 634 (no. 1571).

[5] Elton, *Policy and Police*, pp. 180–82; *LP 6*, nos. 1486–87, 1510.

[6] *Articles* is reprinted in *Records of the Reformation: The Divorce, 1527–1533*, ed. Nicholas Pocock, 2 vols. (Oxford, 1870), 2, 524–31.

Cranmer at Dunstable.[1] The harvest had been abundant in 1533, and the threat of popular disorder was thereby reduced, but even so the Council was taking no chances. For its greatest worry since at least the beginning of 1532 had been that England would be subjected to papal interdict, and that this would fuel coordinated catholic resistance.[2]

Hearing of Cromwell's visit to Rastell, More sent the minister a letter on February 1, 1534, informing him that the rumor was false and that he had written nothing since the *Articles* appeared in print. His latest work was *The Answer to a Poisoned Book*, which was already on sale before Christmas of 1533.[3] Yet More had read the *Articles*, "ones over and never more." In some matters he did not know the law, in others the facts; thus he would not presume to answer the tract, whoever had written it. More continued:

> And then while the matter parteined vnto the Kinges Highnes, and the boke professeth openly that it was made by hys honorable Counsail, and by them put in print with his Graces licens obteined therunto, I verely trust in good faith that of your good mind toward me, though I neuer wrote you worde thereof, your selfe will both think and say so much for me, that it were a thing far vnlikely, that an answer shold be made therunto bi me. . . . Yet suerly if it shold happen any boke to come abrode in the name of hys Grace or hys honorable Counsail, if the boke to me semed such as my selfe would not haue giuen mine owne aduise to the making, yet I know my bounden duety, to bere more honour to my prince, and more reuerence to his honorable Counsaile, than that it coulde become me for many causes, to make an aunswere vnto such a boke, or to counsail and aduise any man els to do it.[4]

Here More offered a statement of principle. He affirmed the distinction between books published "openly" in the name of king or Council and other writings. His duty as a subject precluded his making answer to the king's propaganda.

The trouble was that, by answering *A Treatise concerning the Division* and *Salem and Bizance*, More had already rebutted Henry's propaganda in the eyes of the regime. More and the government were now applying different definitions. Whether its propaganda was "openly" declared as such on its title page was manifestly irrelevant to the Council

[1]*LP* 7, nos. 140, 146, 259, 454.
[2]Guy, *Public Career*, pp. 182–83.
[3]See p. xviii, n. 2, above.
[4]Rogers, pp. 468–69 (no. 194).

in the wake of the schism. More relied, too, on the "anonymity" of St. German and his lack of strict legal "knowledge" of what the Council passed to Berthelet's press at a time when Henry VIII had started to feel haunted by the catholic underground. Some form of collision was inevitable.

On February 21, 1534, the bill of attainder against Elizabeth Barton, the so-called Holy Maid or Nun of Kent, was laid before the House of Lords. Fisher and More, the latter at Henry VIII's own insistence, were named among those who "by the act shalbe atteynted of mysprision and have imprisonament at the kynges will and lose all their goodes."[1] More's name was eventually deleted—the accusation was a sham. Yet why had Henry's affection for his former chancellor—visible at York Place as late as May 1532—turned to malice and hatred a month before the First Act of Succession was on the statute book? One conceivable reason was that More had refused to attend Anne Boleyn's coronation the previous June.[2] But Henry must also have associated More and Fisher as equal partners in the catholic press campaign against his jurisdictional revolution. Nowhere was the juridical aspect of the Henrician schism better defended than in those books of Christopher St. German which were printed by Berthelet. Since *A Treatise concerning the Division* and *Salem and Bizance* were components of the king's secondary line of propaganda, More's *Apology* and *Debellation* were viewed as opposed to Henry's policies. However More perceived his position in law and morality during 1533, Henry VIII believed that his ex-chancellor had overstepped the mark. Within the volcanic recesses of the king's consciousness, Thomas More's mere existence came to pose an intolerable threat.

[1]S. E. Lehmberg, *The Reformation Parliament, 1529–1536* (Cambridge, 1970), p. 194; hereafter cited as "Lehmberg."

[2]R. W. Chambers, *Thomas More* (London, 1935), pp. 292–94.

CHRISTOPHER ST. GERMAN: HIS LEGAL AND POLITICAL CAREER UP TO 1534

Christopher St. German (c. 1460–1541) was Thomas More's most re-doubtable English adversary. He was the respected author of the twin dialogues of *Doctor and Student,* the most distinguished of Tudor legal treatises, a work studied by students of English law until the reforms of the 1870s, when the ancient system of superior courts in England was consolidated into the Supreme Court of Judicature and St. German's account became technically obsolete. Nor were his ideas obviously he-retical, at least in his encounter with More. On the contrary, his doc-trinal orthodoxy and quest for spiritual renewal in the tradition of the *devotio moderna* (Bridget of Sweden was his favorite saint)[1] makes him seem unlikely to have become an antagonist of Thomas More. Why he did so is clear from More's *Apology* and *Debellation:* to More St. German was a dangerous man because his general theory of English law and institutions denied the independent legislative and jurisdictional powers of the church, especially in cases of heresy or property. St. German's desire to attack long-standing clerical abuses head-on by means of journalistic exposés in the vernacular also earned him More's frigid rebuke.[2] Yet St. German was in a position of strength: learned, relentless, concise, and with a razor-sharp mind, he enjoyed the confi-dence of Thomas Cromwell and briefly too of Henry VIII. But he was clearly no intellectual puppet, no hack writer for the propaganda ma-chine of Henry VIII. His stature was that of an independent scholar in contact with, but not a pensioner of, the circle of Thomas Cromwell.

St. German was born about 1460 at Shilton in Warwickshire, the son of Sir Henry St. German by his wife Anne Tyndale.[3] Firm biographical

---

[1]*Doctor and Student,* pp. li, 26–27, 330. It may be noted also that in the *Division* St. German quotes Whitford's translation of the *Imitation of Christ (CW 9,* xlvi–xlvii, lxvi, 205, 339).

[2]See 19/29–20/7, below, and *CW 9,* 60.

[3]For this account of St. German's career, I have drawn on work in preparation for my Selden Society edition of St. German's unpublished legal writings, which contains a full account of St. German's life, legal career, and legal thought (see p. xxiii, n. 2, above). Some earlier accounts of St. German are: John Bale, *Scriptorum illustrium maioris Brytan-niae . . . catalogus* (Basel, 1557–59), pp. 660–61, sigs. Oo₂v–Oo₃ (hereafter cited as

details concerning Christopher's paternal ancestry are lacking. We know for certain only that his grandparents on the maternal side were Sir Thomas Tyndale of Hockwold, Norfolk, and his wife Margaret Yelverton. St. German himself did not marry, and the bulk of his small property was bequeathed shortly before his death in May 1541 to the families of his three sisters, to the children of his cousin, and to charitable uses. Much of our knowledge of his life derives from two wills, his own (which was drawn on July 10, 1540) and that of John Blennerhasset, another cousin, who died in 1532.[1]

In the first part of his will, St. German left bequests to various churches,[2] relatives, and servants. The second part of his will arose from his relationship with John Blennerhasset and the family of Sir Henry Grey. John Blennerhasset had made his will and died in July 1532, naming as his executors his brother-in-law Sir Henry Grey and St. German.[3] As he made his own will eight years later St. German had to deal with bequests by Blennerhasset to his numerous nephews and nieces. Sir Henry Grey had bound himself by indenture to St. German to discharge his coexecutor of these legacies and (as St. German said in his will) "shulde have delyvered unto me an accquitaunce of the payment therof in the name of every one of the saide Childerne." This Sir Henry had failed to do.[4] St. German believed that the bequests to the children had not yet been executed; accordingly, he himself left money to the intended beneficiaries out of his own estate, "so that at the payment therof, every one of the saide childerne delyver unto myne Executour a suffycient accquittaunce of bothe the saide bequestes."

The third section of St. German's will provided bequests to the poor of the parish in which the testator should be buried, together with an annuity of 13s. 4d. to be shared among the poor people of Shilton until 1550 on every St. Andrew's Day, the patronal feast day of their church.

"Bale"), reprinted in St. German's *Dialogus de fundamentis legum Angliae et de conscientia* (London, 1604; STC² 21560), sig. A₂v; Pearl Hogrefe, "The Life of Christopher St. German," *Review of English Studies, 13* (1937), 398–404 (hereafter cited as "Hogrefe"); Franklin L. Baumer, "Christopher St. German: The Political Philosophy of a Tudor Lawyer," *American Historical Review, 42* (1937), 631–32; and J. B. Trapp in *CW 9*, xli–liv. J. L. Barton's brief account in *Doctor and Student* (p. xi) is based on Bale and Hogrefe.

[1] St. German's will is PRO, PROB 11/28, quire 29; Blennerhasset's is PRO, PROB 11/24, quire 16.

[2] Including Shilton, where his parents were buried, and Marylebone in Middlesex.

[3] Hogrefe, pp. 399–400.

[4] His family had been ruined by the unusual wastefulness of his half-brother, Richard third earl of Kent, and Sir Henry had also lost out to the extraordinary rapacity of his courtier-neighbor, Sir William Compton. See G. W. Bernard, "The Rise of Sir William Compton, Early Tudor Courtier," *English Historical Review, 96* (1981), 754–77.

In return, the recipients of St. German's charity were to pray for the testator and his parents; at his burial St. German also wished a sermon to be preached on the subject of the Resurrection, for which he left the preacher the generous remuneration of 10s. St. German's two final instructions are of interest for the light they shed on his last years. The first makes clear that by 1540 he was living in a house in Old Fish Street, London, near the Old Exchange, which his will says was owned by the trustees of the church of St. Mary Magdalen. He had evidently installed windows, doors, and trap doors; these improvements were bequeathed to the trustees, who could either accept them as they stood or restore the house "to the furst fasshion" if they preferred. Second, St. German urged special diligence on his executor to see "suche evydences as I have concernyng other men" returned to their rightful holders. This instruction suggests that St. German, who had probably retired from formal law practice about 1511, had nonetheless continued to act in the interests of his friends until his penultimate year.[1]

From the note appended to the registered copy of St. German's will, we know that the will was proved in the Lambeth office of the Prerogative Court of Canterbury on May 30, 1541: the presumption must be that the testator had died only some few weeks before. John Bale, not always a reliable authority, adds the information that St. German was buried in the church of St. Alphage, Cripplegate. He had also heard that St. German left almost his entire wealth in books, an estimate which is supported by the will. St. German directed that his books, chests, cupboards, presses, and "other stuffe" were to be sold to meet his bequests; Christopher Breteyn, as executor, might choose the books he wanted for himself from the library, but he was to pay a fair price.

Like the executor of his will,[2] St. German was a member of the Middle Temple.[3] On January 29, 1502, he was fined, together with John Rastell, Robert Bowryng, and other "utter barristers," for not

---

[1]Guy, *St. German*, p. 5.

[2]Christopher Breteyn was admitted to clerks' commons at the Middle Temple in 1522; see *Middle Temple Records: Minutes of Parliament*, ed. Charles T. Martin, 4 vols. (London, 1904–05), *1*, 71; hereafter cited as "Martin." See also Richard J. Schoeck, "'That Most Erudite of Tudor Lawyers,' Christopher St. German," *Journal of the Rocky Mountain Medieval and Renaissance Association, 6* (1983), 107–23.

[3]He is mentioned in the *Minutes of Parliament* (which are extant from 1501) under the dates January 29, 1502; November 5, 1504; July 3, 1509; July 4, 1510; and July 4, 1511 (Martin, *1*, 2, 11, 29, 32, 36–37). A mistake by Bale (pp. 660–61) gave currency for centuries to the error that St. German was a member of the Inner Temple. John Hutchinson's *A Catalogue of Notable Middle Templars with Brief Biographical Notices* (London, 1902) strangely omits any mention of St. German.

attending the parliament of the Middle Temple.[1] As an "utter barrister" he was permitted to dispute before the benchers of the Middle Temple at moots and readers' cases and to practice in any of the courts of law (except Common Pleas when sitting in banc) as long as he could obtain clients.[2] Not long after 1511 St. German left the Middle Temple. He is not mentioned in the minutes after that year, and in a letter of 1539 to Cromwell he makes it clear that he was "goon fro the Temple" not later than 1518.[3] Moreover, by 1518 St. German had clearly retired from the active practice of law, for his name does not appear on any of Wolsey's official lists.[4]

The utter barrister Bowryng fined in company with St. German and John Rastell in 1502 was Robert Bowryng, autumn reader at the Middle Temple in 1507, who became a double reader in 1513.[5] Early in Michaelmas term of 1506 Bowryng, Robert Fermour, and Christopher St. German, "gentylmen of yᵉ Mydell Tempull of London," were served with writs of subpoena, returnable in the Court of Chancery on November 25, 1506, at the suit of Richard Pynson of London, "printer of bokes." Pynson's bill in Chancery, addressed to Archbishop Warham, Lord Chancellor, complained that the defendants were in breach of a covenant and bargain by indenture for reprinting 409 copies of *The Abridgement of Statutes.*[6] *The Abridgement,* an alphabetical digest of statutes under titles from "Abiuracion" to "Utlagarie," had first been issued by John Lettou and William de Machlinia, of London, in 1481.[7] Pynson's revised edition had first appeared in October 1499.[8] Pynson's bargain with Bowryng, Fermour, and St. German was for a commis-

---

[1]Martin, *1*, 2. On November 5, 1504, St. German was appointed auditor together with one "More" (Martin, *1*, 11). This More was not St. German's future antagonist but Thomas More of Southampton (*Calendar of Patent Rolls, Henry VII*, 2 vols., London, 1914–16, 2, 658).

[2]*The Reports of Sir John Spelman,* ed. J. H. Baker, 2 vols., Selden Society Publications, vols. 93 and 94 (London, 1977–78), 2, introduction, pp. 129–30; hereafter cited as "Spelman's Reports."

[3]For the text of this letter (PRO, SP 1/152, fol. 249), see Guy, *St. German,* pp. 8–9. St. German tells Cromwell that he left the Temple about the time that Edward Boughton (son and heir of William Boughton) was born. The letter also makes it clear that in 1539 Edward was still a young man, although he was able to inherit and thus over twenty-one.

[4]Nor had St. German returned to the Middle Temple by 1523, when the subsidy for Henry VIII's war in France was collected; the subsidy assessments for the Inns of Court in this year are printed in *A Calendar of the Inner Temple Records,* ed. F. A. Inderwick, 5 vols. (London, 1896–1937), *1*, 455–66.

[5]Martin, *1*, 18, 40.

[6]PRO, C 1/345/4.

[7]STC 9513.

[8]STC 9514.

sioned reprint of 409 bound copies with clasps. He was to be paid £20, and the Middle Templars were to correct the proofs free of charge at Pynson's behest. The printer delivered the books, as he now claimed, but 118 copies lacked clasps. Pynson pleaded an acquittance to discharge him of his obligation to supply all copies with clasps, but this document had been signed only by St. German and not by the other two partners. For his part, Pynson alleged that the Middle Templars had refused to read and correct the proofs and had declined to pay more than £10 for the books. They had also, unconscionably, begun an action of debt at common law against Pynson for a penalty of £40, taking unfair advantage of the fact that the original bargain had, strictly, been unfulfilled because the printer failed to supply all the books with clasps. No further pleadings or proofs in the Chancery case are extant. But the litigation does show that St. German was a member of the enterprising trio which had commissioned the reprinting of this standard work of reference.[1]

St. German's writings now extant in print or manuscript are as follows:

Dialogus de fundamentis legum Anglie et de conscientia (1528)[2]
Dialogue in English betwixt a Doctor of Divinity and a Student of the Laws of England (1530)[3]
A Little Treatise called the New Additions (1531)[4]

---

[1]No extant copy of this reprint is listed in *STC*. For further details of St. German's legal career, including his work in the Court of Requests, see Guy, *St. German*, pp. 11–15.

[2]The first dialogue of *Doctor and Student*, published in Latin in 1528 (*Doctor and Student*, pp. lxix–lxx). *STC*[2] 21559 conflates two separate editions of this work printed by John Rastell. A 1523 edition of the first dialogue is probably a "ghost" created by William Herbert in his edition of Joseph Ames's *Typographical Antiquities* (London, 1785–90), ed. T. F. Dibdin, 4 vols. (London, 1816), *3*, 86. St. German's first dialogue was translated into English in 1531 (*Doctor and Student*, pp. lxx–lxxiii; *STC*[2] 21561, 21567). The authoritative modern edition is by Plucknett and Barton (see p. xix, n. 2, above).

[3]The second dialogue of *Doctor and Student*, written in English and published in November 1530 and in three more editions in 1531 and 1532 (*Doctor and Student*, pp. lxxiii–lxxvi; *STC*[2] 21565–68). The authoritative edition is by Plucknett and Barton (see p. xix, n. 2).

[4]*STC*[2] 21563–64. The printer's date is 1531, which may mean either the year beginning January 1, 1531, or the year beginning March 25, 1531; see William I. Edgerton, "The Calendar Year in Sixteenth-Century Printing," *Journal of English and Germanic Philology, 59* (1960), 439–49. But Berthelet normally used January 1 as the beginning of a new year; see E. G. Duff, *The Printers, Stationers and Bookbinders of Westminster and London from 1476 to 1534* (Cambridge, 1906), p. 179. The authoritative edition is by Plucknett and Barton (see p. xix, n. 2).

Parliamentary draft in PRO, SP 6/7, pp. 55–74 (1531)[1]
[*Replication of a Serjeant at the Laws of England* (n.d.)][2]
A Little Treatise concerning Writs of Subpoena (1532?)[3]
A Treatise concerning the Division between the Spiritualty and Temporalty (1532)[4]
Salem and Bizance (1533)[5]
The Additions of Salem and Bizance (1534)[6]
A Treatise concerning the Power of the Clergy and the Laws of the Realm (1535?)[7]
A Treatise concerning divers of the Constitutions Provincial and Legantines (1535)[8]
An Answer to a Letter (1535)[9]
"A Discourse of the Sacramentes: howe many there are" (1537)[10]
"A Dyalogue shewinge what we be bounde to byleve as thinges necessary to Salvacion, and what not" (1537)[11]

If we compare this list with Bale's (pp. 660–61) and allow for some degree of confusion on his part, it seems clear that we still possess St. German's principal works. We lack three pieces which Bale entitles *Doctrina Bernardi et Brigidae, In Mahumetem et eius sectem,* and *Consilia Romanorum pontificum,*[12] although it is possible that the second of these is *A lytell treatyse agaynst Mahumet and his cursed secte,* which Peter Treveris printed on behalf of an unnamed author at his Southwark shop about 1530, the year that he printed the first edition of the second

---

[1]Printed by Guy, *St. German,* pp. 127–35.

[2]Possibly compiled by St. German; it was not published until 1787. It is printed from St. German's manuscript in Guy, *St. German,* pp. 99–105. I have given the evidence suggestive of St. German's authorship in *St. German,* pp. 56–62.

[3]Printed from St. German's autograph manuscript in Guy, *St. German,* pp. 106–26.

[4]*STC*[2] 21586–87.7. This work was first published toward the end of 1532 or at the beginning of 1533 (*CW 9,* xcii). Reprinted as Appendix A in *CW 9,* 177–212.

[5]Reprinted as Appendix B, pp. 323–92, below.

[6]*STC*[2] 21585. The printer's date is 1534 (either the year following January 1, 1534, or that following March 25, 1534; see p. xix, n. 4, above).

[7]*STC*[2] 21588.

[8]*STC*[2] 24236.

[9]*STC*[2] 21558.5.

[10]PRO, SP 6/8, pp. 1–20. This work has never been printed.

[11]PRO, SP 6/2, pp. 89–168. This work is in the form of a dialogue between a doctor and a student; it has never been printed. For a fuller description see Fox and Guy, *Reassessing the Henrician Age: Humanism, Politics and Reform, 1500–1550* (Oxford, 1986), pp. 199–220.

[12]But St. German does attack Mohammed and his sect in the closing chapters of *Salem and Bizance,* and he does discuss general councils in "A Dyalogue shewinge what we be bounde to byleve," pp. 103–05.

dialogue of St. German's *Doctor and Student*.[1] In particular, we are fortunate that four manuscripts of writings by St. German have survived which are corrected in the hand of their author. Two newly discovered works, "A Discourse of the Sacramentes" and "A Dyalogue shewinge what we be bounde to byleve," were both apparently written in the immediate wake of the debates that took place in June and July 1537 upon the nature and number of the sacraments, and were sent by St. German to Cromwell, vicegerent in spirituals since 1535, who chose not to have them printed.[2]

I have already given the evidence which shows that the works in this list which were written or printed in 1534 or before are by St. German.[3] Of the remaining works, *An Answer to a Letter* (1535) contains a lengthy and complex analysis of the question of the restitution of things to which a man has no right in conscience, and the cases discussed closely resemble learned argument on this topic in *A Little Treatise concerning Writs of Subpoena*, which was clearly written by St. German.[4] In turn, *An Answer to a Letter* shares overwhelming similarities of argument with *The Power of the Clergy* (1535?)[5] and is plainly descended from that work; moreover, five chapters of *The Power of the Clergy* are also strikingly related to passages in the second dialogue of *Doctor and Student* and *New Additions*.[6] Finally, *A Treatise concerning divers of the Constitutions* can be added to St. German's canon because two of its chapters are identical with two chapters in *The Power of the Clergy*,[7] and five of its chapters are strikingly similar to chapters in the second part of *Doctor and Student* and *New Additions*.[8]

St. German's greatest work was *Doctor and Student*. The first dialogue

---

[1]*STC*[2] 17994.5. Dr. H. C. Porter has linked St. German with *A dyaloge betwene one Clemente a clerke of the Conuocacyon, and one Bernarde a burges of the parlyament / dysputynge be/twene them what auctoryte the clergye haue to make lawes. And howe farre and where theyr power dothe extende* (an apparently unique printed fragment, Selwyn College, Cambridge, Q.3.4), but the association, as he notes, is speculative. See Porter, "Hooker, the Tudor Constitution, and the *Via Media*," in *Studies in Richard Hooker*, ed. W. Speed Hill (Cleveland and London, 1972), p. 86.

[2]See pp. 406–14, below. It is possible that the "Dyalogue" was commissioned in 1536; see *LP 11*, no. 84.

[3]See pp. xxii–xxiii above; Guy, *St. German*, pp. 16–18.

[4]Guy, *St. German*, pp. 106–26.

[5]*Answer to a Letter*, chaps. 1–2; *The Power of the Clergy*, chaps. 1, 17.

[6]*The Power of the Clergy*, chaps. 4, 8, 13, 16, 19; second dialogue of *Doctor and Student*, chaps. 32, 45, 55; *New Additions*, chap. 13.

[7]*A Treatise concerning divers of the Constitutions*, chaps. 8, 14; *The Power of the Clergy*, chaps. 4, 8.

[8]*A Treatise concerning divers of the Constitutions*, chaps. 8, 14, 17, 20–21; second dialogue of *Doctor and Student*, chaps. 32, 55; *New Additions*, chaps. 4–6.

was published in Latin in 1528, and a translation was issued in 1531.[1] The second dialogue was written and published in English alone and was on sale in November 1530.[2] By publishing in the vernacular in 1530 and 1531, St. German gained himself a wide readership; both English dialogues were sold in rival editions within a year of first publication.[3] Yet *Doctor and Student* was successful primarily because it was a brilliant, comprehensive, and intellectually satisfying attempt to construct a systematic theory of law within an English context, something far beyond a mere amalgam of existing or separate theories. Within St. German's framework, the universal laws of God and nature were shown to be both rationally antecedent to, and harmoniously coexistent with, English common law (the law of man) and good conscience (equity), even though conscience, as derived from natural reason and moral calculation, might sometimes speak directly contrary to general rules of common law in specific instances. The key to St. German's theory was that equitable interventions in the name of good conscience, which were sometimes necessary to mitigate the rigor of common law, were designed to reinforce, not to contradict, general legal principles. General rules of law could not be expected automatically to take cognizance of every particular human situation, but since positive human law had always originated from the laws of God and nature, it could never be discarded or discounted, but must be interpreted in difficult cases according to the presumed intention of the human legislators. Usually this added element of flexibility, when applied to such difficult cases, could avert any obvious injustice to particular individuals, although St. German conceded that equity must never be allowed to overrule or nullify an accepted maxim of law, even if the application of that maxim might result in manifest injustice.[4]

The effect of St. German's theory was twofold: it created the impression that English common law was a homogeneous corpus, the pervasive logic of which was to produce similar results in similar situations or types of case; and it enhanced vastly the status of English common law as compared with other species of law, especially canon and papal law. A radical feature of St. German's thought was that it showed neither more nor less favor to clergy or laity under the law, a position heavily bolstered by St. German's ancillary account of the historical basis of property rights.[5] According to the first dialogue of *Doctor and*

---

[1]*Doctor and Student*, pp. lxix–lxxiii.

[2]*Doctor and Student*, pp. lxiii–lxxvi.

[3]*Doctor and Student*, pp. lxix–lxxvi.

[4]Guy, *St. German*, p. 116. For some qualifications to St. German's argument see pp. 111–12.

[5]*Doctor and Student*, pp. xxi–xxv.

Student, private property was an institution of human convenience, probably introduced by Nimrod when the world's population had increased to the point where common possession was no longer practicable. It followed that property was not a divine institution, and thus property rights were firmly vested by St. German within the temporal sphere of jurisdiction, where they were subject to regulation by the law of man.[1]

In his second dialogue, St. German led his doctor of divinity and student of common law into debate upon a series of test cases, the purpose of which was to illustrate that there were few, if any, areas of ecclesiastical activity, beyond the exercise of purely sacramental functions, which did not in some sense touch rights of property or privileges, which were another form of property. For example, it pertained to the church to have the probate and execution of wills, but the church, argued the student, was barred from legislating on such issues as the lawful age of majority for the purposes of inheritance:

> the chyrche may not as it semeth determyne what shall be the lawfull age for any persone to haue the goodes for that belongeth to the kynge & his lawes to determyne / & therfore yf yt were ordeyned by a statute of the realme that he sholde not in suche case haue the goodes tyll he were of the age of .xxv. yere that statute were good & to be obserued as wel in the spyrytual lawe as in the lawe of the realme / & yf a statute were good in that case / then a decre made therof is not to be obserued / for the orderynge of the age maye not be vnder two seuerall powers / & one propertye of euery good lawe of man ys that the maker excede not hys auctorytye / & I thynke that the spyrytuall Juges in that case oughte to Juge the full age after the law of the realme seynge that the matter of the age concerneth temporall goodes / & I suppose ferther that as the kynge by auctoryty of his parlyament may ordeyn that all wylles shall be voyde & that the goodes of euery man shall be dysposyd in suche maner as by statute sholde be assygned: that more stronger he maye appoynte at what age suche wylles as be made shall be perfourmed.[2]

In the student's opinion the goods of convicted heretics were temporal property "and belonge to the iugement of the kynges courte."[3] Similarly, covenants made upon gifts of property to churches should be strictly enforceable in both law and conscience; general rules of prop-

---

[1] *Doctor and Student,* pp. 19, 32–35.
[2] *Doctor and Student,* p. 242.
[3] *Doctor and Student,* p. 243.

erty law should be applied, and such issues "muste of necessytye be iuged after the rules & groundes of the lawe of the realme and after no other lawe as me semyth."[1]

Only on matters concerning "the artycles of the fayth," as the student maintained, should men "be bounde to byleue the chyrche," an opinion which St. German later revealed to be his own.[2] It was otherwise in cases in which the church "makyth any lawes wherby the godes or possessyons of the people may be bounde," because when property rights were at stake, the church "may erre and be deceyuyd and deceyue other eyther for syngularytye or for couetyce or for some other cause." Hence St. German exhorted common lawyers to prepare systematic studies of the ecclesiastical laws, to know "whan the lawe of the chyrche must be folowyd and whan the lawe of the realme."[3] But if such inquiries were undertaken in St. German's frame of reference, they would nudge English common law inexorably toward the apex of the jurisprudential pyramid, because St. German had resolved the sixteenth-century conflict of laws in favor of English common law and because he had also insisted that common law should properly govern the consciences of Englishmen in matters of equity.

The collision between More and St. German stemmed unquestionably from St. German's ideas as first mooted in the second dialogue of *Doctor and Student*. Moreover, in 1531 St. German published an appendix to *Doctor and Student* entitled *New Additions*, which was linked to a draft for parliamentary legislation that St. German was permitted to prepare simultaneously. *New Additions* was a blistering review of the issues disputed between church and state in 1531.[4] The subjects treated included the efficacy and legal validity of the statute of mortuaries, which had been enacted in 1529; the question of lay property passing into mortmain; the extent of parliament's jurisdiction over appropriated benefices and sanctuaries; the rights disputed between church and state regarding trees and grass in churchyards; the issues of clerical apparel and dilapidations; parliament's right on behalf of Englishmen to validate the "true" incumbent of the papacy in case of schism; parliament's right to enforce strict observance of liturgical

---

[1]*Doctor and Student*, pp. 252–54.

[2]*Doctor and Student*, p. 309. St. German's opinion, expressed in his "Dyalogue shewinge what we be bounde to byleve as thinges necessary to Salvacion" (PRO, SP 6/2, 163–65), was that a general council of the church was the right body to declare the articles of faith, although a council could not invent new articles but merely clarify and reinforce existing doctrines.

[3]*Doctor and Student*, p. 309.

[4]*Doctor and Student*, pp. 315–40.

worship on idle or slovenly priests and its power to demand mutual respect and good relations between clergy and laity; parliament's power to regulate admissions to the priesthood and religious life; its right to control shrines, pilgrimages, and the investigation of miracles to eliminate clerical rackets, profiteering, and superstition; its power to dictate the assignment of tithes and to oversee the conduct of ecclesiastical visitations. Debating the pros and cons in *New Additions,* St. German was distinctly in favor of unilateral reform by the state against the church in the name of efficiency and good government. Furthermore, almost all the issues raised in *New Additions* were resolved in St. German's parliamentary draft along identical unilateral lines: there can be no doubt whatever that Christopher St. German was at work in 1531 on a program of parliamentary reform and propaganda designed to purchase peace between church and state at the expense of the clergy's traditional privileges and jurisdictional independence, and in favor of the Crown and the laity, who were now to control virtually the whole gamut of ecclesiastical functions save the purely sacramental life of the church.

In 1531 St. German was a special asset to Henry VIII and his advisers because he proffered a general solution to the most intractable problem of the day, that of the limits of parliament's legislative power.[1] For *New Additions* not only promoted the cause of those specific reforms which St. German desired by statute, but also addressed itself by implication to the fundamental issue of statutory competence, the issue that alone blocked immediate action on the question of the divorce between 1530 and 1532. Before May 1532, all the schemes of Henry VIII's men were directed toward a divorce pronounced by an archbishop or committee of bishops and enforced throughout the realm by an act of parliament. The difficult question was: could parliament lawfully legislate in defiance of papal anathema and Roman custom? What were the boundaries of parliament's power? St. German formulated a succession of arguments in favor of the omnicompetence of parliamentary statute in *New Additions,* the most robust of which was that the king in parliament was "the hyghe soueraygne ouer the people / whiche hath not onely charge on the bodies, but also on the soules of his subiectes."[2] Despite Professor Elton's claims for the revolutionary mind and thought of Thomas Cromwell, it was Christopher St. German who, two years before the Act of Appeals and three before the Act of Supremacy, was the first Englishman to articulate the theory of

---

[1]Guy, *St. German,* pp. 21–24, 32–33.
[2]*Doctor and Student,* p. 327.

the sovereignty of the king in parliament—the theory that grounded the English Reformation and finally prevailed.[1]

Yet the most devastating aspect of St. German's work, from the point of view of the church in England, sprang from his parliamentary draft of 1531.[2] Two thirds of it concerned the reform of church and clergy; the remainder dealt with problems of social policy and poor relief. Specific provisions covered a wide variety of topics, but central to both parts of the document was a new governmental institution, a "great standing council" which was to be the main agency of the proposed reforms, exercising authority delegated to it by parliament from time to time. The precise membership of this council was not settled by St. German, a space being left for a full list of names at the appropriate point in the first article, but enough was said to verify that it was to consist of bishops, peers, and other members of parliament, both clerical and lay, together with other persons named by the king who were not already in parliament. As to the council's work, it was first to establish whether popular desire for an English translation of the New Testament sprang from "mekenes and charytye." If it did, the king would allow the council to "have suche parte therof translated in to the mother tonge as shall be thought convenyent by the seid councell."[3] The standing council was next to inquire into the spread of heresy, assuming responsibility for all initial investigations. It would reason with those persons detected or delated, assess the level of seriousness, and hand over only hard cases for trial by the bishops in the spiritual courts.[4] A third proposal began by observing that "many lawes, uses and custumes concernyng the spirituelte and the spirituell iurisdiccion have ben made and used in tyme paste by the spirituell power undre such parcyalytye and with so greate syngularitie to spirituell men that it hathe ben very grevouse to the people to susteyn theym." The great standing council was to review such matters in order to determine which aspects of clerical jurisdiction should be revoked or reformed. The council would scrutinize canon law and custom, reforming those

---

[1]See Elton, *Studies*, 2, 215–35.

[2]PRO, SP 6/7, pp. 55–74 (*LP* 5, 50), printed with commentary in Guy, *St. German*, pp. 127–35. This document was previously discussed by G. R. Elton, *Reform and Renewal: Thomas Cromwell and the Common Weal* (Cambridge, 1973), pp. 71–76 (hereafter cited as "Elton, *Reform and Renewal*"); Lehmberg, pp. 120–22; J. J. Scarisbrick, "Thomas More: The King's Good Servant," *Thought: Fordham University Quarterly*, 52 (1977), 249–68; J. A. Guy, "The Tudor Commonwealth: Revising Thomas Cromwell," *Historical Journal*, 23 (1980), 684–87 (hereafter cited as "Guy, 'The Tudor Commonwealth'").

[3]Guy, *St. German*, p. 26.

[4]Guy, *St. German*, p. 26.

om St. German's Parliamentary Draft: PRO SP6/7, art. 14, p. 61 (reduced).

disputed points deemed to be within parliament's jurisdiction, and reporting the rest to Henry VIII, who would then negotiate directly with his clergy.[1] After this followed draft legislation prohibiting the church courts from hearing pleas of dilapidations, and enabling the successors of wasteful clergy to recover damages in the courts of common law. This last aspect of St. German's first article did not relate directly to the functions of the new standing council, but was a further restriction of spiritual jurisdiction derived from the planned revision of canon law. It had already been proposed by the student of common law in chapter 6 of *New Additions*.[2]

The second article of St. German's parliamentary draft was exclusively concerned with the need to force slovenly or greedy clergy to fulfill their duties in the matters discussed in chapter 8 of *New Additions*. Every parish priest was to conduct a monthly *dirige* and requiem mass, offering prayers for the king and realm and for the living and the dead. All religious houses were to do likewise, praying especially for their founders, and no priest, secular or regular, was to accept payment for saying mass. In addition, parish priests were required to hold burial services for deceased parishioners and others without special payment and were to recite freely the names of the dead from the pulpit on Sundays for a year thereafter to encourage prayers for their souls.[3]

St. German's third article examined a mixture of matters, including those dealt with in chapters 2 and 3 of *New Additions*. First, there were to be no more grants in mortmain of land, tenements, rents, liberties, franchises, or other property except by the king, apart from grants of farms which might lawfully be held by religious houses in accordance with the act in restraint of clerical pluralities and farms passed in the first session of the Reformation Parliament.[4] Second, clergy who held appropriated benefices were to give a minimum of five percent of their incomes to charity, along the lines laid down by 15 Richard II, c. 6 (1391). Third, parish priests were never to deny the consecrated host to their parishioners on account of debts or personal disputes.[5]

St. German's fourth article barred the church courts from deciding cases concerning temporal goods or property in a manner contrary to that prescribed by common law and parliamentary statute. An impor-

---

[1]PRO, SP 6/7, p. 57.
[2]Guy, *St. German*, p. 27; *Doctor and Student*, pp. 324–25.
[3]Guy, *St. German*, p. 27; *Doctor and Student*, pp. 328–30.
[4]21 Henry VIII, c. 13.
[5]Cf. *Doctor and Student*, pp. 320–22.

tant sanction was added to the provision: if a spiritual judge ignored this new rule a party subject to him might obtain a prohibition out of Chancery, commanding the spiritual court not to proceed to judgment upon pain of treble damages to be paid to the party.[1] This remarkable clause was followed by nine detailed measures designed to ameliorate lay resentment against the clergy, the chosen proposals being selected from those canvassed in chapters 2, 9, 10, 11, and 13 of *New Additions*. For "encrease of love, amytie and good agrement betwene the spiritualltye and the temporaltie," both clergy and laity were ordered to stop defaming each other, and priests were to cease forming associations to maintain any worldly privilege, under penalty of punishment as conspirators.[2] Sermons were to be preached at shrines and centers of pilgrimage twice a year to explain the proper purpose of such places, and "tables" were to be set up to instruct literate pilgrims. Owners of shrines were not to divide the relics in their custody among several altars in order to attract multiple offerings. After proper investigation alleged miracles were to be approved by both the ecclesiastical authorities and the *custos rotulorum* of the shire (the latter a layman), and clergymen who had a pecuniary interest in the verification of alleged miracles were not officially to investigate them. Nobody having a share in the profits of a shrine or pilgrimage-center was to enjoy a monopoly of selling candles to pilgrims, nor was he to resell unused candles already purchased by previous visitors. Confessors were not to supplement their incomes by instructing penitents to visit holy places from which they derived a share of the profits, and no one with a pecuniary interest was to require donations to shrines or pilgrimages as a condition of leases or tenancy agreements. Clergymen appointed as visitors of churches or religious houses were forbidden to accept gifts or financial inducements at the time of their visitations. Children under the age of fourteen were not to be allowed to assume the habit and enter religious orders, as had already been provided by statute in 1402 (4 Henry IV, c. 17). Finally, nobody was to impugn parliament's right to govern by claiming that certain reforming acts had been made contrary to the liberty of the church or that their authors should stand in ecclesiastical censure. The controversial acts St. German had in mind were the act concerning tithe on timber called *silva cedua* (45 Edward III, c. 3),[3] the three anticlerical acts passed in 1529, "ne any statute made in this parliament."[4]

---

[1] Guy, *St. German*, p. 27.
[2] See note on 198/6–11.
[3] See note on 195/5–6.
[4] Guy, *St. German*, p. 28; *Doctor and Student*, pp. 320–21, 330–35, 338–40. The anticlerical acts of 1529 were 21 Henry VIII, cc. 5, 6, 13.

This section of the document ended with a list of additional points to be worked out at a later stage, such as "doles to be sent home to the people," "corpus presentes," and "prestes commyng to buryalles and monthes myndes."[1] Apparently St. German had not yet begun to plan the remedial legislation he desired on such minor topics. He had, however, spent considerable time and effort on his response to the fundamental questions of poor relief and social policy with which the remaining third of his parliamentary draft was concerned. In this final part of the document, St. German offered an astute diagnosis of the economic issues facing early Tudor society and proposed legislation for large-scale public welfare.[2]

St. German's first proposal for social reform aimed "to put away the greate multitude of vacaboundes" in England by instituting a centrally organized scheme to create jobs. The great standing council was to devise a national program of state works on the highways, raising the necessary finance partly by voluntary contributions and partly by levying a graduated income tax on all householders, clergymen, and provosts and masters of colleges within the realm. Common chests were to be established in every town, city, and county, with each chest under the management of three independent keyholders. Funds were to be provided for the relief of the impotent poor, in addition to money needed to finance road construction, while Henry VIII himself, we are told, had promised £3,000 in cash for the fund and offered half the income from penal statutes.[3] Two points are immediately obvious from this scheme. First, St. German preserved the usual medieval assumptions about the distinction between the impotent and the able-bodied poor, assumptions derived from the theological concepts of voluntary and involuntary poverty, which had been expounded in the fourteenth and fifteenth centuries from the pulpit and in the writings of such authors as William Langland and Henry Parker. From the concept of "voluntary" poverty came the harsh attitudes to unemployment characteristic of almost all European preindustrial communities. Thus St. German made it a felony wilfully to refuse the employment offered and to persist in vagrancy. Second, St. German sought to combine the authority of the great standing council with a state-controlled system of finance in order to introduce into England an up-to-date, lay-directed scheme for poor relief modeled on projects recently pi-

---

[1]Guy, *St. German*, p. 28.

[2]For a detailed discussion of such issues, see volume 4 of *The Agrarian History of England and Wales*, ed. Joan Thirsk (Cambridge, 1967–); Peter Ramsey, *Tudor Economic Problems* (London, 1968); John Pound, *Poverty and Vagrancy in Tudor England* (London, 1971); and W. G. Hoskins, *The Age of Plunder* (London, 1976).

[3]Guy, *St. German*, p. 29.

oneered in several leading continental cities in the aftermath of the famines of the 1520s. He thought that England should emulate those European cities, both catholic and protestant, which had already implemented poor-relief schemes, among them Mons, Ypres, Lyons, Venice, Wittenberg, Nürnberg and Strassburg.

The secularized reforms of these cities were much discussed throughout the 1520s and 1530s: the reforming ordinances of Nürnberg (1522), Ypres (1525), and Lyons (1531) were published in several editions and languages.[1] Such documents inspired intellectuals to promote and justify further reforms. The most prominent proponent was the Spanish catholic humanist Juan Luis Vives, whose *De subventione pauperum* (1526) was written for the city governors of Bruges.[2] Lay municipal officials, it was increasingly thought, had a fiduciary duty to combine classical models of public service with human intelligence in order to ameliorate the growing animosity between rich and poor, and the method of achieving this goal was to be civic welfare institutions. In fact, the diffusion of these ideas coincided with the spread of the Reformation, and violent controversy inevitably arose upon such questions as whether the creation of lay-controlled welfare institutions and the prohibition of begging and indiscriminate charity constituted heresy and Lutheranism. St. German steered clear of the pitfalls by providing for clerics as well as peers and other laymen on his great standing council, and by omitting any attempt to outlaw begging, as opposed to vagrancy.[3] Manifestly, however, his aim was to find the best way to translate the newly perceived responsibilities of European municipal officials into an English context, making his great standing council the central welfare arm of English royal government. In choosing the weapon of a parliamentary statute, he anticipated Thomas Cromwell, who later in the 1530s made acts of parliament the instruments of serious attempts at social reform and economic renewal.[4]

---

[1] See *Some Early Tracts on Poor Relief*, ed. F. R. Salter (London, 1926), hereafter cited as "Salter"; N. Z. Davis, "Poor Relief, Humanism and Heresy: The Case of Lyons," *Studies in Medieval and Renaissance History*, 5 (1968), 217–75; H. J. Grimm, "Luther's Contributions to Sixteenth-Century Organization of Poor Relief," *Archiv für Reformationsgeschichte*, 61 (1970), 222–34; R. M. Kingdon, "Social Welfare in Calvin's Geneva," *American Historical Review*, 76 (1971), 50–69; Brian S. Pullan, *Rich and Poor in Renaissance Venice* (Oxford, 1971), pp. 239–91; P. A. Fideler, *Discussions of Poverty in Sixteenth-Century England*, Ph.D. dissertation, Brandeis University, University Microfilms (Ann Arbor, 1971); H. Heller, "Famine, Revolt and Heresy at Meaux, 1521–1525," *Archiv für Reformationsgeschichte*, 68 (1977), 133–56.

[2] Salter, pp. 1–31. In England Vives lived for a while with More. Wolsey appointed him to his newly founded lectureship in rhetoric at Oxford.

[3] Guy, *St. German*, p. 29.

[4] Elton, *Reform and Renewal*, pp. 66–97; Elton, *Studies*, 2, 137–54.

In 1531 St. German was an independent scholar who took a keen interest in the cause of ecclesiastical and social reform but who remained doctrinally orthodox. His expertise in jurisprudence and practical law was used by the official party at a time when it was especially interested in such matters. In 1532 Cromwell assumed command of Henry VIII's policy, following the Submission of the Clergy and More's resignation as lord chancellor.[1] One of Cromwell's staff recorded in March 1533 that he had received 13s. 4d. from St. German, presumably as rent for the parsonage of Marylebone, Middlesex.[2] Both Christopher St. German and John Blennerhasset made bequests to Marylebone church in their wills, thus establishing a clear connection between this rent and the author of *Doctor and Student*, but the significance of St. German's payment is that Marylebone parsonage was part of the former possessions of the monastery of St. Laurence, Blackmore (in Essex), dissolved by Wolsey to help endow his college at Ipswich and seized by the Crown in 1529.[3] It is highly probable that St. German was granted this property after its reversion to the Crown; this grant looks very much like a reward for his work on *New Additions* and his parliamentary draft.

Nevertheless, such a reward should almost certainly be viewed as reimbursement for St. German's services in 1531, rather than as a retaining fee to assure the official party of his assistance on future occasions. St. German received no more grants from the Crown, nor did he accept any form of patronage that would have compromised his intellectual freedom and independence from the immediate aims of officialdom during the ensuing Reformation. It is indeed explicitly clear that St. German valued his independence, because in July 1534 he declined to cooperate with Henry VIII's circle of propagandists assembled at Blackfriars, London, when they requested his help. Thomas Thirleby, John Olyver, Edward Carne, and others had met "sundry times" at Blackfriars to discuss matters laid before them by Cromwell but could not "set them forth" without the aid of men learned in the laws of God and of the realm. They informed Cromwell on July 25: "And where we welhopyd to have hadde the assystence and helpe of Master Sayntegerman, he divers tymes spoken unto hathe made answer that he trustyth to be excusyd by your mastershippe in that behalfe, for such consyderacions as he hathe signyfied unto you."[4] Whatever St. German's role may have been in the official propaganda

---

[1]Guy, *Public Career*, chap. 9.

[2]*LP 6*, no. 228 (1).

[3]*LP 4*, nos. 1137 (3), 1833, 1964, 2024 (5), 3537 (1, 4), 3538 (2, 3), 4229 (1, 9), 4473, 5076, 5286, 5304–05.

[4]PRO, SP 1/85, fol. 86 (*LP 7*, no. 1008).

campaign of the early 1530s, it is plain that he would not serve in July 1534, that he himself had told Cromwell the reasons why, and that Cromwell had not dissented.

During the summer of 1534, great unrest was caused by two statutes which had been passed in the fifth session of the Reformation Parliament: the act to reduce Catherine of Aragon to the status of princess dowager and the First Act of Succession.[1] The ecclesiastical implications of these acts were that Cranmer's verdict on the divorce was to be accepted and papal jurisdiction in England denied, and it was partly on the question of the meaning of the preamble to the Act of Succession that More and Fisher were prepared to go to the Tower.[2] The acts had not "made" the divorce, but were designed to enforce Cranmer's verdict and to ensure the succession of the offspring of Anne Boleyn; nevertheless, the preamble to the Act of Succession denounced papal action in the matter of Henry VIII's first marriage as a usurpation of God's law. St. German's reticence in the aftermath of these acts was that of a man anxious to see how the repudiation of papal authority, with its implied doctrine of royal supremacy, would be publicly proclaimed, before he was prepared to lend his pen in unqualified support of the regime. To step into the debates before the theory of royal supremacy had been fully worked out and asserted would have been to repeat More's own error when he accepted the chancellorship.

In any case, St. German's activity between publication of *New Additions* (1531) and 1534 already centered on his controversy with More, which produced in quick succession St. German's *Treatise concerning the Division between the Spiritualty and Temporalty* (1532), More's *Apology* (1533), St. German's *Salem and Bizance* (1533), and More's *Debellation of Salem and Bizance* (1533).

---

[1] 25 Henry VIII, cc. 22, 28. See Lehmberg, pp. 196–200.
[2] See note on 80/6.

THE LEGAL CONTEXT OF THE CONTROVERSY:
THE LAW OF HERESY

More's *Debellation of Salem and Bizance* is his most legal, technical, and intricate book. At times it becomes incomprehensible or unpalatable unless the reader acknowledges the seriousness of the attack upon the traditional law of heresy that More recognized in *Salem and Bizance*. Yet St. German's attack was itself a reflection of ideas that had been mooted among common lawyers and in the House of Commons since 1529. Hence it will be helpful to outline the initial rise of Roman-canonical inquisitorial procedure in heresy cases; the English heresy statutes of 1382, 1401, and 1414; and the attacks upon these laws and procedures in England between 1529 and 1534.

The early history of the repression of heresy was essentially that of the rise of the Inquisition.[1] Catharism and the birth of new evangelical groups such as the Humiliati and Waldensians prompted the papacy to create centralized procedures of investigation and accusation in the late twelfth and early thirteenth centuries. At the Council of Verona in 1184, Lucius III in the presence of Frederick Barbarossa issued the decree *Ad abolendam,* which provided that archbishops, bishops, or their representatives were to examine reliable witnesses on oath in their provinces or dioceses once or twice a year in order to detect suspected heretics or conventicles.[2] Anyone refusing to swear was to be

---

[1]I have drawn upon the following studies: H. C. Lea, *A History of the Inquisition of the Middle Ages* (New York, 1888); Augustin Fliche, Christine Thouzellier, and Yvonne Azais, *La Chrétienté romaine, 1198–1274,* Histoire de L'Eglise depuis les origines jusqu'à nos jours, 10 (Paris, 1950; hereafter cited as "Fliche"); A. G. Dickens, *Lollards and Protestants in the Diocese of York, 1509–1558* (Oxford, 1959); Gordon Leff, *Heresy in the Later Middle Ages,* 2 vols. (Manchester, 1967; hereafter cited as "Leff"); Frederick Pollock and F. W. Maitland, *The History of English Law before the Time of Edward I,* rev. S. F. C. Milsom, 2 vols. (Cambridge, 1968; hereafter cited as "Pollock and Maitland"); *The Concept of Heresy in the Middle Ages,* ed. Willem Lourdaux and D. Verhelst (Louvain, 1976); M. D. Lambert, *Medieval Heresy: Popular Movements from Bogomil to Hus* (London, 1977; hereafter cited as "Lambert"); *Heresy Trials in the Diocese of Norwich, 1428–31,* ed. Norman P. Tanner, Camden Society, 4th Series (London, 1977; hereafter cited as "Tanner"); Ralph A. Houlbrooke, *Church Courts and the People during the English Reformation, 1520–1570* (Oxford, 1979; hereafter cited as "Houlbrooke").

[2]Lambert, pp. 71–73, 76–78, 84–85, 101, 104; Leff, *1,* 37–41. See notes on 110/32–33 and 113/34–36 and Appendix B, 356/24–25, below. See also *CW 9,* 131/31, Commentary at 130/14–15, and 189–90.

deemed a heretic himself, and accused persons might be cited on suspicion only. If the accused would not confess or could not be proved guilty, he was not necessarily to be absolved. He could be required to purge himself by swearing under oath that he was not guilty and by supporting his oath with those of other credible persons willing to swear that they believed him to be speaking the truth. Those found guilty were to be excommunicated and handed over to the secular authorities for punishment.

None of these regulations was new in itself, but *Ad abolendam* fused existing elements into standardized procedure. The clergy henceforward "were systematically to act as inquisitors."[1] In 1199 Innocent III confirmed *Ad abolendam* in his bull *Vergentis in senium* and assimilated heresy to the crime in Roman law of *lèse majesté*, with the concomitant penalty of the confiscation of goods.[2] The Fourth Lateran Council then reaffirmed both bulls.[3] Yet centralized heresy investigations under Innocent were galvanized less by legislation than by case law and by his practice of appointing papal legates with overriding powers. These legates could even depose negligent bishops, as they did in Languedoc.[4]

Pope Honorius III renewed the attack on Catharism, but the significant legislation during his pontificate was that of Emperor Frederick II, who agreed to assist the spiritual arm by burning heretics, partly as a quid pro quo for his coronation by the pope. In fact, capital punishment for convicted heretics can be traced back to the persecution of the Manichaeans.[5] The early Christian emperors had inflicted the death penalty for this heresy and for teaching heretical doctrines or attending conventicles. When cases of heresy burgeoned in France, Italy, and the Low Countries in the early eleventh century, study of the Code of Justinian invited renewed persecution.[6] Heretics were put to death at Toulouse (c. 1022) and Orléans (1022).[7] Since the Council of Verona had not specified the punishment to be exacted by the lay power, exile, infamy, fines, and imprisonment were variously applied. In 1197, however, Peter II, king of Aragon, decreed of heretics "corpora eorum ignibus crementur."[8] In 1220 Frederick II endorsed the Lateran can-

---

[1]Leff, *1*, 37.
[2]Leff, *1*, 38.
[3]Leff, *1*, 41. See 114/1–16 and note, below. See also *CW 9*, Commentary at 130/14–15 and 131/32.
[4]Lambert, p. 101.
[5]Pollock and Maitland, 2, 544–45.
[6]Pollock and Maitland, 2, 545.
[7]Lambert, pp. 24–29.
[8]Fliche, p. 302.

ons, and in 1224 he ordained that convicted heretics throughout Lombardy be punished by death or by excision of their "blasphemous" tongues.[1]

The legislative arsenal of the Inquisition was strengthened by Gregory IX, who in January 1231 commanded that Frederick's Lombard constitution be entered in the papal register. The next month Gregory issued a codifying constitution of his own entitled *Excommunicamus et anathematisamus*.[2] The penalty for convicted heretics surrendered to the lay power after condemnation in the church courts was now implicitly that of burning, and "impenitent" suspects who refused to confess and be absolved were liable to perpetual imprisonment—the so-called wall (*murus*).[3] Sentences of excommunication were reiterated against the Cathars, Patarines, Poor Men of Lyons, and Speronists, their supporters and abettors, and those who communicated with them or failed to denounce them. Suspects who did not satisfactorily purge themselves within a year of accusation were to be punished as heretics. Those convicted of heresy, if they abjured, were still deprived of their legal rights and excluded from public office. All discussions, public or private, between laymen on points of catholic doctrine were forbidden. Christian burial was denied to convicted heretics. The descendants of heretics or their accomplices down to the second generation were excluded from ecclesiastical office. Finally, accused persons in heresy trials were denied advice or legal representation, and no appeals were to be allowed.[4]

Yet legislation is effective only when it is enforced. Gregory IX's use of special legates or inquisitors equipped with plenary powers to detect and condemn heretics in specific regions marked the true origins of the Inquisition on the continent. Since England produced no significant heresy before Lollardy, it did not immediately need a centralized inquisition, and the procedures of denunciation, investigation, and trial as laid down by canon law remained in the hands of the English bishops. But requirements of episcopal inquiry by the oaths of local witnesses were tightened by the Councils of Narbonne (1227) and Toulouse (1229). Inquiries (and trials) could be conducted in secret; in England the bishop was sole judge of the accused's case, legates being relatively rare. When the fifteenth-century English canonist, William Lyndewode, doctor of both civil and canon law, dean of the arches, and

---

[1]Fliche, pp. 300–02. Leff *1*, 41–42.
[2]Fliche, p. 309. Leff, *1*, 42. See 117/19, note on 113/34–36, and Appendix B, 357/6–7, below. See also *CW 9*, Commentary at 130/14–15.
[3]Leff, *1*, 42.
[4]Fliche, pp. 309–10.

compiler of the standard *Provinciale* (completed in 1430), glossed the 1409 constitutions of Archbishop Arundel against the Lollards, he wrote that only the bishop of the area or a specially delegated papal inquisitor had jurisdiction over heresy, though he added that the ordinary could delegate the power to initiate heresy trials (for instance, to his chancellor or commissary), but that he alone should give sentence.[1] Under Innocent IV, the Councils of Narbonne (1244), Béziers (1246), Valence (1248), and Albi (1254) reinforced earlier antiheretical legislation, and the pope's bull *Ad extirpanda* (1252) combined existing machinery with new inquisitorial techniques—for instance, torture might be used on the accused. A half-century later, when the papacy had settled at Avignon, Clement V's decree *Multorum querela* empowered the bishops, acting together with papal inquisitors, to arrest and imprison persons upon suspicion of heresy without formal denunciations by witnesses.[2] *Multorum querela* was validated at the Council of Vienne in 1312, the assembly which suppressed the Templars on flimsy grounds of heresy. Its effect was to make inquisitors both prosecutors and judges.

Ecclesiastical legislation against heretics contradicted evolving principles of common law in England. For in *ex officio* proceedings in church courts summonses might be issued on the basis of accusations by unnamed persons, the presiding official acted ..s both accuser and judge, the accused was bound under oath to answer the charges, and conviction did not necessarily require the accused's confession but resulted from the judge's assessment of the evidence. Moreover, in heresy cases accusers or witnesses could include other heretics or suspects, their names could be withheld if they feared recrimination, and summary procedure could be used.[3] But for the moment there was no clash of systems, precisely because England knew little heresy before Wycliffe.[4] In fact, canon law and Roman-canonical procedures were widely received there. Instance and *ex officio* procedures, purgation, proof by sworn witnesses, and the oaths of calumny or of speaking the truth (*de calumnia seu de veritate dicenda*) were all operative in the English

---

[1] William Lyndewode, *Provinciale seu Constitutiones Angliae* (Oxford, 1679), pp. 296, 304; Henry Ansgar Kelly, "English Kings and the Fear of Sorcery," *Mediaeval Studies, 39* (1977), 210–11. I am grateful to Professor Kelly for these references.

[2] Fliche, pp. 334–40. Leff, *1*, 41–45. See note on 168/28 and Appendix B, 365/18. See also *CW 9*, Commentary at 151/18.

[3] Kelly, "English Kings and the Fear of Sorcery," pp. 211–13, 231. I know of no examples of torture in English heresy cases after 1350, but for apparent torture in two earlier cases of heretical sorcery (one in Ireland), see Kelly, p. 213, n. 20.

[4] Lambert, p. 217.

ecclesiastical courts by the end of the thirteenth century, though to differing degrees.[1] For example, the oaths of calumny and speaking the truth were included in the provincial constitutions of the legate Otto (1237).[2] On the other hand, summary procedure in *ex officio* cases could not have appeared on any scale until it was first authorized in heresy proceedings to all bishops by Boniface VIII and in cases of benefices, tithes, matrimony, and usury by Clement V.[3] Lyndewode wrote that the death penalty for obstinate and relapsed heretics applied in England because Frederick II's constitution had been sanctioned by papal decretals.[4] Yet absence of English lay enactments on the topic meant that Lyndewode was predictably hazy about the source of the secular arm's duty to burn—that is, before 2 Henry IV, c. 15, the statute *De heretico comburendo* (1401).[5]

In fact, few heretics had been burned in England before 1401. An Albigensian was "concrematus" at London as early as 1210; in 1222 an apostate deacon who had turned Jew for the love of a Jewish woman was degraded at a provincial council at Oxford and delivered to the sheriff, who burnt him.[6] Otherwise, the only reported English case was that of William Sawtry, a Norfolk Lollard burnt shortly before *De heretico comburendo* was passed. Sawtry was surrendered in 1401 to the secular arm upon a writ *de heretico comburendo* that itself anticipated the statute then in the process of enactment, a circumstance which vexed scholars by becoming the basis for an erroneous opinion that the writ existed at common law.[7]

Yet it was the lack of English precedent for the doctrinal definition of heresy that was most remarkable in 1401, though Lyndewode pro-

---

[1] *Select Cases from the Ecclesiastical Courts of the Province of Canterbury, c. 1200–1301*, ed. Norma Adams and Charles Donahue, Selden Society Publications, vol. 95 (London, 1981), introduction, pp. 37–103 (hereafter cited as "*Select Cases*"). For an explanation of these legal procedures, see notes on 60/29–30 and 86/3–4, below.

[2] *Select Cases*, pp. 43–44.

[3] Kelly, "English Kings and the Fear of Sorcery," p. 18, n. 18; Pollock and Maitland, 2, 550–55.

[4] *Provinciale*, p. 293; Pollock and Maitland, 2, 546.

[5] Reprinted in *CW* 9, 251–57.

[6] Pollock and Maitland, 2, 548–51.

[7] Pollock and Maitland 2, 551–52. See also John Foxe, *Acts and Monuments*, ed. George Townsend and Stephen R. Cattley, 8 vols. (London, 1837–41), *3*, 221–34. Before and after 1401, burning was the penalty for women convicted of high treason and (sometimes) felony. The legal textbooks *Fleta* and *Britton* and the unreliable *Mirror of Justices* specified burning as a punishment for heresy and sorcery, but their views represented speculation by lawyers as to what ought to be done if heretics were to appear. See Pollock and Maitland, 2, 549; Kelly, "English Kings and the Fear of Sorcery," p. 214.

vided a storehouse of relevant material in books 1 and 5 of *Provinciale*. An act of 1382 against Lollardy (5 Richard II, st. 2, c. 5) condemned "Sermons containing Heresies and notorious Errors" and commanded sheriffs and others to assist the bishops by arresting and imprisoning suspects to be tried in the ecclesiastical courts—the context was the Peasants' Revolt in the previous year.[1] Nothing was said, however, about the theological content of heretical preaching. In 1401, the act *De heretico comburendo* condemned "divers false and perverse People of a certain New Sect" who taught "privily divers new Doctrines"—that is, Lollardy. Unlicensed preaching or writing of books contrary to catholic doctrine, unofficial public instruction, conventicles, or other heterodox activities were prohibited. Books or writings possessed by Lollards or their supporters were to be handed in to diocesan bishops within forty days after the statute was proclaimed; those disobeying the act were to be arrested on suspicion and detained until they had purged themselves of erroneous opinions or had abjured and performed penance. Convicted offenders were to be punished at the discretion of the ecclesiastical authorities by imprisonment or fine, while relapsed heretics and those refusing to abjure their opinions were to be surrendered to the secular arm to be burnt—"that such Punishment may strike in Fear to the Minds of other, whereby no such wicked Doctrine and heretical and erroneous Opinions, nor their Authors and Fautors in the said Realm and Dominions against the Catholic Faith . . . be sustained or in any wise suffered."[2]

It was thus the act of 1401 that directly authorized the burning of heretics in England, while leaving the Roman-canonical procedures of accusation and doctrinal definition of heresy unglossed. The next step was taken in 1414, when the revolt of Sir John Oldcastle led to supplementary legislation and also forged the link in England between heresy, sedition, and treason.[3] The new act (2 Henry V, st. 1, c. 7) required a wide range of secular officers and judges, sheriffs, justices of the peace, and other local and municipal officials to assist the bishops in the task of investigating and suppressing heresy. Their oaths of office were permanently amended to incorporate their newly defined duty "to put out . . . all Manner of Heresies and Errors, commonly called Lollardries, within the Places where they exercise their Offices and Occupations from Time to Time, with all their Power; and that they assist the Ordinaries and their Commissaries, and them favour and maintain, as

---

[1] Reprinted in *CW* 9, 249–51.
[2] See *CW* 9, 251–57.
[3] Reprinted in *CW* 9, 257–60. See notes on 104/35–105/1 and 110/14–18, below.

often as they or any of them shall be required by the same Ordinaries or their Commissaries."[1] The act then declared that the lands, tenements, goods, and chattels of convicted heretics should be forfeit as in cases of attainder or felony, save that no one should lose his lands before he was dead. Finally, justices of King's Bench, of assize, and of the peace were empowered to inquire into heresy by the secular procedures of presentment and indictment in the interests of coordinated investigation, and those indicted were to be arrested and delivered to the bishops or their commissaries for trial in the ecclesiastical courts within ten days after their arrest.[2]

In conjunction with the Roman canons already discussed, the acts of 1382, 1401, and 1414 constituted the law of heresy in fifteenth- and early sixteenth-century England. Yet the medieval canon law was not regarded as absolutely binding statute law. Considerable latitude existed for local custom and variant interpretations within the law, and an English variant in cases of suspected heresy was presented by Lyndewode—one of considerable importance, since More apparently followed it in the *Debellation*. In his *Provinciale*, Lyndewode interpreted the decree *Ad abolendam* to mean that the bishop could inflict "penitential pains" (*poenae poenitentiales*) on suspects by way of purgation.[3] When those remarkably suspect for heresy would not confess and could not be proved guilty, they were not necessarily to be absolved, since the bishop had discretion to order purgation. But according to Lyndewode this "purgation" (*purgatio*) could take the form of *poenae*; suitable acts of penance mentioned by him included abjuration of heresy, confinement in a monastery, building a church or hospital, performing deeds of piety, and so on. Also the bishop was to impose a form of *poenae* appropriate to the suspect's rank and position.[4] In More's words:

> And therfore those wise men that made ye law, left ye thyng in thordinarys discrecion to assigne hym that is proued suspect of heresy, such kynde of purgacyon as the cyrcumstaunces of the person, and the peple and the tyme shall most requyre.
>
> And therfore wyll thordynary to some man so suspecte, somtyme assygne hym . . . that he shall openly confesse y^t those heresyes that the people toke hym to mene, be very false heresyes

---

[1]*CW 9*, 258.

[2]See *CW 9*, 258–60. See also notes on 185/7–8, 185/29–186/4 and 217/29–31, below.

[3]*Provinciale*, p. 290 (gl. v. *Purgaverit*), a reference kindly supplied by Professor H. A. Kelly. See notes on 110/32–33, 116/3–4, 116/32–117/1.

[4]*Provinciale*, p. 290. See note on 116/3–4.

indede / and openly shall deteste them and swere that he so byleueth them to be / and swere that he neither ment to teche theym,
nor neuer was mynded y^t any man shold take hym so, nor neuer
wold afterward teche nor hold heresies, but abiure them for euer.
   And yet for the ferther purgacyon of such suspicion, the ordynary myght also enioyne hym some certayn thynges to do, suche as
maye declare the more clereli, y^t he is not of such mind / as open
prechyng agaynste the selfe same heresyes, & the doynge of some
suche thynges as those heresyes dyd stande agaynste (116/1–19).

Although it is not established by this passage alone that More followed Lyndewode in assimilating *purgatio* to *poenae poenitentiales,* later
comments by More establish that his words "certayn thynges to do"
could amount to *poenae,* and that "abiure" in the sense More uses it in
the quoted passage was probably equivalent to "recant." First, he admitted that the person required to abjure because he was vehemently
suspected but not actually convicted was "in parell to fall into the fyre"
if "he fall after into heresye" (116/33–117/1). According to Lyndewode, the term "vehemently suspected" refers to the case of the suspect who had knowingly visited heretics, or given them alms, or received their books, or defended their persons, but who could not
formally be convicted of heresy. In such a case, however, *demonstrationes leves* ("light proofs") sufficed to justify abjuration (and, in Lyndewode's opinion, penitential pains).[1] Yet burning was never automatic
for a first-time offender in heresy, so that, if More's abjured suspect
was liable to suffer burning the next time he fell into heresy, it appears
that his abjuration as a vehement suspect was counted as the first
conviction, in which case it was closer to recantation than purgation.
   Secondly, More in a later passage repeated that the person proved a
vehement suspect (which implies *demonstrationes leves* but cannot mean
formal conviction) could be compelled to "abiure," admittedly "rather
to purge hym of the suspycyon"—here he made that clear (127/22–
26). But he also commented: "And than for vsyng hym self in such
wyse before [that is, so behaving that he became a vehement suspect]:
though he do penaunce he hath but right" (127/28–29). And he added: "But in all those other cases of suspicion purged, he [the Pacifier]
saith vntrew / for they do no penaunce at all" (127/30–31). These
remarks, however, confirm that More did mean that a vehement suspect might be required to perform penance in the case previously in

---

[1]See note on 116/32–117/1.

question. Moreover, this case of persons remarkably suspect but not formally convicted was the one St. German and More had chiefly been addressing. So to say "though he do penaunce he hath but right" implies that More was all along using the word "abiure" in a penal or quasi-penal sense, and that "certayn thynges to do" might include things other than those he mentioned in the first passage cited. Although More does not refer to Lyndewode by name, he must surely have known his *Provinciale*: the 1483 Oxford edition[1] contained all the relevant glosses, as did the continental editions of 1501, 1505, and 1525.[2] Also More alluded to "such doctours as wryte vpon ye lawes" (114/12–13), though it is not clear which commentaries he had in mind.

Interpretation of *purgatio* to mean *poenae* is, however, striking. For it could be considered a denial of due process of law if, by way of *canonical* purgation, a suspect who could not be proved guilty had first to swear not that he was innocent of heresy but that he renounced the heretical doctrines of which he was accused, and next, at the bishop's discretion, to perform penance.[3] Indeed according to Lyndewode and More, the canon law permitted persons accused of heresy to be put to purgation and penance on suspicion alone, without the clear proof necessary to obtain a conviction in a church court, without the naming of accusers, and without the appearance of witnesses at a public trial if they had reason to fear recrimination. And St. German made much of this, since the literal sense of the canon *Ad abolendam* was that suspects required by the bishop to clear themselves by swearing the oath of innocence (with or without oath helpers) should do so, or otherwise be punished as heretics. In fact, the canon said nothing about purgation through *poenae*.[4]

Historians have not yet established whether acts of penance were frequently assigned to English suspects who could not be convicted of heresy in the church courts. But that the heresy law was enforced in the century before the Reformation is evident from the records of heresy trials in the ecclesiastical courts between 1423 and 1522. We have evidence of 544 trials in this period and know that these resulted in 375 abjurations, 19 canonical purgations, and 29 (possibly 34) burnings. The trials and their outcome are summarized in the following table.[5]

---

[1]*STC*[2] 17102.

[2]*STC*[2] 17107, 17109, 17111.

[3]I am grateful to Professor Kelly for this point.

[4]See notes on 47/14–16, 110/32–33, 111/34–112/2.

[5]I compiled the table from the following sources, omitting duplicate entries: Lambert, pp. 366–70; J. A. F. Thomson, *The Later Lollards, 1414–1520* (Oxford, 1965), pp. 237–38

Heresy trials recorded in England, 1423–1522

Years	Number of trials	Known burnings	Known abjurations	Known purgations
1423–32	81	3	40	14
1433–42	20	[5][1]	—	—
1443–52	9	—	—	—
1453–62	13	—	—	—
1463–72	51	1	27	5
1473–82	14	1	—	—
1483–92	25	—	21	—
1493–1502	58	—	46	—
1503–12	184	11	167	—
1513–22	89	13	74	—

Of course, these figures are minima; the records of the ecclesiastical courts before the Reformation are generally quite defective. But the table makes it sufficiently clear that heresy was not a serious threat to the English church in the period before 1522, that its impact was probably localized, and that heretics constituted but a small fraction of the population as a whole.

Naturally the advent of protestantism in the 1520s disturbed familiar English patterns. By 1529 Lutheran or Lollard sympathizers had been detected in the universities, in the City of London, at the Inns of Court, and even at Henry VIII's royal court in the person of Anne Boleyn.[2] Politics—in particular those of the king's suit for annulment

---

(hereafter cited as "Thomson"); John Fines, "Heresy Trials in the Diocese of Coventry and Lichfield, 1511–12," *Journal of Ecclesiastical History, 14* (1963), 160–74; Tanner, pp. 1–216; and Margaret Bowker, *The Henrician Reformation: The Diocese of Lincoln under John Longland, 1521–1547* (Cambridge, 1981), pp. 57–64.

[1] The executions in 1438 may have been for treason rather than for heresy; see *The Brut or the Chronicles of England*, ed. Friedrich W. D. Brie, 2 vols., Early English Text Society, Original Series nos. 131 and 136 (Oxford, 1906–08), 2, 472.

[2] R. M. Fisher, "Reform, Repression, and Unrest at the Inns of Court, 1518–1558," *Historical Journal, 20* (1977), 783–801; S. E. Brigden, "The Early Reformation in London, 1520–47: The Conflict in the Parishes," Ph.D. dissertation, University of Cambridge, 1979; Guy, *Public Career*, pp. 106–12; E. E. Lowinsky, "A Music Book for Anne Boleyn," in *Florilegium Historiale; Essays Presented to Wallace K. Ferguson*, ed. J. G. Rowe and W. H. Stockdale (Toronto, 1971). Anne Boleyn's religious sympathies are documented by her illuminated psalter, lot 62 at Sotheby's London sale on December 7, 1982; the present location of the psalter is unknown. She may also have owned a copy of Tyndale's translation of the New Testament; see *"The King's Good Servant": Sir Thomas More 1477/8–1535*, compiled by J. B. Trapp and Hubertus Schulte Herbrüggen (London, 1977), pp. 74–75, no. 143, and Maria Dowling, "Anne Boleyn and Reform," *Journal of Ecclesiastical History, 35* (1984), 30–46. See also Eric Ives, *Anne Boleyn* (Oxford, 1986).

of his marriage to Catherine of Aragon—precluded comprehensive counterattack, although Henry VIII himself abominated doctrinal error: throughout his reign he continued to burn those who denied the real presence in the eucharist. Opponents of the royal supremacy were executed after 1534 not for heresy but for treason.[1] English Lutherans, however, remained exceptionally few, and there is no reason to suppose that protestantism would have advanced in Henry VIII's England had it not been for Thomas Cromwell's work as vicegerent in spirituals after 1535.[2] Even Tyndale's first edition of the New Testament (1525) seems to have failed.[3] Yet this view would seemingly make the controversy between St. German and More virtually inexplicable, were it not for the fierce juristic battles between church and state raging within the contemporary legal profession and in the first five sessions of the Reformation Parliament upon the issue of the procedures adopted by the ecclesiastical courts in detecting heretics and conducting heresy trials.[4]

Edward Hall, author of *The Union of the two noble and illustrate famelies of Lancastre and Yorke* and a common lawyer of Gray's Inn, wrote of the beginning of the third session of the Reformation Parliament (1532):

> After Christmas the .xv. daye of Ianuary the Parliament began to sytte & amongest dyuers griefes whych the Commons were greued with, they sore complayned of the crueltie of the Ordinaries, for callyng men before theym *Ex officio:* that is, by reason of ther office: For the Ordinaries woulde sende for men and ley Accusacions to them of Heresye, and say they were accused, and ley Articles to them, but no Accuser should be brought furth, whiche to the Commons was very dredefull and greuous: for the partie so Assited must either Abjure or be burned, for Purgacion he myght make none.[5]

---

[1]G. R. Elton, *Reform and Reformation: England 1509–1558* (London, 1977), pp. 260–83.

[2]There is, however, some evidence of native evangelical protestantism at grassroots level in southeast England; see John F. Davis, *Heresy and Reformation in the South-East of England, 1520–1529* (London, 1983), pp. 1–6, 41–65. Cromwell's work as vicegerent still needs more study, but see A. G. Dickens, *Thomas Cromwell and the English Reformation* (London, 1959), and Guy, *St. German*, pp. 46–47; 52–53. See also pp. 397–98, below.

[3]That is certainly the implication of the story told by Edward Hall in *Chronicle*, ed. Henry Ellis (London, 1809), pp. 762–63; hereafter cited as "Hall, *Chronicle*."

[4]*Spelman's Reports*, 2, introduction, pp. 64–66; Richard J. Schoeck, "Common Law and Canon Law in the Writings of Thomas More: The Affair of Richard Hunne," *Monumenta Iuris Canonici*, Series C, Subsidia, 4 (1971), 237–54; R. L. Storey, *Diocesan Administration in Fifteenth-Century England*, 2nd ed., Borthwick Institute (York, 1972), pp. 22–33.

[5]Hall, *Chronicle*, p. 784.

In other words, *ex officio* procedure, which critics considered to be biased in favor of the clergy, was a key issue in the juristic dispute between church and state that came to focus on heresy trials.

Since Hall was a member of parliament for Wenlock, Shropshire, he was in a position to give a true account of the critics' case in the House of Commons. Hall's version of the Commons' first complaint was that under canon law accusers in heresy trials need not be named or produced in court. Their second complaint is capable of two readings. Either Lyndewode's interpretation of "purgation" to mean *poenae* (that is, abjuration of heresy) was being applied by the bishops against suspects, so that innocent persons suspected of heresy might in practice have to abjure opinions they had never actually espoused or be burned as obstinate heretics, or else the procedure of *canonical* purgation in heresy cases (that is, purgation by swearing the "oath of innocence" with or without "oath helpers") had fallen into disuse. The table on page lvi shows that more burnings and abjurations had indeed taken place since 1503 than before, whereas successful purgation was a rarity after 1472.[1]

The gravamina of the House of Commons against the clergy and church courts were brilliantly exploited by Thomas Cromwell to win his battle for control of Henry VIII's policy in the spring of 1532.[2] Yet a private but vigorous campaign had been under way since 1529 to revise the law of heresy. In 1529 a draft bill was prepared in a legal hand which tradition, doubtless inaccurately, has associated with John Rastell.[3] The bill aimed to restrain the bishops or their commissaries

---

[1]Philip Hughes (*The Reformation in England*, 3 vols., London, 1950–54, *1*, 131) analyzes heresy cases between 1527 and 1532, based on Foxe's purported account of the registers of Bishops Tunstall and Stokesley. He writes: "218 heretics abjured their errors upon conviction in the bishop's court. . . . About a half of the total number of 218 came from places outside London, from towns in close commercial relation with one another." Among these towns were Colchester (20 heretics), Steeple Bumpstead (40 heretics), Birdbrook (44), Halstead (1), Clare (3), and Bury St. Edmunds (2). Between 1527 and 1533 there were eleven burnings: five in London and one each in Maidstone (1530), Exeter (1531), Norwich (1531), Devizes (1532), Bradford, Wilts. (1532), and Chesham (1532). S. E. Brigden, who attempts to verify Foxe, concludes that about 70 people were troubled for heresy in London between 1518 and 1529, but of these only two were burned ("The Early Reformation in London, 1520–47: The Conflict in the Parishes," Ph.D. dissertation, University of Cambridge, 1979, pp. 110–11).

[2]Guy, *Public Career*, pp. 186–201; Elton, *Studies*, *2*, 107–36; J. P. Cooper, "The Supplication against the Ordinaries Reconsidered," *English Historical Review*, 72 (1957), 616–41; M. Kelly, "The Submission of the Clergy," *Transactions of the Royal Historical Society*, 5th Series, *15* (1965), 97–119; Lehmberg, pp. 138–42, 145–53; J. J. Scarisbrick, *Henry VIII* (London, 1968), pp. 297–300.

[3]PRO, SP 2/N, fols. 20–22 (*LP 6*, no. 120 [2]). This draft is briefly discussed by Lehmberg, p. 84, and by Elton, *Studies*, *2*, 68.

from citing or arresting suspects for heresy unless they were free from private grudges, unless there were at least two credible witnesses, unless the accused was handed a "libel" stating the exact charge against him in writing together with the names of his accusers, and unless he was assigned legal counsel for his defense "if it be required." Next, to avoid delays, heresy trials were to be completed within three months of the suspect's arrest. The bishop or his commissary was to allow arrested suspects bail prior to their appearance in the ecclesiastical court, such bail to be upon the surety of not more than two persons in reasonable sums of money. However, the most striking section of this draft bill was its final one. In cases of relapsed heresy, the ecclesiastical authorities were to certify the local justices of the peace.

> yᵉ wholle matter with yᵉ certificate therof under their seale of office, that lyke proces and lawe be used against yᵉ said person or persons as befor this tyme hathe bene used against any person or persons endytid of felony, and that yᵉ certificat of yᵉ same diocesans or there commissaries in that behalfe be taken in as full stre[ng]the and powre as are endytementes at yᵉ common lawe.[1]

In other words, persons condemned in the ecclesiastical courts were not to be executed unless formally sentenced upon conviction in the lay courts.

Since grievances similar to those expressed in this bill were written into petitions preparatory to the Supplication against the Ordinaries and found their way into the Supplication itself in early 1532, we may suppose that the bill of 1529 announced work done in the House of Commons or by a person connected with the Commons.[2] Nevertheless, the bill came to nothing at the time. The Supplication against the Ordinaries was the next step. This document incorporated genuine grievances of the Commons against the clergy and church courts but was manipulated by Thomas Cromwell and his assistant, Thomas Audley, to achieve the Submission of the Clergy on May 15, 1532.[3] Yet the passage relevant to heresy trials in the final draft of the Supplication was plainly derived from the draft bill of 1529 or at least composed by a draftsman with allied opinions, although the last proposal of the 1529 bill was ultimately omitted from the Supplication. In 1532 the Supplication made the following complaint:

> Also divers and many of your said most humble and obedient subjects, and specially those that be of the poorest sort, within this

---

[1]PRO, SP 2/N, fol. 22.
[2]Elton, *Studies*, 2, 68.
[3]Guy, *Public Career*, pp. 186–201, and p. lviii, n. 1, above.

your Realm, ben daily convented and called before the said spiritual Ordinaries, their Commissaries and Substitutes, *ex officio*, sometime at the pleasures of the said Ordinaries, their Commissaries and Substitutes, for displeasure, without any probable cause . . . and sometime, upon their appearance *ex officio* at the only will and pleasure of the Ordinaries, their Commissaries and Substitutes, they be committed to prison without bail or mainprise: and there some lie, as it is reported, half a year and some more ere they can come to their declaration: And when there is none accuser, nor common fame lawfully proved, nor any presentment in the Visitation, yet divers so appearing *ex officio* shall be constrained to answer to many subtle questions and interrogatories only invented and exhibited at the pleasure of the said Ordinaries, their Commissaries and Substitutes: by the which a simple, unlearned, or else a well-witted layman without learning sometime is and commonly may be trapped and induced by an ignorant answer to the peril of open penance to his shame, or else to redeem the same penance for money, as it is commonly used. And if it rest upon witnesses, be they but two in number, never so sore defamed, of little truth or credence, adversaries or enemies to the party, yet in many cases they may be allowed only by the discretion of the said Ordinaries, their Commissaries and Substitutes, to put the party accused or infamed *ex officio* to open penance, and then to redemption for money.[1]

Some evidence from Lincolnshire suggests that the charge that ecclesiastical judges had cited poor laymen for displeasure was topical in pre-Reformation England. The examination on oath in Star Chamber of John Monson, taken about 1509, is extant among the court's records.

John Monson sworn and examined upon his aunswer made to the bill of complaynt of Sir John Segrave preest / seith and deposeth that the seid Sir John was laufully indited for suche offenses as he did to dyvers powre men / whiche powre men for their laufull suyte ayenst the seid Sir John were by hym cited afore spirituall Ordinaries to their greate vexacion and ayenst the kynges prerogatif.[2]

---

[1]PRO, SP 6/1, article 22 (*LP 5*, no. 1016 [1]), printed by Arthur G. Ogle, *The Tragedy of the Lollards' Tower* (Oxford, 1949), pp. 324–30. This is Elton's draft E (*Studies*, 2, 109, 133). My quotation is taken from Ogle.

[2]PRO, STAC 2/32/unlisted fragment in box 2. See also PRO, STAC 2/18/54 for further proceedings in the case.

Complaints against John Segrave caused the attorney general to indict him in the Court of King's Bench.[1] This action has not been traced. What is interesting, however, is Monson's claim before Star Chamber that royal prerogative had been infringed by the spiritual judges. Star Chamber litigants were advised by common lawyers, who practiced there. The intellectual assumptions of the Inns of Court were transmitted by lawyers to their clients. St. German had himself practiced in Star Chamber under Henry VII, as appears from an allusion in *Salem and Bizance*.[2]

In his *Treatise concerning the Division* and *Salem and Bizance*, St. German leveled seven criticisms against the existing law of heresy:[3]

1. Innocent persons might be arrested for heresy and examined *ex officio* upon "light complaints," private malice, or grudges.
2. Accused persons in heresy trials did not necessarily know the names of their accusers, or the witnesses who condemned them, or even the precise charge against them.
3. Bail was not allowed as a right in heresy cases upon reasonable surety found for the accused's appearance in the ecclesiastical court.
4. Suspects in heresy cases languished too long in prison awaiting trial.
5. The evidence of perjured or dishonest witnesses was admissible in heresy trials.
6. Innocent persons might upon suspicion of heresy be driven to purgation or abjuration at the will of the bishops or their commissaries.
7. Those suspects who were assigned *poenae* might be required to pay large sums of money to "redeem" (that is, buy off or compound) their penance.

It is quite clear that, at the very least, St. German was tuned to the same wavelength as the draftsman of the heresy bill of 1529 and the Supplication of 1532. Since *A Treatise concerning the Division* and *Salem and Bizance* were published by Berthelet and constituted the government's secondary line of official propaganda in defense of the Henrician Reformation, it is even probable that these writings of St. German were originally designed to prepare public opinion for a revision of the heresy law. St. German's work owed everything to juristic polemic along the lines of the seven criticisms listed above and almost nothing to the true state of the late-medieval English church and clergy as

---

[1]This action is mentioned in PRO, STAC 2/32/unlisted fragment: "Wherupon informacion was made in the kynges benche by the kynges attourney as apperith by the seid aunswer."

[2]See 391/14–17, below.

[3]*CW 9*, Appendix A, pp. 188–93; Appendix B, below, pp. 351–364.

discerned by modern ecclesiastical historians.[1] His "some says" and other literary ploys may simply have been a fig leaf covering the audacious anticlericalism of Thomas Cromwell's policy in 1532 and 1533.

The maneuvers which culminated in the new heresy law of 1534 (25 Henry VIII, c. 14) began early in the fifth session of the Reformation Parliament, which had convened on January 15 in that year.[2] The Commons took up the case of Thomas Philips, a London leatherseller whom More had suspected of heresy while he was still lord chancellor, and whom he had delivered to Bishop Stokesley for trial in the ecclesiastical court under the acts of 1401 and 1414.[3] Although Philips had denied the charges against him and could not be convicted of heresy by the proofs of witnesses, he was required by Stokesley to make public abjuration. This he refused to do. He appealed to Henry VIII as supreme head of the church—the clergy in February 1531 had acknowledged Henry as supreme head *quantum per Christi legem licet*— and he claimed that Stokesley did not know the difference "betwene an Innocent and a convict, betwene one gyltye and one not gyltye."[4] Stokesley excommunicated Philips, who by refusing to do public penance had incurred the "wall," or (in theory) perpetual imprisonment. At More's suggestion, Philips was sent to the Tower rather than to the bishop's prison: "for bycause I perceyued in hym a great vaynegloryouse lykynge of hym selfe, and a great spyce of the same spyryt of pryde that I perceyued byfore in Rycharde Hunne."[5] Henry VIII dismissed Philips's appeal.

Yet the mood had changed by January 1534. Philips petitioned the House of Commons when it reassembled, reasserting his innocence and claiming that Stokesley "intended nothyng els but to make hym as it were a shep, redye in the bocher's lesure to slaughter when so ever it shuld please the bocher to send for hym."[6] His petition was, however, drafted by an expert common lawyer. For instance, it maintained that the bishops "hade no auctorite to attache any the kynges subiectes or to Judge them in cause of heresye, but only by auctorite of the sayd statute

---

[1]See Peter Heath, *The English Parish Clergy on the Eve of the Reformation* (London, 1969), pp. 49–134, 187–196; Margaret Bowker, *The Secular Clergy in the Diocese of Lincoln* (Cambridge, 1968), pp. 85–154, 179–82; Christopher Haigh, "Anticlericalism and the English Reformation," *History, 68* (1983), 391–407.

[2]Lehmberg, pp. 184–99.

[3]See *CW 9*, 126/11–127/30 and Commentary at 126/12. See also the text and note on 68/3–6 and note on 82/35–83/5, below.

[4]The articles against Philips are PRO, SP 2/P, fols. 139–40 (*LP 7*, no. 155 [1]). Philips's petition to the Commons is PRO, SP 2/P, fols. 142–43 (*LP 7*, no. 155 [2]).

[5]*CW 9*, 126/23–26.

[6]PRO, SP 2/P, fol. 142.

[of 1401] so that the bishop was in thys cause but an inferyor mynyster to our sayd soveraigne lord the kynge"; this argument relied on the juristic implications of the Submission of the Clergy.[1] Second, the petition asked the Commons "to be meanes and intercessors" for Philips in obtaining a writ of *corpus cum causa* to secure the hearing of his case of imprisonment in the Court of Chancery, a radical plea which must have given alert lawyers food for thought. In addition, Philips requested that Stokesley be summoned by subpoena into Chancery to explain his "abuse" of 2 Henry IV, c. 15.[2] This, too, was a topical line of argument, for St. German in his parliamentary draft of 1531 had said that, in certain matters, if "the Juges spirituall wyll not regarde the kynges lawes . . . [the party] may have a specyall wrytte owte of the Chauncery upon thys statute, commandyng theym not to gyve any sentence contrary to the kynges lawes"—and Philips's point was that he had indeed appealed to Henry VIII before Stokesley's conclusion of his case.[3]

The Commons sent Philips's petition up to the Lords on February 7, 1534, but the Lords dismissed it two days later as a frivolous suit.[4] On March 2, the lower house raised the matter again, requesting an answer from Bishop Stokesley, but the Lords refused "una Voce."[5] The Commons accordingly adopted a broader strategy. On March 5

the Comyn house wente before the kyng in to hys palayse and the speker made a preposyssyon to the kyng to and in the name of all hys subgyets, desyryng his grace of reformacon of the acts made by the spiritualtye in the convocacon ayenste hys grace and hys

---

[1]PRO, SP 2/P, fols. 142–43. For the juristic background, see J. A. Guy, "Henry VIII and the Praemunire Manoeuvres of 1530–1531," *English Historical Review*, 97 (1982), 481–503; hereafter cited as "Guy, 'Henry VIII and the Praemunire Manoeuvres.'"

[2]PRO, SP 2/P, fol. 143. Since a subpoena was technically not a writ in the sense that it was not to be found in the *Natura brevium* but was, rather, in the category of "letters missive," it thus did not infringe upon ecclesiastical immunity from secular jurisdiction to serve a subpoena upon a bishop or clerk in holy orders. Philips's plea was radical because a *corpus cum causa* would normally only be granted by Chancery in a case of imprisonment for debt.

[3]The cases are not identical, since St. German spoke of remedy in Chancery when church courts heard pleas upon temporal goods. The theory, however, is similar insofar as proceedings held in church courts which were no longer legitimately empowered to conduct them after the Submission of the Clergy and the concession of Henry's supremacy *quantum per Christi legem licet* rendered the ecclesiastical judges concerned liable to the charge of praemunire.

[4]J. P. Cooper, "The Supplication against the Ordinaries Reconsidered," *English Historical Review*, 72 (1957), 636; Lehmberg, p. 186.

[5]Cooper, "Supplication," p. 636.

subgyets in callyng many of hys subgetts to the corts ex ofycio and
not knowyng there accuser and to cawse them to abyower or ells to
borne them for pure malys and apon there abhomynabyll cursys
takyng of tythes and offryngs contrary to justyse and that they
were juggs and partyes in ther owne cawsys. Therfor at that tyme
hyt was ordeyned that viii of the lower house and viii of the hyer
house and xvi Byshopps with hothyr of the clergye shulde dys-
cusse the mater and the kyng to be umpere.[1]

This quotation comes from the commonplace book of a London
citizen, and the last sentence evidently refers to the Act for the Submission of the Clergy (25 Henry VIII, c. 19).[2] But the Commons persisted
in their attack on *ex officio* proceedings in cases of suspected heresy.
First, copies of the heresy laws (5 Richard II, st. 2, c. 5; 2 Henry IV, c.
15; and 2 Henry V, st. 1, c. 7) were obtained.[3] Next, the contents of
these acts were carefully compared with Magna Carta and other
pre-1414 statutes.[4] On this basis the acts of 1401 and 1414 were
deemed deficient in nine respects because they conflicted with earlier
legislation on subjects' liberties.[5] Third, the act of 1401 was directly
attacked:

In this forsaid acte was forgoten to declare what ys an heretyk /
what be the poyntes of heresy / what ys the determination of holy
chirche / what be called the rightes and liberties of the Chirche /
whiche be called myschevous preachinges / what ys ment by the
canonycall lycence / what yt ys to noryshe heretykes / whiche be
called myschevous bokes / what ye meane by the person defamed
or suspect / what canonycall purgation ys / what ye calle yt to

---

[1]Cooper, "Supplication," p. 636. John Rokewood informed Lord Lisle that on March
5, 1534, "the whole Parliament house were with the King at York Place in his gallery the
space of iij hours, and after that all the Lords went into the Council House at Westminster
and there sat till x a'clock at night"; *The Lisle Letters,* ed. M. St. Clare Byrne, 6 vols.
(Chicago, 1981), 2, 66.

[2]Cooper, "Supplication," p. 637.

[3]PRO, SP 1/82, fols. 63–68 (*LP* 7, no. 60).

[4]PRO, SP 1/82, fols. 67–68.

[5]The conflict was said to be with the following statutes: Magna Carta, c. 29; 3 Edward I,
Westminster I, c. 24 (wrongly cited by the Commons as c. 26); 5 Edward III, c. 9; 25
Edward III, st. 5, c. 4; 28 Edward III, c. 3; 42 Edward III, c. 3; 17 Richard II, c. 6; 4
Henry IV, c. 23 (wrongly cited by the Commons as c. 22). The objections sprang in
essence from Magna Carta and its confirmations. The first article may be cited by way of
illustration: "No freman shalbe taken or ymprisoned or disseased or otherwyse destroyed / nor we shall not goo nor sett upon hym but by lawfull iudgement of his peerys /
or by the lawe of the lande / Magna Carta cap. xxix°/."

abiure after the lawe of the Chirche / what shall be taken for a reasonable excuse that they fynyshe not the premisses within thre monethes / what articles besydes the xij articles of the faithe shalbe obiected to any man to aunswere unto / what ye calle canonicall conviction / In what cases by the canon lawe a man shalbe lefte to the seculer power / for these pointes unknowen the people be soor greyved etc.[1]

These labors were codified in a new heresy bill framed as a Commons' petition.[2] The Lords reworked the Commons' draft, which may have been extensively amended; since the Commons' version is lost, we cannot tell. In any event, the two houses reached final agreement upon 25 Henry VIII, c. 14, which received the royal assent on March 30, 1534.[3]

After a preamble giving the chief points raised by the Commons' research, the heresy act of 1401 was repealed, and those of 1382 and 1414 were confirmed save where they were "repugnant" to the new act. This, we may suppose, was partly a strategem designed to win royal assent. The peroration of the preamble alluded to the "mooste foule and detestable cryme of heresye," which was "utterly [to] be abhorred, detested and eradycate, ne that any heretikes shuld be favored but that they shuld have condigne and sufficient punyshment." Henry VIII and the conservative peers were aligned against sacramental heresy: they were likely to veto legislation that appeared *prima facie* to liberalize the law instead of merely attacking ecclesiastical jurisdiction. The act did in effect liberalize heresy law by six provisions:

1. Accusations in heresy cases were to be made by the presentments of grand juries, or by presentments in sheriff's tourns or leet courts, or upon the testimony of at least two "lawful" witnesses to the bishops or their commissaries.
2. After accusation of heresy in the prescribed form, the suspect was to be arrested and committed for ecclesiastical trial in open court.
3. Those properly convicted of heresy were to abjure and perform "reasonable" penance, if they would. If they refused to abjure, or fell into relapse after abjuration, they were to be surrendered to the lay power.
4. The lay power was to burn obstinate or relapsed heretics, but only upon receipt of a royal writ *de heretico comburendo*.

---

[1]PRO, SP 1/82, fol. 66v.
[2]Lehmberg, pp. 186–87.
[3]*The Statutes of the Realm*, ed. A. Luders et al., 11 vols (London, 1810–28), *3*, 454–55.

5. Speaking against the "pretended power" of the bishop of Rome was not to be heresy.

6. Those arrested on suspicion of heresy were to be allowed bail upon four "sufficient" sureties by two justices of the peace, should the ecclesiastical authorities refuse it, unless the bishop could give the King's Council a reason why bail should be denied.

When these provisions are examined in their procedural context, the extent of practical reform achieved by the Commons is quite apparent. First, juries of presentment hardly ever detected heretics—More drove home this point in his *Debellation*.[1] Second, *ex officio* detection of heresy was now restricted to cases in which admissible evidence could be secured from at least two honest witnesses. More's *Debellation* emphasized that such restriction was likely to cripple heresy trials.[2] Third, trials were to be conducted in open court, thus discouraging confidential denunciations. In reply to St. German, More noted that if secret accusations were prohibited, heresy prosecutions would decline.[3] Fourth, the king's writ became the necessary warrant for burning a convicted heretic; this requirement might occasion delay and the legal or political interference that automatically followed such centralized (and perhaps discretionary) procedure.[4] Finally, bail became normally available, especially to influential protestants, who thus gained the opportunity to muster support for their defense.

We know that the Lords reworked the Commons' draft of the 1534 act: even the finally engrossed version apparently bears the traces of controversy.[5] It looks as if perhaps extreme arguments of the first petition of the Commons were diluted by the Lords, but that the concessions offered by the lower house in the interests of legislation gave little away in terms of the practical effects upon actual heresy trials.

The details of the 1534 act were not identical to St. German's arguments in *Salem and Bizance*, but they achieved essentially the same purpose. They even went beyond St. German by requiring the king's

---

[1] See 138–40, below.

[2] See 90–96, 99/32–37, 100-01, 151–54, 165.

[3] See 90–91, 99–100, 104, 161–62.

[4] William Blackstone, *Commentaries on the Laws of England*, ed. James Stewart, 4 vols., 2nd ed. (Oxford, 1844), *4*, 48 (hereafter cited as "Blackstone, *Commentaries*"). For an example of interference by sympathetic secular officials at the stake where a heretic was to be burned, see British Library, Harleian MS 2143, fol. 7v. The case arose in Mary's reign and led to Star Chamber action.

[5] Lehmberg, p. 187, n. 2.

writ for burning. Of St. German's seven criticisms of the pre-1534 heresy law, four had been fully met, two partly so, and the remaining issue evaporated as the number of heresy trials declined in response to the new, more stringent procedures of accusation.[1] At the very least, ecclesiastical courts had been constrained to observe in heresy trials the "two-witness" rule more strictly, open trials had become a statutory requirement, and the act *De heretico comburendo* had been repealed.[2]

The law of heresy was not totally abolished until 1677 (29 Charles II, c. 9), and the sixteenth century was to see the Act of Six Articles and temporary reenactment by Mary I of the medieval heresy statutes.[3] Yet the 1534 heresy act did more in the long term to undermine the independent, inquisitorial jurisdiction of the ecclesiastical courts and Roman-canonical procedure in England than any other Henrician measure except the Act of Appeals[4] and that which confirmed the earlier Submission of the Clergy.[5] The clash of minds that produced More's *Debellation of Salem and Bizance* marked a major turning point in English legal history.

---

[1] In the list of St. German's criticisms (p. lxi, above), nos. 1, 2, 5, and 7 were fully met; nos. 3 and 4 were partially satisfied; no. 6 remained in effect.
[2] On the "two-witness" rule, see the notes on 73/20–21, 178/24–25.
[3] 31 Henry VIII, c. 14; 1 and 2 Philip and Mary, c. 6 (repealed by 1 Elizabeth I, c. 1).
[4] 24 Henry VIII, c. 12.
[5] 25 Henry VIII, c. 19.

THE ARGUMENT OF THE *DEBELLATION*

More's *Debellation* sometimes produces the bewildering perspectives of a hall of mirrors: it is an answer to an answer to an answer. Hence it is necessary to glance at the earlier stages of the quarrel. The issues that More and St. German debated in 1532–1533 sprang originally from St. German's general proposition in *Doctor and Student* that no greater nor less favor should be shown to clergy than to laity under English law.[1] St. German's *Treatise concerning the Division* had claimed to show why grudges and division had arisen between clergy and laity over the years, and what reforms were needed to restore unity and harmonious relations between church and state.[2] More's *Apology*, in reply, denied the existence of widespread division between church and state and depicted St. German as the misguided associate of those who positively encouraged heresy. More rejected outright the basic premise of *A Treatise concerning the Division* that the law under which clergy and laity were to be equal should be English common law and statute, unless the clergy could prove that an ecclesiastical law rested expressly on divine law. He denied with equal vigor those five of St. German's arguments that derived from this same premise: (1) that the church had historically made laws in its own interests which were beyond its legitimate powers; (2) that these laws were in effect a conspiracy against the laity; (3) that the clergy had exempted themselves from trial in the English courts of common law, to the detriment of clerical discipline; (4) that *ex officio* proceedings in church courts in cases of alleged heresy were unfair, vexatious, and contrary to natural justice, because accused persons were denied their normal common-law rights; and (5) that the clergy used church courts to enforce clerical obligations upon the laity in the matters of offerings, tithes, mortuaries, and probate fees, although they had no lawful authority—as St. German maintained—to touch rights of property, which were temporal matters subject to secular jurisdiction.[3]

More wrote his *Apology* to attack protestant doctrines and their as-

---

[1]See p. xxxvi, above.
[2]*CW* 9, Appendix A, pp. 177–212.
[3]*CW* 9, Appendix A, pp. 185, 188–91, 193–96, 197–203.

sumptions, to justify his own campaign against heretics and heretical books as lord chancellor, and to defend "the very good olde and longe approued lawes, bothe of thys realme and of the whole corps of chrystendome / which lawes thys pacyfyer in his boke of dyuysyon, to thencoragynge of heretyques and parell of the catholyque faythe, wyth warme wordes & colde reasons oppugneth." The quotation is taken from the *Debellation* (9/16–21), and it is important to realize that it was St. German's *Treatise concerning the Division*, not *Salem and Bizance*, which initially provoked the controversy that led to the *Debellation*. As More said, again of the *Apology* but in the *Debellation*, it was necessary to provide "an answere and a defence for many good worshyppefull folke, agaynst the malycyouse slaunder and obloquye so generally sette forth, with so many false some sayes, in that sedycyouse boke" [i.e., the *Division*] (9/12–15). The novelty of *Salem and Bizance*, as we shall see, lay in its detailed efforts to prove that More's knowledge of legal procedure at the grassroots level was flawed.[1] In other respects, the book reinforced *A Treatise concerning the Division*. Thus the *Debellation* cannot be read apart from the *Apology*, which had opened More's attack on St. German. To consider the *Debellation* in isolation would be to distort the author's own perspective. The *Debellation*, however, was written solely to answer St. German, whereas the *Apology* had two declared aims besides that of confuting *A Treatise concerning the Division*. We may therefore here confine ourselves to the briefest outline of the third aim of the *Apology*.[2]

In his *Apology* More denied St. German's accusation that the clergy used canon law to defeat the law of the realm, notably in proprietal and disciplinary matters. He thought this charge reflected St. German's bad faith.[3] He pointed out that canon law was the common law of Christendom: the canons which St. German had singled out for criticism were, in fact, obeyed and observed, without resistance or objection, throughout catholic Europe, and the heresy laws in particular had been ratified by temporal and spiritual powers alike for generations. It was the heretics who feared these laws. Canon law had been enacted in church councils and synods with the assistance of the Holy Spirit, who, according to Christ's own promise, was as much present and was of such assistance as in the time of the apostles.[4] More held that Christians

---

[1]The other new material in *Salem and Bizance* concerned a crusade against the Turks and the destruction of Islam. See p. xx, above.

[2]For a complete summary, see *CW 9*, lxvii–lxxxv.

[3]*CW 9*, 63–76, 95–102, 143–45.

[4]*CW 9*, 99–102.

ought to receive laws made by such authority without grudge or arguments. If the clergy occasionally interpreted canon law partially against the laity, did not laymen also sometimes pursue their own interests in executing common law? St. German did not appreciate that the discovery of one black sheep did not entitle him to condemn the entire English clergy as corrupt or vainglorious. There had been one traitor even among the twelve apostles. Why did St. German expect a perfect clergy?[1] In fact, the English clergy were, in More's opinion, as effective and well disciplined as any in Europe.[2] Thus the real need of the church in England and the best route to peace, unity, and harmony between temporalty and spiritualty would be for the two estates to forge an alliance to extirpate protestants and heretics from church, state, and society. The true faith as practiced for over a thousand years would thus be liberated from such controversies and disputes as those currently being stirred up by St. German.

Concerning *ex officio* procedure in heresy cases in spiritual courts, More branded heresy a heinous crime; heretics were traitors to God.[3] If the law of heresy was altered to admit common-law rules of accusation and evidence, "the stretys were lykely to swarme full of heretykes before that ryght fewe were accused, or peraduenture any one eyther."[4] Secret evidence was necessarily allowed, and More argued that in practice it was admissible, too, in the royal courts in cases of arrest for suspected felony—this, said Henry VIII's ex-chancellor, had been his personal experience. According to More, canon law allowed heresy cases to proceed on suspicion without any witnesses at all, so that a man might be put to canonical purgation and to abjuration and penance on the bishop's authority if he failed in his purgation. But that law, noted More, had been sanctioned by a church council; did St. German deny the authority of general councils?[5] In a few pages, More subjected canon and common law to the sort of precise investigation that was to be the hallmark of his *Debellation*, in order to prove that, if St. German's opinion of natural justice was to be given full credence, English common law and statute would have to be revised quite as thoroughly as ecclesiastical law. Yet More's ultimate argument was the one founded on enforcement. He observed that in every session of jail delivery and in every court leet throughout the realm, the first charge given to the jury was to enquire of heresy. But despite this, very few

---

[1]*CW* 9, 67–70, 108–10, 166.
[2]*CW* 9, 108–09.
[3]*CW* 9, 136.
[4]*CW* 9, 130/29–31.
[5]*CW* 9, 130–33.

presentments had resulted. If *ex officio* procedure were to be disrupted even marginally, heresy would suddenly increase. The catholic faith would be subverted, although the heretics would eventually be confronted directly by God's punishment.[1]

The *Apology* neatly rebutted St. German's propositions that clergymen had conspired against the laity by means of canon law and that the English clergy had exempted themselves deliberately from due process in the courts of common law. More emphasized that the main body of canon law was not English provincial law, but the common law of Christendom, the making of which might not easily be laid at the door of the English clergy, so that it was even more unfair to blame English clerics for the substance of canon law than it was to criticize them for obeying and executing it.[2] In any case, provincial canons, even supposing that these were numerous, were not made at "confederacies" of clergy. More reminded St. German that provincial legislation had been the business of synods lawfully instituted and recognized throughout Christendom since the late Roman empire. In England, moreover, convocations were invariably summoned by royal writ; hence it was untrue to claim, as St. German did, that they and their members formed a law unto themselves. More ended his account of convocation on a humorous note: "For I could neuer wyt theym yet assemble for any great wynnynge but come vppe to theyr trauayl, labour, coste, & payn, & tary and talke & cetera & so gete them home agayne."[3]

St. German's answer to More's *Apology* was his *Dialogue betwixte two englyshe men, wherof one was called Salem, and the other Bizance.*[4] That St. German replied at all owed more to the political and juristic context of the Henrician Reformation than to the intellectual merits of his position. But *Doctor and Student* had already undermined More's principle that canon law was the common law of Christendom. For St. German had conditioned his readers and More's to the a priori notion (as it would have appeared to More) that similar situations and legal cases should result in similar solutions, whether or not these matters were adjudicated before royal or ecclesiastical courts. One law or the other had to yield, and in St. German's system that was canon law.[5] *Salem and Bizance,* however, pressed home with greater force St. German's arguments on heresy and heresy trials in England. After a preliminary

---

[1]*CW* 9, 132, 134–35, 160.
[2]*CW* 9, 143–45.
[3]*CW* 9, 145/9–12.
[4]Appendix B, below.
[5]See pp. xxxv–xxxix, above.

sortie against More's use of terminology and definitions, St. German noted that both he and More had already admitted that heresy trials could at present proceed without the production of witnesses or accusers. But how could such trials ever have begun, if a man's heresy was a secret in his own breast? The suspect must have been denounced or accused by someone, and if that accuser would not appear in court, then his accusation was probably malicious (355/22–33, below). St. German had twice proposed that accusatory procedure in heresy cases should be improved by the King's Council.[1] His idea was in the interests of natural justice, uniformity of practice, and fairness to innocent suspects who were victims of false or malicious accusers, but More had rejected it out of hand. The relaxation of the heresy law was unnecessary and would allow the guilty to escape, in More's opinion (101/21–26, 104/19–105/5, 228/24–37). St. German, however, was adamant that it was essential to protect innocent persons from spiteful, vexatious, and unsubstantiated charges; he believed More's stand to the contrary to be irrational, unreasonable, and illegal (355/22–364/12). In short, St. German abused More for defending an ailing ecclesiastical procedure that encouraged rumor, rancor, and malice.

Yet the kernel of *Salem and Bizance* was St. German's comparison of the admissibility of evidence in heresy cases in church courts with that in cases of suspected felony or wrongdoing in common-law courts. (357/8–359/11).[2] Here St. German attempted to demonstrate flaws in More's knowledge of legal practice at the grassroots level. Persons arrested for felony on suspicion were never arraigned at the bar on suspicion alone; either they were indicted by due process of law, or proclamation was made that evidence be laid, and if no evidence was forthcoming, the prisoner was delivered out of jail without fine or other punishment, even if previously he had been bound over to keep the peace (357/8–34). In contrast, persons suspected of heresy might be required by ecclesiastical courts to undertake canonical purgation or to abjure and perform penance without actual proof of heresy upon the testimony of credible witnesses.[3] In other words, the worst that could happen to suspects at common law, or even in Star Chamber, was less than under canonical procedure. At common law there could be no unjust punishment of innocents, who might temporarily be imprison-

---

[1]*Division, CW 9*, 190; see also St. German's parliamentary draft of 1531 in Guy, *St. German*, pp. 127–35, and note on 32/8, below.

[2]Cf. *Apology, CW 9*, 132–35.

[3]See also notes on 47/14–16, 110/32–33, 111/34–112/2, 116/3–4, and pp. liii–lv, above.

ed upon wrongful arrest or bound over perhaps by local justices of the peace, but who must be released without stain upon their reputations if credible public accusation could not be made (357/8–358/13).

Next, if a man was arrested at common law upon wider suspicion of wrongdoing and bound to good behavior, there could again be no arraignment upon suspicion alone, and if sureties were not forthcoming to guarantee the suspect's future good behavior, then he did not lie long in prison, but the judges at their discretion would issue a writ *de gestu et fama*. And upon the return of information from the suspect's neighbors that he was of good character, he would be freed "as a manne proued to be of good honestie, and to be clered bi his neighbours, of that he was suspected of" (358/6–8).[1] In contrast, the bishops might impose "penitential pains" by way of purgation in heresy proceedings, so that an innocent person might yet be put to penance by the bishop as a suspect, "and so shal he be taken amonge his neighbours, as a man worthye to do that penance for his offences, wherfore it appereth euidentely, that they be nothynge lyke" (358/10–13).[2]

St. German's third example was in reply to More's statement that upon indictments at local sessions, the grand jurors did not reveal their sources of information: "For they may not disclose the kinges counsaile nor their owne" (358/17–18).[3] St. German noted that, while it was true that accusers upon juries of presentment might not name their sources, this was because jurors could not be bound to help the party suspected to his writ of conspiracy "but as they liste to do in conscience" (358/22–24).[4] Proceedings at common law, however, were conducted in open court, and the judges tried no cases of treason or felony save upon presentment or indictment by due process of law. If a grand jury committed perjury, the names of its members were publicly known, and wrongful indictment was no attainder, since it was the business of the petty (or trial) jury to pronounce the ultimate verdict of guilty or not guilty (358/30–40). In contrast to the procedure of the church courts, the judges did not proceed *ex officio* at common law. More had quipped in his *Apology* that he would rather trust the truth of one judge than of two juries, but that was skating on very thin ice, as St. German thought: "I thinke the Iuges wil can hym but littel thanke for that preise: for surely Iuries must nedely be beleued & trusted. And therfore it is not the maner of the iuges to ley vntruth vpon a iurie, ne yet to

---

[1]Cf. *Apology, CW 9,* 132/6–26.
[2]See notes on 47/14–16, 110/32–33, 111/34–112/2, 116/3–4, and pp. liii–lv, above.
[3]Cf. *Apology, CW 9,* 133/ 1–2.
[4]Cf. *Apology, CW 9,* 133/3–5.

commende them that do it, but it be proued afore them of recorde after the order of the lawe" (358/42–359/4).[1] As a former lord chancellor, More should have known better.

More began by writing the first (possibly the first two) chapters of the second part of the *Debellation*, chapters 15 and 16, in which he took up the new material St. German had produced in *Salem and Bizance*.[2] The first part, a preface and fourteen chapters, dealt with matters arising from the former exchange between *A Treatise concerning the Division* and the *Apology*, matters which St. German raised in the first fourteen chapters of *Salem and Bizance*. More proceeded logically and methodically to confute St. German chapter by chapter in his *Debellation*. Typically, he began in quibbling fashion. When More had reported the protestant sermon attacked in chapter 4 of his *Apology*, had the preacher said "poysoned" bread or "moulden" bread?[3] More's opponents insisted on accuracy (5/8–26). However, when *Salem and Bizance* actually appeared in print, "two thynges onely moued me to wryte and medle wyth yt":

> One that I sawe therin folowed and pursewed, the selfe same shrewed malicyouse intent that was purposed in his fyrst boke of diuysyon / that is to wyt to make thordynaryes with fere of slaunder and obloquye, leue theyr dutyes vndone and lette heretyques alone / and ouer that wyth an euyl newe chaunge of good old lawes, labour to putte heretyques in corage, and therby decaye the fayth. (6/7–14)

Yet there was something else. *Salem and Bizance* had misquoted both More and *A Treatise concerning the Division* itself for reasons of tactical advantage (6/22–30). St. German had disguised his literary deceit by "walkynge to & fro, kepynge no maner order, and therwyth makynge me seke so longe for some one place, y^t I saw wel I shold soner answere hym all new, then fynde out for many thynges the place that I sholde seke for" (7/1–5). By this observation, More justified his renewed intervention at book length on grounds of accurate scholarship as much as on grounds of catholic counterattack. He would expose literary error as much as heresy. Readers must "haue all the mater playn and open afore your yien, that ye shal well se that I loue the lyght, no lesse thenne thys pacyfyer wolde fayne walke in the darke" (7/25–27). We

---

[1]Cf. *Apology, CW 9*, 133/28–31.
[2]See pp. xcv–xcvii, below.
[3]Cf. *Apology, CW 9*, 12/4–6.

may suspect that in this passage More was safeguarding himself, at least in part, from any possible hint of political malice aforethought.[1]

In the first part of his *Debellation,* More answered the following criticisms which St. German had expressed in *Salem and Bizance:*

1. That the *Apology* had not suggested suitable reforms to redress the division between temporalty and spiritualty (329/10–330/4).
2. That More had abused the literary genre of apologia in order to attack St. German (327/13–19).
3. That More had contradicted himself in his *Apology* regarding the extent of division between clergy and laity (328/5–329/7, 349/12–39).
4. That More's argument against censuring alleged clerical abuses openly in English was defective (330/7–332/11).
5. That More had addressed his opponents using evil and slanderous terminology (332/13–335/3, 343/27–38).
6. That More would "haue it noysed, that the realme is ful of heretikes" in order to justify persecution (333/28–334/2).
7. That the *Apology* had variously misconstrued or misquoted the text of the *Division* (335/7–338/16, 341/3–14, 347/22–349/10).
8. That More had denied that restitution and charity should take precedence over payments for trentals, chantries, obits, obtaining pardons, or going upon pilgrimages (343/40–345/37).
9. That More had complained that better charity on the part of the clergy would only be resented as hypocrisy by the laity, who would say "that they spende vpon naughtie beggers the good that was wonte to kepe good yomen" (346/12–17).
10. That More should be more tolerant of the faults of others (349/12–49).
11. That More had falsely accused the author of the *Division* of attempting to lower the standing of the clergy in public esteem (350/5–351/25).
12. That More had said that St. German's purpose was to make men believe that the clergy handled suspects cruelly for heresy (352/3–6).
13. That More had denied that simple folk might stray into heresy through ignorance. In St. German's opinion it was only the obstinate defense of heresy that deserved punishment (351/30–352/3, 352/19–353/6).

---

[1]Alistair Fox, *Thomas More: History and Providence* (New Haven and Oxford, 1982), p. 194; hereafter cited as "Fox."

14. That More should consider whether the gentle examination, counseling, and guidance of so-called heretics with the intention of winning them back to orthodoxy was a better method of procedure than putting them on trial *ab initio*. In addition, the seriousness of suspects' alleged heresies should be carefully evaluated before opening heresy trials, and only hard cases should be brought to court. The King's Council should have a supervisory role in pretrial procedure (353/6–355/38).

More replied in his first three chapters that he never accounted himself "for a man mete & able to make a reformacyon, of such two great partes as the spyrytualtye and the temporaltye of this whole realme be" (14/35–15/2). Should he perceive the need for reforming initiatives, he would in any case find a better method of advancing his cause than publishing "sedycyouse slaunderouse bookes" (15/5–6). He would never "put out abrode in prente vnder colour of reformacyon, fawtes that were hatefull and odyouse to here, eyther of the tone parte or of the tother" (15/8–10). Nor would he maliciously proceed to aver "vntrew some sayes," which "vnder colour of ceacynge dyuysyon, excyte and set forth dyuysyon" (15/34–35). Next, More maintained that he had not mishandled the literary genre of apologia, because the rebuttal of the *Division* had been but one of his three goals in the *Apology*—"but an incident . . . and not my pryncypall mater" (8/23–24). If anyone owed his readers an "apology," More thought it was the Pacifier for producing in *Salem and Bizance* an "apology" for what was supposed to be a literary dialogue (10/12–13/5). Third, More affirmed that he had not contradicted himself as to either the genesis or the extent of the division between clergy and laity in England. On the contrary, "ye tyme of such encreace" of division was even shorter than he had originally thought. "For it was growen the greater by thoccasyon of the selfe same boke of the diuysyon" (14/26–29, 62/23–63/26).

In chapter 4, More defended one of the best arguments of his *Apology*, that it was unhelpful to debate the faults of clergy and laity openly in print in English.[1] He reiterated, too, his belief that the Pacifier's purpose in exposing clerical abuses in the vernacular was to put the laity "in remembraunce to mende them" (20/5). More then emphasized how urgent it had become for the bishops to close ranks in the face of anticlerical propaganda and not to shirk their task of repressing heresy for "fere of infamy" (23/11–12).

Chapter 5 of the *Debellation* refuted St. German's allegation that

---

[1] *CW* 9, 59–60.

More had used offensive language in his *Apology*. Attack was here
More's best defense. Was St. Paul a "raylour, when he called hys carleshe kepers dogges" or "when he called the chyef preste a whyted wal"
(24/13–15)? Did Christ rail when he called the scribes and pharisees
"hypocrytes" (24/18)? The fact was that the "blessed bretherne" were
heretics, as St. Paul had named such persons—that is, "all they that
obstinately holde any selfe mynded opynyon, contrary to the doctryne
that the comen knowen catholyke chyrche, techeth & holdeth for necessary to saluacyon" (29/26, 30/4–7). Furthermore, the Pacifier was
himself a slanderous liar. For had he not falsely claimed in *Salem and
Bizance* that More had said in his *Apology* that the realm was full of
heretics in order to justify repression?[1] More had not said this. On the
contrary, the remark had been attributed to him in the first place by the
Pacifier in his *Division*.[2] It was the heretics who exaggerated their
number in order to boost morale. They were few "for all theyr besy
bragyng" (27/17); as More had said in his *Apology*, they were "lyke as a
few byrdes alway chyrkynge and fleyng from bushe to bushe, [that]
many tymes seme a great many."[3]

More confuted next the Pacifier's claim that the *Apology* had misquoted and misconstrued the text of *A Treatise concerning the Division*
for polemical advantage. With self-conscious and deliberate labor,
More cited example after example in chapters 6, 7, 8, and 11 of his
Debellation in order to prove the inaccuracy of St. German's charge. In
doing so, he impugned his opponent's honesty rather than his scholarship, and More even spiced his account with veiled suggestions that it
was St. German, not More, who was guilty of political malice. Chapter
6, in particular, hinted that the Pacifier aimed to curtail Henry VIII's
prerogative by restricting his unequivocal right to license grants in
mortmain to the church (32/8–16); the same chapter linked St. German's ideas with those of a suspected court faction which since 1529
had mooted stripping the English church of its possessions.[4] Henry
VIII could be expected to repudiate the first suggestion and had not
yet espoused the second. This passage illustrates More's profound
political awareness in supposed "retirement."[5]

Chapter 9 consisted of More's denial of the charge that he had urged
people to make payments for trentals, chantries, obits, to obtain par-

---

[1]Appendix B, 333/27–334/2; *Apology, CW* 9, 155/24–156/7.
[2]*CW* 9, 192.
[3]*CW* 9, 159/34–36.
[4]See note on 32/11–16. See also Guy, "The Tudor Commonwealth," p. 683.
[5]Fox, p. 198.

dons, or to go on pilgrimages in preference to making restitution, paying debts, or giving alms to charity. It was not so. More's quarrel with the Pacifier here was not with the material issue but with the slant put upon it, namely St. German's insinuation that "the spyrytualtye were very besye to procure men and to enduce the people, to geue money" (49/24–25) for their own advantage. St. German's case was "labored vnder pretexte of an vntrew report, to brynge the spyrytualtye in slawnder and obloquy amonge the temporaltye" (52/2–4). In addition, whereas *Salem* alleged that More had complained that better charity on the clergy's part would only be resented by the laity as hypocrisy, More had not said that all laymen would so speak (55/11–28). It was perhaps not unreasonable to attribute uncharitable words to a small minority of laymen, especially in the light of the Pacifier's efforts.

Chapter 12 of the *Debellation* developed More's riposte. The Pacifier had said that More, being not infallible, should be more tolerant of the faults of others. Yet the Pacifier's claims in *Salem and Bizance* that More had made mistakes were based on defective citations of More's *Apology*.

> Lo good readers, fyrste he bryngeth forth myne ouersyght, in contradyccyon vsed betwene myne owne wordes / and after wyth good wordes and fayre, excuseth my faute, by suche ouersyght of frayltye as maye soone happen in a man. And then he putteth me after in remembraunce, that I muste bere suche thynges the more charitably in other men, syth I am ouersene lykewyse my selfe. (62/1–7)

St. German's homily was humbug, "For he soyleth hys argument hym selfe agaynste hym selfe, euyn in the makynge therof" (62/20–22).

No better was the Pacifier's argument, demolished by More in chapter 13, that the *Apology* should not have criticized St. German for attempting to lower the clergy's standing in public esteem. More had repeatedly given the Pacifier the benefit of the doubt, saying that the malice of his purpose was that of "some other wyly shrewys / whyche not beynge fully of so good catholyke mynde as I thynke all waye this man is hym self" (64/3–5). Either the Pacifier was malicious, or he was exceptionally naive to suppose that a book like *A Treatise concerning the Division* was not calculated to bring the clergy into disrepute. In any case, St. German's talk of clerical "confederacyes," his innuendo, his fraudulent pretense of "impartiality"—above all, his vicious "some sayes" were hardly excusable (66/1–67/9). St. German should "take recorde of hys owne conscyence" (66/4–5).

In chapter 14, More broached in earnest the central issue of heresy and heresy trials in England that was to dominate the rest of the work. He began by defending the record of the ecclesiastical judges in cases of heresy. The Pacifier had tried to make More seem to abuse him for writing *A Treatise concerning the Division*. More could not abuse him by saying that he labored "to make men wene that the spyrytual iudges in this realme handeled men for heresye so cruelly" (67/13–15). The Pacifier was not "abused," for he had indeed slandered the bishops. Had not the King's Council investigated the "false bylles and complayntes of partyculare persons" and vindicated the ecclesiastical judges (68/5)? Moreover,

> As for his passyon of ignoraunce, he may put vp agayne. For what so euer he say, he shall not fynde I dare warraunt hym whyle he lyueth, but that the thynges that heretykes are punyshed for, be such thynges as be well & openly knowen for heresyes, & to haue ben before condempned for heresyes by the comen knowen doctryne of the whole catholyke chyrch. (68/33–69/2)

The Pacifier had talked of the ignorance of simple folk, but this was unreasonable.

> Now as touchynge hys passyons for frayeltye & for lacke of good aduisement: doth there no man kyll another euyn sodaynly vppon a passyon of angre, for lacke of good aduisement? doth neuer none vnthryftes vppon a passyon of lechery, sodaynly fall together in aduowtry for lacke of good aduisement? (69/3–7)

In heresy, "the wordes be the worke" (69/20).[1]

More noted that his *Apology* had explained that heresy was "treason to god" (70/2).[2] It was easy for the Pacifier to advocate charity, gentle counsel, or "an order of monycyons" upon "pretexte of the gospell of Chryste" (70/22–23). But talking to suspected heretics and privately educating them in the faith before open denunciation would take too long. Furthermore, since the ecclesiastical law gave accused persons leave to abjure their heretical opinions upon the first accusation, this opportunity in itself was "a warnynge as charytable and as larg, as in a cryme so perylous reson can wel bere" (70/14–15). Traitors at common law surely did not receive such gentle admonition.[3] In any case, the overriding need in heresy proceedings was to save from destruction

---

[1]For the list of heretics compiled for the Pilgrimage of Grace in 1536, see *CW* 9, xlvii.
[2]*Apology, CW* 9, 136.
[3]More reiterated the analogy between heresy and treason at 70/30–36 and 153/27–36.

simple souls who had hitherto remained unaffected by error. That was why immediate action was necessary.[1]

Turning to St. German's proposals for more rigorous investigative procedures and for supervision of the ecclesiastical prosecutors by the King's Council in cases of difficulty, More dismissed such ideas as beside the point (72/29–76/29). In fact, they were probably a premeditated distraction by the Pacifier to dilute the real issues in question. So too was St. German's suggestion that only difficult cases of heresy should be sent to the spiritual judges for trial. Throughout a lengthy discussion, More reiterated two points: first, that the King's Council had already probed and rejected the complaints of the critics of inquisitorial procedure in church courts; second, that there were no gradations of seriousness in cases of heresy (76/30–83/7). All heresy was treason. Erroneous opinions of whatever character or degree were equally dangerous. More continued:

> And therfore I saye, that though he neyther defende it obstynately, nor can be precysely proued an heretique in his secrete harte: yet maye his open wordes be suche . . . that for the sore suspycyon that his own wordes hath brought hym selfe into, he maye well and wyth good reason be compelled to abiure. (82/35–83/5)

On these matters More would brook no compromise. For relaxation of the existing law of heresy in even the slightest detail was an unnecessary risk. The peril was real, not exaggerated. The Pacifier's true aim was to destroy *ex officio* procedure in the ecclesiastical courts in cases of suspected heresy. Yet if this was attempted, the streets would indeed "swarme full of heretyques, whyche very lykely were to folowe, though he [the Pacifier] saye naye .xl. tymes" (85/28–29). Upon this prophetic note, More concluded the first part of his *Debellation*.

In his second part, where More actually began writing the *Debellation*,[2] he dissected St. German's case against *ex officio* procedure. The Pacifier "fayne wolde . . . sowe an opinyon in mennes heddes, that it were good to chaunge and put awaye that suit, toward whiche purpose all his boke of diuysyon bendeth" (86/6–9). His purpose was "to brynge the spyrytuall iudges in suspycyon and obloquy, and make the people wene y^t they meruelousely dyd with mych wronge & cruelty mysse handle men for heresye" (86/10–13). He had aimed to prove

---

[1] Cf. *Confutation, CW 8,* 28/17–34.

[2] See pp. xcv–xcvii, below. *Salem and Bizance* is not divided into parts, and the heading "The second part" before chapter 15 may have been a convenience added by Rastell.

three points in chapter 15 of *Salem and Bizance:* (1) that it would not harm the catholic faith to change the heresy law, since suspected heretics could rightly be dealt with by open accusation and public trial as at common law rather than by *ex officio* procedure; (2) that it was a great wrong to leave the law as it stood, since innocent persons might unreasonably be driven to canonical purgation or abjuration; and (3) that More in his *Apology* had misrepresented the issues by comparing *ex officio* procedure favorably with procedure at common law.[1] These matters More investigated at exhaustive length in chapter 15 of the *Debellation.* In fact, this chapter alone makes up almost half of part two, while the seven chapters of part two together occupy half again as much space as the fourteen chapters of part one.

In response to St. German's latest arguments, More explained in chapter 15 how the catholic faith would indeed be harmed by abolition of *ex officio* procedure. First, persons did not willingly accuse their neighbors of heresy in public. There were occasions when up to four or five witnesses of heresy might be prepared to denounce a suspect secretly or to testify in court upon mandatory summonses, but none might be willing to act as an open accuser (90/6–29). Next, it was mere conjecture to suppose, as did the Pacifier, that those with knowledge of heresy who refused to become open accusers were thereby "false or malycyouse" (91/15). It was fallacious, too, to believe that the testimony of one prepared to accuse another of heresy in open court should be better regarded than that of one who gave evidence to the ecclesiastical judge in secret (91/24–30). Nor was the Pacifier correct in his assumption that fear of violent reprisals against accusers or witnesses was the only obstacle to be circumvented if the means of secret denunciations of suspected heretics were to be abrogated. This was "not so in euery case":

> For comenly no man is in such wise angry with them that are in a mater wytnesses agaynst hym, & may seme to witnesse agaynst theyr willys, for the necessyte of theyre othes wherto they may be or may seme to be compelled, as with hym whom he seeth willyngly no man calling him, come forth of his own offre to accuse him. (95/25–30)

Yet in other cases, "when the partye y^t is detected is knowen for myghtye, and for so maliciouse therwith . . . in suche cases the fere maye be such in dede. . ." (95/31–36). But then the risk of intimidation was probably so great that no witness would give evidence, "what so

---

[1]Cf. *Division, CW 9,* 188–91.

euer prouysyon any man sholde deuyse for theyr suertye" (96/3–4). It was for precisely this reason, said More, that the heresy law permitted secret testimony against suspects under *ex officio* procedure.[1]

Concerning the intimidation of witnesses, More also noted that the Pacifier had twice proposed that the King's Council should monitor heresy investigations, particularly in cases in which witnesses were vulnerable to harassment or bodily fear (92/35–93/26).[2] Here his position had been misunderstood by St. German. It was quite right that the Council should do all in its power to assail heresy; law officers from the lord chancellor downward were bound by their oaths of office to do so. More's point, though, was that this intervention of the King's Council should not be enacted as law, either to supplement or to replace the due process of the bishops. The reason was that *ex officio* procedure, based on Roman-canonical law, was the common law of Christendom, which had been devised to fit the circumstances of countries other than England. Was there a royal council in all the territories of Christendom? Not so. St. German's idea would be unworkable and inappropriate, for instance, in Germany (96/13–97/17).

Yet the catholic faith would perhaps take most hurt in situations where, for example, only two persons knew of a case of heresy at first hand. If one of these was himself the suspect, and the other had to be named the accuser, "than were the profe lost" (99/35). "But," continued More laconically, "we shal not nede myche I warraunt you to care for this case. For of them both, you shal haue neyther nother that wyll" (99/35–37). Nor would it help to adduce hearsay evidence from persons with circumstantial knowledge of such cases, since if those would not become accusers "that were present and herde it them selfe: than is it yet lesse lykely that he wyll become the accusour, that hereth it but at a seconde hand" (100/8–10). Furthermore, since St. German had dismissed as malicious those persons who themselves refused to act as open accusers in heresy trials, it was hard to see how he would ever accept them as witnesses (101/7–20). In short, if *ex officio* procedure were replaced by new procedures of public accusation and trial, "it wolde at lengthe come to passe the thyng that I haue sayd, that ye stretes were well lykely to swarm full of heretikes, ere euer that ryght few shold be therof accused, or peraduenture any one heretyke eyther" (104/14–18).

Turning to St. German's second argument in chapter 15, More

---

[1]More later explained that secret testimony was the exception, not the rule, in heresy cases (106/16–26).

[2]See p. lxii, n. 1, above.

firmly resisted the suggestion that the retention of *ex officio* procedure was positively harmful. The disadvantages of the system, if any, were amply compensated for by the benefits: the prosecution of suspected heretics (107/24–108/20). Although innocent suspects might be driven to purgation in *ex officio* proceedings "wythout any offence in hym or be accursed, as yf he be notably suspected & yet not gylty" (111/11–12), More believed that he had answered this objection already in his *Apology.* He reiterated his reply:

> . . . I say that he doth a great offence, & well wurthy were to be dreuen to his purgacyon & to do penaunce to, if he be not able to purge hym selfe / but haue vsed hym selfe so lyke an heretyke in all good folkes opinion, y^t he can fynd no good folke y^t dare in theyr conscience swere that they thynke other wyse. This saye I is a great offence and worthy to dryue hym to this poynte. (111/34–112/4)

More was impatient of St. German's demands that innocent suspects be protected against wrongful purgation or abjuration. In More's opinion a suspect *was* an offender if he "so vseth hym self, y^t none of his honest neighbours dare swere / that in theyr conscyences he is any other than an heretyke" (112/29–31). Such persons were well, not harshly, treated. In any case, the law upon this point had been laid down in papal decrees later ratified by the Fourth Lateran Council.[1] Why should More or the Pacifier "aduise & counsayle this realme in a mater concernynge the conseruacyon of the fayth, to alter and chaunge that law that was made by so great aduyse, by an whole generall counsayle of all chrystendome" (113/9–12)? More then asked pointedly whether purgation at the spiritual judge's discretion was any more unreasonable than the wrongful hanging of a suspected felon convicted at common law upon purely circumstantial evidence by the verdict of a jury (117/2–6).

More naturally devoted space in chapter 15 of his *Debellation* to refuting the new material St. German had introduced in *Salem and Bizance.*[2] He denied the validity of St. German's criticisms of his comparison of *ex officio* procedure in church courts with procedures at common law in cases of suspected felony or other wrongdoing. In reply to St. German's first example, More argued that the public shame of "open bryngyng forth" of suspects in the consistory court or common-law court was identical, save that at common law "myche more people [be] present to gase vppon the tone, than in the consystory

---

[1] See notes on 110/32–33, 111/34–112/2, 113/34–36, and 114/1–16.
[2] See pp. lxii–lxiv, above.

loketh vppon the tother" (124/3–6). Those suspected of felony at common law were not automatically released on bail, but might be "repryed vpon causys from one sessyon to another, and somtyme kepte you se well all the whole yere and more" (124/17–19). Similarly, persons freed at common law upon proclamations that evidence be laid were in the same position as those examined and discharged in the consistory "wythout any other purgacyon" (123/25–26). Neither paid a fine. Yet in both cases the accused were subject to possible stain on their reputations, namely open query as to why they had originally been suspected, since both courts gave them "a good lesson" at their departing (123/34–35).

Concerning St. German's second example, More thought that his opponent had deceived his readers. When a suspect successfully performed canonical purgation and established his innocence in heresy proceedings, penance was not required (127/11–31). At common law, the writ *de gestu et fama* certainly could release a person arrested upon suspicion of wrongdoing if he could find no sureties to his future good behavior, but the writ might not be issued until the suspect had "long lyen in pryson" (127/34–35). Furthermore, this was a discretionary writ, not one of right. If the justices of the peace "let the wrytte alone" (128/12), or if the suspect's neighbors disliked him for any reason, the suspect would rot in jail.

More then turned to St. German's third example. He maintained that, "lyke wise as a man shall in the suyt ex officio for heresye, not knowe his accuser: so may yt also happen many tymes, that no more he shall neyther, when he is at the comen lawe indyghted of felonye" (130/22–25). The Pacifier had argued that, although accusers upon juries of presentment might not name their sources, this restriction was necessary and legitimate because jurors could not be bound to help the accused party to his writ of conspiracy.[1] To this More retorted:

> Nowe good readers all this pretendyd defence, is nothynge ellys in effecte, but a fayre confessyon, that yt is in dede trew the thyng y^t I sayd my selfe, that he whych is endyghted of felony, maye be (as for any aduantage that he can take therby) as ignoraunt somtyme who be his accusers, as he shall in the suyte ex officio. And therby may happen somtyme, that he whyche is fautelesse shall not be all saued harmelesse / and when he hathe hadde his harme, shalbe remedylesse. (131/6–13)

St. German had said that wrongful indictment at common law was no attainder, since it was for the petty jury upon arraignment to pro-

---

[1]Appendix B, 358/14–24.

nounce the verdict of guilty or not guilty. Yet this proved "at the farthest, but y^t the order of the comen law were better, & not y^t the tother were nought" (133/36–134/1). Next, More defended his quip that he would "as wel truste the trouthe of one iudge, as I durst truste the trouth of two iuryes" (134/22–23).[1] The Pacifier's assertion that the judges would give More little thanks for that praise was "not worthe a straw" (134/30). Somewhat feebly, More enquired, "I wolde here wytte of this good man, what disprayse is this to any iury?" (134/36–135/1). He denied that he had meant that the Roman-canonical law of proof was better than jury verdicts, but he added cautiously that the King's Council sometimes undertook pretrial investigations before drafting indictments in cases of treason and notorious felony—enquiries that resembled *ex officio* procedure in certain respects (135/36–136/9).

Yet More recovered his polemical advantage when he concluded his fifteenth chapter by observing that St. German's purported vindication of common-law procedure in *Salem and Bizance* was actually irrelevant to the controversy, because he had not addressed the true point at issue, which was whether or not more people were properly convicted on suspicion of some offense by presentment at common law or by ecclesiastical procedure *ex officio* (138/27–140/14). More thought that five heretics at the most had been detected in some fifteen years by presentments at common law and in leet courts, despite the requirements of 2 Henry V, st. 1, c. 7. He had said so in his *Apology*. The Pacifier had ignored the passage, "as though he were one y^t had as for this point ben born defe & therby dumme" (140/13–14). The proof of the pudding was in the eating. *Ex officio* procedure was not only validated by the whole corps of Christendom; it was also very effective in repressing heresy (144/19–145/12). St. German had for his own reasons adopted the test that an innocent suspect "maye take harme therby" (145/11). But if that test was generally applied, no law at all might withstand it:

> For what lawe can he geue so made in al this world, wherby none innocent can possibly take hurt? But here you se playnely proued agaynst this good man, that by the chaungynge, there wolde surely folowe a nother maner of perell, the decay of the catholyque fayth by thencoragyng of heretikes. . . . Say this good man what he wyll, yf we breke thys lawe so longe approued thorowe crystendome, and take hys deuyse in the stede: his worde wyll neuer so stay the thynge, but that after his wayes ones taken, and by his newe euyll

---

[1] *Apology, CW 9,* 133/28–29.

counsayle the good olde lawes broken, men sholde shortely se wythout any doute great encrease of heretykes / whych, where as they were wonte but to crepe to gether in corners, and secretely scoulke to gether in lurkes lanys, shall sone wax bolde and put oute theyr hornes and flocke and swarm to gether so thycke in thopen stretes, y^t such myschyefe wolde fynally folowe theron, as wo wyll euery good man be that sholde lyue to se yt. (145/12–35)

Chapter 16 of More's *Debellation* continued the debate upon the rules of evidence in heresy trials which St. German had begun in chapter 7 of *A Treatise concerning the Division* and which he had resumed in chapter 16 of *Salem and Bizance*.[1] The chief issue was the canon law rule that perjurers might be admitted in certain circumstances as witnesses against heretics in *ex officio* proceedings. St. German thought this rule was "more lyke to cause vntrew and vnlawfull men to condemne innocentes, then to condempne offenders" (146/17–19). More noted, too, that St. German had attacked other canons which permitted the evidence of excommunicates and even other heretics in heresy proceedings. More complained that his opponent had ignored his arguments on the subject in his *Dialogue concerning Heresies* and *Apology*.[2] The Pacifier had insisted instead that "the makers of the lawes must (as mych as in them is) prouyde that innocentes shalbe saued harmelesse" (147/29–31).[3] But More believed this demand to be unreasonable. In criminal cases at common law, it was common experience (More thought) that murderers and thieves supplied their associates with alibis but later for various reasons confessed their perjury. Given this practical knowledge, the "bare worde" of a former criminal could be "then more trewe, then byfore was hys solempne othe" (148/26–27).

More proceeded to embellish his case in such a way as to impugn the integrity of St. German's stated objection of principle—namely that innocent persons must be protected from the consequences of false testimony. He attempted to demonstrate that judges in both spiritual and secular courts might wisely calculate the credibility of witnesses in the interests of truth and justice (150/21–151/21). His assumptions were, first, that "no man wyl caste awaye his soule for nought"; second, that "no man wyll cast awaye his soule, to do hurt eyther to his owne body or to his frendes"; and third, that "a man reputed good & honest, wyl not for his frendes body nor for his owne neyther, caste hys soule

---

[1]*CW* 9, 188–91; Appendix B, 359/13–364/12, below. Chapter 15, and probably chapter 16 as well, were the first chapters More wrote (see pp. xcv–xcvii, below).

[2]See notes on 146/32–147/17 and 146/33–34.

[3]See note on 147/29–31.

awaye by periury: yet whan hym selfe after sheweth vppon hys seconde othe, that he was periured in the fyrste, the presumpcyon of hys trouth in his fyrst oth, is taken away by the secunde" (152/17–27). These arguments, More maintained, applied to cases of treason and felony as much as to cases of heresy. Consider felony:

> If two or thre wytnessys wold at the barre excuse vppon theyr othes some one man of felony / and afterward whan they were stepped fro the barre happed to be herde rowne and reioyce to gether, that they had geuyn good euidence for acquytayle of theyr felow, with whom them selfe had ben at the same robbery: if they were sodaynly brought agayn to the iudges, the iury not yet departed fro the barre / and beynge seuerally questyoned in that sodayne abashement, seynge y^t god had so vttred theyr falshed, bygan to haue remorce and came forth wyth ye trouth, and agreed in the cyrcymstaunces and told all one tale, confessynge both the prysoner & them selfe gylty, and wold be content to swere that this tale were trew contrary to the othe y^t they sware there byfore: wolde not the iudges trowe you geue them the herynge? yes yes I dowte not, and the iury to. (153/37–154/14)

It was clear, said More, that St. German's claim that canon law rules of evidence clashed fundamentally with those of common law was fallacious (154/17–155/12). The Pacifier had labored to prove that a perjured witness, if admitted to give evidence under the canons, "maye be a wolfe, shewynge hym selfe apparelled in the apparell of a lambe" (156/6–7). Yet a witness who contradicted himself, and thus openly proclaimed his perjury to the world in the interests of justice, was far "lesse lykely to lye & play the wyly woulfe in the lambes skynne, than were an other that neuer was in hys lyfe before neyther forsworen nor sworen" (166/19–21). Moreover, if St. German so feared the harm that might be done to innocent persons from the testimony of villains, he must surely forgo the prosecution of crime generally, because it was only the most unusual criminals who "take honest men wyth theym to bere recorde of it" (164/35). St. German had observed in *Salem and Bizance* that "to fynde a defaute at lawes made by the churche vpon a reasonable consideration . . . and he intendeth no other but to put the rulers in mynde to reforme them by authoritie of the lawe: I thinke it were not only a laufull dede, but also a right good and a meritorious dede, and no offence" (363/38–364/1). More scoffed at such a declaration of good intentions. The Pacifier's complaint against canon law was at best eristic, at worst politically partisan. Nothing in his argument "helpeth hym here in this law [of evidence], agaynst whych he sheweth no reason reasonable, but a reason as vnreasonable as euer reasonable man herde" (167/3–5).

Chapters 15 and 16, the first chapters written,[1] contain the substantive, legal kernel of the book, dealing with the new issues St. German had raised in *Salem and Bizance*. The two other groups of chapters, 1 to 14 and 17 to 21, in whatever order they were written, took up matters already discussed at length in *A Treatise concerning the Division* and the *Apology*, so that the cross-references, quotations and counterquotations, arguments and counterarguments often become tedious or hard to follow. We should remember More's own stated aim in his *Debellation*: to "haue all the mater playn and open afore your yien, that ye shal well se that I loue the lyght, no lesse thenne thys pacyfyer wolde fayne walke in the darke" (7/25–27).[2] Nevertheless, the resumption of such old matters in chapters 17 to 21 was a rhetorical, if not a logical, mistake. Certainly these final chapters are likely to strike most readers as flaccid and anticlimactic. More set the record straight and crushed his opponent on all counts, but at the cost of losing his readers in a welter of mostly repetitious details.

In the last five chapters of his *Debellation*, More demolished the following arguments of St. German:

1. That More in his *Apology* had adopted "a straunge gesting maner" at his opponent's expense, and that although he had rebuked St. German for using the figure of speech "some say," he had actually employed it twice himself in the *Apology* (364/16–28).
2. That More had falsely accused St. German of defaming the spiritual judges (365/34–368/35).
3. That More had ignored St. German's argument that the heresy statute enacted by parliament in 1414 conflicted with canon law (368/39–371/17).
4. That More had misunderstood St. German's point about clerical "confederacies." The term did not apply to the two convocations, but to "confederacies" whereby the clergy defended their privileges and immunity from secular jurisdiction contrary to English law and custom and whereby arbitrary financial exactions were imposed upon the laity (371/20–372/42).
5. That More had misquoted St. German's *Treatise concerning the Division* for polemical advantage (373/2–374/2).
6. That More had claimed in his *Apology* that few passages of *A Treatise*

---

[1]See pp. xcv–xcvii, below.
[2]See p. lxxiv, above.

concerning the Division could stand the test of close scrutiny, but had failed to state more precisely what he meant (377/39–378/3).

In chapter 13 of his *Apology* More had ridiculed the Pacifier's adoption of "some say" as a figure of speech. "And yet bysyde all the fawtes that he bryngeth in vnder *some saye* and *they say* / some that him selfe sayeth without any *some say*, be such as some saye that he can neuer proue, and some they say be playne and open false."[1] More was perhaps unaware at the time that he had twice used the same expression himself in the *Apology*.[2] Upbraided by St. German he replied in chapter 17 of the *Debellation*: "I neither dyd nor wyll fynde fawt that he vse this worde some say . . . For I know well it is englyshe" (167/14–17). The fault lay in the Pacifier's abuse rather than in his use of the figure. The *Division* "abuseth the figure of so many some sayes, to the sedicyous slawnder of yᵉ clergye / and specyally of thordinaryes in the punysshement of heresy, to bryng them in obloquy of the people therby" (167/18–21). Throughout the five closing chapters of the *Debellation*, More emphasized what he had said before, that the King's Council had investigated the critics' complaints and had vindicated the spiritual judges. About this, though, the Pacifier "hath he neuer one Some say therof in al his boke, neyther in yᵉ tone boke nor the tother" (167/24–25).

More then defended his previous charge that in his books St. German had indeed defamed the ecclesiastical judges (169/21–179/13). St. German had repeatedly maintained that the clergy handled men cruelly for heresy. Yet this claim was untrue: the proof, said More, was historical. In the twenty or thirty years before 1533, "very fewe" heresy trials had taken place, except in the dioceses of London and Lincoln. It followed that "the false complaynt of mysse handelynge, could haue lytle colour any farther then those two dyoceses" (170/3–7).[3] More's facts, however, were awry on this point. There had been a minimum of 258 heresy trials in the dioceses of Canterbury, London, Lincoln, Winchester, Salisbury, and Coventry and Lichfield during the twelve years from 1510 to 1522 alone. No fewer than 118 of these trials had taken place outside the dioceses of London and Lincoln.[4] By comparison, some 271 trials had occurred in England in the eighty years

---

[1] *CW 9*, 60/34–37.
[2] See note on 167/13–14.
[3] See also 179/23–25 and *CW 9*, 115–16.
[4] Thomson, pp. 108–10, 237–38.

from 1423 through 1502.[1] The figures are always minima, and in any case an argument based only on statistics cannot invalidate More's complaint that St. German's charge had been asserted but not proved. Yet it seems strange that More had forgotten Bishop Blyth's renowned purge of heresy in the Midlands in the winter of 1511–12, when some fifty heretics were put on trial, not to mention the similar work of Archbishop Warham and Bishop Audley in southern England.[2] The debate between More and St. German, it would seem, was polemical even when it claimed to be historical. More did, however, amply sustain his objection in chapter 17 that St. German had defamed the bishops, when he said in *A Treatise concerning the Division* "vnder the fygure of a great rumour amonge the peple / that spyrytuall men punyshe heresyes rather to oppresse them that speke any thynge agaynste theyre worldely honour and rychesse &c: then for zele of the fayth" (176/21–24).[3]

Chapter 18 of the *Debellation* dealt with St. German's argument that the English heresy statute enacted in 1414 (2 Henry V, st. 1, c. 7) contradicted canon law by commanding secular judges, grand juries, justices of the peace, leet courts, and other lay officials to investigate heresy. St. German's reason was that canon law prohibited temporal rulers and their officers from taking knowledge of or judging heresy upon pain of excommunication. More's reply to this account was decisive. "But thys is not the knowlege that the [canon] law forbedeth: but the knowledge that we call holdynge ple vpon yt, whyche our inquysycyons do not: but onely serue to brynge the mater to the ordynaryes handes, whyche ellys sholde peraduenture not haue herde therof" (185/28–32). More then pressed home his advantage in order to demonstrate his opponent's bad faith. He concluded:

> And where he sayeth that he hath assygned some defautes in the spyrytuall lawes, which I can not tel how they sholde be excused: I answere hym agayne, that . . . these spyrytuall lawes that were made for the repressyng of heresyes, wyth whyche oure temporall lawes are also conformable and concurraunt, wyth whyche thys good wyse man for the ease of heretyques, hath now founden suche fautes as a wyse man maye be ashamed to speke of, I haue

---

[1]Thomson, pp. 237–38 and the table on p. lvi, above. Some evidence for London heresy trials in the 1520s is given by Richard M. Wunderli, *London Church Courts and Society on the Eve of the Reformation*, Medieval Academy of America (Cambridge, Mass., 1981), pp. 125–26.

[2]Thomson, pp. 50, 108–15, 187–89.

[3]See also *CW 9*, 188–91.

> clerely declared that they nede not to be excused / but that for the fyndynge of suche fautes hys foly to be myche accused. (190/22–32)

In this matter, St. German had distorted the words of More's *Apology* to make it appear that "I moue hym to fynde fawtes in the temporal lawes" (192/12–13). But the Pacifier had all along misunderstood the canon law, which "forbedeth laye men to medyll wyth suche maner knowledge of heresye, as sholde be a let and impedement to the ordynaryes, or other the spyrytuall inquisitours / & not suche knowledge as we take by our inquisicyons, that onely serue to helpe the tother forth & bringe ye mater to theyr handes" (194/22–26).

Complaints of misunderstandings and misquotations were dominant also in chapters 19 and 20 of the *Debellation,* as previously in chapters 6, 7, 8, and 11. In chapter 19 More tackled St. German's explanation that by "confederacies" of clergy he had meant those "wherby spiritual men pretend to meyntene the lawes of the church, where they be sometyme ageinste the kinges lawes, and the olde customes of the realme . . . And also of particular confederacies of priestes, as to meinteine obites, and the wages of priestis" (371/35–372/9). More mocked both the Pacifier's reasoning and evasiveness. The issues St. German had raised were not current; they were intrinsically implausible; if clerical extortion ever occurred, there was a remedy at common law (195/19–196/18). In any case, the clerical activities alleged were not "confederacies" in the legal sense unless it were proved that the clergy had assembled "conspyrynge to gether aboute an euyll thynge to be done, wyth a couenaunt and promyse by eche of theym made vnto other, eche to stande wyth other therin" (198/9–11).[1] The Pacifier's claims were childish: his demeanor resembled that of a man who sought to sue his neighbor "bycause his neyghbours horse stode and loked ouer his hedge. For he sayde that he sawe by hys countenaunce that he wolde haue eaten hys grasse yf he coulde haue goten to yt" (199/10–13).

From the misquotations and misunderstandings ventilated in chapter 20 of the *Debellation,* one significant theme emerged. St. German had claimed in his *Treatise concerning the Division* that the clergy pretended to have by divine law what, in fact, was enjoyed only by virtue of human acceptance.[2] The supporting examples of clerical encroachment he adduced were that "the order and disposicyon of the thynges y^t^ are to be disposed of ye chyrch, be to be disposed by the prestes"; that

[1] See note on 198/6–11.
[2] *CW 9,* 197–203.

"all chrysten prynces must subdue theyr execucions to bysshoppes, & not to preferre them aboue them"; that "no charge shold be set vppon clerkes by laye power"; and that "yf a seculare iudge be neglygent in doyng of iustyce, that thanne after monicion to amende it geuen to the iudge, yf he wyl not, than ye spyrytuall iudge may compel hym to it, or ellys supply his rome and here the cause" (209/1–25). More swept these examples aside as irrelevant. Even supposing St. German had stated them accurately (which More doubted), they were not the occasion of social discord. "I neuer knewe grudge or diuisyon ryse here vppon any of them" (209/29–30). No one had even heard of the fourth example until the Pacifier published it. "And therfore by the puttynge in of such thynges: euery chyld as I sayd in myne apologye may sone perceyue that his bokes labour & entende not to quenche but rather to kyndle diuisyon" (210/2–5). St. German was making "an elephant of a gnat" (212/18). It was the heretics who were the true cause of trouble and division in Christian realms.

More then encapsulated his reasons for thinking St. German was dangerous:

> But whyle his bokes go aboute on the tother syde, to make the world wene, that heresyes be no causes of dyuysyon / and to haue heretyques lyue in the lesse fere, wyth many malycyouse some sayes falsely slaundereth the ordynaryes, of cruell wrongfull handelyng of the peple, to dryue them by drede or by shame or other tedyouse besynes, to let heretyques alone / and go aboute wyth balde reasons the beste not worthe a ryshe, to put away the good lawes y^t haue ben made agaynst theym / & vnder colour of a feruour to the faith exhorte men to go wynne the holy land / and in the meane whyle yet wyth suche wyly wayes, labour wyth heretyques, to fyll vp the stretes at home, & by the decay of the crysten catholyke fayth, prouoke ye wrath of god vpon al our heddes, whych our lord rather turne vpon theyrs that so wold haue it: his bokes besyly goyng about this gere, hym self goeth about (ye se well perdye) to make all thynge well. (213/13–27)

The Pacifier had attacked the heresy laws on the ground that "it may somtyme fortune that a man may be punysshed whyche is no heretyke in dede" (220/33–34). More reiterated his objection to such argument. If it were admitted, "it could suffer neyther in thys realme, nor in any realme els any lawe stand in this world . . . for any maner punysshement of vngracyouse folke" (221/2–6).

The final chapter of More's *Debellation* reviewed the faults and merits of St. German's contribution to the controversy (221/15–231/16). In answer to St. German's demand that More state precisely his objections to the supposed superficiality of *A Treatise concerning the Division,* More disarmingly observed that the Pacifier "saith some thynges wel" (222/17–18). He expressed an orthodox belief in the eucharist, prayers for the dead, pilgrimages, purgatory, indulgences, and the veneration of images; he also urged a united effort by Christian princes to recover Jerusalem and Constantinople.[1] "But I mysse lyke mych agayn, that as he wold dylate the fayth, by force of sworde in farre cuntres hense: so he laboreth to chaunge and take away the good & holsome lawes, wherby the fayth is preserued here at home" (222/27–30).

Since St. German was orthodox about a crusade against the Turks, More saw no need to comment on the last three chapters of *Salem and Bizance,* which addressed this topic.[2] Instead he began his peroration. The principal issue of the debate was the Pacifier's desire "to chaunge and put awaye those good lawes / ye chaunge wherof (suche as he deuyseth) the decaye of the catholyke fayth and the encreace of heresyes wolde folowe" (224/9–12). Against this, More had averred the common consent of the realm and of the whole corps of Christendom, together with that of general councils of the church. St. German had proffered nothing more than "his owne reason" (224/15–16).

> And what is hys owne irrefragable reason that he layth agaynst all this? Surely no more as you se, but that by those lawes an innocent may sometyme take wrong. Agaynste this reason we lay hym, that yf this reason sholde stande, than agaynst malefactours there could no law stande. We laye agaynst it also that by his deuyces yf they were folowed, by the encreace of heresyes many innocentes must nedes take mych more wronge. (224/18–24)

Turning to generalities, More remained unconvinced that the Pacifier's purpose had ever been to soothe division between church and state. "I wyll not contende wyth hym vppon hys owne mynde. But surely thys wyll I saye, that yf I hadde ben of the mynde to sow and sette forthe dyuysyon: I wold haue vsed euen the selfe same ways to kyndle yt, that he vsed (as he sayth) to quenche yt" (225/29–33). The Pacifier was at best misguided and naive, despite his "good and playne professyon of the catholyque faythe" (226/33–34). It was astonishing that those who provided the information upon which his "some sayes" were

---

[1]See note on 222/31–33; Appendix B, 383/15–384/8; and Appendix C, pp. 407–08.
[2]For St. German's prophecy of the destruction of Islam, see Appendix B, pp. 383/8–384/8 and above, p. xx, n. 4.

founded unfailingly told him evil and never good. "And of misse handlynge for heresyes haue euer tolde hym lyes, and neuer tolde hym
trew" (227/8–10). Nor had anyone told the Pacifier that the King's
Council had already vindicated the ecclesiastical judges upon investigation. He had not even heard when More had "playnly told hym the
same thynges in myn apologye by writing" (227/20). The Pacifier's
silence was inexplicable. Either it was deliberate or he was the agent of
"some wyly shrewes" (227/25).

Finally, More predicted what would happen if St. German won the
battle to draw conclusions from comparison of the procedures of canon law in cases of heresy with those of common law in cases of suspected crime: he would go on to reform not only canon law but also
common law (228/13–20). This threat should be averted; it would do
more harm than good; "And yf yt happen one innocent to take harme
by the lawe: there shall fyue for one take more harme by the chaunge"
(228/26–28). Once the law was changed, there would be no end of
changes "and neuer cease chaungynge tyll the worlde be all chaunged
at the daye of dome" (229/13–14). The heresy law was affirmed by the
"whole corps of chrystendome, [and] in thys realme ratyfyed specyally
by parlyament" (229/29–30). The Pacifier's goal was to change it, first
by sowing discord in the realm under pretext of appeasing division and
then by a direct assault upon the heresy law on the grounds that an
innocent might take harm under its terms. All this was to be justified by
slanderous "some sayes" in defiance of truth. Yet the liberalization of
the law would cause heretics to "wax bolde" (230/13) and the catholic
faith to "fade and fall awaye" (230/15–16).

Upon the Pacifier's true motivation, More declined to speculate.
Who could read the secrets of a man's heart? As St. German himself
had said, "a wolfe maye loke symply lapte in a shepes skynne." More
would "trust the best, and leue the trouth to god." If the Pacifier was a
fool, "god geue the good man more wytte" (230/30–231/3). Then with
a prayer for Christian unity and men's salvation, More ended his
Debellation.

THE TEXT

The Editions

The textual history of *The Debellation of Salem and Bizance* is fairly simple and straightforward. It was first printed by William Rastell in November 1533 (hereafter designated *1533*)[1] and was reprinted in the *English Works* of 1557 (sigs. N_5-V_1v; hereafter designated *1557*).[2] No manuscripts are known, but the first edition seems to have been printed and corrected rather carefully.

More himself dated the composition of the *Debellation* between September 29 and October 31, 1533 (3/11–12), and *1533* was almost surely printed not long afterward.[3] There are a few indications that it was set from More's autograph, as we would expect.[4] It contains about eight-five minor and usually obvious misprints, most of which were corrected by *1557*, but More himself made one important correction[5] and may well have provided the careful list of errata in *1533*, which often deal with minute or not easily recognizable errors.[6] It would be quite understandable that More should have been especially careful in a work which places such emphasis on exact quotation and verbal precision.

The sequence of signatures shows that chapter 15 was the first to be set in type and hence probably the first to be written. The title page, the declaration of the title, the preface, and chapters 1–14 occupy sigs. a_1–n_8v in an uninterrupted sequence. Beginning with a large heading "The secund part,"[7] chapters 15–21, the colophon, and the errata occupy a new uninterrupted sequence A_1–Y_7v.[8] Had the chapters been set in a regular sequence beginning with chapter 1, there would

---

[1]STC[2] 18081. No. 50 in R. W. Gibson and J. Max Patrick, *St. Thomas More: A Preliminary Bibliography* (New Haven and London, 1961); hereafter cited as "Gibson." Sig n5 of *1533* was missigned "o v."

[2]STC[2] 18076; Gibson, no. 73.

[3]Rastell's colophon gives the year as 1533 (p. 231, below).

[4]See the Commentary at 27/30, 92/2, and 180/18–21.

[5]See Appendix A.

[6]See, for example, the Commentary at 40/32.

[7]There is no corresponding heading for the first part.

[8]Y_8-Y_8v was presumably blank.

have been no reason to begin a new sequence of signatures after gathering n.[1] A new sequence of foliation also begins with chapter 15. More could have known from the outset the places where any of his chapters would begin, because they correspond exactly with St. German's chapters in *Salem and Bizance*.[2] Chapter 15 is disproportionately long[3] and, together with chapter 16, forms the legal kernel of the *Debellation:* a well-organized defense of the *ex officio* procedure and the acceptance of perjured witnesses in heresy trials.[4] In chapters 17–21 More returns to subjects more like those in chapters 1–14: St. German's slandering the clergy and misrepresenting or ignoring More's refutation of *A Treatise concerning the Division*. Throughout the *Debellation* More addresses a plural audience ("good crysten reders") but in chapters 15 and 16 (and only there) he three times uses the singular vocative "syr" (100/2, 115/6, 152/5), as if he had originally addressed this legal treatise to a single person.[5] In chapter 13 More refers his readers ahead to his own chapter 17 as if it were already written (64/30–31), but he could have done so even if it had not yet been written, because he knew what it would contain: it would take up chapter 17 of St. German's *Salem and Bizance*. In chapter 13 More says that if he had time he would bring *Summa rosella* to bear on the question whether a person may speak heresies without being a heretic (83/11–15). In chapter 18 he does discuss *Summa rosella* in some detail, but not on this question, so that chapter 18 could have been already written when More wrote chapter 13. On the other hand, chapters 1–14 had to have been printed when the last part of chapter 21 (sigs. Y$_1$–Y$_5$) was set in type, because the errata for chapters 1–14 are on sigs. Y$_6$–Y$_6$v. More himself says that he originally intended only a brief response, referring his readers to the appropriate pages in St. German's *Division* and his own *Apology*, but that he soon found it more practical to quote not only St. German but also himself (6/31–7/23). More quotes St. German throughout the *Debellation*, but he quotes the *Apology* only in chapters

---

[1]Gathering n is set somewhat more loosely than the preceding gatherings, just as we would expect if the compositor was trying to fill up the eight leaves to reach the new sequence beginning A.

[2]More himself notes that he has replied to each chapter of St. German's book "by row" (223/24).

[3]It is about three quarters the length of the first fourteen chapters combined.

[4]At the beginning of chapter 15 More himself says he will now undertake to answer St. German's main point (86/5–8). In his preface he also wrote that St. German's main purpose was to change the heresy laws by bringing the clergy into disrepute (6/10–14).

[5]All three instances (especially 115/6) could, of course, be merely rhetorical.

as you se fyrst by certain reason put ã
presupposed for a grounde/ã then af
ter that by a certayne order that hym
selfe shortly diuyseth and setted vp
vppon the same.

Hys ground and his foundacion is this, yt is certayn
he sayth that no man may after the law be detected
of heresye/But that there is some man that knoweth
the cause before/why he ought so to be.

¶ Very trouth yt is that no man can
be detected, except a man detect hym
self, but yf some other se some thyng
in hym wherfore he sholde seme
nought, some one thinge or other that
they whych percepue yt suspect hym
therfore them selfe. And therfore as
for this ground this good man and I
wyll not greatly stryue ¶ Then
foloweth his order that he dyuyseth
ã byeldeth vp therupon thus.

And yf any wyll adnow that he knoweth the cause,
and wyll denounce hym an heretyke therfore : then
is yt reason that he be taken as his accuser.

¶ This is a ryght good reason/and
the spirituall lawe wyll not refuse so
to take hym ã accept hym for an accu
ser yf

The Debellation of Salem and Bizance, 1533, sig. A₅v.

that same law and other of old made
agaynste heresyes, yf they had ben in
Almayne dewely folowed in the be=
gynnynge, the mater had not there
gone oute at length to suche an vn=
gracyouse endynge,

℣ These be lo the wordes of myne
apology the .rlii.chappter folio. 232,
Wherof this man taketh holde to say,
that I denye not in myne apology, ꝑ
his deuice is cōueniēt for this realme.
for in these wordes in dede I do not
denye it/ but than you se well I do
not graunte it neyther.

℣ But afterwarde in the self same
chappter, the very nexte lefe after
agaynste the sufficiency of his deuice
write I these wordꝭ folowing.

℣ And on the tother syde, the remedy
that he deuyseth for the suertye of the
wytnesses, sholde not peraduenture
make the men so bolde, as in a cause
of heresie to medle in ꝑ mater against
some maner of man/ but that they ra=
ther wold for theyr owne surety, kepe
theyr own tongys styll, than with all
the

The Debellation of Salem and Bizance, 1533, sig. B₅v.

15–18 and chapter 20. Thus the evidence does not allow us to determine precisely the order in which More wrote all the chapters of the
Debellation, but it is all but certain that he wrote chapter 15 (and probably also chapter 16) first. He might then have gone on to either chapters 1–14 or chapters 17–21, but chapters 1–14 had to have been
written and printed when the last part of chapter 21 was set in type.
Apart from *Utopia* this seems to have been the only time More wrote a
later part of a work first.

Most of the typographical features of *1533* are ordinary enough:
larger type for the title page, the heading "The secund part,"[1] and
proper names and titles in "The declaracyon of the tytle";[2] block letters
at the beginning of "The declaracyon," the preface, and each chapter;[3]
contrasting typeface for the running heads (which give the chapter
numbers), the colophon, page numbers, and the headings of the errata;[4] and smaller type for the errata themselves.[5] But the size and
variation of typeface within the body of the text are distinctive and
probably due to More himself.[6] The usual typeface is bastard 102.
Quotations from St. German are set in a smaller form of the same
typeface, bastard 62. Quotations from More's *Apology* are set in textura
92, which contrasts in appearance but not in size with the Bastard 102
of the main text. Thus typography becomes one way of asserting
More's superiority to his opponent. This typographical distinction dis-
appears in *1557,* which is set entirely in textura 72.[7]

Several variants show that *1557* was set from a copy of *1533.*[8] nor is
there any evidence that a manuscript was used to alter the text. The

---

[1]The typefaces used by William Rastell in *1533* are identified by Frank Isaac in *English
and Scottish Printing Types 1501–35*1508–41* (Oxford, 1930). The title page and heading
are textura 220. The title page border is no. 27 in R. B. McKerrow and F. S. Ferguson,
Title-page Borders Used in England and Scotland 1485–1640 (London, 1932).

[2]Textura 116.

[3]The block letters are followed by one letter in the uppercase form of the predominant
typeface, bastard 102 (Isaac, fig. 74).

[4]Textura 92 (Isaac, fig. 75).

[5]Bastard 68 (Isaac, fig. 75).

[6]See *CW 11,* 89–90.

[7]Isaac, figs. 139, 142. In *1557,* with only a few exceptions, quotations from St. German
begin with a hand pointing right and end with a hand pointing left; quotations from
More begin with a hand pointing right followed by a vertical line with two crossbars and
end with a vertical line with two crossbars followed by a hand pointing left. Quotations
from both are in the same textura typeface as the body of the text.

[8]See the variants at 24/16, 57/2, 72/27, 73/14, 103/18, 114/5, 114/21, 128/7–8, 178/4,
187/32. *1557* also repeats most of the errors corrected in the errata of *1533.*

errata of *1533* were not introduced in the copy-text of *1557*.[1] The compositor of *1557* corrected some eighty-five obvious errors in *1533*, but he also introduced sixty-four substantive errors, including the omission of thirty words; thus it is fortunate that we do not have to depend on *1557* alone for the text.

More's last three polemical works (*The Apology, The Debellation,* and *The Answer to a Poisoned Book*) were printed as small octavos, in contrast to the preceding folios (*Supplication of Souls, A Dialogue concerning Heresies,* and *The Confutation*). The difference stems partly from the relative brevity of the last three works, but they also tend to be more limited in scope, tactical rather than strategic, like frigates protecting the rear of the great galleons.

A Note on the Text

The copy-text of this edition is *1533*, of which five copies have been completely collated.[2] The collation of these copies revealed no stop-press corrections in *1533*.[3] The text and variants are presented in accordance with the norms given in *CW 8*, 1447–50, except that here no letters are capitalized without being noted in the variants.[4] All abbreviations except "yᵉ," "yᵗ," "&," and those indicated by a final period (such as "fo." or "perag.") have been silently expanded. The abbreviation "Iohñ" is expanded as "Iohan."[5] Only substantive variants have been given from *1557*;[6] obvious misprints (such as turned letters) have been ignored. Moreover, the regular changes in *1557*

---

[1]In eleven places *1557* makes the same correction as the errata of *1533*, but these errors are so obvious that the compositor or corrector of *1557* need not have consulted the errata of *1533*. William Rastell did not consistently incorporate the errata of his earlier editions in *1557:* he did so in *A Dialogue concerning Heresies* (*CW 6*, 576) and *The Answer to a Poisoned Book* (*CW 11*, 90) but not in *The Confutation* (*CW 8*, 1434–35) and *The Apology* (*CW 9*, xv).

[2]The copies at the Folger Library and the Beinecke Library at Yale and microfilms of the copies at the Bodleian, Huntington, and John Rylands libraries.

[3]In two places letters were lost during printing: 9/32 the "y" of "poynte" is present in all copies except the Folger copy; at 68/12 the "t" of "it" is present only in the Yale copy.

[4]The font used to set *1533* did not completely lack any capital letters, though occasionally the compositor ran out of capital "W."

[5]See *CW 11*, xci.

[6]For *1557* we have collated the Klein, Larned Fund, and Roper copies at Yale and the facsimile of the copy at Cambridge University (London, Scolar Press, 1978). The only variant among these copies is the absence of all but "9." in the sidenote "Ecclesi. 19." at 226/18 in the Klein and Larned Fund copies.

More, *Dialogue concerning Heresies* (with *Supplication of Souls*), *Confutation*, *Apology*, and *Debellation* (reduced).

The second parte.

The.xv.Chapiter.

The.xv.Chapter concernyng the suite ex officio, begynneth in the xlviij. leafe of hys boke, and holdeth on into the.liiij.

And for as much good christen readers as it may well appeare, that this poynte is the speciall thing þ he sayn would bring about, that is to wit, to sowe an opinion in mennes headdes, that it were good to chaunge and putte awaye that suit, toward which purpose all his booke of diuision bedeth, labouring fyrst with hys so manye some sayes, to bryng the spirituall iudges in suspicion and obloquie, and make the peple wene that they meruaylously dyd de with much wrong and crueltie misseháble men for beresy: therfore I shall in thys poynte here confute hys argumentes so plain & in such wise, that who so liste indyfferentlye to reade both þ partes, shal fynd here causes good and sufficiente why, by hys vnreasonable reasons neuer after to set a stye.

And fyrst because ye shal well sée that I wyl not wrestle in the darke, but brynge the matter into lyghte open and playne at your eyen, I will in this matter leaue you not out one worde of thys hys.xv.Chapiter, but bring forth the hys wordes with mine. And than while you reade the tone fyrst, and the tother euen after hand: there shall neither be nor I, by any slye sleight deceiue you.

But two thinges for this matter will I require you first. One that you reiecte one wyly sleight of hys, with whiche he goeth aboute euen from the begynnyng to corrupt our iudgement that are temporall men, and in the reading to blinde vs with affeccion.

For in all this matter he maketh as there wer two parties. The tone he maketh the spirituialtie. And this cause he so maketh theirs, as though the commoditie of that suite to be kept, wer a thyng that perteined onely vnto them. The to-

ther partie he maketh vs of the temporal-tie, whom he would haue put that same suit awaye. For though that in the parliament be spirituall menne also: yet all wer they all vpon one syde sure, he séeth well they wer to fewe.

But it is necessarye that we consider in this poynt, þ though the iudges be spirituall, yet if þ suit be necessary for preseruacion of the catholike fayth, than is the profit not the spirituall mennes only but that profite and aduauntage is our own to. And if by the change of þ suit ex officio, the decay of the catholike faith shal folow in this realme: than is not þ losse & damage vnto þ spiritualtie alone, but harm is importable vnto þ hole realme.

Therfore haue this point in this matter euer before your eyen, that the chage of that lawe if that law be good, but if he change it into a better, or at the leaste as good, is a comon harme to þ whole realm. And that harme happeneth in the greatest thynge that we coulde possible take harme in, if we be (as I wot well we be and euer entend to be) faithful true christen people.

Loke therfore good readers, both to his reasons and myne, and if you fynde by his reasons that the putting away of that lawe, be better for the keping of the catholike fayth in this lande, yea or better otherwise for this lande without the minithment of the fayth in the same, than am I well content that ye coumpte this good man both for verye wise and for very saythfull to.

But nowe if you finde by mine aunswere on the tother syde, that al hys reasons in this point are not worth one rish toward the profe of any necessary cause of change, but his reason and his argumentes alway such therein, that eyther they be builded vpon a false grounde, or elles, if he make anye that happen to be true, if ye fynde it yet but such as by the selfe same reason if men would vntwysely folowe it, there might no law neither long last, nor yet no law be made: if you fynd I say his reasons against this law but such, ye wil than I doute not thinke it but good reason, for all his royall reasoning to let the law stand.

But than if ye finde farther yet, as I wot well ye shall, that the chaunge that he would make, vnder a nedeles pretece of preseruing innocentes oute of daungeour and perylle, and can not prooue that thys hundreth yere anye one was wronged with it, shoulde cause heretikes

to be

The Debellation of Salem and Bizance, 1557, sig. P$_8$ (reduced).

from "mych(e)" to "much(e)" and from "brethern" to "brethren" and
the interchangeable forms of "than/then" and "thorow/through" have
not been recorded. The errata of *1533* have been incorporated in the
text and noted in the variants; *1557* has no errata. There are no sidenotes in *1533;* the sidenotes of *1557* have been given in the variants.
For More's own cancellation at 12/4 see Appendix A.

The principal typeface of *1533,* bastard 102, appears here as roman.
Bastard 68, which is used for quotations from St. German, appears
here as smaller roman. Textura 92, which is used for quotations from
More's own works, appears here as italic of the same size as the larger
roman type. The block letters which begin each chapter are not reproduced here. Proper names and book titles in "The declaracyon of
the tytle" (sigs. a$_1$v–a$_2$) are printed in textura 116, unlike the text of
"The declaracyon," which is printed in the usual bastard 102; these
names and titles appear here in the usual roman typeface used to
reproduce bastard 102. In the variants the italic typeface used in *1557*
for Latin words is not distinguished from the usual textura; both appear here as roman. In *1533* paragraphs are usually indicated by pilcrows with no indentation, but they are occasionally marked by indentation only.[1] Sometimes a considerable space has been left at the end of
a line but the next line has not been indented; when the context seems
to call for a new paragraph in such places, it has been silently supplied.
In our text paragraphs are uniformly marked by indentation only.

---

[1]The centered headings "The declaracyon of the tytle" (sig. a$_1$v) and "The preface"
(sig. a$_2$v) are preceded by pilcrows, which have been ignored in our text.

The debellacyon
of Salem and Bizance.

2 Bizance.] Bizance made by syr Thomas More. Anno domini .1533. After he had gyuen
ouer the office of lorde Chauncellour of Englande. *1557*

The declaracyon of
the tytle.

Tʜᴇ Debellacyon of Salem and Bizans somtime two great townes, which being vnder yᵉ great turke, were bytwene Easter and Michelmas last passed, thys present yere of our lord, .M.v.C. 5 thyrty & thre, with a meruelouse metamorphosys, enchaunted and turned into two englyshe men, by the wonderful inuentyue wytte and wychecrafte of Syr Iohan Some saye the Pacifiar / and so by hym conuayed hyther in a Dialoge, to defende his dyuy- syon, agaynst yᵉ Apology of Syr Thomas More knyght. But now 10 beyng thus bytwene the sayde Mychelmas & Halowentyde nexte ensuynge in thys Debellacion vainquished: they be fledde hense and vanyshed, & are [a₂] bycome two townys agayne / wyth those old names chaunged, Salem into Hierusalem and Bizance into Constantinople / the tone in Grece, yᵉ tother in Syria / where 15 they may se them that wyll, & wynne them that can. And if the Pacifier conuaye them hyther agayne, & tenne suche other townys with them, embatayled in suche dyaloges: Syr Thomas More hath vndertaken, to put hym selfe in thaduenture alone agaynst them all. But and yf he lette them tary styll there: he wyll 20 not vtterly forswere it / but he is not mych mynded as yet, age now so commynge on & waxynge all vnwyeldy, to go thider & geue thassaulte, to such well walled townys, wythout some suche lusty company as shalbe somewhat lykly to lepe vp a lytell more lyghtly. [a₂v] 25

The preface.

Syr Thomas More to the chrysten readers.

Iꜰ any man meruayle (as I wene some wyse menne wyll) that euer I wold vouchsaufe to bestow any time about makynge an- swere to the pacyfyers dyaloge, consyderynge his faynt & his 30 feble reasonyng: I can not in good fayth wel excuse my selfe

---

22 thider] thyther *1557*.

4 THE DEBELLATION OF SALEM AND BIZANCE, PREFACE

therin. For as I sodaynly went in hande therwyth, and made it in a breyde: so whan I synnys considered how lytell nede it was, I merueyled myne owne selfe and repented to, that I hadde not regarded the boke as it was wurthy, and without any one worde
5 let it euyn alone.

How be it good reders what one thynge or twayne specyally moued [a3] me to make answere to it, and how it happed me to fall in hand therwyth, and to spende and lese a lytell tyme about it, to make the mater the more playne vnto you: that thynge shall
10 I shew you.

As soone as myne apologye was ones come out abrode, anone herde I worde that some were very wrothe therwyth. And yet in my mynde had there no man cause, neyther precher, nor pacyfyer, no nor none heretyke neyther. For I hadde but spoken
15 for my selfe, and for good folke, and for the catholyke fayth / without reproch or reprofe to any mannes person, or wyllyng any man any harme yᵗ were wyllyng to mende. And who so were wyllyng to be nought styll, had cause to be wroth wyth hym self you wote well and not with me.

20 But all this wolde not serue me / for very wroth were they wyth me. Howbeit theyr causelesse anger dyd [a3v] not gretely greue me. For I was not so farre vnreasonable, as to loke for reasonable myndes in vnreasonable menne.

But than herde I shortely that thykke & threfolde the pennys
25 went to wurke, and answeres were a makyng, diuerse, by dyuerse very great cunnyng men. And of this trayuayle of such great mountayne hyllys, I herd myche speche made, almoste euery weke: so ferforth that at laste it was tolde me for trouth, that vnto one lytell pyece, one greate cunnynge man had made a
30 long answere, of twelue whole shetys of paper, wryten nere to gyther and with a smale hande.

But in good fayth I coulde but laugh at that. For as for that pyece, I was very sure that the cunnyngest man that coulde come therto, neyther in .xii. shetes nor in .xii. querys neyther, wryte as
35 nere as he coulde, sholde neuer answere it well. [a4]

For that pyece was the answere yᵗ in myne apologye I make, as

---

34 .xii. shetes nor in .xii.] *1533 corr. err.*, tenne shetys nor in tenne *1533*, tenne shetes nor in tenne *1557*   36 apologye] apology *1557*, apalogye *1533*

you se there vnto certayne sermons, wherin my dyaloge was towched for wrytynge agaynst Tyndals false translacyon. And wherin was also defended agaynst my confutacyon, Tyndals wyse chapyter, in which agaynst my dyaloge he laboreth to proue that the worde was before the chyrche / & in all his chapyter neuer towcheth ye poynt / and the sermon that defended hym, walketh as wyde as he.

It was tolde me as I say that answere was made to that place / and what shyfte there was founde to the remanaunt, that coulde I not here. But to the fyrst poynt I herde saye that there was deuysed, that where as I reherse that the precher spake of poysoned brede, I rehersed hym wrong. For he spake but of moulden brede. And this pyece it was tolde me that in y^t new answere it was reaso[a₄v]ned at length, & set forth very lustely.

But come the boke abrode onys, I shall sone abate that corage. For fyrst syth he taketh recorde y^t he sayd but mouldy brede: yf I brynge wytnesse also that he said poysoned bred, than can his wytnesse stande hym in none other stede, but for to proue for hym that he sayd bothe.

Secundly shall I proue that he sayd poysened brede, by such meanes that men shall se by reason, y^t though the tother were possyble: yet was it farre vnlykely.

Finally shal I ferther proue, that though ye man had sayd not poysened brede but onely moulden brede: yet shall I proue I saye, that as the case stode, that same not poysened brede but moulden brede, was yet for all that a very poysened worde.

Heryng therfore that this gaye boke was made of the .xii. shetys of paper, & lacked but ouerloking, & that many mo were in hand y^t shortly shold [a₅] come out: lyke as an husband, whose wife were in her trauayle, herkeneth euery hande whyle, and fayne wold here good tydynges: so syth I so myche herde of so sore trauayle of so many, so cunnynge, aboute dyuerse answeres, I longed of theyr longe laboure to se some good spede, and some of those fayre babes borne that they trauayled on.

And when these great hyllys had thus trauailed longe, from the weke after Ester tyll as myche afore Mychelmas: the good

---

14 lustely.] *1557*, lustely *1533*   15 But] *no para. 1557*   32 cunnynge,] cunning *1557*   35 And] *no para. 1557*

houre came on as god wold, y^t one was broughte a bed, with sore
labour at laste deliuered of a dede mouse. The moder is yet but
grene good soule, & hath nede of good kepyng: women wote
what caudell serueth agaynst her after throwes.

5   Now after that the boke was out and came into myne handes /
and that I sawe the maner and the fashyon therof: two thynges
onely moued me to wryte and medle wyth yt. [a$_5$v] One that I
sawe therin folowed and pursewed, the selfe same shrewed mali-
cyouse intent that was purposed in his fyrst boke of diuysyon /
10 that is to wyt to make thordynaryes with fere of slaunder and
obloquye, leue theyr dutyes vndone and lette heretyques alone /
and ouer that wyth an euyl newe chaunge of good old lawes,
labour to putte heretyques in corage, and therby decaye the
fayth.

15   This was in dede the very specyall poynte that made me wryte
yet agayne. And yet founde I so lytle reason in hys reasonynge,
that me thought yt sholde not nede. For thys wyste I very well,
that who so euer had wyt, and wold conferre and compare to
gether, the wordes of hys answere wyth the wordes of myne
20 Apologye, sholde sone perceyue that hys answeres were euyn
very dull and dede.

   But thenne was there a nother [a$_6$] thynge that I consydered in
yt / whyche poynte vnprouyded for, myghte soon deceyue the
reader. For all be yt the pacyfyer hath in some places put in myne
25 owne wordes where yt pleased hym: yet hathe he for the moste
parte vsed a prety crafte, to mysse reherse my mater and leue my
wordes oute. Ye and besydes this, the man hath in some places
lefte oute some of his owne, & mysse rehersed them / to make the
reader wene, that in the reprouynge theym, I hadde wryten
30 wronge.

   Now had I supposed to remedy those thinges, & make him an
answere in thre or foure leues, wyth onely poyntynge the reader
to the places, wyth wrytynge in what lefe he shold fynde the
mater. For the wordes ones redde: the trouthe sholde shewe yt
35 selfe.

   But whyle I was thus mynded and went there about: hys an-

---

2 moder] mother *1557*   11 obloquye] *1533 corr. err.*, oloquye *1533*, obloquie
1557   26–27 *Sidenote 1557:* And so doe heretikes most comenly

swere [a₆v] in his dialoge had founden such a way wyth walkynge
to & fro, kepynge no maner order, and therwyth makynge me
seke so longe for some one place, yᵗ I saw wel I shold soner
answere hym all new, then fynde out for many thynges the place
that I sholde seke for.   5
   I made therfore in few days, this answere that you se. And
some suche places yet as I had happed to finde, I haue remytted
the reader vnto in myne apologye / where for his redye findyng,
I haue nombred him the lefe. And yet haue I for some folke
done somwhat more to. For I se wel surely many men are nowe a   10
dayes so delycate in readynge, and so lothe to labour, that they
fare in other bokes as women fare with theyr primer, which
though they be content to saye some tyme yᵉ fyftene psalmys, &
ouer yᵗ the psalmys of the passyon to, yf they fynde them al fayre
sette out in order [a₇] at length: yet wyll they rather leue theym   15
all vnsayde, then turne backe to seke theym out in other partyes
of theyr prymer.
   And therfore leste some readers myghte happe in this boke to
do the same: some places of thapologye myche necessarye and
not longe, that wyth myche sekynge I fortuned to fynd out, to   20
ease the reders labour, & make all open vnto hym, I haue put in
also, into myne answere here. Ye and yet ouer thys in the thynges
of moste weyghte, I haue put into thys boke hys owne wordes to.
And so shall you good readers wythout any payne of sekynge,
haue all the mater playn and open afore your yien, that ye shal   25
well se that I loue the lyght, no lesse thenne thys pacyfyer wolde
fayne walke in the darke. For as the darke is in this mater all hys
auauntage: euen so ys veryly the lyghte in lyke wyse myne. [a₇v]
And where as there are some that commende his answere, for
the compendyouse breuite therof and shortnesse: I nothinge   30
therin enuye the mannes prayse. For lyke as no man can make a
shorter course then he that lacketh both hys legges: so can no
man make a shorter boke than he that lacketh as wel wordes as
mater. And yet when by the places conferred well to gether, the
feblenesse of his answere shall appere: then shall he lese the   35
prayse of shortnesse to. For when yt shall wel be sene, yᵗ he sayth
nothyng to the purpose: then shall euery wise man thynke hys

---

11 *Sidenote 1557:* delicate readers.   35 the] *om. 1557*

boke to longe by all to gether. And that ye may wel perceyue that
so it is in dede, let vs now leue of the preface and fall vnto the
mater. [a₈]

The fyrste chapyter.

5   Iɴ his fyrste chapyter he toucheth two thinges. One that I haue
deceyued hys hope, in that I haue not in myne apologye dyuysed
some conuenyent wayes to reforme and redresse the dyuysyon
betwene the temporaltye and the spyrytualty, to whyche poynte
I wyll answere after in the touchyng of hys seconde chapyter.
10   The tother poynt is, that syth he neuer found any faute in any
worke of myne, of whyche for other lettis he neuer redde none:
he merueleth mych therfore that I make such obieccyon
agaynste his / and namely in that worke whyche I wolde name an
apologye, whyche name sygnyfyeth as he sayth an answere or a
15   defence. [a₈v]
     Now where this good man declareth what thynge an Apologye
ys, and sayth that yt is an answere or a defence / for whych cause
he the more meruaileth, that I wold in that boke wryte agaynste
any treatyse of hys, who neuer hadde any thynge wryten against
20   any worke of myn / as though that therfore my wrytynge
agaynste his worke wold in no wise agre with the name of my
boke: I myghte answere hym that the touchynge of his boke, was
but an incident as I shew in the .100. lefe of my sayde boke, and
not my pryncypall mater / and therfore of many noughty
25   thynges I touche there but a fewe, and suche as were in no wyse
to be dissembled. But now meruaile I myche more, wherfore he
shold so meruayle, that I wold in yᵉ worke which I name an
answere or a defence, wryte agaynst his worke which nothynge
wrote agaynst myn. For if the thynge that I [b₁] wryte agaynst his
30   wordes, be an answere or a defence in dede: thenne though it be
not a defence for my self, yet is the cause of all his meruayle
gone. For in that boke that is called myne apologye, yt is not
requyred by yᵉ nature of yᵗ name, that yt be any answere or
defence for myne owne selfe at all: but it suffyceth that yt be of
35   myne owne makynge an answere or defence for some other.

---

5 two] *1533 corr. err.*, thre *1533*, three *1557*   14 *Sidenote 1557:* Apologye.   26 But]
very slight indentation after a full line 1533, para. 1557

And as these titles Caluicium Sinecii, Moria Erasmi, be names conuenyent for those bokes of theyres, though the maters in those bokes sygnifyed by those names do not onely pertein vnto Sinecius & Erasmus, or peraduenture to neyther of theym both at al: so may my boke well bere the name of an answere or a 　5 defence, yf it be an answere or a defence made by me, though yt were all made for other folke, and not one pyece therof made for me. [b₁v]

So is yt now that myne apology is an answere and a defence, not onely for my formare bokes, wherin the new brethern began 　10 to fynde certayn fautes / but ouer that in the self same parte wherin I touche the boke of dyuysyon, it is an answere and a defence for many good worshyppefull folke, agaynst the malycyouse slaunder and obloquye so generally sette forth, with so many false some sayes, in that sedycyouse boke. 　15

The selfe same pyece ys also an answere and a defence, of the very good olde and longe approued lawes, bothe of thys realme and of the whole corps of chrystendome / which lawes thys pacyfyer in his boke of dyuysyon, to thencoragynge of heretyques and parell of the catholyque faythe, wyth warme wordes 　20 & colde reasons oppugneth.

And finally for as myche as many good vertuouse folke began vpon [b₂] that yll boke of dyuysyon to haue a ryght euyl opinyon of the maker him selfe, whom I for his playne confessyon of the trew faith, toke & take yet for a man good & catholike: therfore I 　25 in many places of myne apology, lay the faute fro the man hym self, vnto some wyly shrewes that deceyued hym. And so was myne apologye an answere also and a defence, for yᵉ person of the pacyfyer hym selfe.

And where he goeth about nowe for to confute yt: there ys not 　30 in all the remanaunt of hys answere one pyece that any thyng appeyreth any poynte of myne Apologye. How be yt of trouthe in thys poynte he goeth moste nere me. For thys answere hathe he made in suche maner wyse, that I shall haue nowe myche more a do then I than hadde, to make any wyse man wene that 　35 euer hym selfe ment well. [b₂v] And yet wyll I not leue yt so / but

---

3 bokes] booke *1557*　　15 false] *1557*, salse *1533*　　24 selfe,] *comma inverted*
1533　　28 and] *1533 corr. err.*, *1557*, an *1533*　　36 And] *para. 1557*

styll wyll putte it from hym to some false wyly shrewes, though the man do as he dothe, saye contrarye therto hym selfe.

And the more the man denieth that thynge hym selfe: the more he maketh yt lykely to be trew. For when in the thynges 5 that so playne appere so nought, he rather taketh the mater all whole vppon hym, then suffreth any parte to be layed from hym, but if the man haue an importune pryde, as by goddes grace he hath not: elles is yt a sure sygne and a good token, that he is suche a good symple soule as soone may be deceyued / while we se that 10 his wit serueth hym no better, but that he wolde rather appere malycyouse then vnwyse.

But nowe that I haue proued hym that the name of Apologye, may serue very well for euery pyece of my boke: nowe wyll I somwhat [b3] se how the maters of his boke agree well wyth the 15 name therof. I mean not here hys boke of dyuysyon. For of that boke the name and the mater agree to gether well / but I meane of hys newe boke that we be nowe in hande wyth, whyche boke as appereth in the fyrste fronte of the fyrst lefe ys named Salem and Bizance. And therin of an hundred and syx leues (for so 20 many be in the boke) there are scante fully fyftene, that any thynge agree wyth the name.

Nowe yf he wyll saye that the communycacyon betwene Salem and Bizance, ys but a bye mater besyde, and that all the rema-naunt bytwene theyre talkynges, ys the very boke: thanne ys yt 25 worse / for then hathe hys booke neuer a name at all.

More ouer yf yt so were: thenne sholde none of the thre laste chapy[b3v]ters bere the names that they do / that is to wytte the .xxii. the .xxiii. and the .xxiiii. chapyter / but lyke wyse as he calleth the begynnyng of theyr communycacyon byfore hys 30 mater, an introduccyon: so sholde he haue called those thre chapyters after his mater, an extraduccyon.

And yet I wote not well what I maye saye therof. For in the begynnynge of the boke, theyre fyrste communycacyon ys called an introduccyon / and so ys it intyteled vpon the leuys. And yet in 35 the very ende of that introduccyon byfore the fyrst chapyter, the man sayeth hym selfe in the persone of Bizance / that he hathe made as yet none introduccyon at all. What he meaneth by thys

¶ But nowe bycause he she weth hym selfe so connynge in greke wordes, that yppon thys worde apologye, he fyndeth the afore sayde faute wyth myne apology, as though I were ouersene and obserued not ý nature of an Apology: lette ẅs se howe well hym selfe that in the begynnynge casteth hys booke a dyaloge, obserueth the nature and propertye of a dyaloge.

¶ In ý thyrd lefe when Saẅ sheweth him seff desyrouse to se the pacifyers answere: Bizance answereth:

I shall cause yt to be wrytten here after in this dyaloge worde for worde, as yt is come to my handes/ and then thou shalt wyth good wyll haue yt. And thou shalt vnderstande that hys answere begynneth at the nexte chappter hereafter ensuynge, and contynueth to the place where I shall shewe the that yt endeth.

¶ Consyder good readers that this introduccyon he doth not bryng in, as a rehersal of a comunicacyon hadde byfore, but as a communycacyon present. And thenne lette hym shewe me where euer he hathe herde in hys

B .iiii.   lyfe

The Debellation of Salem and Bizance, 1533, sig. b₄.

can I not tell / but yf he meane to make men wene that Salem and
Bizance were two Englyshe men indede, and spake those wordes
them selfe wythout any worde of hys. [b₄]

But nowe bycause he sheweth hym selfe so connynge in greke
wordes, that vppon thys worde apologye, he fyndeth the afore 5
sayde faute wyth myne apology, as though I were ouersene and
obserued not yᵉ nature of an Apology: lette vs se howe well hym
selfe that in the begynnynge calleth hys booke a dyaloge, obserueth the nature and propertye of a dyaloge.

In yᵉ thyrd lefe when Salem sheweth him self desyrouse to se 10
the pacifyers answere: Bizance answereth:

I shall cause yt to be wryten here after in this dyaloge worde for
worde, as yt is come to my handes / and then thou shalt wyth good wyll
haue yt. And thou shalt vnderstande that hys answere begynneth at the
nexte chapyter hereafter ensuynge, and contynueth to the place where 15
I shall shewe the that yt endeth.

Consyder good readers that this introduccyon he doth not
bryng in, as a rehersal of a communicacyon hadde byfore, but as
a communycacyon present. And thenne lette hym shewe me
where euer he hathe herde in hys [b₄v] lyfe any two men in 20
theyre talkynge to gether, diuyde theyr present communycacyon into chapytres. This is a poynte not onely so farre fro the
nature of a dialoge, but also from al reason, that a very chylde
wolde not I wene haue handeled the thynge so chyldyshely.

Also that Bizance telleth Salem that the pacifyers answere 25
shall be wryten into theyr dyaloge, that is to wyt into theyr communycacyon: who sawe euer the lyke? who sawe euer any thyng
wryten into a communycacyon, and wrytyng planted in among
wordes spoken?

And what reason hath yt to tell hym where aboute in theyr 30
communycacyon, the pacifyers wordes shal begynne and where
they shall ende? as though Salem talkyng wyth Bizance, hadde
not the wyt to perceyue when Bizance speketh hym self and
when he redeth hym the pacyfyers [b₅] wordes wryten.

19 communycacyon] communicion *1557*   22 chapytres] chapters *1557*   24
chyldyshely.] childishelye. *1557*, chyldyshely *1533*   26 wyt into] *1533 corr. err.*, wyt to
1533 1557   29 spoken?] spoken. *1533 1557*

    Also what a straunge monstrose beste maketh Bizance to Sa-
lem the pacifiers answere, whyle he maketh as thoughe Salem
coulde neyther perceyue the hed nor the tayle, but yf hym selfe
poynted hym to them both with a stycke.

5   Than stand they both styll there as they fyrste mete / and that
is in the strete by lykelyhed (for there folke most comenly mete,
that mete at aduenture as they do) and there is all the answere
perused / the readynge [b₅v] wherof standeth them at yᵉ lest
foure or fyue howres I trow. How be it there I was a lytell ouer-

10 sene. For they stande not there styll aboute the readynge / but
there stande they styll both twayne all the whyle that Byzance is
as you se into theyr talkynge and communicacyon wrytynge it.
And that is but yf Bizance wryte fast, I warraunt the wurke of a
weke. Now than at the wekes ende whan all the .xxi. chapyters

15 are wryten: Bizance in the .xxii. chapyter geueth Salem warnynge, that there is the answere of the pacyfyer ended. And this
was by yᵉ pacifier full prudently deuysed. For ellys wolde Salem
wene that theyr owne talkynge together in the tother thre chapyters by mouth, had ben styll nothynge ellys but onely Bizances

20 wrytynge / and els wold also Salem haue thought that his owne
wordes of exhortacyon agaynst the great turke, and his own [b₆]
rehersynge of that exposycyon of the apocalyps, had bene styll
the pacyfyers wordes agaynst myne apology.

    And finally in the very ende to shew that he could write, not in
25 onely prose: he endeth all the whole booke in this wyse with a
gloryouse ryme, And thus the gloryouse trynite, haue in his kepyng
bothe the and me / and maketh Bizance praye for no mo but for
theym two, after the maner of the good manne Gryme, a mustarde maker in Cambrydge, yᵗ was wont to pray for hym self and

30 his wyfe & his chyld, & grace to make good mustarde & no more.

    And thus you se good readers yᵗ where this man is so cunning

---

4 stycke.] stycke. [*no period 1533*] *para*. More ouer where as Bizance sayth he wyll wryte
it in to theyr dialoge, yᵗ is to wyt into theyr present talkynge as soone as it cometh to his
handes, so that at that word he had it not yet / and than he wryteth it in, euyn by and by,
and neyther goeth any where to fette it, nor maketh any man come thyther to hym to
bryng it: is not this proprely deuysed? *1533 1557* (*see Appendix A*)   6 lykelyhed]
lykelyhode *1557*   14 Now] *para. 1557;* chapyters] chapters *1557*   17 full] *1533*
corr. err., fole *1533 1557*   18–19 chapyters] chapters *1557*   28–29 *Sidenote 1557:*
Grime the musterde makers prayer.

in greke wordes, y^t he can shortely fynd y^e fawt where I fayle in
y^e nature of an apologye: hym selfe in his own dyaloge so well
conserueth the propertye of a dialoge, & expresseth it so naturally, y^t it could neuer be done more naturally, not though he
that wrote it were euyn a very naturall in dede. [b$_6$v]   5

But where he semeth to haue meruayled whan he redde myne
apology, that I wolde make obieccyons agaynst his wurke, whyle
he neuer wrote any thynge agaynste no booke of myne: in good
fayth yf he had, I wolde neuer haue bene the more hasty, but
somwhat peraduenture y^e lesse, leste it myghte haue semed that   10
some desyre of reuengynge myne owne dyspleasure, had ex-
cyted me therto / where as nowe no worldely profyte growynge
to me thereby, there is mych lesse cause for any good man to
thynke, that I wolde take the labour to wryte agaynst a wurke I
wyst not whose, but yf that it had at the leste wyse semed to my   15
selfe, that there were suche thynges therin as god wold geue me
thanke, to geue men warnynge to be well ware of them.

And where he sayeth he wyll not touch euery thyng partycularly, but take an other order all out of order in [b$_7$] answerynge therunto: I can not let him in his own boke to vse what   20
order that beste maye serue his purpose. But me thought and yet
thynke, that I my selfe toke a very playne open way, whan the
chapyters of his whiche I wold answere to, I perused alwaye
euery thynge in order. Whiche order while he foloweth not with
me: how you shall fynd it, your self shall good reders iudge vpon   25
ye ende. But yet in the meane whyle at the fyrste face, it semeth
not that wyth lepynge out of order, he meaneth to make you the
mater very playne.

Nor all, he sayth he wyll not answere neyther / for auoydynge
of tedyousnes. And of trouth yf he haue (as he semeth to sig-   30
nyfye) any other bysynesse: I thynke it be somwhat tedyouse to
hym to answere all to gether.

Finally where he saith that he sup[b$_7$v]poseth to make it appere by hys answeres, and by his consideracyons and his declaracyons, that myne obieccyons are lytell to be pondered: fyrste for   35
his argumentes made agaynste the lawes, wherby the fayth is
preserued, and heresyes kept vnder, those argumentes all his

33–34 appere] *1533 corr. err.*, appere as *1533 1557*

answeres wyll neuer be able to mayntayne. And as to ye remanaunt, in good faith the better that he maye make you his innocent mynde appere, the gladder a greate deale wyll I be therof /
nor nothynge purpose I therin by thys present booke to do
5 ferther, than to make you clerely perceyue, that how well so euer
hym selfe here declare hys good menyng, my selfe was not
causeles there moued to fynd fawte in his wrytynge. [b₈]

The .ii. chapyter.

IN the .ii. chapyter begynnynge in the fyfth lefe, he bryngeth
10 forth ye fyrste consyderacyon, whiche is that I in the 89 lefe of
myne apology confesse that murmur and discensyon agaynst the
clergye was than all redy farre gone onwarde in hys vnhappy
iourney / & that afterwarde in the .106. lefe of the same boke, I
bryng in a very darke sentence, wherby it appereth that I mene
15 that the dyspleasure & grudge bytwene them is in dede neyther
so greate as he maketh it / and yet growen to so greate as it is, but
euyn now of late. But who so loke there in that place, shall I
suppose fynde it nothynge darke / but yf it be suche a man as
lyste not to vnderstande it. [b₈v]
20   And where I saye there, that this dyuysion such as it is, whyche
is no thynge such as this man maketh it, is not growen to so greate
as it is, but synnys that Tyndalys bookes and Frythys, and frere
Barons, bygan to go abrode: therin he wold seme to saye the
contrary, & byddeth me loke better vppon the mater, and I shall
25 fynde it otherwyse. And in dede with better lokyng theron, I
fynd it somwhat otherwyse. For I fynde ye tyme of such encreace
as I speke of, mych shorter than I there assygne, & that by a
greate deale. For it was growen the greater by thoccasyon of the
selfe same boke of the diuysyon, though ye maker as hym selfe
30 sayth and as I truste to, intended it not of purpose. And therfore
where he saith that sith I confesse that there was diuysyon at the
tyme of the makynge of myne apologye, it appereth that I haue
no mynde to haue it ceaced, bycause that [c₁] I seke not out the
causes and deuise the remedyes: veryly good readers I neuer
35 toke & accompted my self for a man mete & able to make a

---

reformacyon, of such two great partes as the spyrytualtye and
the temporaltye of this whole realme be. And veryly yf I knewe
some suche great causes as thys man setteth forth for trewe,
whych I knowe for false / and that I than knewe the wayes to
reforme them to: I wolde vse other wayes towarde it, than se-   5
dycyouse slaunderouse bookes. For as I haue expressely declared in myne apologye, neyther neuer dyd I, nor neuer entende to do, put out abrode in prente vnder colour of
reformacyon, fawtes that were hatefull and odyouse to here,
eyther of the tone parte or of the tother / and specyally so many   10
at onys, as yf they were all trewe, were not all lykely to be remedyed at ones / but the more parte for the whyle re[c₁v]maynynge
lytell remedyed, sholde but make eyther parte to the other more
odyouse, and bothe partes more infamouse, amonge suche
other (yf any suche any where be) as wold be gladde and reioyce   15
to here mych euyl spoken of them bothe.

And thys I saye all though that all were trewe. And now
wolde I mych lesse vse that maner in makyng rehersall of those
thynges, wherof many be false and vntrew, and many other also
very tryfeles / & the very chyefe thynges that thys pacyfyer de-   20
syreth to haue reformed, be lawes all redy well made, whyche
he wold haue made wurse. For where they haue ben by wyse
men well deuysed for the repressyng of heresyes, some by perleament in thys realme, some by the generall counsayle of chrystendome: those deuyseth he so to be chaunged now, as the   25
chaunge whyche he desyreth, though by goddes [c₂] grace he
desyreth not that it so shold, yet out of dowte in dede sholde
turne to thencoragynge of heretykes and encreace of heresyes,
wyth the mynysshement and decaye of the catholyke chrysten
fayth. Wherupon wold not fayle to fal which almyghty god   30
kepe from vs, his greuouse indygnacyon vpon vs. And therfore
god kepe vs from suche reformacyons.

Now to laye to me therfore as a greate fawte, that I blame his
boke in those vntrew some sayes, that vnder colour of ceacynge
dyuysyon, excyte and set forth dyuysyon, but yf my selfe coulde   35
ceace it, whan suche bookes make it: is myche lyke as yf he wold

---

30 Wherupon] 1557, wherupon 1533; to fal] 1533 corr. err., om. 1533 1557   36 it,
whan] it. Whan 1533 1557

say that there ought no man to blame hym that wolde burne vp another mannes howse, but he that wolde buylde it agayne.

And therfore with thys good reason of his, he putteth me in remembraunce of an answere, that a man of [c₂v] myne made ones myche after the same fashyon. I had sometyme one with me called Clyffe, a man as wel knowen as mayster Henry Patenson. This Clyffe hadde bene many yeres mad / but age had taken from hym the rage, so that he was metely well waxen harmlesse among folke. Into Clyffes hed came there some tyme in his madnesse such imagynacyons agaynst images, as these heretykes haue in theyr sadnesse. For lyke as some of them whych after fledde and ranne awaye, and some fell to thefte and were caught, pulled down of late vpon London brydge thimage of the blessed martyr saint Thomas: so Clyffe vpon the same brydge vppon a tyme fyll in talkynge vnto an image of our blessed lady / and after suche blasphemyes as yᵉ deuyll putte than in hys mouth, and now adayes bloweth out by yᵉ mouthes of many heretykes, whyche seme they neuer [c₃] so sad, be yet more madde than he: he sette hande vppon the chylde in her arme and there brake of yᵉ necke. And afterwarde whan honest men, dwellers vppon the brydge, came home to myne howse and there blamed Clyffe before me, and asked hym wherfore he brake of the chyldys necke in our ladys arme: whan Clyffe hadde herde them, he began to loke well and erenestly vpon them / and lyke a man of sadnesse and grauyte, he asked theym, tell me thys amonge you there, haue you not yet sett on hys hed agayne? No quod they we can not. No quod Clyffe by yᵉ masse it is the more shame for you. Why speke you to me of it than?

And euyn thus answereth me now thys good man / whyche where hys sedycyouse some sayes set forth diuysyon, and breke the chyldys necke rekeneth it a shame for me to fynde any fawte wyth hym for yᵉ brekynge [c₃v] but yf my selfe coulde glew it together agayne.

And therfore where he sayth that I sholde haue proued, that all the causes that he layeth as causes of dyuysyon, be no causes of dyuysyon, or ellys I sholde haue deuysed the remedyes: albe it I haue answered hym therin all redy, yet thys I saye therin ferther, that I haue proued wel & clerely, y^t the very chyef cause y^t he layeth, is layd very vntrewly / that is to wytte the mysse handelyng the people to theyr destruccyon vppon suspycyon of heresye. Whyche cause yf it were as trewe as yt ys false, were so weyghty, that it were well wurthy to be layde for a mater of dyuysyon. And whyle it is not trewe: yet by suche bookes beynge blowen aboute in euery parte of the realme for trewe, maye well mysse happe to make a dyuysyon / whyle [c₄] the dwellers in euery quarter aboute by credence geuen to the booke, may at the fyrste face wene, that though it be not so there as they dwell them selfe, yet wene I saye that it were so in al other places. Wherof though they shall by leysoure perceyue the contrary wyth serche: yet they that aske no ferther questyon, shall byleue it styll. And so a rumour onys begonne and spredde abrode, ys not after soone remoued.

Nowe as for hys other causes of thys dyuysyon: dyuerse I haue towched and shewed suffycyentely that they be not suffycyent. But as for me to peruse hys whole booke of dyuysyon thorow, was no parte of my purpose. For yf those thynges that I dyd towche hadde semed to me tollerable: I wolde in good faythe haue bene lothe to haue towched theym eyther. [c₄v] In whyche whyle with hys consideracyons and declaracyons he goeth about now to shew that he than ment none harme: I wyll not therin mych hynder hym, but be gladde rather to forther hym in thexcuse of hys menynge and so dyd I as I haue sayd euyn in myne apologye to. But though I be glad to excuse his own mynde in the menyng: yet can I not excuse his vnwyse folowynge of false wyly counsayle in the doynge.

The .iii. chapyter.

He .iii. chapyter conteynyng hys second consyderacyon, rede and consyder it who so lyste / for I can se nothynge in it to be consydered by me. For in effecte it conteyneth no thynge ellys, but that he wolde the [c₅] clergye shold as myche as they may

---

auoyde all occasyon of murmure and grudge / of the temporaltye towarde them, but yf it be pharysaycal grudge ye and
though the dede that they sholde forbere were good / in whych
poynt bycause that one poynt wolde waxe a longe worke, I wyll
5 fall in no dyspycyons. But in as farforth as he geueth any man
good counsayle and wysheth all thynge well: so farforth shall he
and I not varye / but and he call me to hym, I wyll syt and pray for
yt wyth hym.

But yet where he sayth in thende of the chapiter, that I en-
10 deuour my selfe very myche, to oppresse al them that wyll shew
suche thynges of the spyrytualtye: in dede some suche as haue
made suche lyes, I haue tolde yt theym. But as for any oppressyon let hym proue one, and let hym call that one .xx. And if he
can proue none, as I wote well he can not: then good [c5v] reders
15 let hym be beleued therafter.

More ouer where he sayth that I in my mynde proue yt an
intollerable defaute in the people for mysse iudgynge the clergy,
where as I thinke they haue no cause so to do / and that therin I
leue theym, as though all the whole cause and pryncypall de-
20 faute, were in the temporaltye, wherin he sayth that my iugement is farre deceyued: in this poynte good reder he sayth somwhat to me yf he sayde trew. And sure yf he thought that he
wrote herein trewe / then wysedome wolde he sholde haue
wryten myne owne wordes in. And yf he fered that yt wolde be
25 founden false: then honestye wolde that he sholde haue lefte hys
owne wordes oute. But veryly good readers and he seke thys
seuen yere, he shall in all myne apologye fynde you no suche
wordes of myne. But he shall fynde farre the contrarye. For I do
there [c6] I wote well, in suche places as I shewe that men were
30 vnreasonable that wolde take thys thynge or that thynge (suche
as I reherse of hys bryngynge forthe) for any reasonable cause of
dyuysyon: there I saye in those places that the pacyfyer mysse
sayeth the people, and that the people be myche more reasonable than to take yt so. And therfore here he belyeth me agayne.
35 And also let hym shewe you forth any one place, in whyche I
say that all the whole faute or the pryncypal faute eyther, is in the

---

1 occasyon] occasion *1557*, accasyon *1533*   12 any] my *1557*   34 than] *1557*, that
1533

temporaltye / and than byleue hym the better in another mater.
And in the meane whyle tyll he brynge it forthe, or ellys that you
fynde yt your self: ye may with reason, at the lest wyse in this
mater byleue me better thenne hym / and I wil neuer desyre you
to byleue me one day lenger. For I haue neyther layde the pryn-   5
cypall faute in the tone [c₆v] nor yᵉ tother. And thus hath he
made you of me thre lyes in one chapyter.

The .iiii. chapyter.

Iɴ hys .iiii. chapyter begynnyng in the .viii. lefe, he fyrste
sheweth a diuersyte betwene the sample that I put in yᵉ .94. lefe   10
of myne appologye, of a pacyfyer betwene a man and hys wyfe,
and the thyng that I there resemble it vnto / that is to wytte hys
owne boke, that maketh a lyke pacifycacyon betwene the temporaltye and spyrytualtye.

But surely the dyfference that he putteth semeth to my pore   15
wyt greatly to apayre his parte. For yf it be as he sayth yt is, that
where as the husbande wolde be loth to heare any euyl spoken of
his wyfe, and therfore wil can suche a pacyfyer no thanke, [c₇]
that wyll tell hym suche tales of her before his neyghbours: the
temporaltye wyll be glad to heare harme spoken of the   20
spyrytualtye: then was yt so myche the worse done, to wryte
openly to the temporaltye suche thynges of the spyrytualtye, to
fede and nuryshe any suche euyll delyte: or openly to the
spyritualtye, beynge as he sayde lyke wyse affectyonate, the
fautes of the temporaltye eyther. Howe be yt I can not in good   25
fayth saye, but yf I shold belye hym, that on that syde wyllyngely
he greatly passed his boundes / but of ouersyght vnware, he hath
in some thynges slaundered yᵉ temporalty to.

Then sheweth he farther wherfore he wrote those thynges in
englyshe, though Iohan Gerson wrote theym but in laten /   30
wherin to say the trouth, he layeth a cause suffycyent wherfore
that Iohan Gerson wrote them in latyne. But whyther he laye
[c₇v] cause suffycyent wherfore hym selfe shold not rather haue
let them alone then wryte them in englishe, agaynst the counsayle of Iohan Gerson hym selfe as I touched in myne apology: 35

---

9 .viii.] eight *1557*   28 slaundered] sclaundered *1557*

that I leue your self good readers to consyder. For I wil not
myche stryue agaynste his excuse. For I greatly shall not nede I
thinke, syth al his excuse amounteth to no more, but that he
ment that some laye men redynge the prestes fautes in englishe,
5 myght put them in remembraunce to mende them / specially
bycause he sayth euen in the same chapiter a litle afore, that the
temporaltye so myche delyteth to here of theym.

   Then goth he farther in ye same chapiter / & where as in his
boke of the dyuisyon, he wold haue semed betwene the tem-
10 poraltye and the spyrytualtie to haue spoken indifferently, & to
haue told them theyr fautes on both partis egally: here in the
second syde of the [c₈] .x. lefe, he telleth vs the cause wherfore
he dyd not so, & saith in this wise.

   I haue spoken of defautes and abuses in the spyrytualtye, more then
15 of defautes in the temporaltye / bycause the spyrytualte oughte to be
the gyders and gyuers of lyghte by theyre doctryne & good examples to
the temporalty: & if theyr light be derkenes, where shall the temporaltie then fetche theyr lyghte? trewly I wote not where. And I doute
that then they both shall walke styl in derkenes. And therfore yt is that
20 Iohan Chrysostome sayth vppon Matthew the .xxi. chapyter. That yf
prestehode be holle & sound, all the chyrch florysheth: and yf yt be
corrupte, the fayth and vertue of the people fadeth also and van-
ysssheth away. Lette thys therfore as to thys poynt be the fynall conclusyon for thys tyme, that who so euer proueth defautes to be in the
25 temporaltye, he proueth also defautes to reygne in the spyritualty: &
therfore the defautes in the temporaltye wyl neuer be auoyded, tyll the
defautes in the spyrytualtye be fyrste reformed: and therfore haue I
fyrste spoken of some defautes that be in the spyrytualtye.

   Surely good readers I like wel these wordes. For they be very
30 good & they proue very well, & very trew yt is / nor I neuer sayd
the contrary, but haue in myne apologye playnely sayd the same,
y^t euery faute in a spyrituall man (though ye thyng were of it self
al one) is yet by ye difference of y^e [c₈v] person, farre worse and
more odyouse both to god and man, then yt ys in a temporall

---

1 readers] *1557*, reades *1533*   21 *Sidenote 1557:* Priesthode.; holle] hole *1557*   30
neuer] *1557*, ueuer *1533*   32 *Sidenote 1557:* The faut of a spirituall man.   33 one)]
1557, one, *1533*

man. But yet the worse that euery pryuate spyrytuall mannes faute is, so myche is yt ye more harme to dyffame the corps of the spyritualtye openly in the face of the temporaltye, in suche maner as the boke of dyuysyon doth / of whyche I haue proued those that are weyghtye false, and could (yf I wold now lese tyme about 5 yt whyle that that I haue touched ys suffycyent) shewe the substaunce of al the remanaunt to haue lytle substaunce to.

And therfore the wordes of saynt Chrysostome whyche he layeth for his boke, were in part the very cause that made me wryte agaynste hys boke. For surely as saynte Chrysostome 10 sayth, yf the presthed be corrupt, the fayth and vertue of the people fadeth and vanisheth away / whyche is wythoute any questyon very [d$_1$] trouth for though saynt Chrysostome had neuer sayde it, our sauyour sayth as myche hym selfe: ye be (sayth he to the clergye) the salte of the erthe, & if the salt waxe 15 ones freshe and weryshe, wherin shal any thyng be well seasoned? And you be the light of the worlde. And therfore yf the lyghte that ys in the worlde, be darke: howe darke shall then the darkenes be yt selfe?

But now say I syth that ye prestehed beyng corrupted, yt muste 20 nedes folowe that the fayth and vertue of the people fadeth and vanysheth awaye / and vppon Chrystes wordes yt muste folowe that yf the spyrytualtye be nought, the temporaltye muste nedes then be worse than they: theruppon I conclude vppon the tother syde agaynste the pacyfyers boke, that syth this realme hath (as 25 god be thanked in dede yt hath) as good & as faithfull temporalty, & (though there [d$_1$v] be a fewe false brethern in a great multitude of trew catholike men) as hath for y^e quantite any other countrey cristened, it must nedes, I say folow y^t the clergy, though it haue some such false noughtye brethern to, is not in 30 suche sore maner corrupted, as the boke of diuysyon goth about to make men wene / but as good for theyr part as the temporaltie for theyrs.

And therfore in lyke wyse I saye, that vppon the selfe same wordes of saynt Chrysostome and of our sauyour Chryste: the 35

---

10 *Sidenote 1557:* Corrupt presthode.   11 presthed] priesthod *1557*   13
Chrysostome] Chrisostome *1557*, Chrystome *1533*   15 *Sidenote 1557:* Math. 5.   17
Sidenote 1557: Math 5.   20 But] *no para. 1557;* prestehed] priesthod *1557*   28
trew] *1533 corr. err.*, a trew *1533*, a tru *1557*   34 And] *1533 corr. err., 1557,* A *1533*

sayde boke of the dyuysyon in dyffamynge the spyrytualtie,
diffameth the temporaltye myche more / whyche is the thynge
that as I sayde semeth me neyther honorable nor profytable, in
open prented bokes, for any englyshe man to do / nor veryly I
5 thynke the maker wold not haue done, yf he then hadde thought
so farre.

But now goth he farther and sayth:

And though mayster More can not denye these [d₂] fawtes. (I suppose
you haue herde me denye suche as were the chyefe and proued
10 them I wene vntrewe) yet all the amendementes that he aleyth in hys
Apologye is onely in punyshement of heresyes, as ys sayd byfore:
wherunto he specyally moueth the ordynaryes not to be slacke nor the
more remysse for fere of euyll wordes and sclaunder of the people.
And yf they be therfore the more slacke in callynge attachynge and
15 examynynge, and farther orderynge of heretyques: he sayeth god wyll
not fayle to make fall in theyr neckes the double slaunder of that, fro
whens they fled. And in a nother place he moueth the temporaltye to
ioyn wyth the spyrytualtye eche with other louyngly to represse and
kepe vnder those vngracyouse folke, by whom he meaneth heretykes.
20 Vppon whyche mocyon I shall somwhat shewe my mynde, as hereafter
foloweth in the nexte chapyter.

Here he complayneth agayn yᵗ I deuyse no remedyes, as
though the whole prouysyon for all thynge laye vppon myn
hande. I do some what for my parte, when I praye god to geue vs
25 al the grace spiritual & temporall bothe, to kepe well and obserue
suche prouysyons as god hathe gyuen good men the grace to
make all redye. For yf we kepe theym well: I wene there are
metely many made. And yf we breke the olde: [d₂v] so wil we by
likelihed breke these as wel, yᵗ he wold haue me now dyuyse and
30 studye newe. And somewhat I do better for my parte, whyle I
labour to haue the good olde prouysyons kepte, than thys
pacyfyer dothe for hys, whyle he laboreth to haue them broken,
and namely those lawes that are of yᵉ very beste, and made for
the fayth agaynste heresyes.

35 But then laboureth he as me thinketh, to make the bretherne

7 But] no para. 1557; sayth:] sayth. 1533, saith: 1557   10 aleyth] alegeth 1557   16
slaunder] sclaunder 1557; fro] from 1557   19 heretykes.] heretikes. 1557, heretykes
1533   27 all redye] alredy 1557   29 likelihed] lykelyhood 1557

angry with me / and reherseth and inculketh into theyr eares, y^t I
exhorte both the spyrytualty & the temporaltye to, those to
whome the mater apperteyneth, not to be any thynge the more
slacke in repressynge of heresyes, for any fere of infamye.

Surely good readers what so euer I wrote in that behalfe: I will   5
requyre euery man to haue yt euyn here / for wryten and repeted agayn. For when we se y^t the wordes of his [d$_3$] wrytynge,
whych I haue in myne Apologye rehersed you, how well so euer
he ment therin (as I truste he ment but wel) haue yet y^t playn
open apparaunce in them, y^t they were wel lykely to put such as   10
shold se to the repressyng of heresyes, in doute and fere of
infamy, & to be had among y^e peple as folke suspect of missehan-
deling good folke and of crueltye: I reken yt the parte of euery
good man, that any zele hath to the conseruacyon of the catholyque fayth, to encorage them on the tother side, to the doyeng   15
of theyr dutye therin / and not to sette the respecte of theyr
estymacyon amonge men (whyche yet they shall also mych the
better conserue among all the people saue those few that are
nought) byfore the sauynge of theyr soules, and kepynge the
fauour of god: namely sythe the kepynge of people from here-   20
syes and puttynge the scabbed heretyques oute of the [d$_3$v] clene
flocke, is one of the specyall thynges that thapostle gaue the
byshoppe warnynge of. Let hym fynde oute any worde of myne,
where with I wolde any harme to any man that wolde amende,
and then let hym laye yt to me. And who so euer entendeth   25
neuer to be good: I am wel content that the pacyfyer make hym
not my frende.

The fyfth chapytre.

In the fyfth chapiter he toucheth punyshement of heresyes, &
dyuydeth y^e mater into foure sortes of people / wherin for as   30
mych as he nothynge sayeth that toucheth me, I let them passe all
foure.

After those .iiii. sortes perused: [d$_4$] he speketh of the fyfth,
whyche he very ernestly dysprayseth, that are those whyche take
and hold contrary wayes / to the trewe fayth in dede. But then in   35

---

22 *Sidenote 1557:* Titum 3.   29 fyfth] fyfte *1557*

that part he myche misse lyketh in me, bothe that I call them any
euyll name, as the noughty bretherne or heretyque bretherne,
and also that I call theym good namys to, as the blessed
bretherne and euangelycall bretherne.

5   And for the fyrst in callynge them any suche euyll names: he
sayth I do not as I wolde be done to / as appereth he sayeth in
myne apologye. Surely I suppose he maye therin fynde, that I
force not what suche as they be call me. And I can wryte no worse
worde by theym I wote well, then they wryte many by me.

10   And to as for to geue euyll names to suche folke as are so euyll
in dede: lette hym call yt raylynge at hys pleasure / but howe
[d₄v] so euer yt be in me, I wote well that some other haue done
so, yᵗ yet were no raylours / excepte saynte Poule were a raylour,
when he called hys carleshe kepers dogges, & when he called the
15   chyef preste a whyted wal, whych was a spyghtful word among
them / & except saint Policarpus rayled, when he called the
heretike Marcyon the deuyls eldeste son, & excepte our sauyour
rayled, when he called yᵉ scribes & the pharysyes hypocrytes.

But then yᵗ I cal them agayn good names: this thynge lo this
20   good man rekeneth a very monstrouse maner, to make theym
both good and badde. But this is a monstre lo of euery mannys
makynge. For so call not I them alone, but yᵉ whole people to, in
such maner of spekynge as euery man vseth, when he calleth one
self noughty lad, both a shrewd boy and a good sonne / the tone
25   in the proper symple speche, the tother by the fygure of [d₅]
ironye or antiphrasys. And by a lyke maner figure saint Hierome
agaynst the olde heretyke Vigilantius, calleth hym somtyme
Vigilantius, and somtime agayne Dormitantius / and so he calleth that heretyke two contrary names, as well as I do these.

30   And where he can not tell what I mene by the new broched
bretherhed: that am I content to tell hym / I mene that they be a
barrell of poysen, that the deuyll hath late sette abroche, and
laboreth by them to poysen other men.

And where he can not bere it, that they beynge suche shold be
35   called by the name of euangelycalles: I well allowe the good

---

5 And] *no para.* *1557*   12 me,] me. *1533* *1557*   14–15 *Sidenote 1557:*
Actes .23.   16 called] calleth *1533* *1557*   17 sauyour] sauiour *1557*, souyour
1533   18 *Sidenote 1577:* Math. 23; hypocrytes] hipocrites *1557*, hyprocytes *1533*

mynde of the good man, that he therin sheweth hym self so to
bere to the fayth, that it greueth hym to here heretykes called by
such a good graciouse name. But he must consyder that it is now,
and some yeres al redy passed hath ben, the name by which they
haue bene as commenly [d₅v] called in all the cuntreys catholyke,   5
as by theyr owne very name of heretyke. And thoccasyon therof
grewe fyrst of that that them self toke yᵗ name euangelicall ar-
rogantly to them self both by theuangelycall lyberty that they
pretended, as folke that wolde lyue vnder the gospell and vnder
no mannes lawe besyde / & bycause they wolde also byleue   10
nothynge ferther, than yᵉ very scrypture, all which they take now
vnder the name of the gospell. For yᵉ new lawe they take for no
thyng ellys, but for the declaracyon and perfeccyon of the olde.

Now whan they had taken thys name comenly vpon them self,
the catholikes tellyng them, yᵗ they neyther lyued nor byleued   15
accordynge to the gospell letted not yet to call them by the same
name to / & that not to theyr prayse, but to theyr rebuke &
shame. And some turned in wrytyng yᵗ name of theyrs in scorne,
& in stede of euange[d₆]licos, wrote them pseudo euangelicos.

Now yf this man can not bere it, that I call them as the old folke   20
do: though I wolde my selfe leue it for his pleasure, yᵗ wolde
make ye wote well but a small chaunge. For other folke wyll call
them styll yet by what name they lyst, and neyther I nor he can
lette them.

But to thentent he may be somewhat the lesse discontent with   25
me, for callynge heretykes by a good name: he shal vnderstande
that vpon suche occasyon & such maner, it is no newe begon
thyng so to do. For a certayne sorte there were of the heretikes
that were yᵉ Manicheis, which were fyrst amonge them selfe
called by yᵉ name of Cathari, that is to wyt pure and clene / &   30
afterward the catholikes called them by yᵉ same name. And so
doth saynt Austayne also call theym in his wrytynge. But yet he
declareth bothe theyr false heresyes, & theyr secrete shamefull
lyuyng for such, that [d₆v] though he call them by the name of
pure and clene, as we call now these bretherne euangelycall, yet   35
he ment that they were neither pure nor clene in dede, no more

7 *Sidenote 1557:* Euangelical.;yᵗ] the *1557;* euangelicall] euangelicall, *1533,* evangelical,
1557   19 them] thē *1533 1557 (see note)*   30 *Sidenote 1557:* Cathari.

than these folke in lyuynge or bylyefe, folow the very gospell in dede.

But than cometh he forth vppon me somwhat solempnly with a very foly and with a solempne lye. For lo good readers these are 5 his wordes I warraunt you wyse and trewe.

And now wyll I saye somwhat ferther concernyng thys mater, and that is thys. I meruayle mych, how mayster More durste for offence of hys conscyence, and for drede of the kynges dyspleasure, and of the whole realme, brynge vp such a slaunderouse name in this realme, and put it 10 in prynt, that may lyghtly touche not onely many of the comon people, but also of the greatest of the realme, as well spyrytuall as temporall: yf he and other of hys affynyte lyste to call any of them one of the blessed bretherne, or of the good brethern. And in this poynt it semeth, that he forgate the honour of the realme, whyche he semed moch to regarde, 15 whan he sayd: he coulde not thynke it to the honour of the realme, that other realmes shuld wene, that the whole clergye of this realme shulde be so farre fallen into the grudge and indygnacyon of the whole temporaltye, as he sayth it is spoken to be in the sayd treatyse, whyche he cal[d₇]leth the boke of diuisyon: for certaynly it is more dyshonour to 20 the realme, to haue it noysed, that the realme is full of heretykes, than that the temporaltye grudgeth agaynste the spyrytualty, and so he esheweth and fleeth the lesse sclander, though it were all true that he sayeth and renneth heedlynge into the greater.

And now wyll I saye somewhat ferther concernynge thys 25 mater / and that is thys. I meruayle mych how this man durst for offence of his conscyence & dyspleasure of god, brynge vp suche a slaunderouse lye vppon me, and wryte it in hys boke, that I sholde wryte in myne apologye, that the realme is full of heretykes.

30 If the case were nowe no better vppon my parte, nor no wurse vpon his, but that in myne apologye there coulde no suche sayenge be founden: what rebuke were it yet vnto hym, yf he were a man openly knowen by name? as now the shame cleueth not on hys chekes, but he soone shaketh it of whyle hys name is

not at hys booke. But nowe syth that in myne [d₇v] apologye I playnely wryte the contrary: what wordes wyl there serue to saye to thys man the thynges, that he were in this poynt very wel worthy to here.

Rede good chrysten readers the .xlvii. chapyter of myne apology, begynnynge in the .260. lefe and there shall you playnely se, that I saye playne the contrary. For where as thys pacyfyer dyd in hys boke of dyuisyon vnder the name of some other bylye of lykelyhed some of the spyrytualty than, surmyttynge that they as of polycy noysed that the realme is full of heretykes more than it is in dede / as he now bylyeth me here, surmysynge that I do say the same: ye shall there se that I shewe it to be vnlykely, yᵗ any polytyke spyrytuall man wolde so saye for polycy / syth so to say were for them for the cause that I there shew, very far agaynst good polycy. And there I ferther [d₈] shew, yᵗ some heretykes haue falsely made that noyse, and there I tell for what cause. And afterward in fo. 268. I shew yᵗ for all theyr besy bragyng, they be yet in dede but a few.

Now good readers whan I thus haue wryten there in both the places so open and so playne, that the realm is not full of heretykes, nor hath therin but a few, though yᵗ few be in dede ouer many / & growen mo also by neglygence in some parte, than there hath bene in some late yeres passed: how may this man fynde in his harte for shame, to wryte in this wyse? and as it were with such authoryte so solempnely chekke me falsely, for writyng yᵗ the realm is full, & than excuse his lyke fawte by myne / & yet in the comparison make myne the greater to? But now is all the craft of yᵗ comparyson dyscouered, & the glory of that argument defaced, whyle you se yᵗ his fawt is trew, & that myne he feyneth & fyndeth not in my boke, but playn [d₈v] and expressely the contrary / and that he spynneth that fyne lye without flex, fetchyng it out of his own body as the spider spynneth her cobwebbe. And thus is my fawte fayre wyped awaye, & hys lyeth styll in his necke, and another now layed vnto it.

Now as thys was no lytell foly for hym to lese his credence with

9 lykelyhed] likelyhood *1557*   16 falsely] falselye *1557*, salsely *1533*   19 readers] *1557*, reades *1533*   28 yᵗ] the *1557*   30 my] *1557*, myn *1533* (*see note*)   31–32 without] with *1557*

that open lye, that myght be so soone and so playnely controlled
and reproued: so is his fyrst poynt also no lesse foly than that,
wherin he merueyleth so mych that I dare for my conscyence,
and for dyspleasure of my prynce, & of the whole realme,
5 brynge vp that slaunderouse name in the realme, to call these
heretykes the bretherne / consyderynge that it maye lyghtely
touche not onely any man of ye comen people, but also of the
greatest of the realme, as well spyrytuall as temporall, yf eyther
my selfe or any of myn affinite lyste to call them, one of the [e₁]
10 blessed brethern or of ye good brethern.

   This is forsoth one the most symple sought out foly, that euer I
yet sawe set out with hygh wordes so solempnely. For fyrst as for
to call them by the name of the bretherne, is nothynge of my
bryngynge vppe, but a worde walkynge in euery mannes mouth
15 (whyche thynge I can not byleue but thys man wel knoweth hym
selfe, as straunge as he maketh the mater) and bygonne by the
good blessed bretherne them selfe, as wel appereth vppon theyr
owne letters, inough to be shewed at sondry seasons sent bytwene them.

20 Now touchynge the great fere & perel that he putteth, leste I
or some of myne affynyte may slaunder any of the greatest of the
realme, yf we lyste to call any suche man one of the good
bretherne: the good man maye take his rest I warraunt hym, &
shal not nede to breke his slepe therfore. [e₁v] For fyrst as for
25 myn affynyte is not very great. For I haue none affinyte but as I
thynke hym selfe hath and euery other man, that is to wyt eyther
by gossepred or by maryage / excepte he mene to call all the
trewe catholykes myne affynyte, and all the tother his owne. And
than whyche waye so euer he mene, a lewde slaunderouse worde
30 were as lykely to happen in one of his affinite as in one of myne.
And as for my self the pacifyer hym selfe is (as hys some sayes
shewe) somwhat more set vppon an appetyte of slawnderynge
than am I, whych bere a lytell more reuerence to the great men
of the realme, spyrituall and temporall bothe, and more honest
35 mynd vnto the small also, than wrongfully to dyffame eyther

---

5 slaunderouse] sclaunderous *1557*   10 brethern.] brethren. *1557*, brethern
1533   11 This] *no para. 1557;* one] on *1557*   21 slaunder] sclaunder *1557*   29
slaunderouse] sclaunderous *1557*   32 slawnderynge] sclaunderyng *1557*   35 also]
1533 corr. err., all *1533 1557*

great or small, by callynge eyther the tone or the tother, any of y^e
blessed byched new broched bretherhed / excepte onely such as
by theyr own open wry[e$_2$]tynges, or by theyr open wordes, be
playnly proued heretykes.

But yet consider wel good reders, what a wyse reason thys is y^t 5
he bryngeth forth. For what parell is there of such slaunder,
more by this name of the good bretherne than by the tother
name of heretykes? is not y^e olde name of heretykes, as slaunderouse as this new name of the blessed brethern? what name
can this good man deuyse vs hym selfe to call them by, in whyche   10
name the same parell of slaunder may not fall as well as in this?
Men may by thys wyse reason call them by no name at al, for fere
lest I or myne affinite might yf we liste, call not onely any of the
people, but also y^e grettest lordys both spyrituall and temporall,
by the same name, and so brynge them in slaunder. For the   15
slawnder is all one what so euer the name be, whan the thynge is
all one that is ment and signifyed therby.

And this man vseth hym selfe in [e$_2$v] this place therfore, very
circumspectely for this poynte in this chapyter, where he
speketh of heretykes after his .iiii. sortys of folke before. For he   20
calleth them there by no name at all hym selfe, but sayth of y^e
fourth sort:

These be the wurst sorte of people before all other, excepte onely an
other sorte of people, whiche syre Thomas More in hys apologye calleth somtyme desperate wreches, sometyme starke heretykes, and som-   25
tyme the blessed bretherne, and sometyme the noughty bretherne &c.

So that this good man him self here, lyke a true faythfull man,
affirmeth them nought / & such & so nought, as ther be none
wurse. But name (as it semeth) for fere of occasyon of slaunder,
he durst here none call them hym selfe but sayth they be they,   30
whome I call thus and thus.

Well I wyl make no vow therof as yet / but I wyll peraduenture
at a leysour here after vppon better aduisement, vse the same
cyrcumspeccyon and polycye that I lerne of his ensample here /

---

5 But] *no para. 1557*   6 slaunder] sclaunder *1557*   8–9 slaunderouse] sclaunderous *1557*   11 slaunder] sclaunder *1557*   14 grettest] greatest *1557*   15
slaunder] sclaunder *1557*   16 slawnder] sclaunder *1557*   27 So] *para. 1557*   29
slaunder] sclaunder *1557*

and whan I speke of [e₃] suche maner folke, geue them no name
at all my selfe / but for a token that men maye wytte whome I
mene, I shall saye those fellowes I mene yᵗ saint Poule perdy
calleth heretykes so / & that be all they that obstinately holde any
5 selfe mynded opynyon, contrary to the doctryne that the comen
knowen catholyke chyrche, techeth & holdeth for necessary to
saluacyon.

After all thys in the .xiiii. and the .xv. lefe, he asketh me wyth a
solempne dreuen processe, whyther I wolde not thynke it good
10 and wel done / that all such as haue authoryte to punysh heretykes, shold before they punysh them, amende fyrst theyr own
fawtes. And I thynke yes in good faith, that it were very well
done / and I wold that euery man wolde so do in dede, that
eyther sholde correcte heretyke or any malefactour els.

15 But than agayn I aske hym, that though this were wel done, yf
euery [e₃v] man wolde waxe as good as another good man wolde
wyshe hym, and as hymselfe wold wysshe another man to be: yet
yf there were some yᵗ were not so sodaynly so well dysposed, as to
mende theyr own fawtes so soone as the dewty of theyr offyce
20 wolde requyre of necessyte that they sholde do correccyon vppon the fawtes of some other folke: sholde they not yet do it for
all that in the meane whyle, and other folke to whom it apper-
teyned / be bounden to assyste them therin, though theyr owne
fawtes were not all amended yet.

25 To this question lo he hath in the same place answered me yes,
as I haue hym to the tother. And thus good readers this good
man and I, after our sore conflycte in the tother mater, haue yet
in these two poyntes stryken handes agayn, and be god be
thanked metely well agreed togyther, god holde it. [e₄]

30   The .vi. chapyter.

Hᴵs syxth chapyter begynneth in yᵉ .xvi. lefe, wherin he
shewed that I in myne apologye misse take the letter of his sayd
treatyce / and he telleth which wordes. But he telleth neyther in
what place of his booke his wordes are, nor in what place of my

---

3 *Sidenote 1557:* Titum .3.   19 mende] amend *1557*   20 necessyte] necessyte,
1533, necessitye, *1557*   30 The .vi.] *1557*, The, vi. *1533*

booke you maye fynde myne. Those two thynges he leueth out,
bycause he wolde as he sayd in the begynnynge, not folowe
thorder of my chapyters, but take y^t waye that sholde be best to
the playn openynge of the trouth. But for as mych as me semeth
that to the playn openynge of treuth, the redyer waye is to reade   5
fyrste bothe the places, & than this his answere after: ye may
therfore good readers fynd both hys [e$_4$v] wordes and myne in
myne apologye / his in the lefe .123. / and myne agaynste which
he now reasoneth in his answer ye shall fynd fo. 127. And now
good readers yf you reade and consyder those two places fyrst,   10
and than compare well the wordes of myne apologye there, with
the wordes of his answere here: it shall suffyce for this mater.
For there shal you se wel that I mysse take not ye letter of his
wordes. For I say not nay, but that hys wordes go onely agaynst
spyrytuall men / but his reason runneth out agaynst euery kynd   15
of men spyrytuall & temporall to. And there I shew also, the
reason wherfore and why. And therfore I wene it wyl appere
plain, that I myssetake not the letter of his treatyse at all / & that
his reason runneth out in dede agaynst euery kynde of men. For
there is neyther spyrytuall man nor temporall, but he maye take   20
harme by habundaunce. [e$_5$] But so is there as I there saye,
neyther spyrytuall man nor temporall, but he maye with ha-
boundaunce do good.

But nowe the declaracyon of his mynde in thys answere, men-
deth al the mater. For here he declareth y^t by these wordes of his   25
in a maner stranglynge: he meaneth the mynyshynge of some
feruour, as though a man wolde say that by almost killyng with a
clubbe, he ment the geuynge of a fylyppe in the forhed wyth his
lytle fynger.

But syth that in this .vi. chapiter of hys, his great mortall stran-   30
glyng is nowe strageled away, and tourned into venyall synne: we
shall for this mater trouble you no lenger / but eueryman maye
take haly water and go home to dyner, for seruyce is all done
here for to day.

The counsayle of saynte Bernarde that he there speketh of to   35
the pope Eugenius, is in good fayth as [e$_5$v] me thynketh very

---

7–8 in myne] *1557*, in my *1533*   22 neyther] neyther, *1533*, neither *1557*   33
haly] holye *1557*

well brought in. And I wolde aduyse euery spiritual man to
folowe yt, and to take good temporal men to hym, and let theym
do all hys temporall besynesse for hym. This thynke I good as for
myne owne mynde, but yf there be in any parte any lawes made
5   all redy to the contrarye, by suche folke as yt can not bycome me
to controll. Howe be yt I suppose that myche parte of theyre
temporall besynesse is done by temporall men in dede.

As for his acte of parliament that he speketh of I suppose
veryly that the clergye wolde not be agaynst yt. And suche actes
10   are there all redy made mo then one, good and suffycyent / but
yf he meane to sette an addycyon therto, that the kynges grace
sholde expressely be bounden by the acte, that yf he gaue any
lycence of mortysynge into the chyrche, yt shold be voyde /
excepte such cases as thys [e₆] good man lyste to lymyte and geue
15   hym leue. Syth his hyghnes is now moued by this good man here
therto: his grace may agre to it when yt pleaseth hym.

As for the great mater that he maketh, of that I neuer in all the
tyme that I was conuersaunt in the court, could perceyue any of
the noble men aboue the nombre of seuen, and yet not nowe so
20   many, that euer thought yt good that any possessyons of the
chyrche, sholde wyth oute a lawfull cause be taken awaye there
from: I meruayle mych what he meaneth, and what subtyll conceyte he conceyueth in his wyse breste, that he so mutereth, and
mumbleth vpon that word as though suche communicacyon
25   eyther on the tone syde or the tother, were of suche hygh im-
portaunce, that yt were eyther felonye or some heyghnouse mysprisyon, eyther in tellyng the tale agayn, or els in kepyng yt
counsayle so longe. [e₆v] For I wote nere in good faythe in
whyche of the twayne this good man fyndeth yᵉ faute, or
30   whether he fynde any or none. But yf he fynde any: in which of
the twayne so euer he fynd yt, he fyndeth but his owne foly. For
nowe shall you good readers se, what lytle insyght the man hath
in any thyng that he readeth. Fyrst he reherseth a parte of my
wordes wryten in myne Apologye fo. .139., where I saye that I
35   neuer founde in all the tyme whyle I was conuersaunt in the
courte, of all the nobylyte of this lande, aboue the nombre of
seuen, yᵗ euer I perceyued to be of yᵉ mynd, that yt were eyther

---

6 controll] *1557*, contrall *1533*   33 that he] that 1557   36 lande,] lande. *1533*, land
1557

ryght, or reasonable, or coulde be to the realme profytable, wythout lawfull cause to take any possessyons awaye frome the clergye.

Nowe vpon these wordes ye shall se what he gathereth, by whych ye shal se what wyt and what lernynge the [e₇] man hath. These are his wordes lo.

Syth mayster More sayth that he hath not knowen aboue seuen (wherof he sayth thre are dede) that were of the mynde that yt were reasonable wythout cause to take possessyons fro the clergye / in whyche wordes yt is concluded, that he knew seuen of that mynde, whose opynyons yt lyketh hym to reherse and putte in writynge and in prynte also.

This man hath a special insyght in inclusyues and exclusyues, when he weneth that in my wordes it were included, that I knewe .vii. of that mynde, that yt were reasonable to take awaye possessyons fro the chyrche wythout cause. My wordes were you wote well that I neuer knewe aboue seuen, that wythoute lawfull cause to take awaye possessyons fro the chyrche, thought eyther ryght, or resonable, or that yt coulde be to the realme profytable. What include these wordes now? Do they include as he saith, yᵗ I say that I knew .vii. yᵗ thought yt reasonable? Thys man ys so connynge in hys inclusyues & exclusyues, that he dyscerneth no[e₇v]thynge bytwene copulatyues and dysiunctyuys. This man I se well neuer lerned the rule that almoste euery boy can, that to the veryte of a dysiunctyue, yt suffyseth any one parte to be trew. Let hym now lerne yt therfore / and thenne shall he perceyue that my wordes include no farther, but that I saye that I knewe seuen which among them all thought some one of those thre thynges, that is to wyt, eyther some of them some one, and some of them some other or els al seuen some one of those thre thinges, that is to wyt, eyther ryght, or reasonable, or profytable, wythoute any determynacyon whyche of the thre. And neyther includeth those wordes of myne that I say all seuen thoughte yt ryght, nor that all seuen thoughte yt reasonable, no nor yet that all seuen thought yt profytable. But yt hangeth not vppon hys

---

4 Nowe] *no para. 1557*   16 were] *1533 corr. err., om. 1533 1557*   23 copulatyues] compulatyues *1533,* copulatiues *1557*   24 *Sidenote 1557:* A general rule

determynacyon, but vpon myn own de[e₈]claracyon, which of
these thre thinges whyche of those same seuen thought or
whyche one of the thre they all thoughte / and neuer one of
those thre thynges is determinately included to any one of the
5 seuen. For yf I wolde saye that I neuer knewe in all my lyfe any
man aboue the nomber of seuen, that had ben eyther at Alkayre
or at Salem, or at Bizance: do these wordes include that I saye
that I haue knowen seuen that haue ben at Salem? That am I
sure they do not. But I maye well stande by those wordes, yf I
10 sayde after, that I haue knowen seuen persons that haue ben al
seuen at Bizance / but as for Alkayre or Salem I neuer knewe any
one that hadde ben at any one of them both.

    And in lyke wyse wyll I well stande by myne other wordes and
veryfye theym wyth a good excludyng of this mannes includyng.
15 For I say [e₈v] and very trouthe yt is, that I neuer found any
noble man aboue the nombre of seuen, that wythoute lawfull
cause to take awaye possessyons fro the clergye, thought yt
eyther ryght or reasonable, or that yt coulde be for the realme
profytable. I founde not I saye aboue seuen, that thought any
20 one of all these thre / is not this trew but yf I found seuen, yᵗ
thought all thre? yes forsoth trewe ynough though I neuer
found any one, yᵗ euer thought any two of the thre. And nowe
therfore though I neuer founde any noble man so vnryghtuouse, or so vnreasonable, as to thynke yt ryght or reasonable,
25 wythoute lawfull cause to take awaye any possessyons from the
clergye: yet haue I founde seuen that haue thought, yf ryghte
and reason wolde bere yt, they coulde tell howe that as for
worldely polycye, some of the possesseons taken awaye myght be
to the realme profytable. [f₁] And some one hathe thought that
30 yt wolde be peraduenture profytable to the realme, that the
lordes hadde the landes whose auncestours had mortysed
theym. And peraduenture he that so thought, shold not haue
lost a grote by yt. And some other hathe thought that it wold be
more profytable to put yt into hospytalles of some certayn new
35 fashyoned foundacyon, and therof neyther make prestes the

---

20 but] *1533 corr. err., om. 1533 1557*   29 profytable.] profitable. *1557*, profytable
1533   29–31 *Sidenote 1557:* Many mens thoughtes concerning spiritual landes.
31 mortysed] mortisied *1557*

maysters, nor no laye men neyther, but some good sad honest
vertuouse wydos, that wolde be tendable & tendre to syke folke,
and that shold yerely yelde a compte vnto thordynarye. And
some other haue thought yt better to dyuyde & cant yt amonge
good pore husband men, that shold tyl the ground theyr own   5
handes, & take the lande for theyr labour, with dyuers other
dyuyses mo, euery man after hys own mynde. And what harme
was there nowe in any of all theyre [f₁v] myndes, yᵗ thys good
wise man wold haue my wordes seme so heygnouse, vppon a
sentence that hym selfe includeth in theym / and whyche sen-   10
tence of hys, reason excludeth from theym / and in whyche as
you playnly se proued, thys man woteth nere what he meaneth.
And to thentent yᵗ he shold wel knowe that the mater is nothynge
ferefull: therfore wrote I that thre were dede, bycause he sholde
well wyt that there were yet the more parte a lyue. And therfore   15
yf the good man thynke any great heygnouse offence in the
mater: lette hym come to me hym selfe, and I shall brynge hym
to some of theym, that shall not make yt straunge to say agayne
the same to hym selfe / and than he may vse it at his pleasure as
his hygh wysedome shal thynke conuenyent.   20
    Than sayth he farther in the seconde [f₂] syde of the .xviii.
lefe, yᵗ he can not tel what cause I wold thynke a cause resonable,
to take any possessions from yᵉ chyrche. But yet syth yt is im-
plyed in my wordes, that some cause lawefull and resonable
there may be: he thynketh he sayth, yᵗ peraduenture yf I were   25
asked the question therin, by them yᵗ haue authoryte to do it, I
wolde shewe what I ment therby. There shal in good faith nede
no gret solemne examynacyon of me by men of authoryte for
that mater. For I wyll not stycke to tel yt vnto hym selfe / but haue
tolde yt al redy to hym and euery man ellys that lyste to reade yt,   30
a good whyle a go in my booke of the Supplycacyon of soules /
and there maye thys good man go seke yt yf yt please hym, and
then vse yt as yt lyke hym.
    But fynally after his harte some what eased, he cometh to hym
selfe [f₂v] agayne, and endeth the chapyter very well / wyshynge   35
the clergye the grace that the apostles had, and declarynge that

---

he neuer desyred them thapostles pouertye nor wold them no
lesse then they haue / and exhortyng theym that haue aboundaunce of possessyons, to be well ware so to vse yt as yt be not a let
of the deuocyon that they sholde haue to god, and the charyte
5 that they sholde shewe to theyre neyghbour. In these thre
thynges he sayth as me thinketh very specially well. And I praye
you hartely good readers euery man the rather at my pore request, what so euer he wrote before, thynke now that he ment
then but thus. [f₃]

10 H   The .vii. chapeter.
       Is seuenth chapiter begynneth in the .xix. lefe and therin
vppon a sex leues / he argeweth agaynste a lytle doute that I
moued vpon the begynnynge of his fyrste chapyter of hys dyuysyon / whych wordes of his and myne theruppon begynne in
15 myne apologye fo. 101. And the same poynt is touched agayne
there fo. 106. When you haue there redde what I say: then may
you rede here hys answere, wherin he declareth yᵉ mater, and
argueth it by cases of law, mych after the maner of a motable
case, ful wel fauoredly in good fayth / and wyth longe labour
20 proueth at laste, that yt must be taken in such wyse as he seeth, yᵗ
among other construccions [f₃v] I construed his minde my self,
though I was loth to do so, bycause yᵗ waye was the worste for
hym selfe. But nowe he remedyeth that wyth a lyne or twayne,
wherin he declareth yᵗ he ment not to preferre euery seculare
25 preste byfore those that are in relygyon. Wherin I wold haue
trusted him as well vppon his worde, as vppon the reason that he
layeth for it now / whyche saue for the truste that I haue to his
word, I wold wene he neuer thoughte on whan he wrote the
dyuysyon / but rather ended yᵉ clause in suche wyse as yt hap-
30 ped, wythout any respect peraduenture to thencrease and
growynge of the sentence in the ende.
   I was ones halfe in mynde here to haue kept scoles wyth hym
yet in this poynte ones agayne, euyn all of pleasure / and to haue

---

1–2 nor wold them no lesse then they haue /] *1533 corr. err., om. 1533 1557*   2–3
Sidenote 1557: A godlye exhortacion.   12 sex] sixe *1557*   20 seeth,] seeth
1557   25 Wherin] *1557,* wherin *1533*

broughte yt yet agayne in questyone, whether the cyrcumstaunces of his wordes were [f₄] able to proue, that he ment
otherwise than he now argueth yᵗ it muste nedes be taken. And
then yf the cyrcumstances so dyd, whether commen vsage and
acceptaunce of a worde sholde agaynste the cyrcumstaunces of   5
the mater, haue lyke strength in all other thynges, as yt hath in
maters of law / and whether the reason vsed in the courtes in
maters of law, be of lyke strength in euery other thynge as they
be when they be made in maters of lawe / and of lyke vygour and
force in euery place abrode, as they be in the courtes in whyche   10
they haue ben longe receued and accepted for sure and stable
groundes.

And whyther in this poynte betwene hym and me, beynge no
mater of the law nor perteynyng to the iudgement of any court,
but to be consydered by the whole people in euery mannes rea   15
son at large, the cases of the lawe of thys realme that he [f₄v]
bryngeth in, whyche be iudged and sure, and shold serue the
tone parte in the lawe, though the mater were the weyghte of a
thousande pounde, sholde bycause we be englyshe men, and our
mater wryten in Englande and in Englyshe wordes, stande for a   20
sure and an insoluble argument, though the lawes both ciuyle
and canon that are called the comen lawes of all chrystendome
besyde vs, were as peraduenture they be in the selfe same cases,
full and whole to the contrarye.

And yet wolde I besyde thys a lytle haue assayed, so to shake   25
his cases of London and Mychelmasse, yᵗ peraduenture to many
a man in London betwene this and Michelmas, shold they neuer
haue semed lyke vnto our mater, by that tyme that I had ones
declared them the dyfference.

These poyntes and happely mo to, was I when I redde his   30
answere [f₅] halfe mynded as I saye to haue brought in, and
dysputed wyth hym vpon this mater. For I was waxen with yᵉ
readyng of his answere very mery, and waxen me thought a yong
man agayn / and semed set at a vacacyon mote with hym in some
Inne of the chauncery, bycause of hys comen entendement, and   35
his proper casys of lawe.

---

10 in whyche] is which *1557*   19 bycause] *1533* corr. err., because *1557*, hycause
1533   22 *Sidenote 1557:* The common lawes of christendome.   25 And] *no para.*
1557   31 halfe] half *1557*, halse *1533*

But than I consydered that as I was in the redynge of his
answere mery: so was hym selfe I saw well in the wrytynge wery /
and other readers that were no lawyers, wolde in the readynge
waxe almost as wery. Than sawe I also, that whan hym selfe had
5   all sayed, he lyked not hys owne all the beste / but after all hys
payne taken in the answeryng, seyng that his answere lyked hym
not, he was fayne to fall to another waye, & telleth me that there
nedeth none answere to that poynte at all, bycause [f₅v] that
there is no frute he sayth in that obieccyon.

10   Now therfore yf thobieccyon be frutelesse, and therfore
thanswere nedelesse, and verily frutelesse to: nowe to reply
thereto were labour halfe loste and more. And therfore good
readers for as myche as to the answere made by the maner, no
law putteth vs ferther to reply: yᵉ mater is at a demurrour in
15   thys poynt, and we at your iugement, wherein ye may vse your
wysedome and iuge it euyn as you fynde it. Wherin the best that
he can aske, is but to be dysmyssed, & iudged that he ment not
to preferre the state of chauntry prestes before the state of relygyouse prestes / but ment as he now declareth his minde
20   (whiche very few folke coulde before as I suppose haue gessed)
that the varyaunce bytwen prestes and prestes, that is to wyt
bytwene seculare prestes and seculare prestes, is more to [f₆] be
lamented than betwen other prestes & relygyouse, or bytwene
relygyouse and relygyouse, bycause yᵉ varyaunce bytwene
25   prestes and prestes is more marked and more notable than any
of the tother, bycause the seculer prestes go more abrode.

Now yf this exposicyon of his mynde may serue to quyte hym
now: (which I am content it do) it is all I promyse you that it maye
do. For it wyll neuer serue hym to recouer dammages. For he can
30   neuer blame no man that perceyued not that before, that is skant
credyble yet.

But yet bycause he so myche inculketh the lacke of fruyte in
many of myne obieccyons, and that they be no maters of no
morall vertue: I wyll not answere hym wyth the lyke / and saye
35   that in many of hys pretended causes of dyuisyon is no fruit at

---

1 But] *no para. 1557*   17 iudged] *1533 corr. err.*, iudge *1533 1557*   19 prestes]
1533 corr. err., persons *1533 1557*   23 betwen other] *1533 corr. err.*, bytwene *1533*,
betwene *1557*   26 seculer] *1533 corr. err., om. 1533 1557*   27 Now] *no para. 1557*

all, nor no morall vertue neyther / as in procurynge the people to
[f₆v] byleue vntrewly, that the prelates handle men vncherytably, and for heresyes vexe them wrongfully, & geue occasyon
that some peryshe both in body and soule / whyche yf the ordynaryes had handeled them cherytably, had ben in bothe   5
twayne saued / and that it wylbe very harde to fynd so myche as
any one spyrytuall man suche, as hym selfe deuyseth and
aduyseth, that none but suche sholde be suffred to be iudge in
heresye / and laborynge also the good lawes of thys realme and
of all chrystendome to be chaunged, to the ease of heretykes, yᵗ   10
haue ben made for the repressynge of heresyes / wyth suche
other thynges lyke that are in his boke of dyuysyon mo than I
euer wrote worde of yet / in whiche (as I haue often sayd) for as
mych as I se yᵗ he professeth hym selfe to hate and abhorre these
heresyes, yᵗ these folke now holde, whom saynt poule calleth   15
heretikes (I dare [f₇] not now for hym but whan I forget my selfe
call theym by none other name) I wolde with good wyll that men
shold thynke he ment none hurt. But in the wordes of the wrytynge, taken after the comen vsage and acceptaunce of spekynge,
as he wyll in thys his .vii. chapyter haue me take them, there is   20
neyther morall vertue nor frute, but full vnfrutefull vyce.

But as I sayd, I wyll not in defence of myne, answere hym with
yᵉ fawtes of his. For myne were neuer the better though his be
nought to. But I saye that myne obieccyons in myne apologye be
not frutelesse, bycause they defende the truthe, & make good   25
folke perceyue both what harme it were to byleue suche euyll
lyes, & what dammage it were to put awaye suche good lawes /
and how vnreasonable it were in other mennes fawtes to take
small thynges for very heyghnouse and great / or for them that
in a [f₇v] felesshyp are fawty, not to bere dyspleasure onely to   30
theyr persons, but to be at dyuysyon in generall wyth the whole
company. And this fruit is there also, that though that boke saye
the contrary, straungers such as are here and can rede englysshe, whyche are not ye wote well a few, many yet perceyue by
playne proues in myne apologye, that not onely there is no suche   35
great generall causes of dyuysyon as the booke of dyuysyon sayth
that there is, but also that there is no such great generyll dyuy-

syon thorow the realme in dede. These fruytes are there in many
of myne obieccyons agaynste hys booke in myne apologye.

Now where as some of myne obieccyons peraduenture, lay but
eyther lacke of lernynge in hym, or lacke of naturall wytte, syth
5 his name is not at his boke, but he sp-keth hym selfe vnknowen:
this profyte is there in [f₈] suche obieccyons, that wythout hys
rebuke or shame, the readers may by those fawtes perceyue, that
the wryter was not of any such specyall qualytees, as the booke
wherin so mych euyll was conteyned, sholde be mych lened vnto,
10 for credence and authoryte of the man.

Finally the very selfe obieccyon, wherof he speketh in y^t
seuenth chapyter of his in his new booke, & sayth there is no
profyte in that obieccyon, and that therfore it neded none answere / but he myght graunte me all that euer I saye therin, and
15 yet none effectuall mater were there for all that: therto I saye
that loke who so lyste what I saye therin, and he shall fynde that
yf this man graunte all y^t, he shal graunte in hym self mych more
ouersyghte & mych more lacke of lernyng to, than were requysyte in hym that wold put out bokes abrode / and therfore
20 hys wrytyng the lesse to be [f₈v] regarded, whyle hys person is
vnknowen / where as yf his person were knowen, he myght be
peraduenture perceyued for all that, for suche a specyall man
bysyde, that hys approued wysedome and lernyng well knowen
otherwyse, myght for thestimacyon of his boke, more than coun-
25 trepayse some suche ouersyghtes as at a tyme myght happely to
scape a right wyse man, y^t wolde wryte by candellyght whyle he
were halfe a slepe.

But than I say ferther yet / that in that obieccyon was a mater
of no lytell effect. For takyng that he ment as hym selfe sayth he
30 dyd: his wordes semed playnely to shewe, that he rekened the
state of chauntry prestes, to be a state of more perfeccyon than
the state of relygyouse prestes. And therfore thobieccyon con-
tayned mater of great effecte, and whych he mych neded to
answere and to declare that he ment not so / but that he ment as
35 he [g₁] now declareth, that dyuysyon is bytwene seculare prestes,
more lamentable than bytwene relygyouse, bycause the seculare
prestes be more abrode, and therby theyr varyaunce more

knowen. Whyche exposycyon few men I wene wold haue
thought vpon before. But now that he sayth he ment so: I am
very well content therwyth, and wolde that all folke sholde take it
so to / & yet is it ye wote well but very wynter ware, and a scuse as
colde as a kay.   5

The .viii. chapyter.

H IS .viii. chapiter begynneth in the secunde side of his .xxv.
lefe, and pretendeth to answere my wordes wryten agaynste his,
in the .xix. chapiter of myne apology, whyche begynneth folio .116. [g₁v] And now he sayth that I say there, that I wote not   10
wel what he meneth in that he sayth that the spyrytualtye call the
worldely honour of the chyrche and of spyritual persons, the
honour of god. And therfore he sayeth here, that he wyll, & so
doeth declare therin, what he there ment therby.

But here is now yᵉ crafte: where as I did there shew what I   15
thought he ment therby, and therfore made answere to those
thynges yᵗ I thought he there ment: now the mater beyng
chaunged here, by hys new declaracyon: he bryngeth in myne
answers made there, and confuteth them for insuffycyent now,
whan hys new declaracyon hath made a chaunge in the mater / as   20
though I had than ment to answere this, that I was not than ware
that he wolde now saye, nor I wene hym selfe neyther.

But rede fyrste good readers the .xix. chapyter of myne
apologye be[g₂]gynnyng fo. 116. and there shall you se those
wordes of his suffycyently answered, for the thynge that me   25
thought he ment. And than after that done, consyder hys answere here / in whyche for all hys holy pyece of a sermon, what
doth he tell me. He telleth me that honour is onely dew to vertue, & that no man may couet honour without offence / excepte
it be to the honour of god, and that inordynat appetyte of hon-   30
our is dedely synne / and that yf a spyrytuall man wolde accepte
honour by reason of any spirytuall dygnyte, and that god were
therby dyshonoured, thanne that honour were not to be called
honour but dyshonour / and that yet some laye menne saye that
spyrytuall men call it an honour to god.   35

---

9 chapiter] chapter *1557*   15 crafte:] crafte. *1533*, craft, *1557*   28 *Sidenote 1557:*
Honour dewe to vertue.

All thys whole tale for all thys holy sermon is yet to the mater, in mayntenaunce of hys formar wordes whiche [g₂v] he wold here seme to defende, vtterly tolde in vayne. For fyrste in all this tale he telleth vs not well what he calleth worldly honour, whyche he sayth the spirytualty calleth the honour of god, & which was the thynge that I sayed I wyste nere what honour he ment. For where he wolde seme to declare it: there is hys declaracyon both very bare, & yet agaynst hym to. For in the secunde syde of the .xxvi. lefe, he drybbeth in a worde of spyrytuall dygnite / & thus he sayth.

Then I mene ferther, that yf any spyrytuall man wolde accept a worldly honour, by reason of any spyrytuall dygnyte, & god were therby dyshonored, as it may be by many circumstances, as yf for suche worldly honour charyte be in any maner broken or denyed, iustyce delayed, any of the .vii. sacraments not duely mynystred: or the people not dylygentely and playnely instructed: that then it is not to be called honour to god, but rather dishonour, and that yet some laye men say, they call it an honour to god. And surely the truth is, that many laye men saye, that for the mayntenaunce of such worldly honour, spyrytuall men bothe relygyouse and seculer, be neglygent somtyme in such thinges, as be before rehersed, and that yet they call suche worldly honour the honour of god. [g₃]

Here he hath told vs that yf any spyrytuall man wold accept a worldly honour, by reason of any spiritual dygnite, wherby god were dyshonored, that honour were not honour. But yet he telleth vs not what maner of worldly honour it is that he meneth to be accepted by reason of a spirytuall dignyte / nor yet what maner thynge suche worldly honour is / nor touchyng that spyrytual dignite, he telleth not whyther he mene a desyre in any man to attayne any spyrytual dignite, for some kinde of worldly honour yᵗ he thynketh shold folow theron, or els some worldly honour by reason of any spyrytuall dygnyte, that the man hath all redy.

I let passe his cold and vnsauery tolde tale of cheryte denyed, and iustyce delayed, and some of the seuen sacramentes not duly mynystred, for mayntenaunce of such worldely honour, as some

---

1 All] *no para. 1557*   6 nere] neare *1557*

spyrituall men bothe [g₃v] seculares and relygyouse by reason of
spyrytuall dygnytees accepte, as some laye men saye. A pore tale
and a colde by my faye, to be tolde for a cause of an heyghnouse
vniuersall dyuysyon. For thys were an endeles dyuysyon, yf euery suche fawte of some, sholde vppon euery some saye be layed   5
for a cause of dyuysyon agaynst the generall body.

And yet bysyde all thys, I saye that hys fyrste wordes are
nothynge mayntened wyth all thys mater. For hys fyrste wordes
spake of a consent and agrement, wherin seculare prestes and
relygyous, for all the varyaunce bytwene them selfe for other   10
thynges, yet agre togyther about the mayntenaunce of that
worldely honour that they call the honour of god. And here he
speketh but of another mater that is to wyt yᵗ for the mayntenaunce of worldely honour spyrytuall men both relygyouse and
secu[g₄]lar be neglygent somtyme, & in some maner breke or   15
denye cheryte, delaye iustyce, & do not dewly ministre some of
the seuen sacramentes, nor dylygently & plainely instructe the
peple.

All this tale as you se towcheth yᵉ pryuate fawtes of some such,
as for the mayntenaunce of that worldly honour which they call   20
goddes honour, thus mysse vse them selfe. But thys tale is
nothynge sybbe to hys other tale, that he tolde and I towched
before. For that spake of such agrement all in one, that is to wyt
an holdynge togyther whych sygnyfyeth a maynteynynge eche
of other agaynst other men, in mayntenaunce of that worldly   25
honour that they call the honour of god, in lyke wyse as for
maters of theyr owne, they be one agaynste another amonge
them selfe.

And thus you se playnely good reders, yᵗ this maner of mayntenyng [g₄v] of his formar wordes, is a clene going from them,   30
and a leuyng of them vnmayntened / and (bycause he cometh
vppon me byfore in another place with casys of law) were in the
lawe a very playne departure, and sholde in any of the kynges
courtes yf I demurred vppon it, vtterly marre all his mater.

And so it appereth that some other some, haue sayd this vnto   35
him sinnys to glose his fyrste wordes wythall. And yet I meruayle

---

14 worldely] worldly *1557*, wordely *1533*   15 secular] *1533 1557, catchword* lar,
1533   17 seuen] *om. 1557*

that he coulde thynke theyr sayeng worth the rehersynge
agayne. For who can byleue y^t any spyritual man wold be so
madde, as to call worldely honour vsed to goddes dishonour, the
honour of god. I can scant byleue that any laye man wolde so tell
5 hym / at the leste wyse not wyth that adieccyon, that he now
putteth new therto.

But now yf it so be that vn the tother syde, all spyrytuall men
wold [g5] wyth one voyce to gether, call the honour of god, that
worldly honour that worldely folke do to the chyrche and vnto
10 spyrytuall persons, for the deuocyon that good lay men bere to
god and vnto spyrituall persons for goddis sake, by reason of
theyr holy orders and honorable romes that they bere in
Chrystes chyrche / though some of theym as this man sayth /
sometyme do not theyre dutye therin, but leue some parte of
15 theyr dutyes towarde goddes honour vndone therfore: yet for
the deuocyon of the temporall persons that for goddis honour
do it, they may all well call yt goddes honour in dede. And
therfore is thys good man in that poynte full answered, as solemne a mater as he made therof.

20 But nowe concernynge hys formare wordes of the agrement
of all spyrytuall folke to gether, in ye mayntenaunce of theyr
worldly honour, for [g5v] al theyre pryuate dyspleasures and
dyssensyons in other thynges among theym selfe / wyth whyche
he cometh in after here agayne, and referreth hym to the com-
25 men opinyon of mych parte of the people bothe spyrytuall and
temporal, whether laye men so saye or not: I saye that though al
men so sayde, yet is no man at dyuysyon wyth theym therfore.
For there is no cause wherfore any man shold. For yt is none
vnreasonable thynge, that syth those thynges whych thys man
30 speketh of, that is to wyt those spyrytuall dygnytees to whyche he
sayth suche worldely honour apperteyneth, are lawefully theyr
owne, eche of theym sholde in all laweful ways and such as are by
no law prohybyted, helpe & assyste other to kepe them, though
there be for pryuate maters of theyr owne varyaunce & suyt
35 betwene theym. And thys may they with better conscyence do
eche for other [g6] than eche of them for them selfe. For in thys

_____

7 vn] on _1557_   9 worldly] _1557_, wordly _1533_   22 worldly] _1557_, wordly
_1533_   29 thys] _1557_, thys, _1533_

that they do for other, is there not the synne of ambycyon that
thys man here speketh of. And this is the parte not onely of
spyrytuall men relygyouse and seculare bothe, but of euery good
temporall man to / and not onely to do so for them, but euery
man also for other. And therfore what reason hadde those same   5
some that so tolde this man, yf there were any some suche in
dede, to take thys thynge for any cause of dyuysyon? or why dyd
not he so rather tell theym, than putte theyre fonde tale in hys
boke?

But than one pretie pyece he hath of two partes, by whych he   10
weneth that the spyrytualtye can in no wyse escape but that they
muste nedys be betrapped in the tone. For when he hathe sayde
that the people saye that spyrytuall men be sometyme neglygent
in kepynge or grauntynge [g₆v] charyte, or in spedy doynge of
iustyce or in duely mynystrynge some of the seuen sacramentes,   15
or in playne & dylygent instructynge of the people: then with a
proper pyece of two partes thus he concludeth the mater.

And yf yt be not so as the people saye: then are the spyrytuall rulers
bounden to helpe the people oute of that iugement, or ellys they be not
wythout offence theym selfe. And on the tother syde, yf yt be as the   20
people saye: then are spyrytuall men bounden to reforme yt.

As for thys two handed sworde, some yonge lustye frere wold
boldely bete of wyth a two handed staffe, and tell this man
agayne, that yf the peple as he putteth for the tone parte sayde in
such thynges not trew: than seeth he not nor no man elles nei-   25
ther, what the spyrytual rulers coulde do to put theym oute of
that iudgement, but tell theym, nolite iudicare et non iudicabimini / and so wyll that syde of the sworde do this man lytle
seruyce. And then on the tother syde, yf the people in these
thynges saye trew as [g₇] yt is well lykely they do: than trewe yt is   30
that the spyrytuall men be bounden to reforme yt. But than is yt
as trew agayne, that the thynge beynge but suche as this man
reherseth, that ys to wyt neglygence but in some, in doyenge of
some parte of theyr dutye, and that also but sometyme, is no

8 fonde] *1557*, founde *1533*   22 frere] *1557*, freee *1533*   27–28 *Sidenote 1557:*
Luke .6.   31 spyrytuall] spiritual *1557*, spyrytull *1533*

cause of dyuysyon to sette the whole temporaltye agayne theym all, and that syde of the sworde yᵉ frere wold wyth this ende of his staffe bete harde vnto this mannes own hed.

Now goeth this man farther fo. 27. and sheweth that myne
5 answere to his wordes whyche you reade in the .xix. chapyter of myn Apologye, be very darke, by the reason that I vse therin so often this word (Some saye) whyche is he sayth done after a raylyng fashion. But as you know wel good reders, I haue taken yᵗ word Some say, of his boke, in whyche I redde yt so often / that
10 yt falleth som[g₇v]tyme into my penne ere I be ware.

And as for the raylynge fashyon, yf I durste be bolde to tel so sadde a man a mery tale, I wolde tell hym of the frere, that as he was prechyng in the countrey, spyed a pore wyfe of the paryshe wysperynge wyth her pewfelowe / and he fallynge angrye ther-
15 wyth, cryed oute vnto her alowd, holde thy bable I byd the, thou wyfe in the rede hode. Whyche when the houswyfe herd: she waxed as angry agayn / and sodaynly she starte vppe and cryed oute vnto the frere agayn, that al the chyrch rang theron: mary syr I beshrew his harte that bableth moste of vs both. For I do but
20 wysper a word with my neighbour here, & thou hast babled there al this houre. And surely good readers saue for lettynge of the word of god in this good mannys sermone: I durste well in the same worde (Some saye) be[g₈]shrowe hym and beshrowe hym agayne, that moste hathe rayled therwyth of thys good man or
25 me. For reade my wordes there when ye wyll, and you shall fynde that I wyth that worde do but in a maner playe wyth hym. But by saynte Mary he, how well so euer he ment, hys wordes wyth his many (Some sayes) brynge good men in slaunder and obloquye of the people, and peraduenture in parell to, wyth
30 vntrewe surmysed talys of mysse handelynge folke for heresye / and all coloured vnder some sayes to make the lyes seme some-what lykely. Suche shrewd (Some sayes) lo be no mery sportynge, but be sadde and erneste rude raylynges in dede.

Then he toucheth myne answere made in the sayde chapyter
35 of myne apology, & double confuteth yt, yᵗ I saye that he hath herd some laye men [g₈v] say the contrary. For fyrste he sayth he

---

1 agayne] *1557*, agaynge *1533*   12 *Sidenote 1557:* A mery tale.   14–15 therwyth]
1533 corr. err., therto *1533*, thereto *1557*   21 lettynge] setting *1557*   28 slaunder]
sclaunder *1557*

neuer herd lay man say to hym the contrary / but that al y^e
spyrytual men relygyouse and seculare, holde to gether in the
mayntenaunce of the worldly honour, that they cal the honour
of god, & of the ryches of spyritual men.

Now you wote well I speke in the sayde .xix. chapytre, that of   5
the spirytualtye suche as are fallen from the fayth vnto heresye,
hold not at al wyth that honour that I thoughte he there had
ment, that is to wyt wyth byeldynge and garnyshynge of
chyrches / but be both agaynst that, and tythes, and offeringes,
and obytes, and trentalles, and purgatorye, & masse, and al.   10
And I had went in good fayth that of so great a thyng, and so
mych spoken of, yt had happed hym to heare some lay men
speke, but he sayth nay. Wel we can no farther than, but stand
vnto hys worde, and take an othe of his honesty therin, & yet I
wene as [h$_1$] honeste as he is, what so euer he be, his own hon-   15
este frende / wyll be loth to swere wyth hym therin.

But then sayth he farther, y^t though yt were so: that wolde not
yet answere hys sayeng. It wolde not to saye the soth in very
dede, takynge his worde as I wene he ment yt. But takynge his
worde to the worst (as he taketh alwaye myne) and yet but euyn   20
as he wrote yt (but yf yt be prented false) yt is a confutacyon to yt.
For yf those spyrytuall persones bothe relygyouse and seculares,
that are fallen from the fayth to heresyes holde not wyth the
remanaunt: then perdye though they were fewer then they be, yt
ys not all trewe that he sayeth, that in the mayntenaunce of suche   25
honoure they holde together all. And yet as I haue all redye
shewed you, yt wolde not helpe hys parte of a peny, though they
dyd euerychone seculares and relygyouse, [h$_1$v] catholyques and
heretyques to. And therfore can he not saye but he ys in thys
poynte answered, euen to the very full.   30

Than in the .xxviii. and .xxix. lefe he subtylly fyndeth a faute,
that I saye that there are some suche of the spyrityalty so fallen
vnto heresyes, that yt is pytye that euer they were therof, bycause
he sayth we sholde not dyspayre of theym / but they may repent
and amende. And also though they do neuer amende: yet I   35
sholde not saye so. For men maye not saye by the deuyll, that yt is

---

5 you] ye *1557;* chapytre] chapter *1557*   9 be] he *1557*   17 But] *no para.*
1557   26 together] *1557,* the gether *1533*

pytye that euer he was created, bycause goddes iustyce ys shewed
on hym. We wyl in thys mater kepe no longe scholes. But thys
euery man knoweth, that who so vse a commen worde spoken
amonge the people, ys rekened so to meane therin, as the com-
5 men people meane y^t vse yt. And therfore syth the people that so
speketh, mea[h$_2$]neth not to speke agaynste amendement, but
agaynste the present wreched state that the man standeth in at
the tyme: that worde may by goddes grace be borne metely well
ynough. And as touchynge the deuyll, though men maye not
10 grudge agaynste goddes iuste punyshement: yet peraduenture a
man myght saye wythoute parell of dampnacyon, that yt was
pytye that he so mysse vsed hymselfe / as in theym that are for
theyre heyghnouse offences put vnto paynefull deth, though we
saye they were serued as they well deserued, yet we lette not to
15 saye yt was pytye that they guyded theym selfe no better. And
saynte Chrysostome pytyeth also the deuyll. And our sauyoure
hym selfe pytyed Hierusalem, and for the pytye wept also thereon, for the punyshement that sholde fall theron / and yet was yt
the iuste punyshement of god. [h$_2$v]
20 And though the partyes afterwarde maye mende and do good
agayne: yet for the tyme tyll they mende, ye and after to, we
maye pytye that they were in suche case, as to hurte theym
whome they haue all redy remedelesse destroyed, by theyr false
doctryne dede in the damnable heresyes that they lerned of
25 theym, and lye therfore beryed in hell. And therfore the thynge
that I maye not absolutely pytye: yet in some respectes I may.
Fynally he sayeth that I sholde not call any heretyques desperate wrechys. This is a sore poynte I assure you, to cal a wreche,
suche as he sheweth hymselfe to be / to cal hym desperate, whose
30 lyuynge sheweth no maner hope of amendement. Saynte Cypryane I se well was sore ouersene, whyche in the seuenth pystle
of hys fyrste booke, for lesse thynges than these are, calleth some
[h$_3$] folke desperate. And yet was saynt Policarpus farther ouersene, whyche calleth Marcyon the fyrste begotten sonne of the
35 deuyll. Thys man hathe here as he weneth founde oute proper
fantsyes, wherin I hadde leuer leue hym in the lykynge, thanne
lese myche tyme in answerynge of suche blonte subtyll tryfles.

---

1 shewed] *1557*, sheweth *1533*   11 dampnacyon] dampnacion *1557*, dampnacyom
1533   16–17 *Sidenote 1557:* Math. 23.   33–34 ouersene] *1557*, euersene *1533*

But to the mater good readers concernynge the formare
wordes of hys dyuysyon, all be yt that I haue here more thanne
fully confuted this chapytre of hys, for any defence that he hathe
for hys sayde formare wordes, where aboute ys all our mater:
reade yet the .xviii. chapyter of myne Apologye, wherin you   5
shall se dyuerse other lyke wordes of his / and applye me myne
answere there, to those other wordes of hys whyche he defendeth here / and ye shall se that he shal haue more worke [h₃v] then
ynough, to defende theym well, and to make theym serue hym to
purpose.   10

The .ix. chapyter.

H IS .ix. chapyter begynneth in the .xxx. lefe. And his formare wordes which he therwyth defendeth and myne answere
also therto, ye shall se in the .xix. chapyter of myne apologye fo.
119. Whyche when you haue good readers there ones redde   15
ouer / than forthwyth whyle yt ys freshe in remembraunce /
retourne agayne vnto this, the .ix. chapyter of his dyaloge / and
than iudge whether it any thyng touche the poynte or not. For al
thys chapyter is spent in preachynge of restytucyon, full wel and
ful trewly forsoth / and whych in my pore mynd [h₄] I very well   20
allowe / and wold haue allowed in lyke wyse his fyrste boke very
well, yf there had ben no worse wordes in yt than suche. But
nowe the mater standeth all in thys, that thys man maketh there
as though the spyrytualtye were very besye to procure men and
to enduce the people, to geue money to trentalles, to founde   25
chaunteryes, and obytes, and to obteyne pardons, and to go
vppon pylgrymages, leuynge theyr dettes vnpayed, and restytucyon vnmade, whyche thynges shold be done fyrst / and that thys
ys the maner of the multitude of the spyrytualtie. In this standeth
the questyon. And therfore is now the poynt, not whether dettes   30
be fyrst to be payed, & satisfaccyon of wronges fyrste to be made,
byfore al these other thynges, wherin thys man sayeth here
surely full well / but whyther (as he wolde haue yt seme by his
boke of diuisyon) yᵗ yᵉ mul[h₄v]titude of the spyrytualtie, yᵗ is to
wit eyther al saue a fewe, or at the leste wyse farre the moste   35
parte, do solycyte and labour lay people to the contrarye maner /

8 haue] *1557*, houe *1533*   15 Whyche] *para. 1557*

that is to wyt, to do those other thynges, rather than to pay theyr
dettes or make restitucyon of theyr wrongis. This is I say y^e
point. And of thys poynt wherin al the mater standeth, this man
in this .ix. chapiter of his speketh not one worde. And therfore
5   in this thing, standeth myn answere made in ye sayd .xx. chapiter
of myne apologye clene and clere vntouched, as euery man may
perceyue that readeth yt. And therfore where in ye seconde syde
of his .xxxii. lefe, this man saith thus.

And to thentent I wold haue this mater the better loked vppon: I
10 wolde here aduertyse syr Thomas More, not by waye of argument, but
for clerenesse of conscyence, to consydre whyther ys the more charytable waye, fyrste to make restytucyon and paye dettes, and releue
extreme pouerte, and then to do the tother yf he haue to do bothe / or
elles to do the fyrste and let the tother passe. [h$_5$]

15 For this his good aduertysement I very hartely thanke hym / &
answere hym as hym selfe wolde wysshe I sholde, that surely me
thynketh as he doth, that the more charytable waye of the twayne
were that y^t hym self here moueth.

But than lo by and by, he geueth me another good lesson,
20 wherwith he wolde I sholde amende myne owne fawte, that he
wolde it shold seme I had in myne apologye made agaynst hym.
For than lo thus goeth he ferther forth.

And yf he thynke that this waye that I moue be the more cherytable
waye, that than he helpe it forwarde, rather than the other / and than
25 not to blame any man that maketh that mocyon, as though he were
agaynst trentallys, obitis, & such other. For he is not agaynst them
dyrectely / but onely entendeth to haue them chaunged into a more
cherytable order. For though prayours be ryght expedyent and
helthfull to the soule: yet they serue not in all cases as to dyscharge
30 dettes or restytucyons, where there ys inough to paye them wyth / no
more than there can be founden any one salue, that can hele all maner
of soores.

I neyther haue done that I wote of, nor wyllyngly intende to
do, blame [h$_5$v] hym for any part of this cherytable mocyon / but
35 thynke his mocyon ryght good, and that the fruyte therof yf it be
folowed, wylbe more yet than him selfe sayth he myndeth. For

---

6 apologye] apology *1557*, apolpgye *1533*   19 But] *no para. 1557*

he sayth as you se, that he myndeth but to chaunge obitys and trentallys and those other thynges into a more cherytable order / that is to wytte in to payeng of dettes and recompensyng of wronges in them that haue not of theyr owne bysyde / and in them that haue than to paye the dettes and recompence wronges fyrste, and do the tother after. But me thynketh there wyll come yet a ferther profyte of this order to. For where as here we speke but of hym that payeth his det and recompenseth his wronges, of whiche folke many a man is able well to do y^e tother whan bothe those twayn be done / there is the tother sort of menne also bysyde, to whome those wronges are done, and those dettes [h_6] owynge, of whyche sorte there be many, that yf theyr wronges were ones recompensed them, & theyr dettes payed them, were able and wolde do those other thynges also them selfe, which now for lacke be not able / & so sholde there of lykelyhed be the selfe thynges y^t brynge (as his fyrste boke sayth) rychesse into the chyrch, by this good order encreaced. And therfore not onely haue I no cause, to blame thys good man for the mocyon of this good cherytable order / but also no more haue the multytude of the prestes, whiche myghte of lykelyhed wynne as mych by thys waye as by the tother, and more, excepte the multytude of prestes wolde for y^e redynesse to take it where it is all redy, moue theym that haue it to do these other thynges fyrst, & leue theyr dettes vnpaied & theyr wronges vnrecompensed, which y^t the multitude of prestes do / I neuer herd yet any honest laye man, [h_6v] that wolde for very shame say. For I thynke it were harde to mete with a prest that were so wreched, but that yf he were asked in y^t point his aduice & counsayle, he wold in so playn a point though it were but for very shame well & playnely counsayle the trouth. And if percase there were some founden so shamelesse, that they wolde geue counsayle contrary: yet am I very sure they shulde be farre the fewer parte / and not as thys good mannys fyrste booke sayth, the more parte and the multytude.

And therfore syth this order that this good man here moueth, is so good and so cherytable: I neuer blamed hym for the mo- cyon. But though this mocion in this boke be good: I myght well

---

10 is] *1533 corr. err.*, is to *1533 1557*   21 more,] *1557*, more *1533*

and so I dyd, blame his other booke / not for this mocyon, but for a nother mater, that is bycause it labored vnder pretexte of an vntrew report, to brynge the spyrytualtye in [h₇] slawnder and obloquy amonge the temporaltye, by makynge men wene that of
5 this cherytable order whyche he now moueth, the multytude of the spyritualty induced men to yᵉ contrary.

This is lo the thynge that I blamed. And therfore lyke as thys good man sayeth, that one plaster can not hele all soores: so surely thys same salue of this good cherytable mocion can not
10 serue this good cherytable man, to salue and hele well, this vncherytable soore.

In this mocion, of this cherytable order, thys good manne waxeth so warme, that of a good zele he falleth in remembraunce of the soule (which our lorde perdon) of the moste noble prynce
15 of very famouse memory kynge Henry the .vii. father to the most excellent prynce our souerayne lorde the kynge that now is / wherin after mencyon made of obitys and chauntrees lettyng the dew examy[h₇v]nacyon requysyte for restytucion, sodaynly thus he sayth.

20 How be it the ryght noble prynce of blessed memory kynge Henry the .vii. father of our souerayne lorde the kynge that now is, wylled restytucyons to be made. But how hys wyll was performed I can not tell. How be it what so euer was done therin: I suppose hys good entent suffyseth to hym.

25 What yf thys good man can not tell? By lykelyhed there is nothyng owynge to hym therof. For yf there were: than were it lykely yᵗ he could tell. For he coulde tell than that all the wyl were not performed. I haue herde I wote well that the kyng our souerayne lorde, delyuered great substaunce into thexecutours
30 handes, to fulfyll the wyll wythall. Whyche how they haue bestowed, thys good man maye (yf he haue thauthoryte) call them to the rekenynge. And yf he neyther haue authorite to call for the accompte, nor haue nothyng owyng to hym neyther: the mater than towcheth not hym so nere, nor so specyally per-
35 teyneth vnto hym yᵗ he shold [h₈] greatly nede to geue all the

---

1 this] his *1557*   3 slawnder] sclaunder *1557*   17 chauntrees] chauntrees, *1533*, chauntries, *1557*   25 lykelyhed] lykelyhoode *1557*

worlde warnynge thus, y^t hym selfe is not made of counsayle, how the kynges wyll is performed.

But here wyll this good man say y^t I do but mocke him / wherin I wyl not greately stycke wyth hym. But surely for my pore wyt, me thynketh it somwhat more ciuilite, in some such poyntes as this is, a lytell merely to mokke hym, than wyth odyouse ernest argumentes, seryousely to preace vppon hym. Whyche I wolde also be very loth to do, for chargyng of myn owne conscyence. And therfore in all thynges y^t me thynke are of greate weyght, though I touche his wordes, I accuse not his own mynde & intent. For in good fayth I haue of y^e man good trust, y^t he meneth no wurse, but wold all thyng were well hym self / but euer more my mynde geueth me, y^t some wyly shrewes abuse y^e good mannes simplicyte. [h$_8$v]

The .x. chapyter.

His .x. chapyter begynneth in the .xxxiii. lefe, wherin he towcheth certayne wordes of myne, wryten in the .xxvii. chapyter of myne apologye, that begynneth fo. 162. wherin he varyeth not mych with me, sauynge in that I say that yf the prelates of y^e chyrch wold wythdrawe from theyr worldely contenaunce, as is kepynge of honest ley men in theyr seruyce, and kepynge of a good wurshypfull table, and wold bestow theyr plate & the moste parte of all theyr mouables at ones vppon poore folke, and yerely after the moste of theyr yerely reuenus to (of whiche mynde I sayd I durste warraunt well that some prelates be, yf that wolde as I saye there, amende [i$_1$] all these grudges) that I durste be bolde to warraunt as well also, that yf the prelates so dyd, the selfe same folke that now grudge and call them proude for theyr countenaunce, wold than fynde as great a grudge, & call them ypochrytes for theyr almoyse, and wolde saye that they spende vppon noughty beggers the good that was wont to kepe good yomen, and that therby they both enfeble and also dyshonour the realme.

Vppon these wordes of myn this good man maketh me for-

---

11 intent.] *1557*, intent *1533*   12 thyng] thing *appears only as catchword 1557*   17–
18 chapyter] chapter *1557*   30 almoyse] almes *1557*

sothe a full goodly sermon, in the .xxxv. lefe of his booke / where
he begynneth it with these wordes, I can not se. And veryly yf he
had there left & gone no ferther: it had ben well inough. For as
for the thyng that he speketh of, it appereth by hys wordés he
5   can not se very well in dede.

Bycause chryst commaundeth in the gospell, y^t we shall not
iudge / and [i₁v] that saynt Poule sayth also, who art thou that
iudgest another mannes seruaunt / and agayne byddeth vs that
we iudge not before the tyme / al whiche places are vnderstand
10 of iugyng certayne and determinate persons to do euyll, in the
thynges that we se them do, where the thynges be but indyfferent of them selfe, and maye be done not euyl onely but well
also: this good man therfore layeth these textys to touche me, for
iudgyng that some folke whom I neyther assigne by name, nor as
15 yet knowe not who they be, wyll do euyll hereafter, by mysse
iudgynge other men.

I wene verely that saynt Poule hym selfe, at the tyme whan he
forbode vs to iudge before the tyme, did euyn than iudge, that
some wolde after that misse iudge and iudge before the tyme to.
20 And albe it that our sauyour saith that who so call hys brother
fole: is [i₂] gylty to the fyre: yet he ment not of him y^t wold say,
that there were some folys abrode in the worlde. For yf he so
ment: than wolde there not tenne fyrys be payne inough for hym
that wrote these wordes in the scrypture: There are of folys an
25 infynyte nomber.

And bycause this good man vseth somtyme thys fygure of
examynacyon, I wolde wytte of mayster More this & that, I wolde
nowe wytte thys one thynge of thys good man. Suche fawtes as he
fyndeth wyth the spyrytualty wryten in hys boke of dyuysyon:
30 whyther dyd he than iudge y^t some of the spyrytualtye wolde fall
in them any more after or not? If he iudged that all theyr fantasyes towarde those fawtes were all redy passed before, and that
none of them wolde neuer do more so: than hadde he lytel cause
to write all that wurke vppon theym. [i₂v]
35 And vn the tother syde yf he iudged that some of them wolde

6 *Sidenote 1557:* Luke .6.   7 *Sidenote 1557:* Roma. 14.   8–9 *Sidenote 1557:* i. Corin.
4.   17 I] *no para. 1557*   19 and] *1557,* and, *1533*   20 *Sidenote 1557:* Math
5.   28 fawtes] fawltes *1557,* sawtes *1533*   35 vn] on *1557*

afterwarde do some such thynges agayne, eyther but yf he gaue theym warnynge, or ellys though he dyd, as I dare saye, what so euer hym selfe saye, in some of those thynges he dyd: than syth ye tyme in which he iudged in his mynd, & made hym selfe therof sure, y^t some of theym wolde do some suche euyll thynges after- 5
warde, as were at the tyme of the same iudgement of hys mynde not comen, hym selfe fell as you se by hys owne argument, in the daynger of that prohybycyon y^t hym selfe bryngeth in, by whyche saynte Poule forbedeth and sayth: Nolite ante tempus iudicare. Iudge you not before the tyme. 10

Now yf he say that I tell whom I mene, though not by name: yet by a sygne and a token, in that I saye euyn the same wyll than call theym ypocrytes for theyr almoyse, that [i3] nowe call theym proude for theyr worldely countenaunce: he muste consyder, that I neyther tell nor can tell who be they / nor though I saye the 15
same, I saye not yet all the same. And therfore I no more mysse iudge any man determynately and in certayne, than he that wolde saye thus, as many men saye in dede: Euyn they that go now full fresshe, in theyr garded hosyn, and theyr gaye golden reuen shyrtes, and in theyr sylken sleuys, that nought haue to 20
bere it out but gamynge, wyll ones I warraunt you fall fro gamynge to stelynge, & start strayt out of sylke into hempe. Thus sayeth and thus iudgeth ye wote well many a man / and yet meneth not that it shall so mysse happe them all, but that some shall amende and do better / and that yet hys worde wyll be 25
veryfyed in many, & so doth it proue in dede / and he that so sayth before, is farre inough fro the dayn[i3v]geour of all those textes whych this good man precheth to me.

But than he sayth ferther, that he trusteth that those prelates whom I saye I durste warraunt to be of such mynde, wyll not 30
dyfferre theyr good purpose for no suche suspycyon that hap-pely wyll neuer come, ne yet for no such vncherytable wordes, though they were spoken in dede. And thervppon he descen-deth to the makyng of actys of perleament.

If those prelates that I mene of rekened them self very sure, y^t 35

---

4 y^e] that *1557*   9–10 *Sidenote 1557:* i. Corin. 4.   13 almoyse] almes *1557*   16 I no] *1533 corr. err.*, no *1533 1557*   19 and theyr] and in theyr *1557*   22 Thus] *para. 1557*

all the wytte and the lernynge that is in the worlde, or within this
realme eyther, were eyther in theyr owne hedys, or in this good
mannes and myne / which peraduenture for myne owne mynde
colde agre well with this good man in this poynt, and aduise
5 those prelates that I speke of, to folowe theyr owne mynde
therin, and out of hande euyn so to do: than haue I lytell dowt
[i₄] but that they wold euyn so do in dede. But some of them haue
ofter ben as I suppose than onys, where they haue herde both
wyse and good folke to, and peraduenture yet sholde here
10 agayne yf it were, as thys man wold haue it, spoken of in the
playne open perleament, that wolde not fayle to dyssuade it, and
laye no lytell causes why.

But I wyl not at this tyme with this good man entre in this
mater, into seryouse ernest argumentes. But I shall shew hym a
15 good mery cause wherfore, that though I be of hys mynde
therin, yet I dare not aduise them there to. The cause is, that I se
them haue so greate desyre & feruent concupyscence towarde it,
that I am aferde to counsayle theym folowe it, bycause of the
scrypture that sayth, Post concupiscentias tuas ne eas. After thy
20 concupyscences goo thou not. [i₄v]

I wyll make no lenger tale vpon this mater. For if you rede my
.xxvii. chapyter, in whyche my wordes are that we now dyspute
vppon: I truste you shall not thynke theym so very farre out of
the way, but yᵗ they maye be wryten, without offence of Chrystes
25 gospell well inough.

And also concernynge this word, proude worldely countenaunce, wherof we speke here: vouchesaufe good readers to
rede my .xxx. chapyter of myne apologye, whych begynneth in
the lefe .174.

30   The .xi. chapyter.

H IS .xi. chapyter begynneth in the .xxxvi. lefe / wherin fyrst
he sheweth yᵗ I reherse ryght, and constre a mysse thys worde of
his. And therfore. [i₅]

You shall fynde my wordes good readers vppon these whole

---

7 dede.] *1557*, dede *1533*   10 were,] were *1533*, wer *1557*   19–20 *Sidenote 1557:*
Eccle. 18.

wordes that he reherseth here, in the .xxxiiii. and .xxxv. chapyter of myne apologye / of whyche the tone begynneth fo. 183. / &
the tother begynneth fo. 184.

Here this man declareth that the worde of his boke, whyche
here also he well & trewly rehersethe, do not importe that hym   5
selfe sayeth ye thyng whych I by those wordes, and among other
by thys worde therfore / afferme there that he sayth as of hym
selfe / but he sayeth that the wordes proue playne, that he sayeth
yt, but onely of the reporte of mych other folkes thynkynge, and
not as of hys owne sayenge.   10

Surely neyther nowe, nor in any place of myne apologye, I
neyther haue done nor intende to charge thys man, that his
mynde & purpose was suche in his intent, as the great lykelyhed
of his wordes, wold geue [i$_5$v] men occasyon to thynke. But vn
the tother syde, that the wordes haue geuyn me good occasyon   15
and suffycyent, to saye as I there haue sayde: who so rede the
sayd two chapyters of myne apologye, shal by the whole cyrcumstaunce of the mater very wel I suppose perceyue. And you
shall ouer that, yf after those two chapyters redde, you retourne
to his own declaracyon here in hys .xi. chapyter, wel perceyue   20
also that to kouer slyly that ouersyghte of his (for surely I thynke
yt was none other) he leueth oute properly in one place this
worde therfore wheruppon a good pyece of all the mater hangeth. For in the ende of the .xxvi. lefe lo, thus he handeleth wylyly
the mater.   25

And in that he sayth, that I saye playnely those wordes my selfe / he
sayth playnely agaynste the letter of the sayde treatyse / whyche ys that
they haue punished many persons, which mych peple haue iudged
them to do vppon wyll / and not that I sayd so my selfe.

Now good readers in this reher[i$_6$]sall of hys own worde, he   30
reherseth his own wordes wrong. For here he leueth oute as I
told you the worde that maketh the mater. Whyche he rehersed
hym self in the whole context before. For his wordis were not,
that they haue punished many persons, whych mych peple haue iuged

---

2 the tone begynneth] to tone begyyneth *1533*, two tone beginneeh *1557*   6 y^e] that
1557   13 lykelyhed] lykelyhod *1557*   14 vn] on *1557*   26 selfe] *1557*, seflfe
1533

them to do vpon wyl, but that therfore they haue punyshed many persons / whyche mych people haue iudged them to do vppon wyl &c. Nowe when he sayth hym selfe that they haue punyshed many therfore, that is to wyt for the same cause, and hathe before also
5 shewed a cause of his owne dyuynacyon to, & hath vsed the same word therfore in yᵉ same fasshyon before / and this worde therfore which sygnifyeth for the same cause, hath here in his laste clause no necessarye place to the complement of the sentence folowyng: it appereth that he sayth therin two thynges,
10 bothe that they therfore, that is to say for yᵉ same cause next before spoken of, the cause yᵗ him self ther imagineth, haue [i₆v] punished many / and also that (as he sayth yt so) myche people iudged the same.

And this shall you the more clerely marke, yf you tourne these
15 wordes. And therfore they haue punyshed many whyche myche people &c. in to these wordes (wherof the sentence is all one). And for that cause they haue punyshed many whyche myche people &c.

And therfore, that is to saye for that cause whych I before told
20 you, that is to wyt that you shold not perceyue thys poynte, this man in hys laste rehershall as you haue herde, bryngynge the thynge to the tryall, lefte his therfore oute. But reade my sayd two chapyters / & than as for the sentence of his open wordes, I trust you shall byleue me. As for the secrete meanyng of his mynde, I
25 pray you byleue hym. For so that you byleue not the shrewd wordes of hys [i₇] boke, I wolde to chose you sholde byleue well of the good man hym selfe.

Now where he saith in yᵉ .xxxvii. lefe, that he thynketh I chaunge his mater, bycause I wolde be lothe to haue yt re-
30 ported, that myche people take yt so: veryly I chaunge not his mater. But trouth yt is yᵗ I am loth to haue that thyng so reported about. For trewly yᵉ report abrode is nought all though yt were not vntrew.

And where as for the farther maintenaunce of hys mater, he
35 sayth that yf I make serche therin to knowe the trouthe, I shall

---

3 Nowe] *para. 1557*   8 no necessarye] *1533 corr. err., 1557,* nonecessarye *1533*   16 all one).] allone) *1533,* al one.) *1557*   34 where as] whereas *1557,* were as *1533*

fynde that myche people take yt so, that many whyche haue ben punyshed for heresye, the spyrytualtye haue done yt of no loue but of wyll, for such euyll mynde as in the booke ys there ymagyned of them: he hath of lykelyhed hym selfe made serche to fynde yt so. For as for me though I go not aboute to serche [i₇v] that poynte of purpose: yet I haue talked wyth many one in this meane whyle, & yet I thanke god it is not my fortune to fynde out that same mych people that take yt so. And yf there were myche people that so dyd, yt were theyre owne faute / wherin I can not deuyse what the spyrytualty myght do to chaunge theym, but onely praye god to mende theym. And as for me, yf there were myche people that so toke yt, as I truste in god veryly there is not: I wolde as my dutye were be surely very sorye for theym / but in thys cause of trouth, trewely I wolde not flater theym. For though that sorte of people were neuer so myche in dede: yet is the trouth in that poynt so clere agaynste theym, that yf theyre myndes were suche, yt were bothe great shame for theym to saye yt, and also great synne to thynke yt.

And surely that theyre sayenge [i₈] ys false and noughte in hys owne secrete iudgement: you maye se good reders by this yᵗ he laboureth so sore to put yt from hym selfe, and wolde be so lothe to haue yt taken for hys owne. And therfore whyle hym selfe thought theyre sayeng so false, he sholde not haue told yt after them. Nor nowe sholde he not sende me to serche and seke theym, but to saue hys owne honesty / leste men myght thynke he fayned, he sholde seke out & brynge forthe some of those shrewd sayers hym selfe.

A nother thynge thys man toucheth in the same chapyter, concernynge that seconde sorte of people whome I saye in some places of myne Apologye, that thys man calleth polytyques. And here he declareth that he doth not so / and proueth yt by lyke wordes spoken of a good mannys mouthe by an hypocryte, of whome a man maye say: Thys [i₈v] man vseth hym self as he were a vertuouse man / and yet cal hym not vertuouse. And so myght this man saye yᵗ they spake heresyes as of polycye, and yet call theym not polytyque.

2–3 *Sidenote 1557:* As heretikes doe say.   4 lykelyhed] likelihod *1557*   11 And] *para. 1557*

But here must he now consyder, y^t who so speke suche wordes
in such fashyon by an hypocryte, sayth yt in hys desprayse and in
detestacyon of suche hypocrysye / and therfore he that so
sayeth, sheweth y^t by such wordes he taketh not y^t hypocrite for
5   vertuouse. And therfore reade good readers this mannys whole
processe of hys thre sortes of people to gether, whych you shall
fynde in the .xxi. chapyter of myne apologye fo. 123. / and then
yf you fynd his wordes of theyr spekynge suche heresyes as of
polycye, in lyke maner spoken by hym in dysprayse of here-
10 tyques, as he putteth here his sample of those wordes spoken by a
good man in dysprayse of hypocrites / & not spoken by a way [k₁]
of geuynge theym by that worde as of polycye a colourable excuse
for defense of sewynge theyre heresye: than am I contente, that
euery man take yt that I mysse reporte hym shamefully. And
15 ellys I truste loke in all the places in whyche I speke therof, and
you shal soon iudge, that vppon hys wordes vsed to suche purpose as he there vseth theym: I may wel vse the wordes of hys
polytykes in suche wyse as I vse yt.

And as for the tynkar and the tyler, that he speketh of in the
20 ende of the chapyter / and sayth god forbede but that they were
dysmyssed and wente home aboute theyr besynesse, yf they can
by any reasonable and trewe allegeaunce, so order theym selfe,
that yt maye appere that they oughte to be dysmyssed of iustyce:
therin holde I well wyth hym and god forbede ellys to / for els
25 myghte they lese betwene theym, the tone the [k₁v] pryce of hys
trewell, and the tother of his clouted ketyll. But loke good readers in myne Apology the .xlviii. chapyter, whych begynneth fo.
272. / and that done, I doute not but you shall fynde for the
tylare and the tynkare / for heresy there called in of offyce, this
30 good word so spoken here, but a very vayne worde of offyce /
and that the tynkare wolde haue tynked oute of hys pannes
botome, a reason that wolde at the leste wyse rynge a lytle better
then thys.

2 hypocryte] ypocrit *1557*, hyprycryte *1533*   4 not y^t] not the *1557*   7 chapyter]
Chapter *1557*   13 sewynge] shewing *1557*   16 vppon] vpon *1557*, vpppon
1533   18 yt] yet *1557*   20 chapyter] Chapter *1557*   27 chapyter] Chapter *1557*

The .xii. chapyter.

His .xii. chapiter begynneth in the .xxxviii. lefe / whych by-cause yt ys a good swete sermone & a shorte, made vnto my selfe, to put me in remembraunce howe I shold bere the lyke [k₂] lyght fautes of other men, as I some tyme fall in my self: I shal take his chapyter in here euyn hole. Lo good readers thus yt sayth.

Mayster More in the .217. lefe of hys Apology, speking of defautes, that as he thynketh, shulde haue ben leyde for causes of thys dyuysyon, concludeth thus: If there be such a dyuysyon: wherby it appereth that he doubteth, whether there be any diuysyon or not: for this coniunc-cion, yf, purporteth alway a doubte. And after in the same Apologye, fo. 241. he confesseth playnely, that there is a dyuysyon / and maketh no doute at yt: and he calleth yt there the late spronge dyuysyon. And so in one place to make a doute, whether there be suche a dyuysyon or not / and in a nother place to agre, that there ys suche a dyuysyon / semeth to be a varyaunce and contradyccyon in yt selfe: howe be yt surely I do not intende to laye that varyaunce to hym as for any notable defaute: For a lyke thynge may soon happen in any man by a lyght ouersyght. But the cause why I speke of yt is this, to put hym in re-membraunce / that he hereafter ought the rather to beare suche lyghte defautes of other the more charytably / syth he hym selfe hath lyke wyse ben ouersene. For we be all frayle ignorant and vnstable / though we be estymed and taken as angels in oure conuersacyon. And therfore ys yt sayde in the fyrste boke of the folowynge of Cryste the .xvi. chapyter, that no man is in this worlde wythout defaute, no man wyth-oute burden, no man suffycyent to hym selfe, no man wyse ynough of hym selfe. Wherfore yt behoueth eche one of vs to beare the burden of [k₂v] other, to comforte other, to helpe other, to enforme other, and to instructe and admonysh other in al charytie. And yf we wyll note well the sayde wordes, we shall the sooner lerne thys lesson / to do in al thynges as we wolde be done to: and to do nothyng that we wold not haue done to vs. And that is as I take yt one of the moste souerayne doctrynes that is / to instructe a man how he shall in euery thynge concernynge hys neyghbour, kepe hym selfe in a clere conscyence, lerne yt who so maye.

Lo good readers, fyrste he bryngeth forth myne ouersyght, in contradyccyon vsed betwene myne owne wordes / and after wyth good wordes and fayre, excuseth my faute, by suche ouersyght of frayltye as maye soone happen in a man. And then he putteth
5 me after in remembraunce, that I muste bere suche thynges the more charitably in other men, syth I am ouersene lykewyse my selfe. He fareth in all this tale, as though we sat to gether playeng at post. For fyrste he casteth my contradiccion as a vye, to wyt whyther I wold geue yt ouer with a face. And bycause that wyll
10 not be, falleth after to treatye, [k₃] and wold fayne parte the stacke, and diuide all such ouersyghtes betwene vs. But all this is in vayne / for I am as sure of this game and there lay .xx. li. vppon yt, as he that hathe thre acys in his hande.

For loke good readers in his own fyrste chapyter of thys booke
15 of hys and there shall you se the thyng that shall serue me, suffycyently shewed euyn by hys owne wordes, that there ys no suche contradyccyon in myne. And than loke myne answere to the same / and than shall you se yt yet more clerely. Or ellys yf any man be lothe to tourne the leuys, and loke bakke: ye shall
20 nede to take no besynesse in tournynge bakke at all. For he soyleth hys argument hym selfe agaynste hym selfe, euyn in the makynge therof, and all wyth one worde vnware.

For nowe rede yt agayne / and you shall se that he sayeth hym selfe, [k₃v] in the tone place I saye, If there be any suche dyuy-
25 syon. And so bycause thys coniunccyon If, he sayth inporteth all waye a doute: therfore he sayth that fo. 217. I doute whyther there be any suche dyuysyon or not. And after he sayth that in the tother place I confesse that there ys a dyuysyon / and call yt there the late sprongen dyuysyon. Lo nowe he forgetteth thys
30 lytle shorte worde, this monasyllable, Suche, whych he rehersed fyrste in bryngynge forthe my fyrste place / and then by and by, eyther of forgetefulnes or ellys of wylynesse, leueth oute in hys illacyon that he maketh vppon the same wordes of myne.

Nowe good readers you se well that to saye there is a dyuysyon,
35 and to saye there ys no suche dyuysyon, be nothynge contrarye at all. For I dyd in dede not deny but that some dyuysyon there

---

7 He] *para.* 1557   11 stacke] stake 1557   17 answere] aunswere 1557, auswere
1533   25 inporteth] importeth 1557   27 And] *para.* 1557

was, that ys to wytte [k₄] some lytle varyaunce in some place
begonne, and by some fewe naughtye folke blowne forthe to
farre (For a lytle waye ys to farre in suche a thyng). But than
meane I a dyuysyon such as yt ys, not suche a dyuysyon as thys
man by hys booke maketh yt. I maye well wythoute contradyccyon saye to hym, There ys a dyuysyon / and yet saye that there
ys no suche dyuysyon as he speketh of. For yt is not all one to saye
there ys a dyuysyon, and to saye there ys suche a dyuysyon.

Nowe yf I wolde stycke wyth hym vpon tryflys: I coulde proue
hym that If, dothe not alwaye purporte a doute, as he sayeth that
yt alwaye dothe, but ys sometyme vsed to conferme a certayntye. As yf a man say he that dyeth in dedely synne shal go to the
deuyll, yf goddes word be trewe, douteth not of the trouthe [k₄v]
of goddes worde / but by the trouthe therof, meaneth to conferme the damnacyon of theym that dye in dedely synne.

But I saye not this as though yt sholde be lyke in myne. For I do
not in dede take If there in such fashion. And therfore I wyll not
do here by If, as thys man doth by As, in hys chapyter nexte
byfore, in heresyes spoken as of polycye / vsynge yᵉ sample of
wordes spoken by a good man in reprochynge of hypocrysee, to
be lyke hys owne wordes spoken in the mynyshynge of theyre
blame, that vnder suche pretexte of polycye / wolde speke and
sow aboute playne and open heresye. I nede here no suche
wayes for my wordes. For here haue you sene your selfe by his
owne wordes, that there ys in my wordes, no contradyccyon at
all. [k₅]

The .xiii. chapyter.

His .xiii. chapiter begynneth in the .xxxix. lefe / and by yᵉ
rehersynge of diuerse wordes of his owne in dyuers other places
of his boke, here he declareth his mynde that he entended not in
his boke of diuysyon, to brynge in among the people any hatered
agaynste the spyrytualtye.

Now in dede I do my self declare expressely, in many places of
myne apologye, that what so euer wordes I speke therin, yet I
ment euer more thentent of hys boke and not of hys person. And

---

6–7 dyuysyon / and yet saye that there ys no suche] *om. 1557*

all though that in some places I say the pacyfyer here doth this or
that, to this euyll purpose or that: yet I mene euer, the dede his,
the malyce of the purpose some other [k₅v] wyly shrewys /
whyche not beynge fully of so good catholyke mynde as I thynke
5   all waye this man is hym self (which openly dysprayseth these
new broched heresyes, and with detestacyon of them reherseth
them by name) haue abused his playn simplycyte / makyng him
wene good sowle, yᵗ while he dyd put in of his own good mynde,
these good wordes whych he reherseth here, and with them here
10 & there in some sondry places pretyly powder yᵉ boke, it coulde
not be taken that there were any hurt ment in the hole worke
togyther, how euyll wordes and how malycyouse so euer the sotle
shrewys made hym stuffe vp yᵉ boke with bysyde. Was not that a
synful wily way of them, to begyle a good symple soule so? For I
15 wysse it is eth to se, that yf the good man were not of hym self
very simple & playn, those dowble wyly shrewes coulde neuer
deceyue hym so, as to make [k₆] hym wene that these wordes
whych he reherseth here in his .xiii. chapyter, were any maner
token that his boke of diuisyon, ment not to brynge the clergye in
20 hatered amonge the people.

For who were there that so intendynge, wolde yet for shame
vtterly say that there were none good / and not rather to kepe his
credence in slawnderynge the body, wolde caste in sometyme an
excepcyon of some? In suche crafte is no great sleyght. It is but a
25 comen playne poynt, and as easy to spye as a longe nose vpon a
lytell face / specyally whyle as clerely as he sayth that there be
many good, yet as you maye se folio .238. of myne apology, he
sayth playnely that it is harde to fynde any one, without that
poynt, that (yf he saye therin trew) the very beste is very nought,
30 and as badde as a very beste. [k₆v] And for yᵉ ferther profe of this
point, rede myne answere to hys .xvii. chapyter in thys boke.

And where he speketh here of the fere that he wold euery man
sholde haue of the leste censures of the chyrche, as though he
therin ment myche the fauour of spyrytuall men: consyder the
35 place euyn here in hys new boke, where he speketh of inquysycyons of heresyes in his .xvii. chapyter, and you shall well per-

---

8 yᵗ] yᵉ *1533*, that *1557*   14–15 I wysse] ywisse *1557*   30 And] *para. 1557*   31
hys] this *1557*   36 chapyter] Chapter *1557*

ceyue that they that made hym there put those wordes in, ment
lytell good to ye clergye. For it is there layed in a mater full
chyldyshly to theyr charge / as though they wolde haue all the
iustyces of the peace and all the iuryes of the realme, accursed
for enquyrynge of heresye.   5
    But yet is it of all thynges a very specyall pleasure to se how he
vseth here for a playne apparent profe of hys good mynde towarde the spyry[k7]tualty, that he wisheth wel for them, and
prayeth god to sende them habundauntely zele of sowles, pitye,
good doctryne, and deuowt prayour. And sayth that than a new   10
lyght of grace sholde shortely shyne &c. and that he sayth also,
that it is great pytye and mych to be lamented, that the
spyrytualtye do not faste and praye and do other good dedes, to
ceace the dyuysyon withall / but y^t all that euer they do therin
moste comenly, is that they take it that they that fynde defawte at 15
theyr abusyons and mysse order, loue no prestes / but do all of
malyce that they do, to destroye the chyrche and to haue theyr
goodes and possessyons them selfe / and that therfore the clergye thynke it a good dede to se them punyshed / and therfore
(that is to saye for that same cause) haue they punyshed many   20
persons, which mych people iudge to haue ben done of wyll &c.
And sayth also that they [k7v] do continue styl after theyr old
course, pretendyng by confederacyes, worldly polycye, and
strayte correccyons, to rule the peple / where he vseth these
thynges whyche I haue here rehersed out of his .xiii. chapiter of 25
this his newe boke, and somwhat made them more playne, with
addyng therto his owne other wordes wryten in his diuysyon / as
you maye rede in myne apologye fo. 158. in the .xxvi. chapyter,
and answered there at length, in the same chapyter and diuerse
other in order there ensuyng, of which this man hath answered 30
to some very lytell, and to the moste parte and the chyefe parte
no thynge: now is he so symple, that he vseth the same thynges /
for a profe that he bereth the clergye very good wyll and mindeth not to brynge them in obloquy / whyche he wold we shold
take for a thing playnely proued, bycause he pytyeth & lament- 35
eth theym therin, and so byt[k8]terly prayeth god to make them
good and amende them.

---

11 and] And *1557*   28 chapyter] Chapter *1557*

Thys good man many tymes taketh recorde of his owne conscyence that he meneth well, in suche thynges as his wordes
make many good men wene, that he ment very nought. And
therfore wyll I now be bolde in thys poynt, to take recorde of hys
5 owne conscyence, whyther hym selfe, yf one that knewe hys
name, wold wryte suche a worke so towchynge hym, as hys
wurke of dyuysyon toucheth there the clergye / and wold therin
vnder so many Some sayes, say that he were as euyll as he saith
there that they be (for worse coulde lyghtely no man saye) wolde
10 hym selfe hold hym satysfyed, and thynke that y^t wryter ment
hym none harme, bycause he powdered hys shrewde slaunderouse some sayes, wyth lamentynge and pityenge that the man
is no better. [k$_8$v] And wold he wene by his trouth, that the
wryter ment not to cal him gracelesse, bycause he prayed god
15 habundauntely to sende hym grace? nor to call hym witlesse,
bycause he prayeth god send hym wyt? Surely yf he can thynke
so: than shall he well shewe hym selfe so simple a sowle, as men
may well se that some wily shrewys begyle hym. And on the
tother syde yf he be wyser than to thynke so: than he well
20 sheweth hym self more wily in thys same .xiii. chapyter of hys,
than to meane so well in his wurke of dyuysyon as he wolde here
make men wene.

    Now where he saith these wordes

Also I saye not in all the sayde treatyse, that the spyrytualtye make
25 confederacyes agaynste the temporaltye / but I saye that they contynue
styll after the olde course, in not doynge good dedes / but pretendyng
by confederacyes, worldely polycye, & straight correccyons, to rule the
people.

Who coulde wryte thus, but eyther he that were a man of very
30 innocent symplenesse, or he that entendeth to [l$_1$] mocke of a
shrewd wily dowblenes? For (sauynge that hys worde pretendyng signifyeth not in dede the thyng that he for lacke of language pretendeth here therby) to go aboute not to do good to the
people, but by confederacyes with wylynesse and strayght cor-
35 reccyons, to rule the peple: what thynge calleth he this but confederacyes agaynst the people?

---

13 And] *para. 1557*   29 Who] *para. 1557*   36 people?] *1557*, people. *1533*

How be it syth thys chapyter goth but to the dyschargynge of hys owne personall entent, that he ment not hym selfe maly-cyously what so euer hys booke speke: I wyll not therfore wrestle agaynst it mych, but wolde he were well byleued in that thynge. But yet yf you rede the places of myne apologye, and compare them with such partes of hys boke as I there speke of: ye shall well and clerely se, that though the manne in his own mynde ment it not hym self, yet the thynge that I saye was the [l₁v] menynge of hys boke.

The .xiiii. chapyter.

H is .xiiii. chapyter begynneth in the .xlii. lefe. In the begyn-nyng therof he laboreth to proue that he dyd not (as I in myne apologye, saye that he dyd) go about in his boke of diuysyon, to make men wene that the spyrytual iudges in this realme hand-eled men for heresye so cruelly, that all the worlde had cause to wonder and grudge therat / which thynge that I shold so say, this good man myche meruayleth at.

For I sayed no more (sayth he) but that it were pitie it sholde be so, and that it sholde be trewe that is reported, that there sholde be such a desyre in spyrytuall men to haue men abiure, or to haue men haue extreme punyshement for heresye / as it is sayde that there is.

Rede good reders the .xlv. chapyter of myne apologye be-gynnyng fo. [l₂] 243. and than shall you fynde this answere of his a very bare naked thing. This man answereth here as though he trusted that all the worlde were woodcokkys saue hym self / and that hys fayre fygure of some saye, were so wylyly founde, that men had not the wytte to se therby what his booke meneth, & what wurke it goth about. But this I dowte not, but that yf eyther hym self or such another man, wolde deuise me suche another boke, eyther agaynste the nobylyte of the realme, or agaynste the iudges of the same, or agaynste the hygh court of perleament it self, which were soone done yf a man in lyke wyse lyste to slaunder & to bylye them / nor it could not I wote wel what so euer he sayd therin, be lyghtly wurse or more false thanne that

---

24 thing.] *1557*, thing *1533*   34 lyghtly] *1557*, lyghty *1533*

booke of hys dyuysyon, concernynge the poynt that we speke of,
that is to wyt thys false slaunder of the spyrytuall iudges in mysse
han[l₂v]delynge men for heresye, as it hath ofter than ones before the lordes of the kynges most honorable counsayle vpon
5 lyke false bylles and complayntes of partyculare persons by good
examynacion ben proued / and than if he that wolde make I say
of the nobylyte, the iudges, or the perleament, suche another
boke wolde brynge in all his false talys agaynst them vnder the
selfe same fayre fygure of some say, and many say, & they saye /
10 and than say that hym selfe wold say no piece therof, but onely
that it were pytie that it sholde be trewe, that it were so as many
folke reporte it is so, and than preche and pray god send them
the grace that they do not so: I dare be bolde to saye that there is
no wyse man, but he wolde bothe soone se and saye, that the man
15 wyth suche false lesynges went about to dyffame and slaunder
them, and make the people wene that it were so. [l₃]

Than after this thynge so fetely skused: he declareth hys
wordes agayne, whyche he spake in his dyuysyon of spekynge
heresyes of lyghtnesse, or of a passyon. And bycause I answered
20 hym in myne apologye, yᵗ yf such thynges shold be excused by
lyghtnesse & by passyons, than myght there passe by myche
lewdenesse and myche myschyef to / the begynnynge wherof
groweth of lewd lyghtnesse & of euyll passyons: herin he
sheweth that there is dyfference in dedys, and yᵗ some be more &
25 some be lesse. And bycause I did put for samples, manslaughter
and aduowtry, whiche he thought was to high to be lykened to
spekyng & talkyng heresye: he bryngeth it somwhat agayne to
bace, and putteth other samples of one spekyng an angry worde,
& yet wolde not kyll one / & one yᵗ hath a passion of aduowtry, &
30 yet doth not the dede / & sayth yᵗ his treatise ment not obstinate
dedely [l₃v] passyons, but passyons of ignoraunce & of frayltie, &
done for lacke of good aduisement.

As for his passyon of ignoraunce, he may put vp agayne. For
what so euer he say, he shall not fynde I dare warraunt hym
35 whyle he lyueth, but that the thynges that heretykes are
punyshed for, be such thynges as be well & openly knowen for

---

20 apologye] apology *1557*, apolygye *1533*   26 aduowtry] *1533 corr. err.*, aduowter
1533, aduoutri *1557*   32 lacke of] *1557*, lacke or *1533*

heresyes, & to haue ben before condempned for heresyes by the comen knowen doctryne of the whole catholyke chyrch.

Now as touchynge hys passyons for frayeltye & for lacke of good aduisement: doth there no man kyll another euyn sodaynly vppon a passyon of angre, for lacke of good aduisement? doth neuer none vnthryftes vppon a passyon of lechery, sodaynly fall together in aduowtry for lacke of good aduisement?

Ye wyll this man saye, but these folke do ye dede. That is very trouth in dede. But yet they do the dede, but [l₄] of a passyon of frayltye, for lacke of good aduisement. In y^t aduoutry, the malyce is the lacke of goodnesse in ye wyl to ye kepyng of goddes commaundementes.

ʼAnd yet euyn in those passyons to, though the ferther dede be not done, no man neyther kylled nor stryken, nor none aduowtry done in dede, though the lawes of the worlde for lacke of power to loke into ye harte, can not punyshe the bare entent of suche thynges: yet our sauyour saith hym selfe very sore wordes therin, and sayth that hym selfe taketh theyr wylles for theyr dedys.

But now in heresye the wordes be the worke. For not onely the spekyng, but also the defendyng therof, is in wordes to.

But a man sayth he, maye speke heresye of lyghtnesse, & of a passyon of frayltye, & yet not entende to fall fro the fayth. So may a man speke very lewde and ryghte traytorouse wordes by hys prynce to, of a passyon [l₄v] and of a frayltye, without an inward entent and purpose to procure his destruccyon. But than wyll this man peraduenture say, that than be suche wordes yet no treason, without some maner of ouert & open actuall dede therwith. Whyther they be treason or not, yet in any englysshe boke that I wold put in prente, I wolde as thus aduised, aduise euery man for fere of treason, beware of all suche lewd language / and not vnder colour to teche the iudgys theyr part, go tell the people without necessyte, y^t though they talke traytorouse wordes, yet it ys no treason, as this good man in hys booke of diuysyon telleth them, that to talke heresyes is none heresye.

8 Ye] Yea *1557*   12 commaundementes.] *1557*, commaundementes *1533*   17–18 *Sidenote 1557:* Math. 5.   30–31 *Sidenote 1557:* Good counsayle.   35 heresye.] heresy. *1557*, heresye *1533*

Nowe as I sayed before, concernynge heresye whyche is the treason to god, the outwarde acte therof by whyche men muste iudge whyther the manne fall fro the fayth or not, standeth in the wordes. And [l5] therfore both wysedome and reason wyll,
5 that folke well be ware vpon the parell of heresye, that they forbere all such talkyng of heresye, as maye declare theyr mynde that they byleue suche heresye.

That I wyl well agre wyl this good man say. But than I wolde they sholde be ware, by meane of charytable warnynge geuen to
10 theyr persons. I wolde veryly wene, yᵗ in a matter so heyghnouse and of suche weyght, wherof so mych harme may growe by the sufferaunce, the spyrytuall lawe that geueth hym leue to abiure at the fyrste, and in so great a cryme saueth ones his lyfe, geueth hym a warnynge as charytable and as larg, as in a cryme so
15 perylous reson can wel bere. And yᵗ shold we soon fele, yf we wolde geue the lyke lybertye for ones warnynge, to euery lesse cryme than that / & shal shortly fele it in heresyes, if besydes that we [l5v] geue theym lesse fere and more lybertye in bolde talk-ynge and teachynge without other parel than warnynge.

20 For as for the order of warnynge that this man here pro-uydeth, in this .xiiii. chapyter of his newe boke, takynge a col-oure and a pretexte of the gospell of Chryste, that speketh of an order of monycyons, requyrynge a tracte of tyme, before any open denuncyacyon: I wyl not mych stycke vpon. For I purpose
25 not to make a longe processe vppon euery fonde pyece of his dyuyses, wherin thys good man is content to lese tyme and spyl paper. But I wyl say this and say trouth, that thordinaryes, of this order that he speketh, do vse in dede as myche as may wel be borne, and sometyme I fere me more to.

30 For thys muste thys good man understande, that thys good softe slowe sober order, that he descrybeth here, may not all, & alway, be kept, [l6] neyther in heresye nor treason, nor some other great crymes neyther, wythoute great hurte and damage to the comen weale, and vtter losse and destruccyon of many a
35 good symple soule, that sholde by thys order alwaye kepte, per-yshe in the meane whyle.

1 heresye] heresy, *1557*   6 such] *1533 corr. err., om. 1533 1557*   16 ones] once
1557   22–23 *Sidenote 1557:* Math. 18.   25 vppon] vpon *1557*, vpppon *1533;* fonde]
1533 corr. err., fond *1557,* founde *1533*

Nor our sauyour ment not in hys wordes, that if I wyst one that were walkynge aboute myschyefe, that wolde go geue such drynke about as shold poysen them that dronke therof, that thanne I sholde vse all that tracte of time, rather then cause hym be taken vp by tyme at the fyrst sope that I se him geue any man to syppe vpon. Nor that tract is not therfore to be vsed wyth them, that speke and boldely talke heresyes about, & therby do plainly teche them, though they byd not ye herers lerne them. For (as saynte Poule speketh of suche heresyes) euyl communicacion corrupteth good maners. [l₆v] Whyche wordes though the greke poete Menander ment by the communycacyon of other fleshely lewdnesse: yet the blessed apostle vsed them and applyed theym specially, to the lewd communycacyon of heresyes, whych wyth suche bolde noughty talkynge crepeth forth and corrupteth (as saint Poule also sayth) lyke a corrupt canker. And therfore as I saye, suche a long sober tracte before theyr callyng by the ordynarye course of ye law, ys not alwaye to be vsed of necessyte wyth euery suche maner man, and let theym poysen other good symple soules in the meane season, whyche they may do percase with suche communycacyon, though they neyther mynded in theyr owne harte, to make any other men heretykes, nor to be heretyques theym selfe.

And yet wolde there besyde this, some suche as well wyste theyr myscheuouse dealyng to be suche, and so [l₇] wel able to be playnly proued, as the ordinarye coulde not without goddes dyspleasure let theym after passe vnpunyshed / they wolde at the fyrste worde spoken by the ordynarye to hym at large, flyt oute of that place / and as I haue in myne Apologye sayd, and as we se yt often proued, go kepe lyke scoles in a nother.

But yet because I haue herd say euen whyle I was wrytynge thys, that the myld sober order whych this good man hath here in this chapyter dyuysed, is very wel lyked, and hath bene wel praysed wyth some suche folke as my self haue had some communycacyon with ere this: I wyl therfore not hyde yt nor kepe yt awaye from you, but geue you good reders here euen his owne wordes, fo. 45. he sayth.

And nowe wyll I saye a lytle farther in this mater / concernynge suche
wordes, that ys to say, that yf any man now in thys daungerous tyme,
whyle this dyuysyon contynueth, wyll shew vnto the ordynary [l₇v] that
he herde any speke wordes, that as he thought stode not wyth the
catholyque faythe / and the ordynarye mysse lyketh the wordes also: I
wolde than thynke / that yf he vppon whome the informacyon is made,
be suche a man / that he that complayneth of hym may conueniently
speke to hym wythout daunger / that than the ordynarye shal aduyse
hym to kepe the mater secrete, yf yt be yet secrete / and not openly
knowen: and that he shall than charytably aske of hym / what he ment
by these wordes. And than when the questyon is asked hym, yf he make
so reasonable an answere / that yt soundeth to no heresye / than is the
mater answered. And yf he auowe the wordes / and yet they be in dede
agaynst the catholyque fayth: than yt semeth good / that he that accused hym, folowe the gospell / and take wytnesse wyth hym / and efte
charytably gyue hym monycyon therof. And yf he wyll yet stande styll
opynatyuely in his opynyon / and not accept the good monycyon of the
other: than I thynke it good that he agayne informe the ordynarye
therof / and than yt semeth to be conuenyent that the ordynarye sende
for hym / not as for a man yet notoryousely knowen or detected for an
heretyque / but to knowe farther, whether yt be trew as the other hath
reported or not: and yf he fynde yt trewe by suffycyent profe / or by
hys owne confessyon and he wyll not be reformed, than yt semeth
conuenyent / that he vppon the wytnes of the other / be punyshed as he
hath deserued. And yf he wyll be by the ordynary secretely reformed:
then yt semeth good, yᵗ he depart without any open penaunce: but
what were conuenient to be farther done in that mater, I wyll commytte
yt to other.

Consyder now good readers the commodite of this order. You
se that he [l₈] speketh of one that speketh such wordes, as to the
herers seme heresye. For both he so taketh them that informeth
thordinary of them, and so doth thordynarye to. Nowe may you
perceyue by the progresse of his deuyce, that though there were
mo thann one that herd hym, or mo than twayne, or tenne

---

10 charytably] charitably *Salem and Bizance, 1557,* charytable *1533*   24 conuenyent]
conuenient *1557,* couenyent *1533*   27 be farther] *1533 corr. err.,* be[*new line*] ther
1533, bethere *1557*

eyther: yet wold he not that the ordinary shold send for him / but fyrst assay by some such as herd him, what he wyll saye there to when he ys asked the questyon what thynge hym selfe ment therby. And then if he haue the wyt to say y^t he ment in his wordes but suche a thynge as that meanynge soundeth to none heresies (which wit heretykes ynough haue) than ys all the mater answered. For than ye wote wel a wyly heretyque by this wyse order, may be bolde with gloses redy prouyded, to saye what he wyll and where he wyll. For the ordynarye maye not sende for hym to laye those [l$_8$v] heretycal wordes to his charge, and to consyder vpon the cyrcumstaunce of his dealynge in suche talk- ynge, peraduenture in diuerse places vsed, whether he ment as hym selfe declareth yt, or ment to teache the thynge that he spake, and to kepe his declaracyon in store for a scuse. This fyrst poynte alone of thys good mannys order yf yt were surely ob- serued, were ynough to fyl an whole towne shortely ful of heresyes.

Than goth he farther to a second poynte, that yf he that spake heresyes, wyl when he is asked the questyon auowe theym: yet shal not he that herd hym resorte vnto thordynarye but go fetche wytnesses fyrste, before whome yf the felow be so folysh to con- fesse them, and so frantike as to auow them, than this good man geueth theym leue to go tell thordynarye the tale and accuse hym. But nowe yf he haue the wytte byfore the [m$_1$] wytnesses to lye and saye that he neuer sayd theym, or to saye that he wil saye so no more: then is all the mater yet saufe ynough agayne / it shall neuer nede that euer the ordynary here any more worde of hym / but let hym go forthe and vse that fashyon styll, in as many companyes as he cometh. For that ye wote wel can do no hurt. But and yf euery man to whome he speketh heresye secretly, and secretely wolde make mo heretyques, shold secretely enforme the ordynarye / & that he sholde vpon .xx. suche secrete infor- macyons, afterwarde call hym forthe openly, and after vppon theyre open deposycyons, openly make hym abiure, and beare a fagot or accurse hym for hys obstynacye / and after an whole yeres sufferaunce fynally for his immedicable malyce, as a des-

8 prouyded,] *1533 corr. err.*, proued, *1533*, proued *1557*   12 vsed,] vsed *1533*
1557   14 kepe] hepe *1533*, heape *1557*

perate wreche delyuere hym to the seculare handes, where a
fagotte sholde beare hym: thys were a [m₁v] cruell delynge of the
ordynarye, and a mysse handelynge of a good honest man for
heresye.

5   And yet goeth he farther a lytle, that though he holde yt and
auow his heresyes afore the witnesses: thordynarye sholde not
yet for all that procede agaynst hym openly, but speke with hym
secretely. And though he auow theym before hym selfe to: yet
sholde he not by thys good mannys aduyse, procede agaynste
10 hym by ordynarye meanes openly, but let hym departe wythoute
open penaunce, yf the felowe be so wyse as at laste (rather than
he wolde come therto) saye that he wyl amende and wyll say such
thynges no more.

But than after al this, what were conuenyent to be farther
15 done he wil he sayth remyt vnto other men. And so were yt
myche nede in dede. How be yt yf this order that he deuyseth
here, were wel obserued for so farre [m₂] forthe as he goeth: I
wene all the worlde coulde not well deuyse farther, suffycyentely
to reforme and remedy the myschyefe that hys charytable de-
20 uyse wolde do.

How be it the beste is therin, that he deuyseth not this order
for a thing to stande for euer / but for this tyme now he saith
which is he sayth a daungerouse tyme, whyle thys dyuysyon
contynueth.

25 But nowe so is yt good readers that whether this tyme be so
daungerouse as he speketh of or no, or whether there be in this
tyme suche dyuysyon as he maketh or no: sure it is I saye, that
euyn in this same tyme heresyes begyn to growe a great deale
faster than they haue bene wont in some other tymes past / and
30 therfore is this tyme so mych the worse to vse such order in, than
were a nother time, wherin there were many fewer. For yf this
pacyfyer wyl nowe be so [m₂v] peasyble, as to deuise such an
order yᵗ al myscheuous factyous folke shold be suffered in
peace: he shall wyth his peasyble order (yf yt were obserued)
35 brynge the worlde in that case, that good peasyble folke that
fayne wold lyue in peace, shold not for such inquiete and
vnrestful wreches with out some rufle lyue in peace longe.

---

23 dyuysyon] diuision *1557*, dyuyuysyon *1533*   25 But] *no para. 1557*

Were it not a wise order wene you if he wold in like wise deuyse
for theuys the same softe charytable fashyon that he deuiseth
here for heretikis? that is to wyt that men shold to hym that had
stolen an horse, or robbed an house, go geue hym a monicyon
fyrst and then yf he saye that he dyd yt not or that he wolde do so   5
no more, take all the mater for saufe / and than say that he wolde
not haue that order allwaye kepte, but onely in suche dayngerouse tymes as many folke wolde fall to thefte. For than were
yt good to spare theim and speke them fayre, [m₃] and suffer
theym tyll they wolde waxe fewer of them selfe / and than after   10
that, vse agaynste theym the lawis & the old order again. Wold
not thys wyse waye trowe you do well in thefte? For sothe yt were
a waye as farre vnwyse & as farre agaynst reason in heresy, as
eyther in theft or murder or any other maner cryme.

And surely me semeth yᵗ where he calleth this a dayngerouse   15
tyme: he vseth a very daungerous worde / and to fere the ordynaryes wyth all, wolde make the worlde wene, that heretyques
were here so many and so stronge, that thordynaryes myght not
nowe do theyre dutyes in subduynge heresyes, wythoute great
daungeour. Wherin there is as great daungeour yet, and shall I   20
dout not in the kynges graces days that now is, and longe mote
be, as there ys in the parynge of an apple. Howe be yt I wyl not
denye hym thys in[m₃v]ded, but that yf suche daungerouse
wordes of his dyuysyon, may make thordynaryes aferd of theyre
owne shadow a whyle: yt may grow to some daunger at the laste.   25

But than goeth he farther with a nother remedye, that I truste
in god shall neuer nede. For I truste in god there neuer shall in
thys realme, any suche great personage fall into heresye, as thordynarye dare not procede accordynge to the law agaynste hym.
Howe be yt in case yt shold happen: than this good man pro-   30
uideth for the remedy (to say the trouth) very wel, that is to wyt
that thordynary sholde haue recourse vnto the kynge, that his
hyghnes vppon petycyon made vnto hym, and informacyon
geuyn hym, maye (as no doute were there but he wolde) wyth his
royall assystence, prouyde a meane suffycyent, yᵗ the course of   35
the law myght procede.

---

13 a waye] *1557*, awaye *1533*   14 murder] murther *1557*   25 shadow] *1557*,
shawdow *1533*

This is wel deuised. And here in [m$_4$] he plaieth the good kow, & geueth vs a good galon of mylke. But than shal you se howe he playeth the shrewde kow agayne, and turneth ouer the payle euyn by and by wyth his hele. For vppon this good deuise, he
5   forthwith addeth this shrewd sayeng to yt.

But as longe as there is an opynyon amonge the peple / that the ordinaryes & theyr offycers wil geue lyght credence vppon informa-cyons made to theym of heresye / and that they wyll noyse theym that be complayned on as heretyques / before dew examynacyon in that
10   behalfe: so long wyll the peple grudge and peraduenture the kynge not geue hys assystence so redyly to haue them attached as he wolde do, yf he herde that the ordynaryes noysed no man to be an heretyque wyth-out dew examynacyon, as is before rehersed.

If this good man had as myche wyt as I se wel he lacketh: I wold
15   wax euyll content with hym, that he shold ones conceyue any such opynyon of the kinges graciouse hyghnes, as that his grace wold any thynge be the more remysse to geue royall assystence vnto thordinaries, about y^e attaching of such as are suspect of heresy, [m$_4$v] as longe as hys grace herde that thordynaryes
20   noysed that any man were an heretyque wythoute suche dewe examynacyon as this man afore rehersed. For the kynges hygh prudence very wel perceiueth, that if he sholde forbere tyl that tyme that he sholde here no suche thynge sayde by theym: yt were almoste as myche to say, as he shold geue no asystence
25   agaynste heretykes, tyl al heretykes were gone. For neuer shall there lacke suche a false sedycyouse fame agaynste the or-dynaryes, as longe as there are heretyques here & there to sowe it, and suche sedycyouse bokes of dyuysyon, with such vntrewe Some sayes to blowe yt farther abrode.
30   The vntrouth of such false fame, hath ben before the kinges honorable counsayle of late well and playnely proued all redy, vppon   sondry   suche   false   complayntes   by   the   kinges gra[m$_5$]cyouse commaundement examyned. And all be it that this is a thynge notoriousely knowen, and that I haue also my
35   selfe in myne apologye spoken thereof, and that synnys that boke gone abrode, it hath ben in lyke wyse before the lordes well

---

3 kow] *1557*, know *1533*   7 lyght] lyghte *1557*, lytght *1533*

& playnely proued in mo maters a fresshe / and all be it that this
water wessheth awaye all his mater: yet goeth euer this water
ouer this goosys backe / & for any thynge that any man can do,
no man can make it synke vnto the skynne that she maye ones
fele it / but euer she shaketh such playne proues of with her   5
fethers of Some say and they say the contrary. Is not this a prety
proper way? And therfore thus you se good reders, that this
mannes deuicys in his order to be taken with suche as speke
heresyes, be very vicyouse and haue they neuer so fayre a fleryng
at the fyrste face: yet whan they be consydered well, they be   10
foun[m₅v]den farre worse than nought. And yet was I not mynded as you maye se, to haue examyned them so farre, sauynge that euyn whyle I was in writynge of this chapyter, and
about to leue of: worde was brought me that thys deuyce of his
order for heresye, was with some folke whom my self haue   15
knowen, so specyally well commended.

But yet wyll thys man say, & in effecte so he dothe, mayster
More wyll not say for all thys that euery thynge that a man
speketh whiche yf he obstynately wolde holde he were an heretyke, is inough to iudge euery such man an heretyke, as doth in   20
any maner speke it.

I wyll not at thys tyme varye with this good man for that, nor
dyspute with hym vppon the trouth of yᵗ tale, there be so many
maner waies of spekynge. For a man maye speke therof in
dysprayse therof. But this wyll I saye to hym. That tale and [m₆]   25
such other lyke, were they neuer so trewe, were yet as me semeth
mych better out of his englysshe prented booke than in it.

For yf he thynke it necessary to wryte it, bycause of any folke
whom he thynketh necessary to lerne it: eyther he meneth that
they nede it, whiche are the spyrytuall iudges, or els the comen   30
people. Now as for the iudges, veryly I haue knowen and do
knowe many of them, & yet knewe I neuer none so symple of
wyt, nor so farre vnlerned, but for any wyt or lernyng that I
perceyue in this man, the wurste of theym wyste a greate dele
better what perteyned vnto theyr parte and theyr dutye in suche   35
poyntes as these are, than doth thys good man here.

Than yf he saye he putteth it in, bycause that though they

---

2 wessheth] washeth *1557*   35 vnto] *1557*, vn to *1533*

knowe it they mysse vse it, and do the contrary [m₆v] and so do therby misse handle the kynges people, and put theym to cruell punyshement vniustely: than I aske hym how he proueth that lye to be trew? Therto ye wote well he wyll brynge forth for the
5 playne profe of his playn trouth in the mater his old thre wurshypfull wytnesses whiche stand yet all vnsworne that is to wyt Some saye, and They say, & Folke say. And than hath he now brought forth other two, whome he maketh as me semeth bothe as wytnesses & iudges to, that is the good sely sowle Symkyn
10 Salem, and his ryght honest neyghbour brother Byzance. Well I am content I, yᵗ all his fyue wytnesses be sworen & wel examined, how they know the thynges that they reporte / & than those spyrytuall iudges of whom they shall so speke and proue, let it be layed vnto theyr charges. And yf you fynde of suche so many,
15 and theyr dealynge so cruell or [m₇] vniuste, as this man maketh it, or any thynge well towarde it: than am I content that ye shall for them byleue all the remanaunt the wurse. And yet is yᵗ I wysse somwhat with the most. And than am I content that you byleue also, that this man had for that cause / a necessary occa-
20 sion and a profytable, to put yᵗ tale in his bate makynge boke.
    But in the mene whyle, I laye agaynste hym for yᵗ point, and agaynst all his fyue wurshypfull wytnesses to, the dede & the reporte of yᵉ gretest and the moste honorable temporall lordes of the kynges most honorable counsayle, and other ryght
25 wurshypfull temporall men of the same with them, whiche by the gracyouse commaundement of the kinges hyghnesse, haue examyned dyuerse suche complayntes, at the suit of yᵉ partyes them selfe and theyr frendes, & haue theruppon founden the same complayntes [m₇v] false, & that thordynaryes haue done
30 them but ryght, and that wyth great fauour to.
    And therfore as for thyꝪ poynte, the treuthe beynge so sub-stancyally proued vppon this syde, by all hys fyue forenamed wytnesses on the tother syde sette I not fyue strawes. And ther-fore good reders as for this poynt, his puttynge of that pyece in
35 hys boke of diuisyon, had neyther necessyte nor profyte / ex-cepte it were eyther necessary or profytable to sow a euyll sede

---

7 *Sidenote 1557:* Three sure witnesse I ensure you.   17–18 I wysse] ywisse *1557*
23 gretest] greatest *1557*   33 wytnesses] wytnesses, *1533*, witnesses *1557*

agaynste good folke, of vntrew reprouable slaunder in hys owne
wrytynge, vnder the colour of some other mennes vnproued
wordes.

Than resteth there as farre as I can se but one cause by-
hynde, y^t shold excuse hym. And that is that it was a thynge
profytable for the people, to know that though a man of a
lyghtnesse or of a passyon growynge of ignoraunce or of
frayltye, speke and [m$_8$] talke heresyes at lybertye: yet but yf he
defende it opinatyuely, he shold not be taken for an heretyke
therby. Veryly good readers yf thys tale were trewe: yet wolde I
wene as I sayde, this tale vnto the people as good vnwryten as
wryten, & a great dele better to.

As for thys good man or any man ellys, I can not let theym to
wryte what they lyste, and saye they thynke it good be it neuer so
badde in dede. But I durste in my conscyence no more vse thys
fashyon of wrytynge concernynge heresye, than I wolde vse it in
wrytynge any boke, wherof I wolde speke of eyther treason or
any other felony / excepte some other necessary occasyon sholde
happely dryue me therto, as no good occasyon in hys booke of
dyuysyon droue this good man therto.

If I were agayne to reade in Lyncolns Ine & there were in
hande [m$_8$v] wyth a statute that touched treason and all other
felonyes: I wolde not let to loke, seke out and reherse whyther
any heyghnouse wordes spoken agaynst the prynce, were for the
onely spekynge to be taken for treason or not.

Nor I wolde not let in lyke wyse to declare, if I founde out any
casys in whyche a man though he toke another mannes horse
agaynst the law, sholde yet not be iudged for a felon therby. And
this wolde I not onely be bolde there to tell them, but wolde also
be bolde in such french as is peculiare to the lawys of this realme,
to leue it wyth them in wrytynge to. But yet wold I reken my selfe
sore ouer sene, yf all suche thynges as I wolde in that scole speke
in a redyng, I wolde in englysh into euery mannys hand put out
abrode in prent. For there is no such necessyte therin as is in the
tother. For in y^e places of court [n$_1$] these companies must
nedes be taught it / oute of whyche companyes they must after
be taken that shalbe made iudges to iudge it. But as for the
comon people to be tolde that tale, shall as farre as I se do many
folke lytell good, but rather very great harme. For by per-

ceyuyng that in some thinges were no thynge the perell that
they ferede, some may waxe therin more neglygent / and by
lesse ferynge ye lesse dayngeour, may soone steppe into the
more. And therfore haue I wyste ere thys, the iudges of a great
5 wysedome in great open audyence, where they haue hadde occasyon to speke of hyghe mysseprisyon or of treason, forbere
yet the sayenge of some suche thynges, as they wolde not haue
letted to speke among them selfe.

If any man wold happely thynke that it were well done that
10 euery man were taught all / and wolde aledge [n₁v] therfore that
if he know surely what thynge wolde make hys behauour hygh
treason or heresye, than though he wolde aduenture all that
euer were vnder that, yet wold he be peraduenture the more
ware to kepe hymselfe well from that / as many a man though he
15 byleue that he shall abyde greate payne in purgatory for hys
venyall synnes, dothe for all that no greate dylygence in for-
berynge of them, and yet for ye feare of perpetuall payne in
hell, taketh very greate hede to kepe hym selfe frome those
synnes, that he surely knoweth for mortall.

20 As for suche venyall synnes as folke of fraylty so comenly do
fall in, that no man is almoste any tyme wythout theym, though
the profyte wolde be more yf men dyd wene they were mortall,
so that the drede therof coulde make menne vtterly forbere
theym: yet syth it wyll not be, that [n₂] men wyll vtterly forbere
25 them / the knowlege of the trouth is necessary for them / leste
euery tyme that they do suche a veniall synne in dede, wenyng
that it were mortall, the doyng of the dede wyth the conscyence
of a mortall synne, myghte make it mortall in dede.

But of any such kynde of veniall synnes as be not so mych in
30 custume, and may be more easyly forborne: I neuer founde
any wyse man to my remembraunce, that wold eyther wryte or
teche the comune peple so exactly, as to say though you do thus
farre, yet is it no dedely synne / but wyll in suche thynges syth
the veniall synne it self is a drawyng toward ye dedely, rather
35 leue the people in dowt and in drede of dedely synne, and
thereby cause them to kepe them selfe farre of from it / than by
tellynge theym it is but a venyall synne, make them the lesse

---

11 behauour] behaueour *1557*   26–27 *Sidenote 1557:* Venial sinne maye be made
mortall.

aferde to do it / and so [n₂v] come so myche the nerer to mortall synne, and assaye how nere he canne come to it, and not do
it, tyll he come at laste so nere the brynke, that hys fote slyppeth
and downe he falleth into it. For as the scrypture saith, Qui
amat periculum, peribit in illo. He that loueth perell shall per-   5
yshe in it.

Nowe as for heyghnouse wordes spekynge agaynste the
prynce, or talkynge of heresye agaynste the knowen catholyque
fayth: these are no thynges lyke these commen veniall synnes /
but be thynges bothe twayne, whyche they that do theym, maye   10
myche more easely forbere them. And therfore were it more
profyte vnto the people, to thynke rather the more perell
therin thanne the lesse.

The iudges parte is to se that the punysshement passe not the
grauyte of the offence. And therfore shall the comon people   15
take none harme, [n₃] though them selfe concernynge treason
or heresye, fall not by suche bokes to the myncyng of suche
maters, and dyspute howe farre they maye go forwarde in
theym, wythout the extreme daynger and perell of them / but
shall the better kepe them selfe from the greater, yf for fere of   20
greater, they kepe them selfe well from the lesse.

But surely suche tales tolde vnto the people, and geuyn euery
man and woman at auenture in prented englysshe bookes
abrode, as may geue them suche boldenesse in talkynge, as thys
man here in thys .xiiii. chapyter dothe, and to tell theym that   25
there is not therin so mych perell, as many man wolde wene:
maye be myche harme bothe vnto them selfe and vnto other to.
To them selfe, for with a lytell lesse feare than they had before,
they maye soone fall ferther than they dyd before, or euer wolde
[n₃v] haue done. And than sholde he in whome it so sholde   30
happen, fynde that it were (as holy saynt Hierome sayth) better
to leue some thynges vnknowen, than with perell to lerne theym.

To other men also maye a man do thereby myche harme. For
some man with bolde talkynge heresyes, wherby he maketh

---

4 scrypture] scripture *1557*, strypture *1533*   5 *Sidenote 1557:* Eccle. 13.   14 *Side-*
note 1557: The parte of iudges.   22 vnto] *1557*, vn *1533*   23 auenture] aduenture
1557

other men fyrste to take them for lyght, and lytell and lytell
after to byleue them to (whyle they here him so boldely speke
them, & here hym nothynge reproue them) may do mych more
harme by making many other fal from ye fayth, though he were
5 not fallen from it hym selfe, than he shold do if he hylde his
tonge, though secretely in his harte he were a starke heretyke in
dede.

And therfore surely good reader, what so euer the man ment
in hys owne secrete mynde, the fashyon of his doctrine is yet in
10 my mynde play[n_4]nely a thynge to the people myche more perylouse than profytable / and in his booke of dyuysyon very euyll
putte in, and here euyll repeted agayne.

Now where as he referreth the remanaunt of the mater concernyng heresye, vnto theym that can better skyl / of whom he
15 desyreth me to aske what were to be done, wyth suche as speke
heresyes and are none heretykes in theyr harte: surely yf euer
any suche case sholde happen, as I shold nede to make serche
for that poynte, I wolde wyth good wyll so do. But I loke for no
suche necessyte. For it is inough for me, yf I sholde happe to
20 here any talke heresyes, than to declare it vnto theyr ordynaryes,
to whome the ferther charge apperteyneth, to make therupon
ferther serch suche as he maye / and theruppon as he maye
ferther fynde therof, so ferther do therin. [n_4v]

And as for thys man hym selfe, as he canneth therin for any
25 thynge that I se very lytell skyll, so wolde I that he hadde lesse
medeled therwith, than to tell and teache the peple fyrst by hys
booke of dyuysyon, and afterwarde by thys booke agayne, that
they maye speke and talke heresyes well inough, wythout the
daynger or perell to be for suche spekynge lawfully taken for
30 heretyques. Wyth whiche tale though it were trewe, he doth
them yet lytell good. For the vsyng of such spekyng of heresyes,
yf it fully proue not a man an heretyque, yet may it make hym ye
wote well of heresye in hys harte very ryghte sore suspecte. For
as oure sauyour saythe hym selfe, Ex habundantia cordis os
35 loquitur. The mouth speketh suche thynges as in the harte be
plentuouse and haboundeth. And therfore I saye, that though
he neyther defende it [n_5] obstynately, nor can be precysely

---

5 hylde] helde *1557*   34–35 *Sidenote 1557:* Luke .6.   36 plentuouse] plenteous
1557

proued an heretique in his secrete harte: yet maye his open
wordes be suche (though they were spoken of I can not tel you
what maner passyon) that for the sore suspycyon that his own
wordes hath brought hym selfe into, he maye well and wyth good
reason be compelled to abiure. And therin were there I wysse no 5
great honesty nor no very great profyte neyther. And yet is it al
the profyte that I se can come of thys good mannes doctryne.

And this is the thynge lo that this good man bosteth in this
chapiter, the seconde syde of his .xliiii. lef, that I do not deny / as
though he had goten therby a great ouer hande on me in ye 10
mater. But yet wold I good reders saue for the length, let hym
perceyue hys ouersyghte and ignoraunce, in a nother maner
touchynge the thynge [n₅v] that he so bosteth that I denye hym
not / and wolde make hym loke a lyttell better euyn vppon Summa Rosella, whom he so mych allegeth here hym selfe. 15

And where as in the same lefe and syde, he maketh a certayne
certyfycate (as though I were a bysshoppe, and hadde sente hym
a commyssyon to enquyre) that he knoweth not one heretyke in
all this realm in worde nor dede: mary I wolde meruayle myche
yf he dyd. For yt muste nedes be very long ere he can knowe any, 20
while the man is so lytle suspycyouse in maters of heresye, that
though he sholde here theym talke heresye by hym, yet bycause
though he heare what theyr mouthes speke, he can not yet perdye lo loke in vnto theyre hartes there, and se what they thynke,
nor knoweth not also, whyther yf they were asked [n₆] where 25
they were well aferde, they wolde holde yt opynatyuely / or elles
(rather than be burned or beare a fagotte) say that they sayde yt
al but of a passyon of ignoraunce or frayltye: he can not therfore
lyghtely knowe any one heretyque (as he sayeth he doth not)
neyther in worde nor dede in all thys whole realme. 30

And then for hearynge by report, therin goth he farther and
sayeth.

For howe be yt that I haue herde somtyme reported, that there be
many heretykes / yet I neuer hard so farre profe therin, that I myght
with conscyence iuge or report / that this man or that man is an here- 35

---

5 I wysse] ywisse *1557*   12 hys] *1533 corr. err.*, thys *1533*, this *1557*   31 And] *no
para. 1557*

tyque. And to euery lyght worde a man maye not gyue full credence in
that behalfe / ne reporte yt lyghtly / that any man is an heretyque by
suche lyght tales. And surely thys poynte is myche to be noted of all
men / but moste spycyally of them that dayly mynystre the sacramentes
5 of the chyrche, leste happely thorough suche reportes they mynystre
theym somtyme in dedely synne, and yet wolde not thynke so theym
selfe.

It wolde haue done very well, that thys good man hadde geuen
as lyghte a credence, to suche reportes [n₆v] in mysse hand-
10 elynge of heretyques as some haue made hym of the spyrytualtye
(yf hym selfe therin saye trewe) as he semeth to haue geuen to
theym that haue reported vnto hym that there are many here-
tiques. For than, syth after hys owne preachynge here, a man
oughte to be so well ware howe he lyghtely reporte agayne, any
15 euyll lyghte reportes that he hathe herde to the slaunder of any
one man: hym selfe wold not of lykelyhed so lyghtely haue made
such euyll report in that poynt, to the slaunder and obloquye of
the prelates of the spyrytualtye, therby to brynge theym in
grudge of the whole temporalty, vppon such lyght reportes
20 made vnto hym, by some lyghte symple persones / where as by
the kynges honorable counsayle the trouthe hathe ben so
playnely proued to be contrarie. [n₇]

But yet where as he confesseth that he hathe herde yt sometyme reported, that there be many heretyques: I wolde fayne wyt
25 of hym, whether that suche reporte haue ben made vnto hym by
any of the temporaltye. If he saye naye, but that all that so tolde
hym were spyrytuall men: than may they byleue hym that thynke
hys answere lykely. For I wolde wene in my mynde, that betwene
hym and spyrytuall persones, were not so myche famylyare com-
30 panye, as to come to tell hym that tale. For he semeth not very
metely for spyrytuall men in that mater to make theyr mone
vnto. And than yf he harde yt eyther of temporall men besyde,
or of temporall men onely and no spyrytuall men at all: than dyd
he not very well when he wrote in hys dyuysyon, that spyrytual
35 men make that noyse for a polycye. [n₇v] And yet also wolde I
farther wyt, whether he haue herde any speke heresyes in any
place where hym selfe was present in companye. If he answere

---

16 lykelyhed] likelyhod *1557*   35 And] *para. 1557*

me naye: than wyll I preace no farther vppon hym, but let euery
man as I saide before byleue yt that thynketh yt lykely. But on the
tother syde, yf he answere me ye: than wolde I fayne farther wyt,
whyther euer hym selfe wente so farre wyth theym, as to proue
whether he sholde by hys owne rule in thys chapyter, haue cause   5
to shewe theyr ordynarye of theym, that he myghte sende for
theym / or ellys that herynge folke so speke heresyes by hym, he
toke all to the beste alwaye of his owne specyall goodnesse / and
leste he myghte wyth questyonynge happe to fynde yt worse,
folowed euer in that mater, the good counsayle that saynt Poule   10
gaue in a nother mater, nolite interrogare, pro[n₈]pter conscien-
tiam, aske no questyon, leste you brynge a scruple into your
conscyence. If he vsed any dylygence in questyonynge: than
were yt well lykely that he founde in all thys longe whyle, some
where at the leste wyse some one.   15
    But now yf he herde them speke heresye, & founde no faute
therwyth, nor no questyon asked: then ys yt as I sayde lytle
meruayle, though he neuer no where in al England found one.
And that is euen one of the very thynges, whyle many folke nowe
fall to the same fashyon, to heare heresyes talked and lette the 20
talkers alone, whyche yet wyll (yf they be brought into the court
byfore the iudge) tell than the trouth, and wyl not be so false as to
be forsworen: thys is I say one of the very special thynges, for
whyche in cryme of heresye the suyte ex officio (whyche in the
next chapyter folowyng he laboreth [n₈v] sore to destroye) maye 25
what so euer thys man saye, in no wyse be forborne, but yf we
wolde haue the stretes swarme full of heretyques, whyche very
lykely were to folowe, though he saye naye .xl. tymes. And that
haue I agaynste hys boke of dyuysyon well declared in myne
Apologye. And he hath agayn here in thys boke defended, in   30
that poynte his boke of dyuysyon, as your self shal anon se god
wote wyth myche worke full febly.

---

30 boke] boke here *1557*

The secund part.

The .xv. chapyter.

H IS .xv. chapiter concernynge the suit ex officio, begynneth in the .xlviii. lefe of his boke, & holdeth on into yᵉ .liiii.

5   And for as mych good christen readers as it may well appere, that this poynt is the specyall thynge that he fayne wolde brynge about, that is to wyt to sowe an opinyon in mennes heddes, that it were good to chaunge and put awaye that suit, toward whiche purpose all his boke of diuysyon bendeth / laborynge fyrst with

10 his so many some sayes, to brynge the spyrytuall iudges in suspy-cyon and obloquy, and make the people wene yᵗ they mer-uelousely dyd with mych wronge & cruelty mysse handle men [A₁v] for heresye: therfore I shall in thys poynt here confute hys argumentes so playne & in such wyse, that who so lyste indyf-

15 ferently to rede bothe the partes, shall fynde here causes good and suffycyent why, by his vnreasonable reasons neuer after to set a flye.

And fyrst bycause ye shall well se that I wyll not wrestle in the darke, but brynge the mater into lyght open and playne at your

20 eyen / I wyll in this mater leue you not out one word of this his .xv. chapyter, but brynge forth his wordes with myne. And than whyle you rede the tone fyrste, & the tother euyn after hande: there shall neyther he nor I / by any sly sleyght deceyue you.

25   But two thynges for thys mater wyll I requyre you fyrste / one that you reiecte one wyly sleyght of hys, with which he goth about euyn from the begynnynge to corrupte our iudgement that are temporall men, and [A₂] in yᵉ redyng to blynd vs with affeccion.

For in all this mater he maketh as there were two partes. The

30 tone he maketh the spyrytualtye. And thys cause he so maketh theyrs, as though the commodyte of that suit to be kepte, were a thynge that perteyned onely vnto them. The tother partye he maketh vs of the temporalty, whom he wold haue put yᵗ same

---

5 as it] *1557*, at it *1533*   17 flye.] *1557*, flye *1533*   28 affeccion.] *1557*, affeccion *1533*   29 partes] parties *1557*

suit away. For though that in the perleament be spyrytuall men also: yet all were they al vpon one syde sure, he seeth wel they were to fewe.

But it is necessary that we consyder in this poynt, that though the iudges be spyrytuall, yet yf that suit be necessary for pre-   5
seruacyon of the catholyke fayth, than is the profyte not the spirytuall mennes onely, but that profyte and aduauntage is our owne to. And yf by the chaunge of that suit ex officio, the decay of the catholyke fayth shall folow in this realme: than [A₂v] is not the losse and damage vnto the spyrytualtye alone, but the harme   10
is importable vnto the whole realme.

Therfore haue this poynt in this mater euer before your eyen, that yᵉ chaunge of that law yf that lawe be good, but yf he chaunge it in to a better, or at the leste as good, is a comen harme to the whole realme. And that harme happeneth in yᵉ   15
gretest thyng that we coulde possyble take harme in, yf we be (as I wote well we be & euer entende to be) faythfull trew chrysten people.

Loke therfore good readers both to his reasons and myne, and yf you fynde by his reasons that the puttyng awaye of that   20
law, be better for the kepyng of the catholyke fayth in this land, ye or better other wyse for this land without the minisshement of the fayth in the same, than am I well content that ye compte thys good man bothe for very wyse and for very [A₃] faithfull to.   25

But now yf you fynde by myne answere on yᵉ tother side, yᵗ al his reasons in this poynt are not worth one rysshe towarde the profe of any necessary cause of chaunge / but hys reason and his argumentes alway such therin, yᵗ eyther they be byelded vppon a false ground / or ellys yf he make any that happen to be true, yf   30
ye fynde it yet but such as by the selfe same reason yf men wolde vnwysely folowe it, there myghte no lawe neyther longe laste, nor yet no law be made: yf you fynd I say his reasons agaynst this law but suche, ye wyll than I dowt not thynke it but good reason, for all his riall reasonyng to let yᵉ law stand.   35

---

3 fewe.] *1557*, fewe *1533*   10 but the] but *1557*   16 gretest] greatest *1557*   35
riall] royall *1557*

But than yf ye fynde ferther yet, as I wote well ye shall, that the chaunge that he wolde make, vnder a nedeles pretence of pre-seruyng innocentes out of dayngeour and parell, and can not proue that thys hundred [A₃v] yere any one was wronged with it,

5   sholde cause heretykes to be bolde, take corage, & encreace, and for lacke of this law the catholyke fayth to dekaye: than wyll you not I wote wel let to tell thys man, that he lacketh in this mater, how gay so euer he make it, either wyt, or (which wurse were) loue to the chrysten fayth.

10   The tother thynge y^t I requyre, you shall your selfe se reason-able. For it serueth to the clere perceiuyng of vs bothe, how both he and I bere our selfe in this mater. And I shall not requyre therin parcyally for my parte, but a requeste indyfferent and egall for vs bothe, syth ye shall the clerer therby perceyue where

15   about we bothe goo, and where any of vs bothe swarue a syde fro the mater, and to hyde the trouth out of syghte, slynke into lurkys lane.

My request is no more, but that it maye lyke you to take the laboure [A₄] and payne for perceyuynge of the trowth, from the

20   begynnynge to peruse the whole mater, as farre as perteyneth to the chaunge of this lawe.

Reade fyrste hys owne wordes in his owne boke of dyuysyon. And after reade myne answere in myne apologye, whyche you shall fynde in the fourtyth chapyter, the .218. lefe, and his

25   wordes to therwyth. And whanne those two thynges be bothe fresshe in your mynde, reade thanne this his fyftenthe chapyter of thys booke, wyth myne answeres euery where added therun-to / and than haue I whan this is done lytell dowte of your iudgement, ye shall se the mater proue agaynste thys good man

30   so playne.

In hys .xv. chapyter good readers he wolde make men wene, that he suffycyentely proueth thre thynges. The tone is that it were none hurte to chaunge now this olde lawe. [A₄v] The se-cunde thynge is that it were great hurte to kepe it. The thyrde,

35   that suche samples of the lawes of thys realme as I resembled vnto the suit ex officio, I resemble against reason, they be so farre vnlyke.

---

24 chapyter] Chapter *1557*   30 so] *1533 corr. err., om. 1533 1557*

Into these thre poyntes therfore wyll I deuyde thys chapyter that the reader may the better se in what parte he is.

I shall reherse you fyrst here his whole wordes togyther, that he bryngeth for the fyrste poynte. Lo good readers these they be.

THen to the conuentynge of men before spyrytuall iudges ex officio,   5
and wherupon mayster More sayth in his apology, fo. 219. that yf it were lefte, the stretes were lykely to swarme full of heretikes: Veryly I meruayle right moche at his sayeng therin: and that for this cause: It is certayne, that no man maye after the lawe be detected of heresye, but that there is some man that knoweth the cause before why he oughte so   10
to be. For yf it be secrete in hys owne breste, none can be hys iudge but god onely, that is the sercher of mans herte. And yf any wyl aduowe, that he knoweth the cause, and wyl denounce hym as an heretyke therfore: than it is reason, y^t he be taken as his accuser. [A$_5$] And yf he wyll not aduow to be his accuser, yt ys to thynke that he doth yt of some   15
malyce or crafte rather then for the trouth of the mater. And yf he saye he dare not for fere of his lyfe auow yt, I haue shewed a meane in the .vii. chapyter of the sayde treatyse how the wytnesse maye be saued from daunger, as by shewynge the mater to the kynge and hys coun-sayle, and that then yt is not to suppose nor so to thynke, but that they   20
wyll prouyde suffycyently for the indempnyte of the wytnesse in that behalfe. And this remedye mayster More denyeth not to be conuen-yent for this realme. And yet he wyll not assent, that a lawe be made that yt shall be so. And then yf the wytnesse wil not auow it, but an other wyl geue credence to hym and auow yt: then yt semeth reasonable, that   25
they y^t wyll gyue credence therto, & wyl reporte yt / be taken as ac-cusers: takynge those wytnesse for theyr warraunte, yf yt be denyed.

In these wordes lo good readers you se, howe he proueth hys fyrste poynt, that of the chaunge of this law by puttynge awaye this suyt ex officio, wherin wythoute any specyall accuser of-   30
ferynge hym selfe as party, the suspecte may be called in before the iudge ex officio, that is to wyt by reason of his office: there could none harme growe at all.

---

6 fo. 219.] fo,219. *1533*, Fo.219. *1557*   18 chapyter] Chapter *1557*   30 accuser]
accuser, *1533 1557*

And howe dothe he nowe proue vs this poynt? He proueth yt [A₅v] as you se fyrst by a certain reason put & presupposed for a grounde / & then after that by a certayne order that hym selfe shortly diuyseth and setteth vp vppon the same. Hys ground and
5 his foundacion is this,

Yt is certayn he sayth that no man may after the law be detected of heresye / but that there is some man that knoweth the cause before / why he ought so to be.

Very trouth yt is that no man can be detected, except a man
10 detect hym self, but yf some other se some thyng in hym wher-fore he sholde seme nought, some one thinge or other that they whych perceyue it suspect hym therfore them selfe. And ther-fore as for this ground this good man and I wyll not greatly stryue.
15 Then foloweth his order that he dyuyseth & byeldeth vp theruppon thus.

And yf any wyll aduow that he knoweth the cause, and wyll denounce hym an heretyke therfore: then is yt reason that he be taken as his accuser.

20 This is a ryght good reason / and the spirituall lawe wyll not refuse so to take hym & accept hym for an accu[A₆]ser yf he will / and then wyll they not in that case vse the suit ex officio. For in that case it nedeth not. But nowe what yf he that knoweth it, & secretly detecteth it, peraduenture four or fyue and sometyme
25 mo to, & yet not one of them al, wil openly be called an accuser, but wilbe content to be taken and knowen for a wytnesse, called in by the court & sworen, and to tell the trouth as of an necessyte, & not as accusers of theyr neyghbour of theyr own offre wyll-yngly: what shall the ordynary do then?
30 Agaynst this parel this good man geueth vs this remedy.

If they wyll not be hys accusers, yt is to thynke that they do yt of some malyce or crafte, rather then for the trouth of the mater.

I wene good readers that there is no man but when he hereth

---

2 by a] 1533 corr. err., by 1533 1557   3 by a] by 1557   4 setteth] 1533 corr. err., 1557, setted 1533   4–5 Hys ground and his foundacion is this,] 1533, His ground and his foundacion is thys. 1557, All thys muste be in the great letter 1533 corr. err. (see note)   6 Yt] yt 1533, It 1557   14 stryue.] striue. 1557, stryue 1533

this answere, he wold wene there were yet for the farther remedye some other more mater behynd. For what madde man wolde
thynke that this were a suffycient remedy, so fully prouyded
[A₆v] for thys mater, that yf there were any heretyques they
could not fayle so fully to be detected by thys waye of accusacyon,   5
that there sholde nede no suyte ex officio, bycause they that
knowe yt maye eyther holde theyr peace yf they lyste, or ellys yf
they wyll algates detecte any man, maye be taken and accepted
for accusers / and yf they wyll not openly be taken so, then be
taken for malycyouse and craftye, and therfore byleue theym   10
not, but bydde theym lyke false harlottes hense and go gete
theym home.

But howe shall we do yet for one thynge? For thoughe that
theyre refusynge to bycome open accusers, were a coniecture to
lede vs somewhat to byleue them false or malycyouse: yet were yt   15
not so great a coniecture on that syde, nor so sure, but that we
might be therin deceyued and they bothe charytable and trew,
[A₇] and the man yᵗ they detected a very perylouse heretyque in
very dede. And then for oughte that this man deuyseth yet, we
sholde nede the suyte ex officio to bulte oute this mater better /   20
or ellys that man that they detected shall (yf he be suche as they
sayde he was) teache heresyes styll, and do myche harme a great
whyle.

Also good readers thys good man hathe no suche cause so sore
to mysse truste suche a denouncer, onely bycause that he re-   25
fuseth to be taken of his owne offre for a partye and an open
accuser, consyderynge that he refuseth not to be broughte in by
processe, and depose in yᵉ parties owne presence as a wytnesse,
and wyll be content that his deposycyons hym selfe standyng by
be publyshed, & redde openly byfore yᵉ world. And therfore any   30
wyse man wold wene, yᵗ this good man to proue that we shold
[A₇v] not nede the suyte ex officio, yf he wolde make hys suyte by
waye of accusacyon, suffycyent to serue in the stede, he had nede
to haue diuised some farther thing then this. But this good hoste
of ours, prayeth you for this feste to be mery with such as you   35
haue, for here is al your fare / sauyng that to make vs lyke this

---

4 for] *1557, catchword 1533,* For *1533*   24 Also] *no para. 1557*

meate the better, & fyl our belyes somwhat the better therwyth, he geueth vs one lytle messe of sauce to it, in shewynge vs a cause / wherfore it is good reason, that we shold geue theym no credence that detecte a man of heresy, and yet wil refuse to
5 become his open accusers. And ye cause that he geueth vs is this.

For yf he say (sayth this good man) that he dare not for fere of his lyfe auow yt, I haue shewed a meane in the seuenth chapyter of the sayd treatyse how the wytnesse may be saued from daunger, as by shewyng
10 the mater to the kynge and his counsayle / and that then it is not to suppose nor to thynke, but that they wyll prouyde suffycyently for the indempnyte of the wytnesses in that behalfe. [A₈]

Nowe good readers herde any man euer any reason made for suffycyent, by any man that any reason had in his hedde / and
15 handeled so insuffycyently. By this wyse reason he maketh as though no man detectynge any man of heresye, excepte he surmysed the mater of falshed & malyce, wolde refuse to be hys open accuser for any thynge saue for onely fere / nor for no lesse fere neyther then onely the fere of deth. And then for that fere,
20 he hath as he sayth diuysed suffycyent remedye.

Now that none other thynge can let a man to make hym selfe a partye and an open accuser, but onely fere: I wene there wyll no man graunte hym / and that no lesse fere then onely fere of deth, and adde fere of all bodyly harme thereto, that wyll I wene euery
25 wyse man lesse graunte hym. [A₈v]

But nowe let vs consyder whether the fere that hym selfe graunteth to be suffycyent, to let a detectour from takynge vppon hym to be an accuser, be so suffycyently prouyded for by thys good man, that yt muste nedes be, that by hys prouysyon
30 that fere shall be quyte gone. For yf that yt maye be, that all hys prouysyon not wythstandynge, the mannys fere maye styll remayne in his harte / then may yt also be perdy, that be hys deteccyon neuer so trew, yet he maye for that fere, refuse to make hym selfe a partye and become an open accuser.
35 Consyder nowe therfore what is the remedye that he hath dyuysed in his seuenth chapyter. He reherseth yt here agayne,

---

2 vs one] *1533 corr. err.*, vs therto one *1533*, vs thereto one *1557*   15 By] *1533 corr. err.*, *1557*, Be *1533*   21 Now] *no para. 1557*

that vppon complaynt made to the kynge and his counsayle it is
not to suppose nor thinke, but y^t they wold prouyde sufficiently
for thindemnyte of the wytnesse in that behalfe. [B$_1$]

I am content to graunte hym for the whyle, that they wyll
suffycyently prouyde for thindempnyte of the wytnessys. But
fyrst all this prouysyon is in our case here very nedeles. And his
prouysyon in the seuynth chapyter of his dyuysyon, is brought in
for a nother maner of mater / that ys to witte agaynst a prouisyon
made in the spyrytuall lawe, by whyche yt is there deuysed, that
in some case for drede of perell that may fall to the wytnesses, the
ordynary shall not suffre the partie that is detected, to knowe
who hath wytnessed agaynste hym. And nowe wolde this good
man bygyle his readers in this chapyter, & make theym wene that
that specyall prouysyon in that one specyall case, whych prouysyon I wene was yet in Englande neuer put in vre, were a comen
order in euery mannys case. But consyder good reader that our
case is now, that the man refuseth not [B$_1$v] to be a wytnesse / but
is contente both to be sworen when he is as a witnesse called in,
and to auowe then hys deposycyon trewe, byfore the iudge in the
partyes awne presence / and if he maye so be vsed as a wytnesse,
wyll neyther be afrayed nor a shamed, nor desyre to putte the
kynges counsayle to any busynesse aboute the prouysyon of his
indempnyte at all. And therfore in our case thys good mannys
prouysyon deuysed for wytnesses, shall not nede for our wytnesses, yf he lette the suyt ex officio procede, and receyue them
as onely witnesses.

But on the tother syde, yf this good man putte a way that suyt,
and wyll receyue no man fyrste for a denouncer secretely, and
after that for a wytnesse to, that wyl refuse at the begynnynge to
make hym selfe a partye and bycome an open accuser / but
though they were suche twenty wyll take theym al for false
shrewes and [B$_2$] putte theym to sylence, excepte some one of
theym wyll take vppon hym the name and persone of an accuser:
I saye that his prouysyon dothe not suffyse, not euyn in hys owne
case of fere, to make euery trew man content to accuse an heretyque / but that we muste eyther lette that heretyque alone and

---

4 I] *no para.* *1557*   9 spyrytuall] spirituall *1557*, spyrytull *1533*   20 awne] owne
1557   27 But] *no para.* *1557*

lette hym go make mo, or ellys muste we vse the suyte ex officio
styll.

That is not so sayeth this good man. For yf he bycome an
accuser I haue diuysed a remedye for hys indempnyte. That is
5 well & properly sayde. But we speke not of hys losse but of hys
fere. Why what shold he nede to fere whan he can take no losse?
hath this good man neuer herd in his lyfe that some man hathe
ben wurse aferde than hurt? a man may fere perdy though he
fere causelesse. And yf he so do styl then wil he not by[B₂v]come
10 thaccuser, & angre hym whome he fereth, though the man be
bounden, and ryghte good suertyes with hym, that he shall do
his accuser no bodyly harme at all.

His fere is also for all the prouysyon that can be made by
suffycyent suertye, not all causelesse yet. For he may well and
15 with good reason fere, that he that is bounden may by some
secrete shrewes of hys acquayntauns murdre hym / and that in
such wise as when he doth it, he may wene & haue hope that it
shal neuer be knowen for his dede, nor he therby lese forfaiture
of his bounde.

20 There can no man (ye wote wel) also kyll a nother, but with the
parel of his owne lyfe. And yet is there dayly many a man, that
standeth for al that in drede, that a nother man wil for euyll will
and malyce destroye hym. And the comen lawes of thys realme
so farre forth alowe and ap[B₃]proue his drede, for al that his
25 enimy is vpon losse of his own lyfe bounden to the contrarye,
that vpon his owne othe, they compell the party to be bounden
with other suertyes for hym in certayne sommes of money, that
he shal not. And yet the man yᵗ fered byfore, may peraduenture
be full ferd styll, that his enymye wyll as well aduenture the
30 forfayture of his frendes money, as he before fered that he
wolde aduenture his owne lyfe. But yet bycause yt maye be that
his respecte vnto frendshyppe, wyl temper his respecte of malyce, and make him loth, for hurtynge of one whome he hateth, to
hurte twayne whome he loueth: the man is content syth he can
35 go no farther, to take that maye be goten, and so to sew for such
suertye, to lyue therby, though not in ful suerty, nor clene oute

---

31 But] *para.* *1557*   32 respecte vnto] *1557*, res-[*new line*]specte vnto *1533*

of fere, yet in suerty somwhat the more, and in fere somwhat the lesse. [B₃v]

But now this man yᵗ doth detecte this heretyke, agaynst whom he fereth to make hym self an open aduersary & accuser, is not in the case byfore he become his accuser, but maye sytte styll you se well and hold his peace, and nedeth not to make that heretyque his aduersarye by his wylfull accusacyon / whyche yf he sholde ones do, he wyll neuer after happely whyle he lyueth, reken hym selfe so sure from bodyly harme that he may after hap to haue by him and by his meanes, as he wyl reken to be in yf he accuse him not / nor by such open accusacyon geue hym an open occasion of displeasure / no not for all the prouysyon that all the world can imagine for his suertie / except onely suche suertye as a pore man deuysed ones for him self, when he came to a kyng & complayned how sore he fered that suche a seruaunt of his wold kyll hym. And the king bode hym fere not felow, for I promyse yᵉ if he kyll the he shalbe hanged within [B₄] a lytle whyle after. Naye my lyege lord quod the pore soule I beseche your grace let hym be hanged for it a great whyle afore. For I shall neuer lyue in the lesse fere tyll I se hym hanged fyrste.

Now will this good man happely say, that this maner of rea-sonynge shold proue not onely yᵗ a man for fere wold refuse to be an accuser, but also to be a witnesse / & then were it agaynst my selfe to.

That is not so in euery case. For comenly no man is in such wise angry with them that are in a mater wytnesses agaynst hym, & may seme to witnesse agaynst theyr willys, for the necessyte of theyre othes wherto they may be or may seme to be compelled, as with hym whom he seeth willyngly no man calling him, come forth of his own offre to accuse him. And therfore yᵉ cases be very far vnlyke. But yet in some cases when the partye yᵗ is detected is knowen for mygh[B₄v]tye, and for so maliciouse therwith, that he wyll of lykelyhed hate & myschyefe any man by whome he taketh any harme, though the tother man do yt neuer so myche agaynst his wyll: in suche cases the fere maye be such in dede, that it maye peraduenture cause some that

---

17 yᵉ] yᵗ 1557   18–19 Sidenote 1557: A pore mans aunswere.   21 Now] no para. 1557   33 lykelyhed] lykelihode 1557

ellys wolde tell the trewth yf he sholde neuer knowe them, for
drede of his dyspleasure to be forsworen, rather then abyde
thaduenture, what so euer prouysyon any man sholde deuyse
for theyr suertye.

5   And for suche case yf it happened was ye lawe made, which in
his seuenth chapyter this man so sore complayneth of, that the
party detected shold in suche case be kepte fro the knoweledge
of ye wytnesses / & as (with the prouisyons that are in that law
made farther) very good reason is that he sholde / and therfore is
10   euen here that poynt of his seuenth chapyter of hys deuisyon,
and all that euer he can far[B₅]ther deuyse for the farther defence therof, full answered here by ye way.

But nowe sayeth this good man therto, that I denye not in
myne apologye, that remedye of his dyuyse to be conuenyent for
15   this realme / & yet I wyl not he sayth assent that a law be made
that yt shalbe so.

In this tale this good honest man sayth vntrew. The wordes in
myne apologye wheruppon he taketh hold to say, y^t I denye not
his deuyse to be conuenyent for thys realme be these.

20   *His deuyse though peraduenture yt wolde serue in some one lande,*
wolde yet not serue in some other. And they that made that lawe of the
chyrche, made yt as it myght serue most generally thorow chrystendome /
where as this deuyse though it myght serue in Englande, myght not haue
serued in many places of Almayne that are peruerted synnys / not euen
25   *whyle that mater was in a mamerynge byfore the chaunge was made. But*
surely [B₅v] *that same law and other of old made agaynste heresyes, yf*
they had ben in Almayne dewely folowed in the begynnynge, the mater had
not there gone oute at length to suche an vngracyouse endynge.

These be lo the wordes of myne apology the .xlii. chapyter
30   folio .232. wherof this man taketh holde to say, that I denye not
in myne apology, y^t his deuice is conuenient for this realme. For
in these wordes in dede I do not denye it / but than you se well I
do not graunte it neyther.

But afterwarde in the self same chapyter, the very nexte lefe
35   after agaynste the sufficiency of his deuice write I these wordes
folowing.

And on the tother syde, the remedy that he deuyseth for the suertye of the

---

13 But] *no para. 1557*   30 folio .232.] folio. 232, *1533*, fo.232. *1557*

wytnesses, sholde not peraduenture make the men so bolde, as in a cause of
heresie to medle in ye mater against some maner of man / but that they
rather wold for theyr owne surety, kepe theyr own tongys styll, than wyth
all [B₆] *the suretie that could be founden them bysyde, haue theyr persons*
dysclosed vnto the partye.

Lo good reders the thynge that he sayth I deny not, bycause
that in the fyrst wordes I neyther sayed ye nor nay (for I sayd not
y^t it myght serue in england / but that though it myghte serue in
Englande, yet myght it not serue in Almayne / which wordes I
myght haue sayd, though I had in ye nexte line before, expressely sayd y^t it myght not serue in England) y^t thyng do I (as
you se) forthwith in ye nexte lefe well & playnely denye. And yet
you se y^t he sayth here agayne in thys boke, that I denye it not.
This good man semeth not very shamefast lo, but yf his logyke
lede hym to thynke that this were a good argument. In these
wordes he denyeth it not: ergo he denyeth it not. Which argument is euen as good as this. He denyeth it not in one place, ergo
he denyeth it not in no place. [B₆v]

Now where he sayth that though I denye not his deuyce to be
conuenyent, yet I wyll not assent that a law be made that it shall
be so: surely as mych of his deuice as I thynke conuenyent for the
realme, so myche therof wyll I not be agaynste that a lawe be
made that it shalbe so. For where this good man thynketh it
conuenyent for this realme, that he which is detected or accused
of heresye, sholde be bounden & fynde suretyes, that he shall not
hurt neyther accuser nor wytnesse: I wyll not be agaynst it that a
law be made that it shalbe so. But yet though that law were made
(syth for all that lawe there wold remayne a feare behynde in y^e
mennes hartes, for whose saufe garde suche surtyes sholde be
founden, and perell and dayngeour to, suffycyent to make them
drawe backe from makynge them self in heresye open accusours, and in some case from berynge wyt[B₇]nesse also, but yf
they thought theyr names sholde from the person agaynst whom
they shold wytnesse, be surely kepte close and vnknowen) I
wolde not assent for my parte to put awaye the sayd law that he
speketh of in his seuenth chapyter of his deuisyon, for chaunces
that myght herafter happen. And mych lesse wolde I graunte to

---

16 Which] *1557*, which *1533*   19 Now] *no para. 1557*   27 so.] *1557*, so *1533*

putte awaye the suyte agaynst heretikes ex officio, into his deuice
of onely open accusers, for the harme y^t wold vndowtedly dayely
growe, by the encreace of heretykes & hynderaunce of the catholyke fayth / no more than though I blame not the law, by whiche
5   he that is aferde of kyllyng shall haue his aduersary bounden to
y^e peace, I wolde yet when the tother is so bounden by recogni-
saunce, haue that lawe stande in stede of the tother, by whyche
he shall yf he kyll that man, fall therby ferther into the daynger
of hangynge. [B$_7$v]
10   And yet this his gaye gloryouse deuice, that he deuysed in his
formar boke, and here now repeteth agayne: no man nedeth to
geue him any great thank for. For who knew not that allway, that
who so euer be aferde, may desyre & haue surety for the peace,
yf he fere him self of his lyfe or bodyly harme, & may aske it of
15   course vpon his othe as soone as he is aferd (and soner perdye
this man deuiseth it not) of ye kynges ordinary iustices, without
any other ferther suit, to trouble the kynges grace or his counsayle withall.
     But yet wyll all this surety fyndyng as you se, neuer so take
20   away ye feare of harme from mennes hartes, but y^t they wyll
rather forbere to be accusours, than by the becoming of an open
accusour runne in y^e dedely malyce of that man, by whom for all
his bond & all his suretyes founden, they fere still alway y^t they
shal take hurt.
25   But here wyll happely this good [B$_8$] man tell me nowe, that I
am a man importune, & one whom no reason can satisfye / & byd
me therfore go deuyse some ferther thyng myne owne selfe for
helpe of the mater, and assay also what ferther thynge any other
folke can fynd therin. And if neyther myne own wyt nor no
30   mannes els can fynd no ferther remedy, wherfore shold I than
blame hym whan he deuiseth as full a remedy as any mannes
reason can find. Forsoth I can with any wyt that I haue, nor I
wene no more can no man els / fynd no ferther remedy than he
fyndeth here hym selfe. But yet syth the ferthest that he can fynd
35   is very far vnsufficient, with chaunge of the suit ex officio to kepe
heresyes from great encreace, and preserue ye catholyke fayth: I
can therfore fynd at hand a mych nerer remedy than this that he

---

10 And] *no para.* *1557*   32 wyt] witie *1557*

fetcheth so farre, that is to wyt to let his new deuices passe and let
the old law stand styll. [B₈v]

And thus you se good readers yᵗ this pyece wherein he so
bosteth the prouisyon that he hath deuysed so suffycyent to
delyuer the accusers fro fere, leueth theym so in drede & fere
styll, that though there were no lette but the fere of bodely
harme: yet of many trew men that wyl detecte and bere wytnesse,
ye shold fynde but very few that wolde bycome accusers.

But now though there were founden prouysyon good and
sure, to dryue out of thaccusers harte all fere of bodyly hurt: yet
are there many that dare secretely detecte, and by whome yᵉ
ordynarye shall knowe who can tell more, and wyll also yf they be
called and sworen, and wyll not vncalled and vnsworen, tell no
tale at all / and they them selfe also wyl neyther accuse nor yet
bere wytnesse neyther, nor so myche as haue it knowen that euer
thei spake word therin. And that not for any fere of theyre lyfe,
for [C₁] whiche this good man fyndeth as he sayth a remedy / but
for losse of theyr lyuynge, for whiche he fyndeth none, nor
neuer ones thought theron. And yet is the lyuynge to some folke,
as lyefe almost as the lyfe. And theyr lyuynge they feare vtterly to
lose (yᵗ they gete peraduenture by them whom yet of cheryte for
theyr amendement they detecte) yf they were ones perceyued
any thing to medle in yᵉ mater.

And yet as I sayde before euery wyse man well woteth there
are many other affeccyons bysyde all suche feare, that lette men
to become accusers in heresye, and yet letteth them not to do
otherwyse truely and charytably theyr dewtye, both in secrete
detectyng of them, and also in open berynge wytnesse agaynst
them, whan they be called forth and commaunded by yᵉ court to
depose, that wyll neuer as I sayed of theyr owne offre make
theym selfe a party, and openly be[C₁v]come theyr accuser.

Now what if there were but two wytnesse of the mater, suche as
were well able playnely to proue yᵉ thyng, yf neyther of both
maye be herd but yf the tone shold become thaccusour: whan the
tone were made party, than were the profe lost. But we shal not
nede myche I warraunt you to care for this case. For of them
both, you shal haue neyther nother that wyll.

---

11 secretely] *1557*, secrely *1533*   27 charytably] caritably *1557*

How be it yet hath this good man at last founden a good way for that. For lo syr thus he sayth.

And than yf the wytnesse wyll not auow it, but an other wyll geue credence to hym and auow it: than it semeth reasonable that they that
5 wyll geue credence therto and wyll reporte it, be taken as accusers / takynge those wytnesses for theyr warraunt yf they be denyed.

If he thynke it lykely that none of them wyll become accusours that were present and herde it them selfe: than is it yet lesse lykely that he wyll become the accusour, that hereth it but at a
10 seconde hand. [C₂] And therfore me thynketh that this deuise is not mych wyser, than the deuice that a good felow deuised ones for his neyghbour, that had a greate hylloke in his close / whiche for planynge of yᵉ ground he counsayled hym to haue it away. Mary quod his neyghbour I muste carye it than so farre, that
15 it were lesse losse to me to geue away yᵉ close & all. Mary neyghbour quod the tother, I shall soone fynde a way for that. For I shal deuise a prouision yᵗ it shalbe had away & yet neuer caryed hense. For euen there as it lyeth lo, dygge me a great pytte, & cary it neuer ferther, but berye it euen in that. Where
20 shall I than lay that hepe quod his neyghbour that cometh out of the pytte? At that the tother stodyed a lytle. But whan he hadde well bythought hym: mary quod he euen digge another greate pytte vnder that, and bery me that hepe there. [C₂v]

So this man wyll in any wyse lo, haue awaye this hyllocke, this
25 suyte ex officio, that he sayeth dothe here myche hurte. Howe shall we haue yt away say we without yet mych more hurte? Good remedy sayth this good man shortely shall I deuyse. Putte accusers in the stede of that suyt, and they shall do myche better. Who shall be thaccusers say we? Mary sayth he they that here
30 them. They wyll not say we bycome accusers in no maner case. No wyl they sayeth he, then be they but false shrewes. What remedy then say we to supply the sayde suyt. A redy waye sayeth he, take some other that heareth the tother that herd the heretike speke.

He will myche lesse bycome accuser saye we, then they that
herd yt theym selfe. What hath this good man farther to saye
then, bydde vs take then another that wyll. And euer we folowe
styll & say we shall neuer fynde hym / and that word he denyeth
not, [C₃] but alwaye byddeth vs go gete one. And now yf the
second man were content, or the fyftenth after: yet hath this
man marred all thys mater with one thynge. For you wote well
that yf yᵉ wytnesse that sayth he was present and herd it his owne
eares wyll refuse to bycome thaccusar hym self: this good man
wyll that yᵉ ordynary shall take hym for malycyouse or false.
Now than yf we gete with longe labour some other man to accuse: yet hym that herde it and wold not be thaccuser hym selfe,
syth the bysshoppe must take hym alwaye for malycyouse or
false in the mater, he maye neuer accept hym therin for a wytnesse. For yf we take hym for fraudulent & maliciouse to the
partye / this mannes credence is tenne tymes lesse in all reason,
than his is that afterwarde deposeth to his harme, where he was
fyrst forsworen, whyle he wold fayne haue done hym good /
[C₃v] and that man wolde not this good man byleue after in no
wyse.

And thus bothe for the tone cause and the tother, for lacke of
an accusour and credence of the wytnes, you se playnely good
readers that by this mannes deuice, yf we dygge vp and bery this
hylloke ex officio, we shall whan we haue all done, say he what he
lyste, make & leue that neuer wyll than be voyded, as great an
hylloke of heretykes in the stede.

And this you se good readers that this good man sheweth vs
yet no let but that for any thynge that he sayth here, yf the suit ex
officio were chaunged as he wolde haue it, and in stede therof
truste all vnto accusours, of whyche for any thynge that he deuiseth we were lykely to fynde few, & as I feare me veryly rather
none at all: it were well lykely to come to passe as I sayd, that yᵉ
stretes sholde swarme full of heretykes, ere euer [C₄] they were
conuented and repressed by his way. Of which sayenge of myne
as mych meruaile as he saith he hath: yet sheweth he nothynge
(as you se) wherfore he shold meruaile of it / nor to the thynges

---

2 What] *1557*, what *1533*   24 done,] done *1533 1557*   27 this you] thus you *1557*
(*see note*)   28 ex] *1557*, ef *1533*

that I preue it wyth / he no more answereth, than though he neuer herd them.

Whyche dealynge of his you may clerely perceyue, euyn by the very same lefe, wherin I wrote those wordes of which he mer-
5 uayleth so mych and hath so lytell cause. For there lo my wordes be these.

For surely yf the conuentynge of heretykes ex officio were lefte & chaung-ed into another order, by whyche no man sholde be called, be he neuer so sore suspected, nor by neuer so many men detected, but yf some man make
10 *hym selfe party agaynste hym as hys accusour: the stretes were lykely to swarme full of heretykes, byfore that ryght few were accused, or perad-uenture any one eyther.* [C₄v]

These were lo my wordes in myne apology against which you haue herd what he sayth. Than bycause he shold not nede to
15 meruayle at the mater, I shew by & by what maketh me so to say. For there it foloweth thus.

For what so euer the cause be, it is not vnknowen I am sure, that many wyll gyue to a iudge secrete informacyon, of such thinges as though they be trew, yet gladly he wyll not or peraduenture dare not, be openly knowen
20 *that the mater came out by hym.*

Consyder here good readers that as to bycome open accusars, I speke here of two lettes. One yᵗ men wyll not, another that some men dare not. And yet that they dare not / I put as the more rare & more seldome. Now cometh thys good answerer, and for the
25 more seldome, yᵗ is to wyt where they dare not, he deuiseth a remedy, whych seldome yet or neuer, suffycyently shall serue the mater. And the tother cause that I call moost [C₅] commune as in very dede it is: that cause he neyther denyeth nor any one word speketh of it, but softely slynketh besyde it, as though he
30 hadde neuer redde yt. What maner of answerynge good readers call you this?

More ouer lest he myght deny me that I sayde trewe therin: I layed there for the profe the playne comen experyence, whiche this good man hymselfe I am very sure (but yf he be a recluse and
35 haue ben all his lyfe) knoweth well to be true / and in dede he sayth not nay.

Then go I there farther yet, and I declare what profyte there

---

cometh to the commen weale, to geue suche folke herynge / such
folke I saye as this good man wolde haue reiected backe, and
taken for false or malycyouse, bycause they come secretly and
wyll not theym selfe openly bycome accusers. Therin lo these are
my wordes. [C₅v]   5

And yet shal he sometyme geue the namys of dyuerse other / whyche
beynge called by the iudge, and examyned as wytnesses agaynst theyr
wyllys, both knowe and wyll also depose the trouthe, and he that fyrste
gaue enformacyon also / and yet wil neuer one of theym wyllyngly make
hym selfe an open accuser of the party, nor dare peraduenture for his   10
earys.

This thynge good readers euery man euery where fyndeth
trewe that any order of iustyce hath in his hande. And in these
wordes you se well I tolde hym there ones agayn, not onely that
some dare not, but that though men dare they wyll not (excepte   15
the thynge do pryuately touche theym selfe) for the causes of the
commen weale become open accusers. And as I agayne there
tolde yt hym: so he here agayne forgeteth yt.

Then go I yet forthe a lytle farther, and these are there my
wordes.   20

And this fynde we not onely in heresye, but in many temporall maters
[C₆] *amonge our selfe / wherof I haue had experyence many a tyme and*
oft, both in the dysclosynge of felonyes, and somtyme of myche other
oppressyon vsed by some one man or twayn in a shyre, wherby all theyr
neyghbours sore smarted / and yet not one durste openly complayne.   25

Lo thus I there declared good reders by commen experyence,
that if men shold do as this man here deuyseth, reiecte euery
man for malycyouse & crafty yᵗ wil geue secrete informacion, but
yf he be content to bycome an accuser openly: there sholde
myche harme growe therof / not in heresyes onely, but besyde yᵗ   30
in myche other myschief to. To al this gere you se good readers
that this good man playeth as though he came in in a mummery,
for any one word he sayth / whyche shold not so haue scaped
hym ye may be very sure, but that he sawe full surely that he
coulde neuer answere them. For though he wold haue denyed   35
all [C₆v] that I speke of myne owne experyence, yet in the lyke

thynges so many men of worshyp dayly do proue the thynge
trew that I tell yt for, that he could nothyng wynne in his cause
by al that denyenge. And yet dyd I not myne own selfe my
besynesse in such wyse, but that I can yf nede requyre proue it
5 playne inough. But of thys gere as I sayd he denyeth nothynge,
nor answereth nothyng neyther thervnto. And sure maye you be
y^t if he had coulde, he wold not haue fayled to haue done the
tone.

And therfore good readers my wordes stand styll so sure, that
10 thys good man hath not yet nor neuer shal whyle he lyueth, be
able to voyde them with all the crafte he can, but that yf men
wolde be so farre ouersene as in thys mater to folow hys deuice,
to put awaye thys olde lawe the suit ex officio, and truste that all
wolde be well holpen by meane of [C7] open accusers: it wolde at
15 lengthe come to passe the thyng that I haue sayd, that ye stretes
were well lykely to swarm full of heretikes, ere euer that ryght
few shold be therof accused, or peraduenture any one heretyke
eyther.

And now good chrysten readers syth you se so clerely, that by
20 suche chaungynge of that law, ye catholyke fayth shold decaye: I
care not now greatly what he saye for his second parte, syth he
hath so fowle an ouerthrowe in the fyrste, vppon whiche fyrste
parte all the mater hangeth. For though he coulde in his seconde
parte make you now good profe, not onely that there myght, but
25 also that there dyd & hath done, greate harme grow by that
suyte, whiche he shall neuer proue you whyle he liueth / but at
sundry tymes & that of late where it hath ben so surmysed, it
hath alway be proued the contrary: yet syth you [C7v] se well that
by this chaunge that he deuyseth, while we wold helpe these
30 harmes that he speketh of, that is to wytte that no man sholde be
conuented of heresye causelesse, we shold by the prouydyng for
that harme, be the cause of farre more hurt and harme in the
stede / that is to wyt, that when that suyte were so chaunged, the
catholyque fayth sholde dekaye, and heretyques so sholde en-
35 crease, that by such insurreccions as they haue here byfore
made, not in other countreys onely, but in this realme of Eng-

---

19 And] *no para. 1557*   31 conuented] couented *1557;* causelesse, we] causelesse. we
1533, causeles. We *1557*

The burning of Oldcastle, from John Foxe, *Actes and Monuments* (1563), sig. Dd₁ (reduced).

land haue also attempted y^e same, put yt vppon the parell & assey to robbe spoyle and kyll also myche innocent people openly, and tourne folke from the fayth by force, and worke other maner of maystryes many mo, suche as myne harte abhorreth so myche as to reherse or name. Syth euery man may se I say, that suche harme were in parel to fal by this chaunge of his: [C₈] there wyll I wene no wyse man folow his fonde deuyse in puttyng this law away, all though he proued wel in his seconde parte, that there were harme in the kepynge / whyle he can not defende the contrarye, but y^t there were incomparably mych more harme in the leuynge.

But by what waye he proueth y^t there is great hurt in the kepyng, that shall we now consyder. After whyche well examyned / I shall agayne retourne good readers efte soon vnto the fyrst, that this suyt ex officio taken onys away, the stretes were lykely to swarme full of heretykes. And as clere as you se that pointe alredy, and that this man hath therin neyther answered nor ones touched suche thynges as your selfe se that I sayd therin before: yet shall I make yt you anon, with the farther foly of his deuyse double (ere we departe) so clere.

Concernynge the seconde parte, thus lo thys man begynneth.
[C₈v]

But to putte the partye that is complayned on, to answere, and to condempne hym, yf he saye contrarye to that the wytnesse haue sayde, not knowynge who be the wytnesse, ne who be hys accusers: yt semeth not reasonable to be accepted for a law. For as I haue sayde in the sayd treatyse, yf he that is accused knewe theyr names that accused him, he myght percase allege and proue so great and so vehement cause of rancour and malyce in them that accuse hym, or beare wytnesse agaynst hym, that theyr sayenges by no law ought to stande agaynst hym: as yf there were two men that had sworn the deth of an other: and bycause they can not brynge yt about, they ymagyne howe they maye brynge hym to all the shame and vexacyon that they can, and therupon they apeche hym of heresye: yf he in thys case knewe theyr names, he myght proue theyr rancour and malyce. And bycause he knoweth them not, he can not proue yt. And also the wytnes may be such, as shal

---

4–5 abhorreth] *1557*, abhorret *1533*   12 But] *no para. 1557*   17 pointe] point *1557*, ponte *1533*   21 Concernynge] *no para. 1557*

haue his landes by eschete after hys deth. And yf it be sayde, that these
cases fall so seldome, that yt ought lytell to be pondred: so may yt be
said lyke wyse, that it falleth but seldome, that the wytnesses in heresye
stand in any feare of them, that they accuse. And then to make a
5 generall lawe to prohybyte all men, that they shulde not haue knoweledge of the wytnes in no case, yt is not reasonable.

Now good readers one thynge opened vnto you whiche is
trouth, which thys man of wylynesse hydeth from you, and wold
make you wene the trouth were contrary: deuyde after that
10 knowen all this myschyefe & [D₁] vnreasonabylnes that he telleth
vs here into .xx. partes / & with the bare knowledge of yᵗ one
trouth, nynetene and a halfe of all hys false fayned myschyefes
are gone.

The trouth is good chrysten readers, that except onely one
15 case, wherof he speketh in his seuenth chapiter of his deuysyon,
where to let the partie know the wytnesses were parell, to whyche
I haue answered hym bothe in myne apologye fyrste, and synnys
euen in this same chapyter byfore: elles in all other cases, the
wytnesses, whose deposicions shalbe taken & layed agaynste hym
20 to proue hym an heretyque, and vppon whyche deposycyon
sentence of condemnynge hym for an heretyke shall be gyuen
agaynste hym, he shall se theym and shall here theyre deposycyons to. So that yf there be any suche great causes, as this good
man here ymagyneth that myght happen, of enimyte, [D₁v] or
25 hope of lucre, or any mych lesse either, the iudge both may and
wyll consyder them before the sentence.

But why shall he not know them forthwith, when he is fyrste
conuented? For yt were not well done he shold, no more then the
kynges counsayle that many tymes call malefactours byfore them
30 vppon secrete informacyon fyrste, vse alway there by & by to
dysclose who told them the mater and what / whych if they shold
and by and by brynge hym forth, then though the suspecte wold
confesse happely some thynge therby the sooner: yet sholde it be
but that thynge which he thought the tother knew. Whereas
35 whyle yᵉ thyefe knoweth not who hath gyuen the informacyon,

---

11 into] in *1557*   12 myschyefes] mischiefes *1557*, mychyefes *1533*   27 forthwith]
1557, forth with *1533*   34 Whereas] where[*new line*]as *1533*, Where as *1557*   35
thyefe] chiefe *1557*

and yet thynketh by his examynacyon that among his many felowes though they be theuys all, yet some false shrewes there be,
he mysse gesseth among and weneth yt were one where in dede
yt [D$_2$] was a nother / & so in stede of one felonye, to lyght there
cometh twayne.   5

But at a nother time & in an other place, byfore he shall haue
any iudgement theruppon, he shall commenly se them sworen
and here them speke to.

And here I say commenly, bycause that sometyme percase in
poynt of iugement he shall not haue them brought forth and   10
sworen in his presence, nor peraduenture neuer heare them
speke in the mater. For they may happen to be some, y^t deposed
and died to before hym selfe were taken / and some happely that
were his felowes confessed his felonyes at the galowes, when they
were on the lather. And some peraduenture bycame approuers   15
when they were caste, and called for a coroner / and the lawe
kepynge no store of him but hangyng hym vp forthwith, vseth
yet his informacyon & all these other to, whych may happen to
come so many to gether & so likely to be trew, [D$_2$v] that his lyfe
may go therfore, and be well worthy to, and yet neyther hym   20
selfe nor thenqueste neuer here any one witnesse sworen, neither the fyrst nor the second, neyther at thendyghtynge nor at
hys arreyghnynge neyther.

Nowe maye yt so fortune in lyke wyse and sometyme so doth it
to, that folke some good and honeste depose in cause of heresye   25
agaynst some one man that is detected therof. And happely
there depose also some other of hys owne affynyte / and in
deposynge agaynst that one man detecte by theyr deposycyons, a
nother man of ye selfe same companye y^t is then walked farre of,
no man can tel where, y^t appereth playnly vpon al theyr othes   30
peraduenture the very chyefe heretyke of all. If he happe longe
after when these wytnesses be dede, to come agayne in to y^e
countrey and teache heresyes a freshe, and one or twayne detecte [D$_3$] hym / they shall now be sworen and shall be brought
forthe face to face byfore hym, that he shall obiecte agaynste   35
theym what he can byfore his iudgement passe. But yet those

---

15 lather] lader *1557*   16 when] *1557*, vhen *1533*

olde deposycyons shall not serue for nought, but are adminicula
probationis, though the men be dede. And agaynst all reason
were it that it were otherwyse. Howe be yt what they sayde he
shall here / and also who they were.

5   Lo this is good chrysten readers the maner of that suyte,
wherof this good man wold here make vs wene the contrarye,
and that men were commenly condempned of heresye by deposycyons of those men whome he sholde neuer knowe. And
therfore syth the trouth is in dede, that all the wrong whych he
10   speketh of, he groundeth vpon a playn vntrouth, though he
make not thys lye wyttyngly him self, but hering some folke say
so, we[D₃v]neth that yt were trewe: yet is as I sayde before all his
reason spylt / and as l tolde you the harme yᵗ he layeth in that
poynt if he shold dyuyde it into twenty partes, xix. partes and an
15   halfe were nowe clerely gone. For there remayned but yᵗ one
case which he wolde haue here seme comen, and yet in his
seuenth chapytre of his fyrst boke he declareth hym selfe that
the case is but specyall, that is to wytte, where the witnesses are
kepte away for fere / elles in all the remanaunt this mannys
20   harmes that he layeth here agaynste the law be very clerely gone.

And therfore his two gay cases of swerynge a mannys deth, &
wynnynge a mannys land by eschete, haue place but in the specyall point of that one specyall lawe. And yet are his two cases
suche as well consydered, are of no great effect. For yf we [D₄]
25   shold regard those two cases: yᵉ publyshynge of the wytnesses
names wold seldome remedy the mater. For yt myght then as
well hap, that such folke myghte hyre other that sholde beare
suche false wytnesse as do the thynge theym selfe, and of
lykelyhed so wolde they rather do.

30   But seynge that his cases for the farre fetchynge and lykelyhed
of so seldome fortunynge, were lykely to be taken for fonde: yet
for the fauour of his owne deuysynge he was lothe to scrape
theym out, but excuseth the dyuysynge of them thus.

And yf yt be sayde that these cases fall so seldome that yt ought lytle to
35   be pondered: so may it be sayd lyke wyse that yt falleth but seldome that
the wytnesses in heresye stand in any fere of theym that they accuse.

---

1 adminicula] *1533 corr. err.*, *1557*, admonicula *1533*   18 witnesses] wytnesse
1557   30 lykelyhed] likelyhode *1557*

Nowe yf thys answere of hys were good & trew, y^t it happeth as seldome that the wytnesses stand in any such feare: then he soyleth his owne [D$_4$v] reason hym selfe. For than hathe he no cause to complayne for the law to kepe the wytnesse close, is made but for to serue in that specyal seldome case, where it happeth such feare to fall.

And therfore is hys laste cause veryly not very shamefaste, where he maketh as though the lawe were made generall, to prohybyte all men that they sholde not haue knowledge of the wytnesses in no case.

And as for in this poynte of hys, wheruppon all his whole mater hangeth, to shew you that he sayth playn vntrew, and groundeth all this gere of alwaye kepynge wytnesses close, vppon a playne open lye: I wyll for thys tyme take none other wytnesses agaynste hym but hys owne playne open wordes. For in his seuenth chapyter of hys dyuysyon, lo thus good readers he sayth.

And in the chapyter there, that begynneth Statuta quedam, it is decreed / that yf the byshoppe or other enquerours of heresye, se that any greate daunger [D$_5$] myghte come to the accusours or wytnes of heresye by the great power of theym that be accused: that then they maye commaunde, that the names of the accusours or wytnesse shall not be shewed but to the bysshoppe or enquerours / or suche other lerned men as be called to them, and that shall suffyce / though they be not shewed to the party. And for the more indempnyte of the sayde accusours and wytnes it is there decreed / that the byshoppe or enquerours may enioyne such as they haue shewed the names of such wytnes vnto / to kepe them close vppon payne of excommunycacion, for dysclosynge that secrete without theyr lycens. And surely this is a sore law / that a man shalbe condempned / and not know the names of them that be causers therof.

Now good chrysten readers here you se playnely by his own wordes, that the cause of that law is specyall, & serueth but where as there is feare that the wytnesses myghte stande in dayngeour, by reason that the person detected were a man of great myght and power, which happeth very seld and almost neuer tyll it be well nygh paste remedy. And therfore now you se by these

---

4 is] *1533 corr. err.*, om. *1533 1557*

wordes of hys owne, that those other wordes of his are to sham-
full, where he now sayth here, that ye law is generall, & forbedeth all men [D₅v] that they sholde not haue knowledge of
the wytnesse in no case. Vpon my fayth except this good man se
5 better how to salue this sore than I se: I wolde not haue wryten
such another poynt in my boke, for more than all the paper
coste and the prentynge to.

But nowe as I saye, syth you se that al these greues of his be
gone saue in this one onely case of so great probable feare, whyle
10 he groundeth all the remanaunt vppon a greate open vntrewth:
it is you se well a very seldome gryefe that is lefte. For I neuer
sawe, nor to my remembraunce redde, nor trust in god neuer
shall se the nede, that euer any great man whom folke neded to
fere, was condempned in thys realme for heresye, saue onely syr
15 Hugh olde castle ones in the tyme of kyng Henry the .v. that was
than lorde Cobbam / nor yet he neyther, tyll that thorowe his
heresye he fell to treason to, and [D₆] wolde haue ben the captayne of heretykes in a sodayne traytorouse insurreccyon.

And therfore as for thys harme that this good man telleth vs
20 here, that ryseth by the suite ex officio in heresye, this poynte is
as you se both reasonable yf it happed, and in lawe suffycyently
prouyded fore / and yet besyde y^t so selde happeth here in this
realm, y^t it was foly for hym to speke therof / and yet no more
toucheth in dede the suite ex officio, thanne yf the suit were
25 bygon and pursued by some great man, that wolde & fered not to
professe hym selfe for accuser. And thus is this case vtterly nothing to purpose / & all the remanaunt is (as you se also by his owne
wordes proued) grounded vpon great vntrouth. And therfore
all this y^t he hath sayd set asyde for nought: let vs now se what
30 other harme the good man fyndeth ferther. Lo good readers
therin thus he sayth. [D₆v]

Also syr Tho. More denieth not, but that by reason of the law, ex. de
hereticis ca. Ad abolendam, which is recyted in the .vii. chapyter of the
sayde treatyse y^t a man may be dreuen to a purgacyon wythout any
35 offence in hym, or be accursyd, as yf he be notably suspected, and yet
not gylty, as it may well be: and yet he wyll not condescende, that that

---

4 Vpon] 1557, vpon 1533   16 Sidenote 1557: Lord Cobham   32 ex.] 1557, ex 1533

lawe shulde be chaunged, but sayth in fortyfyenge therof, that veryly
he thynketh, that he whiche can not be proued gylty in heresy, and yet
vseth such maner of wayes, that all hys honest neyghbours wene he
were one / & therfore in theyr conscyence dare not swere that he is any
other / is well worthy to do some penaunce. Truely thys is a meruelous   5
persuasion, that a man shulde be put to hys purgacyon / bycause hys
neyghbours dare not swere that he is no heretyke.

Now good readers bycause thys good man begynneth here to
fortifye hys worde, wyth that that I dyd not in my sayd .xl. chapyter of myne apologye denye, that a man may be dreuen to a   10
purgacyon wythout any offence in hym or be accursed, as yf he
be notably suspected & yet not gylty: I wyll fyrst brynge you forth
myne own wordes wryten in the sayd chapyter / and afterwarde
than shall we se whyther he can take suche greate holde vppon
my wordes, as he wold [D7] it sholde seme. Lo good readers these   15
are my wordes. folio .220.

It may be somtyme (albe it very seld it happeth) that in heresie vpon other
vehement suspycyons wythout wytnesses, a man may be put to hys purga-
cyon, and to penaunce also yf he fayle therof / whyche thynge why so many
sholde now thynke so harde a lawe as thys pacyfyer sayth there do I can not   20
se / nor those wyse men neyther that made the law. And yet were they many
wyse men / and not onely as wyse, but peraduenture many mo also in
nomber, than those that thys pacyfyer calleth many now, that as he sayth
now do fynde the faute. For though it be alledged in the extra. de hereticis:
yet was that law made in a generall counsayle. And veryly me thynketh   25
that he whyche can not be proued gylty in heresye, and yet vseth suche
maner of wayes, that all hys honest neighbours wene he were one in dede,
and therfore dare not swere that in theyr conscyence they thynke [D7v]
hym any other: is well worthy to do some penaunce for that maner of
byhauour, wherby he geueth al other men occasion to take hym for so   30
noughty.

Now good readers where thys man taketh me that I say a man
may be dreuen to his purgacyon wythout offence: you se well I
say not so / but I say that he doth a great offence, & well wurthy
were to be dreuen to his purgacyon & to do penaunce to, if he be   35
not able to purge hym selfe / but haue vsed hym selfe so lyke an

---

30 byhauour] behauiour *1557*

heretyke in all good folkes opinion, y^t he can fynd no good folke
y^t dare in theyr conscience swere that they thynke other wyse.
This saye I is a great offence and worthy to dryue hym to this
poynte. And this good man sayth that I denye not, but that he
5 maye by the law be dreuyn to it without offence.

And where as he sayth I denye not that he may be dreuen
therto without wytnesse: wherfore not I praye [D$_8$] you? For the
suspycyons beyng proued by wytnesses, to be notable and vehement, wyll they not be cause sufficyent to dryue hym to pourge
10 hym selfe of that infamy, or els to do penaunce for bryngyng
hym selfe therinto, but yf there be wytnessys of hys expresse
heretycall wordes? No sayth this good man, & meruayleth y^t I
could thynk this any reason. But why he shold so meruayle at y^e
mater, or why I shold be ashamed to thinke so, therof telleth vs
15 this good man no tale at all, but onely sayth,

Truely thys is a meruelous persuasion, that a man sholde be put to his
purgacyon bycause hys neyghbours dare not swere that he is none
heretyke.

Meruelouse god where was this mannys mynde whan he wrote
20 these wordes? do I say y^t he shall be put to his purgacion, bicause
his neighbours wyl not swere with him? nay I say y^t whan there
be by wytnesses sworen byfore his face, suspicions of heresie
proued vpon hym: than may thordinary [D$_8$v] put hym to such
purgacyon, to proue whyther they wyll swere wyth hym or no.
25 For whan they wyll not but refuse it / what mad man wold say
that he shalbe put to that purgacyon than, whan he hath fayled
therof, and yt all redy paste. This man speketh here as one that
perceyued no pyece of the mater.

For where as I declare that he is in great offence y^t so vseth
30 hym self, y^t none of his honest neighbours dare swere / that in
theyr conscyences he is any other than an heretyke: this man
taketh it as though they that sholde swere wyth hym in his purgacyon, sholde precysely swere that he were none heretyke / where
as theyr othe shall not be what he is in dede, but what them selfe
35 thynke of hys othe / they shall not swere that he is none heretyke,
but that they byleue that he hath sworen trew, in denyeng tharti-

12 No] *para.* 1557

cles layd vnto hys charge. Lyke as [E₁] in the wageour of a lawe, they shall not swere that the defendaunt oweth not the money, but that they byleue that he swereth treuth.

I meruayle in good fayth yᵗ thys good man handeleth thys mater in this maner, & without any tellynge why, meruayleth so mych yᵗ I wold thynke that law reasonable. But surely though he coulde make me a proper reason for his part, and my selfe another for the same syde also: yet wolde I thynke my selfe ryght vnreasonable, yf I shold vpon his reason & myn, aduise & counsayle this realme in a mater concernynge the conseruacyon of the fayth, to alter and chaunge that law that was made by so great aduyse, by an whole generall counsayle of all chrystendome / wherin there were (I dowte it not) men that had as good zele to kepe innocentes out of trouble, as any of vs twayne / and mych more reason also [E₁v] than we both haue to. But that point that I shewed hym in my apologye, that the same prouisyon that is made in yᵉ law ad abolendam, was also made in a generall counsayle: yᵗ tale he letteth go by, as though he herde it not.

But than he cometh forth wyth a worde or two of a ferther fawte in the law, which eyther the man vnderstandeth not what it meneth, or ellys is it herd for any man to thynke yᵗ he meneth wel. These are his wordes lo.

And veryly the law is that theyr othe in that case shulde not be accepted: for the sayde chapyter Ad abolendam, is that yf a man be notably suspected of heresye, that he shall purge hym selfe after the wyl of thordynarye or be accursed: and so the purgacyon of hys neyghbour wyll not serue: Lette euery man therfore consyder, whether the sayd law be indyfferent or not. And yf it be not, lette them put to theyr hande to haue it broken. And I thynke veryly, they shall deserue great thanke of god, yf they tourne it to a more indyfferent waye, then it is at nowe. For vnder thys maner the moost innocent man that is, may of malyce be reported to be suspected of heresye and be not so in dede, and so be dreuen to hys purgacyon or be accursed: and then there is another law, that yf he in that case of an indurate mynde stande so accursed a yere, he shalbe punished as an heretike and that is by the law, Extra. de hereticis, ca. Excommunicamus. [E₂]

---

15 than] that *catchword 1533*   21 herd] harde *1557*   22 lo.] *1557*, lo *1533*   36
Extra.] *1557*, Extra *1533*

This prouysyon good readers y^t he speketh, whyche is in the lawe ad abolendam, recited in the .v. boke of the decretalis in the tytle de hereticis y^t such as were suspecte shold purge them selfe at the arbitrement & discrecion of thordynary, was as I before

5　haue sayed, afterward loked vppon & alowed in the generall counsayle called consilium latranense, as euery man may soone perceyue that wyll well consyder the paragraffe excommunicamus afterward in the same tytle. For where as y^t law there saith, Qui inuenti fuerint sola suspitione notabiles, nisi statim

10　innocentiam suam congrua purgatione monstrauerint: these wordes congrua purgatione be referred vnto the tother law ad abolendam therof made byfore, as bothe appereth by such doctours as wryte vpon y^e lawes / & also to hym y^t wyl consider it wel it wel appereth by y^e self text. For in y^e paragraf Excom. be

15　rehersed [E$_2$v] part of the very wordes of the lawe ad abolendam, wherby we may se y^t the counsayle there loked vpon that lawe. And so was I saye that prouisyon which this man calleth so vnreasonable, not onely made by pope Lucius the .iii. but after also made agayne by ratificacyon by pope Innocent y^e .iii. in an

20　hole generall counsaile. And rede the stories who so wyll, and he shall fynde bothe by Platina and Cronica cronicarum to, that both this pope Lucius and thys pope Innocent were very vertuouse men. And here had it ben reason now therfore, y^t this good man sith he fyndeth in this point so gret a fawt in y^e wittes

25　of both these good popes, & in al them y^t were membres of that generall counsayle, and in all the wyttes of al chrysten regyons that haue vsed and allowed y^t lawe for good euer synnys: reason wolde I say / that he sholde at the leste haue layed some reason [E$_3$] here, wherfore y^e lawe can not please hym, that he whiche

30　though he be not proued gylty of the dede, is yet proued suspecte, shold purge hym selfe after tharbitrement of thordynarye, that is to wytte in suche maner wyse as thordynary sholde thynke conuenyent, vpon the qualytees of y^e person & cyrcumstaunces of ye cause consydered.

35　Suppose now y^t there were none other maner of purgacion, but by his neyghbours swerynge wyth hym, & that those wordes

---

5 sayed, afterward] sayed afterward, *1533 1557*　　21 Platina] Platiua *1533 1557*
22–23 vertuouse] verteouse *1557*　　24 wittes] wytnes *1557*

BARTHOLOMAEVS PLATINA
HISTORICVS.

Pontificum vitas, & mores scribo: bonumᵍ
Edoceo ciues nobile nosse bonos.

BARTHO·

Bartolomeo Platina, from Nicolaus Reusner, *Icones* . . . (1589), sig. C₅v (reduced).

Veius tertius, natione Tuscus, Luca vrbe, gente nobili oriundus, omniū *178.Pont.* confenfu eo tempore pōtificatum inijt, quo Andronicus Græcus, quem diximus Alexio pupillo tutorem datum, pulfis Latinis, qui puero fauebant, Conftātinopolitanum imperium vfurpauit, necato in vndis puero, dum laxandi animi caufa paruo nauigio huc illuc temere dilabitur. Pręterea verò ne facinore partam tyrannidem amitteret, facinus haud paruum addidit. Nam proceres omnes quorum virtutum fufpectam habebat, breui interfecit. At verò Guillelmo Longafpata Hierofolymis mortuo, Balduinus rex nepoti confulturus, Sibyllam nouo marito collocat Guidoni Lufigniano è Pictauorum gente oriundo, hac tamen lege, vt fe mortuo Guido pro nepote Balduino quoad pueritiam fupergrederetur, regnum gubernaret: illudq; deinceps nepoti traderet. Agebantur hæc omnia Lucij pontificis auctoritate, qui ad Chriftianam remp. pertinere arbitrabatur, principes Afiæ quàm maximè inter fe beneuolentia & affinitate connexos effe, quò facilius Sarracenis & Turcis in bello refifterent. Is tamen ex vrbe eijcitur, dum fauentibus quibufdam ciuibus Romanis, abolere confulum nomen annititur. Fautoribus eius in vrbe deprehenfis, effofsi oculi funt. Accepta autem tam infigni contumelia pontifex Veronam profectus, cōcilio habito, & Romanorum licentiam ac fuperbiam improbauit, & principes omnes Chriftianos adhortatus eft, vt noftris in Afia pro fide Chrifti laborantibus fuccurreretur: maximè verò cum feditione principum noftrorum hoftes freti, duce Saladino Hierofolymitanum agrum popularentur. Nam pulfo Guidone Lufignano ab adminiftratione regni ob fuperbiam, Bertrādo comite Tripolitano tutore defignato, ad arma ciuilia res ipfa fpectare videbatur. Non deftitit tamen pontifex & literis & nuncijs eos adhortari, vt pofitis fimultatibus, vna mente, eodemq; animo tam diu hoftibus refifterent, quoad nouæ copiæ in fupplementum militiæ fubmitterentur. Iam enim inftante Heraclio patriarcha Hierofolymitano, qui primo Veronam eius rei caufa ad Lucium venerat, deinde ad Philippum Franciæ regem acceflerat, milites cruce fignati ad tantam expeditionem mittebantur. Verùm Guillelmus Siciliæ rex, in iquo tempore iniurias Latinis ab Andronico Conftantinopolitano imperatore illatas vlturus, cum armato exercitu in Græciam traijciens, omnia perturbauit. Nā & Theffalonicam Macedoniæ vrbem vi cæpit, & multas Græciæ Thraciæq; ciuitates va rijs calamitatibus affectas partim cæpit, partim diripuit: nufquam occurrente Andronico, & dijs & ciuibus fuis infefto, propterea quòd multos occiderat, plerofq; exilio damnauerat. Hac verò necefsitate impulfi & coacti Conftantinopolitani ciues Ifaacium quendam regia progenie ortum, è Peloponnefo ad imperium vocant: qui Andronicum prælio fuperatum & captum, varijs cruciatibus interfecit. Quo fublato, Lucio pontifici haud difficile fuiffet. Guillelmum regem pace cum Ifaacio compofita, impellere pollicitationibus, & præmijs, vt in Afiam traijceret. Verùm dum ob hanc rem nuncij vltro citroq; mitterētur, Lucius vir optimus pontificatus fui anno quarto, menfe fecundo, die xviij. Veronæ moritur: fepeliturq; magna adhibita pompa ante altare cathedralis bafilicę. Hic autem pontifex non immemor patriæ fuæ, eam multis muneribus, tum diuinis, tum humanis ante mortem ornauit. Ab imperatore enim Frederico, quo cum in pace vixit, obtinuit, ne Etrufci alia quam moneta Lucenfi vterentur, quemadmodum Longobardi folam Papienfem admitterent fignatam imperatoria nota. Nam Cifalpinos iam antea pontifex imperatori cōciliauerat. Scribit Ptolemæus Lucenfis & Petrum Comeftorem, qui hiftoriam vtriufq; teftamenti confcripfit, & Ioachimum abbatem in Calabria apud monafterium Florisab eo conditum, in pretio tum fuiffe, doctrina & diuinandi arte, quam fub ambagibus quibufdam præ fe ferebat.

A N N O T A T.

Lucius ifte Lucæ ortus, ex nobili gente, quæ Allucingula dicebatur, tertio pontificatus fui anno Veronam patriam meam florentißimam tunc Italiæ vrbem ciuili feditione vrbe à fenatoribus (non vt Platina fcribit, confulibus)
Q 3

The story of Pope Lucius III, from Bartolomeo Platina, *Historia . . . de vitis pontificum* (1574), sig. Q₃ (reduced).

Linea summoꝛ pontificũ
Lucius tercius

Urbanus tercius

Gregoꝛius octauus

Anno mundi. 6 5 8 4 ¦   Anno xpi. í í 7 4 ·

Lucius eius nois tercius papa natione tuscus luca vꝛbe ꞇ gẽte nobili oꝛí undus. Cũ Alexander põfex romanus gloria magis ꝗ annis plenus diem obijt oim ꝑsensu põtificatum inijt, cõsules aũt a romanis deponi cura/ uit. multo eñ ex nobilitate populoꝗ ro. ope ꞇ auxilio quos iam diu ea tira~ nis ad rapinam omia ꝗuertes fastidisset innitebat. sed adeo cõsularis factio preualuit vt lucio vꝛbe deturbato in fautoꝛes suos crudeliter sit seuitum. No~ uo eñ apud romanos exemplo quotꝗt põtifici studuisse comptum est. qui fu ga sibi tardius ꝑsuluerint effossis oculis sunt cecati. ꞇ põtifex fuge sue necessi tate ad bonũ ꝗuersum ꝑsilium quod rome destinauerat veronam ꝗcilium cõ~ uocauit. rebus iherosolime titubãtibus suppecias allaturus. veronaꝗ ꝑfect⁹ cõcilio habito ꞇ romanoꝗ licentiam ac supbiam impꝛobauit. ꞇ principes om nes xpianos adhoꝛtat⁹ est vt in asia laboꝛãtibus succurreret. verũ dũ ob hãc rem nunꝗ vltro citroꝗ mitterent. lucius vir optimus põtificatus sui anno ꝗr to mense secundo die decimooctauo veroñe moꝛif sepelit ꝗ magna adhibita pompa ante altare cathedralis basilice. hic ante moꝛtem nõ immemoꝛ patrie sue eam oꝛnauit. Ab Friderico imperatoꝛe quo cum in pace vixit obtinuit ne hetrusci alia ꝗ moneta lucensi vterentur.

Urbanus tercius papa patria mediolanẽsis patre Johanne e gente cri bella põtificatũ iniens quo tpe fridericus occidẽtalis ro. impatoꝛ bein/ ricum filiũ ꝑuicijs ꞇ vꝛbibus quas de italia romanũ tũc possidebat imperiũ ꝑfecit. Qui ꝗ pꝛimũ põtificatum inijt reuocare ad cõcoꝛdiam xpianos princi pes pꝛimo annixus est. ne dissidentes a barbaris opprimerent. At vrbanus quẽ audita Guidõis lusiniaci regis noui ꞇ tripolitani comitis dissidia. ꞇ quẽ Saladini virtus fama principio sui pontificatus terruerat oꝛbem xpianoꝛꝗ generali edicto de mittẽdis in asiam copijs monuerat. Idcꝗ quũ serius negli gentiusꝗ ardore sui animi quo ferebat fieri cerneret. venetias petere cõstitu erat xpianã eo militia festinãtius copiosiusꝗ sua ꝑsentia cõuocaturus. Jáꝗ ferrariã attigerat quũ i felicis plñ rumoꝛe pꝛimũ. post cercioꝛe. atꝗ ꝗ erat ma ioꝛe xpianaꝝ rex exterminij nūcio ad se plato febꝛe ꞇ doloꝛe coꝛreptus ẽ. ex ꝗ bꝛeui mest⁹ ferrarie i itinere moꝛif põtificat⁹ sui anno pꝛimo mese. x. die. xxv

Gregoꝛius octauus papa patria beneuentanus summo oim cõsensu põ tifex creat⁹. ꝗ ardore animi par suo pdecessoꝛi. sed tpe acceleratioꝛe ba buit moꝛtis euentum. ꞇ statim nūcios ꞇ litteras ad pꝛincipes xpianos mittit eos cohoꝛtatus vt viribus omnibus vna secũ cõparato exercitu terrã mariꝗ hierosolimam ab hostibus captã recuperarent. ꞇ cũ ad mittẽda in terras san/ ctam xpianoꝛ militum auxilia totis animi coꝛpoꝛisꝗ viribus insudat. pisas se ptulit. quo pisanos inter. ꞇ genuenses acerrimo cõtẽdẽtes bello pacem faci lius cõponeret ꞇ vtrumꝗ populũ bello maritimo ꝑpotentem in sanctam exp/ peditionem excitaret. pace aũt plane cõposita adiecta vtriꝗ parti cõditionem vt classe armata in barbaros duceret xpianos in asia vexãtes dũ hec intẽtoꝛ cura vir sanctissimus agit pisis moꝛif põtificatus die sui quinꝗgesimoseptio.

Joachim abbas calaber ad vrbanũ põtificem veroñe accessit. Js maxime do ctrine ꞇ excellentissimi ac ꝑpe diuini ingenij vir hac ipa tẽpestate apð guil belmum regem ꞇ calabꝛos omnes clarus ꞇ inclitus fuit. qui spiritu pꝛophetie (vt aiunt) repletus futura quasi ꝑsentia differebat. cũ pꝛius nõ multũ ab homie doctore didicisset donum intelligentie vt ferunt diuinitus accepit. adeo vt facũ de scripturaꝝ difficultates enodaret. ꞇ cum plurimũ eruditus esset nõnullos in sacris codicibus edidit cõmentarios. ꞇ ꝗ maxime in apocalipsim. vbi ꞇ multa pꝛedixit. ꞇ potissimum de oꝛdinibus medicantium. Item cõtra petrus lumbar dum theologũ librum cõposuit. qui postea damnat⁹ ꞇ repꝛobat⁹ fuit. sicut pz i pꝛicipio libꝛi decretaliũ. Fert ꝗꝗ mlta scripsisse. libꝛosꝗ suos dño pape emẽ dandos obtulisse. ꞇ ei multa de futuris reserata aũt de duob⁹ regibus francie et anglie apud messanam hiemantibus aliꝗ interrogatus quid sibi de expedi tione sarracenoꝝ sperandũ esset respondit nõ dum adesse tempus quo iherusa lem recuperari posset. Sup his aũt que scripsit de futuris tempoꝛibus nos rex incertarum ꝑsagiũ relinquere conuenit iudicio posterioꝛ. alia quoꝗ ꝑpulcra scripto mandauit.

Joachim abbas

Linea summoꝝ pontificũ
Innocentius tercius

Anno mundi. 6403. Anno christi. 1204.

Innocentius tercius papa natione campanus patria anagninus patre trasi-
mũdo e familia comitum. vir certe in omni genere vite ꝓbatissim⁹ atq̃ doctissimus. q̃ a primeua etate parisius lr̃is operã dedit. Is añ põtificatũ doctria
et moribus insignis. a celestino in numero cardinaliũ refert. quo mortuo in ei⁹
locũ oĩm consensu põtifex sufficit. Q̃tũ autem fuerit gloriosus põtifex opa eius
ostẽtant. q̃ si omnia scribenda forent ingens volumẽ efficerent. q̃ cũ exosaȝ ba-
beret venalitatẽ edicto statuit vt nullus curie officialis quicq̃ ab alieno exigeret
preter scriptores ac bullatores. q̃bus modũ p̄fixit. hostiarios quoq̃ a notario-
rum cameris amouit vt liber esset aditus. statim quoq̃ vbi magistratũ iniit bello asiatico animũ adijciẽs germanos ꝓpter Heinrici mortẽ in asia tumultuãtes
retinere in officio lr̃is. nuncijs. premijs. pollicitationib⁹ conat⁹ ẽ. verum id fru-
stra tentauit. at vbi videret sarracenoꝝ potẽtiam in asia concrescere apud lateranum maximum conciliũ celebrat. cui interfuere plures viri p̄stãtissimi. Postmo-
dũ multa libroꝝ volumia composuit. inter que extat liber de miseria cõditionis
humane. ⁊ libros de sacramẽto eucharistie. de sacrameto baptismi. habuit item sermones temporibus ⁊ so-
lennibus diebus accomodatos. Decretales quoq̃ antiquas composuit quas obseruari mandauit. Vir doctissimus ⁊ omi ornatissimus virtute. eo pontificatu sese dignũ breui ostendit. nam inter ceteras decretales
quas extantes reliquit tres eo põtificatus sui initio edidit. Primã q̃ de inducijs habet. Quotiẽs orbis p̄n-
ceps alter in alterũ delinqueret correctionẽ ad põtificem romanum spectare. Et venerãdos esse principib⁹
q̃tũuis maximus sacerdotes secundam. Terciã que extra de electiõe habet singularis fuit. Iuuere hui⁹ põ-
tificis virtutẽ ⁊ doctrinã beati Dñici ⁊ Francisci assistatis sanctitas. Improbauit p̄terea abbatis Ioachim li-
bellum quẽdam nõ sanam doctrinam p̄ se ferẽtem. Damnauit ⁊ errores almerici heretici qui postea parisi⁹
cũ sectatoribus suis exustus est. qui affirmabat ydeas que sunt in mente diuina ⁊ creare ⁊ creari. cũ in eo nil
nisi eternũ ⁊ incommutabile sit. dixerat p̄terea in charitate constituto nullũ peccatũ imputari. Nec Innocentius opera pietatis in tanto pontificatu p̄termisit. Extant etiam rome duo huius pontificis opa situ. vtilita-
te ⁊ vsu longe distantia. hospitale sanctispũs in Saxia a longobardis ⁊ Saxonib⁹ ibi solitis habitare ap-
pellatum. quod in vaticani suburbio celebre ⁊ ditissimũ hospitalitati amplissime deseruit vnũ. Et alteꝝ tur-
ris appellata comitis vrsani operis. que muro oĩm totius vrbis rarissimo sublimitate surgit eximia. Estq̃
ad forũ olim neruẽ ad veteris subure principiũ que p̱ etatẽ nostrã ⁊ diu ante inhabitata nulli omnino vsui
est aut fuit. indeq̃ basilicam sancti sixti que extat in auentino celebris tũc dirutam instaurauit. Verũ dũ Pe-
rusij tollende discordie causa (que inter Genuenses ⁊ pisanos vigebat) ꝓfectus fuisset morit. pontificatus
sui anno decimooctauo mense septimo die. xvi. Cuius vita adeo ꝓbata fuit vt post eius mortẽ nil earum re-
rum que in vita egerit laudauerit improbaueritq̃ immutatũ sit. hic quoq̃ primũ ordinẽ diui Augustini he-
remiticum sub tutela apostolica suscepit.

Sinodus maxima hoc anno apud lateranum ab
Innocẽtio põtifice p̄dicto ꝓ recuperanda ihe-
rosolima celebrat. cui interfuere mille ⁊ trecenti p̄la-
ti cum iherusolimitano ⁊ constãtinopolitano patriarcha. Metropoli septuaginta. Episcopi quadringen-
ti duodeciȝ. Abbates. priores. cõuentuales octingẽ-
ti. Greci ⁊ romani imperij legati. Regum vo iherusalem. francie. hispanie. angli e ⁊ cipri oratores. Vene-
re multa tum quidem in cõsultationem nec decerni tamen quicq̃ aperte potuit. q̱ ⁊ pisani ⁊ genuẽses maritimo ⁊ cisalpini terrestri bello inter se certabant. verum decreta ibi ꝓlata fuere quibus tam laicorum q̃
clericorum mores componerentur.

Iohãnes bon⁹ ordinis heremitaꝝ diui augustini
instaurator natiõe Mantuanus his temporib⁹ i
flaminia ⁊ vmbria vitam religiosissimam ac sanctissi-
maȝ duxit. multa monasteria ibi erexit. Inde fratres
zãbonite vulgo appellati sunt. Tandem cum vir san-
ctus. 50. ãnis in flaminia ꝯmorat⁹ fuisset i patriã re-
uersus plen⁹ dieꝝ ⁊ opib⁹ bõis. ãno a natiuitate dñi
1222. migrauit ad dñm. Cuius corp⁹ translatuȝ in
mõasterium ordinis sub titulo sancte agnetis fabre-
factũ summo seruetur honore vbi indies fiunt miracula.

Concilium lateranense

Hartmann Schedel, *Liber chronicarum* (1493), fol. 206v (reduced).

ad arbitrium episcopi were not writen in the law: were it yet
reason to accepte his oth in what so euer maner the man wolde
hym selfe deuyse it? and with as few handes as hym selfe lyste
appoynt? and with what maner folke so euer hym selfe wolde
brynge?

Nay syr. For it may so be, y^t there shalbe good cause why
somtyme and in some place, that thordynary sholde not putte
some man to that kynde of [E$_3$v] purgacion which yf he dyd,
were he neuer so noughty, he shold be sure of compurgatours,
peraduenture mo than inough.

For it hath ben sene in many cuntreys ere this & somtyme in
england to, that some euyll precher prechyng playne open heresyes, shold yet (if he myght haue ben put to such purgacyon)
haue lacked none handes to lay on the boke with hym, that he
neuer spake suche wordes. How be it where ye wordes are open
& playn heresye, ye law hath prouided an other way for ye remedy good inough.

But than haue there ben some prechers such ere this, y^t tech-
yng playne heresies to theyr familiars secretely, wold prech in
such wyse abrode, that theyr wordes shold haue two senses, &
one bote serue for eyther legge like a shypmans hose / & so shold
be tempered as the peple shold haue occasyon alway to take
them to the wurst / and hym selfe yf he were examined wold say
before thordinary & swere to, that [E$_4$] he neuer ment but the
beste.

Now whan it shold by good wytnesses appere, y^t his maner
was such the peple toke mych harme therby, & alwaye toke his
wordes so that they thought he so ment them, y^t he purposed
by them to set forth & aduance those thynges y^t were stark
heresies in dede: yf thordinary shold than appoint him with
other compurgatours to purge this suspicion, were these suspicions neuer so vehement, he shold lacke no compurgatours to
purge hym self euery weke, & than do as he dyd before. And
many good symple folke takyng him euen as he ment, shold fall
into his heresyes ye while / & wene while he preched so styll, y^t
to byleue y^t way were no perell.

And therfore those wise men that made ye law, left ye thyng in
thordinarys discrecion to assigne hym that is proued suspect of
heresy, such kynde of purgacyon as the cyrcumstaunces of the
person, and the peple and the tyme shall most requyre. [E₄v]

5   And therfore wyll thordynary to some man so suspecte, somtyme assygne hym (to purge his suspycyon y^t with his lewd maner of prechynge he is fallen in, to the greate hurte of his herers)
that he shall openly confesse y^t those heresyes that the people
toke hym to mene, be very false heresyes indede / and openly

10   shall deteste them and swere that he so byleueth them to be / and
swere that he neither ment to teche theym, nor neuer was mynded y^t any man shold take hym so, nor neuer wold afterward teche
nor hold heresies, but abiure them for euer.

And yet for the ferther purgacyon of such suspicion, the or-

15   dynary myght also enioyne hym some certayn thynges to do,
suche as maye declare the more clereli, y^t he is not of such mind /
as open prechyng agaynste the selfe same heresyes, & the
doynge of some suche thynges as those heresyes dyd stande
agaynste. [E₅]

20   And now by this purgacyon thys good shall he do, that yf he
wolde after preache the same thynges agayne though he vsed
agayne such a nother wyly fashyon: yet wolde his audyence then
thynke thus (as many as hadde any mynde to be good) eyther this
man meaneth not nowe by his wordes to teache vs that poynt that

25   hym selfe hath abiured, and then lette vs not lerne the thynge of
hym that he wolde in no wyse we shold / or elles he meaneth to
teache yt vs styll for al his abiuracion. And then wherfore sholde
we be so madde to byleue a false wreche, y^t wolde make vs byleue
now, that that thynge were trewe / whyche hym selfe hath openly

30   confessed and sworen to be false.

But then wyll happely this good man say, that this abiuracyon
is perylouse for iubardye of the relapse. The parell of deth by
relapse is not vppon euery abiuracyon. But of [E₅v] trouth he
that is abiured vppon such thynges proued, as maketh hym not

35   sleyghtly but very vehemently suspected, yf he fall after into

---

7 in, to] in-[*new line*]to *1557*   9 false] *1557*, salse *1533*   11 theym] thym *1557*
24 not] *1533 corr. err.*, om. *1533 1557*   32 iubardye] ieopardy *1557;* The parell] *para.*
1557

heresye, putteth hym selfe in parell to fall into the fyre. And very good reason yt is that yt be so. And a man may sometyme be so suspecte of felony by reason of sore presumpcyons, y^t though no man saw hym do yt, nor hym selfe neuer confesse yt, but saye and swere to that he neuer dyd yt: yet may he be founden gyltye 5 of yt, and theruppon hanged for yt, and haue no wronge at all.

And thus this prouysyon for purgacyon at the dyscrecyon of the ordynarye, is not I truste so vnreasonable, nor they so vnreasonable that made yt, nor they so vnreasonable y^t ratified it, nor al they so vnresonable y^t thys two or thre hundred yere 10 haue accepted and allowed yt, but that yt maye nowe stande by thys good man[E_6]nys leue at this daye as well as yt hath standen all this whyle before. But yet is there one thing y^t he taketh for a thing very sore. For than is there (sayth he) a nother law that if he that is so proued suspect, refuse to pourge hym self at the discrecyon of 15 thordynary, and be for hys contumacy excommunycate: that in that case yf he of an obdurate harte stande so accursed an whole yere, he shalbe punyshed as an heretyke. And that ys (as he sayth) by the law Extra. de hereticis, capitulo Excommunicamus.

This prouisyon was made as I tolde you in the sayde generall 20 counsayle. And where he bringeth it forth as though yt were a very sore thyng and a cruell: yt is in dede very fauorable. For sauynge that I wyll not do as he doth, go fynd fautes in their doynges, that were so many so mych better, and had so myche more wytte then I: elles could I lay a lytle better cause to proue 25 that prouysyon ouer fauorable, then euer this good man shall fynde whyle he lyueth, to proue that prouysyon to sore. And surely he that beynge proued [E_6v] suspect, and refuseth in such reasonable maner to purge hym self therof, as his ordynarye shall by his dyscrecyon assygne hym, whych must both by lawe & 30 all reason be his iudge and not hym self, sheweth hym self lytle to force or care, though folke wene he were an heretyque: whych thyng sore aggreueth the suspycyon that he veryly is one in dede. And then when he wyll rather be ones accursed, then of suche suspycyon yet to purge and clere hym selfe: he yet encreaseth y^t 35 suspycyon twyse so sore. But fynally when rather then to purge

---

5 dyd] *1533 corr. err.*, hadde *1533*, had *1557*   19 Extra.] *1557*, Extra *1533*   28 he that beynge] that being be *1557*

that suspycyon, he contynueth excommunycated all the whole
yere, and neuer wyll be purged in the whyle, but yf he maye haue
yt accepted in suche a faynte fashyon as hym selfe lyste to offre:
the suspycyon of his heresyes from sore and vehement, tourne
5 by suche dealynge into pleyne open and vyolent, so that he can in
reason be [E7] none other rekened but a playne heretyque in
dede, whome to tolerate so longe doth somtyme lytle good. And
then syth the law is, that such as the fauour of the chyrche shall
preserue from the temporall handes, shold by the lawe be onely
10 those, which vpon theyr deteccyon, tourne of theyr own offre
mekely by and by, and shewe good tokens of ryghte harty repen-
taunce: I wyll let no man from thinclinacyon towarde pytye, in
preseruynge the lyfe of any man / when so euer he seme peny-
tent. But yet surely when the chyrch receyueth agayne that
15 man, that by his obstynate dealynge, wyth abydynge excomuni-
cate and contempnyng the great curse all the whole yere, rather
then he wolde purge the suspycyon of his heresye, but yf he
may purge it after his own swete wyll, proueth hym self at last,
to haue ben an heretyque so longe, & all that whyle wold not
20 retourne but [E7v] euer more drawe bakke: yf thordynary for
all that receyue hym to grace agayne, and kepe hym styll and
preserue him from the seculare handes: I wyll not saye that he
doth wrong / but fyndynge hym yet repentaunte, fayne wolde I
se hym saued.
25   But yet wythout doute as farre as I can se, thordynarye to saue
the mannys lyfe of pytye, strecheth out wyth his teth the lawe and
reason both, so farre that euyn scantely can any of the both
holde.
    And therfore these lawes beynge suche as they be, made and
30 ratyfyed by whole generall counsayle, accepted and vsed so
longe thorow al chrystendome: when thys good man cometh
now forth, and vppon his own bare reason as bare as euer I herd
yet in all my lyfe, bycause onely that an innocente may somtyme
take harme, whyche may happen vppon any lawe that euer all
35 the world can [E8] make, wherby there shalbe deuysed any
punyshment for the euyl folke, he byddeth euery man consyder
nowe whyther the law be iuste or not, & if it be not, byddeth
euery man put to theyr handes to haue yt broken and make a
better, and sayeth that he thynketh they shall haue great thanke

of god therfore: his request is now no better, but in effecte euyn
this, that agaynste euery wyse mannes reason well approued
hytherto, euery man shold in this mater now, eyther trust vnto
his, or els at the lest wise euery man to his owne / and in stede of a
better old law, make a new mych worse. For if his deuise were   5
folowed: it appereth playnely so there sholde / and heresyes
sholde grow vp on heyght, and the catholyque fayth decaye. And
then god saue vs frome that thanke of god that shortely we shold
wyth such dealynge deserue.

Thus haue I good readers as you se clerely confuted this good   10
man[E$_8$v]nys answere in bothe the pryncypall poyntes, of
whyche the tone was wherin he mynded to shewe that in heresye
the suyte of offyce myghte be lefte, and that by the leuyng there
shold none harme folow to the catholyque faythe / bycause heretyques myght as well come to correccyon by the waye of open   15
accusers as by that maner suyte.

But in this poynte you haue sene clerely, that his deuyse wolde
neuer so serue the mater / but that yt were very lykely so to
mynyshe in thys realme the catholyque fayth with encrease of
heresyes, that thindygnacyon of god were sore to be fered therby   20
to folowe theron: and the realme to fall in trouble and besynesse,
with insurreccion of the same rebellyouse heretyques, that by the
chaunge of that law had so bene suffred to grow as other countreys haue ben of late, and this realme was ere this so nere [F$_1$]
lyke to haue ben / that for thauoyding of the lyke parell to fall   25
afterwarde, yt was prouyded by parlyament of great polycye /
for the better repressyng of heresyes, to fortyfye that lawe and
gyue thordynaryes yet greater power to maynteyne yt / and wyth
temporall assystence to make yt more strong.

His secunde poynte was to shew that of the kepynge of that   30
law, there sholde growe great harme / bycause the law is so
vnreasonable he sayth, that innocentes may come to trouble
therby wythout offence.

This parte howe properly thys good man hath proued, that
haue you sene also / and that he therin is so full and whole   35
confuted, that when he readeth yt agayne, I suppose he will not
now greatly lyke it.

---

10 Thus] Thys *1557*   26 was] *1533 corr. err., om. 1533 1557*

Now these two thus handeled he cometh to the thyrde poynte, whyche though I graunted hym all to gether, yet were he neuer the nere. [F_1v] For y^t poynt is suche as yf I wynne it, thanne it maketh my parte more playne: but on the tother syde yf I loste it & he wanne it, yet were myne playne inough. And stronge inough were my part wyth the fyrste poynt alone. For yf by the leuynge of the suit of office shold folow thencreace of here-tikes, as euery man I thynke that wyt hath, may well se that there wolde / than though there wold some other harme hap-pen somtyme therof, yet must that other harme in reason, rather be borne than that.

But now to come good readers vnto the thyrde poynt, whyche yf he wan all together coulde very lytell serue hym / ye shall se hym yet by goddes grace, wynne hym neuer a pyece.

The thyrde poynt good readers in myn apology you se well your self entendeth nothynge ellys, but by ensemple of the com-en lawes of thys [F_2] realme, to shew that the same spyrytuall law, whyche this man wolde proue vnreasonable, is not in dede proued vnreasonable by thys thyng that he here putteth for the profe / that is to saye, bycause that by that lawe sometyme yt myght happe that a man myght fall in parell of a cryme whyche he commytted not. For yf yt so were nowe, that in all the cases that I rehersed of the commen lawe, there coulde neuer no man that hadde not done the dede, take any harme so myche as a phylyppe / yet though I hadde myssed in those ensamples, the thynge myghte yet be trewe. For there myghte be for all that, other ensamples ynough, bothe in other good lawes and in the same to, that a lawe were not vnreasonable, nor to be put away, though there myght happe somtime some man take some harme that neuer dyd the dede that [F_2v] were layde to his charge. And of trouth this conclusyon is so clere that yt nedeth no profe at all. And therfore though he wanne al that poynt / yet hadde he loste the mater. But let vs now a lytle se whether he wynne thys poynte or no.

And bycause the effecte of all hys answere lyeth all waye in this, that he sayeth all waye that the sample of the comen lawe that I laye, is not lyke the thynge that I resemble yt vnto in the

32 al] at *1557*

spyrytuall lawe: I shall fyrste reherse you myn owne wordes in
myne apologye / and then shall I reherse you hys wordes here,
that when you haue herd bothe twayne, whether they be lyke or
vnlyke ye maye the more surely iuge. These were lo good readers my wordes.

*And veryly me thynketh that he whych can not be proued gyltye in
heresye, and yet vseth suche maner of* [F₃] *wayes that all hys honeste
neyghbours wene he were one, and therfore dare not swere that in theyr
conscience they thynke hym any other / is well worthye me thynketh to do
some penaunce for that maner of byhauour, wherby he geueth all other
folke occasyon to take hym for so noughtye.*

*And by the comen law of this realme, many tymes vppon suspycyon the
iuges a warde write to enquyre of what fame and behauour the man ys in
his countrey / and hym self lyeth somtyme styll in pryson tyll the retourne /
and yf he be returned good, that is to wyt yf he be in a maner purged, then
is he delyuered / & yet he payeth his fees ere he go. And yf he be retourned
noughte / then vse the iuges to bynde hym for hys good aberynge, and
somtyme suertyes wyth hym to, suche as theyr dyscrecyon will allowe. And
then to lye styll tyll he fynde theym, is somtyme as myche penaunce to the
tone, as the spyrytuall iudge in* [F₃v]*ioyneth to the tother. For the tone
cometh to the barre as openly as the tother to the consystorye / and somtyme
hys feters waye a good pyece of a fagotte, bysydes that they lye lenger on the
tone mannys legges, then the fagotte on the tothers sholdre. And yet ys
there no remedye but bothe these must be done, both in the tone court and
in the tother / or ellys in stede of one harme (whych to hym that deserueth yt
not happeth seldome, and as seldome I am sure in heresye as in thefte, and
myche more seldome to) ye shall haue tenne tymes more harme happen
dayly to folke as innocent as they / and of innocentes many made nocentes,
to the destruccyon of theym selfe and other to, bothe in goodes bodye and
soule.*

To thys pyece lo good reader thys is this good mannys answere. [F₄]

Then he goeth further for mayntenaunce of the sayde suyte Ex
officio, and resembleth it to arestyng for suspecyon of felonye, and to
the suertye of good aberynge, and to indytementes: wheruppon men
be put to answere at the commen lawe. And how farre these re-

---

13 behauour] behaiuour *1557*   23 And] *para.* *1557*   31 reader] readers *1557*

semblances varye from the suyte Ex officio, he in some place openeth yt hym selfe. But yet for a more playne declaracyon therin, l shall saye a lytle farther in that mater. Fyrst as to the arrestynge for suspycyon of felonye, yt is in dede an olde lawe of thys realme, that for suspycyon of
5 felonye, a man may be arrested, so that he that doth arreste hym, vppon a reasonable cause doth suspecte hym: but yt is a generall rule, that he shall neuer be put to answere vpon that arreste, but proclama-cyon shalbe made that yf any man wyll lay any thynge agaynst hym, that is so suspected, that it shal be herde: & yf none such come he shalbe
10 delyuered without fine or any other punyshment, with a good exhorta-cion of the iudges, that he shall take good hede howe he ordereth hym selfe in tyme to come. And then mayster More lykeneth the penaunce of suche a man that hath ben in pryson vppon suspycyon of felonye, and so delyuered by proclamacyon, to the bearynge of a fagotte for
15 heresye. For he sayth, that the one of them shal come as openly to the barre as the other to the consystory: And that sometyme his fetters shall wey a good pece of the fagot, besydes that they lye lenger on the one mannys legges, then the fagotte on the other mannys shulder: but he reherseth not howe they lye many tymes lenger in pryson for here-
20 sye, then they do eyther for suspycyon of felonye or for good aberynge. And ouer that I dare say, that there are but few, but that they hadde wel leuer abyde the payne to be thryse acquyted by proclamacyon, and peraduenture ofter, then ones beare a fagot for heresy. [F₄v]

Howe goeth nowe good readers thys answere of thys good
25 man vnto the purpose, to proue the trouble of hym that ys ar-rested vppon suspycyon of felonye, to be vnlyke to the trouble of hym that ys sued ex officio for heresye, touchynge the poynte that I resemble theym for?

The point ye wote wel for whyche I speke of tharrestyng for
30 suspycyon of felonye, is to shew, that lyke wyse as yt may happen a man for heresye to fall in trouble sometyme though he were none heretike in dede: so may yt happen a man somtyme to be troubled vppon suspycyon of felonye, though he be no felon in dede: and yet bothe the tone lawe necessarye and the tother to /
35 and neyther of bothe maye be forborne. Hathe this good man

---

5 hym,] hym *Salem and Bizance, 1533*, him 1557   6 cause] cause, *Salem and Bizance, 1533 1557*

proued vs the contrarye of this? that you se well he hath not. And
then hathe he not perdye proued [F₅] them vnlyke.

He weneth he sayth somewhat, whan he telleth vs that vpon
tharrestynge vppon suspycyon of felonye he shall not be put to
answere tyll he be indighted. What is hys trouble the lesse for
that? If he lye in pryson tyll the sessyon as he maye happe to do,
were it not more his ease to be putte to answere before and
acquytte, yf he be not fawty (for of suche folke we speke) than for
lacke of puttynge to answere lye styll in pryson yᵉ lenger?

As for that, that in conclusyon yf no man laye nought to his
charge at the sessyons, he shall be delyuered by proclamacions /
so shall he that is suspected of heresye to: For yf there be
nothynge founden agaynste hym, he shall neyther be dreuen
to abiuracyon nor purgacion but be deliuered quyte, how so
euer that eyther thys man myssetake or wolde make other men
myssetake the mater to the contrary. [F₅v]

And as to that, that the tone shall pay no fyne / no more shall
the tother neyther.

Yf this man wyll peraduenture say, syth that thordinary fyndeth the man not suspect in the ende, why dyd he take and arreste
hym for suspecte in the begynnynge. Bycause that in the begynnyng the man semed vpon good consyderacyons suspecte, and
semed lykely to fle, and vppon his examynacyon the mater full
serched out, the causes of suspycyon so well auoyded, that thordynary declareth hym for dyscharged wythout any other purgacyon. But yet hath it myshapped hym to haue some harme the
meane whyle / and so hath it hym also that was arrested vppon
suspycyon of felony that neuer was after indyghted, but delyuered forth fre vpon the proclamacyon.

I se no great dyfference bytwene these two men in all this
mater yet, [F₆] saue that the tone lyeth at his owne fyndynge, the
tother at the bysshoppes coste.

For where as this man sayth, that he whyche is delyuered by
proclamacyon, hath alwaye geuen hym by the iustyces a good
lesson at his departing: yf the bysshoppe geue not the tother a
good lesson at hys departynge to, than is he somwhat to blame in

dede / but in good fayth I here saye that he doth so to. And
therfore where is this dyfference yet? I loke alwaye for that. For
as for the shame of open brynging forth, is both one as I said /
sauynge that the sessyon hath comenly myche more people pres-
5 ent to gase vppon the tone, than in the consystory loketh vppon
the tother.

And where thys man sayth, that they lye lenger in pryson for
heresye, than they do eyther for suspycyon of felonye or for
good aberynge / yf he speke of those whyche are in conclu-
10 [F₆v]syon founden in no more fawte concernynge heresye, than
those are that are deliuered by proclamacion be founden at the
sessyon concernynge felony / I dare be bolde to tell hym nay.
And I am very sure the trouth wyll proue so to. But now yf he
speke of those that appere vppon thende in suche fawte that by
15 the law they be bounden to abiure / than is it good reason that
they lye lenger in dede. And so lye there as reason is sometyme
some for felonye to, repryed vpon causys from one sessyon to
another, and somtyme kepte you se well all the whole yere and
more. And that somtyme such as are in conclusyon neuer in-
20 dyghted neyther, but after all that delyuered by proclamacyon,
and yet good causes in yᵉ meane whyle why they were kepte so.
And therfore where as this man sayth, that they be in worse case
that bere a fagotte, very trouth it ys somewhat and so is it reason
they be. [F₇] For they be not fawtelesse but conuicted of the
25 fawte. And our dyspycyons is of innocentes that happen by the
lawe, the tone lawe or the tother, to take harme without theyr
fawte. For yf he wolde compare the fawty with the fawtye, than
must he compare the tone berynge the faggotte, with the tother
at the very fyrste tyme borne vppe wyth the rope.

30 And therfore I dyd in that place, not onely shewe that he that
is innocent, maye by arrestynge for felonye happe to haue as
myche harme, as he yᵗ is innocent and arrested for heresye: but
that he maye happen to haue sometyme also as mych harme, as
he that for the fyrst tyme is founden fawty in heresye and
35 playnely conuycted therof. And surely saue for the ferther perell vppon hys ferther fawte, so maye it happe in dede and yet as I
sayed in my apologye the lawe muste nedes be kepte, [F₇v] but yf

---

10 no] *om.* *1557*   37 apologye] *1533 corr. err.,* dyaloge*1533,* dyalogue *1557*

you wyll by the chaunge haue fyue theuys for one. And thus as
for this pyece of arrestynge for suspycion of felony, the case hath
he not proued vnlyke, towchynge the purpose that I putte it for,
but for my parte very stronge. And so hath thys good man in thys
fyrst pyece of the thyrde point a very great fall.   5

Than cometh he nexte vnto another case that I spake of also,
that is to wyt arrestynge vppon good aberynge. And where as in
myne apologye that pyece is the thyrde, y^t pyece in hys answere
he maketh the second / and I se why well inough. For syth hym
selfe seeth that he answereth it so slenderly, he wrappeth it vp in   10
the myddes, bycause it sholde be the lesse marked, and wold
ende with another pyece wherin hym selfe weneth that he sayth
somwhat better.

Now as for this good aberynge, to thende y^t ye may se the
better how [F$_8$] gayly this good man answereth it, I shall fyrste   15
reherse you the wordes of myne apology that he maketh this
answere to.

After that I haue shewed there, that y^e iudges of the spyrytuall
court be not so folysshe, but that they had leuer not medle with
any man, saue onely vppon some suche open inquisycyon as are   20
indyghtementes of felonye for auoydynge of obloquy, sauyng
that necessyte compelleth them to take thys way, for feare that
with sufferaunce of heresyes to go forth & grow, all myghte at
length thorow goddes displeasure very farre grow to nought / I
say there farther thus folio .225.   25

Necessyte somtyme causeth also both the temporall iuges and the kynges
counsayle, to put some folke to busynesse or dyshonestye somtyme, wythout
eyther iury or bryngynge of the accuser to the profe of the mater in the
partyes presence. [F$_8$v]

For yf the iudge knowe by sure enformacyon, that some one man is of   30
such euyll demeanure amonge his neyghbours, that they may not bere it /
and yet that the man is bysyde so vyolent and so iuberdouse, that none of
them dare be aknowen to speke of it: wyll there no iudges vpon many
secrete complayntes made vnto them, without makynge the party preuye
who tolde hym that tale, bynde that busy troubleouse man to good aber-   35
ynge? I suppose yes, and haue sene it so to / and wronge wolde it be some
tyme wyth good pore peasyble folke in the countrey, but yf it were so done

---

18 shewed] *1533 corr. err., 1557,* sheweth *1533*   30 For] *no para. 1557*

amonge. And my selfe whan I was chauncellour, vpon suche secrete
enformacyon haue put some out of commyssyon and offyce of iustyce of the
peace, whyche els for mych money I wold not haue done, & yet yf I were in
the tone rome styll and they in the tother agayne, but yf they be mended
5   *(wherof I neyther than sawe nor yet here any lykelyhed) I wold put them*
out agayne, and neuer tell them who [G₁] *told me the tales yᵗ made me so*
to do.

Lo good readers here you se, that in thys pyece I mene
nothynge els, but that where as this good man fyndeth a fawte
10 that the spyrytual iudge sholde medle wyth any man for heresye
without an open accusour complaynyng to hym, or an open
presentement in yᵉ begynnyng / I shew there that necessyte is the
cause, and forthwyth afterwarde I proue it, whiche thys good
man dyssembleth here and inuerteth here thordre for the
15 nonys. And I shew that necessite (lest mych more harme sholde
grow theron) causeth the temporall iudges & the kynges honorable counsayle to, to putte some man to busynesse somtyme and
some to dishonesty both, without eyther indyghtement, or open
accusour, or suffryng hym to make answere eyther / and thus be
20 they fayne to do, but yf they shold suffre many great harmes to
growe. Now marke well I re[G₁v]quyre you how substancyally
thys good man answereth thys. These are hys wyse wordes lo.

And then as to the arrestynge for good abearynge, trouth it is, that a
man by commaundement of the iustyces may so be arrestyed, but he
25 shall neuer be put to answere vppon that arrest, but onely bounde, and
suretyes with hym of his good aberynge. And yf he can no suche surety
fynde, and he haue lyen there longe in pryson, then the iuges by theyr
dyscresyon may sende a wrytte to enquere of hys fame, and of hys
behauour, whyche is called a wryt de gestu et fama, wherof syr Tho.
30 More maketh mencyon in hys apologye: and yf it be founde for hym
vppon that wrytte, that he is of good fame and behauour, then he
shalbe delyuered. Wherby mayster More sayth, he is in a maner
purged, and by that sayenge it semeth that hys meanynge is, that that
delyuerye shulde be resembled to hys purgacyon vppon the suspycyon
35 of heresye, as is sayd before. But how ferre they be vnlyke, it appereth
thus: when a man is delyuered vppon the sayd wrytte De gestu et fama,

---

17 counsayle] chunsayle *1557*   18 some] *1533 corr. err.*, so *1533 1557*

he is delyuered as a man proued to be of good honestye and to be
clered by hys neyghbours, of that he was suspected of. And when he is
purged vpon the suyte Ex officio, or for suspicion of heresye, he is put
to penaunce by thordynarye, as a man suspected, wherof he is not
clered, and so shall he be taken amonge his neyghbours, as a man   5
worthy to do that penaunce for hys offences, wherfore it appereth
euydentely, that they be nothynge lyke.

In this answere good reader one piece he answereth with an
vntrouth [G₂] another piece he leueth halfe vnanswered, and to
another pyece he maketh none answere at all.   10

For where as he saith, that he that is purged of heresye in the
suyte ex officio, is put vnto penaunce by the ordynary as a man
suspecte, wherof he is not clered: this man sayth vntrewe, and
woteth not also what he meneth. For the spyrytuall iudge not
onely (as I haue sayde) though he were sore suspected in the   15
beginnyng whan he toke hym, yet yf he fynde in thexamynacyon
those suspicyons clered: he putteth hym to no ferther busynesse
at all, but also yf it be not so fully clered, but that there remayne
some tokens of suspycyon, of whych he thynke it good to pourge
hym by yᵉ othe of hym self & some other compourgatours with   20
hym, he putteth hym after yᵗ purgacion vnto no penaunce
neyther. But now yf it so be, yᵗ there be wel proued such suspicions as are so [G₂v] vehement, that though they proue not
precysely yᵉ dede, yet make euery man that hereth them, that he
can none other wyse thynke: there wyll the ordynary cause hym   25
to abiure / and yᵉ rather to purge hym of the suspycyon that he
were styll nought and afterwarde styll wolde be nought, than yᵗ
he was not such before. And than for vsyng hym self in such wyse
before: though he do penaunce he hath but right.

But in all those other cases of suspicion purged, he saith   30
vntrew / for they do no penaunce at all.

Now concernynge the good aberynge awarded by the iustyces:
he answereth yᵗ it is trew / but it is he sayth vnlyke vnto this
mater, bycause the iustyces (sayth he) whan he hath long lyen in
pryson, maye by theyr dyscrecyon (yf he can fynd no suertyes)   35
award a wrytte de gestu et fama.

This is but half an answere, nor scant so mych neyther. For
fyrst hym [G₃] selfe sayth that this wryt they maye sende out after
that yᵉ man hath long lyen in pryson / so that than the man yet
wythout presentement or open accusour hath had that longe
lyenge in pryson in the meane whyle for hys euyl demenure at
home among hys neyghbours, wherof they durste not openly
make complaynt. And thys doth as you se thys good man not
deny, whych is for my purpose inough.

But than saith he ferther for me, in that he sayth they may
award that wrytte yf they wyll. Wherin he implyeth that yf they
wyl not, they may vpon good dyscrecyon lette hym yet lye styll &
let the wrytte alone. And so hath he therfore putte in one poynt
ferther for me.

But yet hath this good man one stoppe gappe for me styll, to
proue alwaye that my sample is not lyke / and that is that where
as in the suyte ex officio, men be put to answere, vpon [G₃v] this
arreste and imprysonment vppon good aberynge, the man shall
neuer be putte to answere.

For answere of this euasyon I wyll aske this good man this, that
he which is in pryson vpon good aberyng shall neuer be put to
answere, whyther is it his profyte or his losse? If his losse: than
his not puttyng to answere, maketh yᵉ mater of my resemblyng,
mych the more strong for me. And yf this good man dare answere me yᵗ it is his profite: than wyll I no more but praye hym to
put the felow in choyse / & than yf hym selfe chose it for the
better, let hym lye styl for me.

This you se good readers that this man sayth not nay, but that
vpon good aberynge by dyscressyon of the iustyces, for all the
wrytte de gestu & fama, a man maye lye longe in pryson & some
peraduenture euer, how be it of trouth I trow it happeth not so.

And yet can neither this good man [G₄] say, nor I suppose no
man ellys, but that it maye somtyme happe by possybylyte, that
all that informacyon were wronge. But that is a thynge not lykely
to happe so often, but that yf we sholde for suche may happys,
put away yᵗ ordre whiche order very necessyte brought vp: there

---

7–8 not deny] deny *1533*, denye *1557* (*see note*)   9 But] *no para. 1557*   10 Wherin]
1557, wherin *1533*   16 answere,] answere *1533*, aunswer *1557*   17 impryson-
ment] imprisonment *1557*, imprysoment *1533*   19 For] *no para. 1557*   31 And] *no
para. 1557*

wolde mych myschyefe grow, & many great harmes wold there than happe indede.

Now as towchyng that I sayde, that the kynges counsayle vsed also somtyme vppon great secrete informacion to put some folke to busynes and to some dishonesty to / and I letted not to laye some sample in myne owne dede whyle I was chauncellour my self, by puttyng some out of commyssyon in theyr contreys / which dishonesty saue for such secrete informacyon, I wold not for an hundred pound haue done them, & dare yet vpon such secret informacion very well auow the doyng / & dowt not but y^t yf I sholde [G₄v] declare the cause openly, bothe good men & wyse men wold allow my dede: to all thys poynte lo this good man sayeth nothynge at all, but letteth it go by his eares as though he neuer herde it.

And thus as I tolde you, concernynge thys pyece of good aberynge: thys good answerer hath here borne hym selfe so wel, that some parte he answereth with vntrouth, some part he answereth a greate deale lesse than halfe, and some parte neuer a deale. If men be content to take this fashyon for answerynge: let any man make than agaynste me as many bokes as he wyll, and putte in what mater he lyst, and I shall neuer nede to study mych for an answere, but may make answerys to theym all shortely and shorte inough, and answere a longe boke in space of one paper lefe.

But now lette vs se how he handeleth this thyrde piece of endyghte[G₅]mentes at the sessyons. For that pyece he setteth in the rere warde, to staye therwyth all the felde. But nowe that you may se what strength he hath in that warde: I shall fyrste brynge you forth that warde agaynst whyche yt fyghteth. In myne apologye fo. cc.xxii. these are mye wordes lo.

And bycause thys pacyfyer taketh yt for so sore a thynge in the spyrytuall lawe, that a man shall be called ex officio for heresy, where he shal not know his accuser: yf we sholde chaunge the spyrytuall lawe for that cause, then hadde we nede to chaunge the temporall to, in some suche poyntes as chaunge yt when ye wyll, and ye shal chaunge yt into the worse for aughte that I can se, but yf yt be better to haue mo theuys then fewer.

For now yf a man be endyghted at a sessyons, and none euydens geuen

---

15 And] *no para.* 1557   25 But] *no para.* 1557; this] his 1557

openly at the barre (as many be, and many maye well be. For thendytours
[G₅v] may haue euydence gyuen them a parte, or haue herde of the mater
ere they came there, and of whome be they not bounden to tell, but be
rather bounden to kepe yt close, for they be sworen to kepe the kynges
5 *counsayle and theyr owne) shall then the partye that is endyghted be put*
vnto no besynesse aboute his acquytayle? And who shall tell hym there the
names of his accuser, to entytle hym to his wryte of conspyracye? This
pacyfyer wyll peraduenture saye, that the same twelue men / that are hys
endyghtours are his accusers, & therfore he may know them. But what
10 *helpeth that his vndeserued vexacyon yf he were fauteless? For amendes*
the law geueth him none agaynst any of them, nor it were not well done he
sholde / but may when he is after by other .xii. acquyte, go gette hym home
and be mery that he hath had so fayre a day / as a man getteth hym to the
fyre and shaketh his hatte after a shoure of rayne. And nowe as yt often
15 *happeth, that a [G₆] man cometh into a shoure by his own ouersyght,*
though somtyme of chauns and of aduenture: so surely though somtyme yt
happe that a man be accused or endyghted of malyce, or of some lykelyhed
whyche happed hym of chaunce and not his faute therin yet happeth yt in
comparyson very selde, but that the partye by some demeanure of hym selfe
20 *gyueth occasyon that folke haue hym so suspected.*

In this pyece my purpose is good reders as you se, to shewe
that lyke wise as a man shall in the suyt ex officio for heresye, not
knowe his accuser: so may yt also happen many tymes, that no
more he shall neyther, when he is at the comen lawe indyghted
25 of felonye. And I shewe also therin as you se, that though yt
maye sometyme happe eyther of malyce or chaunce: yet yt seldome happeth for all that, that the partye so falleth in trouble
without some defaute of hym selfe, and that the commen [G₆v]
generall lawe maye not for such seldome specyall happes be
30 forborne. To this pyece lo this good man answereth me thus.

And then mayster More sayth yet farther, that vppon indytementes
at sessyons, the indyters vse not to shewe the names of theym that gaue
them informacyon. And he sayeth farther, that they may not shewe
theyr names. For they may not dysclose the kynges counsayle nor theyr
35 owne. But as I take yt that prohybycyon of openynge of the counsayle
in this case is onely to be vnderstande of theyr own counsayle amonge

22–23 *Sidenote 1557:* For heresye a man shall not know hys accusers.   26 sometyme]
somtime *1557*, tometyme *1533*   31 farther] further *1557*

them selfe, after that they be sworne / but for openynge of the names of theym, that gaue them informacyon before they were sworn, I know no prohibicyon. And yf they wyl not shew theyr names, they be not bounden to do yt / for they be not bounde to helpe the partye to his wryt of conspyracy, but as they lyste to do in conscyence. 5

Nowe good readers all this pretendyd defence, is nothynge ellys in effecte, but a fayre confessyon, that yt is in dede trew the thyng y^t I sayd my selfe, that he whych is endyghted of felony, maye be (as for any aduantage that he can take therby) as ignoraunt somtyme who be his accusers, as he shall in the suyte ex 10 officio. And therby may happen somtyme, that he [G$_7$] whyche is fautelesse shall not be all saued harmelesse / and when he hathe hadde his harme, shalbe remedylesse. And yet for all that the lawe not vnreasonable, nor for auoydynge of myche more harme may not be forborne. And therfore as for my purpose 15 euen at that poynte myghte I haue left, and neded to go no farther. And then as you se this good man had ben quyte answerelesse.

But yet went I farther where me neded not, and that this good man sayth that I dyd of necessyte, wherof for this mater I hadde 20 of trouth no nede. And yet wolde I not nowé but I so hadde done in dede. For I haue therby the better broughte to lyghte, what lacke thys good man hath of any suffycyent answere. For these are there lo good readers therin my farther wordes.

Nowe yf thys pacyfyer saye, that yet here ys at the leste wyse in a 25 *tem*[G$_7$v]*porall iuge an open cause apperyng, whereuppon men maye se that the iudge calleth hym not, but vppon a mater broughte vnto hym / where as the spyrytuall iudge maye call a man vppon his owne pleasure yf he bere the partye dysplesure: thys is very well sayde as for the temporall iudge. But what sayth he now for the temporall .xii. men? For ye wote well* 30 *they maye do the same yf they were so dysposed / and then hadde I as leue the iudge myght do it as they. For in good fayth I neuer saw ye day yet, but that I durste as well trust the trouth of one iudge as of two iuryes. But the iudges be so wyse men, that for the auoydynge of obloquye, they wyl not be put in the truste.* 35

And I dare saye the ordynaryes be not so folyshe neyther, but that they

*wolde as fayne auoyde yt to yf they myghte / sauynge that very necessyte
leste all sholde fall to noughte, compelleth theym to take this waye.*

Here you se that I meane in this [G₈] wordes, that though the
pacyfyer wolde tell me that the temporall iudge hath by suche
5 endyghtement at the leste wyse, an open cause apperynge
wheruppon a man maye se that the iudge calleth hym not of hys
owne mynde, but vppon a mater broughte vnto hym: I wolde
then graunte hym that thys is in dede a good ease to the temporall iudge, to kepe hym oute of obloquye. And the spyrytuall
10 iuges be not so vnwyse, but that they wold be glad of such a
nother pauyce sauynge that they be bounden to take the tother
waye, and suffre them self euyl peples obloquye, for auoydyng
of the harme yᵗ ellys wold folow, by the decay of Cristes catholyke faith. Whyche thynge I there proue well to, as you shall
15 after se. This as I saye wolde I haue graunted allway thys good
man. But then I wold allwaye therwythall haue tolde hym to, that
yet all that tale of hys [G₈v] hadde nothynge touched the poynte /
but that alwaye for all this tale, the man that was indyghted, yf
the mater were in dede vntrew, was neuer the nerer the knowl-
20 edge who were his accusers, to gete any amendes therby, no
more then he that is called of offyce for heresye byfore a
spyrytuall iudge. And here nowe what he sayth to this, and
whyther we be by his answere for the poynt yᵗ was ment by me,
any one ynch yet the nerer. Lo good readers this is hys proper
25 answere.

And then bycause he can none otherwise do, but confesse a great
dyuersyte betwyxte them that be put to answere ex officio, and them
that be putte to answere before the kynges iustyces vppon indytementes at the common lawe: for there the iudges haue suffycyent and
30 apparant mater to put theym to answere vppon, and in the other there
is none, but that the spyrytuall iudge vppon a dyspleasure may do yt ex
officio, yf he wyll. Therfore he goeth yet farther and sayeth, that
the .xii. men maye yet do the same, and make a man to be called that is
not gyltye, yf they were so dysposed. And trouth yt is, they may indyte a
35 man, that is absent, and that is also not gyltye, and be vntrewe, yf they
wyll: but yet in suche case the .xii. men be knowen that do yt, and be

---

8 then] *1533 corr. err.*, *1557*, them *1533*   17 nothynge] nothing *1557*, nothyge
1533   22 here] heare *1557*   35 vntrewe, yf] vntrue. If *1557*

also com[H₁]pelled to be vppon the inquyrye: for they maye not be
vppon it, but they be therto assygned: and also the partye vppon theyre
verdyte shall not be put to answere before theym, as yt is vpon the suyte
Ex officio, but before the kynges iudges, before whome the indytement
is no atteynder to the partie: but that he maye be founde not gyltye, not   5
wythstandynge that indytement. And though mayster More saye, that
he neuer saw the daye yet, but that he durste as well truste the treuth of
one iudge as of two iuryes: I thynke the iudges wyll can hym but lytle
thanke for that preyse: for surely iuryes must nedely be beleued and
trusted. And therfore it is not the maner of the iudges to laye vntrouth   10
vppon a iurye, ne yet to commende theym that do yt, but yt be proued
afore them of recorde after the order of the lawe.

Here you se good readers yᵗ touchynge the poynte that we
spake of, all thys tale helpeth nothynge, but goeth all aboute a
nother mater, to proue a nother dyfference betwene yᵉ suyte of   15
offyce and indyghtementes, as though I had sayd there were no
difference betwene them at all. But I was neuer yet so madde to
be of that mynde. For then must I say they were both one. And
then were euery endytement a suyte of offyce, & euery suit of
offyce an indyghtement, yf there [H₁v] were no dyuersytees   20
betwene them at all.

And therfore yf his dyuersyte shall serue aughte for the purpose: he muste make yt appere that the suyte of offyce bycause
of that dyfference, and bycause yt is not lyke indyghtementes in
that poynte, is therfore in heresye eyther very clerely nought, or   25
ellys that at the lest wyse yt were somwhat better, that they sholde
neuer put any man to answere in heresye, but eyther vppon
open accusacyon or presentement had byfore. For els if he wene
to wynne this poynt of me with shewynge forth a dyfference: if
his difference proue me no such thyng as I tel you, he may for   30
the mater as wel brynge vs forth any verse dyfference at aduenture, that he lerned at grammer scole.

Now when he hath layed al his dyuersyties on an hepe, & wold
theruppon conclude, yᵗ bycause of those diuersyties, yᵉ suyte of
office were nought [H₂] and vnresonable: I say yᵗ foloweth noth-   35
ing: For it proueth yet no farther at the farthest, but yᵗ the order

---

of the comen law were better, & not y^t the tother were nought.
For it myght well be for al that, y^t the commen law might be good
ynough, though they y^t secretly or openly come now & enforme
the queste, came either secretly or openly, and lykewise en-
5   formed the court.

   And now saw I well, that to this poynte was there none answere
for this good man agayne / but to tell me y^t in such thinges as they
now trust the questes, it were parell in stede of iuryes so myche to
truste the courte, by cause the iuges myght then fayn mater
10   agaynste men, and say they were secretely enformed. To this
syth I saw what truste the realme must nedes put in y^e iudges
handes, so farre aboue the wheyghte of the fyrste endyghtement, that serueth for nothynge but for an informacyon and
seynge also what maner of men they [H$_2$v] be that be chosen to
15   be iudges, so that there is nothynge of so great weyght but that yt
well may be put in theyre handes: I rekened theym of suche
trouth, that saue for euyll folkes obloquye, to them selfe warde /
elles to the people there sholde come none harme, though the
truste that we put in thendytours, were in stede of them put in
20   the iudge hym selfe. This I there sayde lo, and this I thynke in
dede. For as I sayde there, I neuer saw yet the day, but y^t I durst
as wel truste the trouthe of one iudge, as I durst truste the trouth
of two iuryes. What hath this good man answered me nowe to
this? To all this gere here is lo his worshyppefull answere.

25   I thynke the iudges wyll can hym but lytle thanke for that prayse. For
surely iuryes must nedes be beleued and trusted. And therfore yt ys not
the maner of the iudges, to lay vntrouth to a iurye / ne yet to commende
them that do yt. But yt be proued afore them of recorde after the order
of the lawe.

30   This answere of trouthe is not worthe a straw. For as for y^t he
sayth [H$_3$] the iudges wyll for that prayse can me lytle thanke:
that word were somwhat, yf I hadde sayde it for theyr thanke.
But I sayd it in good fayth, not for theyr thanke at al, but bycause
yt is very trouth, y^t I neuer saw the day yet in dede, nor neuer I
35   truste in god I shall, but that I may wel and so wyll I do in dede,
trust the trouth of one iudge, as well as the trouth of two iuryes. I
wolde here wytte of this good man, what disprayse is this to any

---

24 worshyppefull] worshipful *1557*, worsyppefull *1533*   32 somwhat] som[*new
line*]what *1553*, somewhat *1557*

iury? what vntrewth is there here layed vnto them, or to any one man of them, I wyll vse one worde now this ones, whych this good man vseth often. For now wyll I saye a lytle farther, and that is this (though this man maye happe to thynke the sayenge straunge) I wyll not let to beleue the trouth of some one man, of whose trouth I make my selfe sure & doute nothyng at al, euen as wel as the trouthe of a great many at ones, [H₃v] though they be all suche as I beleue euery one of theym as well as I beleue hym selfe. And I also byleue some one iuge alone, not in connynge but in trouthe, as well as I wyll beleue both hym selfe & all his felowes to. For some one man may be suche, that if he shold tel me a tale as of his own perfyt knowlege: I wold so litle doute yt to be trew, yᵗ I could beleue yt no better, though all the town told yt with hym. Lo what a great vntrouth I lay here to the iuryes.

And this I say for my selfe. And now wyll I with this good mannys leue, saye yet a lytle farther, and I wene I shall not say so alone. I suppose veryly that there be very few, but so that it myghte make a fynall ende in theyr mater, excepte happely some such as trust more in the fauour of the countrey then in the trouthe of theyr cause: they wold rather be content to put yt whole into the iudges handes, then trouble the countrey [H₄] wyth callynge vppe of the iuryes, whose trouth yet many tymes deceyueth them, that in an euyl cause haue very great truste vnto theym.

And yet in all this saye not I that the commen order and longe contynued law of this realme, to trye the maters by iuryes, & in felony or treason neuer to procede but vpon endyghtementes, is not good / nor that the contrarye waye were better. Mary two thynges I saye, that in treason and felonye this ordynarye lawe of endyghtementes is many tymes fayn to be holpen forth by a nother meane, myche lyke in many thynges to the suyte ex officio / and that ys by dylygent polytyque serche and examynacyons bysyde, both by the kynges honorable counsayle, & the iuges, & iustyces of peace, euery man for theyr parte in euery parte of the realm / & els wold there many such mischiefes passe by & by indightement neuer wold be founden. [H₄v] And some

great and clerely proued felonyes byfore dyuerse and ryghte
worshypfull of the kinges counsayl, haue I wyste ere thys, that
neuer coulde be goten to be founden by endyghtement in theyre
countreys, for all that. How be yt suche examynacyons hathe
5 caused yet many myscheuouse people to be brought to theyre
punyshement / and haue put also many suche other vnthryftes
in fere, & made them refrayn fro theuyng and drawe them selfe
to thryfte / or elles not wytstandyng that there are yet theuys
ynough, there wold be wythout doute many mo.
10   The tother thynge that I wyll say is this, that all these
dyfferences & dyuersyties that this good man putteth here, betwene indyghtementes & the suyte ex officio, proue yet nothing
that the suyte ex officio is not good / but onely at the very vtter-
most, that the ordre not to procede wythoute an [H5] open pre-
15 sentement were better. For as I sayd before, though this lawe by
endyghtementes be better in felony now: yet were not the tother
waye nought, yf the lawe were so that the iudges myght procede
and put felons to answere without endyghtementes / as in treason is vsed in thys realme by the lawe marshall vppon warre
20 rered, as we sawe by experyence in captayne Quintyn, captayn
Genyn, Corbet and Belke. And yet is that lawe not euyll, thoughe
that oure owne comen law be better, and that though we truste
the iuryes neuer so well, yet myght we truste the iudges as well.
And this maye I saye me thynketh without any dysprayse or
25 fawte fyndynge in the iuryes at all. For let him assygne me two
iuryes of very well knowen good men / & than yf he wyll aske me
what fawte fynd you syr in these men: I wyll answer hym, Mary
syr no fawte at all I. I [H5v] take them all for good men & trewe,
and thynke they wyll not saye but treuth / nor I neuer sayd nor
30 thought otherwyse. But than wold I assygne hym by name one of
oure iudges agayne / and say now syr that I truste the trouth of
your two iuryes well, what fawte is that that you fynde in thys
iudges trouth, that maketh you to chekke me so bycause I wyll
trust hym no wurse than I wyll truste them. For that is ye wote
35 well al that euer I sayde, that I wolde trust the iudge as well, and
not that I wolde truste hym better. And yet yf I had sayd I wolde

---

12 proue yet] *1533 corr. err.* proueth *1533 1557*   20–21 Quintyn, captayn Genyn,]
Quintyn, captein Genyn, *1557,* Quintyn captayn Genyn *1533*

of the bothe truste the iudge better: I hadde not by that word neyther, dyspraysed the trouth of iuryes. For he that sayth he wyll better byleue .xxiiii. than .xii, dysprayseth not the trouth of the petit iuries, but byleueth theym well also, saue suche as be founden false. And thus I haue shewed you that I may well [H₆] say the wordes that I sayd, without any fyndynge of any fawte in any iuryes. And it appereth also metely well, that hym selfe can not well say the contrary, that is to wyt that he wil not trust a iuge so well: thys can he not saye wythoute some maner of dystrust in theyr trouth. And yet syth theyr wurshyppys be so well knowen that this good mannys dystruste can not apayre it: they wyll I dare saye forgeue hym. How be it sith the iudges wold (as this man sayth, and as I dare also saye they wolde) be sore dyscontent wyth me, yf I dystrusted the trouth of the iuryes: the iuryes may now no lesse do agayne of courtesye, than for his wurse opinion of the iudges trouth some what be angry wyth hym.

Nor herin se I none other shyfte for this good man, but for the mayntenaunce of hys mater to saye, that in the comen law, the law wold be good inough in felonye, though the truste were put in the iudges, to putte tray[H₆v]tours and felons to answere wythout indyghtement / but in heresye it coulde not be good before an ordynarye / and wolde laye for hys cause a dyuersyte bytwene the tone iudge & the tother, and saye that oure iudges be good men and worshypful, & euer haue ben and euer shall / and that the ordynaryes be, and euer haue bene, & shalbe, very false & nought. Other shyfte hath this man none that I se than euyn to saye thus. And veryly his boke of diuisyon, saue that it saith nothynge to the prayse of temporall iudges that I now remember: yet to the dysprayse of the spyrytuall, for those algates that be now, saith euyn in effecte as mych, ye and rather yet wurse to, saue that yᵉ colour of some say saueth hym from sayenge it hym selfe.

But now yf he defend hym selfe with that fasshyon agayne: what the iuryes wyll say that can I not tell / [H₇] for the panellys be not yet called. But as for oure iudges, I knowe theyr wyse-

---

8–9 contrary, that is to wyt that he wil not trust a iuge so well: thys can he not saye wythoute] *1533 corr. err.*, contrary without *1533*, contrarye withoute *1557*   12 hym.] *1557*, hym *1533*   25 bene] *1557*, beue *1533*

doms and theyr wurshyppys such, that I am very sure in his so
sayenge and his so lyenge vppon the spyrituall iudges, they
wolde can hym no thanke at all.

And veryly that the spyrytual ordinaryes be not at these dayes
5 lykely to be such, ye temporall iudges beyng so good as they be:
there is amonge many other one lykelyhed this, that he hath
chosen the tone that hath chosen the tother, the kynges gracyouse hyghnesse hym selfe / whiche hauyng on both sydes very
good to chose of, hath I dare say ben as cyrcumspecte in chos-
10 ynge of thordynaryes, as of ye iudges. And yet leste in theyr absence the offycers of theyr owne choyse might happe to misseordre ye maters: his grace kepeth not two bysshoppes of all the
realm out of theyr diocises, nor to say the trouth not so myche as
[H7v] one. For he whose attendaunce hys grace vseth moste, is
15 far the moste parte of the yere in hys owne dyocise euery daye.

And therfore as I sayd before, all these verse dyfferences, and
all these dyuersytees, whiche thys good man layeth bytwen the
suit ex officio in heresye, & the not procedynge with out indyghtementes vpon treason or felony, proueth at the very fer-
20 theste not that the suit ex officio is noughte, but that not to
procede but vpon a presentement were the better a way. And
than I saye that it is a pore tale and a colde, yf a man wolde come
forth & labour vs to breke euery olde lawe longe vsed in this
realme, whyche he could not proue but that it were good
25 inough / but yet wolde nedes haue it chaunged, bycause that if it
were now to make, hym selfe coulde he sayth make it better.

But now wyll I come a lytell [H8] nerer vnto this good man,
wyth the tother poynte y^t I towched before / y^t is to wytte that it is
not in thys mater inough for this good man, to proue vs that not
30 to procede wythout open accusacion or presentement is the better waye, bothe vppon treason and felonye, but yf he proue vs
ferther, that the same waye were also better in heresye.

But thanne haue I shewed byfore in myne apologye, that in
heresye that waye wyll not serue. And that haue I there proued
35 by the playneste profe that in suche maner thynges any man can

---

make, that is to wytte by comon open experyence / wherunto
thys good man of polycy wolde geue none eare, but in hys answere he hath left it quyte out.

And therein he fareth lo lyke a geste, that maketh hys rekenynge hym self without his hoste / which is [H₈v] therfore
after fayne to reken agayn / as I shall nowe brynge in here one
peny more into this good mannes rekenynge, whyche I perceyue
well hym selfe wold very fayne forgete. Lo thus wrote I ferther
good readers towchynge thys poynte in that selfe same chapiter
of myne apology folio .226.

But yet wyll peraduenture thys pacyfyer saye, that sometyme in some very
specyall case, he coulde be content that the spyrytuall iudge shold vpon hys
dyscrecyon call one for suspycyon of heresye ex officio / but he wolde not
haue men comenly called, but eyther by accusacyon or presentement in
theyr senys or endyghtementes at the comon lawe. I had as lyefe for any
thynge that I se, that thys pacyfyer sholde say thus: By thys way that they be
called I wolde not haue them called / but I wolde haue them called after
suche an order as they myght be sure that than sholde they neuer be called.
[I₁] For as for accuse folke openly for heresye, euery man hath experyence
inough, that ye shall seldome fynde any man that wyll / but yf the iudge
shold set an officer of the court therto wythout any perell of expensys / and
than were thys way and that way all of one effecte. And as for presente-
mentes and endyghtementes, what effecte wolde come of them concern-
ynge heresye, ye se the profe I trowe metely well all redy.

For thys is a thyng well knowen vnto euery man, that in euery sene,
euery sessyon of peace, euery sessyon of gaole delyuery, euery lete thorough
the realme, the fyrste thynge that the iury haue gyuen them in charge is
heresye. And for all thys, thorow the whole realme how many presente-
mentes be there made in the whole yere? I wene in some seuen yere not one.
And I suppose no man dowteth, but that in the meane time some there be. I
wyll not be curiouse about the serchyng out of yᵉ cause, why it is eyther
[I₁v] neuer or so very selde presented, not fyue in fyftene yere. But thys I
saye that syth some wyl not, some can not, and none doth / yf he sholde put
a way the processe ex officio, the thyng shold be lefte vndone / and than
shold soone after with heretykes encreaced and multyplied, the fayth be
vndone / and after that thorough the stroke of god reuengyng theyr

5

10

15

20

25

30

35

25–28 *Sidenote 1557:* Heresye in al sessions is the firste thynge that is charged.   32
yere] *om. 1557*

malyce and our neglygence, sholde by sedycyon, & trouble, and derth, &
deth, in thys realme many men bothe good and badde be vndone. And
therfore for conclusion of this pyece, my pore aduyce & counsayle shalbe,
that for heresye, and specyally now thys tyme, men shall suffer the pro-
5   *cesses ex officio stande / and for as many other synnys also as are onely*
reformable by the spyrytuall law, excepte there be any such synnys of theym
as ye thynke were good to growe.

What hath this good man good readers sayd vnto this pyece?
what shall we good reders say now to this [I₂] good man? yᵗ in this
10 goodly answere of his, whiche he wolde were taken for so
stronge, vnto this piece vppon whiche great part of the mater
hangeth, sayth not so mych as mum / but letteth it slippe euyn by,
as though he were one yᵗ had as for this point ben born defe &
therby dumme.

15   And now concernynge this poynt, I wyll yet saye a lytle ferther,
that in places mo than one, good euidence haue ben geuen vnto
questes of playn & open heresye, whych yet wolde not fynde it /
yᵗ wold vpon mych lesse euydence, haue shortely presented
felony.

20   And one of these maters wyth the prest yᵗ preched it whan I
was chauncellour, was brought vnto me by ryghte wurshupfull
folke, yᵗ before me aduowed it in his face. And yet coulde not all
they cause the quest to present it, but some folke bygan to fal to
fauour hym / & had he not ben taken by good wurshypfull
25 temporall men, many wold haue flocked after hym, [I₂v] & haue
folowed hym about for pleasure of hys new fasshyon prechynge.
And yet for all that flockyng, though they had made .ii. or .iii.
hundred as they sholde happely within a whyle yf a few good
men had not letted it: they had ben yet but an handfull to theyr
30 good catholyke neyghbours / and yet by such flockynge togyther, and folowynge on a plumpe, they sholde haue semed in
folkes eyen farre the more parte / and at length peraduenture yf
they went on & were not letted, they myght grow to it in dede.

That preste I delyuered vnto his ordynary, and that with good
35 and playne profe of his heresye / whyche was in dede soone after
that abiured. But for this I tell it you, that yᵉ iury wolde not fynde

---

1–2 *Sidenote 1557:* The plages that folow vpon heresy.   4–5 processes] *1557,* pre-
esses *1533*   13 as though] as thoughe *1557,* asthough *1533*   28 happely] haply
1557, hahpely *1533*   36 abiured.] *1557,* abiured *1533*

it for all the good folke that gaue them open euydence. And that
this is not in one case, nor a thynge that happeth seld, as I sayd in
myne apology, playne experyence [I₃] proueth. Wherby you
maye se, that in heresy yf the iudge sholde not ex officio procede, tyll the mater were presented by yᵉ iuryes: heretikes myght   5
be bolde to procede on a pace and so they wold I warraunt you,
and multyply full faste.

And thus you se good readers, yᵗ concernyng this pyece, this
good man hath in euery point a gret ouerthrow.

And therfore now the last clause of this .xv. chapyter of his, is   10
clerely wrested awry. For as though he had all proued, where all
is dysproued: he fynysheth hys chapyter thus.

And thus it appereth, that mayster More can neyther proue the suyte
Ex officio to be lyke to the arrestynge of men for suspycyon of felonye,
or for good aberynge, to puttynge of men to answere vpon indyte-   15
mentes, ne yet to them that may be accused by .xii. men, and knowe not
of it, and that for the causes before remembred. Wherfore it semeth,
that though it were clerely putte awaye, the stretes shulde not swarme
full of heretykes neuer a whyt.

This good man sayth here I can not proue any of al these   20
thynges like. But euery man may wel se, that lyst [I₃v] to loke
backe and rede it, that there is not any one piece of all these that
he speketh of, but I haue very playnely proued it very lyke, for yᵉ
purpose & entent that I resemble it for. And this shall euery man
clerely se, that wyll aduise pyece by pyece.   25

And therfore whyle vpon dyfferences & dyuersytees that he
putteth bytwen them, such as let them not to be lyke in the thyng
that I lyken them for, he bosteth in conclusyon yᵗ I can not proue
them lyke: I shall shewe you what thyng now this bost of his is
lyke.   30

If it had come in this good mannes hed, to diuise a law and
wryte a boke therfore, to kyll vp all the band dogges thorow out
all yᵉ realme (wherin his tyme as vnwysely as it were bestowed,
had not yet ben so ill spent as it hath ben in this) and than wold
lay for the cause, yᵗ bandogges do spende vitayle, & wyll som-   35
tyme byte folke [I₄] to: yf I wolde than wryte agaynste his wyse

---

boke, and say that he myght by that reason kyll vp houndes and grayhoundes & all, for they must eate to, and wyll somtyme byte chyldren to / but lykewyse yet as they maye not yet for all that be forborne, bothe for the pleasure that they do, and also for that
5　they helpe to take vs some suche bestes of venory as men eate, and hunte and kyll also suche other bestes and vermyn, as ells wolde destroye mych vytayle / so the banddogges may not be forborne neither, for they both defende husband mennes howses fro theues, & helpe folke home with theyr bestes to som-
10　tyme, such as wold not ellys come home: now myghte this good man by this reason y^t he vseth here, write agayne & defend his polytike deuice agaynst bandogges / & therin answer me thus. Fyrst y^t for defence of folkes houses there shal nede no bandogges at all / [I₄v] for men may make theyr seruauntes watche,
15　or make fast all theyr dorys / and whan theues wolde breke in, defende theyr howses them selfe. And as for suche bestes as wold not come home, yf they be not ouer heuy they may bere them home / and those that be to heuy to be borne home, taye ropes to there taylys and drawe theym home. And than myght he saye yet
20　a lytell ferther / and that is this, that he merueiled mych y^t I could for shame and fere of myne own conscyence resemble & lyken together, gentle houndes or goodly greyhoundes, to such il fauored mastyffes. And than to proue them very farre vnlyke put his dyfferences & his dyuersitees, and saye a mastyffe hath
25　you wote well a great iolte hed, & a great mosel & a thycke boystuouse body / where as a greyhound hath a proper hed, with a goodly smal long snowt, & fayre long slender sydes / & the houndes yet mych lesse lyke to. [I₅]

　　And theruppon myght he there conclude (as he nowe con-
30　cludeth here) and saye thus.

　　And thus it appereth that maister More can neyther proue ye mastyfes to be lyke to ye greyhoundes, nor to the tother gentle houndes neyther, and that for the causes before remembred. Wherfore yt semeth that though all bandogges and mastiffes
35　were clerely putte awaye: yet mennys houses sholde be defended well inough, and theyre bestes broughte home well ynough to, so they sholde lo.

---

28 to.] *1557*, to / and *catchword 1533*　　29 And] *no para. 1557*　　34 Wherfore] Wherfore *1557*, wherfore *1533*

Nowe yf he ryally tryumphed vppon this, and thought he had auoyded me well: I could no farther go therin in good fayth, but let him take that glorye to hym. And surely wyth any wyse man that readeth ouer here in this chapyter, both hys wordes and myne, and one after a nother consydereth wherfore I resemble 5 theym to gether: shall fynde I dare boldely [I₅v] warraunt, that wyth his dyfferences and hys dyuersytees, he wynneth lyke wor-shyppe in thys.

But now to turne agayn as I promysed to the fyrste poynte, that ys to wyt his deuise of open accusers: consyder well this good 10 chrysten reader, that where as this good man in his boke of diuysyon, where he wold haue the suit ex officio left of: he then reserued vs yet both open accusacyons and presentementes, to put heretyques to answere vpon. But nowe in this .xv. chapiter of his, in his boke of Salem & Bizance, for fauour towarde the 15 catholyque fayth, he dyuyseth no more agaynst heretyques but open accusers alone / and sayeth that open accusers shall suffy-ciently serue the mater. And vnto yᵗ here yᵗ I say, and that euery man seeth, that no man wyll in heresy make hym self a partye by way of open accusyng: therto saith thys good man nothynge. [I₆] 20

He seeth perdy very well, that in many thynges forboden by sondry statutes for the comen weale, as agaynste the great excesse of apparell and some such other thynges: yᵉ law dothe inuyte and hyre euery man to thaccusynge of the brekers of yᵉ same by geuynge theym the tone halfe of the forfaytoure. And 25 yet for all that as longe & as many lawes, & as sore as haue ben made agaynste suche excesse of apparayle, and as myche as some men myght haue wonne by the suyt: yet howe fewe folke haue ben founden that haue taken those accyons and therby accused those offenders, the kynges courtes can declare, and 30 the lytle amendement may shew.

Ryottes be open thynges and enquyrable, with paynes also set vpon yᵉ concelours, yet many great ryottes go by vnfounde & yᵉ concelours neuer spoken of / & a statut was there fayn to be made, yᵗ it myght be pursued, & punished by the kinges coun- 35 sayle without [I₆v] presentement, and that euen by suyte in man-er ex officio to. For though the partyes that made the ryot, and the partye vppon whome yt was made, were so well agreed

4 chapyter] chapter *1557*   25 forfaytoure] forfaiture *1557*

agayne, that neyther nother wolde by theyre wylles haue the
mater moued or any more spoken of it: yet may the kynges
counsayle vpon secrete informacion, cause the kynges atturney
to make a byll of the ryot, and put the partyes to answere, and
5 sende for what wytnesses they wyll.

Nowe thys man wyll not be so madde I trowe to lay me for a
defference, that in the suyte ex officio there is none accuser, and
that here the kynges atturney is. For as I haue sayde byfore yf the
spyrytuall courte sholde assygne in lyke wyse an offycer of
10 theyre owne wythoute eyther parell or coste: what wolde y^t
auayle the partye?

If this good man had therfore dy[I$_7$]uised rewardes for accusers, & great paynes of forfaytours for them that wolde con-
ceyle and hyde: yet wolde not all that haue holpen well the mater
15 in heresyes. And weneth he then y^t his bare diuise of open accusers alone, neyther compelled nor hyred, wyll helpe yt? Nay
not and take endytementes and presentementes to them, wyth
paynes set vppon the conceylours to.

And this hathe all chrystendome good chrysten reders per-
20 ceyued / and therfore in euery good chrysten countrey, do they
vse the same suyt of offyce (whyche vppon a lyghte reason this
man calleth vnreasonable) and haue vsed many longe yeres.
Thys lawe also whych this good man thus impugneth vppon his
owne vnreasonable reason, was thoughte a lawe ryght reason-
25 able as I tolde you in a generall counsayle at Rome there holden
by pope Innocent the thyrde [I$_7$v] and many great wyse & well
lerned vertuous men there at. There were thembassyatours of
all the realmes and countreys chrystened / & amonge tother
thembassiatours of England. There were thembassiatours of
30 both the emperours, y^t is to wyt of Almayne & Grece. There were
also y^e .iiii. gret patriarches / y^t is to wyt ye patriarche of Anti-
ochia, & the patriarche of Alexandria by theyr deputies / & the
patriarche of Constantinople, & the patriarche of Hierusalem in
theyr own proper persons. In this great ful & whole counsayle of
35 crystendome, was this lawe agreed & approued. And from y^e

---

13 forfaytours] forfaitures *1557*   27 thembassyatours] thembassitours *1557*   28–
29 tother thembassiatours] thother thembassitours *1557*   29 were thembassiatours]
were thembassitours *1557*   30 of] *1533 corr. err., om. 1533 1557*

fyrst makyng al cristen countreys receiued yt / & haue by the
contynuall vse euer syns alowed it. And this realm hath found it
so necessary, y^t by statutes yt hath strengthed it. And al trew
cristen countreis to this day styll obserue it / nor no countrey
hath there any where left & forsaken it, except such places [I$_8$]   5
onely as haue lefte and forsaken the fayth of Chryst wyth all /
whose ensamples I truste thys realme is to faythfull to folowe,
vpon such good reason as this good man here bryngeth / wherof
the very whole summe when it is gathered to gether, amounteth
to no more, but that yt may some tyme happen, that an innocent   10
maye take harme therby / a reason that ones receiued, may
suffre no law to stand. For what lawe can he geue so made in al
this world, wherby none innocent can possibly take hurt? But
here you se playnely proued agaynst this good man, that by the
chaungynge, there wolde surely folowe a nother maner of per-   15
ell, the decay of the catholyque fayth by thencoragyng of heretikes / whiche wold be well content that we made lawes to burne
theym twyse when they be proued heretykes, so y^t the good
counsayle of this good man be folowed, that the suyte ex officio
maye be chaunged into suche open [I$_8$v] accusers, as in seuen   20
yere shall neuer one come forth, nor one heretyque of lykelyhed
ones be put to answere / with a nother good counsayle of thys
good mannys also dyuysed for theyr farther saufegard agaynst
arrestyng of them, wherof we be to speke afterwarde in a nother
chapyter. Say this good man what he wyll, yf we breke thys lawe   25
so longe approued thorowe crystendome, and take hys deuyse in
the stede: his worde wyll neuer so stay the thynge, but that after
his wayes ones taken, and by his newe euyll counsayle the good
olde lawes broken, men sholde shortely se wythout any doute
great encrease of heretykes / whych, where as they were wonte   30
but to crepe to gether in corners, and secretely scoulke to gether
in lurkes lanys, shall sone wax bolde and put oute theyr hornes
and flocke and swarm to gether so thycke in thopen stretes, y^t
such myschyefe [K$_1$] wolde fynally folowe theron, as wo wyll
euery good man be that sholde lyue to se yt. And yet wolde god   35
of his goodnes turne at length the chief harme vppon theyre

6 Chryst with all /] *1533 corr. err.*, Chryst / wyth all *1533*, Christe, wyth all *1557*   21
lykelyhed] lykelyhod *1557*   32 lanys] *1533 corr. err.*, lanes *1557*, lauys *1533*

heddes. But better folke sholde fyrst fele so mych therof, that it
were better for bothe, that by these good lawes well kepte
whyche thys good man wolde breke, these heretyques be well
repressed, and kepte vnder by tymes.

5   The .xvi. chapyter.

HIS .xvi. chapyter begynneth in yᵉ .liiii. lefe, wherin he fyrste
recyteth agayne hys own wordes writen in his boke of diuisyon
wherin he disputed agaynst the lawe in the chapyter Accusatus,
perag. Licet, wherby yt is ordyned yᵗ though one beynge accused
10 & sworne [K₁v] confesse nothyng, and yet afterward he confesseth bothe of hym selfe and other, such thynges as it may wel
appere, that yf he were not forsworen in the secunde, he was
forsworen in the fyrste, and yet that lawe there admytteth hym
for a witnesse in yᵗ same court and in that mater of heresye, yf
15 there appere manifeste tokens that he doth it not of lightnesse of
mynde, nor of hatered, nor for other corrupcyon / whych he
sayth is therfore a daungerouse law, and more lyke to cause
vntrew and vnlawfull men to condemne innocentes, then to condempne offenders.
20   And you shall vnderstand good reders, yᵗ in his boke of diuisyon, he not onely dyd impugne the law that he speketh of here /
but also a nother chapyter In fidei fauorem, bycause that therby
suche as are accursed, & suche as are partyes to the same offence,
shalbe wytnesse in heresye.
25   This reason of his good reader, all be yt that me then thought
and yet [K₂] thynke so vnresonable, that I rekened yt lytle worth
the answeryng, as a reason reproued by yᵉ comen law & by the
course & vsage of all realmes chrystened, and in other crymes
bysyde heresye playnely reproued, and yᵉ contrary wel vsed in
30 this realm here also: yet in yᵉ .xli. chapiter of myn apologie fo.
cc.xxviii. in this maner wyse I answered hym.
This pyece concernynge the testymonye of knowen euyll persons to be
receyued and taken in heresye / I haue somewhat touched in the thyrde
chapyter of the thyrde boke of my dyaloge / where syth they maye reade yt
35 *that wyll, I wyll make here no longe tale agayne therof. But well he woteth*

---

14 yᵗ] the *1557*

that heresye, wherby a Chrysten man becometh a false traitour to god is in
all lawes spyrytuall and temporall bothe, accompted as great a cryme as is
the treason commytted agaynst any worldely man. And then why sholde
we fynde so great a faute, that suche wytnesse sholde be recey[K₂v]ued in
a cause of heresye, as are receyued not onely in a cause of treason, but of
murder also, and of other more syngle felonye / not onely in fauour of the
prynce, and detestacyon of such odyouse crymes, but also for the necessyte
whyche the nature of the mater wurketh in yᵉ profe. For syth euyl folke vse
not to make good folke of counsayle in doynge of theyre euyll dedes / those
that are done, shold passe vnpunyshed, and mo lyke be commytted a
freshe, but yf they were receyued for recordes to theyre condempnynge,
that were of theyre counsayle and perteners to the doynge. Whyche kynde
of folke wyll not lette to swere twyse nay, before they confesse ones ye / and
yet theyr one ye more trewe vppon theyr bare worde, then theyre twyse naye
vppon a solempne othe / and yet confesse they not so symplye, but that it is
commenly holpen wyth some suche cyrcumstaunces as make the mater
more clere. [K₃]

Nowe as to those thynges that I wrote in my dialoge concernyng great crymynouse wytnesses to be taken in great criminall
causes, he answereth wyth no worde at all. How be yt to say the
trouth he the lesse neded. For he geueth ouer here, al that faute
that he founde in the chapyter In fidei fauorem, as a thynge
wherin hym self seeth now that he was ouersene than and therfore he letteth that here passe by, as though he hadde neuer
spoken therof, and stycketh onely vppon yᵗ one case of hym yᵗ is
ones forsworen.

But now let vs se what he sayth here concernynge this selfe
same case. Fyrst he saith yᵗ yᵉ lawes, though they must deuyse
suche ways as euyll persons maye be punyshed: yet the makers of
the lawes must (as mych as in them is) prouyde that innocentes
shalbe saued harmelesse. This is very trew as myche as in them
is / the tother poynt beynge prouyded for to, [K₃v] that offendours maye be punyshed. But then say I yᵗ yt is not in all the
wittes of the world, for punyshement of myscheuouse wreches,
to dyuyse a lawe in suche wyse, that men maye be sure that none
innocent can take harme therby. And then yf he graunt me this

---

1 *Sidenote 1557:* Heresye.   8 For] *1533 corr. err.,* But *1533 1557*   12 Whyche]
Whych *1557,* whyche *1533*

(whyche whyther he graunt or no, yet very trew yt is) then say I
that his onely reason agaynst the suit ex officio, and agaynst this
lawe to, that is to wytte that innocentes maye take harme therby,
ys such a reason y^t yf it were folowed in euery law wherby mysse-
5 guyded folke are punyssed, there shold no law stand for theyr
punyshement at al, but lest it myght missehappe that some innocent myght take harme, we sholde lette all myscheuouse folke
alone, & therby suffre many mo good innocent men take harme.
But then goeth this good man ferther & sayth y^t the punishe-
10 ment of an offender must be by a dew & a reaso[K$_4$]nable order.
And y^t is very trew also / & therfore we shal agre well in that. But
than goth he ferther and sayth,

I can not se what dew or resonable order of tryal it is that he y^t vpon his
oth hath fyrst clered hym self & his neyghbour of heresyes, sholde after
15 contrarye to his fyrste othe, be receyued agayne as a wytnesse, to condemne hym that he clered byfore, and that in the same courte, and in
the same mater.

Though this good man can not se yt: other men can se yt / and
haue sene it, & dayly do se it to wel ynough. I haue sene suche
20 thynges as thys is my selfe proued, I can not tell howe often, that
in the excuse of a thefe some haue taken an othe, that the felon
was with hym in hys owne house at suche tyme as the felonye
sholde be done in a nother place. And a man wolde haue wente
he hadde ben credyble and sayd trouth. And yet afterwarde
25 hathe hym selfe confessed that the felon and hym selfe also were
at the robberye bothe twayne / and hys bare worde then more
trewe, then byfore was hys solempne othe. [K$_4$v] And euery man
that hathe medeled myche wyth suche examynacyons, hath a
sure experyence, that this ys a commen fashyon of murderers
30 and theuys and such as are theuys receyuours / of whome at the
fyrste face some seme honest men, & are so some tyme reputed,
and come forth for declaracyon of them that are suspected and
in trouble, and depose for them / and yet after vppon some other
occasyon in examynynge of the mater, begynne to be suspected
35 theym selfe, and afterwarde confesse yt to, bothe of them selfe

---

4 ys] *1533 corr. err.*, is *1557*, if *1533*   6 punyshement] punishment *1557*, punyshe-
nent *1533*

and theym whom they came to clere by theyr periury before.
And I am very sure there be not a fewe that haue herd suche
euydence, geuen in causes of felony dyuerse tymes to the iurye.

But hereuppon bycause I spake in myne apologye of suche
witnesses in felonye: thys good man maketh here a doute / what   5
maner wytnesses [K₅] I mene / whyther I mene yᵉ .xii. men that
are the iury, or other wytnessys that are brought into the court
for to enforme them. And than fyrst if I mene the .xii. men, than
he answereth me certayn thynges, to shew that he can skyll of the
law. But veryly as for me, I shal put hym out of that dowt, that I   10
ment not them. For I neuer toke the .xii. men for wytnessys in
my lyfe. For why shold I call them witnesses, whose verdycte the
iudge taketh for a sure sentence concernynge the facte, without
any examynacyon of the cyrcumstaunces, wherby they know or
be ledde to byleue theyr verdicte to be trew?   15

And also wherfore shold I mene to call them wytnesses,
whome I se desyre wytnesses at the barre to enforme them in the
mater, as wytnessys enforme a iudge? He myghte therfore haue
spared hys labour in yᵗ pyece well inough. For I neyther [K₅v]
ment the iurye, nor neuer toke theym for wytnesse.   20

If he wyll aske me what they be than: I saye they be the iury.
And yf he wyll wyt ferthermore what person they represent of
those yᵗ are vsuall in other courtes wherin there be no iuryes
vsed: that can I metely wel tell hym to yf the tale were as necessary as it wolde be longe.   25

But than cometh he to the tother parte and sayth,

And yf mayster More by that terme, witnesse, mene suche wytnesse, as
be somtyme brought into the kynges courtes, to geue euydencys to an
enquest, than is that wytnesse no suche wytnesse, as the wytnesse bene
in the spyrytuall courte, that shall acquyte or condempne the partyes: 30
for of those wytnesse so brought into the kynges court to geue euydence to an enqueste at the comon lawe, no mencyon shall be made in
the recordes, ne the iury be not bound alway to folow tho wytnesse. For
yf the iury of theyr owne knowlege or otherwyse know the trouth
agaynste the sayenge of suche wytnesse, they be bounden to fynde   35

12–15 *Sidenote 1557:* The verdicte of .xii. men, is vnto the iudge a sentence.   24 that]
1533 corr. err., than *1533,* then *1557*   33 tho wytnesse] the wytnesse *1557*

accordynge to the trouth, and let tho wytnes go. And yet yf it hapned, that such collaterall wytnes fyrst testyfyed upon theyr othe, that the partye were not gylty: and after it were informed the iudges, that they reuoked theyr fyrst sayeng, and wold saye that the partye were gylty: I

5 can not thynke, [K₆] that the iudges wolde any more calle them to here theyr sayenge therin. And though they wolde, yet as I sayd before, it were farre vnlyke to thys case. For theyr sayenge there, is but as an euydence, whiche the iury sholde not be bounde to byleue, but as ye truth is. I can not se therfore, how mayster More can proue his

10 sayenge, that suche wytnesses, that is to say, suche as be periured in the same court, shulde be afterward receyued as wytnes in any of the kynges courtes.

 Now good readers euer more remember this, that it is not inough for hym that wyl auoyde a resemblaunce bytwen two

15 thynges, it is not inough I saye for hym to proue that in some poyntes those two thynges are vnlyke / (for so muste euery two thynges nedes be, for ellys were they not two but one) but he muste proue that they be vnlyke in the self same point wherin, and to the self same purpose wherfore, they were so resembled

20 to gether.

 And now I say that in that poynt for that purpose for whyche I resemble them, I say that they be lyke. I dyd not say that they were lyke in the maner of the examynacyon, and [K₆v] puttynge of theyr names and theyr deposycyons in the recorde, in whych

25 thynges this man sayth & I confesse that they be vnlyke / but I sayde that they were lyke in this point, that lyke as he that hath bene sworne and clered one as farre forth as in hym was of heresy, may yet be receyued sworen agayn & herd, and by his new contrary deposycyon may hurt the same party whom he dyd

30 clere, before the same spyrytuall iudge, whyche lawfully may geue credence vnto hym vppon certayne cyrcumstaunces by his wysedome well wayed / so maye in lyke wyse he that hath ben sworn, and by his othe clered a man as myche as in hym was of felony, be yet receyued and sworne agayne and herd, and by hys

35 new contrary deposycyon maye hurte the same partye whom he dyd before clere in a temporall court, before the selfe same

---

1 tho wytnes] the wytnes *1557* 26 sayde that] sayde *1557*

iudges / by the reason that the iury maye lawfully byleue hym in the seconde othe, vppon [K₇] certayne consyderacyons by theyr wysedoms wysely wayed, notwithstandyng his formar othe in the same court to the contrary.

And all be it that here before I thought vppon no ferther than vpon such wytnesses taken before the kynges counsayle, or iustyces of yᵉ peace men of wurshyppe in the cuntrey, & afterwarde those deposycyons with such contrary othes and all the cyrcumstaunces therwith geuen in euydence to the iury at the barre, in the face of the kynges ordinary court, syttynge vppon the deliueraunce of the prysoner: yet syth this good man dissymuleth that poynt, and draweth me forth before the iudges, I am well content to wayte vpon hym thyther. And I nothynge dowt but that euyn there he shold, the case myght so fal, fynde it trewe that I tell hym.

That is not so sayth this good man. For yf it happened that such col[K₇v]laterall wytnesses, fyrste testyfyed vpon theyr othe that the party were not gilty / and after it were enformed the iudges that they reuoked theyr fyrst sayenge, and wolde say that the party were gylty: I can not thynke that the iudges wolde any more call them to here theyr sayenge therin.

Here you se good reders that he proueth thys poynt by none other thynge, than onely by his owne thynkyng. Now albe it yᵗ against his thinkynge that they wolde not, it were inough for me to saye that I thynke they wolde: yet wyll I not leue it so bare, but I wyll shew some cause wherfore in some case they sholde / & I wyll also put you some such case, whiche if the case happed I nothyng dowt but they wolde.

Fyrst the cause wherfore a person ones periured is repelled from beryng wytnesse agayn, is bycause the lawe presumeth that he setteth not so mych by an othe, but that his oth notwith[K₈]standyng he were likely inough to lye.

Now syth this presumpcyon is the generall let, and therfore the reason of the generall law: yf the case happen that this presumpcyon be more than countrepaysed with a contrary pre-

---

8 deposycyons] deposicions *1557*, deposycyous *1533*; othes] *1557*, ohtes *1533*   29–
32 *Sidenote 1557:* why a periured person is repelled from bearyng wytnes agayne.

sumpcyon vpon the tother syde, there is ye contrary presumpcyon a reason sufficyent, to make in y^t case a contrary law, or a
law that shalbe for that case an excepcyon out of that generall
rule.

5 Now syr as he y^t on his oth clereth hym self & his felow to,
eyther in heresye or in felonye, doth after confesse & swere also
the contrary: yf we wold not byleue him in ye secund oth, bicause
we fynde hym therby periured in the fyrst / than in that we iudge
hym in y^e fyrst to haue sworen false, it implieth that euyn therby
10 we iudge hym in the secunde to say trewe.

If we wyll refuse his secund oth, and not thynke hym worthy to
be byleued, bycause that he sware the con[K$_8$v]trary byfore, &
therby presume hym a false shrewe whan he sholde by the secunde othe proue hym selfe ones periured, and than we could
15 not tell in whyther othe of the twayne: here I say the fyrste
presumpcion is ouerborne wyth the secunde. For it is an other
presumpcyon that no man wyl caste awaye his soule for nought.
And yet a greater presumpsyon that no man wyll cast awaye his
soule, to do hurt eyther to his owne body or to his frendes.

20 Now loke me than vppon this mannes two othes, his fyrst othe
and his secund. And though there be a comon presumpcyon
therin also, wherupon the credence of all othes resteth, that is to
wyt that a man reputed good & honest, wyl not for his frendes
body nor for his owne neyther, caste hys soule awaye by periury:
25 yet whan hym selfe after sheweth vppon hys seconde othe, that
he was periured in [L$_1$] the fyrste, the presumpcyon of hys
trouth in his fyrst oth, is taken away by the secunde.

Now the secund if it be to thaccusynge of hym selfe & his
frende both, whome his fyrste othe excused, hath these other
30 two presumpcyons for to bere agaynst the fyrst presumpcyon
generall of his vntrouth for his periury. The tone, that though it
be presumed in the law, y^t he wolde be false and forsworen for
somwhat: yet is it presumed that he wyll not be forsworen for
ryght nought. And yet as I sayed it is more strongely presumed
35 that he wyll not be forsworen to the hurt of hym selfe and hys
frend. And therfore hath hys secunde othe inough to bere it

---

agaynste the fyrste, syth in the fyrste he sware for his frendes
aduauntage and his owne, for whiche (syth he nowe appereth
false in the tone othe or the tother) he was than lykely to be
forsworen. [L₁v] And in the secunde yf he were forsworen, it
were to theyr both harme. And therfore is that othe presumed to   5
be trewe, though the man hym self be presumed false.

This is I trowe to no man any dowt, but that though a man had
ben openly periured thryes: yet yf the worlde myght (as it may
not) be sure that in another mater he wold for all that swere
trewe, the worlde wolde receyue his othe. Now for as myche as of   10
no mannys oth any man can be so sure, but that he maye be by
possybylyte deceyued: the law goth as farforth as it can, and
taketh theyr othes for a profe, whych are in that case by presumpcyon lykely to swere trewe. And syth that he therfore
whom the respecte of his frendes saufgarde & hys owne, gaue   15
occasyon to be forsworen in the fyrst, in the secund swereth
contrary wyse to theyr bothe parell & harme: therfore in yᵗ case
reason [L₂] bereth yᵉ law, yᵗ in such heyghnous crimes his secund
oth shold be receyued.

Here haue I shewed you a reason whych semeth me sufficient,   20
that bothe in heresye and felony, the iudges sholde be content
not withstandyng the fyrste othe, in some case to suffer hym
swere the contrary.

But now for the temporal courtes, let vs put some case for a
sample, to se whyther yᵉ iudges wolde yf yᵉ case happed so, here 25
yᵉ witnes again or not.

I wyl not put the case in treason, wherin there wolde I wene be
no dowte / but that yf after his euydence gyuen vppon his othe in
clerynge there the prysoner, he happed euyn sodaynly there at
the barre to repent hym selfe, & say that he was hyred to be   30
forsworen, & that he was forsworen in dede, & than wolde tell
another tale far contrary to yᵉ fyrst, ere euer he went fro the
barre: wold his tale not be herd trow you? yes and (the iury [L₂v]
so desyrynge as peraduenture they wold) the iudges wolde swere
hym to I suppose / and very good reason wolde bere it that they   35
sholde.

But as I say let treason go, and come but euyn vnto felonye. If

6 the] yᵗ 1557   26 not.] 1557, not 1533   37 treason] reason 1557

two or thre wytnessys wold at the barre excuse vppon theyr othes
some one man of felony / and afterward whan they were stepped
fro the barre happed to be herde rowne and reioyce to gether,
that they had geuyn good euidence for acquytayle of theyr fel-

5   ow, with whom them selfe had ben at the same robbery: if they
were sodaynly brought agayn to the iudges, the iury not yet
departed fro the barre / and beynge seuerally questyoned in that
sodayne abashement, seynge y^t god had so vttred theyr falshed,
bygan to haue remorce and came forth wyth y^e trouth, and

10 agreed in the cyrcymstaunces and told all one tale, confessynge
both the prysoner & them selfe gylty, [L$_3$] and wold be content to
swere that this tale were trew contrary to the othe y^t they sware
there byfore: wolde not the iudges trowe you geue them the
herynge? yes yes I dowte not, and the iury to.

15   And thus you se clerely good readers, y^t in this poynt if this
man had wysely wrought, he sholde haue geuen it ouer.

    And now albe it y^t here I myght ende this chapyter, and haue
no nede at all to go any ferther: yet to the ferther openyng, how
lytell holde there is in the causes that he layeth of dyssymilitude

20 & vnlykenes, bytwene the wytnessys brought into a spirituall
court, & the wytnesses brought in to y^e temporal for informacyon of the iury / I meruayle mych yf hym self know not that lyke
as the iury may yf they se cause why, way the wytnesses at lyght,
and quyte the prysoner for all the wytnesses wordes, so may the

25 or[L$_3$v]dynary do to. For in his estymacyon the power lyeth, to
way and consider the qualytees of the wytnesses / and all suche
other cyrcumstaunces as may mynysshe or encreace theyr
credence.

    Ye and vnto the tother syde, the wytnessys are not in the

30 temporall courtes wayed and estemed so lyght, but that the iury
shall yf they byleue them not, be somtyme dreuyn to yeld a good
rekenynge why. For though the wordes of the wytnesses be not
entred in the recorde, yet in attaynt they shall agayne be geuen in
euydence agaynst the petyt iury, and be testyfyed by the court

35 and by the othes of them y^t before herde them depose.

---

11 to] to to *1557*   17 chapyter] chapter *1557*   18 any ferther] any further *1557*;
the ferther] the farther *1557*   32 wytnesses] witnesses *1557*, wytnestes *1533*   34 be
testyfyed] *1533 corr. err.*, testyfye *1533*, testifye *1557*

And thanne yf it appere vnto the graund iury in theyr conscyence, that the petyt iury wylfully of some corrupte mynde
regarded not the wytnessys, and therfore in the geuyng of theyr
verdycte passed agaynste theyr owne conscyence: euery man
well [L4] woteth that they shalbe attaynted.   5

And necessyte hath also dreuen the kinges grace & his counsayle for ye sure punyshment of felons, to prouide y^t yf the iury
lykewyse regard the wytnessys so sleyghtly, y^t the iudges thynke
they quyte the felon agaynste theyr own conscyence: they bynde
them sometyme to appere before the kynges counsayle. And   10
there haue there dyuerse iuryes bene proued so to haue myssevsed them self therin, that they haue ben punysshed therfore.

Now wyll I good readers come vnto that piece, which (as a
thyng all redy confuted & of it self vnworthy to be touched) I
wold haue passed ouer & not ones vowchsafed to write one word   15
therin, sauyng y^t I se him to haue taken such labour therabout, y^t
he semeth to wene y^t he hath defended it well / whiche whither
he haue well defended or not, your selfe shal good readers
iudge. [L4v] These were his wordes in his boke of diuision.

Thys is a daungerous law, and more lyke to cause vntrew and vnlawful   20
men to condempne innocentes then to condempne offenders. And it
helpeth lytell, that yf there be tokens, that it is not done of hatered nor
for corrupcyon of money: that it shold be taken: for somtyme a wolfe
may shew hym selfe in the apparell of a lambe. And yf the iudge be
parcyall, such tokens maye be soner accepted then trewly shewed.   25

To thys pyece these were my wordes in myne apology
folio .229.

Syth euyll folke vse not to make good folke of theyr counsayle in doynge
of theyr euyll dedes / those that are done, sholde passe vnpunyshed, & mo
lyke be commytted a fresshe, but yf they were receyued for recordes to theyr   30
condempnynge, that were of theyr counsayle and parteners to the doynge.
Whyche kynde of folke wyll not lette to swere twyse naye before they
confesse ones ye / and yet theyr one ye more trewe vppon theyr bare worde,
than theyr twyse naye vppon a solempne oth / and yet confesse they not so

---

11–12 myssevsed] mysse-[*new line*]vsed *1533*, mysse vsed *1557*   32 Whyche] Which
1557, whyche *1533*

symply, but that it is comenly holpen with some suche cyrcumstaunces [L₅]
as make the mater more clere.

    Nowe se you well that as hym selfe sheweth, the lawe prouydeth well
agaynste all lyght receyuynge of such confessyon. And yet thys pacyfyer
5 *sayth that all that helpeth lytle, bycause the iudge may be parcyall, and* the
wytnesse maye be a wolfe, shewynge hym selfe apparelled in the apparell of a lambe, *whych apperynge in apparell, pore men that can not*
apparel theyr speche with apparell of retoryke, vse comenly to cal a woulfe
in a lambes skynne.

10   *But what order may serue agaynst suche obieccyons? what place is*
there in this world spyrituall or temporal, of whyche the iudge maye not
haue some saye that he is, or at the lest wise (as he sayth here) maye be
parcyall? And therfore not onely such wytnesse shold be by this reason of
his reiected in heresye, treason, murder, or felony / but also by his other
15 *reson of a woulf in a lambes skynne, all maner of wytnes in euery mater.*
For in euery mater may it happen, yᵗ he yᵗ semeth a lambe, may be in dede a
wolf / and be nought [L₅v] *where he semeth good / & swere false where he*
semeth to say trew. And therfore this patche of this pacifyer concernynge
witnesse / euery wyse man may bere wytnesse that there is lytle witte
20 *therin / and lesse good wolde growe therof, yf folke wolde folowe his*
inuencyon, and make of the lawes a chaunge.

    Now that you haue good reders herd what we saye bothe
before. Now shall you se how substancially this man defendeth
his fyrst wordes agayne. These are lo in this .xvi. chapyter of hys
25 newe boke hys wordes.

Nowe by reason of this obieccyon I wyll speke somwhat farther in thys
mater, then I dyd in the sayde treatyse. And fyrste I wyll saye thus, that
yt ys to me a great meruayle, to se mayster More so farre ouerseen, or
ellys yf he be not ouerseen therin, that then he wolde yf he coulde,
30 deceyue other and make theym so farre ouerseen, to byleue that yt
shulde be one lyke reason of a periured wytnesse, that wyll loke lyke a
lambe, and saye contrarye to [L₆] that he hathe deposed before, and of
a wytnesse that cometh to depose in a matter that he was neuer yet
sworne vppon. For when a wytnesse ys broughte in, that was neuer
35 sworen vppon the mater byfore / the iudge maye not by the lawe refuse
hym, nor iudge any defaulte in hym / oneles he knowe a suffycyent

---

26 farther] *Salem and Bizance, 1557,* father *1533*

cause hym selfe in that behalfe / or that the partyes do alledge yt: but he
muste byleue / that he ys honeste, good and indyfferent / tyll the
contrarye be shewed / as euery man ys in charytye bounde to do of hys
neyghbour. But when a wytnesse hathe deposed in the courte / and
then wyll offre hym selfe to depose to the contrarye that he sayde   5
byfore: the iudge maye wyth good conscyence mystruste and thynke,
that he doth yt of lyghtnes of mynde, hatered, or for corrupcyon of
money.

   If I were in thys poynte ouersene, I nede not greately to be
ashamed of the ouersyghte. For then hathe there bene many   10
suche other men ouersene also, as I wolde not wyshe to be wyser.
And I no more entende to deceyue other men in thys mater,
thanne many other haue entended, that vsed and allowed thys
thynge that I defende [L$_6$v] now byfore / such men as wyth the
condycyon that I were neuer worse, I wolde neuer wyshe to be   15
better. This man maketh as though it were great shame for me,
to liken to gether a person ones periured, and a person that was
neuer yet ones sworen. I wolde in dede be a shamed to lyken
theym to gether in euery poynte, all though there were no more
dyfference betwene theym, but that the tone had a longe nose   20
and the tother a shorte. But I am not mych ashamed to say that
for some purpose, where he speketh of the tone I maye speke of
the tother, and lyken them well ynough to gether. For I may say
(as I said) that lyke wise as he that hath forsworen hym selfe, may
fayne hym selfe to saye trew, and loke lyke a lambe, and yet be a   25
woulfe in dede: euyn so I saye maye he that neuer was sworen
byfore.
   Ye sayth thys man, but yet these [L$_7$] two be not lyke. For he
that was neuer sworen, there is no cause to mystruste nor presume that he wyl play the woulf in a lambes skynne. But he that   30
hath bene forsworen, is of reason to be mystrusted / and yt is to
be presumed, y^t he wyll play the woulfe in a lambes skynne.
   Marke yet in the meane whyle, y^t yf I could make no farther
answere: yet hadde I wonne and he loste. For his fyrst wordes
were in his boke of dyuysyon, that he that confesseth hym selfe   35
forsworen, shold in no case be receyued to swere agayne the

---

14 defende] defind *1557*   33 farther] *1557*, father *1533*

contrarye / bycause that though there seme a good cause to byleue hym in his seconde othe, yet yt maye be that he dothe but fayne / and I sayde so may he to fayne and dyssemble, that neuer was sworen byfore. And then yf the onely power and habylyte to
5   fayne, were a cause suffycient to put any one man from berynge witnesse [L₇v] vppon his othe: euery man were by that reason repelled / for euery man ys able to fayn. This was as you se yᵉ thynge that I then sayde. Whyche thynge neyther this man nor any man elles is able to confute, nor proue the forsworen man
10   and the man vnsworen vnlyke in the poynte that I lykened them / that is to wit in powre and abylyte to fayne. And farther then that, went not I. For I had no farther cause in answerynge hym there, whyle he wente no farther there, nor sayde none other, but that he that was forsworen may fayne. And nowe
15   reade your selfe his wordes, and loke whyther I say trewe.

But nowe thys beynge proued as yt is proued playne, that he hathe a fall in those wordes whyche he spake byfore: let vs a lytle se whyther wyth thys leysour after hys mater agayne consydered a freshe, he haue caughte any better holde [L₈] now. And surely
20   me thynketh not one whyt.

For where hys newe reason resteth in thys, that he whyche confesseth hym selfe ones forsworen, is by reason mystrusted, as one not onely to be able to swere false, and wylyly cloke hys falshed vnder a colour of trouthe, but also presumed that he so
25   wyll do in dede: to thys I saye that he sayeth trouthe, as longe as there is no greater presumpcyon on the tother syde to serue for hys seconde othe. But when the case happeth that there is, as yt happeth in the case of this lawe: than ys the presumpcyon that he wyll swere false gone, as I shewed you byfore. And then that
30   presumpcion by a greater presumpcion beyng purged: this man forsworne and the man vnsworn are in the thynge that I resembled them for, waxen well lyke agayne. [L₈v] And that the sayde presumpcyon ys purged: I shewed you byfore, in that it is now a greater presumpcyon for his seconde othe, that he wyll
35   not forswere hym selfe, to the parell of his frende and hym selfe to.

---

5 one] *1557*, oue *1533*   6 that] *1533 corr. err., om. 1533 1557*   24 falshed] falsehood *1557*   31 forsworne] *1557*, forworne *1533*

Then goeth he farther, and enforceth his reason with the reason of the lawe before y^t peragraph Licet was made. And therin thus he sayth.

In so mych that byfore that parag. Licet was made the iuge myght none otherwise haue done of iustyce, but to haue refused to haue taken any farther examynacyon of hym. And yf he hadde, and the other had sayde contrarye to that he hadde sayde byfore: hys saynge hadde ben voyde in the lawe.

And thys thynge wherwyth he thynketh his reason made the strenger, maketh his reason a great deale febler. For whyle the generall rule of refusynge suche wytnesse in all cases, was made so longe byfore: it appereth playnely that necessyte found the faute, and caused oute of the generall rule this case to be made an excepcyon / and so the lawe made by bet[M$_1$]ter delyber-acyon.

And in such other horible crymes, the same lawe is vsed in temporall courtes, and was also before that law made by the chyrche.

But agaynste all thys yet, thys man maketh me this reason.

What the makers of the sayde peragraph ment, to put into the dyscre-cyon of the iudge, that yf he saw by euydent tokens that yt is not done of lyghtnesse of mynde, nor of hatered, nor for corrupcyon of money, that hys sayenge shall stande as well agaynste hym selfe as agaynste other: I can not tell. For I can not se how there can be any euydent token in any suche case, but that there myght be in suche a periured wytnesse sometyme inwarde hatered or corrupcyon that the iudge can not knowe, so that he can not iudge of certayntye that there ys none.

Consyder now good readers that all the strength of this reason hangeth in this, that the iuge can not surely se somtyme, whether the periured wytnesse do it for the trouth, or haue an hatered in his breste so secret that the iudge can not se yt, & therfore he can not certaynly iuge that he hath none. Consyder here now y^t he sayth not y^t [M$_1$v] yt is presumed, or must be presumed, that the periured wytnesse hath so / (for yf he so sayde, he sholde saye to

10 strenger] stronger *1557*   16 And] *no para. 1557*   20 What] *1557*, And what *Salem and Bizance*, what *1533*; paragraph] Peragraph *1557*, Perag. *Salem and Bizance*, peragragh *1533*

no purpose. For as I haue shewed you how that presumpcyon maye be ouer wayed wyth greater presumpcyons to the contrary) but he sayeth that it may be in dede, that the forsworen wytnesse hath so. And then saye I yet agayne, yf we go to the
5 possybylyte of the dede, and not vnto the presumpcyon and lykelyhed / he that was neuer sworen byfore, may haue a secrete hatered whyche the iuge can not se, as well as he maye that was twyse sworen byfore. And theron I saye also yet agayne, that yf the iuge were charged to geue no sentence but suche as he knew
10 of certaynetye sure to be trewe: he coulde neuer vppon any wytnesses in this worlde geue any sentence at all. For no wytnesse were there but he myght swere false & y^e iuge myght wene he sware trew.

Now yf this man wold saye y^t he [M$_2$] meaneth no farther
15 certayntie, then onely a sure thynkynge in the iudges owne conscyence, and that therfore he modered all his other wordes with this worde conscyence, sayenge that the iuge could not with conscyence iuge of certaintie y^t there were no hatered: this meanyng were a very marryng of al y^t he goeth about there to
20 proue. For though the periured witnesse might haue (and happely hadde in dede) a secrete hatered in his own breste, as an other witnes myght haue (& happely had in dede) that neuer was swore byfore: yet myght the iuge beyng induced by certayn tokens & lykelyhedes haue a sure & a certayn persuasyon &
25 bylyefe in his own conscyence, y^t neyther the tone nor y^e tother had any hatered at y^e time, but onely deposed y^e trouth. And therfore if he wold say y^t he ment thus: he marred all his mater.

But it appereth playn y^t he ment in y^e tother maner vpon which there must [M$_2$v] nedes folowe (yf he were not in his
30 sayeng deceyued) that euery iudge in euery sentence y^t he shold geue vpon any witnesses, were they neuer so honest in apparence, were in a daunger ineuytable. And that he meaneth in that maner, that the bylyefe of his owne conscyence induced reasonablye thereto, coulde not excuse the iudge yf he were deceyued
35 and the thynge other wyse in dede: he declareth farther by the wordes that next ensewe, where he goeth farther thus.

---

1 presumpcyon] presumpcion *1557*, presumpcyou *1533*   6 lykelyhed] likelyhod *1557*, lykelyked *1533*   21 dede)] dede *1533 1557*   23 swore] sworn *1557*   24 lykelyhedes] likelihodes *1557*   33 induced] *1557*, iuduced *1533*

And therfore me semeth that the makers of the said peragraph layd
ouer great a daunger to the iudges, that they sholde haue lybertie to
accept yf they wold the sayeng of hym that so offreth hym selfe agaynst
hys fyrste othe / for so myche as the iudge can not be sure to saue hys
conscyence therin, but yf he clerely refuse to accepte any thynge that   5
the wytnesse wold saye contrarye to hys fyrst othe. For yf the iudge dyd
otherwyse, & therupon the witnesses testyfy agaynst the partye, & yet
the partie not gylty in dede: I suppose verily y^t the iuge were party to
the same offens.

And I suppose not the contrarie, but am very sure of y^e con-   10
trarye. For I am very sure, that where the iuge [M$_3$] seeth suche
tokens as seme vnto him manyfeste and open tokens, to proue
that his seconde othe is not offred of any corrupt effeccion, but
of remorse of his periurye and of a mynde to amende his faute
and saye trewe: he falleth in no daungeour of conscience,   15
though the trouthe be otherwyse in dede. For yf there neuer
hadde lawe bene made at all to refuse any wytnesse bycause he
was ones periured: ye iuge had ben clere at libertie vpon resons &
lekelyhedes ledyng his conscience, to haue receyued him again
without any perell of his own conscience at al, where so euer hym   20
self had thought greater lykelyhed that he wolde saye trouth at
the second othe, then he dyd before at the fyrste. And then syth
he was now letted to receyue hym, and his lybertye therin re-
strayned but by a lawe made: what parell can he more fall in
when a seconde lawe hathe set hym at large, then yf the [M$_3$v]   25
formare lawe hadde neuer made the restraynte?

Also where the lawe there prouydeth, that the iudge shall styll
reiecte that witnesse, which offreth to tel the trouth vpon a second oth contrary to his fyrste, but if there appere manyfest
tokens that he do it not of any corrupt effeccion: it meaneth   30
none other but that yf the tokens seme suche vnto the iudge, that
they induce hym in his conscyence so to byleue & thynke and not
that he shalbe certayne & sure that ye thynge is so in dede, by
lokyng into the secrete corners of the mannes harte / no more
then the kynges iuges at the comen lawe, by what wordes so euer   35
they geue thenqueste an oth, nor by what precyse wordes so euer

---

13 effeccion] affeccion *1557*   19 lekelyhedes] likelihodes *1557*   20 own] *om.*
1557   21 lykelyhed] likelyhod *1557*   26 restraynte?] restraynte. *1533 1557*   30
effeccion] affeccion *1557*

they receyue theyre verdycte, meane not to charge theym vppon
parell of theyre soules to say none other wyse thenne the trouthe
of the thynge shal be in dede / but as the trouthe shall seme to
theym to be, vppon suche [M₄] thynges as they shall perceyue
5 eyther by the euydence geuyn theym at the barre, or otherwyse
ere they came there. Nor the iudges theym selfe in the iudgynge
of a matter of lawe, neuer meane precisely that the lawe is so. For
then yf other iudges after reuersed that iudgement or iudged
the same case otherwyse in a nother tyme bytwene other men,
10 the tone iudges or the tother hadde putte theyr soules in parell,
doynge bothe twayne theyre beste to iudge as well as they coulde.

But syth no man can se farther then his eyen wyll serue hym,
no nor no man can se farther then his own reason can vppon the
mater thorowly debated perceyue: yf eyther the .xii. men or the
15 iuges, neyther neglygent nor corrupt, iuge as they thinke trew,
theyr soules are saufe ynough / as saufe as is the soule of the
carpenter, that putteth in hys frame no [M₄v] tymber but such as
is good & sounde as farre as men can se / and yet some of yt
secretely may be suche in very dede, as soon after shall fayle and
20 fall downe all the rofe. His soule is saufe ynough, though his
purse may happe to swete, yf he bounde hym selfe to prouyde
the tymber at hys owne parell. But so byndeth hym selfe neyther
iudge nor iurye for the wytnesse on parell of theyre owne soules,
that the tother shall swere trewe.

25 And thus you se good reders that the iudge is oute of parell,
vsynge dylygence and trouth, though the witnesse be false and
haue hatered in his harte / where the iudge weneth none vpon
tokens yᵗ he thynketh manifeste, al though the witnesse were
forsworen before. And thus is this good man in this mater all
30 gone quyte awry.

But yet beynge sore troubled wyth the wylde woulfe, that
maye [M₅] swere false and seme trew, nothyng mystrusted by-
case he cometh lapped in a lambes skynne: thys good man goeth
ferther yet and therin thus he sayth.

35 And where I sayde in the sayd treatyse, as before appereth, that somtyme a wolfe may shew hym self in the apparell of a lambe, and that yf
the iudge be parcyall, suche tokens maye soner be accepted then truely
shewed: It is euydent inough, that by those wordes I note no iudge to
be parcyal, but I say that yf the iudge be parcyall, suche tokens may be

sooner accepted then truely shewed. As who sayth, the iudge may accepte such a token to be true, though there appere some suspycyon of vntruth in the wytnes. In whyche acceptaunce he shal more lyberally and wythout offence of the lawe do wronge to the party that is accused / then he could do by acceptyng of any other wytnesse agaynste the law,   5 that were neuer sworne before. For yf he accepte any suche wytnes contrary to the rules of the lawe, it appereth to all theym that knowe the lawe, that he doth agaynst the law therin: and that wyll sounde som-what to hys rebuke, and that wyll make hym the more loth to do it. But yf the iudge accepte suche a periured wytnesse where there is no   10 suffycyent token to proue that he doth it not for lyghtnesse of mynde, hatered, corrupcyon, nor such other: yet he breketh no lawe therin. For all is commytted to his dyscrecyon. And that may hapely gyue a boldnes to some iudge to accepte suche a periured wytnes where he ought not to accepte hym. And though the sayde Peragr. say that yf   15 there be suche tokens as before [M₅v] appereth, that then in fauour of the fayth hys wytnes shall be taken: yet I can not se, yf the party accused be gyltlesse in dede, as he maye be for all that wytnesse, how it can be taken in fauour of the fayth, to accepte the wytnesse. For it can not be sayd in fauour of the fayth to condempne an innocent.   20

All thys tale whan it is all tolde, wayeth vnto no more, but that yf the iudge be parcyall, than he may abuse the lawe, and than that lawe in that case may do harme in heresy.

Now besyde that the quest herynge the same wytnesse sworne fyrste, and after contrarye, maye yf they be parcyall, do lyke   25 harme in felonye: what lawe was there euer made, wherein the iudge coulde do none harme yf he wold be parcyall? what lawes maye there serue, yf the mynystres wolde be false? Thys man is content that to a mannes condempnacyon, the presumpcyon shall serue that the wytnesses wyll swere but trewe, suche wyt-   30 nesses at the leste wyse as are not proued false [M₆] before / and yet maye they marre all yf they be false and parcyall. And whan he presumeth suche indyfferencye in a wytnesse: why fereth he so sore parcyalyte in a iudge? yf he saye he mystruste the iudges, bycause of some Some sayes: thanne muste he mystruste wyt-   35 nesses, iuryes, and iudges, and all togyther. For suche Some sayes there lacke not that can say well by no man.

36 all togyther] altogether 1557

Thys reason of hys dothe but putte a suspycyon in mennys heddes agaynste the iudges, for euery thynge that is putte in theyr dyscrecyon. But surely (as I haue often harde that greate wyse and ryghte wursshypefull manne syre Johan Fineux say,
5 late chyefe iustyce of the kynges benche) who so taketh from a iustyce the order of hys dyscrecyon, taketh surely frome hym more thanne halfe hys offyce. If thys realme sholde mystruste iustyces: [M₆v] it must in the lawes than make many suche chaunges, as I neuer sawe nede yet, nor truste I neuer shall.
10 What harme myghte any iustyce of the peace do, yf he were dysposed to be false and parcyall? And euer shall be able to do, make what lawes men wyll, but yf men wolde vtterly put awaye that offyce. And than in stede of one harme that maye happe, we shall haue an hundred happe in very dede.
15   Consyder also good readers, that by the lawes afore made, there was not onely forboden to bere wytnesse, he that appered to be ones forsworen, but also many other maner of cryminouse persons, for the generall presumpcyon that they were vnworthy credence / and yet haue bene by other lawes after made, re-
20 ceyued to bere wytnesse agaynst them selfe & theyr felowes in heresye & in treason both, for the necessyte as I haue sayd and [M₇] vppon presumpcions more probable that they were in that case wel likely to swere trewe.
     Now yf this good man for fere of suche harme as maye by
25 possybylyte fall vppon an innocent, wyl put one of these frome witnessynge: he must repell them all. For as the latter lawes haue synnys receyued all: so the formar lawes generally dyd fyrste refuse them all. For the generall rule is naturally before hys partycular excepcyons.
30   And than yf he wold in lykewyse repell them all, than for one harme yᵗ may happe, and happely neuer shall: he sholde haue many myschyeuouse people very bold, whyle they myght be sure they muste nedes passe vnpunyshed, bycause theyr priuy my-schief coulde neuer well be proued, but yf they wold whan they
35 went about it, take honest men wyth theym to bere recorde of it. [M₇v]

4–6 *Sidenote 1557:* Note this saying.   11 do,] dooe, *1557,* do *1533*   13 offyce.] office. *1557,* offyce *1533*

And thus you se good readers very clere and playne, that this good man hath hytherto brought you forth no reason. And I thynke he saw that hym selfe / and therfore he thought he wolde saye beter at last, and not leue it so. For thanne goeth he ferther and sayeth.

And ferthermore it appereth also, that the wordes of the sayd treatyse extende no ferther, but to suche as be iudges, where there is before them suche a periured wytnes, and not to al iudges. And in lykewyse those wordes, that a wolfe maye shew hym selfe in the apparell of a lambe, stretche onely to suche a periured wytnes. For there is no other wytnesse spoken of in the sayd treatyse in that place.

Thys man goeth to his wordes and forgetteth what I saye / whyche is that though his wordes go no ferther, yet the reason of his wordes (yf it were reason as I haue proued it none) wolde stretche so farre farther that it wold marre all. And this point haue I proued you very clere and playne.

And therby is ment, that suche a periured wytnesse maye haply shewe hym selfe to denye that he sayde before, of a compuncte harte and of a new knowlege [M₈] of the treuth, and of a very zele vnto the fayth: and yet do it in dede of couetyse, falshod, rancoure, and malyce to the party. And so as the gospell sayth, he may happe outwarde to appere in the apparell of a shepe, and withinforth be a raumpynge wolfe. And suche one maye that periured wytnesse be, that is spoken of in the sayde treatyse. And of suche a wytnes in heresye the sayd treatyse speketh onely there and of none other witnesse, as to the readers wyll appere. And therfore as me semeth, mayster More fyndeth defaute in thys behalfe, where he hadde no cause reasonable so to do.

Now good reders where as this man sayeth, that he ment that suche a forsworen wytnesse maye happely play the woulfe in a lambes skynne: I graunt that he ment so. But as I graunte yᵗ to hym: so muste he graunt thys agayne to me, that so maye he playe to, that was neuer sworen before. And than whyle he goeth no ferther, but that the tone happely may, and can not hym selfe

---

3 thought] *1533 corr. err.*, *1557*, though *1533*   21 *Sidenote 1557:* Math. 7.   22 withinforth] withinfurth *1557*, within forthe *Salem and Bizance*, within forth *1533*   26 defaute] default *1557*

saye naye but that the tother happely maye so to: there foloweth
vppon that the thyng that I sayd before, whyche this man sayth
he merueyleth mych y^t I wold say, that ys to wytte, that by that
[M$_8$v] wyse reason there sholde be receyued in suche crimynall
5 causes, no maner wytnesse at all.

    Now yf he leue his may happely and say that it is lykely, that
the forsworen witnesses wyll say false, and the tother trew that
neuer was sworen before / and that the witnesse ones forsworen
afore, is in his secund othe contrary to his fyrste, more lykly to
10 playe the wyly woulfe in the lambes skynne, than suche a playne
symple man as was neuer sworen before: I wyll be so bolde for
thys ones as in some case to tell hym boldely nay. For where he
sayd a lytell afore, y^t he coulde not se how there coulde be any
suche euydent token in any suche case, but that such a periured
15 wytnes myghte do it of a secrete hatered, and seme charytable,
and so play y^e wyly woulfe in the simple lambes skynne: I can se
well inough, y^t in some case there may be an euydent token, that
[N$_1$] some suche wytnesse as was so fyrst forsworen, were after in
his secunde othe swerynge the contrary, lesse lykely to lye & play
20 the wyly woulfe in the lambes skynne, than were an other that
neuer was in hys lyfe before neyther forsworen nor sworen.

    For yf he that was before vppon his oth examyned both of hym
selfe & his sone, or of hym self & his father, or his other specyall
knowen frende, & on his othe clered them all, do at an other
25 tyme vppon a new oth confesse them all gyltye, and hym selfe
also / and where peraduenture hym selfe must to the fyre, bycause he was abiured before, & they maye turne yet in tyme & be
but abiured: were not thys an euident token that he doth it not of
any secrete hatered, nor playeth not the wyly woulf in a lambes
30 skynne? For iwys to confesse hym selfe gylty in such case and
puttyng hym self in worse case than hys felowes, were [N$_1$v] but a
pore poynt of a wyly woulfe. And as I putte thys case for ensample: so may there be many other. For the tokens myght be playne
inough though they were lesse playne thanne thus. And therfore
35 to conclude in this mater, this man hath no reason in this worlde
to defende hys fyrste booke wythall.

    And therfore where he spendeth a patche in the ende, about

---

18 were] wer *1557*, where *1533*   32 woulfe.] woolfe. *1557*, woulfe *1533*

his declaracyon, that it may be lawfull for hym to fynde defaute
at lawes made by the chyrche, so that he fynde them vppon a
suffycyent reason, bycause all that poynt nothyng helpeth hym
here in this law, agaynst whych he sheweth no reason reasonable,
but a reason as vnreasonable as euer reasonable man herde: I   5
shall I saye therfore let that piece passe by, and here make an
ende of hys .xvi. chapyter. [N₂]

The .xvii. chapyter.

Hɪs .xvii. chapyter begynneth folio .lxii. In yᵉ begynnyng
wherof he merueileth that I speke so ofte in myne apology, of his   10
vsyng this word Some saye. And he sheweth that in a tale tolde
hym by other folke, there is good reason that he so sholde say /
and that I vse the same worde my selfe to sometyme, and telleth
two places where, fo. 77. and fo. 100. I neither dyd nor wyll
fynde fawt that he vse this worde some say / nor I wyll not let   15
(where the case requireth) to saye my selfe, yᵗ some say this or
that. For I know well it is englyshe. But the fawte that I founde
and yet fynd, is that hys booke of diuysyon abuseth [N₂v] the
figure of so many some sayes, to the sedicyous slawnder of yᵉ
clergye / and specyally of thordinaryes in the punysshement of   20
heresy, to bryng them in obloquy of the people therby. And
where as vppon complayntes made the maters haue late ben
examined, & the treuth hath ben playnely proued contrary: yet
hath he neuer one Some say therof in al his boke, neyther in yᵉ
tone boke nor the tother / but all hys Some sayes euer more saye   25
euyll, & neuer a Some say well. This is the fawte that I fynde. For
yf he made a boke with fiue times as many good Some sayes, as
his Some sayes in that boke be nought: I wold fynd in his Some
sayes no defawt at all. For some say is (as I saye) good englysshe.
But whan a booke is full of shrewde Some sayes: there do some   30
men saye, that Some saye is as shrewd englysh, as any dowch
woman speketh. [N₃]
But now to shew that in all hys Some sayes he meneth none

---

1 defaute] defaulte *1557*   15 fawt] fault *1557*   17 fawte] faulte *1557*   26 fawte]
fault *1557*   29 defawt] defaulte *1557*   31 englysh] *1533 corr. err.*, an englysh *1533*,
an english *1557*

harme, he goeth ferther, and for a sample he bryngeth forth
one, whych is in very dede a very malycyouse noughty pestylent
Some saye, wherof the pretence is the sauegarde of innocentes /
theffecte is the dekaye of the faythe by the boldyng of heretykes,
5 the instrument is a false imagyned slaunder agaynst the ordynaryes. And as wylyly as those shrewys that begyle hym haue
holpe hym to inuolue and intryke the mater: I shall vse so playne
and open a waye therin, that euery man shall well se the trouth.
Lo these are thys good mannes wordes.

10 And one of the (some sayes) that he fyndeth defaute at is thys: I saye in
the .viii. chapyter of the sayde treatyse thus: And here some saye that
bycause there is so greate a desyre in spyrytuall men, to haue men
abiured or to be noted wyth heresye: And that some as it were of a
polycye doo noyse it, that the realme is full of heretykes, more then it is
15 in dede, that it is very peryllous, that spyrytuall men shulde haue
auctoryte to arreste a man for euery lyght sus[N₃v]speccyon or complaynt of heresye, tyll that desyre of punyshement in spyrytuall men be
ceassed and gone but that they sholde make processe agayne them, to
brynge them in vppon payne of cursynge: and then yf they tarye .xl.
20 dayes, the kynges lawes to bryng them in, by a wrytte of Excommunicato capiendo, and so to be brought forth out of the kynges gayole
to answere. And it foloweth in the sayd .viii. chapiter thus: but surely as
it is somwhat touched before in the .vii. chapyter, it semeth that the
churche in tyme past haue done what they coulde to brynge about, that
25 they myght punysh heresy of them self, wythout callynge for any helpe
therin of the secular power. And therfore they haue made lawes that
heretykes myght be arrested, and put in pryson, and stockes, yf nede
were, as appereth in Clementinis de hereticis, Cap. Multorum querela.
And after at the specyall callynge on of the spyrytualty, it was enacted
30 by parlyament, that ordynaryes myght arest men, that preche, holde,
teche, or enforme other in heresye, there prohybyte, or that therof
holde any conuentycles or scholys. For some men thynke that the sayd
Clementine was not of effect in the kynges lawes to arrest any man for
heresye. But yf a man were openly and notably suspected of heresye,
35 and there were suffycyent recorde and wytnes agaynste hym, and
there were also a doubte, that he wolde flee and not appere, wherby he

---

myght infecte other, it semeth conuenyent, that he be arrested by the body, but not vpon euery lyght complaynt that full lyghtly may be vntrue. And that it wyll be ryght expedyent that the kynges hyghnes and hys consayle loke specyally vpon thys mater, and not to cesse, tyl it be brought to moore quietnes then it is yet: and to se with great dylygence that pryde, couetyse, nor [N₄] worldly loue be not iudges, nor innocentes be punysshed ne yet that wylfull offenders go not wythout due correccyon.

And when mayster More in his apologye hath recyted the sayd wordes of the sayd treatyse: then he endeuoyreth hym selfe very moch, to make it appere that the mocions that be made in the sayd treatyse in the place before rehersed be vnreasonable, & can not be brought aboute: or els that yf they were brought aboute they sholde do hurte and no good. And to make hys sayenges the more acceptable / he layeth sometyme defaute in my sayenges and sayth that I therby defame the iudges spyrytuall, where I defame them not / but say onely that it is expedyent that the kynges hyghnes and hys counsayle se / that pride couetyse nor worldly loue be no iudges. And whether thoo wordes amount to that effecte / that mayster More sayth they do / that is to saye that I defame all spyrytuall iudges it appereth euydentely they do not.

Now good readers to the entent that you may the more playne-ly perceyue, both the good mynde of thys good mannys fyrst boke of dyuysyon, and also his secunde boke here in defence of yᵉ same: take yᵉ labour to rede the .xlvi. chapyter of myne apolo-gye fo. 232. And than shall you thynke I suppose, yᵗ all hys defence is so faint that I lytell nede to reply. [N₄v]

For fyrst where he sayth, that I saye that in those wordes, he dyffameth the iudges spyrytuall: I wold he had rehersed my wordes with whiche I saye so. For I am sure inough my wordes be no larger than yᵉ treuth. But that is hys vsuall crafte to leue out for the more part, both my wordes & the place, bycause men myght wene it were in some part of my boke though they re-member not where.

But now bycause he sayeth, that it is euydent that those wordes of his do not amounte vnto the dyffamacion of the spyrytuall iudges: I haue shewed and proued in dede in one or two places

---

1 other,] *1557*, other *1533*   30–32 *Sidenote 1557:* And so doe al heretykes.

of myne apologye, that all the great mater of his complaynt,
vppon the crueltye of the spyrytuall iudges, in handelyng men
for heresy, syth there hath bene very fewe troubled therfore in
any dyocise in Englande or Walys / by y^e space of these .xx. yeres
5   or .xxx. laste passed / except [N$_5$] onely Lyncoln and London /
and that therfore the false complaynt of mysse handelynge,
could haue lytle colour any farther then those two dyoceses / and
yet to saye the trouthe neuer complaynt broughte forth by any
suche man but in London dyocese, nor yet not but in London
10 and some pyece of Essex alone / and the complayntes vppon
examinacyon hadde by the kynges honorable counsayle, alwaye
founde causelesse and false: syth thys is I saye so clere, that no
man can saye the contrarye, but that thys is trew, I declare and
shew in my sayde appologye, that where wyth hys false some
15 sayes he defameth and laboreth to brynge in obloquye of the
people, all the spyrytuall iudges in the realme: of wrong and
cruell handelynge men for heresye, all the men y^t his false some
says (if they were trew) dyd touche, were yet in dede so few, that
he myght in a [N$_5$v] maner as well speke of them by name. And in
20 very dede so few they be. For they be as few or fewer, then are
the iuges eyther of the tone benche or the tother.

And therfore when he cometh now forthe vnder shadowe of a
shrewed some saye, and sheweth that the spyrytualle men haue a
great desyre to put men to abiuracyon, and to haue men noted of
25 heresy, and that therfore tyll they leue that condycyon, it were
well done they sholde haue lesse authorytie / & that yt wyll be
ryght expedyent that the kynge and hys counsayle loke specyally
vppon thys mater, and to se wyth great dylygence, that pryde,
couetise, nor worldly loue be not iudges, nor innocentes pun-
30 nyshed, nor yet that offenders go not wythout dew correccyon:
ys not this a lewde colored slaunder and (wythout any such
thynge proued) a shamelesse dyffamacyon?

If thys good man wold in lyke [N$_6$] wyse wryte and put in prent
a nother boke, and there in speke fyrst of iustyces in generall, as
35 it myght seme to touche all the iudges of euery base court, &
iustyces of the peace to / and then by some certayn cyrcumstaunces restrayne it in such wyse, that euery man may se that he
meaneth onely the kynges iuges at westmynster, & say, y^t some
say that specially of late the maters of comen plees be euyll

handeled by the iudges / and y^t in writtes of errour & in plees of
the crowne the iudges mysse handle the people sore and do
mych wrong / & that some say that they haue this euyl desyre, &
y^t / & y^t tyl they haue left them, it were wel done that they had
lesse authoryte. And then after such a false folyshe some saye,   5
com forth with his sayeng, & in approbacyon of his other sayng,
conclude & saye thus myche farther, it wyll be ryght expedient
therfore, that the kynges hyghnesse and hys counsayle [N_6v]
loke specially vppon this mater, and to se wyth great dylygence
that pryde couetyce, nor worldely loue be not iuges &c, were this   10
wyly folyshe handelynge no false dyffamacyon at all?

And nowe when he handeleth the spyrytuall ordynaryes wyth
lyke wordes for heresye, and his somesays false ymagyned lyes /
and though hys boke of dyuison laboreth to draw that false
suspicyon farther / yet hym selfe seeth by experyence that whyle   15
there hathe in long whyle but in two dyoceses very fewe bene
punyshed for heresye, the slaunder that he soweth toucheth
some very few, no lesse then though he wrote in theyr names.
How can he therfore for very shame saye that yt is no dyffamacyon? Weneth he the reders of his worke were all such folys, that   20
he myght auoyde his playne open dede wyth his bare bolde
worde, where he sayth yt appereth euydentely nay, where euery
[N_7] wyse man that readeth yt seeth well hym selfe that yt well
appereth euydently yes.

Nowe goeth he farther wyth a nother pyece and sayth.   25

Nor yet my wordes proue not that I wolde haue al spyrytuall iudges
chaunged. For the spyrytuall iudges that be nowe, maye be iudges styll,
and haue al the propertyes before rehersed, as well as other, for any
thyng that I haue sayd. And yet mayster More taketh yt otherwyse, and
sayeth / I wolde haue such iudges, as haue no spyce of any of the sayd   30
poyntes. And he sayth, that tyll suche iudges may be founde, heretykes
may make mery for a lytle season / whyle men walke aboute and seche
for such iudges / which he weneth wyll not be done in a wekes worke.

Here he leueth oute agayne the place of myne that he toucheth. For when that is ones redde, all hys gay tale is gone. For   35
there shall you se that I consyder hys wordes, and declare two

---

wayes that the good man myght meane / of whyche twanne he
taketh here the tone, and the tother he letteth slype. And yet in
takynge his wordes as he wolde nowe seme: my wordes whyche
he dyssembleth [N₇v] here, turne vppe all his tale / and that the
5   man sawe full well / and therfore wynked at theym. But I shall
brynge theym in agayne here, and repete theym for hym. Lo
good readers in yᵉ .xlvi. chapiter fo. 253. after hys wordes rehersed at length, thus I begynne myne owne.

In thys processe lo good readers this pacyfyer declareth, that he wold
10 *haue the kynges hyghnes and hys counsayle so specyally loke vppon thys*
mater, that neyther innocentes sholde be punyshed, nor yet wylfull offend-
ers go wythoute dewe correccyon. Who could ende and conclude all hys
mater more frutefully?

But now the specyall ways wherby he dyuyseth, that the kynges
15 *hyghnesse and his counsayle sholde bryng this thynge about be twayne.*

The tone is, yf they prouyde that neyther men that be proude nor
couetouse, nor haue loue to the worlde, be suffred to be iudges in a[N₈]ny
cause of heresye.

The tother ys, that the byshoppes shall arreste no man for heresye, tyll
20 *the desyre that spyrytuall men haue to cause men abiure heresyes, and to*
punyshe theym for heresyee, be ceased and gone.

And surely I thynke that his two dyuyses wyll serue suffycyently for the
tone parte / that ys to wytte that none innocentes shall be punyshed. But I
fere me very sore, that they wyll not serue halfe so suffycyently for the
25 *tother parte, that ys to wytte that wylfull offendours go not withoute*
correccyon.

For now to begynne with his fyrst dyuyse, that none be suffred to be
iudges in cause of heresye, yᵗ are proude or couetouse, or haue loue to yᵉ
world yf he meane of suche as haue none of these affeccyons wyth notable
30 *enormyte, then tyll he proue theym that are all redy worse thenne he*
proueth them yet / that is to say tyll he proue yt otherwyse by some of theyre
out[N₈v]ragyouse dedes in the dealynge and myshandelynge of men for
heresy, yᵗ he here defameth them of, then he hath yet proued, and that he
proue theyre cruell wrongful dealynge, otherwyse then by somesayes, or by
35 *hys owne sayenge: the kynges hyghnes & hys counsayle can se for all hys*

---

1 twanne] twain *1557*   7 chapiter] Chapter *1557*   12 Who] *1557*, who *1533*   13
frutefully?] fruitfully? *1557*, frutefully. *1553*   17 loue] *1533 corr. err.*, any loue *1533*
1557   32 myshandelynge] missehandling *1557*, myslandelyuge *1533*

holesome counsayle, no cause to chaunge those iudges that are all redy,
but to leue them styll / and then serueth that dyuyse of nought.

And on the other syde, yf he meane that the kynges hyghnesse shal suffer
none to be iudges in cause of heresye that hath any spyce at all, eyther of
pryde, or of couetyse, or any loue at all vnto thys worlde: heretykes may syt 5
styll and make mery for a lytle season, whyle men walke about and seke for
such iuges. For yt wyl not be lesse then one whole wekes worke I wene both
to finde such, and to be sure that they be suche.

Here haue you herd good reders a resonable cause why that I
sholde take hym that he wolde haue the [O₁] spyrytuall iudges, 10
such as shold haue no spice of pride, couetouse, nor worldly
loue. For either he must meane so / or elles (as I sayde) he must
meane on the tother maner which I reherse fyrste, and whych he
wold now seme to mean. But then (as I haue sayd) yf he ment in
the fyrst fashyon as he wolde now seme: all his tale is ouerturned. 15
For then hadde he no cause of any suche complaynte. For he
neyther hadde hym selfe when he wrote nor any man elles,
preued by any of theym the contrary. And then neded he not to
spende oute hys profounde wysedome, in makynge suche ex-
hortacyons to the kynges hyghnesse and his counsayle, to se with 20
so great dilygence (as though they had be so long neglygent) to
the thyng that him self could not say nay, but yᵗ it was metely well
ynough all redy. And thus you se good reders that he lefte oute
and dissembled that fyrst part of my wor[O₁v]des, bycause he
wyste nere what to saye therto. And therfore syth, except he 25
ment in the fyrst maner (which he could not do without the
marryng of all his mater) you se well that him self droue me to
thynke, that he wold haue the kynges grace and his counsayle, se
dylygently that there shold be no spyrituall iudges, but they yᵗ
had no spice of pryde, couetise, or worldly loue at all. And then 30
myghte heretyques as I sayd (whyle suche iudges were in
sekynge) make mery for a lytle whyle. And I kepte my selfe
metely well wythin my boundes. For where I sayde yt wolde be a
wekes worke to seke theym: I wene yt wold be fourtenyght ful
ere we founde them. 35

---

2 then] *1533 corr. err., 1557*, them *1533*   10 the spyrytuall] the spirituall *1557*, the
spy [*new page*] spyrytuall *1533*   11 pride, couetouse,] pride, couetous, *1557*, pride
couetouse *1533*   34 be] *1557*, he *1533;* fourtenyght] fortnight *1557*

But then gooth he farther somewhat aboute to shewe, that I haue mysse handeled his wordes, & wyth ioynynge myne owne vnto his, haue made yt seme that he sayeth myche [O₂] worse by the spyrytualtye then he eyther sayde or ment. But when you
5 haue herde all hys tale and myne to, you shall well se good readers that he shall neuer whyle he lyueth conuey this gere so clene. For these are fyrste his wordes here.

And he sayeth / that yt wyll be the more harde to fynde suche iuges. For he sayth, that I haue putte that mater oute of doute / that where
10 as men wolde haue wende soneste to haue founde theym, that there I saye / yt wyll be meruaylouse harde to fynde any one of theym / eyther prelates, seculere prestes or relygyouse persons. For he saythe that I saye playnely / that haue they neuer so many vertues besyde / that yet I saye, yt wyll be harde to fynde any one spyrytuall man / but
15 that he ys so infected wyth desyre and affeccyon to haue the worldely honour of prestes exalted / that he is thorough suche pryde farre fro suche indyfferency and equytye, as oughte and muste be in suche iudges / whych as he saythe, I assygne to be suche, that they muste haue no spyce of pryde couetyse nor loue towarde the worlde.
20 As to thys laste rehersed sentence of master More this is yᵉ trouth therin / I say in an other place of the sayde treatyse, other then that / that mayster More hath rehersed here / that is to say, in the .vii. chapyter of the sayde treatyse, that though many spyrytuall men maye be founde, that haue many great [O₂v] vertues, and great gyftes of god /
25 as chastyte, lyberalytye, pacyence, sobernesse, temperaunce, connynge and suche other: yet yt wyll be harde to fynde any one spyrytuall man that ys not infecte wyth the sayde desyre and affeccyon / to haue the worldely honour of prestys exalted. And there my sentence endeth, as to thys purpose. But then as yt appereth before, mayster More in hys
30 sayde Apologye addeth immedyatly to those wordes of myne, wordes of his own puttynge in / whyche be these: That he ys through such pride ferre fro such indifference and equyte / as ought & muste be in the iuges, whyche he sayth I assygne. And he combyneth tho wordes to myne / in suche maner as though I spake theym my selfe. So that they
35 that shall rede theym, can none otherwyse take theym, but as my wordes: wherby he peruerteth clerely my meanynge and my sentence

---

25 temperaunce,] *1557*, temperaunce *1533*   28 exalted] *Salem and Bizance, 1557*, axalted *1533*   36 peruerteth] *1557*, peruerteh *1533*

therin. For my sentence, ne yet my meanyng therein / is not but that
iudges spyrytuall maye haue some spyce of pride couetyse and worldly
loue, and yet be meate iudges in heresye / as the frayltye of man
suffereth. For we be no angelles but synners, that lyghtlye may fall and
be deceyued. Ne I meane not, ne yet my wordes amount not to yt, but
that a man may haue a desyre and affeccion / to haue the worldly
honour of prestes exalted / and yet be a mete iudge in heresye. For I
suppose / that a man may haue that desyre in some degree, and to some
entent / and not offende therin / specyally dedely. How be yt he may
also lyghtly offende therin, yf he be not ryght well ware.

If thys good man here saye trew in these aforesayde wordes of
hys And there my sentence endeth as to this purpose: [O₃] then am I
content to confesse, that he sayth well, and I wronge. But on the
tother syde nowe, yf he saye not trewe, but that in the defamynge
and slaunderynge of the spyrytualty, his sentence ended not
there, but wente there myche farther forth, and so far forthe
also / as amounted vnto as myche as I saye that he sayde, & vnto
myche more to: then wyll euery man bere me recorde, that I
mysse reporte not hym but he me.

Now shall you good reders sone se thys tryed bytwene vs. For
hys whole wordis as they lye there to gether, I shall nowe reherse
you here. Lo these they be as you shall fynde them bothe in hys
boke of dyuysyon, and in myne Apologye fo. 237.

And though many spyrytuall men may be founde, that haue ryghte
many great vertues and great gyftes of god, as chastyte, lyberalytye,
pacyence, sobernesse, temperaunce, connynge, and suche other / yet yt
wyll be harde to fynde any one spyrytuall man that is not infecte wyth
the sayde desyre and affeccyon to haue the worldely honour of prestys
exalted [O₃v] and preferred / & therfore yf any lay man reporte any
euyll of a preste / though yt be openly knowen that yt is as he sayeth /
yet they wyll be more dylygent to cause the laye man to cease of that
sayenge / then to do that in them is to reforme that is a mysse in the
preste that it is spoken of / takyng as it were an occasyon to do the
lesse in suche reformacyons / bycause laye men speke so myche
agaynst theym: But surely that wyl be none excuse to spyrytual rulers

---

11 here] *1557*, her *1533*   16 forth] furth *1557;* forthe] furth *1557*   26 pacyence,]
pacience, *1557*, pacyence *1533*

afore god / when he shall aske accompt of hys people / that were commytted vnto theyr kepynge.

Now you se good reders, how vntrew it ys y^t this man telleth
you. For here you se y^t his sentence leueth not where he sayth yt
5 lefte as to that purpose: but you se that yt goeth forth farther
aboute that purpose styll, to shewe that it wyll be harde to fynde
any one spyrytuall man iuste & indyfferent, but that the desyre
and affeccyon to haue y^e worldly honour of prestes exalted and
preferred, hath so farre infected them, that yf a lay man reporte
10 any euyll of a preste, though it be openly knowen y^t it is as he
sayth, yet they wyl not onely rather put the lay man to sylence,
then any thynge [O$_4$] amende the preste: but that they will also
do the lesse to the amendment of y^e preste, because the lay men
speketh of yt. Whyche affeccyon can not be but a very proude
15 dampnable frowardnesse.

And therfore whyle this good pacifyer there sayth, that all the
prestes be so farre infecte wyth such a proud damnable desyre of
theyre worldely exaltacyon, that yt wylbe harde to fynde any one
of them any other, and then a lytle byfore those wordes (as you
20 may se in hys sayde chapyter in myn apologye fo. 235.) he sayth
vnder the fygure of a great rumour amonge the peple / that
spyrytuall men punyshe heresyes rather to oppresse them that
speke any thynge agaynste theyre worldely honour and rychesse
&c: then for zele of the fayth: these wordes of his beyng there
25 such, iudge nowe good reader whether I might not well say y^t
this good man saith it [O$_4$v] wyll be harde to fynde any one
spyrytuall man, but that he is so infected with the desyre and
affeccyon to haue the worldely honour of prestes exalted, that
he is thorough suche pryde farre fro such indifferencye & equy-
30 te, as oughte and muste be in suche iudges as him selfe assygneth
to be such as they muste haue no spyce of pryde couetyse or loue
toward the worlde. I am very sure y^t hys wordes mayntayne
myne and more to.

---

5 forth] furth *1557*   13 men] man *1557*   14 Whyche] Which *1557*, whyche
1533   18 worldely] worldlye *1556*, wordely *1533*   19 other, and] other. And *1533*
1557   20 fo. 235.)] fo. 235. *1533*, Folio .235. *1557*   23 thynge] thing *1557*, thynke
1533   26 saith] *1557*, saiyh *1533*   28 worldely] worldly *1557*, wordely *1533*

Naye (sayth he) for I do not meane that they shold haue no spyce therof. For they may haue some spice therof: and yet maye be iudges in heresye well Inough. For they may haue that desyre in some degree and some entente, and not offende therin, specyally dedely.

But I haue agaynste y^t proued afore that he muste meane so: or ellys muste haue lefte hys tale vntolde. Fo yf he ment to be contente wyth folke of meane condycyons wythoute notable enormyties, suche they were all redy, and then had his great exhortacyon lytle place. [O$_5$]

Also this pryde with whyche hys wordes saye that they be all so sore infected, that it wylbe very harde to fynde any one other / is a very pestylent pryde / and in an hygh degre, and suche as he coulde not well deuyse a more dedely dyffamacyon of the hole spyrytualtye / than those wordes be, whyche yf they were trew (as they be false) playnely proued, that in all the hole clergy it were hard to fynde any one good honest man, or mete to be a iudge, eyther in heresye or in any thynge ellys. And so wold he by this deuyce of his, take awaye as I sayd frome examynacyon of here-sye, all the spyrytuall iudges, and leue them none at all.

And yet good readers to thende that you maye the better perceyue, what those wordes of this man amount vnto / whyche he wolde make you wene here that I both mysse reherse and mysseconstre: wouchsaufe to rede [O$_5$v] my wordes that I wryte vpon them in myne apologye folio .238.

But now this good pacyfyer perceyuynge, that it wylbe harde to bere it, but that his wordes clerely take away fro the clergye, all suche indyferency and iustyce, as hym selfe assygneth to be re-quyred of necessyte, in euery man that shold be suffred to be iudge in heresy / he falleth to another shyfte to saue the mater vpryght. And therin thus he sayth.

And farthermore though it were as mayster More taketh it to be / that my wordes shuld sounde to that effect that the iuges y^t were then, were through such pryde farre fro the indyfferencye and equytye that I assygne: yet that proueth not / but that they be now indyfferent and

---

13 hole] whole *1557*   15 hole] whole *1557*   23 mysseconstre] misseconstrue
1557   32 then, were] *Salem and Bizance*, thē were, *1533*, then, wer *1557*

ryghtwyse. For they myght syth the makynge of the sayde treatyse, bycome through grace, indyfferent, ryghtwyse, meke, lyberall, and louynge to god and theyr neyghbour / though they were not so then. And yf they be so, then heretykes shall not make mery for lacke of
5 iudges a weke ne yet a daye. For the same iudges may sit styll wythout chaungynge / to here and examyn theym whan nede shalbe. Thus as me semeth, it appereth euery waye / y^t the excepcyon that mayster More taketh of chaungyng of spyrytuall iuges is but of smal effecte.

This reason hath lo some sotylty: but it hath no substaunce.
10 For yf [O$_6$] they were all so noughty so late, as this good man saith they were, it wyl be but hardely byleued, that so many of them, vppon so shorte a sermon of this poore precher, sholde be so well chaunged so soone, but that as I said, theretykes were well lyke, yet one weke lenger to make mery, before men myghte
15 haue so sure experyence as to put theym so sone in truste to be iudges in heresye, whom thys pacyfyer hadde perswaded to be so farre vnmete for the mater so late. And therfore it appereth euery waye that thys good mannys inuencyon is towarde euyll of very great / towarde good of very small effecte.
20   Than goth he forth·on with the mater and thus he sayth.

Then sayth mayster More ferther that yf some say be no suffycyent profe / then is my tale all lost. And to these wordes I wyll answere thus. I wyll agree that my sayenge that some saye thys or thys / is no profe / neyther to proue that some saye so / ne yet to proue that it is so. For in
25 euery profe must be two wytnesse at the leste: but yf two wyll saye it is so: then it is a proffe. [O$_6$v]
    And surely yf mayster More wyll inquere for the truth in thys mater, he shall fynde that there be many mo then two that say so. And veryly yf many men saye so, though the treuth be not so, yet the tale is not all
30 loste to say that some men say so. For then it shall put the byshoppes and rulers spyrytuall in mynde, that they are bounde in conscience to helpe them that saye so all that they can, fro the daunger that they ronne in by that sayeng. And yf it be true, then may the spyrytuall rulers order the mater as they shall se cause, and reforme it in suche

---

charytable maner that none shall say so hereafter: but they wyll of
malyce do it, and renne into the slander of the Pharyseis: and that
wolde charytably be examyned, whether it be so or not.

Thys is a prety pyece, and suche as I haue seldome sene y^e
lyke, come out of any wyse mannys mouth. For though that in   5
iugement, men muste presume a thynge is trewe, whyche two
good honest persons sworen and examyned depose and testyfye,
that themself haue sene the dede, or herde the wordes spoken,
by the mouth of the person whyche for suche dede or sayenge is
accused: yet sayth no man for all that / that bycause two men say   10
it and swere it to, therfore it is so. For as to the necessary consequence [O_7] of the dede / this argument is very faynt that thys
man maketh. Two men saye it is so, ergo it is so.

Than vpon thys argument such as you se, he sendeth me to
inquere and than I shall he sayth fynde, that there be many mo   15
than two that saye so. That maye well happe now, by occasyon of
his boke of dyuysyon. But what yf I enquered of them, and I
shold happe to fynd not onely many mo than two, but also many
mo than two hundred, that wold say that the spyrytuall men for
such euyll affeccyons as this good pacyfyer surmyseth, haue   20
great desyre to abiure men or note theym of heresye: yet whyle
all they coulde amonge them all ley no profe at all / but alway the
trouth proued contrary, both by that, that in farre the moste
parte of thys realme, and take Walys therto, there haue not ben
before his boke of diuysion, fiue men abiured in fiftene yere,   25
[O_7v] and in those that haue bene / rigour hath not ben vsed
more than necessary: but there hath ben vsed more than necessary fauour / & that this hath ben al redy proued ofter than ones,
before the kynges honorable counsayle, I wold not esteme the
bablyng of two hundred, no not though they were two thousand,   30
& yet many mo to, the mountenaunce of .ii. strawes / for any
thyng that I wold regard any good man ye wurse. But I wold for
theyr owne partes be sore ashamed to here them, & clerely perceyuynge y^t they so lewdely lyed: I wolde be sore ashamed to tell
the tale agayn after them. And this I say yf I sholde with inquery   35

---

17 and] *1533 corr. err.*, that *1533 1557*   18–19 two, but also many mo than] *om.*
1557   25–26 yere, and] yere. And *1533 1557*

thus happe to fynde, as I veryly trust I shold not yf I dyd enquere.

But now his Some say beynge so false as it is, it is a world yet to se what a fonde shyfte he fyndeth, that he wolde not yet by hys
5 wyll haue that lye loste. For he sayth, [O₈] that though the treuth be not so, yet the tale is not loste to say that some men say so. For (he saith that) then it shall put the byshoppes and spyrytuall rulers in mynde, that they are bounde in conscience to helpe theym that saye so all that they can, fro the daungeour that they ronne in by so sayeng.
10 What good I praye you can thys false Some saye do? For what can yᵉ spyrytuall men do for theyr helpe yᵗ so bylye them? any other than aduise them to leue suche lyeing? And that had ben a better parte for thys good pacyfyer to haue played hym selfe, & so to haue told them vpon whose tale he wrote it: than to yᵉ
15 reproch & rebuke of so many good worshypfull men make a boke of diuisyon, & therin write euery lewde worde, that any lewde folke, or any false shrewes wolde tell hym. Whose euyll tonges the spyrytualtye can neuer appease: but yf to please them they sholde dysplease god / and without lettynge heresyes growe
20 and go forth, shold them selfe rather do euyll than let lewde folke speke euyll. [O₈v]

And now to thentent good reders that you may the more clerely se, to how lytell purpose the pacifyer hath in thys poynt answered me / ye shall vnderstande that my wordes in myn
25 apology whiche he wold seme to answere well here, were these .fo. 257.

But yet is thys pacyfyer not so fauourable towarde folke suspected of heresye, as to take away the power of the byshoppe for euer, of arrestynge them, and to dryue the ordynaryes for euer to sue cytacyons agaynst
30 *heretykes and processe of excommunicacyon / but wyll haue he sayeth the bysshoppes power of arrestynge no lenger suspended, thanne as longe as spyrytuall menne haue that great desyre to cause menne abiure or to haue theym punysshed for heresye / as though he hadde well proued that they haue so, bycause he sayeth that some men say so.*

35 *But now yf Some say be no suffycyent profe / than is hys tale lost. For than he sheweth no cause why that [P₁] power of theyrs sholde in any case be more suspended now, than in any time here before. And on the tother*

---

syde, yf some say be a good profe / than the suspendynge wyll be as longe as
a depryuynge for euer, syth there shall neuer be any tyme in whyche there
shall lacke one or other some saye to saye more than trouth.

Lo good readers here you se, that vnto the secunde parte of
these wordes of myne, he answereth nothynge at all. And than   5
haue you sene before that vnto the fyrste, hys answere is so feble,
that it had ben better for him to haue done therwyth as he dothe
wyth the tother, leue it vnanswered to.

But nowe goeth he ferther and saith,

Then sayth mayster More yet ferther, that which is a lyghte suspycyon   10
and whyche is a heuy, and whyche wytnes be suffycyent, and whych
not, must be weyed by the spyrytuall iudges, and vppon theyr weyinge
of the mater for lyght or heuy, to folowe the arrest of the party, or the
leuynge of the arrest. [P₁v] Now veryly in thys poynt me thynketh that
mayster More maketh a ryght good mocyon, that is to saye, that the   15
mater shulde be examyned before the arreste. For it hath ben sayd in
tymes paste, that in suche case the arrest hath many tymes gone before
the examynacion. Neuerthelesse vnder what maner the examynacyon
and the arrest shulde be made in suche case, I wyll make no deuyse at
this tyme: For happely mayster More wold anone fynde a defawt at it,   20
and therfore I wyll leaue it to them that haue auctoryte, to treate
ferther of it, and to dyuyse how to auoyde the mase that mayster More
speketh of in hys sayd .xlvi. chapyter.

Now good readers this man maketh here, as though I hadde
geuen hym in my wordes, some greate aduauntage to grounde   25
some great mater vppon. And therfore I shall reherse you what
my wordes were, that your selfe maye se how sore I ouersaw my
selfe therin, and what he meneth by the mase that he nameth
here. These are lo my wordes in myne apologye fo. 257.

Yet is he content at the laste, leste euery man myghte spye the perell of   30
hys deuyce, to temper hys deuyce in suche wyse, that tyll the spyrytualty
[P₂] haue lefte theyr cruell desyre of abiurynge and punysshynge folke for
heresye, they sholde not be suffred to arreste folke for euery light suspy-
cyon, or euery complaynt of heresye. How be it he graunteth that where
one is openly and notably suspected of heresye, and suffycyent recorde and   35

---

20 defawt] defaulte *1557*   21 auctoryte] authoritie *1557*   23 chapyter] Chapter
1557   29 here.] *1557*, here *1533*   30 Yet] *1557*, yet *1533*

wytnes agaynst hym, & bysydes all that, a dowte that he wolde fle wherby
he myghte enfecte other: than he graunteth it conuenyent that he shold be
arrested by the body. And therin he bryngeth in the Clementine and the
statute, by which the ordinaries haue power to arrest folke for suspycyon of
5 *heresye / and wold as farre as I perceyue, haue the kynge reforme them*
after hys deuyce. But yet syth whych is a lyght suspycyon, and whych is an
heuy / and whych is a lyght complaynt, and whych is an heuy / and whych
is an open suspycyon, and whyche but a preuy, and whyche suspycyon ys
notable, and whyche is not notable, and whyche wytnesses be suffycyent,
10 *[P₂v] and which be not suffycyent, be thynges that must be wayed by the*
spyrytuall iudges / and vppon theyr wayenge of the mater for lyght or
heuy, muste folowe the arrestynge of the party or the leuynge of the
arreste: we be come agayne as in a mase to the poynt where we beganne,
that be the mater greate or smale, lest all the whyle they be cruell they shold
15 *iudge lyghte heuy and smale greate, theyr arrestynge of any at all muste be*
susspended fro them, and sende them to sue by cytacyon, tyll men se that
same mynde of theyrs of desyryng mennes abiuracyon and punysshement
vtterly chaunged and ceace / that is to say tyll there be no man lefte that
wyll so myche as saye, that some men saye that they haue not lefte that
20 *mynde yet, and make a lye agayne of theym than, as those some haue done*
that haue so sayde all redy to syr Iohn some say now. And longe wyll it be I
warraunt you ere euer all suche folke fayle. [P₃]

   And therfore syth in the mean season by thys pacyfyers good deuyse,
heretykes may go vnarrested / I can not byleue that yf his way were
25 *folowed, it wold be any good meane to make that wylful offenders in*
heresy shold not passe vnpunysshed, as faste as bothe in the ende of thys
chapyter & the tother before also, he calleth vpon the kynges hyghnes and
hys counsayle and hys parleament, to loke vppon thys mater after his good
aduertysement, and neuer ceace tyll they brynge it to effecte.

30   Here you se good readers, bycause thys man wyth hys deuyces
bryngeth hym selfe into a mase, out of whyche he can not se how
to gete, he wold now set other folke to study there about. And
wolde make theym very carefull, aboute a thynge lytle nedefull.
For it hath well appered, & well ben proued to, that the spyritual
35 iuges haue yet hytherto in arrestyng for heresy, ryght well examyned and [P₃v] considered, fyrst bothe the cause, and the necessyte, & haue ben rather therin many tymes to slow / than any

---

19 not] *om.* 1557   27 chapyter] Chapter 1557

tyme ouer hasty. And therfore I maye and wyll say here agayn as
I sayd there, that I lytell dowte but that yf the kynges hyghnes do
as I dowte not but his hyghnes wyll do, maynteyne and assyste
the spyrytualty in executyng of the lawes, euyn those y^t are all
redy made agaynst heresyes / & commaunde euery temporall   5
officer vnder hym to do ye same for his part: though ther were
neuer mo new laues made therfore, yet shall both innocentes be
saued harmelesse well inough, & offendours punyshed to.

To thys commeth forth this good man in this wise.

Now veryly to those wordes of mayster More I dare say thus, that   10
mayster More or he had spoken tho wordes, had occasyon by reasonable coniecture to haue doubted more at the mater thenne he hath
done, and to haue thought it very lyke, that yf the same lawes shulde
stonde as do nowe in euery poynt concernynge heresye, that many
innocentes that be not gylty, myghte vppon suspeccyon of heresye be   15
dryuen to pourge theym selfe, after the wyll of the ordynarye, and yet
be not gylty. Ye and ouer that [P$_4$] mayster More myghte haue reasonably doubted, & as I suppose in conscience he ought to haue doubted
more then he hath done, that somtyme innocentes myghte happen
vppon the suyte Ex officio, or vppon lyght complayntes by fauour of   20
offycers, or vppon malyce or dyspleasure, be arrested before examinacyon, and yet mayster More hym selfe assenteth, that the examynacyon
shulde be before the arreste. And he myghte haue doubted also, that
some innocentes myght by suche periured persons, as be aboue rehersed in thys chapyter be somtyme condempned. And therfore the   25
sayde wordes of mayster More wherby he taketh vppon hym to saye, as
it were in hys owne auctoryte to performe it, that innocentes by the
same lawes as be all redy made for heresye, shalbe saued harmelesse
well inough, myght happen to be of small effect to helpe an innocent
man or woman that shulde happen to be wrongfully troubled in tyme   30
to come agaynst hys wordes before rehersed.

Now verily to all these wordes of this good man, I dare say
thus, that I whan I wrote the wordes had & yet haue very good
coniecturs to put litle dowt therin. For though I myghte thynke

---

8 well inough] wel ynough *1557*, wellinough *1533*   9 forth] furth *1557*   17 Ye]
Yea *1557*, ye *1533*   25 chapyter] chapter *1557*   27 auctoryte] authoritie
1557   28 harmlesse] harmeles *1557*, harme lesse *1533*   31 rehersed.] *1557*, rehersed *1533*

y^t this harme and this harme myghte happe: yet syth I haue well
sene it proued, y^t the spyritual iudges haue vsed them self in
these maters, not onely so truly, but ouer y^t also so fauorably / y^t
no man can proue in this realm suche harmes to haue happed
5   yet / [P$_4$v] but where as such thynges haue ben of late surmysed,
the trouth hath ben well proued contrary byfore the kynges
honorable counsayle / I had and haue very good cause to thynke,
that as they haue done well hytherto, so shall they well do
hereafter.

10 And syth all thys good mannes grownd is no more, to take
away wel approued lawes with, but y^t harme maye happe sometyme, to some good man therby, whyche reason he maye make
agaynst the beste lawe that all the worlde can make: I dare be
bold to warraunt, that that colde reason so feruentely sette
15 forthe in suche a weyghty mater, is not well worthe a ryshe.

And yf men wolde go aboute to chaunge these old long
proued lawes: I wolde as my duyte is, praye god geue them y^e
grace to make the chaunges good / but for that lytle wyt that I
haue, I veryly byleue and thynke [P$_5$] that yf any chaunges be
20 made rather more slacke then streighter: then shal the chaunges
be made rather farre worse then better. And thus ende I good
readers this good mannys .xvii. chapyter.

The .xviii. chapyter

H IS .xviii. chapyter begynneth, fo. lxix. Wherin he beginneth
25 first wyth the ca. vt inquisitionis negocium & li.vi. wherby yt
appereth, that all lordes and rulers temporall, be prohybyted
that they shall not in any maner take knoweledge or iuge vppon
heresye. And vppon this hym self addeth vnto it in his boke of
dyuysyon, that he y^t enquyreth of heresy, taketh knoweledge of
30 heresy, and y^t him selfe sayth [P$_5$v] not so alone, but that Summa
Rosella sayth so to. And hereuppon he concludeth, that yt sholde
seme, that all the iustyces of the peace be excommunycate, and al
stewardes in letys, & all enquestes to, as many as medle wyth all.
For whether in letys they may or not: that he sayth he dowteth,

---

15 forthe] furth *1557*   24 chapyter] Chapter *1557*   26 prohybyted] prohibited
1557, prohyhyted *1533*

nos. de his que fi. a pte. imo quod non est gestuz
nomine meo possum p nouum consensum ratifi-
care. pro hoc glo. in.c. cum ad sedem. de resti. spo.
Et ad materiam ratibabitiōis vide Panoz. in. c.
j. de cōuer. insi. vbi dicit q̊ ratihabitio retrotrahi
tur ex fictione iuris. Sed ad hoc vt fictio pcedat
requirit q̊ ambo duo extrema sint habilia ad illū
actum perpetrādum. scz tempus in quo act? fuit
gestus z tempus ratibabitionis. Si enim deficit
alterum istorū non pcedit fictio: quia non causae
sup impossibili. Pone exemplū. Quidam interse-
cit hominē nomine infantis: demū infans maior
factus habet ratum. Certe hec ratibabitio nō tra-
bitur retro: quia impossibile erat illum infantem
tunc temporis mandare delictum. ergo nō potest
retrotrahi: cum nō debeat plus posse fictio q̊ veritas. Et istud appellatur extremū ad quod. Pone exemplū in extremo a quo. Debebam termi-
num ad certum quid agēdum: amicus meus nomine meo illud egit: ego post terminū habui ratū
nūquid sufficiat: Dic q̊ non: cum post terminuz
nō potuissem ego vere facere. ergo nec ficte. Ideo
ad hoc vt possim ratum habere quod est gestum
nomine meo. requirit q̊ illo tempore ego potuissem facere vere: quo fuit gestum. Ad hoc vide q̊
notat He. in. c. cum quis. de sen. excō. li. vj. q̊ non
sufficit ad hoc vt quis censeatur cōmisisse malefi-
cium habeat ratum quod est gestum nomine suo
quādo. lex requirit maleficiū z p prius tractatum.
Pro hoc allegat glo. zibi per Jo. an. in dicto. c.j.
Pone exemplum. Quis nomine mulieris machinatus est in morte viri sui: z mulier ratum habuit. nūquid poterit cōtrahere matrimoniū cum
illo qui machinatus est. Glo. ibi videtur dicere q̊
sic. Idem panoz. q̊ lex nō solū requirit maleficiū:
sed etiā p prius tractatum. Ideo q̊uis sit gestum
nomine mulieris: tamē habēdo ratum nō censet
cōmisisse homicidiū quo ad impediendū matrimoniū. Secus qn lex requirit solum factum. Et
tunc ratibabitio faceret incurrere penam ipsum
ratificantem.

¶ Excommunicatio .j.

Cōmuniter quid sit: Rn. sm Panoz.
extra eo. sup ricā. q̊ excōicatio est cen-
sura a canone vel a iudice ecclesiastico plata: pri-
uans cōmunione sacroz et q̊uz hominuz. Et sic
sm materia nostrā due sunt species excōicatiōis
scz maioz: z illa priuat ptici patiōe sacroz z cōmunione hoīm. Quedā est minoz. z illa priuat ptici-
pati one sacroz. nō aut pmuniōe fideliuz. vt in. c.
si. de cle. ex. mi. Item minoz excōicatio fert q̊uz a
iure. q̊uz potest ferri ab homie. licz nūc nō sit in
vsu. Ite excōicationū. Alia est iur?. s. qua quis incurrit ipo iure delicto cōmisso: vt si quis iniiciat
manus violētas in clericū. xvij. q̊. iiij. si q̊s. Alia ē
iudicis. s. que irrogat a iudice: potestatē habēte p
pcessum iudiciariū. extra eo. nup.

¶ In quibus casibus incidit quis excōmunicatione maiorem ipo facto: Rn. in multis casibus.
Multos habes s. Absolutio pmo et scdo. Sunt

z alij casus. Primus cum quis incidit in heresim
iam damnatā. xxiiij. q.j. c.j. et. ij. Et glo. ibi i sum-
mario dicit: siue vetere: siue nouam sequat heresim est excōicatus. Item credens: receptatoz vel
fautoz hereticoz. extra de here. excōicamus. Et
casus hodie est papalis per pcessum curie. Et intellige predicta sm glo. singularē in cle. j. de here.
etiā si sit oīno occultus. Et facit regulā q̊ ecclesia
ligat crimen oīno occultum quo ad penas excōicationis z suspensiōis. Et nota illud verbū oīno
quod denotat solum actum interiorem z non ali-
quod signum exterius. De hoc vide diffuse supra
Absolutio primo.

¶ Qui aūt dicant credētes hereticoz: Rn. do.
An. q̊ quidā sunt credentes hereticos ee bonos
z istis nō imponit pena hereticoz. Quidam sunt
credentes hereticoz erronibz. z tales sunt heretici
Pe. aūt de anch. in. c. quicūq̊. de here. li. vj. dicit
q̊ credentes dicitur qui se dicunt credere eorum
erroribus. de pe. di. j. potest. Item qui in orationi-
bus sequūtur eorum ritum: z cōmunione ab hereticis recipiūt: vel similia que ad eoz ritum pti-
nent. Et ideo tales dicitur credentes: quia pru-
mitur affectus ad eos esse quoz opera sequūtur.
Defensores autē sunt qui psonam defendunt: vt
aduocati pstando patrocinia. vel tabelliones fa-
ciendo instrumēta: vt iuuando in causa. Qui aūt
non psonam sed heresim defendit: heresiarcha ē.
Receptatores vo sunt: qui in domo vel in terra
sua eos recipiūt. semel vel pluries: publice vel pri-
uate. Fautores sunt qui aliqd fauent facto: mitte-
do alimoniā vel huiusmodi. Aliqñ verbo vt di-
cendo. Isti sunt boni homies: z iniuste agit pctra
eos. Item omissione. qn quis potestate fungitur
in capiēdo. z als non fauet inquisitoribz sicut debent. omnes isti sunt excōicati ipo facto. Item qui
in potestate existens omittit facere qd debet. licz
nihil exterius agat excōmunicatione incurrit: q̊
ad idem iudiciū ptinet habit? z puatio.

¶ Secūdus casus. Quicūq̊ hereticos: credētes: receptatores: vel fautores eorum scienter pre-
sumpserit ecclesiastice tradere sepulture: vsq̊ ad
satisfactionē idonea. excōicationis sententie se
nouerit subiacere. nec absolutiōis bñficiū mereat
nisi prijs manibus extumulet publice z proiiciat
huiusmodi corpora damnatoz: z locus ille perpe-
tua careat sepultura. extra de here. ca. Quicunq̊.
libro. vj.

¶ Tercius rectores impediētes vel non iuuantes episcopos z inquisitores in inquisitione here-
ticorū z credentiū eis z fautorz z receptatoz: sut
excōicati. extra eo. vt inquisitionis. li. vj. Et quia
pape nō reseruat absolutio: ordinarij poterit absoluere. Nota sm Pe. de an. super cle. de vsu. et
graui. q̊ actus fenerādi non sapit heresim: nec p-
tinet ad inquisitorem. z tamen ptinaciter asserere
hoc non esse peccatū: est hereticū. Rōnem collige ex glo. ibi. Et quo collige decisionē huius. q̊
Quidam in publicis pdicationibus predicando
z concitando turbam et seditionem contra cleru
asseruit q̊ laici non tenebantur soluere. decimas.

Baptista de Salis, *Summa casuum conscientiae* [*Summa rosella*] (1488), sig. o₁v (reduced).

nec eis confiteri:nec oblationes dare. et ꝙ pecca̅
bant cōtrarium faciendo:cum essent omnes cleri
ci mali ꝝ d ecclesijs remouendi. Querebaꝶ an ista
ꝝ plura alia essent heretica:ꝝ procedi possit contra
eum tanꝗ hereticum. et firmatū fuit per omnes
theo.ꝝ doct. vtrinsꝗ iuris ibi existe̅tes ꝙ sic:quia
sapiebat heresim ꝝ ꝑtinaciter tenebat diuersas et
friuolas opiniones reprobatas per sacros cano-
nes.Et pau.clarius loque̅s dicit hereticus est:nō
solum qui male sentit de articulis fidei ꝝ sacrame̅-
tis ecclesie:sed etiā qui falsam ꝝ extortam expositi
one in scripturis diuinis ponit cōtra id qd tenet
ecclesia.Et quia sunt nōnulli casus:in quibus ꝓ-
babiliter dubitatur vtrum in isto vel in illo casu
sit vsura. nō esset hereticus qui teneret opinione̅
etiā forte nō verā.Iudei aut ꝗuis affirment vsu-
ram nō esse peccatū: nō possunt dici heretici; nec
taliter ꝓtra eos procedi potest: qꝝ in eis nō cadit
heresis.Et cum nō sint de gremio ecclesie diuisi
one ab ea facere nō possunt.Si tame̅ errorem suū
dogmatizarent.ꝝ si nō vt cōtra hereticos:tame̅ ꝑ
alios modos possent ꝑ ecclesiam puniri.sicut ꝝ in
alijs casibus qn offendunt fidem.Nota etiā fm
Pan.i dicta cle.ex graui.ꝙ dicere ꝑtinaciter vsu-
ram esse peccatum:sed facta restitutione nō esse cō-
fitendū.Sicut qui est obligatus ex contractu lici-
to:est hereticus.

¶ Quartus dūī tempales qui cognoscu̅t de offi
tio inquisitiōis:aut captos liberarent:excōmuni-
cati sunt.extra eo.vt inquisitiōis.li.vj.Et hoc in-
tellige:siue principaliter:siue incide̅ter cognoscāt.
puta qꝝ de causa principali cognoscentes; faciunt
capi hereticū.Incide̅ter. puta quia fecerunt eum
capi alia de causa. sed incidenter de hoc inquisie-
runt.Item nota.ꝙ dantes auxilium ꝓsilium vel
fauorem eis sunt excōmunicati: si scienter hoc faciunt ꝝ ordinarius absoluere poterit.

¶ Quint⁹ inquisitores: ꝝ ipoꝝ seu episcopoꝝ vl̉
ꝝhonicoꝝ sede vacante:sup hoc deputati cōmis-
sarij:si sub pretextu officij inquisitiōis quibusuis
modis illicitis ab aliquib⁹ pecuniā extorque̅t.aut
scienter attēptant ecclesiarū bona ob clericoꝝ delictum ꝑdicti occasione officij fisco ecclesie applica
re sunt excōmunicati ꝝ absolui nō possunt ꝑterꝗ
in mortis articulo donec illis a quib⁹ extorserint:
plene satisfecerint de extortis. ꝝ nullis priuilegijs
pactis:aut remissionib⁹ super hoc valituris. vt in
cle.nolentes eo.ti. Et Jo.an. super verbo ecclesie
dicit multominus sibi psis; vel officialib⁹ vel fisco seculari: cui applicata sunt ipso iure bona lai-
coꝝ damnatoꝝ d heresi.

¶ Sextus est de quadā excōmunicatiōe que po
nitur in.c.primo.de scis. Et ibi Panor. dicit ꝙ in
tribus casibus quis incurrit illam excōmunicati
onem. Primus quādo quis emit rem ecclesiasti-
cam:vel aliter acquirit a scismatico. Et sic nota ca
sum in quo emens rem ecclesiasticā est ipso facto
excōmunicatus.Al's aute̅ regulariter etiam occu
pans rem ecclesiasticā nō est excōmunicatus: sed
excōmunicādus. vt in.c.cōquestus.de fo.compe.
Secūdus qn quis tenet beneficium a scismatico.

Tertius qn quis initiatur ordinationi facte ꝑ eu̅
ꝝ nota fm Hosti. illos esse scismaticos tn̅: qui
se extollunt contra romanam ecclesiam ꝝ ab illa se
separant.Et isti sunt excōmunicati cum adheren-
tibus.Et dicitur tales heretici. Illi vo qui volu̅t
cōtra episcopū aliquem insurgere: ꝝ episcopatum
suum tollere: ꝝ clericos suos facere; excōmunica-
di sunt. Item nota. ꝙ scismatici ꝑut in dicto.c.ſ.
sunt illi qui sunt diuisi ab vnitate ecclesie ꝝ qui cō
nantur sibi episcopos: pſbyteros ꝝ ꝑstitutiōes cre
are. vij.q.j.nouacian⁹. Sed nūquid omnes tales sint heretici? Hosti.tenet ꝙ nō. dūmodo re
cognoscant romanā ecclesiā:qꝝ tunc non sunt ab
vnitate diuisi.Vnde duo licꝝ ꝑtendāt se esse pontifices romanos:nō ꝓpter hoc heretici sunt:qꝝ cre
dunt vnam ecclesiā:licꝝ quilibet credat se eius spō
sum esse.Sꝝ siquis se papam ꝑtenderet:quia crederet ecclesiam duos posse habere pontifices: eēt
heretic⁹ quia crederet duas ecclesias.Et ex predi-
ctis patꝝ ꝙ greci hucusꝗ fuerunt excōmunicati:
qui fuerūt diuisi ab eo qd ecclesia ꝑ articulis fidei
determinauit.

¶ Septim⁹.Qui asserit ꝑtumaciter romanā ec-
clesiā nō esse caput ecclesiaꝝ: ꝝ nō posse cōdere canones: ꝝ ei etiam tanꝗ capiti nō esse obediendū.
excōmunicat⁹ est.xix.dist.nulli.Et no.ꝙ illud.c.
loquitur de contēptorib⁹ canonū ꝝ transgresso-
ribus.Et fm Vg.ibidem dupliciter dicitur quis
ꝑtēptor canonū. Vno modo qui apostolicā sedē
contumaciter negat esse caput ecclesiaꝝ. ꝝ habere
potestatē cōdendi canones ꝝ decreta: ꝝ statuta ei⁹
nō esse obseruanda.et talis est excōmunicatus et
heretic⁹ ꝝ scismaticus. ꝝ sic intelligiꝝ dictū capms
nulli. Et est canon late sente̅tie. Idem dicit In-
noc.Jo.an. ꝝ Host.Secūdo mo dicitur qs cō-
tēptor ꝝ transgressor canonū: qui ipsa mandata
canonū nō seruat ꝗuis credat ꝝ dicat esse seruan-
da.Et hic nō est scismaticus ꝓrie nec excōmunicatus. Et sic de huiusmodi intelligendo est canē
ferende sentētie.

¶ Octauus excōicati sunt oēs violatores ecclesiastice libertatis. Et ꝑsertim qui contra sacroꝝ
canonū instituta ecclesijs: ꝝ ecclesiasticis personis
sine licētia speciali romani pontificis collectas vl̉
alia onera aut queuis grauamina realia: vel ꝑso-
nalia imponu̅t.aut exigunt. aut erigi faciunt vel
ꝓcurant. ꝝ est hodie papalis ꝓ ꝑcessum curie.

¶ Quero nūquid clerici teneātur ad aliqua one
ra? Dic ꝙ persone ecclesiastice nō debent granari
an gartijs vel pangartijs. puta ad fossata faciend●
ꝝ huiusmodi.vt in.c.nō minus.de imu.eccle.nec
ad collectas vel talleas.siue exactiones qualscūꝗ.
vt in.c.aduersus.de imu.eccle. Nec pro domib⁹
predijs. vel quibuscūꝗ possessionibus ab eisdem
ecclesijs vel ꝑsonis ecclesiasticis legitime bacten⁹
acꝗsitis vel imposteru̅ acquirendis.vt.c.j.de im-
mu.eccle.li.vj.

¶ Sed dubitaꝶ.nūquid ecclesia vel clerici tene-
a̅tur soluere onera ꝓ possessionibus eis collatis
que prius erānt tributarie? Rū. Panor. in.c.fi.
de vi.et bone.cle. post multa concludit ꝙ aut illa

o ij

Baptista de Salis, *Summa casuum conscientiae* [*Summa rosella*](1488), sig. o₂ (reduced).

but he sayth y^t I say they may, but he telleth not where I say so,
nor as I veryly thynke he neuer founde yt in any boke of myne. I
saye in myne apologye, fo. 227. that in euery lete they do so,
whyther they lawfully so maye do or not thereof speke I nothynge / all be yt I thynke they may well ynough, bothe wythout   5
offence of the kynges lawe, or parell of cursynge eyther.

For I lytle doute, but that there were of the clergye at the
makynge of the statute mo men then one, y^t vnderstode Summa
Rosella, as well as thys good man dothe, yf Sum[P$_6$]ma Rosella
were then made and in mennys handes.   10

And I doute also as lytle, but y^t there were at those days in the
clergye mo then one, that were of counsayle in the makynge of
the statute, that vnderstode the chapyter vt inquisitionis, as wel
as this man doth, and as well as he that made Summa Rosella to.
And that they well vnderstode that the sayde chapyter ment of   15
suche inquysytours, and suche inquysycyons, as they make that
are in the corps of the lawe called Inquisitores heretice
prauitatis / of whyche there are in some places specyall offycers
to enquyre, procede, and do therin as thordynaryes do: and
ment not of such inquyrours and suche inquysycyons, as do   20
none other wise inquyre, but onely by way of informacyon to
brynge the mater to the ordynaryes knowledge.

For as for the minour of this good mannys argument, that he
that enquy[P$_6$v]reth of heresye, taketh knowledge of heresye, so
dothe euery denouncer, euery accuser, and in a maner euery   25
wytnesse to, take vppon theym knowledge of heresye in some
maner wise: for they take vppon theym as they well maye that
thys thynge or that thynge is heresye. But thys is not the knowlege that the law forbedeth: but the knowledge that we call holdynge ple vpon yt, whyche our inquysycyons do not: but onely   30
serue to brynge the mater to the ordynaryes handes, whyche
ellys sholde peraduenture not haue herde therof.

And for thys cause, to be sure that by these inquysycyons no
man shold fall in daunger of any excommunycacyon yt was substancially prouyded in the sayde statute, y^t thynquisicyon and   35

---

11 doute] *1533 corr. err.*, doute not *1533*, doubte not *1557*   14 man] *1557*, mam
1533   24 enquyreth] *1557*, enqnyreth *1533*   26 heresye] heresy *1557*, herelye
1533   34 excommunycacyon] *1533 corr. err.*, examynacyon *1533*, examinacion *1557*

the endyghtement of heresye, shold serue the ordynarye
nothynge to the procedynge in the mater: but that he shold
begynne hys processe agaynste the [P₇] partye a freshe, wythoute layenge that endyghtement vnto hys charge.

5   And therfore where as this good man, by the hygh authorite of
Summa Rosella denounceth here al the iustyces of peace accursed, I dare be bold by the hyghe authoryte of Summa Angelica to denounce them all assoyled agayne. And therfore
where as this good man wenynge that he had well wonne hys
10   spurrys in thys poynte tryumpheth vppon me and sayeth.

And to thys lawe mayster More answereth not, but passeth yt ouer, as
a thynge that as yt semeth he lytle regardeth / but onely that he sayth,
that the lawes of thys realme, and of holy chyrche in heresyes maye well
stande to gether, for oughte that he seeth: And yet yt appereth, that
15   vppon thys lawe they do not agree nor stande to gether. And therfore
me thynketh yt wolde not be so lyghtly passed ouer as mayster More
doth passe yt ouer. For yt is a daungerous thynge to fall into the leste
censure of the chyrche.

There were two causes for whyche I answered hym not / one a
20   generall cause, concernynge all hys maters of lawes of the
chyrche, wherin [P₇v] he fyndeth fautes, of whych I shall speke
afterwarde. A nother specyall cause there was concernynge thys
excommunycacyon. And that was that me thought & yet thinke,
that he spake therin so chyldyshely that I was ashamed on his
25   byhalfe to medle with yt / and to make open hys chyldyshe
handlynge therof.

But nowe syth I se hym compte for so great a conqueste, that
he put me to sylence therin, what purpose can he dyuyse for
whyche I sholde haue answered any thynge to that poynt? had I
30   made any professyon to proue euery worde wronge that he sayd
in all hys boke? he knoweth that I sayde not that I wolde medle,
but wyth those certayne thynges that I there speke of.

But now suppose that there were in that law such faute as he
allegeth what could myne answere amende the mater, or his
35   boke of diuisyon either? [P₈] If men were accursed as he mysse

---

6–7 accursed,] accursed. *1533 1557*   21 fautes] faultes *1557*   33 faute] fault *1557*

taketh it, could my boke or his boke take away the curse? No, but
we may put the parlyament in mynde to make a lawe. His boke
alone is as able to put theym in remembraunce therof as hys and
myne to gether. And yet for that poynte neyther nedeth myne
nor hys neyther. For the parlyament hath made all redy a lawe   5
for these inquysycyons. Whych yf they myght lawfully make in
such forme as they haue (as I am sure they myght) then am I sure
y^t they fall not in excommunycacyon for it. Now if they myghte
not laufully make it, & therby fel therin, what could the parlyament farther adde vnto it, that might deliuer them of yt? And   10
therfore I can not in good fayth se to what purpose he wrote of
that poynte hym selfe.

No but thys lawe is one great cause of dyuisyon betwene the
spyrytualtye and the temporaltye. That [P$_8$v] wolde I very fayne
wyt howe. For temporall men be not I wote well so farre ouer-   15
sene, as to be angry wyth the spyrytual men here now, for that
lawe that a pope made at Rome ere they were borne. And the
spyrytuall men haue also as lytle cause agayn of any grudge
agaynst the temporaltye for the mater. And therfore why he
sholde put yt in hys boke of dyuysyon, for a cause of diuisyon I   20
can dyuyse no reason. For as for that, that he wolde shold seme a
cause here, is to vnresonable where he sayth.

As long as that law standeth so vnrepelled / some prestes that se yt, wyll
saye that they that do agaynste yt / be accursed: and so may lyghtly fall
therby into a wrongfull and vntrew iudgement / whych though yt be no   25
great offence, oneles yt be of pryde / by dyspysynge of the temporall
power in that behalfe, yet yt wolde be eschewed. And also yf they that
be so noysed to be accursed / here of yt, they wyll be dyscontented. And
so grudges and varyaunces maye ryse and encrease by occasyon of yt.

Thys is a very colde tale, & as dede as euer was dore nayle. For   30
before hym selfe broughte in thys babe[Q$_1$]lynge of his owne
about that lawe / (whych babelyng is yet (as I haue shewed you) to
no purpose at all) I neuer herd any man talke any such worde of
that lawe in my dayes, nor in good fayeth no more I wene dyd he
neyther.   35

---

6 they] *1557*, thy *1533*   21 For as] *1557*, Foras *1533*   32 yet (as) yet] as *1533 1557*;
you) to] you (to *1557*

Nor I dare saye he hereth no where yet any prestes saye, that the iustyces of the peace be accursed for enquyrynge agaynste heresyes / none I dare saye but suche prestes as be heretyques. And therfore thys whole tale of his, saue for the malice that yt

5 meaneth / ys euyn a very tryflynge.

For as for ye mocyon y^t he maketh so often to haue that lawe repelled, bycause yt is he sayth agaynst the lawes of the realme: excepte he mokke I wote nere what he meaneth. For yf the realme here may repell yt: then by y^t the law is here made to the

10 contrarye (yf yt were contrary as yt is not) [Q₁v] yt is repelled all redy. And yf he thynke that the realme here can not repell yt / thenne whereto wryteth he and prenteth that pyece in his boke of dyuysyon, as a thynge for whyche the temporaltye & the spyrytualty of thys realme sholde fall in varyaunce for, where

15 neyther the makynge nor the repellynge lyeth in neyther nother of theyr handes.

But surely the repellyng though yt be the thyng that is spoken of, is not yet the thynge y^t ys ment in thys mater as yt appereth in these wordes.

20 And therfore me thynketh yt wolde not be so lyghtly passed ouer as mayster More doth passe yt ouer. For yt is a daungerous thynge to fall into the leste censure of the chyrche. And yf yt be sayde, that the sayde lawe ys voyde, bycause the chyrche hadde no authoryte to make yt: And that yt is therfore not to be fered. And I wyll yet say therto, that

25 though yt were voyde / that yet as longe yt standeth so not repelled, yt were good to eschewe it, and not to fal wylfully into the daunger of yt: and therfore yt were better to repelle yt then to lette yt stande styll, and rather do hurte then good.

Here you may se good readers, that where as otherwyse to

30 repell [Q₂] that law then it is repelled, lyeth not in oure handes yf oure lawe were agaynste yt / and where as of trouthe yt nedeth no repellynge at all, but the lawe of the realme standeth therwyth well ynough, he maketh as though al the iustyces of peace were accursed there by, as ofte as they geue the iuryes in charge to

35 enquyre of heresye: therfore leste they sholde wylfully fal into

---

12 whereto] wherto *1557*, wereto *1533*   14 varyaunce] variance *1557*, varyaunce
1533   18 appereth] appeareth *1557*, aypereth *1533*   25 longe] long as *1557*

the censures of the chyrche, wherof as he sayth the leste is a
daungerouse thyng, ye may playnly se that these wyly shrewes
whych abuse his labour, meane in all thys mater nothynge ellys,
but that they wolde not haue heresyes enquyred of. And yet they
nede not so greatly to care therfore, for any great thinges y^t by   5
such inquisycions are in heresyes presented. But yet thus declare
they theyr good wylles these wyly shrewes y^t thus deceyue this
good symple soule, & set hym so euyll a worke.

If he fere so·myche y^e censures of [Q$_2$v] the chyrche as he
maketh for, and vnderstande and byleue Summa Rosella so   10
surely as he pretendyth: yt hadde ben better for hym to examyne
well hys boke of dyuysyon, and thys his seconde boke also by the
tytles of Summa Rosella, and se well whyther hym selfe varye not
fro Summa Rosella, & be by ye sentence of Summa Rosella fallen
in the censures of the chyrche hym selfe, by some such maner of   15
wrytynge as hys sayde bokes haue.

But now cometh this good pacifier forthe wyth a goodly pyece
& to declare hym selfe indyfferent, and to shewe also a great
ouersyght vsed vppon my parte: thus the good man Some say
sayth.   20

And therfore yt semeth ryght expedyent that the sayd law be repelled. And in lyke wyse it were good to repelle all suche lawes
spyrytuall, as be made contrarye to the kynges lawes and the custome
of the realme. And yf yt be sayde, that yt were good also / that suche
statutes and lawes / as be made and vsed by the temporall power to the   25
grefe of the people were also reformed / and that yf I were in-
dyffe[Q$_3$]rente / I wolde make some mocyon so to haue yt: And so it
semeth mayster More doth partely moue, that I ought to haue done, &
to haue founde as wel defaute in the temporall lawe as in the spyrytuall
lawe: How be yt bycause he wolde beare no blame of the temporall lawe   30
in that mocyon, yt semeth that he somwhat mytygateth hys sentence
therin and sayeth / that yf I do so / and that then I handle theym / that
ys to saye, the temporall lawes and fynde defautes at them / as trewly as
I do at these, that is to saye at the spyrytuall lawes: that then I shulde
make two lyes for one / and yet as I suppose, I haue assigned some   35

---

1 chyrche] churche *1557*, chyrhe *1533*   17 forthe] furth *1557*   29 defaute] defaulte *1557*   30 he] *1557*, be *1533*
(*see note*); defautes] defaultes *1557*   33 ys to] is to *Salem and Bizance*, *1557*, ys *1533*

defautes in the spyrytuall lawe / whyche mayster More can not tell howe they shulde be excused.

As to hys repellynge, I se as I haue sayde no substaunce in hys wordes. For we repell theym as farre as I se we can, when we
5 kepe theym not but make our owne lawes to the contrary. And therfore as farre as I se all that he speketh of these repellynges, saue onely for settynge forth of his dyuysyon, is ellys but a very vayne tale.

But nowe where he sayeth that I wolde haue hym and seme to
10 moue hym / to fynde fautes in the temporall lawe to: I wote nere [Q₃v] whether his wordes haue herein more falsed or more foly / but surely they haue both twayn, and eyther the tone or the tother double.

For fyrste euery man maye se by his owne wordes euen here,
15 that I moue hym not to vse as for indyfferencye, to fynde fautes in the temporall lawes as he hath done wyth the spyrytuall lawes, when hym selfe here sheweth that I saye that yf he so dyd, he sholde make double lyes. This sheweth that he vseth in thys saynge playne and open vntrouthe. And syth hys owne
20 vntrouthe appereth vppon hys owne shewynge, thys sheweth also, that he vseth open foly.

And where he sayeth that he hath assygned some defautes in the spyrytuall lawes, which I can not tel how they sholde be excused: I answere hym agayne, that vnto all lawes, or all maters
25 that he lyste to bable of, [Q₄] am I not bounde to medle wyth / but of these spyrytuall lawes that were made for the repressyng of heresyes, wyth whyche oure temporall lawes are also conformable and concurraunt, wyth whyche thys good wyse man for the ease of heretyques, hath now founden suche fautes as a wyse
30 man maye be ashamed to speke of, I haue clerely declared that they nede not to be excused / but that for the fyndynge of suche fautes hys foly to be myche accused. Thys haue I proued so playne, that he can fynde no great cause of glorye when he loketh backe vppon yt.

---

1 defautes] defaultes *1557*   7 forth] furth *1557*   10 fautes] faultes *1557;* to:] too: *1557,* to. *1533*   15 fautes] faultes *1557*   22 defautes] defaultes *1557*   28 concurraunt,] concurraunt *1533,* concurrant *1557*   29 fautes] faultes *1557*   32 fautes] faultes *1557*   34 loketh] looketh *1557,* lokath *1533*

But nowe to thentent you maye good readers se, that eyther
this man is not so symple in hym selfe as he semeth, or els that
some wyly shrewes shamefully do deceyue hym: I beseche you
consyder a lytle eyther the foly or the crafte that the man vseth
here. [Q₄v]

He hathe brought you forth wordes of myne whych I speke he
sayth of the lawes, where as of trouthe I speke theym not of the
lawes at all, as your selfe shall well se. For though he dyssemble
the place bycause he wolde not haue you reade yt: yet haue I
soughte yt oute for you, in the .99. lefe of myne Apologye / and
there lo these are my wordes.

*And thys pacyfyer aggreueth (as myche as in hym lyeth) the clergye of
Englande, for vse of the lawes not made by theym selfe, but be commen
lawes of all chrystendome. If he wyll saye that he blameth but theyr abuses
therof, the trouth appereth in some place otherwyse in hys boke. And yet
syth he proueth that poynte but by a some say / he myght wyth the same
fygure lay lyke fautes in the temporaltye concernynge the lawes of thys
realme, and proue yt in lyke wyse wyth a greate Somme [Q₅] say to. And
therin he sheweth him self not indyfferent whan he bryngeth in the tone
and leueth the tother out. And on the tother syde, yf he brynge in the tother
to / than shall he make two fawtes for one. For yf he handle them as truely
as he handeleth these / than shall he make two lyes for one.*

Lo good readers consyder here I bysech you the maner of thys
good man. To the fyrst piece of these wordes of myne, in whyche
case is also the law that we be now in hand with al, vt inquisitionis,
wherwith he wold in hys boke of dyuysyon aggreue the clergye
of this realme whych neuer made the lawe: he answereth not in
all his boke one word. And yet in his such maner of aggreuynge
he vseth a very synfull, and in hys not answerynge, a very sham-
full waye.

Than in the remanaunt you se good readers your self, that I
speke not of the lawes. For whan I saye [Q₅v] thus, yf he wyll say
that he blameth but theyr abuses therof: yet syth he proueth that
point but by a Somsay / he myghte by the same fygure laye lyke
fawtes in the temporalty to, concernyng the lawes of this realme:

---

6 forth] furth *1557*   17 fautes] faultes *1557*   20 And] *para. 1557*   21 fawtes]
faultes *1557*   22 one.] *1557*, one *1533*   28 word. And] word, and *1557*   35
fawtes] faultes *1557*

is it not here playne that I laye blame in hym, for hys bylying of
the mynistres of the spyrytuall lawes vnder a figure of Somsay, as
though they abused the spyrytuall lawes in myssehandelynge of
heretykes wherof I speke more after. And I saye that by a lyke
5 figure of Some say, he might dyffame all the temporall mynistres
to, and brynge theym in grudge and obloquy of the peple wyth
lyke lyes of abusyng the temporal lawes to.

Now consyder good readers, eyther how falsely thys honest
man hath hym self, or ellys how folyshly he hath suffered false
10 shrewys, to make hym turne and chaunge the sentence of my
wordes fro the men to [Q₆] the lawes, to brynge in his maters
vppon, and say that I moue hym to fynde fawtes in the temporal
lawes and put them in prente abrode as he doth in the tother,
where as you playnely se I speke not of the lawes but of the
15 mynistres / nor yet aduise hym to vse suche fasshyon wyth the
temporall mynystres neyther, leste he make two lyes for one.

Is not now thys chaunge of my sentence that he maketh here a
very shamelesse dealynge, eyther of hym selfe, or of some
shrewed counsayle of hys?

20 And now knytteth he to this handelynge the remanaunt of the
sayde .xviii. chapyter, and sheweth that he speketh fyrste of the
spyrytualtye, bycause the causes of the dyuysyon specyally be
growen by theym / and layeth forthe a sorte of gryefes, some
parte very tryfles, and some parte remedyed before hys booke of
25 [Q₆v] dyuisyon made, and some parte very folyshe, & some part
for all hys some sayes vndowtedly very false.

He hath there two leuys in the ende of that chapiter which any
wyse man that readeth them, shall I suppose, iudge a very
dreamynge tale. And therin it semeth that as he hath bygonne
30 wyth the spyrytuall lawes, so he wyll after procede in the temporal lawes to. And fayne wold yᵉ man make me so fonde as to be
hys felow therin / and saith yf I know any such made, as the
perleament had none authoryte to make, or wheruppon the
people haue iuste cause to complayn: it were well done that I
35 shold shew them. And so he thynketh verily that cheryte shold
compell me to do, seynge that I am he sayth lerned in yᵉ lawes of
the realme.

Veryly yf I knewe any suche: yet wold I not folow neyther this

good mannys holy exhortacyon, nor hys [Q₇] godly sample
neyther, to do in yᵉ tone as he hath done in the tother, but yf I
lyked hys doynge a lytell better than I do.

And yf I be lerned in the temporall lawes, the lesse wyll I
folowe his counsayle. For the better that I were lerned in them   5
the lesse wolde I wene it wold become me, to prent and put
abrode amonge the people, a slawnderous boke of them to
shame theym.

And vnto this point good readers I haue answered and shewed
my mynde in myne apologye byfore, wherto thys man geueth a   10
defe eare alwaye. And here, vppon a soughte occasyon with a
fonde wyly chaunge of my wordes, exhorteth me to the thynge to
whyche I made answere all redy. And what I before sayde therin,
that he dyssembleth, and sayth not one worde therto. But in
myne apologye good readers, the .159. lefe [Q₇v] these were in   15
this poynt my wordes.

Hys other murmours & grudges that he sayth he can not now reherse,
he reherseth after many of them in his other chapyters / whych I wyll passe
ouer vntowched, bothe for that the more parte of them be suche as euery
wyse man wyll I suppose answere them hym selfe in the redynge, and   20
satysfye hys owne mynde wythout any nede of myne helpe therin / & for
that some thynges are there also therin, that are very well sayed / and some
also that be they good or badde, I purpose not to medle myche wythall, as
are the thynges yᵗ towche any lawes or statutes all redy made, be they of the
chyrche or of the realme, defende them I am content to do, yf I thynke them   25
good. But on the tother syde yf I thinke them nought / albe it that in place
& tyme conuenyent I wold geue myn aduice & counsaile to the chaunge,
yet to putte out bookes in wrytynge abrode amonge the people agaynste
theym, that wolde I neyther do my[Q₈]*selfe, nor in the so doynge com-*
mende any man that doth. For yf the lawe were suche as were so farre   30
agaynste the lawe of god, that it were not possyble to stande wyth mannes
saluacyon / than in that case the secrete aduyse and counsayle may become
euery man / but the open reprofe and redargucyon therof may not in my
mynd well become those that are no more spyrytuall than I. And sure yf the
lawes maye be kepte and obserued without perell of soule, though the   35
chaunge myght be to the better: yet out of tyme & place conuenyent to put
the defawtes of the lawes abrode amonge the people in wrytynge, and

---

18 chapyters] chapters *1557*

wythout any suretye of the chaunge geue the people occasyon to haue the
lawes in derysyon, vnder which they lyue, namely syth he y^t so shall vse to
do, may somtime missetake the mater & thynke the thyng not good wherof
y^e chaunge wold be worse: y^t way wyll I not as thus aduised neither vse my
5 *self nor aduise no frend of myne to do.* [Q$_8$v] *And therfore I wyll as I saye*
leue some thinges of his boke vntouched, whyther he say well or euyll.

Here you se good readers myne answere to thys poynt,
concernynge the fyndynge of fawtes and puttyng theym abrode
in prente: whiche answere he dyssembleth, & agayne prouoketh
10 me to the same, as though he had neuer herd it / whyche answere
I wyll therfore be had as repeted in euery place where he prouoketh me hereafter to the same poynte. And thus you se good
reders, that where as he hath not in any one chapyter of hys,
brought forth any reason yet: yet hath he brought forth leste in
15 this hys .xviii. in whiche he bosteth moost. For by thys hath he
playnely declared, that he neyther vnderstandeth the law vt inquisitionis, that he allegeth, nor so mych as the pore summe
called Summa rosella neyther. For that good man y^t made it,
vndowtedly [R$_1$] neuer ment of suche inquisicions as ours are, of
20 whyche maner he hadde happely neuer knowen none. And as
for the law, the very fyrste wordes therof to hym that vnderstondeth them and consydereth them well, suffycyently do declare,
that that lawe forbedeth laye men to medyll wyth suche maner
knowledge of heresye, as sholde be a let and impedement to the
25 ordynaryes, or other the spyrytuall inquisitours / & not suche
knowledge as we take by our inquisicyons, that onely serue to
helpe the tother forth & bringe y^e mater to theyr handes.

And therfore syth I se well, that this man in the laten lawes and
Summes, hath so lytell vnderstandynge: I shall be the more con-
30 tent in his lawes & his Summys, so mych the lesse to dyspute or
medle wyth hym. [R$_1$v]

The .xix. chapyter.

I$_N$ his .xix. chapiter he declareth what he meaneth by confederacyes of the spyrytualtye / and sayth he meneth con-

---

5 do.] dooe. *1557*, do *1533*   21 the very] *1557*, they very *1533*   23–26 *Sidenote*
1557: How the law forbedeth lay men to meddle with the knowledge of heresye.   33
chapiter] chapter *1557*

federacyes wherby spyrytuall men pretende to mayntayne some
suche lawes of the chyrche, and some such constytucyons prouincyall, as are agaynste the kynges lawes and the olde customes
of the realme / and putteth for a sample, the puttyng of prestes
to answere afore temporall iudges, & the statute made de Silua   5
cedua, and the statute of Mortuaryes.

As for conuentyng of prestes before seculare iudges, trouth it
is y^t one tyme thoccasyon of a sermon made the mater come in
communicacion before the kynges hyghnes. But neyther any
tymes synnys nor many yerys afore, I neuer herd y^t there was   10
any bysynes about it. And yet was y^t [R_2] mater ceaced long
before any worde sprange of this great generall dyuision, that
his boke maketh as though there were such, in a maner generall
thorow the whole realme.

And diuerse statutes haue there sinnys ben made, concern-   15
ynge y^e same poynt. And many prestes conuented as they were
wont to be byfore / and no bysynes made by the spyrytualty
therfore y^t I here of, nor I trow him self neither.

And in lyke wise men cutte downe theyr woodes euery yere, in
one place & other of the realme / & eyther is there not asked the   20
tythe agaynst the statute / or yf some person wold with good wyll
gete it, & therfore aske yt, he geteth yt not yet in dede.

For where he sayeth that yf I wolde remember my self well,
how often the constitucion prouincial, made agaynste the statute
de Silua cedua, hath ben put in execucyon of late dayes, to the   25
gryefe of many lay [R_2v] men: I wolde not haue sayde so generally that there is not any one constytucyon prouinciall that he
speketh of, to any mannes gryefe or grudge put in execucyon in
the tyme of any of the prelates that are now lyuyng / and affermeth that the same constytucyon hath of late in the tyme of   30
dyuerse of the same prelates that nowe be, ben put in execucion,
to the gryefe and grudge of many persons within this realm.
Fyrst as towchyng myne owne rememberaunce: in good faith I
can not remember one. And as to his owne remembraunce, vpon
which he affermeth it to haue ben done so lately, to the grudge   35
and gryefe of so many: he shall perdon me though I byleue hym
not tyll he proue it, or at the leste wyse name them that haue had
the wynnyng, & them also y^t haue borne the losse / so that I may
my self proue whyther it be trewe or not. For excepte he do the

tone, ellys haue I [R₃] good cause in yᵉ meane whyle, in this poynte to gyue no greate credence to hym.

For fyrste I can scantely byleue that vppon the persons bare worde, for allegacion of the constytucyon prouyncyall, his par-
5 yshen wold let hym haue it. And yf there happed any man that wold: yet am I sure they were so few, that it were dowble foly to lay that for any cause of diuisyon, which were done bothe but by a few, and also not without the parties wyll, and rather of his own pryuate deuocion, than for any fere of compulsion.

10 Now if the person wold take it of hys parishon by force: I se the comen experyence therin suche: that I dare boldely saye the whole paryshe wold not suffre hym. And yet yf it were taken in dede: neyther sholde the person enioy yᵉ profyte, nor the par-yshen bere the losse / but sholde at the kynges comen lawe re-
15 couer a ryght large a[R₃v]mendes. For well ye wote his dam-mages sholde be taxed hym, not by .xii. prestes, but by .xii. temporall men, & his costes by the kynges iudges that are no prestes neyther.

Now yf this man wyll saye, that many of the personys haue in
20 yᵉ tyme of the prelates that now be lyuynge, or that were lyuyng at the tyme that hym selfe wrote those wordes, recouered in any of the spyrituall courtes, the tythe of such woodes, agaynst the statute, by force of that prouinciall constytucyon: I wyll se this man proue it ere I byleue hym in it. For the dayngeour of that
25 suit may be peraduenture more, than I suppose the person wyll put in perell for his tythes. And also the paryshen maye soone stoppe the suit in the begynnyng by yᵉ kynges prohybycyon / wherby yᵉ kynges iudges shall se whyther the person sewe for suche tythes or not, & wyll not therin suffre hym to procede. [R₄]

30 And therfore tyll thys good man make me better proues of this mater than hys owne bare sayenge: he geueth me no cause agaynste so many lettes to the contrary, therin to byleue his word. But I durst well warraunt it, that if he come ones to the namyng of the partyes, so that the specialtyes of the maters may
35 be sought out and made appere: you shall surely fynd it vntrewe.

Now than to mayntayne withall hys great word of con-federacyes: he bryngeth forth that some prestes say styll, that

---

6 dowble] *1533 corr. err.*, so dowble *1533*, so double *1557*   36 Now] *no para. 1557*

those tythes & mortuaryes also, for al the statutes be theyr dew-
tyes styl, & that they which pay them not be accursed. I haue
espyed thys good man is a man of sadnesse, & no great gamener.
For yf he were he wolde neuer be angry for an angry worde,
spoken by a man that is on the lesynge syde. Hit is an olde   5
courtesye at the cardys perdye, to lette [R₄v] the leser haue hys
wordes. And in good fayth in thys mater I here no suche talkyng
at all. And veryly this deuyce of his to put thys for a cause of
diuisyon, is in my mynde a very chyldyshe thynge.

But thanne goeth he ferther that prestes make partycular   10
confederacyes, to mayntayne obytys, & prestes wages, and to
haue more at byryalles than they haue bene wont to haue or ellys
to shewe them selfe not content, that is to saye to aske more than
they can gete / and bycause they can not gete it, shewe them selfe
not content / that is to wytte lowre and loke angerly, and say they   15
be not pleased. Be not these hygh maters and mete for that
heyghnouse name of confederacyes?

And yet goeth he ferther wyth an other heyghnouse confederacy, that yf a preste haue a besynesse to do in some countreys:
other prestes wyll as it is sayde so confeder wyth hym at arbytrementes   20
and other metynges / or ellys [R₅] make theym suche frendes pryuyly,
that the tother partye though he be of right good substaunce & haue
also good ryghte / yet shall he sometyme haue mych a do to obtayne yt.

Is not here good readers a wonderfull heyghnouse worke, and
well worthye yᵉ name of confederacies of the spyrytualte / that   25
but in some countreys, nor there neyther of any certayntye, but
as some saye, some prestes in the besynesse of a nother preste,
wyll, and yet but somtyme neyther, at arbytrementes confedere
wyth theyre good worde to helpe forthe theyr felowe, or ellys to
make hym frendes? Ye and thenne what a myschyefe he sheweth   30
that enseweth therupon? The tother party hath he sayth myche a
do to obteyn his ryght and yet that but somtyme neyther. But as
for lese his ryght by theyre meanes, he sayeth not that any man
dothe. Be not these heyghnouse confederacyes, & thynges mete
for thys man to make a boke of diuysyon for? And yet as though   35

---

he had very well [R₅v] acquyte hym selfe: he knytteth yt vp wyth
these wordes.

And these be some of the confederacyes of prestes that I ment of /
and not the gatherynge to gether of the clergye at the conuocacyons.

5   In good fayth I sawe not howe he sholde meane any other
thynge, nor that neyther well. For the name of confederacyes
taken to an euyll parte as thys man taketh yt, dothe sygnyfye a
metynge and gatheryng to gether, and a determynacyon of certayne euyll folke, conspyrynge to gether aboute an euyll thynge
10   to be done, wyth a couenaunt and promyse by eche of theym
made vnto other, eche to stande wyth other therin. Nowe where
as at conuocacyons good men come to gether to do good, and
therfore he coulde not call theym confederacyes as he nowe
sayeth he ment not to do: yet I douted somewhat whyther he so
15   ment or not, bycause the conuocacions be at the leste wise comen
assemblies to gether, wher[R₆]of he myght hap I thought to geue
a good thyng an euyl name. But these maters yᵗ he now speketh
of, I could not ymagyne that euer he ment to cal them confederacyes, wherin he neyther seeth assemblies, nor can assygne
20   and proue any conspyracy & mutuall promyse, in assystynge
eche other about the procurement of any thynge at all good or
bad. For where as he sayth yᵗ these be some of the confederacyes
that he ment: I am sure no man douteth but that these be eyther
all the confederacyes that he fyndeth, or ellys at the leste wyse
25   the greatest. And thenne are those that he calleth here partyculare confederacyes, so chyldyshe that in good faythe I myche
meruayle, that his herte could serue hym for very shame to
speke of them. And then the tother yᵗ he taketh for generall
confederacyes / he neither seeth nor assygneth so mych as any
30   assembly about theym, or promyse or abettement to procure and
pursue theym. [R₆v] And therfore though some prestes wold
here or there speke of them as theyr owne affeccyon ledeth
theym: this is farre fro the nature and name of confederacye.
         And yet when he hath al to gether done, whyle he proueth
35   nothynge at the vttermoste (though all that he layeth were as

---

1 hym selfe] himselfe *1557*, hm selfe *1533*   6 *Sidenote 1557:* The name of confederacies   28 he] *1557,* be *1533*

trew as yt is not) but that they wolde fayne haue the tythe of
tymber styll, and that they wolde fayne haue the mortuaryes
styll, and that some wolde fayne haue greater wages, and some
wolde fayne haue more money at the beryalles, then for all
theyre fayne wyllynge they can gete / when they wold onely fayn   5
haue yt, and yet in dede gete nought of yt, nor other folke
nothynge lese: to make now so great a mater of this and call yt an
hyghnouse name of confederacyes, ys as me semeth somewhat
lyke to hym, that wolde nedes haue an accyon agaynste his
neygh[R₇]bour bycause his neyghbours horse stode and loked   10
ouer his hedge. For he sayde that he sawe by hys countenaunce
that he wolde haue eaten hys grasse yf he coulde haue goten to
yt. For as for that, that the hedge letted hym, was lytle thanke to
hym / for hys wyll was neuer the lesse. And thus hys .xix. chapyter you se good readers howe lytle reason is in yt.   15

The .xx. chapyter.

H<small>IS</small> .xx. chapyter begynnynge in yᵉ .lxxvi. lefe, hath so lytle
effecte & substaunce in it, and so faintly defendeth his formare
mater whyche yt pretendeth to defende, that I purpose to make
no longe worke aboute yt. [R₇v]   20
   For yf you rede fyrste his wordes as they lye in mine Apology
fo. .159. in the seconde syde begynnynge at these wordes, *And
here me thynketh I myghte saye:* ye shal there good readers fynde,
that I reherse those wordes of his euyn whole, wyth those wordes
in them, which he wold in the begynnynge of this his .xx. chap-   25
yter, make men byleue that I had wythdrawen / as though they
were wordes of suche substancyall effect, that I wold not haue it
appere in my boke that he had wryten so piththely.
   Afterwarde in a nother place where they be rehersed again fo.
162. the prenter of lykelyhed left them out of ouersyght & hast.   30
And surely they be not of so great weyght, but yᵗ if the authour
had hym selfe left them out in his boke of dyuysyon, yt had made
lytle mater. And yf he had ouer that left out the whole clause:
then hadde he lefte in hys boke one lye the lesse, [R₈] and hys

---

19 purpose] *1533 corr. err., 1557,* puroose *1533*   29 Afterwarde] *no para. 1557*   30
lykelyhed] likelyhod *1557*

boke the better by so myche. For wherby proueth he that the
spyrytuall rulers pretende theym selfe to be so clene and pure,
that there ys no defaute in theym, but all in the people alone, and
in theym selfe no maner faute at all? Where herde he euer any
5 spyrytuall man saye thys, by the whole spyrytualtye or by any one
man therof?

They confesse theym selfe to be men and synners. And they
confesse and knowledge also, that the very cause of thys chyefe
myschyefe that nowe begynneth to make dyuysyon, that ys to
10 wytte the execrable heresyes, whyche myschyefes thys good
mannys euyll dyuyses with chaunge of good lawes were lykely to
mayntayne, yf men wolde folowe theym: dyd bothe begynne,
and ys also sette forthe & auaunced forward, by those vngracyouse folke that are suche amonge the spyrytualtye, as Iudas was
15 amonge thapostles / & thys not [R₈v] in thys realme onely, but in
other countreys to. As by frere Luther, and preste Pomerane,
Otho the monke, and frere Lambert, frere Huskyn, and
Swynglius / & here in Englande Tyndale, frere Barns, George
Ioy, & some other suche, as with the sede of sedycyouse heresye,
20 haue sowen and set forth dyuysyon.

Thys thynge the spyrytualtye bothe knoweth & knowledgeth.
And therfore they do not pretende as thys pacifier sayth they do,
that there hath ben no faute amonge theym, but all amonge the
people. And therfore this good man where he sayeth that I lefte
25 out thre wordes in that clause of his (which yet I did put in in
dede): hym selfe hadde somwhat amended hys mater with leuyng in of one lye the lesse, yf he had left out the whole clause all
to gether.

As to that yᵗ he sayth I chaunged his wordes in yᵉ ende from
30 these wordes [S₁] the lyghte of grace that ys spoken of before
wyll not appere, into these wordes the lyghte of grace that ys
spoken of byfore, be wyth you now and euer more amen: therin
he sayeth very trewe. For syth he was fallen into preachynge, I
not onely in the fyrst place rehersed hym as he spake hym self,
35 but afterward also in the seconde place I toke the payne for hym

---

17 *Sidenote 1557:* A worthy company.   18 Barns,] Barns *1533 1557*   19 Ioy] Iay
1557   25–26 in in dede):] in in dede: *1533*, in dede) *1557*

to mende his collacyon in that poynt, & make yt ende some what
more lyke a sermon with a good gracyouse prayour.

Then goeth he forthe, and in the same lefe and the next
folowyng, he maketh a suspicyouse mater, and can not tell what
mynde I was of, in chaungynge his worde spyrytuall rulers, into   5
this worde prelates. But loke good readers vppon the place, and
you shal se that I dyd yt of good cause. For I do not there saye
that he sayth prelates, but I saye there [S₁v] that peraduenture
he wyll saye so. And also besydes this that there ys no very great
dyfference betwene these wordes, the prelates and the spirytuall   10
rulers: the chaunge from this worde the spyrytuall rulers into
this worde prelates, semed me the more mete and more proper
for the mater that the pacifier speketh in that place, where he
speketh of authorite yᵗ they pretende, and obedyence that they
clayme.   15

Howe be it rather then I wolde geue any cause of dyuysyon
agaynst me, to hym that vseth to make great dyuysyons vpon
smale groundes / I shall be content to geue hym his own worde
agayne. And therfore I pray you good readers euery of you
mende your bokis / & in the stede of prelates in that place, put in   20
spyrytual rulers. And when you so haue done, yᵉ chaunge shal
for the mater not be very great / & yet so myche as it shalbe, shal
more [S₂] serue me then hym.

But yet to make me sory, yᵗ euer I was so farre ouersene, as to
take away his gay golden worde of spyrytuall rulers from hym,   25
he begynneth as it were with a great thret & sayth.

What mayster More meaneth to chaunge these wordes spyrytuall
rulers into prelates, I can not tell. But nowe by occasyon of the wordes
that mayster More hathe spoken, I wyll saye farther in the mater then I
hadde thought to haue done.   30

Howe happy was I lo, yᵗ I had not the grace to let his owne
worde stande. For now wyll he saye farther in the mater thenne
euer he hadde thoughte to haue done. And that ys (sayth he)
this.

That I thynke veryly that if so great an ouersyght fell in to prelates and   35
spyrytuall rulers, that they wolde take vppon them to preache heresy,
that they wolde that the people sholde byleue theym therin / and to

take yt to be catholycall that they preached. For who wolde preache any
thynge but suche as they wold haue theyr audyence byleue?

Byleue me good readers, that thys man weneth he sayeth well
fauoredly in this point / wherin he taketh such pleasure, that
5   afterwarde fo. [S₂v] lxxix. he falleth into the same agayn, and
sayth thus.

Mayster More goeth about onely to proue, that all my tale ys loste,
bycause prelates pretende not to be byleued yf they preache heresye as
he taketh yt that I sholde saye they do. And yet I sayde not so in dede.
10   And yf I dyd say so / I sayde but trewly. For yf they dyd preache
heresye, yt is certayne that they wolde loke to be byleued as I haue
sayde byfore / ye and yf they wolde preache and saye that yf they
preched heresye, that they wolde the people sholde not byleue theym:
yet yf they dyd after preache heresye in dede, they wolde loke that the
15   people sholde byleue theym. For they wolde saye that they were no
heresyes that they preached. For who wyll confesse that he preacheth
heresye?

Nowe good readers here haue I ioyned you to gether this good
mannis gaye wordes in two places, wherin I perceyue he pleaseth
20   hym selfe ryght well. But to thentent that you may se whether he
haue so good cause as he weneth, consyder well his wordes and
myne byfore, wheruppon he cometh to thys poynte. For he
maketh as though, I wythoute occasyon geuyn of his wordes,
hadde writen that the prelates pretende not to be byleued yf they
25   wolde preache he[S₃]resye. Wherin whether he saye trew or not
you shall se by hys owne wordes, whyche are these.

The lyghte of grace wyll not come, as longe as the spyrytuall rulers
pretende that theyr authoryte is so hygh and so immedyate of god, that
the people are bound to obay them & to accepte all that they do and
30   teache, wythoute argumentes resystence or grudgynge.

Nowe good readers fyrst consyder well here in these wordes of
his, what wysedome the man hath shewed, in makynge suche a
mumblynge of chaungyng spyrytuall rulers into prelates. For
when he saith here, that the spyrytuall rulers pretende that theyr

---

2 byleue?] byleue. *1533*, belyeue. *1557*   17 heresye?] heresye. *1533*, heresy.
1557   28 authoryte] aucthority *1557*   31 readers] redes *1557*

authoryte is so hyghe: what doute is there but though he meane
other rulers mo besyde whom he calleth no prelates: yet he
meaneth prelates to / ye & prelates specyally to. And then when
he sayth that the prelates & the other spyritual rulers pretende
this or that: may I not wel say that he sayth y⁰ prelates pretend   5
this? yes veryly that I may. And yet in so [S₃v] chaungyng his
worde: I chaunge it to his aduantage & not vnto myne, in yᵗ I
make his odyouse sayenge myche lesse, and nothynge more.
And thus fyrste you se good readers this mannys myche ouersyght in fyndynge of that faute.   10

Now consyder farther good readers yᵗ he sayth in those
wordes, not that the spyrytual rulers, yᵗ is to saye both the prelates & all the remanaunt to, pretend theyr authorite to be so
hygh and so immedyatly deryued fro god, that the peple are
bound to obey them in this thynge or that thynge, one, or   15
twayne, or tenne, or twentye / but vtterly to accept and obaye not
onely all theyr teachynges, but also al theyr doynges to / and
neyther argue resyst nor grudge at any maner thyng, that they
wold eyther teache or do.

This generall thynge he saythe. And therfore though I deale   20
as you se so fauorably with him in my .xxvii. [S₄] chapyter of myn
Apologye, as to dyuyde y⁰ mater, & aske whether he ment yt by
theyr whole authoryte or part: I myght well vpon these wordes
of his haue taken it, yᵗ he had very shamfully belyed them, & had
sayde yᵗ they had pretended to haue theyr whole authoryte im-   25
medyatly of god euery whit. For if I wold so haue sayd / his
generall wordes wolde well haue warraunted myne. Also syth his
saynge is so generall, and extendeth vtterly not onely to all theyr
techynges, but also to al theyr doynges to / & sayth that they
pretend, yᵗ by goddes immediate ordynaunce the people shold   30
accepte all to gether, both al yᵗ euer they say, & all yᵗ euer they
do: by how many maner thynges myght I haue confuted his
saynge, and haue proued it false?

But yet his sainge beyng such, I toke but one thyng / & yᵗ was
such, as for y⁰ mater yᵗ we both specially spake of was next at   35

---

1 authoryte] aucthoritie *1557*   11 Now] *no para. 1557*   13–14 so hygh] *1533 corr.*
err., hygh *1533 1557*   23 authoryte] aucthoritie *1557*   31 all to gether] altogither
1557

hand. And therfore I [S$_4$v] sayde / that they pretende not to haue
suche an authoryte that men sholde obay theym in all thynges /
for they pretende not to haue authorite to bynde men to byleue
and obay them, yf they wolde preache heresyes. But they playnly
5 professe that if they so wold, men shold not byleue theym nor
obey them therin.

   Here you se that where he sayth that he ment not that the
prelates wolde preache heresye: he speketh all besyde the purpose. For I sayde not that he eyther so sayd or so ment. But I
10 sayde and yet saye, that in those wordes he sayde, that yf they
wolde preche heresies, they do now pretende, that by the authorite whyche god hathe geuyn theym, the people were thenne
therin bounden to beleue and obey theym. And in hys so sayenge
I there sayde and yet saye, that he sayth very farre vntrewe, and
15 that they pretende yt [S$_5$] not, but playnely pretende the contrary. And thus in this poynt that he maketh a mater without
grownd or cause, and that hym selfe with his owne wordes gaue
me good occasyon to wryte the thynge that I wrote: this you se
good readers proued very playne.

20   But now consyder his other wordes, wherin he lyketh hym
selfe so well, and weneth y^t he proueth y^t the spyrytuall rulers of
the realme pretende, that yf they wolde preche heresye, the
people were by goddes ordynaunce bounden to byleue & obey
them therin, bycause they wold than say y^t it were none heresye.
25 In thys poynt hys reasonynge hath I promyse you a lytell more
subtylte than substaunce / and yet but symple subtylte neyther.

   Fyrste as for his case, that yf all the spyrytuall rulers wolde
preche heresye: yf he had ment of the spyri[S$_5$v]tuall rulers of all
chrystendome, I wolde haue admitted his case none otherwyse,
30 but as men put & admitte a case impossyble, to se what myghte
ensew theron yf it were possyble / as saynt Poule putteth the case
that yf an angel came from heuyn & preched a contrary gospell,
yet the same angel shold not be byleued. But now syth he putteth
it but by the spyrytuall rulers of one realme, I admytte the case as
35 possyble / but yet as suche a case, as I truste in god this good man
shall se the skye fall fyrste and cache larkes ere it happen, though

---

2 authoryte] aucthority *1557*   3 authorite] aucthoritie *1557*   5 wold,] wold *1533*,
would *1557*   31 *Sidenote 1557: Ad Gala. 1.*

it maye be lykely inough to happen in some one or twayne, or some fewe, agaynste whome the remanaunt shall preche and teche the trouth.

But now sayth thys good man thus. If it so happened in them all: than wolde they all pretende, that by theyr authoryte gyuen them of god, the people were bounden therin to [S₆] byleue and obaye theym. For they wolde than saye that theyr heresyes were none heresyes.

I am content lo to graunte hym all thys / and I aske hym now what than? For all thys good readers proueth (you se very well) no more, but that yf that case happened that they al so preched, they wolde thanne al so pretende. But all this proueth neuer a whyt, that the spyrytuall rulers eyther now do, or at any tyme haue done, pretended theyr authoryte such. Now consyder than for what purpose he speketh of suche pretendyng. He layeth (you wote well) theyr pretendynge of theyr authoryte to be so great, that the people shold obay them without argument, grudge, or contradiccyon in all yᵗ euer they eyther say or do. This he layth I say for so sore a cause of this diuision, which he maketh in his boke, yᵗ he sayth the lyght of grace wyl not come to ceace it, tyll they ceace so to pretende. [S₆v]

And therfore good readers syth thys is the thynge yᵗ he sayth, and the purpose that he sayth it for, makyng it a cause of dyuysyon present: how can he maynteyne hys sayenge with a case fayned, wherby it may be that they wyll so pretende hereafter / where as euer hytherto hym selfe sayth not naye, but yᵗ they bothe haue pretended and yet pretende the contrary? Can he mayntayne yᵗ the temporalty is at dyuision wyth the spyrytualty now all redy, bycause it maye peraduenture happe here after by a farre fet possybylyte, that they maye than, no man woteth whan, pretende peraduenture a thynge, wherof they presently pretende the contrary / and protest also that yf the case sholde so mysse happe hereafter, they desyre now for than yᵗ no man sholde therin than byleue theym? Saw you euer good readers any man with suche a symple subtyltye, caste all his mater [S₇] in the dust so shamfully?

2 fewe,] fewe, [*comma inverted*] *1533*, few *1557*   11 al so] also *1533 1557*   12 al so] also *1557*   14 authoryte] aucthorite *1557*   16 authoryte] aucthoritie *1557*   17 the] *1557*, they *1533*

Now where he sayth to mayntayne hys mater here withall, that
it is not to suppose y^t spyrytuall rulers wyll pretende that such
authoryte as they haue of the graunte of prynces, is immedyately
of god: I say that therin he sayth trouth, and y^t I suppose that
5 they wyll not. But yet let hym selfe loke wel in his own boke of
diuision, & he shall fynde that hym selfe sayth ye contrary there,
of that he now sayth here / and sheweth some thynges whiche he
bothe sayth that they haue but by the meane of prynces and the
good mynde of the people, and yet sayth also that they pretende
10 to haue the same thynges immedyately of god. As for ensample
both theyr authoryte to haue y^e tenth part for tythe, and the
thynge whyche they enioy by the name of y^e lybertyes of y^e
chyrch, wherby theyr persons be in many thynges pryuyledged
in this realme [S$_7$v] byfore y^e person of a lay man. These thynges
15 hym self sayth y^t they haue but by a meane and not immedyately
of god. And yet he sayth in this same .xx. chapyter, that the
thynges whych they call the lybertyes of the chyrch, they pretende to haue immedyately of god / and for all that he sayth now
that it is not to suppose y^t they wyll pretende so. And thus you
20 maye se good readers, that for the defence of thys place, he is
dreuyn to a shrewde narow streyte, whan to defende one fawte
he is fayne to make twayne.

Now where as he saith I myght haue satysfyed my selfe wel
inough, and y^t the letter of his wordes were playne: you se that in
25 the rehersynge agayne of hys own wordes fo. lxxx. he is fayne to
suppresse & stele away these hys owne generall wordes, all that
they do or teche, to make hys wordes seme playne. For as you se,
they standynge styll, his wordes are playne [S$_8$] agaynst hym. For
hym selfe now confesseth y^t they pretende not to do by authoryte
30 immedyate fro god, suche thynges as they do by authoryte gyuen
them by prynces.

But bycause I wold fayne fully satysfye hym: I shall now shew
you y^t with his new declaringe y^t his wordes were well inough, he
hath made his mater out of all measure wurse.

35 For now rede his wordes agayne fo. lxxx. & there you shall se
y^t he saith y^t he meneth onely of such authoryte as ye spirituall

---

1 Now] *no para.* *1557*   11 authoryte] aucthoritye *1557*   29 confesseth y^t] confesseth, *1557*   30 authoryte] aucthorite *1557*   36 authoryte] aucthorite *1557*

rulers pretende to haue immediately of god. And yet after he declareth it ferther & better on yᵉ secunde syde of the same lefe in yᵉ .xiiii. lyne, yᵗ he meneth onely such authoryte, not as they pretende to haue, but as they haue in dede immediately of god. And to thentent men myghte se yᵗ he meneth not of authorite falsely pretended, but truely had immediatly of god, he putteth for yᵉ sample theyr authoryte in ministracyon of yᵉ sacramentes. [S₈v]

Thys is hys owne exposicyon of his owne wordes, whyche he wolde haue taken for so playne, that he is angry with me that I could not spye it, and so satysfye my selfe before.

Well go to now: let vs reherse his owne wordes agayne as hym selfe for his owne aduauntage folio .lxxx. reherseth them, & let vs plant in hys owne exposicion with them, to make his sentence yᵉ more clere / & than shal we se to what good conclusion he bryngeth all in conclusyon. For than commeth hys whole tale to thys.

As longe as the spyrytuall rulers wyll pretende, that theyr authoryte is so hygh and so immedyately deryued of god, in suche thynges as they haue theyr authoryte immedyately of god in dede, (as in the minystra-cyon of the sacramentes and such other thynges lyke) that the people are bounden to obay them wythout argument or resystence: so long the lyght of grace wyll not appere.

Now good readers here be now hys owne wordes wyth hys owne exposycion therin. And how lyke you them now? For now the sentence hath [T₁] he brought at last with myche wurke to none other, but that the lyghte of grace wyll not appere, as longe as the spyrytuall rulers pretende to be obayed and not resysted in the mynystracyon of the sacramentes & suche other thynges lyke, bycause they haue theyr authoryte therin immedyately of god in dede. But than on the tother syde, whan so euer they wyll not pretende theyr authoryte so hygh therin, nor so imme-dyately deryued of god, as to be obayed therin, but wyll be con-tent that men grudge and argue and resyste them therin, and

---

3 authoryte] aucthoritye *1557*   5 authorite] aucthorite *1557*   18 authoryte]
aucthorite *1557*   20 authoryte] aucthoritye *1557*   30 authoryte] aucthoritie *1557*

pull them from the awter, and suffre them to mynyster no sacramentes nor any such other thynges lyke: than shal by thys good
mannes newe declaracyon the light of grace appere by and by.
Hath not thys pacyfyer here good readers, wyth myche laboure
5 at last brought thys mater to a wyse conclusyon? [T₁v]

If he wyll nowe go fro thys agayne, and put in his other generall wordes agayne / whyche for his aduauntage he lefte out in
that place: than is all gone agayne that he goeth aboute / and all
myne answere made (as I haue shewed you) good, and all his
10 owne wordes nought.

In the lefe also .lxxxi. these are hys wordes.

Where I saye that as longe as the spyrytuall rulers wyll pretende that
theyr authoryte is so hygh and so immedyately deryued of god, that the
people are bounde to obaye them wythout argument or resystence &c.
15 By these wordes I confesse that they haue authoryte immedyately
deryued fro god. But as I sayd before in the seuenth chapyter, mayster
More hath a ryght greate and a ryght inuentyue wytte, wherby he can
lyghtly turne a sentence after hys appetyte. And so he doth here &c.

What hygh wytte or inuentyue I haue to turne a sentence, let
20 yᵉ reders iudge. But surely the heygth of my wyt can not reche so
hygh, as to perceyue in those wordes of his, the sentence that
hym selfe turneth them to / nor I trow no mannes els / tyll these
[T₂] wordes, They haue authoryte, and these wordes, They pretende to haue authoryte, be bothe one thynge, whyche they were
25 neuer yet. And therfore before his confession that he now
maketh here new: I myght than well take that excepcion which I
haue brought there, to a litle better effect, than he doth his here,
whiche wyth all hys wrestelynge and al hys new declaracyons,
bryngeth all togyther euer the lenger vnto the wurse conclusyon.
30 For nowe to colour this his ouersyght with all, he telleth vs
whiche maner of pretences he ment in those wordes, which he
wold here so fayne defende. And than in stede of pretendynge
to be by goddes ordynaunce byleued & obayed in all thynges as
well wordes as dedes, he bryngeth forth here a few amountyng
35 in a some totall to the infynyte number of foure.

---

1 awter] aulter 1557   6 If] no para. 1557   11 In] no para. 1557   12 Where] 1557,
where 1533   15 authoryte] aucthorite 1557   20 heygth] heyght 1557   27 he]
1533 corr. err., om. 1533 1557

The fyrst is, that the order and disposicyon of the thynges y^t are to be disposed of y^e chyrch, be to be disposed [T$_2$v] by the prestes: whyche poynt to put as for a mater that hath made dyuysyon bytwene theym and vs, is a poynt of smal reason as farre as my reason can geue me. For I remember not of any varyaunce that euer arose bytwene them & vs for that poynt.

The secunde is, that all chrysten prynces must subdue theyr execucions to bysshoppes, & not to preferre them aboue them. I can not tell you whyther there be any suche lawe made or not. But I can tell you well that though there be, this poynt wyll not serue his purpose ye value of a blew poynt. For I am sure he neuer sawe in hys dayes any bysshoppe in thys realme, vse that pretence agaynst the kynge, or that euer there arose any diui- syon theruppon.

The thyrde is, y^t no charge shold be set vppon clerkes by laye power. I neuer herde yet any dyuision ryse vppon thys poynt in my dayes / nor [T$_3$] he neyther in his I dare saye. For I neuer saw the day yet nor he neither, but that whan any nede of the kyng & the realm requyred it, they haue euer more ben redy to set taxes vpon them selfe, as lyberally and as largely as any man well myght wyth any good reason requyre.

The fourth is he sayth, that yf a seculare iudge be neglygent in doyng of iustyce, that thanne after monicion to amende it geuen to the iudge, yf he wyl not, than ye spyrytuall iudge may compel hym to it, or ellys supply his rome and here the cause.

If I shold loke now for these .iiii. lawes, it myght peraduenture happen that I sholde fynde, that thys man had mysse taken some of them, as well as he hath mysse vnderstonden some of the other that he hath spoken of before. But syth that I neuer knewe grudge or diuisyon ryse here vppon any of them, me nedeth neuer to loke [T$_3$v] more for the mater. For sith this man neuer saw that any spyrituall iudge hath interprysed, in defawt of iustyce to geue any such monicion, or to supplye the rome: were that law neuer so vnreasonable, yet to say that vpon that lawe the temporaltye hath here conceyued such grudge as it hath ben a cause of diuisyon, this pacifier of diuisyon may be mych ashamed y^t euer he deuysed it. For I dare say that as well this fourthe cause, as many of all his other be suche, as the people

---

2 disposed of] dysposed of *1557*, disyosed of *1533*

neuer neyther talked of nor thoughte vppon / nor before his own boke, had neuer redde nor herde of. And therfore by the puttynge in of such thynges: euery chyld as I sayd in myne apologye may sone perceyue that his bokes labour & entende not
5 to quenche but rather to kyndle diuisyon.

And therfore verely with his leyenge here euyn in the ende and conclusyon suche causes of his dyuisyon, [T₄] whych causes but by hym selfe the peple neuer herde of: I maye well saye onys agayne good readers, is not this gere by this good pacyfyer
10 brought vnto a wyse conclusyon?

To those wordes wryten in myn apology the .169. lefe, this good man answereth thus.

And now to thys conclusyon of mayster More I wyll say thus, that I beseche almyghty god, that the ende of all these maters may come to
15 thys conclusyon, that the very groundely causes of these dyuisyons, that now be not onely in thys realme, but also in maner through all chrysten realmes, maye come to perfite knowledge. For surely I do not take it, that they began eyther by heresyes, or apostasyes as mayster More in his apology meaneth that they shulde do.

20   Here you may se good readers yᵗ this good man wold be loth yᵗ it shold appere, that yᵉ diuision, parel, & harme haue any where sprongen vpon heresies begon & set forth by false apostatase, wedded freres & monkes, as clerely as it is knowen yᵗ by thocca-sion therof, there haue ben slayn in Almain within these very
25 fewe yeres, aboue .lxxx .M. persons in one somer & yet synnys [T₄v] among the Swychis whan zuynglius was slayne, many thou-sandes killed to / and the warre bygonne by the heretykes, and the lashe by goddes great goodnes layed in theyr own neckys / as falsely as Fryth bylyeth the catholykes, and agaynst the playne
30 and open knowen trouth, wolde wyth shame inough to hym self make men wene yᵗ the catholikes began yᵉ warre.

But than goth he ferther & saith.

And yf mayster More wyll nedyly endeuour hym selfe to hyde the truth therin, as it semeth he hath done in this chapiter, and dyuerse other
35 places of his apologye, by kepynge secrete suche abusyons and pre-

---

34 chapiter] chapter *1557*   35 his] her *1557*

tences, as in my conscyence haue ben moste pryncypall causes of thys dyuysyon, wherof parte be recyted in the sayd treatyce, and part in thys answere but not all.

Of these there had nede in dede to be mo, & some more trew, and some of a lytell more substaunce to, than be the most parte of these y^t this good man hath layed forth yet.

Now here he sayeth that I kepe secrete such abusyons and pretences as be the pryncypall causes of the [T₅] dyuysyon, wherof hym selfe hath he sayth shewed some: eyther he mean-eth that those which I kept secrete, be those that hym seĩfe hath wryten, or other besyde theym. If he meane other: then eyther hym self knoweth theym or not. If he knowe them not: how knoweth he that I know them, or that there be any suche at all? If hym selfe knowe theym and shewe them not: then he hydeth theym and kepeth theym secret hym self as wel as I. Nowe yf he meane but those that hym selfe hath wryten: how can I kepe those secrete that he hath writen? Can I bothe gather vppe all hys bokes and go hyde theym, and also make them y^t haue redde them go vnreade them agayne, or forgete what they haue redde?

But now after this, lyke wyse as he is wonte when reason fayleth hym to fal to preachyng: so here, bycause reason faileth hym, he falleth to pray[T₅v]enge / and therin thus he sayth.

I beseche almighty god that he haue no power to do yt, but that the trouth may come to lyghte therin, though he resyste yt all that he can. For yf yt were knowen / and the fautes charytably reformed: all these dyuysyons wolde shortely haue an ende.

Nay perdye, this man seeth well ynough that though the fautes of the spyrytualtye were neuer so fully reformed, yet could not all that suffyse to brynge all dyuysyons to an ende, but yf one thyng be done / whych wyl neuer be done, wherof (which he forgeteth) I gaue hym warnynge in the .116. lefe of myne Apolo-gye in these wordes.

But now if thys pacyfyer to cease and quenche thys dyuysyon, coulde fynde the meanes to make all the whole clergye good: yet for all that, syth

---

19 vnreade] vnredde *1557*; redde?] *1557*, redde. *1533*   27 ynough] *1557*, ynought *1533*

he layeth for causes of this dyuysyon that some men saye thys by the clergye,
and some men saye by them that / were all the clergye neuer so good in
dede, and serued god neuer so wel, this diuisyon by his own tale, [T₆] yet
could not for all that cease / except he coulde prouyde farther, that no
5 *pytuouse pacyfyer sholde in lamentynge of dyuysyon, putte forthe a boke*
and saye, that some lay men say that some of the clergye be noughte, and
loue theyre ease and theyr welth / and that some saye that those that seme
beste and take moste labour and payne, be but hypocrytes for all that, and
serue god but for vayne glorye to gete theym selfe laude and prayse
10 *amonge the people.*

　　Also yf defautes sholde be charytably reformed, as this man
sayth he wolde haue theym: yt wolde be nede then to sette a lytle
more charytable folke about yt, then those haue ben, that haue
begyled thys good man wyth euyll counsayle in hys bookys / and
15 haue made hym vnder pretexte of pacyfyenge dyuysyon, sette
forthe and encrease dyuysyon, wyth dyuysynge and spredynge
abrode causes of murmure and grudge, [T₆v] makynge in some
of them an elephant of a gnat, and for olde grudges bryngynge
forth some suche, as the people neuer had herd of tyll they
20 redde his bokes and some of the very worst, whyche were most
effectuall causes yf they were trewe, bryngyng forth by hepes
wyth a fygure of some say, and very playn lyes in dede. Is this the
way good readers for a pacifyer to make peace wyth, and put
awaye dyuysyons?

25 　　And nowe hym selfe handelynge the mater thus / he taketh of
his charyte great thought, leste I go about to hynder hys holy
purpose. And therfore sayth.

I doute me very sore, that maister more goeth about rather to marre
all, then to endeuoyr hym selfe to make all well.

30 　　Whyche be the lykelyheddes now good reders that lede this
good man into this gret fere? Bycause I make open the shrewde
mynde of hys demure countenaunce, and the harmful [T₇] intent and purpose of his holy holesome wordes. Bycause I wolde
haue the temporaltye and the spyrytualtye as the bodye and the
35 soule of one man, loue well to gether and agree and neyther of

---

5 pytuouse] piteouse *1557*　　11 charytably] *1533 corr. err.*, charitably *1557*, charyble
1533　　17 grudge] *1557*, grndge *1533*　　34 *Sidenote 1557:* Exceding good counsail.

theym be glad to here euyll of other, nor to geue eare to false
sedycyouse slaunder, but the good folke of eyther parte, drawe
bothe by one lyne, accordynge to both the lawis, to represse and
kepe vnder the bad / and among other vyces, specyall suche
pestylent heresyes, as elles wolde oppresse the catholyque fayth,   5
& prouoke the dyspleasure of god, and fyrste sow deuysyon, and
afterwarde rere rebellyon in ye realme, as they haue done byfore
thys tyme both here and in other places / and y^t I to thys entent
geue myne aduyce to kepe styll those good lawes that bothe thys
realme and all the corps of chrystendome haue long vsed and   10
approued. Bycause I thus do lo: [T₇v] therfore this good man
fereth that I go about to marre all.

But whyle his bokes go aboute on the tother syde, to make the
world wene, that heresyes be no causes of dyuysyon / and to haue
heretyques lyue in the lesse fere, wyth many malycyouse some   15
sayes falsely slaundereth the ordynaryes, of cruell wrongfull
handelyng of the peple, to dryue them by drede or by shame or
other tedyouse besynes, to let heretyques alone / and go aboute
wyth balde reasons the beste not worthe a ryshe, to put away the
good lawes y^t haue ben made agaynst theym / & vnder colour of   20
a feruour to the faith exhorte men to go wynne the holy land /
and in the meane whyle yet wyth suche wyly wayes, labour wyth
heretyques, to fyll vp the stretes at home, & by the decay of the
crysten catholyke fayth, prouoke ye wrath of god vpon al our
heddes, whych our lord rather turne [T₈] vpon theyrs that so   25
wold haue it: his bokes besyly goyng about this gere, hym self
goeth about (ye se well perdye) to make all thynge well.

But now wyll I fynyshe vp his .xx. chapiter, wherin he goeth
forwarde thus.

And in thys chapyter mayster More layth dyuers other obieccyons to   30
proue the sayde letter vnreasonable, whych were very tedyouse to
reherse at length. And therfore I shall as shortely as I can / touche
some of theym.

Ye knowe well ynough why they be tedyouse to reherse. Surely
bycause they be very tedyouse to answere. But where he sayth he   35
wil reherse some of them: he begynneth first to shew y^t I had no

---

11 lo:] so *1557*   27 well] *1533 corr. err.*, euyll *1533*, euill *1557*   28 fynyshe] *1533*
corr. err., fyrste fynyshe *1533*, fyrst finishe *1557*

cause to doute of his wordes wherin he sayth that the spyrytuall
rulers pretende theyr authorytye to be so hygh & so immediately
deryued from god &c. I hadde sayth he no cause to doute of
what authoryte he ment. For he sayth that his wordes were playn
ynough, y^t he [T$_8$v] meaneth onely of suche authoryties, as they
pretende to haue immedyately from god.

To this I say playnly, that than are his wordes playne false. For
hys wordes be, that they pretende that theyr authoryte is so hygh
and so immedyately deryued from god, that the people are
bounde to obay them and to accept all that they do and teache,
wythout argument resystence or grudge. Now knoweth euery
man very wel y^t they do not pretende to haue authoryte immedyately from god, to do all thynge that they now lawfully do and
may do, in whyche the people are now bounde to accept and
obey them. For as I sayde in myne apologye, in many suche
thynges they pretende & claym theyr authoryte deryued from
prynces. And therfore ye se that and he labour about yt thys .vii.
yeres: he can neuer defende his wordes, but [V$_1$] that I answered
hym trewly / & with the necessarye dystynccyon that I there
made, answered euery parte. And this hym self seeth wel inough /
and therfore in the .lxxx. lefe in the begynnynge of the seconde
syde, where he reherseth hys wordes agayne, he leueth out these
wordes of his owne. and to accepte all that they do and teache.
Vppon whyche wordes the poynte of the mater hangeth. And
therfore here you se nowe, that where as in the begynnynge of
this chapyter, he wolde make yt seme that I stele two or thre
wordes of hys, whyche I neyther dyd nor neded for any strength
that was in them: here was hym selfe fayne to stele awaye hys
owne wordes, to begyle the reader vppon the readyng of the
place, and make hym passe ouer hys faute for the whyle
vnmarked.

And thus good reader you se, that to saue his owne wordes
vpryghte, [V$_1$v] and to impugne myne: in those two leuys .lxxx.
& .lxxxi. he bestowed his labour in vayne.

---

4 authoryte] aucthoritye *1557*   5 authoryties] aucthorities *1557*   11 Now] *para.*
1557   12 authoryte] aucthoryte *1557*   23 teache] theache *1557*   24 Vppon]
para. 1557   33 vpryghte] vp ryghte *1533*, vp ryght *1557*

But then goeth he farther & toucheth these wordes of myne Apologye, wryten in my sayde .xxvii. chapyter fo. 165.

Surely in suche thynges as the whole clergy of cristendome teacheth & ordereth in spyrytuall thynges, as be dyuerse of those lawes which this pacyfyer in some places of this boke toucheth, beynge made agaynste heretyques / and all be yt that they be & longe haue bene thorowe the whole corps of crystendome both temporaltye and spyrytualtye, by longe vsage and custome ratyfyed agreed and confyrmyd, yet he layeth some lacke in theym callynge theym very sore / in those thynges I saye, that syth I nothynge doute in my mynde / but in that congregacyon to goddes honour gracyousely gathered to gether, the good assystence of the spyryte of god [V₂] is accordynge to Chrystes promyse as veryly present and assystente as it was wyth his blessed apostles, men oughte wyth reuerence and wythout resystence, grudge, or argumentes to receyue them. And yf a prouyncyall counsayle erre / there are in Chrystes chyrche ordynarye wayes to reforme yt. But in suche thynges as any spyrytuall gouernours after a lawfull order and forme, dyuyse for the spyrytual weale of theyr soules that are in theyre charge, and whyche thynges are such as good folke may soon perceyue them for good / in these thinges at the leste wyse sholde the good not geue eare to the badde folke and frowarde, that agaynst the beste thynge that can be deuysed can neuer lacke a fonde frowarde argument. To these wordes this good man answereth me thus.

Then to shew my mynde in some thynges that mayster More hathe touched yet farther in the sayde chapiter: I wyl fyrst agree wyth mayster More / yᵗ in suche thynges as the hole clergye of crystendome teacheth and ordreth in spyrytuall thynges / and whyche of longe tyme haue ben by longe vsage and cu[V₂v]stome thorough the hole corps of crystendome spyrytualtye and temporaltye, ratyfyed agreed and confyrmed, ought wyth reuerence to be receyued: but yet yf the same thynges thorough longe contynuance and thorough abusions that ryse by occasyon of them, proue hurtefull & ouer greuous to the peple to bere: then may the people grudge and complayne lawfully to theyr superyours / and desyre that they maye be reformed / as lawfully as they may do to haue temporall lawes reformed when nede requyreth.

---

2 Apologye] *1557*, Apololye *1533*   22 To] *para. 1557*   26 spyrytuall] spirytuall *1557*, syrytuall *1533*

As vnto thys, bycause he ys so gentle to agree with me, I shall as
gently agre wyth hym agayne / but yet he getteth nought therby.
For sith the lawes agaynste whyche he wryteth, made for the
correccyon of heretyques, as I haue in the .xv. xvi. and .xvii.
5 chapyter playnely proued agaynste hym, and reproued his
obieccyons therin, be good and very reasonable / and that abusyons (by occasyon wherof he wold make yt now seme, that in
long contynuaunce they become hurtfull) he proueth not one in
this worlde, but by false slaunderouse some sayes surmysed
10 agaynst the ordynaryes, and dyuers tymes [V₃] founde false byfore the kynges honorable counsayle: this answere here of his,
helpeth nothyng his mater.
    Then goeth he farther and sayth vn thys wyse.

    I wyll also agre that in the congregacyon of the clergye, to goddes
15 honour gracyously gathered to gether: the good assystence of the
spyryte of god, accordynge to Chrystes promyse / wyll be as veryly
present and assystente wyth them, as yt was wyth hys blessed apostles /
yf they order them selfe in mekenesse and charyte and put all theyr
truste in god, as the apostles dyd. But yf they wyl trust in theyr own wyt
20 and in worldly polycye: then may they lyghtly lese the spyryte of god.
And whether yt were so at the makynge of the lawes, which mayster
More speketh of concernynge heresye or not, I can not tel: but this wyll
I say, that yf they were not good and reasonable in them selfe at the
fyrste makyng, that they were neuer made by the assystence of the
25 spyryt of god. And surely I can not then se, how the vsage and longe
contynuaunce of them can ratyfye or confyrme them. For as yt is of an
euyll custome, that the lenger yt is vsed, the greater is the offence: so is
yt of an euyll lawe. And lyke as an euyll custome ys to be put awaye, so yt
is of an euyll lawe.

30   Of what strength the generall counsayles be, & whether we
may in any of them by lauful order gadered to geder, put any
diffydence or mystrust / and yf we may then in what maner [V₃v]
thinges, and in what wise they bynd, & whom, & how long: I shal
not nede for thys mater to dyspute wyth this good man. And all
35 his doute concernynge the sayd lawes, whyther they be reasonable or not, and whether the contynuaunce of them be good or

13 vn] on 1557   31 them] 1557, thee 1533; gadered] gathered 1557

not: in all these thynges haue I so confuted thys good man all
redye, yᵗ these wordes of hys can serue of noughte. But yet to
make it seme that he sayd some what / and that no lawe of the
chyrche whyche he hath here impugned, made agaynst heretyques, was eyther ratyfyed or approued in thys realme: ye shall   5
heare how properly he proueth. Lo good readers these are his
wordes.

   And the lawes affermed by vsage and agremente of the people be the
lawes of fastynge and kepynge of holydayes, and suche other as the
people of theyr free agremente accepte and agree vnto: but these lawes   10
made for punyshement of heresyes were neuer agreed by a comen
assente of the people, but that some partyculare persons / wherof some
haue ben gyltye / and some peraduenture not gyltye / haue ben
punyshed therby ryghte sore agaynste theyr wylles. [V₄] And that can
not be a confyrmacyon of them that so agree against theyr wyl. But as to   15
them yᵗ do the correccyon, yt ys a confyrmacyon: for they do it wᵗ theyr
good wyll. And though that correccyon were a suffycyent confyrmacyon, as agaynst theym that be so punyshed: yet yt can not be a confyrmacyon to make the lawe approued for all the resydue of the people.
   I can not se therfore that any ratyfyeng, agreyng, or confyrmynge of   20
the people can be proued in tho lawes, concernynge the correccyon for
heresye:

   Dyd euer any man good readers here suche a nother reason as
thys is? He denyeth not but that the suyte ex officio, and the
order taken in the generall counsayle, and the other farther   25
procedynges agaynste heretyques, accordynge to the comen receyued spyrytuall lawes, haue bene vsually longe accustomed in
thys realme / & by the princes of yᵉ same & generally by all the
people by comen vsage accepted / and ouer that, by playn parlyament lawes and orders made for all temporall offycers to assyste   30
the ordynaryes therin, and to put the offenders in execucyon
therupon and knowynge wel all thys, he [V₄v] dyssymuleth yt
euery whytte, & sayth not one worde therto / but argueth that yt
was neuer ratyfyed in thys realme, bycause the heretykes yᵗ are
for heresye punyshed, be burned agaynste theyre wyll, and   35

---

2 But] *para. 1557*   6 properly] *1557*, properly[*new line*]ly *1533*   20 I] *no para.*
1557   21 tho] the *1557*   26 procedynges] proceding *1557*

agree not them selfe therto. This reason wyl I neuer labour to confute. For if any man be so mad to lyke yt, I were almoste as madde as he yf I wolde reason wyth hym.

After this he resorteth agayne to the vnreasonablenes of the
5 lawes / and proueth theym vnreasonable, by the sentence of hys owne conceyte. For these are his wordes.

And then whether the lawes in them self be good & indyfferent or not, I wyll remytte the iugement in that behalfe to theym that haue authoryte. But to shew my conceyte therin, I shall wyth good wyll euen
10 as my conscyence meueth me to / & that is, that I coulde neuer se, that yt was reasonable to be accepted as a lawe / that a man shulde be accused & knowe not his acuser. And that yt is yet more vnreasonable that a man shuld be condempned / and know not the wytnesse that condemned hym. Also that a man vpon suspeccyon shuld be dryuen to
15 make his purgacyon at the wyll of the ordinary, or be accursed: Or [V₅] that a periured wytnesse shulde condempne hym, that he had clered afore: That a greate offender and a lesse offender shulde haue one lyke punyshement, yf they renunced: or be a lyke arrested and put in pryson: I neuer saw no indyfferencye in it.

20 Now good readers as for the conceyte that the good conscience of this man hath conceiued, is of very trowth but euyn a very pore conceyte / as in the sayed chapyters the .xv. the .xvi. and the .xvii. euery man maye soone perceyue.

How be it in the laste poynt that he fyndeth so great a fawte,
25 that a greater offender and a lesse offender, sholde haue one lyke punysshement, thys man loked not well about hym whan he wrote that worde. For whan the thynge is well loked on / yᵉ weight of his reason wyll fall vppon the wronge syde, and all agaynst hys mynde. For where so euer a greater offender and a
30 lesse offender be bothe punysshed alyke: yf the greater offender haue no more payne than the lesse hath deserued, there is the order [V₅v] somewhat lesse sharpe than it sholde be / but yet not vnryghtuouse. For yf it were, than were the lawes of this realme vnlawfull, that hange vppe hym that doeth but robbe a man, as

---

9 authoryte] aucthoritie *1557*   10 meueth] moueth *1557*   12 *Sidenote 1557:* Note these iiii. pointes.   13 the] *1557*, the [*new line*] the *1533*   33 vnryghtuouse] vnrighteouse *1557*

well as hym that robbeth hym and kylleth hym to. Now so is it in
the spyrituall law, that whan two do both renounce theyr heresye, and abiure and bere faggottes bothe, yf the tone hylde .x.
heresyes and the tother but twayne, the greater offender hath no
more payne than the lesse deserueth. And therfore yf this man   5
in that case complayne: thys complaynt (as I sayd) turneth vn the
tother syde / and fyndeth the fawte in that, that where the lesse
offender bereth one faggot, the greater bereth not fyue, yf theyr
bodyes be lyke of strength.

    How be it good readers all thys tale of hys is to no purpose at   10
all. For in the spyrytuall law, they waye the offences / and consyder the cyrcum[V$_6$]staunces, and enioyne the penaunce after
the weygth or grauyte of the trespas / and for emprysonynge vse
to put no man to it, but where good reason wolde not suffre hym
walke abrode. And therfore I suppose / that whan the man was   15
wrytynge thys / hys wytte was walkynge towarde the holy lande.
For yf he wolde saye that he meneth by the lesse offender and
the more offender, suche twayne as abiure bothe, and bere
fagottes bothe, where the tone was worthy and the tother not
worthy at all: I saye that neyther his wordes wyll mayntayne any   20
such menyng (for he speketh generally of the lesse offender &
the more) nor also he proueth none suche but by his slaunderouse some sayes, whyche haue ben playne proued false.

    Than goeth he ferther and knytteth vppe all the chapyter
wyth this goodly conclusyon. [V$_6$v]   25

And yf any man wyll saye that these reasons wyll gyue a boldenesse to
heretykes: trewly I wyll not fully make answere therto. But thys wyll I
saye, that I thynke veryly that they wyll gyue a boldenesse to trewth and
trew men. And veryly I haue herd say, that it were better to suffre an
offender go vnpunyshed, than to punyshe hym vnryghtuousely and   30
agaynst dew order of iustyce.

    Marke good reders here for our lordes sake, what maner of
reason thys is. The thynge that hym selfe very well perceyueth to
be the very weyght and pyth of all the mater, & therfore at laste
obiecteth it agaynste hym selfe, as a thynge that had nede to be   35
soyled, what answere doeth he make vnto it? He sayth he wyll not

---

6 vn] vnto *1557*   26 man] *om. 1557*   30 vnryghtuousely] vnrighteousely *1557*

answere it fully. In fayth that is spoken very dully: well, syth so
greate weyghte hangeth on it, yf he wolde not answere it fully, he
sholde haue answered at the leste wyse halfe. If not halfe, a
fourth part yet, or a fyfth parte at the lest. For thys y^t he sayth,
answereth no parte at all. For two thynges he sayth / one that
though he can not saye naye, but that his reasons [V$_7$] yf they be
folowed, shall gyue a boldenesse to heretikes: yet he thynketh
they shall also gyue boldenesse to trowth and trew men. And by
my trowth I thynke veryly vn the tother syde, y^t yf heretykes
haue boldenesse gyuen them, and (as they therby soone shall)
take corage and myche encreace, they shall make the trowth
shrynke, and many trew men aferde. And yf the geuynge
boldnes to falsed, shall geue boldenesse to trouth / assaye than
and geue boldenesse to theues / and than loke whyther trewe
men shall wax the bolder by it.

The secunde thynge that he saith is thys, whyche yet he dothe
not afferme but sayth he hath herd it sayd, that it were better to
suffre an offender go vnpunysshed, than punyshe hym vnrightuousely
and agaynst dew order of iustyce.

Thys were somewhat pretely sayd, yf thys good man had
proued y^t heretykes myght not be punyshed by those lawes, but
vnryghtuousely [V$_7$v] and agaynst the order of iustice. But than
how hath he proued that? By no meane in thys world but twayne.
The tone, that it is not ryghtuouse nor indyfferente, that a greater offender and a lesse offender sholde be punyshed, em-
prisoned, or arrested lyke / whych vnreasonable reason oppugneth playnely in all crimynall causes almost, all the lawes of thys
realme and yet helpeth not hys mater, but impayreth it mych, as
a lytell here before I haue well & clerely proued.

His other reason is his generall reason y^t is his whole grounde,
whervppon he buyldeth agaynst all those lawes all his whole
mater / that is to wytte, that by those lawes whyche are made for
punysshement of heretykes, it may somtyme fortune that a man
may be punysshed whyche is no heretyke in dede.

---

7 *Sidenote 1557:* Giue no boldnesse to heretykes.   9 veryly] verely *1557*, weryly *1533;*
vn] on *1557*   14 to theues] *1533 corr. err., om. 1533 1557*   18 vnrightuousely]
vnrighteously *1557*   22 vnryghtuousely] vnrighteousely *1557*   24 ryghtuouse]
righteouse *1557*

Now is thys reason so vnreasonable to be layed for a reason to take [V$_8$] awaye a lawe, that yf it were admytted for reason, it could suffer neyther in thys realme, nor in any realme els any lawe stand in this world, that all the wyttes in this world coulde imagyne or deuyse, for any maner punysshement of vngracy- ouse folke. And albe it that of such lawes some maye be reformed from the wurse vnto ye better / though neuer fully to suche poynt, but that an innocent may take harme: yet both by reason and experyence it appereth playnely, y^t these lawes whyche he wolde haue chaunged and made more easy, can neuer haue any good chaunge, but by makynge them more streygth.

And thus hath this good man sore ouersene hym selfe, more I trowe than .xx. tymes in hys .xx. chapyter. [V$_8$v]

The .xxi. chapyter.

I$_N$ hys .xxi. chapyter begynnynge in the .lxxxiiii. lefe, bycause I sayd in myne apologye y^t there be fewe partes in his boke of diuysyon, that shall yf they be well consydered, appere so good at length, as they seme to some men at the fyrste syght and at superfycyall readynge: he prouoketh me to shew what other fawtes I fynde therin. And than to prycke me forwarde, he bryngeth forth two or thre thynges, whych he sayeth it semeth moste lykely that I shold meane. But wherfore it shold be moost lykely that I sholde meane those thynges / therof sheweth he no thynge / but leueth folke occasyon to thynke, that hys owne mynde mysgeueth hym in those thynges. For me hath he neuer herd make any bu[X$_1$]synes of them.

And afterwarde in the lefe .91. agayne he prouoketh me to the same. And there he recyteth how many chapyters of his I medle not withall / wherin he myghte haue made a shorter worke yf he wolde haue let them stande that I towched not / and haue spoken of them onely that I towched. For they were very few, as he that was very vnwyllynge to haue towched any one at all, saue for the mych euyll that couertely was cloked in them. And for the with- drawynge of that cloke that men myght the better se what it ment: I towched the fyrste chapyter for a shew, and the .vii, and

33 them.] *1557*, them, *1533*

the .viii, for that they labored to the great decay of the catholike fayth, to put awaye or chaunge in to wurse ye moste specyall good lawys, bothe of the whole chyrche and of this realm, that haue bene made and obserued longe for the preseruacyon therof. [X₁v] And the fyrst chapiter was in effecte nothynge ellys, but by false slaunderouse surmyses agaynst the ordynarys (as though they myshandeled men for heresye) a shrewde pre-paratiue to it. And therfore leuynge his other tryfles alone: I answered in effecte onely these, of whych so mych harme myght growe. Whych thynges yf they had ben out of his boke, all ye remanaunt good and bad togyther, sholde haue gone forth for me / and therfore yet so shall they: For I purpose not to embysye my selfe with confutynge of euery fawte that I fynd in euery mannes boke. I sholde haue than ouer mych a do.

Nor I wyll not dysprayse or depraue any thyng that I thynke good eyther in his boke or in any mannes ellys. And therfore I haue in myne apology sayd expressely, that he saith some thynges wel. But for as mych as there be many thynges nought to: [X₂] I geue therfore the reader warnyng not to walke awaye with theym ouer hastely, but rede them with iudgement and aduise them well / and not byleue euery spyryt, but proue whyther it be of god or not / and that that is good take / and that that is euyll, lette it go to the deuyll.

I well allow therfore and lyke not a lytell the great good mynde of Salem toward the vaynquysshyng of the great turke / and conquerynge of the holy lande, wherin he spendeth the tother thre chapiters of his boke. But I mysse lyke mych agayn, that as he wold dylate the fayth, by force of sworde in farre cuntres hense: so he laboreth to chaunge and take away the good & holsome lawes, wherby the fayth is preserued here at home.

I lyke also meruelousely well, that suche poyntes of the cath-olyke fayth as heretykes nowe labour to [X₂v] destroye, as prayenge to sayntes, pylgrymage, and purgatory, & the sacra-mentes, and specyally the blessed sacrament of the awter, wherof in the .lxxxvi. lefe he speketh so well, that as helpe me

---

10 Whych] Which *1557*, whych *1533*   12 embysye] *1533 corr. err.*, embusie *1557*, embuse *1533*   21–22 *Sidenote 1557:* 1. Iohn .4.   24 well] will *1557*   34 awter] aulter *1557*

god it dyde me good to rede it: this I saye lyketh me meruelousely well, that the ryght fayth of these poyntes he confesseth so well and so fully for his owne person. But the better
opynyon that I haue of his owne person therin, the more sory am
I to se, y^t his bookes are by some shrewde counsayle handeled in   5
such wyse, as if they were folowed / wolde make the faythe
decaye and peryshe in many other folke. Thys is the greate
thynge that in his bokes greueth me.

For as for the poynt that he spoketh of in the lefe .91, of that
that the prestes shold eate no flesshe fro quinquagesime to East-   10
er: I take it for a mater as small as he dothe I. [X$_3$] But than he
asketh me wherfore in y^e .xxxi. chapiter of myne apology begynnyng in the .175. lefe, I make so greate a mater of it. Who so lyste
to reade the chapyter, shall se that I wrote it not all in vayne, nor
shewe my selfe vnwyllynge that the prestes sholde do it neyther,   15
though they be not bounden to it. But the lesse that the weyghte
of the mater was / the more cause this man gaue me to speke
therof. For the more was he to blame to put that and other suche
smal maters as that is, for causes of so great a diuisyon, as he
surmyseth y^t this is. This was lo y^e cause that made me to speke   20
therof. Whych cause this man gaue hym selfe / and therfore
nedeth not to meruayle as he doth, wherfore I spake therof.

And therfore thus haue I good readers now replyed to euery
chapyter of his boke by row, saue onely y^e last thre which go
about a good viage [X$_3$v] into the holy lande, a great way farre of   25
fro me. And I haue not leped to & fro, now forwarde, now
bakward, in such maner as he playeth in his answere made vnto
me, without eyther order kepte or cause apperynge wherfore,
saue onely the cause that euery man may spye, that he wold not
haue it sene what places he lefte vntowched. Which is in a maner   30
the moste parte of all togyther, that in my boke ys towched of the
thre chapyters of his. And I haue on the tother syde not lefte any
one pyece vnproued, that my selfe spake of before, or that any
thynge perteyned vnto me.

And therfore where as in the begynnyng of the .xxii. chap-   35
yter, Symkyn Salem geueth hys sentence vppon the sayde an-

---

21 Whych] Which *1557*, whych *1533*   31 all togyther] altogyther *1557*; ys towched of]
1533 corr. err., towched *1533*, touched *1557*

swere to the sayde apologye, and alloweth the sayd answere well:
me thynketh that yf he consydered not onely how myche he hath
lefte vnanswered, & how mych [X₄] of his owne wordes vnde-
fended, whyche he nothynge hath towched at all / but ouer that
5 how febly he hath defended those thynges that he hath towched
here: Salem beynge indyfferent, had ben like to haue allowed it
but a lytell.

For settynge asyde for the whyle all the remanaunt, yf he go
but to the very pryncypal poynt alone, wherin he laboreth to
10 chaunge and put awaye those good lawes / yᵉ chaunge wherof
(suche as he deuyseth) the decaye of the catholyke fayth and the
encreace of heresyes wolde folowe: in that poynt alone, I say we
laye agaynst hym, the comen consent of this realm. And he
layeth his own reason agaynst it. We laye agaynste hym the con-
15 sent of yᵉ generall counsayle. And agaynst this he layeth his owne
reason. We lay agaynst hym the generall approbacion of all
chrysten realmes. And agaynst this he layeth his own reason.
[X₄v] And what is hys owne irrefragable reason that he layth
agaynst all this? Surely no more as you se, but that by those lawes
20 an innocent may sometyme take wrong. Agaynste this reason we
lay hym, that yf this reason sholde stande, than agaynst malefactours there could no law stande. We laye agaynst it also that by
his deuyces yf they were folowed, by the encreace of heresyes
many innocentes must nedes take mych more wronge.

25 To thys answereth he, that he wyll not answere that. And nowe
when Salem seeth that he can not answere that, & seeth that al
the weigth of the mater hangeth vpon that: than Sym Salem
geueth sentence that he hath answered very well. But surely yf
suche answeryng be well / I wote not whyche way a man myght
30 answere yll.

And therfore where as Symkyn Salem sayth, that yf this good
man [X₅] wyll, he wyll cause a frende of hys answere all the
remanaunt: he may do this good man a myche more frendly
tourne, yf he make hys frende answere this better fyrst, that this
35 good man hath answered all redy. How be yt yf they lyste thus to

---

5 thynges] thing *1557*   25 To] *no para. 1557*   30 yll.] ill. *1557*, yll *1533*   34 make]
made *1557*

geue ouer thys, and assaye what they can saye better to any other
pyece: let theym a goddes name hardely go to for me. And yf
they saye any thynge metely to the mater, I wyll put no frende to
payne to make them answere / but at leasure conuenient shal
answere them my selfe. And where they say well / I wyll not let to   5
saye so. And where they say wronge / I wyll not lette to tell
theym. But on the tother syde yf they go no better to worke, nor
no nerer to the mater, then thys man hath done: I shall peraduenture let them euen alone / and lette them lyke theyr wrytynge
theym selfe, and no man ellys. [X₅v]   10
    But now lettynge passe all the specyall poyntes: I shall answere
yᵉ generaltyes yᵗ thys good man speketh of. For in the lefe .xc.
these are hys wordes.

And now shall I saye somwhat farther in a generalytye, as mayster
More hathe done / and that ys this: that al that I speke in the sayde   15
treatyse, was to appeace this diuysyon / and not to begynne any, ne to
contynue yt. And therfore how they can saue theyr conscyence / that
saye I dyd rather intende a dyuysyon then agrement, I can not tell /
theyr owne conscyence shall be iudge. And I entended also somwhat to
moue that myght be occasyon to put awaye abusyons, euyll examplys,   20
and heresyes: and not to encrease theym or maynteyne theym I dare
boldely saye.

    To this I answere, that yt neyther was nor is my mynde, that
men shold thynke yᵗ he ment euyl him self, as I haue in many
places of myn apology testified. But verily I thought & yet   25
thinke, yᵗ by some wyly shrewis his boke was so mysse handeled,
that yt ment nought, though he ment wel. For where as he sayeth
that wyth hys boke of dyuysyon, all hys purpose was to appease
dyuysyon: I [X₆] wyll not contende wyth hym vppon hys owne
mynde. But surely thys wyll I saye, that yf I hadde ben of the   30
mynde to sow and sette forthe dyuysyon: I wold haue vsed euen
the selfe same ways to kyndle yt, that he vsed (as he sayth) to
quenche yt.
    Thenne goeth he farther and sayth.

---

11 all the specyall] *1533 corr. err.*, all specyall yᵉ *1533*, al specyall the *1557*   19 owne]
own *1557*, one *1533*   30 But] *para. 1557*

And farther as mayster More knoweth better then I, mentire est contra mentem ire, that is to say to lye ys when a man sayeth agaynste hys owne mynde / & in good fayth in all that treatyse, I speke nothynge but that I thought was trew.

5   To thys I answere, that in dede suche a thynge I haue redde, and as I remembre in Aulus Gellius. Whyche thynge though I haue now no leasure to loke for: yet two poyntes I remembre therof. One that yt ys there mentiri and not mentire / whyche infynytyue mode in what boke of grammer this good man hath founde, I can not tell. I was aferd yt had ben ouersene in the prentynge. [X₆v] But I haue loked the correccyons, and there fynde I no faute founde therin.

The tother poynte I remembre that there ys a dyfference putte betwene mentiri & mendacium dicere, that is as we myghte saye / betwene hym that wyttyngly lyeth, and hym that telleth a lye wenyng that it were trewe. And there yt is sayde, wittyngly not to tell a lye, perteyneth to a good man. And not to tell a lye vnware, is the parte of a wyse man. And surely syth the scrypture sayeth that he that shortely byleueth is ouer lyghte: thys good man to byleue so many lyes so soon, and wyth so many some sayes to set theym forthe in prent, to the rebuke and slaunder of the spyrytual iudges, and make men wene they mysse handeled men for heresyes, though the mannys innocent mynde made the synne the lesse, yet was the thyng at the lest no lesse, [X₇] then a very great lyghtnesse, ye and also a great profe towarde the reprofe of his wordes that folow next, where he goeth farther thus.

And farther I wyll acertayne mayster More as farre as in me is, that I neyther hadde any sotle shrewes counsayle, ne any euyll counsayle at the makynge of the sayde treatyse, whyche he calleth the boke of dyuysyon (as ys sayde before).

To thys I answere, that all be yt thys good man and I be at myche varyaunce here in dyuerse thynges: yet for the good and playne professyon of the catholyque faythe that I fynde in hym, in good fayth I mych better loue hym then in that poynt to beleue

---

16 there] *1533 corr. err.*, here *1533 1557*   18 *Sidenote 1557:* Ecclesi. 19.   28 acertayne] a certaine *1557*   29 shrewes counsayle] *1557*, shrewes counlayle *1533*   31 before).] before) *1533 1557*

hym. For yf he sayde therin trew, then were all the fautes onely
hys owne / in whyche as I haue often sayde, I myche rather
thynke, that some sotle shrewes haue deceyued hym.

And besyde sondry other thynges that lede me so to thynke,
one very stronge thynge ys thys, that euery [X₇v] man maye well 5
se by hys boke, that all suche as haue resorted to hym to tell hym
any suche thynges, as vnder some sayes he put oute agayne, haue
alwaye tolde hym euyll / and neuer told him good. And of misse
handlynge for heresyes haue euer tolde hym lyes, and neuer
tolde hym trew. For where as the punyshement for heresyes 10
hathe ben very lytle any where, saue euen here at hande, and
here but ryght done to them, and that wyth myche fauour to:
they haue made hym good sely soule beleue, that ordynaryes
mysse handle men for heresye in maner thorow oute the realme.

Also where as such slaunderouse clamour hath bene sondry 15
tymes of late in al yᵗ euer complayned, playnly proued false
before the kynges most honorable counsayle, not one man cam
to tell hym nothynge therof, nor not one some say therof wryten
in all his [X₈] boke / and ouer this where as myne owne self haue
playnly told hym the same thynges in myn apologye by writing: 20
yet (which most meruayle were of all, saue for such wyly shrewes)
euery man may well se that he neuer redde yt. For he sayth not
one worde therto. And therfore yt is eth to perceyue what so
euer hym selfe saye whych is loth of his goodnes to put other
folke in faute, yᵗ there be some wyly shrewes so myche about 25
hym, yᵗ they neyther suffer hym any thyng to here but yᵗ them
self lyst to tel him, nor yet any thinge to rede, but where them
selfe lyste to turne hym.

And nowe syth I haue here answered these generalytyes of
hys: I wyll not longe encumbre you with any generaltyes of myn 30
own, but generally I wold yᵗ al were well. And so helpe me my
sauiour & none other wise, but as I wold wishe none heretike one
halporth harme, yᵗ had clerely [X₈v] lefte hys heresye, and were
well turned to god. But on the tother syde, who so sticke styl
therin: rather wold I wyshe hym sorowe to his synne, wherby 35
there are many folke many tymes amended, then prosperousely
to procede in hys myschyefe to the losse of his own soule and

---

35 *Sidenote 1557:* A good wysh.

other mennys to. And towarde that poynte, agaynste all malefactours in the spyrytualtye and the temporaltye to, wold I wyshe all
good folke of bothe partes to agre, and eche loue other wel, and
stycke faste to the fayth, whyche were like sore to decay by the
5   chaunge of these good lawes that thys good man goeth aboute to
destroye. For whose vnreasonablenesse therin the better to be
perceyued, wyth the daungeour and parell that wolde ensewe
theron: I wyll desyre you good readers to resorte to myne Apologye / and begynnynge at the lefe .270, rede vnto the lefe .287.
10 wherin you [Y₁] shall I truste be well and fully satysfyed. And
vnto all that euer ys in all that spoken: thys man hath nothynge
sayd.

  And where as in confutynge the fautes that thys man fyndeth
in the suyte ex officio, and the lawes made agaynste heretyques, I
15 haue vsed some examples of the comen lawe, whyche this man
hathe labored to proue vnlyke / and I haue therin clerely confuted hym a freshe: yt maye peraduenture happen that he wyll
now take a nother waye therin, and saye that in such poyntes
those spyrytuall lawes maye be reformed, and those tempo-
20 rall to.

  How be yt yf he so saye, but yf men forgette what hath ben
sayd before: ellys shall they se that his sayenge wyll not serue
hym.

  For fyrste as I haue sayed ofter then ones all redy, the same
25 thynges [Y₁v] in the comen lawe be not to be chaunged. For yf
they be: there shall come therof more harme thanne good. And
yf yt happen one innocent to take harme by the lawe: there shall
fyue for one take more harme by the chaunge.

  More ouer yf we sholde for that cause chaunge those tem-
30 porall lawes, that ys to wytte bycause some innocent maye somtyme take harme by them: we must chaunge by the same reason,
all that olde vsed lawe that a man maye be arrested and remayne
in pryson tyll he fynde suertyes for the peace, vppon the bare
othe of hys enmye that sayth he is a ferde of hym. For by that law
35 may some tyme an innocent take harme to. And yet muste that
lawe stande yf we do well. For ellys shall there by the chaunge,
mo innocentes take more harme. [Y₂]

25–27 *Sidenote 1557:* By the change of lawes commeth greate harme.   34 enmye]
enemye *1557*

What trouble haue there many men in Walys, by that they be compelled to be bounden to the peace, bothe for them selfe and for theyr seruauntes and other frendes to? And yet is the order there so necessary that in many lordshyppes yt maye not be forborne.

And surely yf we fall to chaungynge lawes vpon y^t symple ground: we muste then chaunge so many that it wolde not be well.

Bysydes thys yf men sholde reforme and chaunge a lawe, bycause that an innocent maye somtyme take harme therby: then must they when they haue chaunged it, chaunge yt yet agayne / & after that chaunge, yet chaunge yt agayne / & so forth chaunge after chaunge and neuer cease chaungynge tyll the worlde be all chaunged at the daye of dome. For neuer can all the wyttes that are in yt, make [Y$_2$v] any one penall lawe / suche that none innocent may take harme therby.

How be yt yf a newe lawe were drawen and putte forthe to be made agaynst any such myschiefe as wold els do mych harme: good reason yt were to take an excepcyon to the byl, and shewe that innocentes myghte be myche harmed by thys poynt or that / and therwyth prouyde the remedye and putte it in the lawe, and stoppe as many such gappes as then coulde be spyed. Ye and yf after the law made men found notable harme, that good folke were myche wronged by it / and the lawe suche that it eyther myghte be forborne, or els the meanes founde to be chaunged to the better: good reason wold it to make prouysyon for it.

But surely to come forth as thys man cometh here, agaynste so good lawes, so well made, and by so great [Y$_3$] authoryte, so longe approued thorow the whole corps of chrystendome, in thys realme ratyfyed specyally by parlyament, and that vppon a profe not wythout great grounde & cause, euer synnys founden so profytable for preseruacyon of the fayth, and proued so necessary vpon thys mannes own deuyces, that without great encreace of heresyes they can not be forborne / nor neuer can be chaunged but eyther to the strayghter or ellys to the wurse: to come now forth and for appeasynge of dyuysyon, sowe fyrste a

5

10

15

20

25

30

35

---

14 dome.] *1557*, dome *1533*   32–33 so necessary] *1557*, se necessary *1533*

slaunder that maye make dyuysyon, and than labour to chaunge
those lawes, vpon none other ground but onely that an innocent
may happe to take harme by meane of false iudges, and than
proue not any wronge done, but by false some sayes onely,
5 agaynste whyche false some sayes the trouth is proued contrary,
bothe [Y₃v] by iuste examynacyon before the kynges counsayle,
and ouer that playnely by thys one poynte also, whyche no man
can denye, that there ys no lawe prouyded agaynste so great a
cryme, by whyche lawelesse people haue in thys realme be
10 punyshed: therfore to come nowe thus as thys good man dothe,
and procure the chaunge of these lawes, so olde, so good, and so
necessarye, and to make theym more easy, wherwyth heretyques
wolde wax bolde, whyche thynge hym selfe (as you se) denyeth
not in the ende: what is this good chrysten readers, but to pro-
15 cure that the catholyque chrysten fayth, myght fade and fall
awaye?

And yet as for thys man hym self to tell you for conclusyon
what I thynke / all be yt there are as you se ryghte euyll and
perylouse thynges in hys bokes, wyth deuyces that [Y₄] wolde
20 make heresyes encrease: yet syth he professyth so playnely the
catholyque chrysten faythe, and by his exhortacyon also towarde
the conqueste of the holy lande, declareth hys mynde zelouse
and feruent toward yt, I rather byleue though hym selfe therto
saye naye, that in those thynges whyche he wryteth so perylouse
25 and so noughte, some wyly shrewes begyle the good innocent
man, than that hym selfe in hys own mynde, meane all that
harme.

But yet for as myche as in thys poynt, wythout syght of mannes
hart we can but go by gesse / & who so goth by gesse, may be
30 deceyued (For (as hym selfe sayth) a wolfe maye loke symply
lapte in a shepes skynne) I shall therfore trust the best, and leue
the trouth to god. And concernynge suche euyll wrytynges, syth
yt must nedes be, that he wrote them eyther [Y₄v] deceyued by
some shrewys, or ellys but of hym selfe / I can no more do for
35 hym, but hartely praye for hym thus. If shrewys deceyue hym:
god sende theym shortely from hym. If he wrote them of his own
mynde: thanne syth the thynges be noughte, he wrote theym

---

1 slaunder] sclaunder *1557*   9 lawelesse] lawe lesse *1533*, lawe[*new page*]lesse *1557*

eyther of euyll wyl, or of ouersyght. If he wrote theym of malyce /
god geue the euyll man more grace. If he wrote theym of folye:
god geue the good man more wytte.

And thus I beseche our lorde sende vs euerychone, bothe the
spyrytuall and the temporall to, bothe wytte and grace to agre to   5
gether in goodnes, and eche to loue other, and eche for other to
praye / and for those y^t of both partes are passed into purgatorye, and there praye for vs as we praye here for theym, that
they and we bothe thorowe the merytes of Chrystes bytter passyon, [Y$_5$] maye both wyth our own prayours, and the interces-   10
syon of all holy sayntes in heuyn, auoydynge the eternall fyre of
hell, haue pyty powred vpon vs in the very fyre of purgatorye,
whyche in those two places veryly burneth soules. And fynally
for our fayth and good workes, whych his grace (workynge wyth
the wylles of those y^t wytte haue) geueth eche good man here: 15
god geue vs in heuen to gyther euerlastynge glorye.·.[Y$_5$v]

Prynted by W. Rastell in
Fletestrete in saynte
Bridys chyrch
yarde, the   20
yere
of
our lorde.
1533.
Cum priuilegio.·.   25

---

5 *Sidenote 1557:* A charitable praier.   7 y^t] that *1557,* y^e *1533*   15 those] thoses *1533*
1557   16 god] God *1557,* good *1533*   17–25 Prynted . . . priuilegio.:] *om. 1557*
17 W.] w. *1533*

COMMENTARY

COMMENTARY

The following bibliography includes works and abbreviations cited frequently in the Introduction and the Commentary. The titles of works referred to only once or occurring only in a brief cluster of references are given in full as they occur. References to the Bible and Latin quotations from it are from the Clementine Vulgate.

BIBLIOGRAPHY AND SHORT TITLES

ASD. See Erasmus, Desiderius.

Blackstone, William. *Commentaries on the Laws of England,* ed. James Stewart, 4 vols., 2nd ed., Oxford, 1844. Cited as "Blackstone, *Commentaries.*"

CCSL. Corpus Christianorum: Series Latina. Turnhout, 1953–. Vols. numbered to 176, of which 92 had been published by 1984.

CIC. Corpus Iuris Canonici, ed. Emil Ludwig Richter and Emil Albert Friedberg, 2 vols., Leipzig, 1879–81.

CW. See More, Thomas.

Doctor and Student. See St. German, Christopher.

Elton, G. R. *Policy and Police: The Enforcement of the Reformation in the Age of Thomas Cromwell,* Cambridge, 1972. Cited as "Elton, *Policy and Police.*"

———. *Studies in Tudor and Stuart Politics and Government,* 3 vols., Cambridge, 1974–83. Cited as "Elton, *Studies.*"

Erasmus, Desiderius. *Opera omnia Desiderii Erasmi Roterodami,* ed. J. H. Waszink et al., 8 vols., Amsterdam, 1969–. Cited as *ASD.*

EW. See More, Thomas.

Fitzherbert, Anthony, and R. Crompton. *L'Office et Aucthoritie de Justices de Peace,* 2nd ed., London, 1584; *STC* 10979. Cited as "Fitzherbert and Crompton."

Fox, Alistair. *Thomas More: History and Providence,* New Haven and London, 1982. Cited as "Fox."

Gibson, R. W., and J. Max Patrick. *St. Thomas More: A Preliminary Bibliography of His Works and of Moreana to the Year 1750,* New Haven, 1961. Cited as "Gibson."

Guy, J. A. *The Cardinal's Court: The Impact of Thomas Wolsey in Star Chamber,* Hassocks (Sussex), 1977. Cited as "Guy, *Cardinal's Court.*"

———. *Christopher St. German on Chancery and Statute.* Selden Society, Supplementary Series, vol. 6, London, 1985. Cited as "Guy, *St. German.*"

———. "Henry VIII and the Praemunire Manoeuvres of 1530–1531," *English Historical Review,* 97 (1982), 481–503. Cited as "Guy, 'Henry VIII and the Praemunire Manoeuvres.'"

———. *The Public Career of Sir Thomas More,* New Haven and Brighton, 1980. Cited as "Guy, *Public Career.*"

———. "The Tudor Commonwealth: Revising Thomas Cromwell," *Historical Journal, 23* (1980), 681–87. Cited as "Guy, 'The Tudor Commonwealth.'"

Hall, Edward. *Chronicle,* ed. Sir Henry Ellis, London, 1809. Cited as "Hall, *Chronicle.*"

Heresy Trials in the Diocese of Norwich, 1428–31, ed. Norman P. Tanner, Camden Society, 4th Series, London, 1977. Cited as "Tanner."

Hogrefe, Pearl. "The Life of Christopher St. German," *Review of English Studies, 13* (1937), 398–404. Cited as "Hogrefe."

Houlbrooke, Ralph A. *Church Courts and the People during the English Reformation 1520–1570,* Oxford, 1979. Cited as "Houlbrooke."

Kelly, Henry Ansgar. "English Kings and the Fear of Sorcery," *Mediaeval Studies, 39* (1977), 206–38.

Lehmberg, Stanford E. *The Reformation Parliament, 1529–1536,* Cambridge, 1970. Cited as "Lehmberg."

LP. Letters and Papers, Foreign and Domestic, of the Reign of Henry VIII, ed. J. S. Brewer, James Gairdner, and R. H. Brodie, 21 vols. and *Addenda,* London, 1862–1932; reprint, Kraus, Vaduz, 1965.

Lyndewode, William. *Provinciale seu Constitutiones Angliae,* Oxford, 1679. Cited as *"Provinciale."*

More, Thomas. *The Yale Edition of the Complete Works of St. Thomas More:* Vol. 2, *The History of King Richard III,* ed. R. S. Sylvester; Vol. 3, Part 1, *Translations of Lucian,* ed. C. R. Thompson; Part 2, *Latin Poems,* ed. C. H. Miller et al.; Part 3, *In Defense of Humanism,* ed. Daniel Kinney; Vol. 4, *Utopia,* ed. E. L. Surtz, S. J., and J. H. Hexter; Vol. 5, *Responsio ad Lutherum,* ed. J. M. Headley, trans. Sister Scholastica Mandeville; Vol. 6, *A Dialogue Concerning Heresies,* ed. T. M. C. Lawler et al.; Vol. 8, *The Confutation of Tyndale's Answer,* ed. L. A. Schuster et al.; Vol. 9, *The Apology,* ed. J. B. Trapp; Vol. 11, *The Answer to a Poisoned Book,* ed. S. M. Foley and C. H. Miller; Vol. 12, *A Dialogue of Comfort against Tribulation,* ed. L. L. Martz and Frank Manley; Vol. 13, *Treatise on the Passion, Treatise on the Blessed Body, Instructions and Prayers,* ed. G. E. Haupt; Vol. 14, *De Tristitia Christi,* ed. C. H. Miller; New Haven and London, 1963–. Cited as *CW* followed by the appropriate volume number.

———. *The Correspondence of Sir Thomas More,* ed. Elizabeth F. Rogers, Princeton, 1947. Cited as "Rogers."

———. *The Workes . . . in the Englysh tonge,* London, 1557; *STC*² 18076. Cited as *EW.*

OED. The Oxford English Dictionary, 13 vols. and supplements, 1933; 1972–1986.

PG. Patrologia Cursus Completus, Series Graeca, ed. J. -P. Migne, 161 vols., Paris, 1857–1866.

PL. Patrologiae Cursus Completus, Series Latina, ed. J.-P. Migne, 221 vols., Paris, 1844–1903.

Pollock, F., and F. W. Maitland. *The History of English Law Before the Time of Edward I,* rev. S. F. C. Milsom, 2 vols., Cambridge, 1968. Cited as "Pollock and Maitland."

PRO. Public Record Office. C 1, Chancery, Early Chancery Proceedings.

_____. C 54, Chancery, Close Rolls.

_____. C 85, Chancery, Significations of Excommunication.

_____. C 244, Chancery, Files, Corpus cum causa.

_____. PROB 11, Prerogative Court of Canterbury, Registered Copy Wills.

_____. SP 1, State Papers, Henry VIII, General Series.

_____. SP 2, State Papers, Henry VIII, Folio Volumes.

_____. SP 6, State Papers, Henry VIII, Theological Tracts.

_____. STAC 2, Star Chamber Proceedings, Henry VIII.

Provinciale. See Lyndewode.

The Reports of Sir John Spelman, ed. J. H. Baker, 2 vols., Selden Society Publications, vols. 93–94, London, 1977–78. Cited as *"Spelman's Reports."*

Rogers. See More, Thomas.

St. German, Christopher. See also Guy, J. A., *Christopher St. German.*

_____. *An Answer to a Letter,* London, 1535; STC^2 21558.5.

_____. *Doctor and Student,* ed. T. F. T. Plucknett and J. L. Barton, Selden Society Publications, vol. 91, London, 1974. Cited as *"Doctor and Student."*

_____. *A Treatise concernynge the diuision betwene the spirytualtie and temporaltie,* London, 1532; reprinted in *CW 9,* Appendix A. Cited as *"Division."*

_____. *A Treatyse concerninge the Power of the Clergye, and the Lawes of the Realme,* London, ca. 1535; STC^2 21588. Cited as *"The Power of the Clergy."*

Select Cases from the Ecclesiastical Courts of the Province of Canterbury, c. 1200–1301, ed. Norma Adams and Charles Donahue, Selden Society Publications, vol. 95, London, 1981. Cited as *"Select Cases."*

Spelman's Reports. See *The Reports of Sir John Spelman.*

STC. *A Short-Title Catalogue of Books Printed in England, Scotland, & Ireland and of English Books Printed Abroad 1475–1640,* comp. A. W. Pollard and G. R. Redgrave, London, 1926.

STC^2. Revised edition of *STC,* comp. W. A. Jackson, F. S. Ferguson, and K. Pantzer, 2 vols., London, 1976–1986.

Tanner. See *Heresy Trials in the Diocese of Norwich, 1428–31*.

Thomson, John A. F. *The Later Lollards, 1414–1520*, Oxford, 1965. Cited as "Thomson."

Tilley, Morris P. *A Dictionary of the Proverbs in England in the Sixteenth and Seventeenth Centuries*, Ann Arbor, 1950. Cited as "Tilley."

Visser, F. T. *A Syntax of the English Language of St. Thomas More*, 3 vols., Materials for the Study of the Old English Drama, New Series, 19, 24, 26, Louvain, 1946–56. Cited as "Visser."

Whiting, Bartlett J. *Proverbs, Sentences, and Proverbial Phrases from English Writings Mainly before 1500*, Cambridge, Mass., 1968. Cited as "Whiting."

3/4 **ye great turke.** The impact of the Turkish threat against Christendom was felt on both a literal and a symbolic level. See *CW 12,* cxx–cxxxv and Fox, pp. 223–42.

3/8 **Syr . . . Pacifiar.** In his *Apology* More had variously used the ironical epithets "Sir John Some-say" and "the Pacifier" to describe his opponent St. German, whom he claimed to believe to be an obscure country priest. See *CW 9,* xl–xli and Commentary at 42/4, 60/2. In chapter 17 of *Salem and Bizance,* St. German had objected to More's "straunge gesting maner" in mocking his use of "some say" as a figure of speech and pointed out that in the *Apology* (*CW 9,* 48/4, 60/5, 60/36) More "vseth the same termes hym selfe in dyuers places" (Appendix B, 364/16–28). More replied at 167/9–32. See the Introduction, pp. lxxxix.

3/9 **Dialoge.** *Salem and Bizance* by St. German; Appendix B, below.

3/9–10 **dyuysyon.** *A Treatise concernynge the diuision betwene the spirytualtie and temporaltie* by St. German; *CW 9,* Appendix A, pp. 173–212.

3/10 **Apology . . . knyght.** *CW 9,* 1–172.

4/1–2 **For . . . breyde.** See 7/6, where More says that he wrote the *Debellation* "in few days." See also the Introduction, pp. xcv–xcvii.

4/24 **thykke & threfolde.** Tilley T100.

4/26 **dyuerse . . . men.** That is, lawyers.

4/26–27 **trayuayle . . . hyllys.** Cf. Horace, *Ars poetica* 139.

4/30–31 **wryten . . . hande.** From this remark we may question whether More knew the identity of his anonymous opponent when writing the *Debellation.* It is not clear that More is directly describing and engaging with St. German in this passage—the matter must remain open, though there is other evidence that More knew his adversary's identity. See the Introduction, pp. xxii–xxiv. More scrupulously maintained his posture of ignorance concerning his antagonist; the present passage, however, gives a perfect description of St. German's handwriting. See the illustration facing p. xxiv and St. German's holograph letter to Thomas Cromwell of July 1539, PRO, SP 1/152, fol. 249 (*LP 14,* 1,1349). This letter is discussed in Guy, *St. German,* pp. 8–9.

4/34 **shetes . . . querys.** In a manuscript a full sheet usually yielded four leaves; a quire (normally four sheets), sixteen leaves. The manuscript of *Salem and Bizance* to which More refers had forty-eight leaves.

4/36 **answere . . . make.** *Apology, CW 9,* 10–39.

5/1 **my dyaloge.** *A Dialogue concerning Heresies, CW 6.*

5/3 **my confutacyon.** *The Confutation of Tyndale's Answer, CW 8.*

5/12 **poysoned brede.** *Apology, CW 9,* 12.

5/35–6/2 **great . . . mouse.** Cf. Horace, *Ars poetica* 139.

5/35–36 **from . . . Mychelmas.** The *Division* was first published about the end of 1532 or the beginning of 1533. More's *Apology* was printed by William Rastell about Easter 1533. The colophon in *Salem and Bizance* reveals that it was printed in London by Thomas Berthelet in 1533. Earlier More remarked that *Salem and Bizance* was composed between Easter and Michaelmas 1533 (3/4–10). Here More affirms more precisely that St. German's riposte to the *Apology* was published about a week before Michaelmas 1533. In other words, the book appeared about September 22.

6/4 **caudell.** A warm drink consisting of thin gruel mixed with wine or ale, sweetened and spiced, given chiefly to sick people, especially to women in childbirth.

6/9 **fyrst . . . diuysyon.** See above, note on 3/9–10.

6/10 **thordynaryes.** The bishops.

7/6 **in few days.** See note on 4/1–2 and the Introduction, pp. xcv–xcvii.

7/12 **as women . . . primer.** Primers or books of hours consisted mainly of the Office of the Virgin, together with other offices such as that of the cross, of the conception of Mary, and of the dead. They also contained various prayers and groups of psalms (the seven penitential, the fifteen gradual, and the ten passion psalms) which occurred after the offices. It was thus necessary in saying the office to turn to the back of the book to find the appropriate psalms. More's own prayer book is a typical primer arranged in this fashion (*Thomas More's Prayer Book,* ed. Louis L. Martz and Richard S. Sylvester, New Haven and London, 1969, pp. xxvi–xxvii). See also Charles C. Butterworth, *The English Primers (1529–1545)* (Philadelphia, 1953; reprint, New York, 1971), 2–3, 9–17.

7/26–27 **I loue . . . darke.** Cf. Eph. 5:8.

8/14–15 **apologye . . . defence.** The word *apology* is not attested before More's use of it as a title (*OED*, s.v.).

8/23 **but . . . boke.** "But for as mych as the touchynge of ye boke is here not my principal purpose" (*CW 9*, 61/7–8).

9/1 **Caluicium . . . Erasmi.** Synesius of Cyrene, bishop of Ptolemais around the turn of the fourth century, wrote *Calvitii laus* (*The Praise of Baldness*). The Greek original of this work, with a Commentary by Beatus Rhenanus and a Latin translation by John Free (Phreas), had been printed together with Erasmus' *Moriae encomium* nine times by 1529 (*Moriae encomium, ASD 4/3*, Commentary at 74/49).

Seneca's *Apocolocyntosis* was also printed with Erasmus' *Moria*. See Genevieve Stenger, "*The Praise of Folly* and Its Parerga," *Medievalia et Humanistica*, New Series, 2 (1971), 97–117.

9/10 **new brethern.** Cf. More's mockery of the "newe named brethren" in the *Letter against Frith* (Rogers, no. 190, p. 440, line 5) and Frith's reply (*The Whole workes of W. Tyndall, Iohn Frith, and Doct. Barnes*, London, 1573; *STC²* 24436, sig. RR₃v). See *CW 9*, Commentary at 14/23. More referred ironically to the "badde bretherne" and "blessed bretherne" throughout his *Apology*. See, for example, *CW 9*, 3, 7.

9/16–21 **an answere . . . oppugneth.** More here expresses the primary aim of his literary platform in 1533. His concern that the unity of the whole corps of Christendom should be defended is reiterated in his later letters (Rogers, pp. 498–99, 558). See the Introduction, p. lxix.

9/24–25 **whom I . . . catholike.** Since St. German remained an orthodox catholic on major doctrinal, as opposed to jurisdictional, issues until his death in May 1541, he proved to be a singularly difficult adversary. See Appendix C, pp. 407–8, 416–17.

9/27 **vnto . . . hym.** Unable to accuse St. German directly of heterodoxy, More argued in the *Apology* that "yf the man meane well hym selfe (as by goddes grace he doth) than hath some other sotle shrew that is of his counsayle deceyued him" (*CW 9*, 60/38–61/1). See the Introduction, pp. lxxviii, xciii.

10/27–28 **the .xxii . . . chapyter.** Appendix B, 383/7–392/8.

10/34 **vpon the leuys.** The running head on A₂–A₃ of *Salem and Bizance* is "Thintroduction."

10/35–37 **the man . . . at all.** Appendix B, 326/37–39.

11/12–16 **I shall . . . endeth.** Appendix B, 326/31–37.

11/21–22 **diuyde . . . chapytres.** More's own dialogues (*A Dialogue concerning Heresies* and *A Dialogue of Comfort, CW 6* and *CW 12*) were divided into chapters, but the speakers themselves never refer to chapter divisions as St. German's Bizance does.

12/4 **stycke.** More canceled a short passage after this word. See the variants and Appendix A.

12/20–21 **owne . . . turke.** Appendix B, 383/16–25.

12/21–22 **own . . . apocalyps.** Rev. 13:18. Appendix B, 384/26–387/33.

12/26–27 **And thus . . . me.** Appendix B, 392/7–8.

12/28–30 **Gryme . . . more.** We have not been able to find any other references to Gryme or to this anecdote.

13/12–17 **where . . . them.** More's claim to be writing for altruistic motives is fully justified, but his persistent claim not to know the identity of his opponent is disingenuous. See the Introduction, pp. xxii–xxiv.

13/18–21 **And . . . purpose.** Appendix B, 327/41–328/2.

13/29–30 **for . . . tedyousnes.** Appendix B, 327/34–35.

14/9 **In . . . lefe.** Appendix B, 328/5–12.

14/10–11 **in the . . . apology.** *CW* 9, 54/35–55/1.

14/13 **in the . . . boke.** *CW* 9, 64/24–26.

14/22–23 **but synnys . . . abrode.** William Tyndale (c. 1494–1536), who was not ordained, was the chief proponent of Lutheranism in England. See John Foxe, *Acts and Monuments,* ed. George Townsend and Stephen R. Cattley, 8 vols. (London, 1837–41), 5, 114–34; *CW 8,* 1157–1268; *CW 9,* 64/26–27 and 302–03. John Frith (1503–1533), a young collaborator of Tyndale, wrote a treatise denying the real presence in the eucharist which More answered (Rogers, pp. 439–64). See *CW 6,* 883; *CW 8,* Commentary at 9/11; *CW 9,* 351–52; and Hall, *Chronicle,* pp. 815–16. Robert Barnes (c. 1495–1540) promoted some Lutheran teachings in England; see *CW 8,* 1367–1415; *CW 9,* 304; and Foxe, 5, 414–38. As lord chancellor More had issued proclamations and waged a Star Chamber campaign against heretical books. See Guy, *Public Career,* pp. 171–74; *Tudor Royal Proclamations,* ed. P. L. Hughes and J. F. Larkin, 3 vols. (New Haven, 1964–69), *1,* 181–86, 193–97.

15/8–16 **put out . . . bothe.** More had complained in the *Apology (CW 9,* 60) that St. German had not helped matters by quoting at length, and in the vernacular, accusations against the clergy supposedly copied from Jean Gerson. In fact, St. German relied heavily on the *Declaratio compendiosa defectuum virorum ecclesiasticorum* by Henry of Langenstein, though in More's time this piece was wrongly attributed to Gerson. See *CW 9*, xlvi–xlvii, lvi, lxxiv, 60–61 and Appendix A, pp. 181–83. See also the Introduction, pp. xix and lxxvi, above.

15/23–24 **some . . . realme.** The heresy statutes are reprinted in *CW 9*, Appendix C, pp. 249–60. See the Introduction, pp. li–lxvii, above.

15/25–28 **those . . . heresyes.** For details of St. German's proposed revisions of the heresy laws in 1531 see note on 39/9–10.

15/34 **vntrew some sayes.** See *CW 9*, 56–57, 60–61.

16/6 **Clyffe . . . Patenson.** Clyffe has not been identified, but Henry Patenson was More's domestic fool, pictured with the rest of the household in the Holbein family portrait. See *CW 8*, 900–01, 1689; R. W. Chambers, *Thomas More* (London, 1935), pp. 179, 220, 311.

16/11–14 **some . . . Thomas.** We have not been able to discover any other information about this incident.

17/15–16 **rumour . . . remoued.** For the serious impact of rumor on Henrician England, see Elton, *Policy and Police*, pp. 46–82.

17/31 **The . . . consyderacyon.** Appendix B, 329/8–330/4.

17/34–18/2 **shold . . . them.** Cf. St. German's proposals of 1530–31 in Guy, *St. German*, pp. 127–35.

18/9 **thende . . . chapiter.** Appendix B, 329/35–36.

18/29–34 **in suche places . . . agayne.** For example, *CW 9*, 64–72, 92–93, 96–97.

19/9 **In hys . . . lefe.** Appendix B, 330/5–332/11.

19/10–11 **in yᵉ . . . appologye.** *CW 9*, 59–60.

19/18 **wil can . . . thanke.** That is, "will acknowledge no gratitude to" (Visser, *1*, 154–55).

19/30 **though . . . laten.** See note on 15/8–16.

19/34–35 **agaynst . . . apology.** *CW 9*, 60/12–20. Cf. *CW 9*, 105/28–31.

20/9–11 **he . . . egally.** *Division*, *CW 9*, 177–80, 183–85, 187–88.

20/11–12 **in . . . lefe.** Appendix B, 331/26–41.

20/19–23 **And therfore . . . away.** Homilia 38 of the pseudo-

Chrysostom's *Opus imperfectum in Matthaeum:* "Ita si sacerdotium integrum fuerit, tota ecclesia floret: si autem corruptum fuerit, omnium fides marcida est" (*Opera D. Ioannis Chrysostomi* . . . , 5 vols., Basel, 1530, *3,* sig. k*k₂; *PG 56,* 839). The passage is also given in Aquinas' *Catena aurea* on Matt. 21:12 (vol. 11 of *Opera omnia,* 25 vols., Parma, 1852–73; reprint, New York, 1948–49). On the *Opus imperfectum* see *CW 8,* Commentary at 933/1–18.

20/20 **Iohan . . . chapyter.** Cf. *Division, CW 9,* 182.

21/8–14 **saynt . . . sayde it.** St. John Chrysostom, bishop of Constantinople (c. 347–407), was one of the Greek fathers More knew best. See *CW 8,* 933–36, 1683–84.

21/14–19 **ye be . . . selfe?** Matt. 5:13–14.

22/8 **And . . . fawtes.** Appendix B, 331/41–42.

22/10–21 **yet all . . . chapyter.** Appendix B, 331/42–332/11.

23/8 **whych . . . you.** *CW 9,* 109/7–110/5, 128/29–129/23.

23/22–23 **thapostle . . . of.** Titus 3:10.

23/30–31 **foure . . . me.** Appendix B, 332/13–333/16.

24/2–4 **noughty . . . bretherne.** See note on 24/35–25/19.

24/6 **I do . . . done to.** Appendix B, 333/21–22. The rule that a man should "do as he would be done to" (Matt. 7:12) was one of St. German's favorite texts. Such demeanor was the mark of good intentions and a clear conscience. See 61/30–35 and cf. *Doctor and Student,* p. 95.

24/10 **And to.** In More's time *to* (in the sense "also, moreover") was rarely used at the beginning of a clause (*OED,* s.v. "too"). More may have written "so" or "lo."

24/13–14 **saynte . . . dogges.** Phil. 3:2.

24/14–16 **when . . . them.** Acts 23:3. In a long note on this passage in his *Novum Testamentum,* Erasmus remarks: "quandoquidem in pariete dealbato manifestum convitium est" (*Opera omnia,* ed. Jean Leclerc, 10 vols., Leiden, 1703–06, *6,* 522).

24/16–18 **saint . . . hypocrytes.** Matt. 23:13, 14, 28; Luke 12:1. The parallelism with "called" in lines 14 and 18 makes it clear that "calleth" in line 16 is a misprint for "called." A similar misprint occurred at 48/1 and the opposite error at 71/15 and 90/4.

24/16–17 **Policarpus . . . son.** In his *Epistle to the Philippians*, Polycarp, bishop of Smyrna (d. 155), said that if anyone claimed there was no resurrection or judgment, he was "the firstborn son of the devil" (*PG* 5, 1012). Polycarp's phrase was especially well known because his encounter with the heretic Marcion in Rome was described by Irenaeus (*Contra haereses* 3.3.4; *PG* 7, 853) and by Eusebius (*Historia ecclesiastica* 4.14; *PG* 20, 339–40): "Once Polycarp met Marcion, who said to him, 'Do you recognize me?' Polycarp replied, 'I recognize you as the firstborn of the devil.'"

24/26 **ironye or antiphrasys.** The *OED* gives this as the first use of *irony* in the sense of saying one thing and meaning the opposite. Bede (and some Greek rhetoricians before him) wrote that when the irony was limited to one word, it might be called *antiphrasis*, as when Christ said to Judas in the garden, "Friend, why have you come?" (Heinrich Lausberg, *Handbuch der literarischen Rhetorik*, Munich, 1960, pp. 303, 450). The *OED* gives this as the first use of *antiphrasis*.

24/26–28 **saint . . . Dormitantius.** Jerome attacked as a heretic Vigilantius, whom he ironically styled Dormitantius because he disparaged the cults of saints and martyrs and questioned the celibacy of the clergy. See *CW 8*, Commentary at 694/32–36.

24/30–31 **new . . . bretherhed.** Cf. *CW 9*, 14/23.

24/35–25/19 **euangelycalles . . . pseudo euangelicos.** More had rung ironical changes on the name of the "counterfayte euangelycalls" in the first book of his *Confutation* (1532); see *CW 8*, 29/14–20, 32/7–12. In January 1530 Erasmus published a book entitled *Epistola . . . contra quosdam, qui se falso iactant Euangelicos*, in which he heaped scorn on the "libertatem euangelicam" of the reformers (*ASD 9/1*, 294/307–296/351, 338/240–45, 362/748–50). Tyndale had adopted "euangelyon" in place of "Word of God" in *A pathway into the holy scripture* (*STC²* 24462), an expanded version of the prologue to the 1525 Cologne New Testament; *A pathway* was in print before September 1531 (*CW 8*, 1090–91). Tyndale called the New Testament the "euangelyon or gospell / to saue those that beleued them [God's promises] / from the vengeaunce of the lawe" (sig. A₆v).

25/10–12 **they . . . gospell.** See note on 24/35–25/19. Luther and Tyndale held that nothing necessary to faith was outside the scripture. Tyndale and his English followers even went as far as to regard "scripture" and the "gospel" as synonymous. For a summary of More's attack on such opinions, see *A Dialogue concerning Heresies, CW 6*, 152–82.

25/19 **them.** The reading of *1533* and *1557* ("thē") might also be expanded as "then." But it is far more likely that More intended "them" (see *OED*, s.v. "write" *v.* 8a).

25/28–32 **heretikes . . . wrytynge.** Augustine mentions that the elect among the Manichaeans were sometimes called "Catharistae," that is, "purgatores" (*De haeresibus* 46; *PL 42,* 36). He also lists the Novatians under the name "Cathari," a name they use "propter munditiam" (*De haeresibus* 38, *PL 42,* 32; and *De agone christiano* 31, *PL 40,* 308). "Cathari" is a transliteration of καθαροί, "pure."

26/6–23 **And now . . . greater.** Appendix B, 333/27–334/2.

27/5–6 **the . . . se.** *CW 9,* 155–63.

27/10–11 **noysed . . . dede.** See *Division, CW 9,* 192.

27/17–18 **And . . . few.** *CW 9,* 157–62.

27/30 **my boke.** The reading "myn" in *1533* probably resulted from More's original intention of writing "apologye." When he changed to "boke" he forgot to change "myn" to "my." See the variant at 31/7–8.

28/7–8 **the greatest . . . temporall.** A few powerful persons at Henry VIII's court were in fact protecting heretics for political reasons; see Guy, *Public Career,* 105–12, 141–47, 175–92, and Guy, "The Tudor Commonwealth," p. 683. See also the Introduction, pp. lvi–lvii, and Lehmberg, pp. 117–18.

28/11 **one . . . foly.** In More's time the pronoun *one* was used with superlatives, where we would now say "one of the most simple folies" (*OED,* s.v. "one" 26).

28/12–14 **as for . . . vppe.** See note on 28/24–25.

28/16–19 **bygonne . . . bytwene them.** For example, the letter which Frith wrote from prison on June 23, 1533, begins "I doute not deare brethern" (printed at the end of Frith's *A boke . . . answeringe vnto M mores lettur, STC² * 11381, sig. L₄). In his letters to Frith, Tyndale addressed him as "Dearely beloved brother" (*The Whole workes of W. Tyndall, Iohn Frith, and Doct. Barnes,* London, 1573; *STC² * 24436, sigs. CC₃–CC₄).

28/24–25 **For fyrst . . . great.** The absence of a pronoun subject such as *it* in sentences beginning "as for" was quite common and idiomatic in More's time (Visser, *1,* 33–34).

28/25–27 **affinyte . . . maryage.** A person has the relationship of affinity with his spouse's blood relatives. He has spiritual affinity ("gos-sepred") with his sponsor (or *gossip*) at baptism.

30/3–4 y^t . . . heretykes. Acts 24:14; Titus 3:10.

30/4 so. Perhaps More wrote "to" ("too"), which would make better sense. See note on 24/10.

30/8 in . . . lefe. See Appendix B, 334/9–18.

30/20–21 requyre . . . folke. The comma after "necessyte" in *1533* and *1557* makes it hard to realize that the clause "that . . . folke" is the object of "requyre."

30/31 His . . . lefe. See Appendix B, 335/7.

31/7–9 both . . . fo. 127. See *CW 9*, 74–75, 77–78, 178–79.

31/26 in . . . stranglynge. *CW 9*, 75 and 179. See also Appendix B, 335/35–38, below.

31/33 take haly water. That is, as he leaves the church after mass.

31/35–36 The counsayle . . . Eugenius. In chapters 5 and 6 of *De consideratione* (*PL 182*, 734–36), which is addressed to Pope Eugenius III, St. Bernard advises him to leave judgments about property and possessions to temporal judges and princes so as to be able to devote himself to judgments about spiritual matters and to contemplation. But Bernard also makes it clear that, the world being what it is, Eugenius cannot be expected to follow this advice strictly and completely.

32/8 his acte . . . speketh of. See Appendix B, 336/40–337/2. St. German had included precisely such a proposal in his parliamentary draft of 1531. The relevant passage reads: "Also for asmoche as the great substaunce of the inherytaunce of the realme wolde in contynuaunce come into mortmayn besyde that that is come into it in tyme paste, if remedie be not provydede in that be half, it is therfore enacted that no mans landes, tenementes, rentes, nor libertyes, fraunches nor other enhereditamentes, what so ever they be, shall not hereafter upon payn of forfayture therof come into mortmayne in fee symple, fee tayle, for terme of lyf, terme of yeres, by tytle of statute marchaunte, statute staple, elegit, lease ne otherwyse, by lycence nor withoute lycence, excepte suche fermes as it is lawfull for howses of religion to take by the statute made in the xxj yere of oure reygn [that is, 21 Henry VIII, c. 13], by feoffement, fyne, recovery, wyll nor otherwyse, in use ne in possession; and the forfayture therof to go to the lordes of whom the londes be holden in suche maner as is conteynede in the seid statute de

religiosis; and all lycences, realeses, and confirmacions, and other wrytynges hereafter to be made to extincte or advoyde the seid for-
[f]ayture, to be voyde, aswell aganste the kyng and lordes and theyr
heyres, as ageynst all other, excepte only that yf it please the kynges
grace heraftre to make any new foundacion for hym self or his pro-
genitors and to gyve therto any landes, tenementes and heredytamentes of his owne, that that gyfte and foundacion shall stonde good
and perfyte for ever. And yf he make any foundacion hereaftre, and
gyve any landes, tenementes and heredytamentes to any such foundacion that shalbe conveyede unto hym by other for that intente, that that
gyfte and foundacion to stonde voyde in the lawe, and that it shalbe
lawfull to hym of whom the londes be holden to entre in lyke maner as
they shuld have doon upon the statute de religiosis; and if no such re-
entre be made by the lordes, that then the kynge for the tyme beying
shall have the tytle of entre therin fro tyme to tyme for ever, any
pardon, graunte, relaxation, confirmacion or other discharge made to
the contrary notwithstandyng." See Guy, *St. German*, pp. 129–30, and
Sandra Raban, *Mortmain Legislation and the English Church, 1279–1500*
(Cambridge, 1983). See also *New Additions* in *Doctor and Student*, pp.
320–21.

32/9–10 **suche . . . suffycyent.** More refers to the statutes of mortmain, namely 7 Edward I, st. 2; Westminster II, 13 Edward I, c. 32; 34
Edward I, st. 3; 15 Richard II, c. 5; 23 Henry VIII, c. 10. An alienation
in mortmain was the permanent transfer of lands or tenements into the
"dead hand" of a guild, corporation, or religious house, a transaction
held to be illegal without the king's license and that of the lord of the
manor, or of the king alone if the land was held in chief of him. The
principal statute, 7 Edward I, st. 2, which was called the Statute of
Mortmain, or *De religiosis*, had prescribed that no religious or other
persons should without license buy or sell any lands or tenements, or by
gift, lease, or any other title receive the same, or otherwise appropriate
them into mortmain, on pain of forfeiture to the lord of the fee, or on
his default to the next immediate lord, or on default of all these lords to
the king.

32/11–16 **that . . . hym.** The statute given in *Salem and Bizance* (Appendix B, 336/42–337/1) speaks of "any fundacion, that the kingis grace
wolde make of his owne mere mocion." In his parliamentary draft (see
note on 32/8) the phrase "of his own mere mocion" is explained as
preventing the king from placing in mortmain lands given to him by
others for that purpose. More's point is: who is to decide whether the
king places land in mortmain of his own will or because others want

him to? Is St. German to decide the point? More interprets St. German's proposal to mean that Henry VIII's royal prerogative to alienate in mortmain would be subjected to unprecedented statutory restriction. He does so in order to insinuate that the king would be reduced by St. German to the status of a subject, his regality infringed, and his prerogative and dispensing power vulnerable to future statutory erosion should Henry be so unwise as to throw in his lot with the political reformers. More aims to drive a wedge between Henry VIII and St. German, exploiting his inside knowledge of their differing attitudes to parliamentary functions. See also Fox, pp. 197–98.

32/17–22 **in all the tyme . . . there from.** Appendix B, 336/17–25. See note on 28/7–8.

32/34 **myne Apologye fo. 139.** *CW* 9, 84.

33/7–12 **Syth . . . prynte also.** Appendix B, 336/23–27. But St. German wrote "includid," not "concluded," and since More places stress on "included" in the following analysis, "concluded" may well be a misprint.

33/13 **inclusyues and exclusyues.** The *OED* cites this place for the meaning "an exclusive proposition or particle" and gives only 33/22 for the meaning "an inclusive proposition or particle." Quantifiers such as *omnis, aliquis,* and *nullus* were discussed by medieval logicians but not under the names of inclusive or exclusive (William and Martha Kneale, *The Development of Logic,* Oxford, 1962, pp. 231–32). Peter of Spain's logic book, perhaps the most popular of all in the universities of More's day, discusses such words as problems of distribution (*Tractatus Called Afterwards Summule Logicales,* ed. L. M. De Rijk, Assen, 1972, pp. 209–32) but does not use the terms *inclusive* or *exclusive.* The *OED* gives a legal meaning under the year 1515: "Fra þe xiiij day forsaid inclusiue to xx day of þe samyn exclusiue" (s.v. "exclusive" 3 and "exclusive" 4b).

33/21–25 **Thys man . . . trew.** Peter of Spain (*Tractatus,* p. 9) gives the rules: "Ad veritatem copulative [propositionis] exigitur quod utraque pars sit vera, ut *'homo est animal et Deus est.'* Ad falsitatem eius sufficit alteram partem esse falsam, ut *'homo est animal et equus est lapis.'* Ad veritatem disiunctive sufficit alteram partem esse veram, ut *'homo est animal uel equus est asinus.'* Et permittitur quod utraque pars sit vera, sed non ita proprie, ut *'homo est animal vel equus est hinnibilis.'* Ad falsitatem eius oportet utramque partem esse falsam, ut *'homo est asinus vel equus est lapis.'*"

33/33 **includeth those wordes.** The use of a singular verb with a plural subject was not uncommon in More's time (Visser, *1*, 46–48).

34/6 **Alkayre.** Cairo (Arabic, El-Kahirah). More's form seems close to the etymology which derives the name from "El Kir," *the* city. In his translation of Ptolemy's *Geographia* (Basel, 1540) Sebastian Münster calls the city "alcayr" (*Index memorabilium regionum . . . ,* sig. *₁); in the *Appendix geographica* (p. 185) he remarks "Memphis hodie Cayrum, uulgo Alkair"; and in book 4 (p. 72) he says "Babylon Babu-lis . . . Alcayrum siue Cayro nunc vocant." But Münster's maps of Africa III and Africa XVIII (Nova tabula) give only the name "Cayrum." George Sandys mentions "this great, and then strong City, which he names *Elchairo* (*Sandys Traviles: containing . . . a Description . . . of Egypt . . . Armenia, Grand Cairo . . . ,* 6th ed., London, 1658, p. 92; first published in 1615). Milton called the city "Alcairo" (*Paradise Lost* 1.718).

34/22–29 **And nowe . . . profytable.** More interprets his statement to mean that none of the seven thought it right or reasonable to take church lands but all seven thought it might be profitable to the realm. This interpretation is technically valid, but if that is what he meant, why bother to include the first two alternatives at all?

34/29–32 **And some one . . . mortysed theym.** The legal theory be-hind this suggestion had been mooted by the student of common law in St. German's *New Additions,* chap. 2: "I suppose it may be enacted by the parliment, that no landes, ne other enheritaunce, shall hereafter be gyuen in to mortemayne, by licence nor without licence, but that all feoffementes, fynes, leasses, and recoueries, by couyn or by assent of the parties hereafter made or had for mortmayne, or to the vse of mortmayne, shal be voyde, and that the house shal take no interest by hit: but that it shall remayne stylle with the feaffours or gyuers, or to suche other vse, as the parlyament shall appoynte. For lyke as the parlyament maye ordeyne / that all feoffementes and fynes, made to any maner of persone shall be voyde, and that euery man shall stande styll seysed of his lande, without makynge of any alteracion of posses-sion therof to any other, more stronger hit may ordeyne, that no altera-tion of possession shall be made in to mortemayne" (*Doctor and Student,* p. 320).

34/33–35/3 **And some other . . . thordynarye.** For discussion of wel-fare proposals and reforms that coordinated, consolidated, or ra-tionalized money, institutions, or property dedicated to pious uses in the early sixteenth century, see R. M. Kingdon, "Social Welfare in

Calvin's Geneva," *American Historical Review, 76* (1971), 50–61; N. Z. Davis, "Poor Relief, Humanism, and Heresy: The Case of Lyons," *Studies in Medieval and Renaissance History, 5* (1968), 217–75; M. Fosseyeux, "La taxe des pauvres au xvi⁰ siècle," *Revue d'histoire de l'église de France, 20* (1934), 407–32; B. Pullan, *Rich and Poor in Renaissance Venice* (Oxford, 1971), pp. 239–86.

35/5–6 **theyr own handes.** For the idiomatic omission of the preposition, see Visser, *1*, 121, and 101/8–9, above.

35/21–23 **in the seconde . . . chyrche.** See Appendix B, 336/30–32.

35/31 **a good whyle . . . soules.** *Supplication of Souls, EW,* sig. v₄v.

36/11–16 **His seuenth . . . fo. 106.** Appendix B, 337/20–340/43; *Division, CW 9,* 177–80; *Apology, CW 9,* 61–66. The idiom "vppon a sex leues" means "on some six leaves" (*OED,* s.v. "a" *adj²*).

36/18–19 **a motable case.** At moots within the Inns of Court after dinner, the junior barristers debated with, or in front of, the benchers and perhaps even sometimes the serjeants-at-law and judges. The juniors learned in this manner both techniques and legal expertise, gaining the ability to distinguish between accepted learning and areas of doubt. The procedure at moots was described by Thomas Elyot in *The Book Named the Governor,* bk. 1, chap. 14 (ed. S. E. Lehmberg, London, 1962, pp. 53–54): "It is to be remembered that in the learning of the laws of this realm, there is at this day an exercise wherein is a manner, a shadow, or figure of the ancient rhetoric. I mean the pleading used in Court and Chancery called moots, where first a case is appointed to be mooted by certain young men, containing some doubtful controversy, which is instead of the head of a declamation called *thema.* The case being known, they which be appointed to moot do examine the case, and investigate what they therein can espy, which may make a contention, whereof may rise a question to be argued, and that of Tully is called *constitutio,* and of Quintilian *status causae.*

"Also they consider what pleas on every part ought to be made, and how the case may be reasoned, which is the first part of rhetoric, named *invention;* then appoint they how many pleas may be made for every part, and in what formality they should be set, which is the second part of rhetoric, called *disposition,* wherein they do much approach unto rhetoric; then gather they all into perfect remembrance, in such order as it ought to be pleaded, which is the part of rhetoric named *memory.* But forasmuch as the tongue wherein it is spoken is barbarous, and the stirring of affections of the mind in this realm was never used, therefore there lacketh *elocution* and *pronunciation,* two [of] the principal

parts of rhetoric. Notwithstanding some lawyers, if they be well retained, will in a mean cause pronounce right vehemently. Moreover
there seemeth to be in the said pleadings certain parts of an oration,
that is to say for *narrations, partitions, confirmations,* and *confutations,*
named of some *reprehensions,* they have *declarations, bars, replications* and
rejoinders, only they lack pleasant form of beginning, called in Latin
exordium, nor it maketh thereof no great matter; they that have studied
rhetoric shall perceive what I mean. Also in arguing their cases, in my
opinion, they very little do lack of the whole art; for therein they do
diligently observe the rules of confirmation and confutation, wherein
resteth proof and disproof, having almost all the places whereof they
shall fetch their reasons, called of orators *loci communes,* which I omit to
name, fearing to be too long in this matter." For modern commentary
see *Spelman's Reports, 2,* introduction, pp. 132–33. See also W. C. Richardson, *A History of the Inns of Court* (Baton Rouge, La., n.d. [1976?]),
pp. 131–38, 168–70, 416–18.

36/32–37/12 **I was ones . . . groundes.** The "science" of Tudor legal
argument has been thoroughly analyzed by Baker in *Spelman's Reports,
2,* introduction, pp. 142–59. The difficulty of legal jargon was noted by
Elyot: "It may not be denied but that all laws be founded on the deepest
part of reason, and, as I suppose, no one law so much as our own; and
the deeper men do investigate reason the more difficult or hard must
needs be the study. Also that reverend study is involved in so barbarous
a language, that it is not only void of all eloquence, but also being
separate from the exercise of our law only, it serveth to no commodity
or necessary purpose, no man understanding it but they which have
studied the laws" (*Governor,* bk. 1, chap. 14, Lehmberg, p. 51). The
need to apply equitable interpretation in appropriate circumstances in
order to ameliorate the injustice caused by too rigorous adherence to
express legal terminology was discussed by St. German in the first
dialogue of *Doctor and Student,* chaps. 16–17 (pp. 95–107). Modern
commentary is supplied in Guy, *St. German,* pp. 19–21, 67, 71–73, 77,
81–94.

37/25–29 **And yet . . . dyfference.** For St. German's hypothetical cases
see Appendix B, 339/40–340/22.

37/34–35 **at a vacacyon . . . chauncery.** At the "grand vacation moots"
in the Inns of Chancery, senior barristers and readers as well as novices
attended open debates outside the legal terms. The atmosphere was
perhaps informal, and the occasions provided opportunities for intellectual exchange between the houses. The Inns of Chancery provided
board and residence, preparatory studies, and learning exercises for

novices prior to their admission to clerks' commons in one of the four
Inns of Court. More's own Inn of Chancery was New Inn. See *Spelman's
Reports*, 2, introduction, pp. 127–29. He lectured at Furnivall's Inn (an
Inn of Chancery) and was autumn reader at Lincoln's Inn (an Inn of
Court) in 1511 and Lent reader in 1515 (Richard O'Sullivan, "St.
Thomas More and Lincoln's Inn," in *Essential Articles for the Study of
Thomas More*, ed. R. S. Sylvester and G. P. Marc'hadour, Hamden,
Conn., 1977, pp. 161–68). See also Richardson, pp. 117 (n. 92) and
417.

38/12 **labour ... more.** Tilley L9.

38/13 **answere ... maner.** That is, "by the manner of pleading in the
court in question." Cf., for example, Isaac Cotton's use of the ex-
pression in his title "The Grounds, Rules and Proceedings of the Hon-
ourable Court of Starre Chamber, with the Course and manner of
Prosecution of Causes from the originall Subpoena to the end of the
Cause" (St. Edmund Hall, Oxford, MS 3; British Library, Lansdowne
MS 639, fols. 1–22; British Library, Stowe MS 418; British Library,
Additional MS 26,647, fols. 151–203).

38/13–15 **no law ... poynt.** A demurrer was a pause or stop put to a
legal action upon a point of difficulty which had to be determined by
the court before litigation could continue. Normally it took the form of
a defense plea seeking discharge with costs on the grounds of technical
or legal insufficiency in the plaintiff's argument, or on grounds of lack
of jurisdiction by the court. By this allusion More means that he rests
his argument on the issue in question as stated by St. German, denying
that St. German has made a valid case.

38/29 **For it wyll ... dammages.** Damages were awarded by the courts
in certain cases as recompense for what the successful party had suffered through the wrong done to him by his opponent. By saying that
St. German's case was too feeble to win damages, More implies that he
has done St. German no wrong.

39/9–10 **and laborynge ... heretykes.** More almost certainly knew
that St. German had "labored" to modify the investigatory procedures
in cases of heresy in his parliamentary draft of 1531. The relevant
passage, which includes St. German's proposal for a New Testament
translation, reads: "For asmoche as it hathe ben reported to the kynges
highnes, and to the lordes temporall and to the commons in this pres-
ente parliament assembled, that many of his temporall subiectes be
moche desirous to haue the new testamente in the mother tonge, and
that in manner the hoole spiritueltye hath resystyd it: therfore the

kyng by auctorytye of his parliament aforeseid hathe named certayn
lordes and other persons hereafter folowyng, some now beyng of this
present parliament and some other also, to whome he hath geuyn full
auctorytie to here the reasons and opynyons of all theym that wyll say
that it were good to haue it in to the mother tonge. And yf the seid
lordes and other so assignede by his highnes may see and perceyve that
the seid desire commethe of mekenes and charytye of the people, and
of a love that they haue to vertue and to knowelege of the trouthe, and
so do make reporte vnto the kynges highnes, his grace wilbe content-
ede that they shall haue suche parte therof translated in to the mother
tonge as shall be thought convenyent by the seid councell, to stirre
theym to love vertue and fle vice, and to enduce theym therupon to
desyre to haue ferther knowlege and enformacion therin by theym
that haue more [word illegible] lernyng then they have. And the seid
auctorytye is gevon to: [blank]. And theyre auctorytye to contynue vnto
the later ende of the next parliament, and they to be callede the great
standyng counsayll. And the seid councell to haue auctorityе to enquere by whom and by what occasyon the noyse hath risen that there
shulde be so many heresies in thys realme as are noysede to bee. But it is
not the intent of ye kyng ne of his parliament that the seid councell
shulde enprison, abiure or attente any man before theym of heresye,
but that they may examyn such as compleynt shalbe made on in that
behalf, and theyr examynacion to serve oonly to this intente: to let all
theym knowe that wyll holde any opynyon contrary to that that the seid
councell shall thynke to stonde with the fayth of Criste, that they shall
not haue the favour of oure seid soverayen lorde the kynge, ne of his
parliament, as his trewe catholicall subiectes haue, and so to enduce
theym by the moste charytable and fauorable [means] that they can to
leve the oppynyons. And if they can in no wise brynge theym to yt, then
to let theym knowe also that his grace wyll then put to his hande to see
theym punysshed accordynge to iustice withowte favor, but they wyll
amende and reforme theym selfe fro the oppynyons. And if they wyll
forsake the same oppynyons, then they to departe with favour, without
ferther troble or punyshment in that behalf. And that no ordynarye
upon the peyn, etc., by fore the ende of the next parliament arest ne
put any man to answere byfore hym, ne before non other, for heresye,
but suche as shalbe fyrst examynyd byfore the seid councell, and that
they haue certyfyed the ordynarye that he is obstynate and wilnot be
reformyd. And yet that certyfycat not to be a condempnacion, but only
to be a warrant to the ordynarye that he may procede without offend-
yng of this estate." See the Introduction, pp. xl–xliv, above, and Guy,
St. German, pp. 127–28 (except that here the original spelling has been
completely preserved).

39/15–16 **saynt poule calleth heretikes.** 1 Cor. 11:19, Titus 3:10.

39/16–17 **(I dare . . . name).** That is, "Except when I forget myself I dare not, because of St. German, call them by any other name than 'heretic.'" See 23/33–26/2, above.

39/30–31 **to theyr persons.** That is, "to them as individuals."

39/34 **many.** Perhaps a misprint for "may."

39/35–36 **there is . . . causes.** A singular verb with a plural subject (especially when the verb is preceded by "there") is not uncommon in More and in writers before and after him (Visser, *1*, 46–47).

40/4–24 **syth his name . . . otherwyse.** For the evidence that More knew his opponent's true identity, see the Introduction, pp. xxii–xxiv, and note on 4/30–31.

40/32 **prestes.** The correction from "folke" shows that More was choosing his words very carefully. The state of an unordained brother in a religious order is not as perfect as that of a secular priest.

41/4 **wynter ware.** That is, "poor stuff," like the cattle or produce of winter (*OED*, s.v. "ware" *sb.*³ 3c–d, 4; and "winter" *sb.*¹ 3).

41/4–5 **as colde as a kay.** Whiting K16 and K16a, Tilley K23. More was fond of this proverbial expression (*CW 6*, 205/32, *CW 12*, 13/8, 242/24, 248/19, 313/4).

41/7–10 **His .viii . . . folio .116.** Appendix B, 341/1–343/38; *CW 9*, 71.

42/8–22 **For . . . god.** Appendix B, 341/27–38.

43/23–25 **that is . . . other men.** More here suggests that St. German was alluding to the legal definition of maintenance, that is, the unlawful supporting, assisting, or financing of legal actions in which the maintainor himself had no personal interest. The offense was akin to conspiracy to pervert the course of justice.

43/29–30 **mayntenyng.** A pun on the legal and argumentative meanings of *maintain*.

43/34 **yf I demurred vppon it.** See note on 38/13–15.

45/8 **fonde.** At 70/25 the misprint "founde" for "fonde" was corrected in the errata of *1533*, but it was overlooked here.

45/18–21 **And yf . . . reforme yt.** Appendix B, 341/38–42.

45/22–23 **As for . . . bete of.** For the absence of a pronoun as an object of "bete of," see Visser, *1*, 31.

45/27–28 **nolite . . . iudicabimini.** Luke 6:37: "Judge not and you shall not be judged."

46/5–8 **whyche you reade . . . fashion.** Appendix B, 342/15–17; *CW* 9, 71–72. See also note on 3/8.

46/34–36 **Then he . . . contrary.** Appendix B, 342/5–10; *Apology, CW* 9, 72/12–25.

47/10 **obytes.** An obit is a ceremony or office (usually a mass) performed in commemoration or on behalf of the soul of a deceased person on the anniversary of his death.

47/10 **trentalles.** A trental is a set of thirty requiem masses said on the same day or on different days.

47/14–16 **othe . . . therin.** The "oath of honesty" ("oath of innocence," with or without "oath helpers") was part of the procedure of compurgation. The defendant protested his innocence, and the compurgators swore that they believed his oath to be true. (Canon law discouraged the more primitive procedure by which the compurgators or "oath helpers" swore to the truth of the actual defense case rather than the defendant's oath, on the grounds that this practice often led to perjury.) In the ecclesiastical courts canonical purgation was probably the normal method of supporting a defendant's denial of the charge in *ex officio* proceedings other than for heresy (see note on 111/34–112/2). In the secular courts the "oath of honesty" was part of the procedure known as wager of law (see note on 113/1–3). The tradition of waging law was especially strong in the civic courts of London, where More had begun his legal career. See Pollock and Maitland, *1*, 116, 443–44; 2, 214, 600–01, 610, 633–37; and *Select Cases*, introduction, pp. 57, 80, 92, 95.

47/26 **together.** The misprint "the gether" in *1533* was rightly corrected to "together" in *1557*. Cf. "holdynge togyther" at 43/24 and "holde to gether" at 47/2.

47/31 **Than . . . faute.** Appendix B, 342/41–343/10; *Apology, CW 9*, 72/16–18.

48/2 **kepe . . . scholes.** See note on 71/29.

48/16 **saynte Chrysostome . . . deuyll.** Needless to say, pity is hardly part of Chrysostom's usual attitude toward the devil, and More is partly teasing St. German with this startling allusion. But in *De Sancto Babyla, contra Iulianum et gentiles* (*Opera D. Ioannis Chrysostomi . . .* , 5 vols., Basel, 1539, *3*, sigs. ggg₄–ggg₆v; *PG 50*, 554–58) Chrysostom does tell a story about a discomfited demon whom he addresses with ironical pity. The episode had occurred at a temple and oracle of Apollo at Daphne, a park near Antioch, and Chrysostom and many of his auditors had firsthand knowledge of it. Under Christian emperors the temple had been abandoned, but young people began to hold wild parties in the park. So the emperor had the body of St. Babyla, a martyred bishop of Antioch, moved to Daphne to render it more venerable and curb the disorder. The plan was apparently successful, but when Julian the Apostate became emperor he reopened the pagan temples and personally made lavish sacrifices to the Apollo-demon at Daphne. But when he asked the demon for an oracular prediction, the demon, who was ashamed to admit that he was mute and powerless because of the presence of St. Babyla's body, could only come up with the lame excuse (ridiculed at length by Chrysostom) that he could not speak because many bodies were buried nearby. Julian gave the game away by immediately going to the tomb of St. Babyla and ordering it to be taken back to Antioch. Chrysostom mockingly tells the demon he should have taken refuge in the usual enigmas of oracles or told the truth to the pagan priest who would have kept his secret. He goes on to ask the demon: "What made you, poor devil, fall into such an obvious and shameful ruse?" *De Sancto Babyla*, translated by Germain de Brie, was included in Erasmus' 1530 edition of Chrysostom's *Opera omnia*.

48/16–19 **And our sauyoure . . . god.** Luke 19:41–44. The sidenote in *1557* refers to Matt. 23:37–39, which also presents Christ's lament for Jerusalem but does not mention his weeping.

48/30–33 **Saynte Cypryane . . . desperate.** Writing to the bishop and people of Assuras in Tunisia, Cyprian exhorts them to dissociate themselves from Fortunatianus, their former bishop, who had worshiped idols during persecution but now wished to resume his bishopric. He speaks of the "desperatorum delictis" of Fortunatianus and his followers. He also urges lapsed laymen to do penance and to obey their bishops in order to be received back by the church. He says that, if they refuse to do this and follow after "desperatos et perditos," they will have to account for it at the Last Judgment (*Epistolae* 1.7, *Divi Caecilii Cypriani . . . Opera*, ed. Erasmus, Basel, 1530, sig. e₄; Ep. 64 in *PL 4*, col. 405, and in *Corpus Scriptorum Ecclesiasticorum Latinorum*, 88 vols. Vienna, 1866–, *3/2*, 725–26).

48/33–35 **saynt Policarpus . . . deuyll.** See note on 24/16–17.

49/5 **reade. . . Apologye.** *CW 9*, 67–71.

49/8 **haue.** The misprint "houe" was rightly corrected by *1557*. The *OED* gives no spellings of any form of *have* with an o.

49/12–17 **His .ix. chapyter . . . dyaloge.** Appendix B, 343/39–345/37; *Apology, CW 9,* 72–74. More wrongly refers to chapter 19 of the *Apology,* but he gives the correct ".xx. chapiter" at 50/5.

49/18–19 **For al . . . restytucyon.** For full discussion of the subject of restitution by St. German, see *An Answer to a Letter (STC²* 21558.5), chap. 6, reprinted as an appendix to Guy, *St. German,* pp. 139–43.

49/33–34 **(as he wolde . . . diuisyon).** *CW 9,* Appendix A, p. 178.

50/9–14 **And to thentent . . . passe.** Appendix B, 345/22–28.

50/23–32 **And yf . . . soores.** Appendix B, 345/27–37.

52/14–19 **the moste . . . sayth.** By his will dated April 10, 1509, Henry VII instructed his executors *inter alia* to purchase 10,000 masses in honor of the Trinity, the Five Wounds, the Five Joys of Our Lady, the Nine Orders of Angels, the Patriarchs, the Twelve Apostles, and All Saints, to be said one month after his death at 6d. each, making £250 in all, and also to distribute £2,000 in alms. The king's debts were to be paid, and reparations for his wrongs made by his executors at the discretion of a select committee headed by William Warham, archbishop of Canterbury. Additional funds were left to complete hospitals at the Savoy, beside Charing Cross, and in York and Coventry, and £2,000 was to be provided for the repair of roads and bridges from Windsor to Richmond manor, from thence to St. George's church beside Southwark, and thence to Greenwich manor, and from there onward to Canterbury. PRO, E 23/3 (*LP 1,* 1, 1) and Thomas Astle, ed., *The Will of King Henry VII* (London, 1775).

52/20–24 **How be it . . . to hym.** Appendix B, 345/18–22.

52/28–30 **I haue herde . . . wythall.** Henry VII's will establishes that this king had himself deposited £8,916 13s. 4d. in ready money by indenture with the abbot of Westminster and with the dean and chapter of St. Paul's to cover the masses, alms, and hospital buildings. The executors were presumably to fund the remaining bequests, some of which were very considerable, from the estate. However, enfeoffments of the duchy of Lancaster had been arranged in 1491–1492 and 1504 in order to furnish income for the fulfillment of the will.

52/31–32 **call . . . rekenynge.** The will required representatives of the executors to assemble at least four times a year for twelve days and to declare annually their account to the archbishop of Canterbury as supervisor of the will. Yet St. German was perhaps right to hint that the executors might have found "reparations for wrongs" done by Henry

VII hard to achieve in full. A favorable view of the reign is taken by G. R. Elton ("Henry VII: Rapacity and Remorse" and "Henry VII: a Restatement," in *Studies*, *1*, 45–97). However, see J. P. Cooper's reply to the first of these papers in *Historical Journal*, 2 (1959), 103–29. See particularly C. J. Harrison, "The Petition of Edmund Dudley," *English Historical Review*, 87 (1972), 82–99. Harrison argues that, according to Dudley, one of Henry VII's trusted ministers and executors, the king had dealt too harshly with his subjects on at least eighty-four occasions. See *CW* 3/2, notes on 19/26–29.

53/16–18 **His . . . fo. 162.** Appendix B, 345/38–347/19; *Apology*, *CW* 9, 97–102.

54/2 **I can not se.** Appendix B, 346/38–39.

54/6–7 **yᵗ we shall not iudge.** Matt. 7:1: Luke 6:37. See note on 45/27–28.

54/7–9 **saynt Poule . . . tyme.** Rom. 14:4; 1 Cor. 4:5.

54/20–21 **who . . . fyre** Matt. 5:22.

54/24–25 **There are . . . nomber.** Eccles. 1:15.

54/27 **I wolde . . . that.** See, for example, Appendix B, 334/9–10.

55/9–10 **saynte Poule . . . tyme.** See note on 54/7–9.

55/22 **hempe.** That is, the hangman's rope.

55/34 **the makyng . . . perleament.** See Appendix B, 347/15–19.

56/19–20 **Post . . . thou not.** Ecclus. 18:30.

56/22 **.xxvii. chapyter.** *CW* 9, 97–102.

56/28–29 **my . . . lefe .174.** See *CW* 9, 104–05.

56/31 **His . . . .xxxvi. lefe.** Appendix B, 347/20–349/10.

56/33 **And therfore.** Appendix B, 347/36–348/4.

57/1–3 **in the . . . fo. 184.** *CW* 9, 110–16.

57/2 **the tone.** The syntax shows that "to" in *1533* was a misprint for "the." The opposite misprint occurred at 47/26.

57/24 **.xxvi. lefe.** The passage begins at the end of the verso of the thirty-sixth leaf.

57/26–32 **And in that . . . the mater.** See *Division, CW* 9, 180; *Apology, CW* 9, 111–12; *Salem and Bizance*, Appendix B, 348/4–8, below.

57/34–58/2 **that they . . . vppon wyl.** Appendix B, 348/6–7.

58/6–9 **and this worde . . . folowyng.** More apparently means that St. German's "therfore" must refer to the preceding sentences, not to a following clause or sentence, as the word sometimes could. In his *Life of John Picus* More wrote: "Howe disceitfull these worldlye honoures; whiche therefore lyfte vs vp: that they might throw vs downe" (*EW*, sig. b₁). Cf. also *CW 11*, 85/19–20. The *OED* gives the following example from about 1300: "þerfor is he cald trinite For he es anfald godd in thre." John Donne wrote (probably in 1623): "Therefore that he may raise the Lord throws down" ("Hymn to God my God, in my Sickness," line 30).

58/26 **I wolde to chose.** The use of the full infinitive form with *to* was still possible in More's time, especially when *would* had strong volitional force (Visser, 2, 590–91).

58/28–30 **Now where . . . take yt so.** Appendix B, 348/8–11.

59/29–30 **concernynge . . . polytyques.** Appendix B, 348/30–33; *Division, CW 9,* 179–80; *Apology, CW 9,* 85, 90.

59/32 **of a good . . . hypocryte.** That is, "by a good man's mouth about a hypocrite."

60/7 **.xxi. . . . fo. 123.** See *CW 9,* 74–76.

60/19 **tynkar . . . tyler.** Appendix B, 349/1–10.

60/27–28 **myne Apology . . . fo. 272.** *Apology, CW 9,* 163–66.

60/29–30 **for heresy . . . offyce.** A bishop (or his chancellor or commissary) could summon into court for trial a person suspected of heresy without confronting him with any accuser. He could do this *ex officio,* by the very nature of his task or duty. See *CW 9,* Commentary at 130/3, and note on 86/3–4, below. See also *Select Cases,* introduction, pp. 57–59.

60/30 **worde of offyce.** That is, "a helpful or serviceable word" (*OED,* s.v. "office" 1). See note on 60/29–30.

61/2 **His .xii. . . . lefe.** Appendix B, 349/11–39.

61/25–29 **no man . . . charytie.** *Ioannis Gerson parisiensis Cancellarij: doctorisque moralissimi: de imitatione christi: de mundi: & omnium uanitatum contemptu . . .* (Venice, 1524): "Nunc autem deus sic ordinauit: vt discamus alter alterius onera portare: quia nemo sine defectu: nemo sine onere sibi sufficiens: nemo sibi satis sapiens: sed oportet nos inuicem portare: inuicem consolari: pariter adiuuare: instruere: & admonere" (sig. B$_4$v). Chapter 16 of book 1 is entitled "De sufferantia defectuum aliorum." St. German seems to be quoting from Richard Whitford's translation, published in at least five editions about 1531 (STC^2 23961– 23964.3): "for in this worlde no man is without defaulte: no man without burden / no man suffycyent to hym selfe / nor no man wyse ynoughe of hym selfe / wherfore it behoueth eche one of vs to bere the burden of other / to comforte other / to helpe other / to enforme other / and to instructe & admonysshe other in all charytie" (STC^2 23961, sigs. d$_1$v–d$_2$). Except for the inversion in the opening clause, St. German's phrasing matches Whitford's translation word for word, a fact that More's quotation slightly obscures by omitting St. German's "ne" in the phrase corresponding to Whitford's "nor no man wyse ynoughe of hym selfe." St. German's dependence on Whitford's translation is also shown by his inclusion of Whitford's phrase "in all charytie," which has no corresponding phrase in at least eleven Latin editions published before 1530 (Augsburg, 1473, 1488; Venice, 1483, 1486, 1488, 1500, 1518, 1524; Paris, c. 1490; Gerson's *Opera*, Cologne, 1483–84; Thomas à Kempis' *Opera*, Nürnberg, 1494). The phrase is also absent in one German translation (Ulm, c. 1480) and three Italian translations (Venice, 1491; Florence, 1494, 1505). St. German also quotes Whitford's version of the *Imitatio* in the *Division;* see *CW 9*, xlvi–xlvii.

61/30–35 **thys lesson . . . maye.** See note on 24/6. Cf. Whitford's translation of *Imitatio Christi* (STC^2 23961, sig. d$_1$v): "studye alway that thou be pacyent in sufferynge of other mennes defaultes for thou haste many thyngys in the that other do suffre of the / and yf thou can not make thy selfe to be as thou woldest / howe mayst thou then loke to haue another to be ordred in all thynges after thy wyl. . . . Thus it apperyth euydently that we seldome pondre our neyghboure as we do our selfe." This passage from the *Imitatio* immediately precedes that quoted by St. German at 61/25–29.

62/8–13 **post . . . hande.** In the card game called "post" each player is dealt three cards. After each card the players "vye" or bet on their hands. A player loses if he is not willing to match the bet. Thus a "vye" is often equivalent to a bluff or "face" (*OED*, s.v. "post" *sb*. 4, "face" *sb*. 10 and *v*. 16). In the first round St. German tries to bluff—unsuccessfully. In the second round, he begins to negotiate ("falleth . . . to treaty"), suggesting that they consider their hands equal and divide the stakes ("stacke"). But More refuses because he is sure his hand will be unbeatable in the third round ("thre acys").

62/14 **fyrste . . . booke.** More intended to refer to the chapter of *Salem and Bizance* entitled "The fyrste consideration, the seconde Chap." (Appendix B, 328/3–329/7).

62/17–18 **myne answere to the same.** See 14/9–30, above.

62/24–29 **in the tone place . . . dyuysyon.** See *Apology, CW 9*, 129, 144.

63/17–23 **And therfore . . . heresye.** See 59/28–60/33.

63/28 **His .xiii. . . . lefe.** Appendix B, 350/1–351/25.

63/33 **many places.** For example, *CW 9*, 55/3–9, 63/11–19, 74/20–26, 92/17–20, 102/35–103/4, 115/35–116/5, 128/11–14, 129/29–34, 163/12–14, 167/1–3, 168/5–21.

64/1 **some places.** For example, *CW 9*, 60/5–11, 60/17–23, 60/38–61/5, 64/30–34, 87/11–17, 88/18–31, 102/35–103/4, 110/6–111/13, 116/29–117/2, 168/5–8.

64/3–5 **some other . . . hym self.** See note on 9/27.

64/5–7 **dysprayseth . . . name.** See notes on 222/31–33 and 222/34–223/1.

64/25–26 **easy . . . face.** Cf. Tilley N215: "As plain as the nose on a man's face."

64/27 **folio .238. . . . apology.** See *CW 9*, 142–43.

64/28–29 **without that poynt.** That is, without the qualification that many clergymen are good.

64/31 **myne answere . . . boke.** See 167/8–184/22.

64/32–34 **he speketh . . . men.** Appendix B, 350/23–26.

64/35–36 **he speketh . . . .xvii. chapyter.** Appendix B, 365/34–367/18.

65/2 **mater.** The sentence probably means: "In [discussing a certain] matter, they are accused, as if. . . ." But it is possible that "mater" was a misprint for "manner." The same misprint occurred in *CW 11*, 69/8, and "maner" was substituted for "mater" in *CW 11*, 108/32. The phrase "in a maner" means "almost entirely" (*OED*, "manner" *sb.*[1] 10).

65/8–24 **he wisheth . . . peple.** Appendix B, 350/39–351/14.

65/19–20 **therfore . . . cause).** More is teasing St. German once again about the proper use of "therefore" (see 56/31–58/27).

65/26–28 **with addyng . . . .xxvi. chapyter.** See *CW 9*, 95–97.

66/24–28 **Also I . . . people.** Appendix B, 351/7–14. More rearranges St. German's wording.

66/31–33 **pretendyng . . . therby.** St. German used *pretend* to mean "intend" or "endeavor," a valid meaning when he wrote (*OED*, s.v. "pretend" *v.* 8 and 9). More wrongly claims that it must mean "claim or profess falsely," also a valid meaning at the time (*OED*, s.v. "pretend" *v.* 3b). In line 2 More uses the word in the sense he claims for it when he says that St. German "pretendeth" or claims falsely that *pretend* means what St. German's context requires.

67/12–16 **he laboreth . . . grudge therat.** *Apology, CW 9,* 145–50; *Division, CW 9,* 191–93.

67/18–21 **For I sayed . . . there is.** Appendix B, 352/10–13.

67/18–19 **and that.** That is, "if."

67/22 **.xlv. chapyter . . . apologye.** *CW 9,* 145–50.

67/25 **woodcokkys.** Whiting W565, Tilley W746: "As wise as a woodcock" (that is, "foolish").

68/3–6 **as it hath . . . proued.** In the *Apology* More had discussed the cases of Thomas Philips and some other unnamed persons who complained unsuccessfully to the king and his council, protesting about the way they were treated after their arrest for heresy (*CW 9,* 126–28 and Commentary at 126/12 and 127/25). See the Introduction, pp. lxii–lxiii, above.

68/17–20 **he declareth . . . apologye.** *Division, CW 9,* 192–93; *Apology, CW 9,* 147–50; *Salem and Bizance,* Appendix B, 352/19–37, below.

68/27–28 **bryngeth . . . to bace.** That is, "to bring to a low point" (*OED,* s.v. "base" *sb.*[1]), in contrast to "high" (line 26). Cf. "to bring base" in the sense "to bring low" (*OED* s.v. "base" *a.* 6b).

68/33 **As for . . . agayne.** See note on 28/24–25.

69/18–19 **and sayth . . . dedys.** Matt. 5:28.

69/27–29 **that than . . . dede therwith.** On treason by words prior to the legislation of 1534 (26 Henry VIII, c. 13), see J. G. Bellamy, *The Law of Treason in the Later Middle Ages* (London, 1970); I. D. Thornley, "Treason by Words in the Fifteenth Century," *English Historical Review, 32* (1917), 556–61; S. Rezneck, "Constructive Treason by Words in the Fifteenth Century," *American Historical Review, 33* (1928), 544–52; Elton, *Policy and Police,* pp. 288–92. Elton's view is that "the judges could declare that a man might commit treason by speaking it, even if they preferred to support the charge with some other overt act if they could find one."

70/9–10 **to theyr persons.** That is, "to them in person."

70/12–13 **the spyrytuall . . . lyfe.** First-time offenders in heresy trials were permitted to abjure their opinions after making their confessions or being proved guilty. The accused swore an oath on the gospels to abide by his abjuration, and might be required to subscribe the record of his abjuration with a cross. After abjuration in court, he was absolved and enjoined a public penance, part of which was normally to be performed in a local marketplace and part in his own parish church. The essential element in such penances was the public admission of the offense. Abjured heretics sometimes appeared in their shirts in the marketplace to be publicly flogged, and then in church to offer a lighted candle. Faggots were often to be carried, and heretical tracts and translations of the Bible, if involved in the man's heresy, would be thrown onto a public bonfire. Abjured heretics were increasingly subjected to geographical restrictions on their movements in the early sixteenth century. They were either to remain in their village or forbidden to leave the diocese. There are occasional records of abjured heretics being branded or ordered to wear a faggot badge embroidered on their clothes. At the time of abjuration, the authorities advised the offender of the consequences if he were later found to be guilty of relapse into heresy. The penalty in such a case was burning. See Thomson, pp. 230–34; Houlbrooke, pp. 224–25; Guy, *Public Career,* pp. 165–74; *CW 9,* 376–77.

70/17 **besydes that.** That is, "in addition to the first warning."

70/20–24 **For as for . . . vpon.** See note on 28/24–25.

70/22–23 **gospell . . . monycyons.** Appendix B, 353/17–354/3. St. German modeled his suggested procedure with heretics on Matt. 18:15–17: "Si autem peccaverit in te frater tuus, vade, et corripe eum inter te, et ipsum solum: si te audierit, lucratus eris fratrem tuum: si autem te non audierit, adhibe tecum adhuc unum, vel duos, ut in ore duorum, vel trium testium stet omne verbum. Quod si non audierit eos: dic ecclesiae. Si autem ecclesiam non audierit, sit tibi sicut ethnicus et publicanus."

71/9–13 **saynte Poule . . . heresyes.** 1 Cor. 15:33: "Noli seduci: corrumpunt mores bonos colloquia mala." Menander, *Thais* 218K. Paul cites Menander in the course of arguing against those who deny the resurrection of the body. Cf. *CW 11,* 4/3–5.

71/14–15 **suche bolde . . . canker.** 2 Tim. 2:16–17: "Profana autem, et vaniloquia devita: multum enim proficiunt ad impietatem: et sermo eorum ut cancer serpit." Paul gives as examples of those to be avoided two men who subvert the faith by teaching that the resurrection has already happened. Cf. *CW 11*, 4/29–32.

71/23–29 **And yet wolde . . . a nother.** The main elements of the sentence ("wolde . . . some . . . flyt") are so widely separated by straggling phrases and clauses that the structure breaks down, nor does the repetition of "wolde" (line 26) or the addition of "they" by the errata do much to repair the damage.

71/28 **as I haue . . . sayd.** See *CW 9*, 154/13–155/22.

71/29 **kepe lyke scoles.** Here and at 48/2 and 168/32 "to keep or hold schools" means "to give private and unauthorized religious instruction," though the *OED* does not give this specific meaning under the appropriate definition (s.v. "school" 1d). The heresy statutes enacted under Henry IV and Henry V show that religious and unauthorized instruction is the intended meaning (*CW 9*, 251–52, 255, 259).

72/1–28 **And nowe . . . to other.** Appendix B, 353/18–354/3.

72/15 **the gospell.** See note on 70/22–23.

72/15 **wytnesse.** The uninflected plural of this word was frequent in More's time (*OED*, s.v. "witness" *sb.* 4). See 99/32, 109/20, 146/24, 147/4, 149/20.

73/9–12 **For the ordynarye . . . talkynge.** Cf. the procedure outlined in St. German's parliamentary draft of 1531 (see Introduction, p. xl). See Guy, *St. German*, pp. 127–28. Preliminary investigations by the ecclesiastical authorities were undertaken before heresy trials. Information was received by the authorities in the form of private reports or denunciations, by common fame, from private enquiries or news from other bishops, or by means of formal presentments at visitations. Accused heretics were often kept in the bishop's prison during preliminary investigations. However, the secret suspicion of the bishop was not sufficient to begin proceedings without better proof, while for an ecclesiastical judge to proceed to sentence on suspicion alone was a mortal sin. See Lyndewode, *Provinciale*, book 1, title 2, "De officio Archipresbyteri," gl. v. *Perversa judicia* (p. 61): "cum aliquis Judex procedit ex suspicione sola ad aliquem condemnandum: et hoc pertinet ad injusticiam. Unde est peccatum mortale." I am grateful to Professor Henry Ansgar Kelly for this reference.

73/14 **kepe.** *1557* failed to correct the obvious misprint "hepe" in *1533*.

73/20–21 **but go . . . fyrste.** Witnesses were not necessary in English heresy trials before 1534, and if they were produced, their depositions were seldom incorporated in the trial record. But More does include "open deposycyons" (line 34) in the current process, which he supports. The medieval heresy laws empowered bishops to arrest suspects on suspicion or common fame alone, and it was not until 1534, by the statute 25 Henry VIII, c. 14, that the ecclesiastical courts were required to act only upon the evidence of at least two witnesses, and suspects were to answer in open court. See Houlbrooke, pp. 216–17, 224. See also the Introduction, pp. lxv–lxvi.

73/30–31 **and secretely . . . heretyques.** Awkwardly elliptical: "and [whom he] secretely wolde make [to be] mo heretyques." On such ellipses in More's prose, see Joseph Delcourt, *Essai sur la langue de Sir Thomas More d'après ses oeuvres anglaises* (Paris, 1914), pp. 220–28.

74/10–13 **but let . . . no more.** See Guy, *St. German*, pp. 127–28.

75/22 **the parynge of an apple.** Whiting P29: "Not to give the paring of a pear." See also *OED* (s.v. "paring" 3).

76/6–13 **But as longe . . . rehersed.** Appendix B, 354/10–17.

76/23 **by theym.** That is, "about them [the ordinaries]."

76/30–35 **The vntrouth . . . thereof.** See note on 68/3–6.

77/2–6 **goeth . . . contrary.** Whiting W67.

78/17–18 **And yet . . . most.** That is, "And yet, indeed, that [remnant] is something larger [than any bad ones they could find]" (*OED*, s.v. "somewhat" B 4).

78/20 **bate makynge.** That is, "strife-causing" (*OED*, s.v. "bate" *sb.*[1] 2).

78/22–30 **the dede . . . fauour to.** See 76/30–35 and note on 68/3–6.

78/33 **sette . . . strawes.** Whiting S807, Tilley S917.

78/36 **to sow . . . sede.** Cf. Matt. 13:24–30.

79/21 **If I were . . . Lyncolns Ine.** See note on 37/34–35. More was autumn reader in 1511 and Lent reader at Lincoln's Inn in 1515. He would have addressed the assembled society in Hall over a period of four weeks on each occasion, expounding some statute or legal doctrine which interested him. His readings are not now extant. Lent readings were invariably "double" readings; that is, they were the second course of lectures which a reader gave normally some five to ten years after his first reading. First readings normally took place in August. See Guy, *Public Career*, p. 5; *Spelman's Reports*, 2, introduction, p. 133; and W. C. Richardson, *A History of the Inns of Court* (Baton Rouge, La., n.d. [1976?]), pp. 98–127.

79/23–25 **whyther . . . treason or not.** See note on 69/27–29.

79/29–31 **but wolde . . . wrytynge to.** Oral pleadings in the courts of common law and learning exercises in the Inns of Court were still conducted in law French in the reign of Henry VIII. Readings were recorded in law French. Spoken French survived in the Inns as late as the seventeenth century, but in More's time oral pleadings in the Westminster courts were declining in favor of written documents in Latin or English. Writs and entries had always been in Latin, and so continued. Litigants pleading in person were allowed to speak English. Numerous written-up versions of readings, moots, and reports of cases are extant in law French. *Spelman's Reports*, 2, introduction, pp. 92–100, 142–50, and introduction, chaps. 4 and 6.

79/32–34 **yf all . . . in prent.** Cf. *Confutation, CW 8*, 179/8–17: "I saye therfore in these dayes in whyche men by theyr owne defaute misseconstre and take harme of the very scrypture of god, vntyll menne better amende, yf any man wolde now translate Moria in to Englyshe, or some workes eyther that I haue my selfe wryten ere this, all be yt there be none harme therin / folke yet beynge (as they be) geuen to take harme of that that is good / I wolde not onely my derlynges bokes but myne owne also, helpe to burne them both wyth myne owne handes, rather then folke sholde (though thorow theyr own faute) take any harme of them, seynge that I se them lykely in these days so to do."

79/35–37 **For in yᵉ places . . . iudge it.** Readings (especially Lent ones, which were "double" readings; see note on 79/21) "were the major events in the educational cycle, and were often attended by those judges and serjeants who had once been members of the inn. They provided excellent opportunities for learning, debating, and perhaps even making, law. At the end of each day's lecture, the barristers were supposed to pick out potential errors in what they had heard, and the debate would be taken up by the benchers, and by the serjeants and judges" (*Spelman's Reports*, 2, introduction, pp. 133–34).

79/37–39 **But as for . . . harme.** See note on 28/24–25.

80/6 **hyghe mysseprisyon.** Misprisions of treason or of felony were offenses less than capital but bordering thereon. Misprision of treason consisted in the bare knowledge or concealment of treason, failure to reveal it to the king, his council, or a justice of the peace in cases where the person accused knew it to have been committed, but always where there was no specific assent to high treason on the part of the accused. Misprision of felony was likewise the concealment of a felony which a person knew about, but to which he had not directly assented. Punishments for misprision were laid down by statute and at common law, and normally took the form of perpetual imprisonment, together with fine or loss of property.

In 1534 the First Act of Succession (25 Henry VIII, c. 22) defended Henry VIII's divorce and enforced the validity of his second marriage to Anne Boleyn. The same act vested the succession to the throne in Henry's male heirs by Anne or (failing them) in those by a subsequent wife or (failing them) in Anne's daughter Elizabeth and her heirs. The act provided that if any persons after May 1, 1534, "by writing or imprinting or by any exterior act or deed" impugned its terms, they were to be considered guilty of high treason. To impugn the Boleyn marriage by words only was to count as misprision of treason. All subjects, however, could be required to take an oath "truly, firmly and constantly without fraud or guile [to] observe, fulfil, maintain, defend and keep to their cunning, wit and uttermost of their powers the whole effects and contents of this present act." Anyone who failed to comply was to be "taken and accepted for offender in misprision of high treason." More refused the oath, which was tendered to him on April 13, 1534. He said, "I coulde not sware, without the iubardinge of my soule to perpetuall dampnacion" (Rogers, p. 502). The reason was that, while he could accept the revised terms of succession to the throne, which were within the agreed competence of parliament in 1534, he believed that to swear to the illegality of Henry's marriage to Catherine of Aragon, which he had long held to be valid, was to commit perjury. Though not convicted in court of misprision of treason under the act, More was sent to the Tower. His imprisonment was regularized in November 1534, when he and John Fisher were attainted of misprision of treason by separate acts of parliament for refusing the oath (26 Henry VIII, cc. 22, 23). More was convicted of high treason under the Treason Act of 1534 at his trial on July 1, 1535. See Lehmberg, pp. 198–99; Elton, *Policy and Police*, pp. 222–27, 263–92, 400–419; Anthony J. P. Kenny, *Thomas More* (Oxford and New York, 1983), pp. 70–72.

81/4–6 **Qui amat . . . in it.** Ecclus. 3:27.

81/31–32 **Hierome . . . theym.** In several places Jerome warns against excess in the pursuit of knowledge (for example, *Commentarius in*

Ecclesiasten 6.10 and 7.14, *CCSL* 72, 299–300 and 305–06). One passage from his commentary on the Epistle to the Ephesians (*PL 26*, col. 504) was particularly well known because it had been quoted by Aquinas in his discussion of the vice of curiosity (*Summa Theologica*, II^a–II^ae, q. 167, a. 1). The passage which comes closest to More in stressing the danger of seeking knowledge beyond human capacity seems to be Jerome's comment on "ne quaeras amplius ne obstupescas," Eccles. 7:17 (*Commentarius in Ecclesiasten 7.17, CCSL 72*, 308): ". . . mentem nostram scit perfectam comprehendere non posse sapientiam et mensuram fragilitatis nostrae iubet nos scire debere. Denique et Paulus ei, qui plus quam homo scire poterat, requirebat dicens: *Quid adhuc queritur? Voluntati enim eius quis resistit?* Respondit: *O homo, tu quis es, qui respondeas Deo?* et cetera. Si enim causas quaestionis ille, qui interrogans introducitur, audisset ab apostolo, stupore forsitan torpuisset et gratiam sensisset inutilem. Quia est et donum iuxta eumdem apostolum, quod non prosit ei cui datum est."

81/33 **To other . . . harme.** Cf. *Confutation, CW 8*, 28/17–29/29.

82/19–20 **yf I sholde . . . ordynaryes.** For More's detection of heresy in cooperation with John Stokesley, bishop of London, see Guy, *Public Career*, pp. 166–67.

82/24–25 **canneth . . . skyll.** The form was usually *can skill*, but as in the phrase *can thanke* the verb was often taken to be a different, weak verb and inflected accordingly (*OED*, s.v. "can" *v.*[1] B 1c and B 10). Cf. "wold christ haue cannid her mich more thanke" (*CW 12*, 185/12–13).

82/34–36 **Ex habundantia . . . haboundeth.** Luke 6:45.

82/36–83/5 **I saye . . . abiure.** The passage expounds More's hard-line position on heresy suspects. Even if a suspect did not defend obstinately any heretical opinion, nor could be proved to be sympathetic to, or an accessory of, known heretics, More believed that "for the sore suspycyon" he might well and on good reason be compelled to abjure. In this opinion he went beyond even some of Henry VIII's bishops, who occasionally allowed suspects to merely take warning to avoid in the future the possession of heretical books and contact with other suspected heretics. Yet More apparently followed Lyndewode, who argued that the bishop could inflict "penitential pains" (*poenae poenitentiales*) on suspects. See the Introduction, pp. liii–lv, and notes on 110/32–33, 116/3–4, 116/32–117/1, 123/12–14, 127/22–31; Houlbrooke, p. 224; Thomson, pp. 230–31. The enforced abjuration of suspected heretics against whom no specific heretical opinion could be proved was already controversial in More's lifetime. See the cases of Thomas Bilney and Thomas Philips, discussed by Guy, *Public Career*, pp. 169–71, and in *CW* 9, 372–73. See the Introduction, pp. lxii–lxiii, above. The church had from Augustine's time onward regarded the "obstinate defense" of heretical opinions as the occasion for discipline, rather than the initial deviation itself. See Augustine, *De civitate Dei*, book 18, chap. 51.

83/9 **the seconde . . . .xliiii. lef.** Appendix B, 352/14–37.

83/14–15 **Summa Rosella.** This was a manual for confessors, compiled by Baptista de Salis (Trovamala), O.F.M., first published in 1489 and many times reprinted. St. German cited it in *Doctor and Student, Division,* and *The Power of the Clergy.* See *CW* 9, xxxix–xl, xliii, xlvi, xlviii, lxiv, lxxxi, 138, 145–46, 190, 192, 298, 382, 384–86; *Doctor and Student,* pp. xxviii, 237, 240, 247, 248, 251, 252, 254, 258, 259, 261, 263, 273, 274–79. See note on 184/30–31, below.

83/33–84/7 **For howe be yt . . . theym selfe.** Appendix B, 353/9–18.

84/20–22 **where as . . . contrarie.** See note on 68/3–6.

85/11–13 **nolite . . . conscyence.** 1 Cor. 10:25, 27.

85/27 **the stretes . . . heretyques.** Cf. *CW* 9, 130/29.

86/3–4 **the suit . . . yᵉ .liiii.** *Salem and Bizance,* Appendix B, 355/21–359/11; *Division, CW* 9, 188–91; *Apology, CW* 9, 129–35. Cases in the ecclesiastical courts were procedurally of three types: instance cases between party and party; *ex officio* cases which represented the corrective action of the bishop, his chancellor, or commissary; and probate cases. *Ex officio* cases were themselves of two types: *ex officio mero,* in which the judge acted alone of his "mere motion," and *ex officio promoto,* in which he was acting on the information of an individual who promoted his action and was supposed to bear the costs if the charge proved unfounded. Heresy cases were almost invariably *ex officio mero,* in which the judge acted inquisitorially on the basis of information obtained during visitations, from denunciations or private reports, or on the basis of common fame. Once cited and accused, the suspect in heresy cases would be examined on oath that he would truthfully answer everything preferred against him. This oath, founded on Roman-canonical procedure, had become controversial in the eyes of such common lawyers as St. German, John Rastell, Edward Hall, Thomas Cromwell, and others. Whether it had become controversial in itself or as an excuse to sweep away the heresy laws and independent ecclesiastical jurisdiction is difficult to determine. It is certainly true that the Court of Star Chamber demanded answers and depositions on oaths taken beforehand, and Chancery in company with all the other courts of equitable jurisdiction took the depositions of witnesses on oath. These oaths in equity courts did not become controversial until the seventeenth century. Once examined, the first-time suspect in heresy proceedings might be admitted to purgation or acquitted (extremely rare but it happened occasionally), or, if convicted, urged to abjure his heresy (see note on 70/12–13). If he refused to abjure, he was surrendered as an obstinate heretic to the secular arm for punishment under the heresy statutes (see *CW 9*, Appendix C). Convicted second-time offenders were automatically surrendered to the secular arm for burning as relapsed and perjured heretics. St. German had objected that in *ex officio* trials summonses were issued on the basis of accusations by unnamed persons; the presiding official acted as both accuser and judge; the accused was bound on oath to answer the charges; and conviction did not necessarily depend on the confession of the accused, but on the judge's assessment of the evidence. Also in heresy trials other heretics or suspects could serve as witnesses or accusers; names of accusers could be withheld from the accused if the judge believed fear of recrimination was present; summary procedure could be used; and torture was permissible. See Kelly, "English Kings and the Fear of Sorcery," pp. 211–13; Thomson, pp. 220–36; Houlbrooke, pp. 38–54; G. R. Elton, *The Tudor Constitution,* 2nd ed. (Cambridge, 1982), pp. 218–35; Hall, *Chronicle,* p. 784; *CW 9,* 376–78. See also the Introduction, pp. xlvii–lxvii.

86/16–17 **to set a flye.** Whiting F344–45.

87/1–3 **in the perleament . . . to fewe.** More's allusion is to the composition of the House of Lords, which during the course of the Reformation Parliament (1529–1536) comprised a total of 107 members. Of these, 50 were lords spiritual and 57 lords temporal, but not all 107 were eligible to sit at any one time. In 1529 the House consisted of 49 lords spiritual and 51 lords temporal; in 1534 there were 50 lords spiritual and 55 lords temporal. The clerics thus formed a minority, but a substantial one. Hence the outcome of a debate could in practice depend on who had turned up on that day. The detailed breakdown for the Reformation Parliament was as follows: archbishops, bishops, and custodians of spiritualities, 21; abbots and priors, 29; dukes, 3; marquises, 2; earls, 13; viscounts, 1; barons, 38. See Lehmberg, pp. 36–38.

87/27 **not worth one rysshe.** Whiting R250, Tilley S918.

88/16–17 **slynke into lurkys lane.** This sounds proverbial but we have not been able to identify it as such. It does not appear as a real lane in

John Stow's *Survey of London,* ed. C. L. Kingsford, 2 vols. (Oxford, 1908). See also 145/32.

88/22–25 **Reade . . . therwyth.** *Division, CW 9,* 188–91; *Apology, CW 9,* 129–35.

89/5–27 **Then to the conuentynge . . . denyed.** Appendix B, 355/22–356/4.

89/12 **god . . . herte.** See Sap. 1:6.

90/4–5 **Hys ground . . . this.** In *1533* these words of More, which introduce the sentence of St. German, were wrongly printed in the small type regularly devoted to quotations from St. German. The corrector noted that they should be in the larger type devoted to More's words ("All thys muste be in the great letter"). The compositor who set the errata of *1533* simply repeated the corrector's words as if they were to be substituted for More's. *1557* ignored this puzzling correction and wrongly included More's words between the pointing hands which it used to mark off St. German's words.

90/6–8 **Yt is certayn . . . so to be.** Appendix B, 355/25–28.

90/17–19 **And yf any. . . accuser.** Appendix B, 355/29–31.

90/20–22 **and the spirituall . . . ex officio.** More's observation is somewhat ambiguous. It is not clear whether he means that persons could indirectly promote suits brought by ecclesiastical judges as accusers in heresy cases, rather than relying on the judges themselves to initiate proceedings (in which case he refers to suits *ex officio promoto* as opposed to *ex officio mero*) or whether he means that heresy proceedings might result from actions *ad instantiam partium.* No instance case of heresy proceedings is known to me, though such cases might theoretically be possible. We should note Houlbrooke's remark that "the course chosen in a particular case was determined to a great extent by the custom of the court in question, the volume of business, the standing of the parties, and the way in which the matter had come to the judge's notice" (p. 38). Yet on the whole More's purpose is probably to draw attention to the availability of procedure *ex officio promoto.* But More does repeatedly speak of such an accuser as a "party" (89/31, 91/26, 92/22, 92/34).

90/31–32 **If . . . mater.** Appendix B, 355/31–33.

91/29–30 **and wyll . . . world.** The depositions of witnesses were, however, rarely put on record in the act books of the ecclesiastical courts. See Houlbrooke, p. 224.

92/2 **vs ... to it.** The presence of "therto" in *1533* (canceled in the errata) suggests that it was an alternative for "to it" which More neglected to cancel. See note on 27/30.

92/7–12 **For yf ... behalfe.** Appendix B, 355/33–38.

93/7 **in the seuynth ... dyuysyon.** *Division, CW 9,* 188–91.

93/8–12 **a prouisyon ... agaynste hym.** A provision for secret testimony had been devised during the proceedings against the Albigensians, who had support among the ruling classes. The canon "Statuta quaedam" (*Sexti Decretales* 5.2.20, *CIC* 2, 1078) provided that if a bishop saw that the accusers or witnesses in a heresy trial of powerful persons would be in grave danger if their names were known, they could testify secretly in the presence of the bishop or his vicar and the inquisitors. The testimony also had to be revealed to some other persons, prudent, honest, and skilled in the law, who were to give their advice before sentence was passed. They were subject to excommunication if they revealed anything secret without the permission of the bishop and the inquisitors. Once the danger was past, the names of the accusers and witnesses were to be revealed, just as in other trials. The bishops and inquisitors were cautioned to be very scrupulous in not declaring such danger when there was none or in ignoring it when it was real. See *CW 9,* Commentary at 137/12.

93/14–15 **whych prouysyon ... vre.** Thomson says, "there is no evidence ... that this weapon of a secret trial was ever needed against the later Lollards" (p. 228).

94/10–12 **though the man ... harme at all.** St. German had proposed that a witness might be saved from personal danger by showing his evidence to the King's Council, who would then take surety for his safety. This procedure of "indemnity" from "bodily harm" may be seen at work in the *corpus cum causa* files, where the *contra brevia* of sureties taken in the King's Council and Chancery were kept. For example, on October 7, 1526, Thomas Strangways, controller of Wolsey's household, was bound in £1,000 to keep the peace, especially against Thomas Cromwell and his servants, and to do them "no bodily hurt" (PRO, C 244/169/19). This procedure, however, was not available in ecclesiastical cases.

94/18–19 **nor he ... bounde.** The considerable penalties due on forfeited conciliar bonds were exacted by actions on writs of *scire facias* in the exchequer.

95/17 **ye.** That is, "thee."

95/18 **quod.** The abbreviation ꝙ in *1533* and *1557* may stand for either of the equivalent forms "quoth" or "quod." Both the abbreviation and the full form "quod" appear frequently in the early editions of *A Dialogue concerning Heresies.* The abbreviation first appears at 16/27.

96/20–28 **His deuyse . . . endynge.** *Apology, CW 9,* 138–39.

96/37–97/5 **And on . . . partye.** *Apology, CW 9,* 139.

97/9 **Almayne.** Germany. More's reason for supposing that St. German's alternative would not serve there must have been that a number of German princes had already embraced Lutheranism. Moreover, territorial fragmentation meant that the German princes or the Imperial Diet could not offer the centralized governmental controls provided in England or France, for example, by the King's Council or *Conseil du Roi.* See *CW 9,* Commentary at 138/38, and the Introduction, p. lxxxii, above.

98/13–18 **surety . . . withall.** For this procedure, see Fitzherbert and Crompton, sigs. N_4–O_4.

99/25–26 **lette . . . letteth.** The plural and singular forms of the verb, both with a plural subject, are inconsistent. But in More's time a singular verb could be used with plural subjects. See note on 39/35–36.

99/32–35 **Now what if . . . lost.** Two witnesses were required for proof and only one would be left because the party or accuser could not be a witness. See note on 178/24–25.

100/3–6 **And than . . . denyed.** Appendix B, 355/40–356/4.

100/10–23 **this deuice . . . hepe there.** In *The Courtier* (book 2, chap. 51), first printed at Venice in April 1528, Baldassare Castiglione told a similar story: "You will not have forgotten the foolishness of that abbot of whom the Duke was telling not so long ago, who was present one day when Duke Federico was discussing what should be done with the great mass of earth which had been excavated for the foundations of this palace, which he was then building, and said: 'My lord, I have an excellent idea where to put it. Give orders that a great pit be dug, and without further trouble it can be put into that.' Duke Federico replied, not without laughter: 'And where shall we put the earth that is excavated in digging this pit of yours?' Said the abbot: 'Make it big enough to hold both.' And so, even though the Duke repeated several times that the larger the pit was made, the more earth would be excavated, the man could never get it into his head that it could not be made big enough to hold both, and replied nothing save: 'Make it that much bigger!' Now you see what good judgment this abbot had" (trans. Charles Singleton, New York, 1959, pp. 151–52.).

100/14 **quod.** See note on 95/18.

100/16 **quod.** See note on 95/18.

100/20 **quod.** See note on 95/18.

100/22 **quod.** See note on 95/18.

101/8–9 **his owne eares.** See note on 35/5.

101/16–20 **this mannes credence . . . in no wyse.** St. German rejected the use of forsworn witnesses, who were accepted at the discretion of the judges in trials for heresy (and treason). Thus the testimony of a witness who had perjured himself to protect the defendant might be accepted when he reversed his testimony. See 146/6–19 and the Introduction, pp. lxxxvi–lxxxvii.

101/27 **this.** An adverbial form of the demonstrative pronoun, meaning "thus" (*OED*, s.v. "this" *adv.* 1).

102/7–12 **For surely . . . eyther.** *Apology, CW 9*, 130/25–31.

102/17–20 **For what . . . by hym.** *Apology, CW 9*, 130/32–36.

102/34–35 **(but yf . . . lyfe).** St. German had been something of a recluse since about 1511. See the Introduction, p. xxxi–xxxii. See also *CW 9*, 94/3–5.

103/6–11 **And yet . . . his earys.** *Apology, CW 9*, 130–31.

103/10–11 **for his earys.** That is, "for fear of great harm," an allusion to the loss of ears as a punishment (*OED*, s.v. "ear" *sb.*[1] 1f).

103/15–18 **they wyll . . . forgeteth yt.** More alludes to the reluctance of private citizens to become involved in criminal prosecutions unless they had a personal interest in the case. In early Tudor England the difficulty of enforcing criminal law was exacerbated by the lack of a formalized prosecutional function at common law above and beyond the presentments of grand juries and proceedings upon informations or criminal appeals of private citizens. Unless justices of the peace were especially assiduous, it was difficult to combat crime and offenses against the common weal effectively. This structural defect in the legal system was addressed by two Marian statutes of 1554–55 (1 and 2 Philip and Mary, c. 13; 2 and 3 Philip and Mary, c. 10), which further developed the pretrial prosecutional role of the justices of the peace.

See J. H. Langbein, "The Origins of Public Prosecution at Common Law," *American Journal of Legal History, 17* (1973), 313–35, and his *Prosecuting Crime in the Renaissance* (Cambridge, Mass., 1974), pp. 1–125, 202–09, 248–51. Clerks of assize increasingly played a role in coordinating criminal prosecutions. See J. S. Cockburn, *A History of English Assizes, 1558–1714* (Cambridge, 1972).

103/21–25 **And this . . . complayne.** *Apology, CW 9*, 131/5–10.

103/32 **playeth . . . mummery.** Mummers, as distinct from maskers, did not speak (See *CW 11*, Commentary at 13/1–10).

104/35–105/1 **by such . . . yᵉ same.** More refers to the Oldcastle rebellion of 1414. Sir John Oldcastle was a Herefordshire knight of baronial rank who had fought for Henry IV against both Scots and Welsh rebels led by Owen Glendower. "He probably incurred suspicion first in 1410 although it seems likely that by that date he was already recognized as a leader of the Lollards, as he wrote letters to a Bohemian noble who favoured Hus, to King Wenceslas of Bohemia, and to Hus himself. However, he remained in royal favour until the start of Henry V's reign, when clearer evidence of his heresies led to accusations against him in convocation. Archbishop Arundel approached the King, who made an unsuccessful attempt to bring Oldcastle back to orthodoxy. After a foolish defiance he was arrested and brought to trial. There he proved obstinate, and was handed over to the secular arm. The King, presumably hoping he would recant, granted a respite of forty days before execution and sent him as a prisoner to the Tower, from which he escaped and made an attempt to raise a rebellion against the King in January 1414. Lollard agents roused supporters in various parts of the country and plans were laid to seize the King at Eltham in Kent and to occupy London. The principal rendezvous was to be at St. Giles's Fields, north-west of Temple Bar. The plot failed when some of those concerned betrayed its details to the King, who had some of the leaders arrested and laid a trap for those who were to join Oldcastle at the rendezvous. The royal victory was easy; a considerable number of prisoners were taken, although Oldcastle himself escaped, and a few were killed. On the royal side the victory appears to have been bloodless" (Thomson, p. 4). See also M. Aston, "Lollardy and Sedition, 1381–1431," *Past and Present, 17* (1960), 1–44. See *CW 6*, Commentary at 409/24–410/6. For background on European heresy, see the works cited above, p. xlvii, n. 1. See also *CW 9*, 162/5–10.

105/1–2 **put yt . . . robbe.** This long sentence, which does not end until "leuynge" (line 11), breaks down at this point: "put" requires some subject such as "they would" and the meaning seems to be "heretics would become so numerous that . . . they would take the risk and make the attempt to rob."

105/23–106/6 **But to putte . . . reasonable.** Appendix B, 356/4–23.

105/23–26 **to putte . . . law.** See note on 93/8–12.

105/36–106/1 **the wytnes . . . after hys deth.** The feudal doctrine of escheat provided that the lands and tenements of a man of property reverted to his lord by way of forfeiture, either on the man's death without issue, or on account of his attainder for felony. Such forfeiture was extended to the lands of relapsed heretics in 1414; see the Introduction, p. liii. St. German's argument is that persons may secretly conspire to give false witness against a man for heresy in order to obtain his lands on forfeiture. (See Appendix B, 356/7–18). The precise terms under which forfeitures in heresy cases operated were dictated by the 1414 statute. *CW* 9, 258–59.

106/17–18 **I haue answered . . . byfore.** See notes on 93/7 and 93/8–12 and *CW* 9, 137–40.

106/28–34 **no more then . . . knew.** The King's Council, especially sitting as a court in Star Chamber, regularly exercised its inherent jurisdiction to examine suspects and investigate crime and offenses prejudicial to law enforcement and public justice. See Guy, *Cardinal's Court*, pp. 60–65.

107/15 **lather.** That is, "ladder."

107/15–17 **approuers . . . forthwith.** An approver was one who, confessing to felony committed by himself, accused others of being guilty of the same crime. He did so normally upon his arraignment, before any plea was entered (a plea of not guilty disabled a potential approver). He first confessed the indictment against him to be true, and then took an oath to reveal all treasons and felonies known to him, praying a coroner to enter his appeal or accusation against those that were his partners in the crimes mentioned in the indictment. Since approvers were invariably executed regardless of their services as informers for the Crown, it is a mystery why any was to be found, save for reasons of deathbed repentance or personal malice.

108/1–2 **adminicula probationis.** That is, an "adminicle" (aid, help, or support) of proof. Cf. the statute 1 Edward IV, c. 1. The system was not dissimilar to the taking of depositions in Chancery *in perpetuam memoriam.*

108/16–17 **his seuenth . . . boke.** *Division*, *CW* 9, 188–91.

108/22 **wynnynge . . . eschete.** See note on 105/36–106/1.

108/32–33 **scrape theym out.** The usual way of erasing words on parchment and paper was to scrape them off with a knife.

109/11 **And.** *1557* has no indentation here, but the very long white space in the preceding line suggests that a new paragraph was intended.

109/16–31 **seuenth chapyter . . . therof.** *Division, CW 9*, 189.

109/18 **Statuta quedam.** See note on 93/8–12.

109/28 **wytnes.** See note on 99/32–35.

110/6–7 **for more . . . prentynge to.** Although we should not read too much into More's remark about the costs of his literary campaign against St. German, the implication is that he had to provide William Rastell with subventions in order to secure publication.

110/14–18 **saue onely . . . insurreccyon.** See note on 104/35–105/1 for Sir John Oldcastle's rebellion. For Oldcastle's possible contacts, see Thomson, pp. 5–19. Oldcastle's Christian name was John, not Hugh.

110/32–34 **Also syr . . . treatyse.** *Salem and Bizance,* Appendix B, 356/24–35; *Division, CW 9,* 189.

110/32–33 **ex. de hereticis ca. Ad abolendam.** The canon "Ad abolendam" (*Decretales Gregorii IX,* 5.7.9; *CIC* 2, 780–82) provides for the punishment of heretics (particularly concerning the sacraments) and of princes and cities which fail to aid the church in prosecuting heretics. But it also contains the following sentence concerning those remarkably suspect for heresy: "Qui vero inventi fuerint sola [ecclesiae, *CIC*] suspicione notabiles, nisi ad arbitrium episcopi iuxta considerationem suspicionis qualitatemque personae propriam innocentiam congrua purgatione monstraverint, simili sententiae subiacebunt" (*CIC* 2, 781). In other words, if the suspect would not confess and could not be proved guilty, he was not necessarily to be absolved. At his discretion the judge might, on his own account or at the instigation of the suspect, order purgation. More, however, apparently followed Lyndewode in interpreting the canon to mean that the bishop could inflict "penitential pains" (*poenae poenitentiales*) on suspects by way of purgation. While this may have reflected current practice in the ecclesiastical courts, what *Ad abolendam* really meant was that unless suspects could clear themselves by *canonical* purgation (that is, by the oath of innocence with or without oath helpers), they were to be convicted and punished as heretics. The "similar sentence" of the canon was that the suspect be handed over to the secular authorities for appropriate punishment as a heretic. See Lyndewode, *Provinciale*, p. 290 (reference kindly supplied by Professor Henry Ansgar Kelly); the Introduction, p. liii–lv; *CW9*, commentary at 130/14–15; and notes on 47/14–16, 111/34–112/2, 116/3–4, 127/22–31.

111/17–31 **It may be . . . noughty.** *Apology, CW 9,* 131–32.

111/34–112/2 **I say . . . other wyse.** When the case against a suspect in heresy proceedings remained unproved, he could be required to purge his name with the support of a specified number of compurgators (that is, "oath helpers"). In William Alnwick's proceedings in Norfolk (1428–1431), six was the commonest number, and most purgations required fewer than ten compurgators. Yet elsewhere as many as twelve or sixteen might be required, and if the suspect was a clerk his compurgators might also need to be in orders. Such large numbers of compurgators would have been hard to muster, and the number of accused allowed to purge their names was, in any case, a very small minority of those charged. Most recorded cases of heresy against first-time defendants ended in the abjuration of a confessed or convicted "heretic." If a case was half-proved and the accused denied the charge, he could theoretically be tortured under canon law. See Thomson, pp. 230–31; Lyndewode, *Provinciale*, p. 305; Kelly, "English Kings and the Fear of Sorcery," p. 213; the Introduction, pp. lv–lvi, above; and note on 47/14–16.

112/16–18 **Truely . . . heretyke.** Appendix B, 356/33–35.

113/1–3 **Lyke as . . . trueth.** Wager of law was customarily used in actions of debt upon a "nude" pact or simple contract without writing, and also in actions of detinue for goods or chattels left with the defendant. The defendant swore in court in the presence of his compurgators that he owed the plaintiff nothing or that he had not detained the goods, and the compurgators swore that they believed his oath to be true. The reason for this procedure was that the defendant might have paid the debt in private or before witnesses since deceased. See note on 47/14–16.

113/11–12 **that was made . . . chrystendome.** See note on 114/1–16.

113/23–36 **And veryly . . . Excommunicamus.** Appendix B, 356/35–357/7.

113/24–26 **the sayde chapyter . . . accursed.** See note on 110/32–34.

113/34–36 **another law . . . Excommunicamus.** The second provision of the canon "Excommunicamus" (*Decretales Gregorii IX*, 5.7.13; *CIC* 2, 787–88) is as follows: "Qui autem inventi fuerint sola suspicione notabiles, nisi iuxta considerationem suspicionis qualitatemque personae propriam innocentiam congrua purgatione monstraverint, anathematis gladio feriantur, et usque ad satisfactionem condignam ab omnibus evitentur, ita, quod, si per annum in excommunicatione perstiterint, ex tunc velut haeretici condemnentur." This canon had been approved by the Fourth Lateran Council in 1215 under Innocent III (Giuseppe Alberigo, ed., *Conciliorum oecumenicorum decreta*, 2nd ed., Basel, 1962, pp. 209–11). See the Introduction, p. xlix.

114/1–16 **This prouysyon . . . lawe.** The canon "Ad abolendam" had been approved by the Council of Verona in 1184 and was quoted in the canon "Excommunicamus" not only in the sentence mentioned by More but also in another sentence (Alberigo, p. 211, n. 1) so that the Fourth Lateran Council could be said to have given "Ad abolendam" implicit approval. We have consulted several commentaries on the decretals of Gregory IX that were current in More's time without finding any that notes the dependence of "Excommunicamus" on "Ad abolendam." But the dependence has been pointed out by modern scholars: see Jean Guiraud, *Histoire de l'inquisition au moyen âge* (Paris, 1935), p. 413; Helene Tillmann, *Papst Innocenz III* (Bonn, 1954), p. 205, n. 3. See the Introduction, pp. xlvii–xlix.

114/12–13 **such doctours . . . lawes.** One such doctor was William Lyndewode, whose opinions and glosses More apparently follows throughout. See *Provinciale*, especially pp. 61, 93, 290, 302–03, 312; these references were kindly supplied by Professor Henry Ansgar Kelly.

114/19–20 **ratificacyon . . . counsaile.** The Fourth Lateran Council was summoned by Innocent III (1198–1216). Its *capitula* were included in the later collection known as the *Decretales Gregorii IX* and hence in the *Corpus Iuris Canonici* (see *CW* 9, Commentary at 130/14–15). Gregory IX (1227–1241), like Innocent III, had studied canon law at Bologna, and his collections, which were intended to supplement the *Decretum* of Gratian, began the so-called *Liber extra* (that is, the constitutions *extra Decretum Gratiani*).

114/21 **Platina.** Bartolomeo Platina (1421–1481) studied Greek under Argyropoulos in Florence and became papal librarian under Sixtus IV. In his *Historia . . . de vitis pontificum romanorum* (Cologne, 1574; there were also editions in 1512 and 1518) he describes Pope Lucius III (1181–1185) as "vir optimus" and details his efforts at the Council of

Verona to settle quarrels among the crusaders in the Holy Land and to get the kings in Europe to send them help (sig. Q$_3$). Platina calls Innocent III "vir etiam ante pontificatum doctrina & moribus insignis" (sig. Q$_5$v) and asserts "constat eum in quouis genere vitae probatissimum fuisse, dignumque, qui inter sanctos pontifices censeatur" (sig. Q$_6$v).

114/21 **Cronica cronicarum.** Richard J. Schoeck ("The 'Cronica Cronicarum' of Sir Thomas More and Tudor Historians," *Bulletin of the Institute of Historical Research, 35* [1962], 85) points out that More here is referring not to the abridged *Cronica cronicarum* (Paris, 1521 and 1532) but rather to Hartmann Schedel's *Liber cronicarum* (Nürnberg, 1493), which says that Innocent III "decretales quoque antiquas composuit quas obseruari mandauit"; it describes him as "vir doctissimus et omni ornatissimus virtute" and "vir certe in omni genere vite probatissimus atque doctissimus" (fol. 206v). This chronicle also sets out the good deeds of that "vir optimus," Pope Lucius III (fol. 204v).

114/25–26 **them . . . counsayle.** The Fourth Lateran Council was remarkable for the extraordinary number of prelates and ambassadors of temporal kings who were in attendance. Both Platina (*Historia,* sigs. Q$_6$–Q$_6$v) and Schedel (*Liber cronicarum,* fol. 206v) record that it was attended by 1,300 prelates (including the patriarchs of Jerusalem and Constantinople), 70 metropolitan bishops, 412 bishops, 800 priors and abbots, the legates of the Greek and Roman emperors, and the ambassadors of the kings of Jerusalem, France, Spain, England, and Cyprus. See note on 144/24–34.

114/31–115/1 **after tharbitrement . . . episcopi.** More is following the wording of the canon closely (see note on 110/32–33).

115/15–17 **where ye wordes . . . inough.** That is, through the testimony of other unprejudiced witnesses.

115/21 **like a shypmans hose.** Cf. Tilley C599: "A conscience as large as a shipman's hose."

116/3–4 **such kynde . . . requyre.** In this passage More conflates under the term *purgation* the strictly distinct procedures of purgation and abjuration. See Houlbrooke, pp. 223–30. Cf. "abiure" (116/13) and "abiuration" (116/32–117/1).The reason is that More apparently follows Lyndewode (gl. v. *Purgaverit, Provinciale,* p. 290), where "purgation" by various penances is described. Such penances include abjuration of heresy, confinement in a monastery, building a church or a hospital, poor relief, or other pious works. The bishop is to impose a form of penance appropriate to the suspect's rank and position, and if it is not properly performed, the suspect may be condemned as a heretic. This reference was kindly supplied by Professor Henry Ansgar Kelly. See the Introduction, pp. liii–lv.

116/13 **abiure.** See notes on 70/12–13, 82/35–83/5, 127/22–31.

116/32–117/1 **The parell . . . fyre.** If an abjured heretic was later found to be guilty of relapse into heresy, the penalty was that of mandatory burning (see note on 70/12–13). Burning was never automatic as a punishment for a first-time offender in heresy. More's point, however, is that it was not unreasonable to fall into the jeopardy of subsequent burning if, on the first occasion that a suspect was in trouble for "heresy," he was "very vehemently suspected." According to Lyndewode, the term *vehementer suspectus* refers to the case of the suspect who had knowingly visited heretics, or given them alms, or received their books, or defended their persons, and so on. In such cases *demonstrationes leves*, or "light proofs" sufficed to justify penitential pains or abjuration of heresy, but not to demand conviction as a heretic. See Lyndewode, *Provinciale*, gl. v. *Vehementer suspecti*, pp. 302–03. I am grateful to Professor H. A. Kelly for this reference. See Introduction, pp. liii–lv.

117/14–19 **For than . . . Excommunicamus.** Appendix B, 357/4–7. More does not quote accurately here, although no violence is done to St. German's meaning.

117/19 **Extra. . . . Excommunicamus.** See note on 113/34–36.

117/27 **And.** *1557* has no indentation here, but the very long white space in the preceding line suggests that a new paragraph was intended.

117/36–118/2 **But fynally . . . the whyle.** Although More describes the legal position at canon law, namely that an unconvicted suspect required to purge himself of suspicion of heresy could delay his purgation for a year before being required to abjure, during which time he was excommunicated, no case is recorded in which such extended delay occurred in the immediate pre-Reformation period. On the contrary, Tanner's evidence from Norwich heresy trials of the period 1428–1431 suggests that such purgations as were permitted were quickly effected, and if successful the accused was then restored "ad pristinam famam." See Tanner, pp. 8–10, 39–40, 210–16.

118/4 **suspycyon . . . tourne.** The use of a plural verb with a singular subject because of the attraction of an intervening plural noun was common in the sixteenth century and earlier (Visser, *1*, 49).

118/29–31 **made . . . chrystendome.** See note on 114/1–16. Cf. More's arguments in his letter to Cromwell of March 5, 1534 (Rogers, no. 199, pp. 498–99).

119/6 **there sholde.** That is, "there should be a worse law made."

119/10 **se clerely confuted.** The adverb "clerely" should probably be taken with "se" rather than "confuted" (cf. 119/17).

119/26–27 **yt was . . . that lawe.** More refers to the statutes against heretics enacted in 1382, 1401, and 1414 (see *CW* 9, Appendix C).

120/14 **wynne . . . pyece.** The metaphor is drawn from chess.

120/15–16 **in myn apology . . . nothynge ellys.** See *Apology, CW* 9, 129/29–137/10.

121/6–30 **And veryly . . . bodye and soule.** *Apology, CW* 9, 131/33–132/26.

121/13 **write . . . behauour.** The writ *de gestu et fama* was awarded at common law by the judges or justices of the peace at their discretion to inquire into the character of an imprisoned suspect in his own locality. If the suspect's neighbors returned that he was of good character, he would not be required to provide sureties for his future good behavior. However, if they replied that he was of low repute in his neighborhood, the suspect would remain in prison until he had found such sureties as were demanded and bound himself in a recognizance to keep the peace or to be of "good abearing" (that is, good behavior)—all this at the judge's or justice's discretion. See William Lambard, *Eirenarcha: or of the office of justices of peace* . . . (London, 1588; *STC*² 15165), book 4, chap. 14. See the Introduction, pp. lxxiii, lxxxiv.

121/17 **to bynde . . . aberynge.** For precedents and examples of circumstances in which men were bound to good behavior and to keep the peace, see Fitzherbert and Crompton, sigs. N_4–O_4.

121/33–122/23 **Then he goeth . . . heresy.** Appendix B, 357/8–34.

121/35 **indytementes.** An indictment was a bill or written declaration accusing one or more persons of some criminal or penal offense. It was laid before a grand jury, upon whose oath it was found to be true (*billa vera*) or groundless (*ignoramus*). No person at common law might be arraigned or put to trial for a capital offense except on a criminal appeal (that is, a private accusation demanding punishment on account of the particular injury suffered by the appellor) or on indictment. For appeals, see C. Whittick, "The Role of the Criminal Appeal in the Fifteenth Century," in J. A. Guy and H. G. Beale, eds., *Law and Social Change in British History* (London, 1984), pp. 55–72. For proceedings in treason other than at common law, see note on 136/18–20.

122/7–8 **but proclamacyon . . . agaynst hym.** The common-law procedure St. German outlined in this passage operated as follows in Henry VIII's reign. A person might be arrested on bare suspicion of felony on reasonable cause known to the person making the arrest. Such a suspect could not be arraigned or put to trial without any appeal or indictment, but was to be held in custody pending the next quarter sessions. Although any person who suspected another might make the arrest, it was well established by the sixteenth century that the overall responsibility was that of the justices of the peace. A technical difficulty was that the person making the arrest had personally to hold the suspicion, and there was a case in 1522 in which it was said that the local justice of the peace had acted illegally by making an arrest on the information of another. A more substantial difficulty, however, was that a private citizen making an arrest on suspicion and keeping a suspect prisoner pending the sessions was liable to be sued for false imprisonment. Hence in practice justices of the peace increasingly acted on information received. The jurisdiction of the justices of the peace had been prescribed by many statutes. They were empowered by legislation of 1328 and 1330 to punish offenders and receive presentments; these powers were enlarged in 1333, 1337, 1343, 1344, and 1361. By 34 Edward III, c. 1, justices of the peace were "to take and arrest all those that they may find by indictment, or by suspicion, and to put them in prison." In 1363 they were ordered to hold their sessions four times a year. By 1 Richard III, c. 3, and 3 Henry VII, c. 3, justices of the peace were permitted to bail prisoners arrested on suspicion of felony, on condition that the persons released on bail undertook to appear before them at the next quarter sessions. When the sessions opened, the grand jury was required not only to validate indictments (see note on 121/35) but also to make presentments of any offenses known to them from their own observations, without any bill of indictment laid before them. In this way, those suspected of felony in the neighborhood might be lawfully detected, and the clerk to the justices would be required to frame an indictment in the wake of any presentment. The person presented and indicted would then be put to answer at the assizes. The alternative course in Henry VIII's reign, which is noted by St. German in this passage, would be for the justices of the peace to make a written or oral presentment on their own account and to make public proclamation on the king's behalf that if anyone would offer evidence concerning the suspected felony, he should come and be heard. The form of words was: "A. B. prisoner standeth heere at the barre, if any man can say any thing against him, let him now speake, for the prisoner standeth at his deliveraunce [that is, he will otherwise be set at liberty]." For these words, see Sir Thomas Smith, *De republica Anglorum* (London, 1583; *STC*[2] 22857), p. 76. If nobody came forward, the suspect was discharged without fine or punishment except for payment of his jailer's fees; if evidence was proffered, the case was remitted to the assizes, where the accused was put to trial on an indictment framed by the clerk of assize or his assistant.

123/12–14 **For yf . . . deliuered quyte.** Although such a case was theoretically possible, we know of none in which an accused in a heresy trial during the immediate pre-Reformation period in England was acquitted without purgation, but More is presumably referring to pretrial investigations. At that stage suspects were often quizzed on the articles of faith by the bishops or their commissaries; any incriminating evidence gathered was used to level a specific charge later. The King's Council used comparable methods in serious criminal cases, chiefly alleged treason (see note on 135/32–35). Yet some bishops, and especially Cardinal Wolsey may, in heresy cases, have examined suspects privately, counseled them, and released them prior to a formal trial. See A. F. Pollard, *Wolsey* (London, 1929), pp. 213–15; H. C. Porter, ed., *Puritanism in Tudor England* (London, 1970), pp. 26, 37–38; and Guy, *Public Career,* pp. 104–05.

123/31 **saue . . . fyndynge.** Persons held in secular prisons in Tudor England were obliged to pay for food, clothing, and services.

124/3 **as for . . . both one.** See note on 28/24–25.

124/17 **repryed.** A variant form of "reprieved," meaning "sent back to prison."

124/25 **dyspycyons is.** The use of a plural subject with a singular verb was common both before and after More's lifetime (Visser, *1,* 46–48).

125/7–8 **And where . . . thyrde.** *Apology, CW* 9, 133–34.

125/26–126/7 **Necessyte . . . so to do.** *Apology, CW* 9, 133–34. Under the statute 4 Henry VII, c. 12 More had been empowered as lord chancellor to dismiss justices of the peace as described here. For "good abearing" see note on 121/13 and Fitzherbert and Crompton, sigs. N_4–O_4 and AA_2v–AA_3v.

126/12 **presentement.** That is, an accusation by a grand jury, by justices of the peace, or by parish officials.

126/23–127/7 **And then ... nothynge lyke.** Appendix B, 357/35–358/13.

127/22–31 **But now yf ... at all.** The significance of More's admission that a vehement suspect might be required to perform penance is discussed in the Introduction, pp. liii–lv, above.

128/7–8 **not deny.** Although *1533* and *1557* have only "deny," the sense clearly requires a negative. The errata of *1533* caught such a missing "not" at 127/28. See also 128/27–30.

128/27 **This.** See note on 101/27.

129/7 **contreys.** That is, "counties."

129/26–27 **setteth in ... warde.** That is, "brings in the rear guard." A "warde" referred in general to any of the three divisions of an army, front, middle, or rear (*OED*, s.v. "ward" *sb.*^{2} 13).

129/31–130/20 **And bycause ... suspected.** *Apology, CW 9*, 132–33.

130/6–7 **And who ... conspyracye?** The word *conspiracy* in the reign of Henry VIII usually meant in strict legal terminology that two or more persons had agreed falsely to indict another or to procure his indictment for felony. The writ of conspiracy lay against the "conspirators" in a civil action after the acquittal of the person unjustly indicted. See 33 Edward I, st. 2; 7 Henry V, c. 1; 18 Henry VI, c. 12. More's point is that the writ lay against named persons, whom the person they had unjustly indicted would have to identify positively in order to seek his civil remedy. This issue was addressed by Star Chamber in the sixteenth and early seventeenth centuries, whence sprang much of the modern criminal law in this area. See P. H. Winfield, *History of Conspiracy and the Abuse of Procedure* (Cambridge, 1921); and G. O. Sayles, *Select Cases in the Court of King's Bench,* 7 vols., Selden Society Publications, vols. 55, 57, 58, 74, 76, 82, 88 (London, 1936–1971), *3,* liv–lxxi. Alan Harding, however, has recently emphasized that the crime of conspiracy was not invented by Star Chamber and the seventeenth-century courts but was acknowledged in England in the fourteenth century by parliament ("The Origins of the Crime of Conspiracy," *Transactions of the Royal Historical Society,* 5th Series, *33,* 1983, 89–108). See note on 198/6–11.

130/31–131/5 **And then ... conscyence.** Appendix B, 358/14–24.

131/25–132/2 **Nowe yf ... this waye.** *Apology, CW 9,* 133.

132/3 **this.** Frequently used as a form of "these" from the twelfth to the sixteenth century (*OED,* "these" *dem. pron.*).

132/11 **pauyce.** That is, "shield." See *CW 12,* 105/24–106/26.

132/26–133/12 **And then ... lawe.** Appendix B, 358/24–359/4.

133/4–5 **but before ... not gyltye.** St. German means that the accused upon whose bill of indictment the grand jury had found *billa vera* was nevertheless not put to trial before them, but remitted for trial at the assizes, where another (petty) jury would give its verdict under the supervision of the trial judges. See J. S. Cockburn, *A History of English Assizes, 1558–1714* (Cambridge, 1972).

133/8–9 **wyll can ... thanke.** See note on 19/18.

133/31–32 **verse ... scole.** Perhaps More is referring to mnemonic verses like those beginning "Barbara Celarent" to distinguish the different moods and figures of syllogisms (though logic was not usually studied in grammar schools); see *CW 8,* Commentary at 346/6–7. Or perhaps he merely refers to the differences between various kinds of Latin verse. In *De inventione dialectica,* Rudolph Agricola has a chapter (1.27) entitled "De differentibus," referring to arguments based on things which differ but are not opposite or contrary to one another (Cologne, 1523; reprint Frankfurt am Main, 1967; sigs. X_1–Y_1); but only a few of the examples of such arguments are in verse. "Differentia" is also one of the predicables discussed by Porphyry in *Isagoge,* but it does not seem to be associated with verses. In his *Apology* (*CW 9,* Commentary at 59/5) More uses "pars verse" in a similarly disparaging context. See also *CW 11,* Commentary at 168/31–169/5.

134/3–4 **enforme the queste.** That is, "give evidence to the grand jury."

134/25–29 **I thynke ... lawe.** Appendix B, 358/42–359/4.

134/30 **not worthe a straw.** Whiting S815, Tilley S918.

135/2–3 **I wyll vse ... often.** More refers to the phrase "some one man" (line 5), alluding to St. German's frequent use of phrases such as "some men say."

135/18–20 **excepte ... theyr cause.** For attempts to influence locally based jurors or arbitrators in favor of parties to litigation and for remedial action by Star Chamber, see Guy, *Cardinal's Court*, pp. 32–33, 60–63, 75, 97–104, 137.

135/19–21 **countrey ... countrey.** See note on 129/7.

135/32–35 **by dylygent ... realm.** The pretrial investigatory function of the King's Council, judges, and justices of the peace is described in Elton, *Policy and Police*, pp. 10–11, 55, 111, 163, 253, 303, 312, 319–20, 337, 342, 381; Guy, *Cardinal's Court*, pp. 61–65; J. H. Langbein, *Torture and the Law of Proof: Europe and England in the Ancien Régime* (Chicago, 1977), pp. 79–82; M. L. Zell, "Early Tudor J.P.s at Work," *Archaeologia Cantiana*, 93 (1977), 125–43.

136/4 **countreys.** See note on 129/7.

136/4 **examynacyons hathe.** See note on 124/25.

136/18–20 **as in treason ... warre rered.** The exception to the rule that proceedings for treason and felony must be begun upon indictments (apart from appeals of felony—see note on 121/35) was in cases of treason when persons were declared traitors (normally posthumously) by parliamentary acts of attainder, or when martial law was proclaimed. See M. H. Keen, "Treason Trials under the Law of Arms," *Transactions of the Royal Historical Society*, 5th Series, *12* (1962), 85–103; his *The Laws of War in the Later Middle Ages* (Oxford, 1965); Elton, *Policy and Police*, pp. 263–64, 292, 297–98.

136/20–22 **by experyence ... be better.** Martial law had been proclaimed in June 1487 and May 1513, the former instance being the occasion of the Cornish rebellion and the latter being the time of one of Henry VIII's invasions of France. More's present remark concerns the pretender Perkin Warbeck's attempted invasion at Deal in Kent during July 1495. The greater part of his forces landed while Warbeck himself remained on board ship, but some 200 of his men were captured, and Warbeck hastily retreated to Ireland. Warbeck's defeated force was led by English captains named Moundford, Corbet, White, and Belt, and (among others) "Capteyn Genyn" a Frenchman, and Captain "Quyntyne" a Spaniard. They and many of their followers were executed as traitors, and their heads exhibited on poles upon London Bridge. More's memory of this episode is slightly erroneous. The relevant London chronicle (British Library, Cotton MS. Vitellius A.xvi, fols. 154v–156v) indicates that the majority of invaders (that is, most of the Englishmen) were arraigned on indictment at common law, Captain Corbet died "of Goddes Visitacion" and his wounds, and only the two foreign captains and Belt seem to have been tried by martial law and beheaded. See C. L. Kingsford, ed., *Chronicles of London* (Oxford, 1905), 205–07; *Tudor Royal Proclamations,* ed. P. L. Hughes and J. F. Larkin, 3 vols. (New Haven, 1964–69), *1,* 14–15, 106–20. All this goes to prove More's actual point (shared by Elton—see note on 136/18–20) that the Tudors invariably preferred the ordinary machinery of statute and common law to the extraordinary procedures of the law of arms when dealing with Englishmen. But aliens could not be indicted at common law unless they had been naturalized as "denizens." There was, however, a more cynical motive for adhering to statute and common law: martial law did not secure the forfeiture of the victim's lands to the Crown.

136/27–28 **I . . . I.** On such emphatic repetition see *CW 9,* 42/28–29 and Commentary.

138/7–10 **the kynges . . . iudges.** There may be a note of irony in this passage. The Tudors since 1485 had transformed the bench of bishops into a body predominantly curial rather than pastoral, and legal training together with loyal service to the Crown had become the key qualifications. Historians have even spoken of "this secularization of the bench." See R. J. Knecht, "The Episcopate and the Wars of the Roses," *University of Birmingham Historical Journal, 6* (1957–58), 108–31; and M. M. Condon, "Ruling Elites in the Reign of Henry VII," in *Patronage, Pedigree and Power in Later Medieval England,* ed. C. Ross (Gloucester, 1979), 109–12.

138/12–15 **his grace . . . euery daye.** The two nonresident aliens occupying English bishoprics in 1533, when the *Debellation* was written, were Lorenzo Campeggio, bishop of Salisbury *in commendam* (1524–1534) and Geronimo de' Ghinucci, bishop of Worcester (1522–1535). If More's allusion to "he whose attendaunce hys grace vseth moste" referred to a particular bishop, it is unlikely to have been Stephen Gardiner, bishop of Winchester, who in 1533 was still in disgrace in the wake of his answer to the Supplication against the Ordinaries in 1532. If John Stokesley, bishop of London, was meant (still possible in 1533), it is obvious why he was resident "far the moste parte of the yere" in his own diocese, and the same applies to Thomas Cranmer, archbishop of Canterbury since March 1533, though Cranmer is unlikely to be the bishop in question, since his early advancement owed as much to Anne Boleyn as to Henry VIII and since he was not yet a member of the inner ring of attendant councillors.

138/16 **verse dyfferences.** See note on 133/31–32.

139/4–6 **geste . . . agayn.** Tilley H726.

139/11–140/7 **But yet . . . growe.** *Apology, CW 9,* 134/19–135/19.

139/15 **senys.** That is, "synods" (*OED,* s.v. "sene" *sb.*³).

139/19 **For as for accuse.** The phrase "as for" is equivalent to "as to" (Visser, *1,* 331).

139/21 **perell of expensys.** That is, without any danger of having to pay costs if the person accused were acquitted. A private plantiff who failed to prove his case normally had to pay his opponent's legal costs, court fees, and travel and lodging expenses. Damages might also be payable for "wrongful vexation" (see note on 38/29).

139/26–27 **euery . . . realme.** Leets or courts-leet were manorial courts of record held once or twice (and sometimes three times) a year before the steward of the lord. They dealt mainly with small crimes, misdemeanors, public nuisances, and personal actions such as defamation. They invariably handled noncapital offenses. If the jury of presentment at a leet found evidence of a serious crime, the steward was obliged to return the presentment to the justices of *oyer et terminer* or of jail delivery. See Westminster II, 13 Edward I, c. 13; 1 Edward III, st. 2, c. 17. See also M. K. McIntosh, "Social Change and Tudor Manorial Leets," in J. A. Guy and H. G. Beale, eds., *Law and Social Change in British History* (London, 1984), pp. 73–85. For an example of a draft charge to be given to the jury of a leet in 1539, see PRO, SP 1/156, fol. 186 (*LP 14,* 2, p. 370). This charge still included "Item, if any do keep erroneous opinions against the Sacrament. Item, if [any say that] priests [may have] wives or that they who have avowed chastity may marry, [or say that] masses and auricular confession [be] unnecessary."

140/17 **questes.** That is, juries of presentment.

140/20–36 **And one . . . abiured.** Since this episode ended in the suspect's abjuration, it did not become a *cause célèbre* and has not been traced. It was probably a case in the diocese of London. For More's work against heresy as lord chancellor, see Guy, *Public Career,* pp. 165–74, and *Confutation, CW 8,* 28–40.

140/26 **new fasshyon.** The *OED* does not give this phrase used as an adjective. The word "of" may have been omitted after "fasshyon" on the analogy of such phrases as "this manner man."

141/13–19 **And thus . . . neuer a whyt.** Appendix B, 359/5–11.

141/32 **band dogges.** A dog tied or chained up, either to guard a house or because of its ferocity, usually a mastiff.

142/25 **iolte hed.** A heavy, clumsy head. The origin of the phrase is obscure, and More's use is the first recorded example (*OED*, s.v. "jolt head").

143/11–12 **in his boke . . . left of.** Division, *CW 9*, 188–91.

143/14–15 **.xv. chapiter . . . Bizance.** Appendix B, 355/21–359/11.

143/21–25 **that . . . forfaytoure.** Actions on penal statutes were begun by the attorney general, royal informers, or private persons. These statutes invariably prescribed fines or forfeitures of which half went to the Crown, and the other half to the informer. See DeLloyd J. Guth, "Exchequer Law Enforcement, 1485–1509," Ph.D. dissertation, University of Pittsburgh, 1967; G. R. Elton, *Star Chamber Stories* (London, 1958), chap. 4. The statutes against excess apparel were numbered among the sumptuary laws. See, for example, 10 Edward III, st. 3; 24 Henry VIII, c. 13.

143/34–144/5 **& a statut . . . they wyll.** More refers to the statute 3 Henry VII, c. 1. For proceedings against rioters by information before the King's Council in Star Chamber under Henry VII, see Hobart, Attorney General *v.* Brandesby et al., PRO, STAC 2/2/164–65, 204, 209; STAC 2/20/27; STAC 2/22/134, 286. See also C. G. Bayne and W. H. Dunham, eds., *Select Cases in the Council of Henry VII*, Selden Society Publications, vol. 75 (London, 1958), pp. lix, cxxx–cxxxiii; and Guy, *Cardinal's Court*, pp. 18–19 and 149, n. 155. Bayne believed that Hobart, Attorney General *v.* Brandesby et al. was a prosecution taken before a special conciliar tribunal established by 3 Henry VII, c. 1, rather than before the King's Council. The distinction is negligible, since the examinations in this case were, without exception, taken down by Robert Rydon, clerk of the King's Council in Star Chamber. Previous statutes against riot were 17 Richard II, c. 8; 13 Henry IV, c. 7; 2 Henry V, st. 1, c. 8; 8 Henry VI, c. 14. It was unusual, however, for the Crown to initiate Star Chamber prosecutions for riot or any other offenses before the middle of the sixteenth century. "Even in cases in which the law gave the Council specific jurisdiction, it often preferred to leave the trial and punishment of rioters to the courts of common law" (Bayne and Dunham, p. cxxxii). For procedure in Star Chamber by official information in the reign of Henry VIII, see Guy, *Cardinal's Court*, pp. 72–78.

144/17 **to them.** That is, "in addition to the accusers."

144/24–34 **was thoughte . . . persons.** See notes on 114/1–16, 114/19–20, and 114/21. The patriarchs of Constantinople, Jerusalem, Anti-

och, and Alexandria were represented, but the Greek bishops gener-
ally did not attend. Innocent III had previously stressed that the resto-
ration of the ecclesiastical unity of East and West could be achieved
only through submission to Roman obedience. See A. Luchaire, *Le
Concile de Latran et la réforme de l'église* (Paris, 1908), pp. 10–11; A.
Fliche, C. Thouzellier, and Y. Azais, *La chrétienté romaine, 1198–1274*
(Histoire de l'église, *10*, Paris, 1950), pp. 194–96; *The Councils of the
Church*, ed. H. J. Margull (Philadelphia, 1966), pp. 140–45.

145/2–3 **And this realm . . . strengthed it.** See the heresy statutes in
CW 9, Appendix C.

145/32 **lurkes lanys.** See note on 88/16–17.

146/6–7 **His .xvi. chapyter . . . diuisyon.** *Salem and Bizance*, Appendix
B, 359/13–32; *Division, CW 9*, 188–89.

146/8–9 **the lawe . . . perag. Licet.** *Sexti Decretales* 5.2.8 (*CIC 2*, 1072).
"Licet vero periuri a testimonio etiam post poenitentiam repellantur, si
tamen ii, qui, coram inquisitoribus iurantes tam de se quam de aliis
super facto haeresis dicere veritatem, eam celando deierent, et
postmodum velint corrigere dictum suum, contra se ac alios suos com-
plices deponendo: quum crimen huiusmodi sit exceptum, si ex man-
ifestis indiciis apparuerit, tales non animi levitate, aut odii fomite, seu
corruptione pecuniae, sed zelo fidei orthodoxae dictum suum velle
corrigere, ac modo quae prius tacuerant revelare: in favorem fidei, nisi
aliud obsistat, stari debet tam contra se quam contra reliquos attesta-
tionibus eorundem." See *CW 9*, Commentary at 135/23–24.

146/22 **chapyter In fidei fauorem.** *Sexti Decretales* 5.2.5 (*CIC 2*, 1071).
"In fidei favorem concedimus, ut in negotio inquisitionis haereticae
pravitatis excommunicati et participes vel socii criminis ad testi-
monium admittantur, praesertim in probationum aliarum defectum,
contra haereticos, credentes, fautores, receptatores et defensores
eorum, si ex verisimilibus coniecturis, et ex numero testium aut per-
sonarum tam deponentium, quam eorum, contra quos deponitur,
qualitate, ac aliis circumstantiis sic testificantes falsa non dicere praesu-
mantur." See *CW 9*, Commentary at 135/21.

146/24 **wytnesse.** See note on 99/32–35.

146/32–147/17 **This pyece . . . more clere.** *Apology, CW 9*, 136/5–28.

146/33–34 **I haue . . . dyaloge.** See *A Dialogue concerning Heresies, CW
6*, 260–64.

147/4 **wytnesse.** See note on 99/32–35.

147/6 **other . . . felonye.** That is, "other single felonies as well." One
would expect "felonye" to be plural, but the preceding adjective seems
to have attracted it to the singular.

147/29-31 **yet the makers . . . saued harmelesse.** The source of St.
German's thought upon the rights of innocent persons in chapter 16 of
Salem and Bizance (especially 360/9-361/25, below) was probably Sir
John Fortescue. In *De laudibus legum Anglie* Fortescue compared certain
points of English and Roman law to demonstrate which of them was
superior. Fortescue criticized defects in the Roman procedure of proof
by witnesses and claimed that these evils were avoided in the English
common-law system of accusation and trial by sworn juries. In chapter
27 he argued that procedure in English criminal cases was neither
cruel nor inhuman, and that it assured the maximum protection to the
innocent. After outlining the procedure, Fortescue opined: "Who,
then, in England can die unjustly for a crime, when he can have so
many aids in favour of his life, and none save his neighbours, good and
faithful men, against whom he has no manner of exception, can condemn him? I should, indeed, prefer twenty guilty men to escape death
through mercy, than one innocent to be condemned unjustly. Nevertheless, it cannot be supposed that a suspect accused in this form can
escape punishment, when his life and habits would thereafter be a
terror to them who acquitted him of his crime. In this process nothing
is cruel, nothing inhuman; an innocent man cannot suffer in body or
members. Hence he will not fear the calumny of his enemies because
he will not be tortured at their pleasure. Under this law, therefore, life
is quiet and secure." *De laudibus legum Anglie*, ed. and trans. S. B.
Chrimes (Cambridge, 1949), pp. 63-65. The *De laudibus* was not
printed until Edward Whitechurch's edition of 1545-46: *Prenobilis
Militis Forescu de Politica Administratione et Legibus Civilibus Florentissimi
Regni Anglie Commentarius* (London, *STC* 11193). The treatise was,
however, circulating in manuscript at the end of the fifteenth century
and in the early sixteenth century (Chrimes, pp. lxxvii–lxxxv). We may
reasonably assume that St. German would have read the work in a
manuscript copy at the Inns of Court. See also Richard Marius, *Thomas
More* (New York, 1984), pp. 410, 436-37.

148/13-17 **I can not se . . . same mater.** Appendix B, 360/17-21.

149/4-5 **But hereuppon . . . felonye.** See *Apology, CW 9*, 136-37.

149/11-15 **For I neuer . . . be trew?** It was, however, occasionally argued up to Henry VII's reign that the jury was supposed to proceed
upon its own knowledge if the evidence presented at the bar was in-

complete, although the chance that jurors would have private knowledge was becoming small. See *Spelman's Reports*, 2, introduction, pp. 109–12.

149/20 **wytnesse.** See note on 99/32–35.

149/27–150/12 **And yf . . . courtes.** Appendix B, 361/5–25.

149/29 **enquest.** The inquest at common law (Latin *inquisitio*) was an inquiry by jurors in civil and criminal cases. The jurors were regarded not as witnesses, but as judges of fact. Upon evidence adduced on either side concerning the facts the matter was referred to their decision, which was reported to the court as the verdict of the jury. Judgment was then pronounced in accordance with the verdict. No one was supposed to give evidence to jurors except openly at the bar.

149/33–150/1 **tho . . . tho.** More correctly reproduces St. German's somewhat archaic form meaning "those" (*OED*, s.v. "tho" 3).

150/2 **collaterall wytnes.** This is not a technical legal term, but a term of convenience used by St. German to distinguish witnesses in the modern sense from jurors, who in the Middle Ages were regarded as witnesses, as St. German had already pointed out in *Salem and Bizance* (Appendix B, 360/27–33). More expressly states in the *Debellation* that jurors were not to be regarded as witnesses, but as judges of fact (149/4–20). By "witnesses" he did not mean jurors, but St. German had been using the word *witness* to mean both "juror" and "witness." To clarify his meaning in *Salem and Bizance,* St. German had qualified "witness" in the modern sense by the word "collateral" (Appendix B, 360/27–361/25). It is this usage that More here quotes twice in the *Debellation.* "Collaterall wytnes" is used by St. German to signify witnesses descended from the same stock as jurors, but who are not judges of fact, as jurors are. Like collateral kinsmen, they descend from the same stock, but differ because they spring from a different branch of that stock. Blackstone wrote of collateral consanguinity: "collateral relations [agree] with the lineal in this, that they descend from the same stock or ancestor; but differing in this, that they do not descend one from the other." (*Commentaries*, 2, 242). A "collaterall wytnes," a person giving testimony to a court of law, and a juror are equally descended from the "jurors" of the medieval period who informed the inquest or gave verdicts from their own knowledge, thus acting as "witnesses."

151/5–10 **And all be it . . . court.** For examples of this procedure as described by More, see Guy, *Cardinal's Court,* pp. 61–63; Elton, *Policy and Police,* pp. 317–21.

151/16–21 **For yf . . . sayenge therin.** Appendix B, 361/15–19.

151/17 **collaterall wytnesses.** See note on 150/2.

153/18 **bereth.** That is, "supports."

153/27–28 **I wyl . . . dowte.** The rules of evidence in treason trials in Henry VIII's reign are admirably described by Elton, *Policy and Police,* pp. 293–326.

153/37–154/2 **But as . . . felony.** For notes of cases of open perjury at the bar reported to the Court of Star Chamber, see Ellesmere MS 2652, at the Huntington Library, fols. 10v, 11, 17v, 18v.

154/24–28 **so may . . . credence.** See note on 146/8–9.

154/32–155/5 **For though . . . attaynted.** Attaint was the remedy at common law when a petty (that is, trial) jury gave a verdict contrary to the evidence. Its application was originally limited but was extended by the following statutes: Westminster I, 3 Edward I, c. 38; 1 Edward III, st. 1, c. 6; 5 Edward III, c. 7; 28 Edward III, c. 8; 34 Edward III, c. 7. The aggrieved party obtained a writ of attaint, upon which the allegedly false verdict was tried by a new jury of twenty-four more substantial persons. If this jury found the verdict false, it was reversed and the original jurors punished by "perpetual infamy" and fines to be divided between the Crown and injured party. This punishment was prescribed by 11 Henry VII, c. 24, revived by 23 Henry VIII, c. 3, and made perpetual by 13 Elizabeth I, c. 25. These statutes ameliorated earlier stricter punishments at common law. Juries might be attainted whether they found contrary to the evidence or beyond its reasonable boundaries. Yet actions were difficult and expensive; in 1522 a defendant who sought relief in Chancery against a verdict claimed that "atteynt . . . is soo chargeable that your seid oratour is not able to sue the same atteynt." J. H. Baker notes that "many attaints were begun, but so far only one successful attaint has been noticed in the early sixteenth century" (*Spelman's Reports,* 2, introduction, pp. 118–19). Attaints were not akin to modern appeals: the party was not allowed to reopen his case at large on the facts, because he could adduce in evidence only what had already been given in evidence during the initial action.

155/8–12 **yᵗ the iudges . . . punysshed therfore.** See Guy, *Cardinal's Court,* pp. 17, 18, 20, 32–33, 52, 53, 60–61, 63, 75.

155/20–25 **Thys is . . . shewed.** See *Division, CW* 9, 189.

155/28–156/21 **Syth euyll folke . . . chaunge.** *Apology, CW* 9, 136/19–137/10.

156/8–9 **a woulfe . . . skynne.** Whiting W474, Tilley W614. Cf. Matt. 7:15.

156/26–157/8 **Nowe . . . money.** Appendix B, 361/39–362/14.

159/4–8 **In so mych . . . lawe.** Appendix B, 362/14–18.

159/4 **parag. Licet.** See note on 146/8–9.

159/20–27 **What the makers . . . there ys none.** Appendix B, 362/18–27.

161/1–9 **And therfore . . . offens.** Appendix B, 362/27–35.

162/35–163/20 **And where . . . innocent.** Appendix B, 362/36–363/18.

164/3–7 **But surely . . . offyce.** John Fineux (O.E. and O.F. *fenix* for "phoenix") was a Gray's Inn lawyer, appointed king's serjeant on October 17, 1489, and chief justice of King's Bench on November 24, 1495. He died on November 17, 1525, and was buried near the altar of St. Thomas in Canterbury cathedral. See *Spelman's Reports*, 2, introduction, pp. 358–59, 386. For his influence on King's Bench justice and his contacts with More's family group, see *Spelman's Reports*, 2, introduction, pp. 54–57. The statement here attributed by More to Fineux found an echo in Manley's case (1544), when one Saunders, serjeant at law, said that "the office of a judge is to execute justice according to his conscience" (*Spelman's Reports*, 2, introduction, p. 41). The legal context is discussed in *Spelman's Reports*, 2, introduction, pp. 37–43. See also More's remarks in William Roper, *The Lyfe of Sir Thomas Moore, knighte*, ed. Elsie Vaughan Hitchcock, Early English Text Society, Original Series no. 197 (Oxford, 1935; reprint, 1957), p. 45.

164/15–19 **the lawes . . . credence.** Canon law prohibited not only perjurers and those who had given false testimony from being witnesses but also various other sorts of criminals such as murderers, thieves, rapists, and adulterers (*Gratiani decretum* 2.3.5.9; *CIC 1*, 516). A later canon allowed reformed criminals of good behavior to be witnesses, unless they had been convicted of perjury (*Decretales Gregorii IX*, 2.20.54; *CIC 2*, 340).

165/6–11 **And ferthermore . . . that place.** Appendix B, 363/19–24.

165/17–27 **And therby . . . so to do.** Appendix B, 363/24–35.

165/21–22 **And so . . . wolfe.** Matt. 7:15.

166/37–167/3 **where he spendeth . . . reason.** Appendix B, 363/36–364/1.

167/9 **His .xvii. . . . folio .lxii.** Appendix B, 364/13–368/35.

167/13–14 **and that . . . fo. 100.** *Apology, CW9*, 48/4, 60/5, 60/36.

167/22–23 **where as . . . contrary.** See note on 68/3–6.

168/10–169/20 **And one . . . they do not.** Appendix B, 364/40–366/3.

168/10–11 **in the .viii. . . . treatyse thus.** *Division, CW 9*, 191–93.

168/20–22 **by a wrytte . . . answere.** Excommunication was akin to ecclesiastical outlawry. If citations failed to produce an appearance in an ecclesiastical court, the offender was publicly excommunicated. If that had no effect, the lay power came to the aid of the church. When the excommunicate had not sought absolution within forty days, the ordinary would signify this to the Crown (see PRO, C 85/1–217), and a writ *de excommunicato capiendo* was directed to the sheriff to arrest the contumacious excommunicate. The offender was then kept in prison until he made his submission. This procedure was settled by the twelfth century. See Pollock and Maitland, *1*, 478–79.

168/28 **Clementinis . . . querela.** *Clementinae* 5.3.1 (*CIC* 2, 1181–82), approved by the Council of Vienne (1311–1312). The canon was intended to prevent both laxity and excess in the suppression of heretics. It provided that either the bishop (or his delegate) or the papally appointed inquisitors, acting independently, could summon, arrest, detain (using shackles or manacles if necessary), and investigate heretics. But both the bishop and the inquisitors had to act together to place them in strict confinement ("Duro tamen tradere carceri sive arcto, qui magis ad poenam quam ad custodiam videatur"), to subject them to torture, or to pass sentence on them. The canon also made provisions to ensure the character and behavior of guards in prisons for heretics. Finally, it provided automatic excommunication for anyone, and three years' suspension for a bishop, who either neglected to prosecute a suspected heretic or falsely charged anyone with heresy. See the Introduction, pp. xlix–l.

168/29–32 **it was enacted . . . scholys.** This refers to 2 Henry IV, c. 15. See Houlbrooke, pp. 216–17; and *CW 9*, Commentary at 151/18–19, and *CW9*, Appendix C.

168/32 **holde . . . scholys.** See note on 71/29.

169/9–10 **in his apologye . . . treatyse.** *Apology, CW 9*, 150–55.

169/24–25 **take . . . fo. 232.** *Apology, CW 9*, 151–55.

170/3–5 **syth . . . London.** See the Introduction, pp. lvi, lxxxix–xc, and *CW 9*, 115–16.

170/10–12 **and the complayntes . . . false.** See note on 68/3–6.

170/20–21 **For they be . . . the tother.** There were two puisne justices of King's Bench in addition to the chief justice until 1522, when a third puisne justice was added to bring the bench to the same size as that of Common Pleas. See *Spelman's Reports*, 2, introduction, p. 352.

170/35 **base court.** An inferior court of justice, one that is not a court of record—for example, a court baron.

171/1–2 **and yᵗ in writtes . . . crowne.** If a litigant could find an error in "the record, process or giving of judgment" against him, he could obtain a writ of error to remove the record of his case into a superior court for further examination. See *Spelman's Reports*, 2, introduction, pp. 119–23. The pleas of the Crown were criminal proceedings on indictments or on appeals of felony and embraced the most serious criminal offenses, namely treason, homicide, arson, rape, robbery, burglary, grand larceny, and escape from prison. See Pollock and Maitland, 2, 453–511; *Spelman's Reports*, 2, introduction, pp. 299–300; W. Staunford, *Les Plees del Coron* (London, Richard Tottell, 1557; *STC²* 23219).

171/26–33 **Nor yet . . . worke.** Appendix B, 366/3–11.

172/9–173/8 **In thys processe . . . they be suche.** *Apology, CW 9*, 151–52.

172/30–31 **proue . . . yet.** That is, "until he proves the present judges worse than he has shown up till now."

174/8–175/10 **And he sayeth . . . well ware.** Appendix B, 366/11–367/6.

174/22–23 **that is to say . . . treatyse.** *Division, CW 9*, 188–91.

174/31–33 **That he ys . . . assygne.** *Apology, CW 9*, 153.

175/24–176/2 **And though . . . kepynge.** *Division, CW 9*, 191; *Apology, CW 9*, 142.

176/19–24 **and then . . . fayth.** *Division, CW 9*, 190–91; *Apology, CW 9*, 140.

177/1–4 **Naye . . . dedely.** Appendix B, 367/1–5. More here paraphrases St. German's words.

177/23–24 **wouchsaufe . . . folio .238.** *Apology, CW* 9, 142–43.

177/31–178/8 **And farthermore . . . effecte.** Appendix B, 367/7–18.

178/21–179/3 **Then sayth . . . so or not.** Appendix B, 367/18–35.

178/24–25 **For in euery profe . . . at the leste.** St. German refers to the Roman-canon law of proof in criminal cases where blood sanctions (death or physical maiming) could be imposed. The rules were three-fold: (1) the court could convict and condemn an offender on the evidence of two eyewitnesses to the gravamen of the crime; (2) if there were not two eyewitnesses, the court could convict only on the basis of the accused's own confession; (3) circumstantial evidence was insufficient for conviction and condemnation, no matter how compelling (J. H. Langbein, *Torture and the Law of Proof: Europe and England in the Ancien Régime*, Chicago, 1977, pp. 4–5, 49–50). Although English law permitted traitors, and occasionally felons, to be convicted on the testimony of a single witness—a fact proved well enough at More's own trial—normally the Crown "did not like to proceed on so slender a basis" (Elton, *Policy and Police*, pp. 308–10). See the Introduction, pp. lxv–lxvi.

178/33–179/2 **And yf it be true . . . Pharyseis.** That is, "if it is true that men wrongly say the clergy are corrupt, clergymen can correct and eradicate that error, as long as ("but") they do not maliciously slander the laity and hypocritically justify themselves like the Pharisees." For the Pharisees' malicious slander against Christ and his disciples, see Matt. 9:34; 12:2, 24; 15:1–2.

179/8 **that themself . . . spoken.** See note on 178/24–25.

179/23–25 **that in farre . . . fiftene yere.** More's statement is hardly borne out by the available facts, though it is unclear what is meant by "in farre the moste parte." See the Introduction, pp. lvi, lxxxix–xc, and *CW* 9, 115–16.

179/31 **the mountenaunce . . . strawes.** Whiting S810–13, Tilley S917. See note on 134/30.

180/5–9 **that though the treuth . . . sayeng.** Appendix B, 367/27–31.

180/11 **theyr helpe . . . them?** That is, "to help those that belie them."

180/18–21 **can neuer . . . euyll.** The sense requires that "without lettynge heresyes growe and go forth" mean "without hindering heresies from growing and going forth," though More and the writers of his time would regularly write "to" before "growe" (Visser, 2, 460; *OED*, s.v. "let" *v.*² 1b). Or "without" could be a misprint for "with." Perhaps the sentence originally ended simply "can neuer appease without lettynge heresyes growe and go forth" and "without" was not changed when the prepositional phrase was combined with the new ending "but yf . . . they sholde dysplease god / and . . . shold them selfe rather do euyll than let lewde folke speke euyll."

180/27–181/3 **But yet . . . trouth.** *Apology, CW* 9, 153–54.

181/10–23 **Then sayth . . . .xlvi. chapyter.** Appendix B, 367/36–368/6.

181/29–182/29 **These are lo my wordes . . . effecte.** *Apology, CW*9, 154–55.

183/10–31 **Now veryly . . . rehersed.** Appendix B, 368/14–35.

184/6–7 **the trouth . . . counsayle.** See note on 68/3–6.

184/15 **not . . . ryshe.** See note on 87/27.

184/19–21 **that yf . . . better.** The law was changed in March 1534 by 25 Henry VIII, c. 14. See the Introduction, pp. lxii–lxvii.

184/24 **His .xviii. . . . fo. lxix.** Appendix B, 368/36–371/17.

184/25–28 **the ca. vt inquisitionis . . . heresye.** *Sexti Decretales* 5.2.18 (*CIC* 2, 1077). The relevant part of this chapter is as follows: "Prohibemus quoque districtius potestatibus, dominis temporalibus et rectoribus eorundemque officialibus supra dictis, ne ipsi de hoc crimine, quum mere sit ecclesiasticum, quoquo modo cognoscant vel iudicent, sive captos pro eodem crimine absque dictorum episcoporum sive inquisitorum, aut saltem alterius eorundem licentia vel mandato a carcere liberent, aut exsecutionem, sibi pro huiusmodi crimine a dioecesano vel inquisitoribus seu inquisitore iniunctam, prompte, prout ad suum spectat officium, facere seu adimplere detrectent, vel alias dioecesanorum aut inquisitorum iudicium, sententiam seu processum directe vel indirecte impedire praesumant." The chapter goes on to excommunicate secular rulers who obstruct the bishop and the inquisitors in the prosecution of heresy.

184/28–29 **And vppon . . . dyuysyon.** *Division, CW* 9, 190–91.

184/30–31 **Summa Rosella sayth so to.** According to Baptista de Salis (Trovamala), *Summa [rosella] casuum [conscientiae]* (Nürnberg, April 14, 1488), sig. o₂, the fourth case incurring excommunication is as follows: "Quartus [casus]. domini temporales qui cognoscunt de offitio inquisitionis: aut captos liberarent: excommunicati sunt. extra eo. vt inquisitionis .li. vj. Et hoc intellige: siue principaliter: siue incidenter cognoscant. puta quia de causa principali cognoscentes: faciunt capi hereticum. Incidenter. puta quia fecerant eum capi alia de causa. sed incidenter de hoc inquisierunt." See note on 83/14–15 and *CW 9*, Commentary at 138/16–17 and 146/29.

184/32–33 **al stewardes in letys.** See note on 139/26–27.

185/2–3 **I saye . . . they do so.** *Apology, CW 9*, 134–35.

185/7–8 **at the makynge. . . statute.** That is, 2 Henry V, st. 1, c. 7. See below, note on 185/29–186/4. The *Summa rosella*, which was written and published in the last two decades of the fifteenth century, was not available to the enactors of the statute.

185/15–22 **the sayde chapyter . . . knowledge.** This is quite clear from the very chapter cited by the *Summa rosella* and by St. German. The opening sentence requires secular rulers, in the defense of the faith, to obey diocesan bishops and the inquisitors for the crime of heresy appointed by the pope and, at the request of the bishop or inquisitors, to seek out heretics, arrest them, turn them over to the bishop for trial, and to punish them if they are convicted: "universos saeculi potestates . . . requirimus et monemus, ut . . . pro defensione fidei dioecesanis episcopis et inquisitoribus haereticae pravitatis, a sede apostolica deputatis aut in posterum deputandis, pareant, et intendant in haereticorum . . . investigatione, captione ac custodia diligenti, quum ab eis fuerint requisiti, et ut praefatas personas pestiferas in potestatem seu carcerem episcoporum aut inquisitorum . . . ducant vel duci faciant sine mora, ubi per viros catholicos a praefatis episcopis seu inquisitoribus . . . teneantur, donec eorum negotium per ecclesiae iudicium terminetur . . ." (*CIC* 2, 1076–77). Indeed, the *Summa rosella* (see note on 184/30–31) cites this earlier part of the chapter immediately before the fourth case of excommunication cited by St. German: "Tercius [casus]. rectores impedientes vel non iuuantes episcopos et inquisitores in inquisitione haereticorum et credentium eis et fautorum et receptatorum: sunt excommunicati. extra eo. vt inquisitionis .li. vj." (sig. o₁v).

185/29–186/4 **but the knowledge . . . charge.** By 2 Henry IV, c. 15, sheriffs, mayors, and bailiffs were to assist the spiritual judges against heretics, and 2 Henry V, st. 1, c. 7 expressly commanded King's Bench justices, assize judges, and justices of the peace to initiate routine investigatory proceedings in their courts against heretics and their abettors.

However, any resulting indictments for heresy validated by grand juries were not to be taken in evidence when the accused was duly surrendered to the jurisdiction of the ecclesiastical courts, but were to be "for Information before the Spiritual Judges against such Persons so indicted, but that the Ordinaries commence their Process against such Persons indicted in the same Manner as though no Indictment were, having no Regard to such Indictments" (*CW 9*, Appendix C, pp. 259–60). See the Introduction, pp. lii–liii, 139/25–28, and note on 139/26–27.

185/29–30 **holdynge . . . vpon yt.** That is, "having jurisdiction, trying an action."

186/5–8 **by the hygh . . . Angelica.** *Summa angelica*, like *Summa rosella*, was a favorite source of St. German's. It was a confessor's manual compiled by Angelus Carletus de Clavasio. See *CW 9*, xl, xliii, xlvi, and Commentary at 146/29; *Doctor and Student*, pp. xxviii, 237, 241, 242, 245, 252, 265, 271, 274–79. More's irony here stresses that such practical handbooks for parish priests are hardly the best sources for the clarification of canon law.

186/11–18 **And to thys . . . chyrche.** Appendix B, 369/14–22. St. German resumed his argument on the conflict of laws in *A Treatise concerning divers of the Constitutions Provincial and Legantines*, published in 1535 (*STC²* 24236).

187/5–6 **For the parlyament . . . inquysycyons.** That is, 2 Henry V, st. 1, c. 7. See *CW 9*, Appendix C, pp. 257–60.

187/13 **No but . . . dyuisyon.** That is, the canon law prohibiting lay courts from taking jurisdiction over heresy cases. See note on 184/25–28.

187/21–22 **For as for that . . . vnresonable.** See note on 28/24–25.

187/23–29 **As long as . . . occasyon of it.** Appendix B, 369/28–35.

187/30 **as dede . . . nayle.** Whiting D352, Tilley D567.

188/20–28 **And therfore . . . good.** Appendix B, 369/19–28.

189/9–16 **If he fere . . . bokes haue.** More is suggesting that the Pacifier is a person who impedes or does not help the bishops and inquisitors in searching out heretics and thus falls under excommunication according to the *Summa rosella*. See note on 185/15–22.

189/21–190/2 **And therfore . . . excused.** Appendix B, 369/35–370/9.

189/33 **to saye.** The reading "saye" in *1533* is a misprint for "to sey" in *Salem and Bizance*, Appendix B, 370/5.

190/24–25 **vnto all lawes . . . medle wyth.** Though "vnto" can mean "with regard to" (*OED*, s.v. "unto" 19), the construction combining "vnto" and "wyth" seems mixed, as if More had originally intended "respond vnto."

191/12–22 **And thys . . . lyes for one.** *Apology, CW 9*, 60/21–33.

192/32–35 **and saith . . . shew them.** Appendix B, 371/11–15.

193/17–194/6 **Hys other . . . euyll.** *Apology, CW 9*, 96/20–97/13.

194/21–27 **the very . . . handes.** See note on 185/15–22.

194/33–195/6 **In his .xix. chapiter . . . Mortuaryes.** Appendix B, 371/18–372/42.

195/4–5 **the puttyng . . . iudges.** The conventing of criminous clerks exclusively before ecclesiastical judges in cases of murder or felony was a privilege the English church had secured against royal law in the wake of the Becket dispute. If an accused was claimed as an ordained clerk by the ordinary, the secular judge was to surrender him to undergo the process of canonical purgation. However, the privilege was under attack from common lawyers in the fourteenth and fifteenth centuries, and directly from the Crown after 1485. In particular, a statute of 1512, 4 Henry VIII, c. 2, withdrew the privilege of ecclesiastical trial from clergy not in the three higher orders of priest, deacon, and subdeacon in cases of murder and robbery in a church, highway, or dwelling-house. This act was acclaimed by common lawyers as the means to bring criminals to justice, but it provoked the most heated clash between church and state in England before the Reformation. See note on 195/7–9.

195/5–6 **& the statute . . . cedua.** That is, 45 Edward III, c. 3. See *Doctor and Student*, pp. lxiv–lxvi, 300–14; *CW 9*, xlv–xlvi, 198–99, and Commentary at 144/18–19. St. German later discussed this statute in *The Additions of Salem and Bizance* (London, Berthelet, 1534: *STC²* 21585), sig. B₅; *A Treatise concerning the Power of the Clergye and the Laws of the Realme* (London, T. Godfray, [1535?]; *STC²* 21588), chap. 4; *A treatise concerning diuers of the Constitutions Prouincial and Legantines* (London, T. Godfray, [1535]; *STC²* 24236), chap. 14. See Guy, *St. German*, pp. 28, 133. Tithes of timber had been a long-standing area of legal dispute in England. On this question, J. L. Barton is the authority: "It was all very well to prohibit the exaction of such tithes by statute, but the convenient ambiguity of the term *silva caedua* rendered any such prohibition extraordinarily difficult to enforce effectively. *Silva caedua* had been defined by Archbishop Stratford, following the Accursian Gloss, as all wood grown for cutting: a definition which might be construed, according to the needs of the moment, to comprehend only such wood as was specifically grown in order that it might be cut, or to include all wood which the landowner might regard as available for cutting if he should have need of it—in effect, all wood whatsoever. When in 1348 the Commons complained of Stratford's constitution for the payment of tithe of *silva caedua*, the clergy informed the King, somewhat disingenuously, it is to be feared, that the constitution was only applicable to tithes of underwood. Lyndewode is quite clear that *silva caedua* includes timber, and the repeated complaints of the Commons suggest that the English canonists had adopted this opinion at a much earlier period. Whether or not *silva caedua* included timber, however, it certainly also included a great deal that was not timber on any possible view of the question. . . . In 1410, counsel can cite the statute of *Silva Caedua* as an example of a statute which may be regarded as invalid because it has never been put in force. Whether or not this statement be strictly accurate, it could hardly have been made unless the statute had been very generally disregarded, and the amount of space which St. German devoted to the controversy shows that the issue was still a live one in his day. To make the statute effective required a procedural change, which came some ten years after St. German wrote. The King's Bench held that the respondent to a libel for tithe of *silva caedua* might obtain a prohibition by averring against the libel that he was in fact being sued for tithes of timber" (*Doctor and Student*, pp. lxiv–lxv).

195/6 **the statute of Mortuaryes.** That is, 21 Henry VIII, c. 6. The act established scale-fees for mortuaries. A mortuary was a sort of ecclesiastical heriot, the church claiming the best article belonging to the deceased as a burial fee. See Lehmberg, pp. 91–92; Guy, *Public Career*, pp. 117–21, 139.

195/7–9 **As for conuentyng . . . hyghnes.** Leo X declared in the Fifth Lateran Council on May 5, 1514, that according to the law of God as well as that of man, laymen had no jurisdiction over churchmen. In early February 1515 Richard Kidderminster, abbot of Winchcombe, preached a sermon at Paul's Cross claiming that the 1512 act limiting ecclesiastical immunity in England (see note on 195/4–5) was against the law of God and the liberties of the church, and that its makers, both ecclesiastical and lay, were subject to censure (that is, possible excommunication if they were obdurate). This is the "sermon" which More says "made the mater come in communicacion before the kynges hyghnes." He refers to the important debates at Blackfriars and Baynard's Castle in November 1515, terminated when Henry VIII himself declared: "By the ordinance and sufferance of God we are king of England, and the kings of England in time past have never had any superior but God alone. Wherefore know you well that we shall maintain the right of our crown and of our temporal jurisdiction as well in this point as in all others." Henry had studied the maxim that a king who does not recognize a superior is free from outside jurisdiction. Yet the material point here was that he spoke in the context of a judges' opinion that the writ of *praemunire facias* ran against all members of convocation who appealed to Roman canons not demonstrably based upon divine law or approved in advance by the king. In other words, Henry defined an aspect of his royal power in 1515 in terms of his right to monitor the reception of canon law, so that his "superiority" was already deemed to embrace denial of the pope's right to infringe his territorial sovereignty on the basis of the Petrine commission. The issue of criminous clerks thus anticipated the main jurisdictional disputes of the 1530s. See Pollock and Maitland, *1*, 441–56; R. Foreville, *L'église et la royauté sous Henri II Plantagenet, 1154–1189* (Paris, 1943); C. R. Cheney, "The Punishment of Felonious Clerks," *English Historical Review, 51* (1936), 215–36; *Spelman's Reports, 2*, introduction, pp. 327–34; A. F. Pollard, *Wolsey* (London, 1929), pp. 27–52; Guy, "Henry VIII and the Praemunire Manoeuvres," pp. 497–98; *CW 9*, Appendix B, pp. 225–37; Richard J. Schoeck, "Common Law and Canon Law in the Writings of Thomas More: The Affair of Richard Hunne," *Proceedings of the Third International Congress of Medieval Canon Law, Monumenta Iuris Canonici*, Series C, Subsidia *4* (1971), 237–54.

195/15–16 **And diuerse statutes . . . poynt.** The statute 4 Henry VIII, c. 2 (see note on 195/4–5), was reenacted and confirmed by 22 Henry VIII, c. 2. More rigorous legislation was then passed in 1532. By 23 Henry VIII, c. 1, the existing law was tightened, and ordained offenders were allowed to be admitted to purgation in ecclesiastical courts only on condition that two sureties for their future behavior were taken before local justices of the peace. Otherwise they were to suffer life imprisonment. In addition, the bishops were empowered and encouraged to degrade criminous clerks and to surrender them back to King's Bench as laymen for sentence of death. By 23 Henry VIII, c. 11, it was made a felony for convicted clerks to break prison. These rules were continued, reinforced, or perpetuated by 25 Henry VIII, cc. 3, 6; 27

Henry VIII, c. 4; 28 Henry VIII, cc. 1, 2, 6, 15; 32 Henry VIII, c. 3. Complete equality before the law came in 1536 by 28 Henry VIII c. 1, the final section of which enacted that ordained persons "shall from henceforth stand and be under the same pains and dangers for the offences contained in any of the said statutes . . . as other persons not being within holy orders." See *Spelman's Reports, 2,* introduction, p. 334.

195/24–25 **the constitucion . . . Silua cedua.** This constitution had been promulgated in 1342 by John Stratford, archbishop of Canterbury. See Lyndewode, *Proviniciale,* book 3, title 16, "De decimis." Cf. *CW 9,* Commentary at 144/18–19.

195/26–34 **I wolde not . . . remember one.** The issue of tithes of timber, however, was far more sensitive than the number of actual cases in the courts might lead us to suppose. See *Doctor and Student,* pp. lxv–lxvi. In fact, tithe litigation generally in the church courts had shrunk to a mere trickle by the middle of the 1530s, but increased in the wake of 27 Henry VIII, c. 20 and 32 Henry VIII, c. 7. See Houlbrooke, pp. 120–21, 146–47, 273–74. See note on 195/5–6.

196/15–29 **For well ye wote . . . procede.** More's assumption is that an action would lie in the King's Bench against tithes wrongly demanded, and that a party sued for nonpayment in an ecclesiastical court contrary to 45 Edward III, c. 3 could obtain a writ of prohibition or bring an action on the Statute of Winchester, 16 Richard II, c. 5. The latter course, if successful, not only led to damages but also to the severe penalties of *praemunire.* See *Spelman's Reports, 2,* introduction, pp. 66–67. See notes on 195/5–6 and 195/26–34.

197/11–13 **to mayntayne . . . not content.** Cf. St. German's draft legislation on these matters in Guy, *St. German,* pp. 128–33.

197/19–23 **yf a preste . . . obtayne yt.** Appendix B, 372/12–17.

197/19 **countreys.** That is, "counties."

197/20–21 **arbytrementes . . . metynges.** That is, arbitrations and meetings to compromise disputes or litigation. See Guy, *Cardinal's Court,* pp. 97–105; E. Powell, "Arbitration and the Law of England in the Late Middle Ages," *Transactions of the Royal Historical Society,* 5th Series, *33* (1983), 49–67.

198/3–4 **And these . . . conuocacyons.** Appendix B, 372/17–19.

198/4 **conuocacyons.** The two convocations of Canterbury and York were the provincial councils of the English church, each being separated into two houses, the bishops, abbots, and priors forming the upper house and the archdeacons and proctors the lower. The convocation of Canterbury by custom met concurrently with parliament; acts of convocation required the assent of both houses and were subject to royal review after the Submission of the Clergy in May 1532. See Lehmberg, pp. 64–75, 151.

198/6–11 **confederacyes . . . therin.** The word *confederacy* in the reign of Henry VIII meant in strict legal terminology that two or more persons had combined with mutual promises to do some damage or injury to another person or to perform some unlawful act. It was necessary to prove that the confederacy had been declared or substantiated by mutual promises or bonds between the participants at a preparatory meeting and also that the confederacy was false and malicious in intent and was directed against an innocent person. Confederacy was part of the criminal law and was an offense against the public authority of the state. It thus did not apply to civil cases in which a writ of conspiracy was applicable (see note on 130/6–7). Confederacy, however, sprang from Roman and Carolingian legislation against conspirators so that the English word *conspiracy* could sometimes be synonymous with *confederacy*. Confederacy was punishable before as well as after the unlawful acts proposed had been committed. Some instances of actual sixteenth-century cases were in Star Chamber for "confederacies" against landlords (Huntington Library, Ellesmere MS 2652, fol. 6). See also Alan Harding, "The Origins of the Crime of Conspiracy," *Transactions of the Royal Historical Society*, 5th Series, *33* (1983), 89–108.

199/13–14 **For as for that . . . to hym.** See note on 28/24–25. The phrase "that, that" means "the fact that."

199/17 **His .xx. . . . .lxxvi. lefe.** Appendix B, 373/1–377/36.

199/22–23 **And here . . . saye.** See *Apology, CW 9,* 96/9–19; *Division, CW 9,* 180.

199/29–30 **Afterwarde . . . hast.** See *Apology, CW 9,* 97–98.

200/16–19 **As by frere Luther . . . & some other suche.** Cf. the similar passage in *A Dialogue concerning Heresies, CW 6,* 434/14–18: "and seeth on ye other syde none other doctours of this new secte but frere Luther & his wyfe / prest Pomerane & his wyfe / frere Huiskyn and his wyfe / prest Carlastadius & his wyfe / dan Otho monke & his wyfe / frere Lambert & his wyfe / frantyke Colyns / & more frantyke Tyndall y^t sayth all prestes monkes & freres must nedes haue wyues."

Martin Luther (1483–1546) was an Augustinian friar.

Johann Bugenhagen (1485–1558) was born at Wollin in Pomerania (hence "prest Pomerane"). He was ordained in 1509 and became an adherent of Luther in Wittenberg in 1521. More attacked him in a blistering letter about 1526 (Rogers, pp. 323–65). See Rogers, p. 324; *CW 6*, 715–16.

"Otho the monke" was Otho Brunfels (c. 1488–1534). He took an M.A. at Mainz, joined the Carthusian house at Strassburg, but left the order before August 1521. He became a supporter of Luther, though he eventually made his peace with Erasmus. See *CW 8*, 1505–06, and *CW 9*, 354–55.

"Frere Lambert" was François Lambert (1486?–1530), a friar of the Franciscan Observants. He left his order in 1522 to follow the reformers and married the next year. In 1524 he attacked celibacy. See *CW 8*, 212/31, 868/31, 1543.

"Frere Huskyn" was Johannes Oecolampadius (Huessgen, Hussgen, Hausschein, actually "little house" but similar to "house-light"). A Brigittine friar, Oecolampadius (1482–1531) directed the evangelical movement in Basel and attached himself to Zwingli. See *CW 6*, 354/3, 461–63, 530, 559, 701; *CW 8*, 41/13, 868/31, 1203, 1267, 1475; and *CW 11*, xlviii–liv and Commentary at 106/10–107/6.

Ulrich Zwingli (1484–1531), ordained in 1506, led the Reformation in Zurich, beginning in 1518.

On William Tyndale (c. 1494–1536) and Robert Barnes, see note on 14/22–23.

George Joye (c. 1490–1553), ordained in 1515, was a biblical translator who spread Lutheran and Zwinglian teachings in England. His *Supper of the Lord,* a Zwinglian tract which denied the real presence in the eucharist, was refuted by More in *The Answer to a Poisoned Book (CW 11*, Appendix B). See the Introduction, pp. xxv–xxvi, above, and *CW 9*, Commentary at 117/32.

201/3–9 **Then goeth ... saye so.** Appendix B, 373/17–22. See *Apology, CW 9*, 101, but cf. *CW 9*, 97.

201/27–30 **What mayster More ... to haue done.** Appendix B, 373/24–28.

201/35–202/2 **That I thynke ... byleue?** Appendix B, 373/28–33.

202/7–17 **Mayster More ... heresye?** Appendix B, 374/42–375/10.

202/22–30 **For he maketh ... grudgynge.** See *Division, CW 9*, 180; *Apology, CW 9*, 97–102; *Salem and Bizance,* Appendix B, 375/40–376/9.

204/31–33 **as saynt Poule . . . byleued.** Gal. 1:8–9.

204/36 **the skye . . . larkes.** Whiting H314, Tilley S517: "When the sky falls we shall catch larks."

206/10–14 **As for ensample . . . lay man.** *Division, CW 9,* 195–96, 199–202.

206/16–18 **And yet . . . of god.** Appendix B, 374/3–8.

206/24–27 **in the rehersynge . . . seme playne.** Appendix B, 375/23–39.

206/35–207/7 **For now rede . . . sacramentes.** Appendix B, 375/23–39.

207/18–23 **As longe . . . wyll not appere.** Appendix B, 375/28–31, 37–38.

208/12–18 **Where . . . doth here &c.** Appendix B, 376/6–13.

208/32–35 **And than . . . foure.** See Appendix B, 374/3–14; *Division, CW 9,* 198–204. Cf. Appendix B, 380/9–382/8.

209/11 **blew poynt.** A point was a tagged lace for attaching hose to doublet. A "blew point" designated something of trifling value (*OED,* s.v. "point" *sb.*[1] B II 5). See *CW 8,* 705/32, Whiting P285, Tilley P456.

210/9–10 **is not this . . . conclusyon?** *Apology, CW 9,* 102/6–7; *Salem and Bizance,* Appendix B, 374/24–25, below.

210/13–19 **And now . . . shulde do.** Appendix B, 374/26–32.

210/24–25 **in Almain . . . somer.** More and other catholic apologists (such as Cochlaeus) frequently accused Luther of stirring up the Peasants' Revolt in Germany in the summer of 1525 and then stirring up the princes to slaughter the peasants. See *CW 6,* 545–48; *CW 8,* Commentary at 56/25–31 and 59/28–60/4. He gives various estimates of the number of peasants killed: more than 70,000 in *Letter to Bugenhagen* (Rogers, no. 143, line 1454); more than 60,000 in *Supplication of Souls* (*EW,* sigs. v5 and v8v); more than 80,000 in *Confutation* (*CW 8,* 56/30).

210/25–27 **& yet synnys . . . heretykes.** Zwingli died fighting with the Swiss protestant troops at the bloody battle of Kappel on October 11, 1531. The battle resulted from the attempt by Zwingli and the protestant cantons to blockade the five catholic cantons located in the Alpine regions (*CW 8,* 483/35–484/6 and Commentary at 484/4–20). In his *Letter against Frith* More had mentioned Zwingli and others as heretics on the eucharist, noting "what maner folke they be, is metely well perceiued and knowen / & god hath in parte with his open vengeaunce declared" (*EW*, sig. G$_5$v). In *A boke* . . . *answeringe vnto M mores lettur* (1533; *STC*^{2} 11381; Anthea Hume, "English Protestant Books Printed Abroad, 1525–35: An Annotated Bibliography," *CW 8*, 1083–84, no. 30) Frith defended Zwingli, claiming that "he was slayne in batayle in defendynge hys cytye / and comen welth agaynste the assaute of wycked enemyes / which cause was moste ryghtwyse. And yf his mastership meane that / that was the vengeaunce of God and declared hym to be an euyll parson because he was slayne. I may say nay / and shewe euident examples of the contrarie. . ." (sig. B$_8$v).

210/33–211/3 **And yf . . . but not all.** Appendix B, 374/32–37.

211/23–26 **I beseche . . . haue an ende.** Appendix B, 374/37–41.

211/33–212/10 **But now . . . people.** *Apology, CW 9*, 70–71.

212/17–18 **makynge . . . gnat.** Whiting E66; Tilley F398; Erasmus, *Adagia* 2027 (*ASD 2/5*, 55–56).

212/28–29 **I doute . . . make all well.** Appendix B, 375/17–19.

213/2–3 **drawe . . . lyne.** Whiting L303, Tilley D584.

213/6–8 **and fyrste . . . in other places.** See notes on 104/35–105/1 and 210/24–25. Cf. *CW 8*, 29–32, 484–85.

213/19 **not . . . ryshe.** See note on 87/27.

213/30–33 **And in thys chapyter . . . some of theym.** Appendix B, 375/20–22.

214/8–11 **that they pretende . . . grudge.** *Division, CW 9*, 180.

214/15–17 **For as I sayde . . . prynces.** *Apology, CW 9*, 97–102.

214/21–23 **and therfore . . . teache.** See Appendix B, 375/28–31.

215/3–21 **Surely . . . argument.** *Apology, CW 9*, 99/31–100/16.

215/23–34 **Then to shew . . . requyreth.** Appendix B, 376/20–31. The mixed construction "in suche thynges . . . ought wyth reuerence to be receyued" is present in St. German's sentence.

216/9 **but.** That is, "except."

216/10–11 **dyuers . . . counsayle.** See note on 68/3–6.

216/14–29 **I wyll . . . an euyll lawe.** Appendix B, 376/32–377/3.

216/30–34 **Of what strength . . . this good man.** For More's views about councils see R. C. Marius, "More the Conciliarist," *Moreana, 64* (1980), 91–99; his "Henry VIII, Thomas More, and the Bishop of Rome," in *Quincentennial Essays on St. Thomas More,* ed. M. J. Moore (Albion, N.C., 1978), pp. 89–107; Brian Gogan, *The Common Corps of Christendom* (Leiden, 1982), pp. 341–70.

217/8–22 **And the lawes . . . heresye.** Appendix B. 377/3–18.

217/18 **agaynst.** St. German wrote "anenst," meaning "with regard to."

217/21 **tho.** This form in *Salem and Bizance* is either an old form of the plural of the article *the* (*OED,* s.v. "the" *dem. adj. and pron.* A II 6) or (more probably) a misprint for "the" or "those."

217/29–31 **and ouer that . . . ordynaryes therin.** See *CW 9,* Appendix C, pp. 249–60.

218/7–19 **And then whether . . . indyfferencye in it.** Appendix B, 377/18–30.

218/9 **to shew . . . I shall.** That is, "I shall show. . . ."

218/20–22 **as for the conceyte . . . conceyte.** See note on 28/24–25.

218/33–219/1 **lawes . . . kylleth hym to.** In *Utopia* Hythlodaeus argues against the justice of such laws (*CW 4,* 60/5–74/11).

219/16 **walkynge . . . lande.** More refers to the last part of *Salem and Bizance* (Appendix B, 383/16–391/35), where St. German urges Christian princes to unite in order to win back the Holy Land from the Turks.

219/26–31 **And yf any man . . . iustyce.** Appendix B, 377/30–36.

220/9 **veryly.** The "weryly" of 1533 is a misprint: More is ironically echoing St. German's "I thynke veryly" (219/28).

220/17–19 **that it were better . . . iustyce.** Appendix B, 377/34–36.

220/21 **but.** That is, "except."

221/15–19 **In hys .xxi. . . . readynge.** Appendix B, 377/37–383/6. Cf. *Apology, CW 9,* 54–57, 167–70.

221/27–29 **And afterwarde . . . I medle not withall.** Appendix B, 382/23–33.

221/35–222/1 **I towched . . . .viii.** See *Division, CW 9,* 177–80, 188–93.

222/21–22 **not byleue . . . take.** A conflation of 1 John 4:1 and 1 Thess. 5:21.

222/24–27 **I well allow . . . of his boke.** Appendix B, 383/16–391/35. Cf. *Additions of Salem and Bizance,* chap. 5.

222/31–33 **I lyke . . . purgatory.** In *Division (CW 9,* 179) St. German explicitly accepts the orthodox doctrines of purgatory, indulgences, pilgrimages, prayer for the dead, and the veneration of images, though he emphasizes that, according to some persons, the doctrines have been abused and disordered in practice.

222/34–223/1 **and specyally . . . to rede it.** Appendix B, 379/5–35. For St. German's orthodox doctrine on the eucharist in 1537, see Appendix C, pp. 407–08.

223/9–11 **For as for the poynt . . . as he dothe.** Appendix B, 382/31–36.

223/12–13 **wherfore in y^e .xxxi. . . . mater of it.** *Apology, CW 9,* 105–06.

223/36–224/1 **Symkyn Salem . . . apologye.** Appendix B, 383/11.

223/36–224/1 **sayde answere . . . sayd apologye . . . sayd answere.** More is mocking St. German's frequent use of the legalistic qualifier "the sayde." At this place in *Salem and Bizance* St. German refers to "the said(e) Apologie" twice, within one sentence.

224/31–33 **that yf . . . remanaunt.** Appendix B, 383/13–15.

225/14–22 **And now . . . boldely saye.** Appendix B, 381/42–382/8.

225/24–25 **many places.** See note on 64/1.

225/26–27 **y^t by some wyly shrewis . . . he ment wel.** Cf. *Apology, CW 9,* 60/38–61/5. St. German had denied in *Salem and Bizance* that he had "any subtil shrewes counsell, ne any euill counsel at the making of the said tretise, which he [More] calleth the boke of diuision" (Appendix B, 382/13–16). See the Introduction, pp. lxxviii, xciii–xciv, and notes on 63/33 and 64/1.

226/1–4 **And farther . . . was trew.** Appendix B, 382/9–12.

226/1–2 **mentire . . . ire.** St. German was probably thinking not so much of Aulus Gellius (see note to 226/6–18) as of Cassiodorus' *Explicatio psalmorum* 17.46: *"Mentiri* enim est contra mentem loqui et illud

lingua promere quod unumquemque constat in animo non habere"
(*CCSL* 97, 166). Ambrogio Calepino (*Dictionarium*, Paris, 1519, sig. C₂v)
and Niccolò Perotti (*Cornucopia*, Venice, 1513, col. 877) give the same
derivation. See also *CW 4*, Commentary at 40/28–29.

226/6–18 **Aulus Gellius . . . wyse man.** Aulus Gellius (11.11.1–4)
gives the sayings of the grammarian Publius Nigidius about the distinction between *mentiri* and *mendacium dicere:* " 'Inter mendacium dicere et
mentiri distat. Qui mentitur ipse non fallitur, alterum fallere conatur;
qui mendacium dicit, ipse fallitur.' Item hoc addidit: 'Qui mentitur,'
inquit, 'fallit, quantum in se est; at qui mendacium dicit, ipse non fallit,
quantum in se est.' Item hoc quoque super eadem re dicit: 'Vir bonus,'
inquit, 'praestare debet ne mentiatur, prudens, ne mendacium dicat;
alterum incidit in hominem, alterum non.' " The only precedents for
mentire as an infinitive are Priscian's mention of it as an obsolete form
and a few minor manuscripts of a few passages in the New Testament
(*Thesaurus Linguae Latinae*, 18 vols., Leipzig, 1900–, 8, 776, lines 60–
65).

226/19 **that he . . . lyghte.** Prov. 14:15.

226/28–31 **And farther . . . (as ys sayde before).** Appendix B, 382/
13–16. See note on 225/26–27.

227/16–17 **playnly proued . . . counsayle.** See note on 68/3–6.

227/33 **halporth.** That is, "halfpennyworth."

228/8–10 **I wyll . . . satysfyed.** *Apology*, *CW 9*, 163–72.

229/1–5 **What trouble . . . forborne.** Wales was not subject to English
common law or its procedure until the Acts of Union (27 Henry VIII,
c. 26; 34 and 35 Henry VIII, c. 26). However, violence and disorder
had to be suppressed, so that the marcher Lords were bound in "in-
dentures of the marches" which obliged them to exercise control over
their officers and servants who were bound by recognizances to good
behavior. See Stanley B. Chrimes, *Henry VII* (London, 1972), pp. 251–
52; J. B. Smith, "The Legal Position of Wales in the Middle Ages," in
Law-Making and Law-Makers in British History, ed. A. Harding (London,
1980), pp. 21–53. More's point is that Welshmen's constitutional liberties sometimes had to be infringed in the interests of policy and good
government, but that this did not mean that the law as a whole had to be
changed.

229/14 **chaunged . . . dome.** Cf. 1 Cor. 15:51–52.

229/23 **after the law made.** For the idiomatic use of a phrase plus a participle where we would expect a finite verb ("[was] made"), see Visser, *1,* 376–78.

230/30–31 **(as hym selfe . . . skynne).** See note on 156/8–9. The phrase "loke symply" may mean "gaze innocently" or (if "symply" is a misprint for "symple") it may mean "appear harmless."

231/16 **god.** The word was not spelled with two *o*'s; "good" is a misprint caused by the preceding "good man."

APPENDIX A

*More's Correction of His Own Error
in the* Debellation

APPENDIX A

More's Correction of His Own Error
in the Debellation

T HIS appendix gives the text of four pages (the first of which is signed ⁊) added by More to the *Debellation* to correct an error in sig. b₅ by canceling ten lines. The same pages (with a few necessary changes in the opening lines) were also printed between the errata and the colophon of *The Answer to a Poisoned Book* (sigs. N₄–N₆).[1] They were also reprinted, with a new heading and adjustments in page, line, and column numbers, on an extra leaf tipped in after the end of *The Answer to a Poisoned Book* in some copies of the *English Works* of 1557.[2] We have removed the lines from our text of the *Debellation* (12/4) and placed them in the variants. In this appendix we give the text of More's note from the copy of the *Debellation* of *1533* in the Huntington Library, together with the variants from *The Answer to a Poisoned Book* (designated *PB*) and the *English Works* of 1557.[3] In this reprint as in the *Debellation* itself, textura is reproduced as roman and the reduced size

---

[1]Of fifteen known surviving copies of the 1533 *Debellation*, five (one each at the Huntington and John Rylands libraries, two at Cambridge University and one of the three in the Bodleian Library) contain the extra two leaves, and ten (at the Newberry Library, the University of Illinois, the University of San Francisco, the Folger Shakespeare Library, Princeton, the British Library, Lambeth Palace, and Corpus Christi College at Cambridge) lack the correction.

[2]In *1557* the leaf is tipped in between pp. 1138 and 1139 (sigs. CC₅v–CC₆). This position suggests that in 1557 the printer's copy for the *Debellation* lacked the supplementary leaves containing the addendum. The added pages were present in the printer's copy for *The Answer to a Poisoned Book*, since they are an integral part of the last gathering; nevertheless they seem to have been added in *1557* as an afterthought.

[3]Collation of the Huntington copy with that in the Bodleian Library reveals no stop-press corrections. For the *Answer to a Poisoned Book* we have collated the copies at Oscott College; Trinity College Dublin; the Bodleian Library; the British Library; and the Huntington Library; they also reveal no stop-press corrections. The extra leaf appears in the Larned Fund and Roper copies of *1557* at Yale and in the Cambridge University Library copy reprinted by Scolar Press (London, 1978); the Klein copy at Yale lacks it. Collation of the three copies that have it reveals no stop-press corrections.

bastard in smaller roman. An arrangement of three dots at the end has been replaced by a period.

At 321/25–28 More says that after the *Apology* he had declared that Tyndale had "somewhat amended and aswaged" his teaching about satisfaction. In the *Debellation* itself there is no such acknowledgment of Tyndale's "amendment," and in the *Poisoned Book* there is only a grudging recognition that Tyndale's reliance on "feeling faith" as including good works is not as foolish as that of the Masker (*CW 11*, 120/37–121/2). But More may be referring to some oral remark rather than to a printed statement.

The analogy of the stumbling horse in the final paragraph (322/9–32) is based on the proverb "It is a good horse that never stumbles" (Whiting H515, Tilley H670), with allusions to several related proverbs:

> The best-shod horse does slip sometimes. (Tilley H633)
> A good horse draws himself and his master out of the mire. (Tilley H647)
> A horse may stumble on four feet. (Whiting H514, Tilley H663)
> Dun is in the mire. (Whiting D434, Tilley D643)
> To bite and plain (whine [whinny]) like a horse. (Whiting H530)

¶The Debellacyon of
Salem and Bizance made by syr
Thomas More. Anno domini. 1533.
After he had gyuen ouer the
office of lorde Chaun-
cellour of Eng-
lande.
(∴)

¶The declaracion of the tytle.

The Debellacion of Salem & Bizans sometime two great townes, which being vnder the great Turke, were be-twene Easter & Michelmas laste passed, this present yere of our lord. M.v.C.thirty and thre, with a meruai-louse metamorphosis, enchaunted and turned into twoo englishe men, by the wonderfull inuentiue witte and wich-crafte of syr John Some say the Paci-fier, and so by him conuaied hither in a Dialogue, to defende hys deuision, a-gainst y Apology of syr Thomas More knight. But now being thus betwene the sayd Michelmas and Halowentyde next ensuing in this Debellacion bain-quished : they bee fledde hense and va-nyshed, and are become twoo townes

agayne with those olde names chaun-ged. Salem into Hierusalem. Bizance into Costantinople, the tone in Grece, the tother in Siria, where they may see them that wyll, and winne them that can. And if the Pacifier conueie them hyther againe, and tenne suche other townes with them, embatailed in such dialogues : Sir Thomas More hath vndertaken, to put himselfe in thaue[n]-ture alone against them all. But and if he let them tary still there: he wyll not vtterly forswere it, but he is not muche minded,as yet. age now so comming on and waring all vnwieldye, to goe thy-ther & giue thassaute, to such well wal-led townes, withoute some such lustye company as shalbe somewhat lykely to leape vp a little more lightly.

¶The preface.

¶Syr Thomas More to the christen readers.

If any man meruail (as I weene some wyse men wyll) y euer I would vou-chesafe to bestowe anye tyme aboute making aunswere to y pacifyers dia-logue, considering his faint and hys feble resoning: I can not in good fayth well excuse my selfe therin. For as I sodainely went in had therewith, and made it in a breide:so wha I since considered how lyttle nede it was, I meruailed mine own self and repeted to, that I had not regarded the booke as it was worthy, and withoute any one worde let it euen alone.

Howebeit good readers what one

thing or twaine specially moued me to make aunswere to it, and howe it hap-ped me to fall in hande therwith,and to spende and lese a little time about it, to make the matter the more plaine vnto you:that thing shal I shew you.

As soone as mine apologie was ones come out abrode, anone herde I worde that some were very wrothe therwith. And yet in my minde had there no mat cause, neither preacher nor pacifier, no nor none heretike neyther. For I had but spoken for my selfe, and for good folke,and for the catholike faith, with-out reproche or reprose to any mannes person,or willing any man any harme that were willing to mende. And who so were willing to be nought still, had cause to be wroth w himselfe you wote well and not with me.

But all thys would not serue me,for very wroth wer they with me. Howbeit they

The Debellation of Salem and Bizance, 1557, sig. N₅ (reduced).

And yet I wote not wel what I may say therof. For in the beginning of the booke, their first communicaciō is called an introduccion, and so is it entitled vpon the leaues. And yet in the very ede of that introduccion befoze the firste chapyter the man sayeth hymself in the person of Bizance, that hee hath made as yet none introduccion at all. What he meaneth by this can I not tell, but if he meane to make men wene that Salē and Bizance were twoo Englishe mē ßin dede, and spake those wozdes thē selfe without any wozde of hys.

But now because he sheweth himself so cunning in greke wozdes, that vpon this wozde apologye, he findeth ß afoze said sawte with myne apologye : as thoughe I were ouerseene and obserued not the nature of an Apology: let vs se how well hymselfe that in the begynning calleth hys booke a dialogue, obserueth the nature and pzopertye of a dialogue.

In the thirde lease when Salem sheweth himselfe desirouse to se the pacifyers aunswere: Bizance aunswereth:

I shal cause it to be wzitten here after in this dialogue wozde foz wozde, as it is come to my handes, and then thou shalt wyth good will haue it. And thou shalte vnderstande that hys aunswere begynneth at the nexte chapiter hereafter ensuyng, and continueth to the place where I shal shew thee that it endeth.

Consider good readers that thys introduccion he dothe not bzinge in, as a rehearsall of a communicacion hadde befoze, but as a communicion pzeset. And then let hym shewe me where euer to hath herde in his lyfe any twoo men in theire talking togither, deuide their pzesent communicacion into chapters. This is a point not onely so farre fro ß nature of a dialogue, but also from all reason, that a very childe woulde not I wene haue handeled the thyng so childisshelye.

Also that Bizance telleth Salē that the pacifiers aunswere shal be wzytten into their dialogue, ß is to wit to theyz communicacion: who saw euer the like Who saw euer any thing wzitten into a communicacion, and wziting planted in a mong wozdes spoken.

And what reason hath it to tell hym where about in theire communycacion, the pacifiers wozdes shall beginne and where they shal ende: as thoughe Salē

talking with Bizance, had not ß wytte to perceiue whē Bizance speaketh himselfe and when he redeth him the pacifiers wozdes wzitten.

Also what a straunge monstrouse beast maketh Bizance to Salem the pacisters aunswere, while he maketh as though Salem coulde neither perceiue the hed noz the taile, but if himselfe poited him to them both with a sticke.

Mozeouer whereas Bizance sayeth he will wzite it into their dialogue, that is to wzite into their pzesent talking as soone as it cometh to hys hādes, so that at that wozde he had it not yet, and than hee wziteth it in, euen by and by, ß nether goeth any where to fet it, noz maketh anye man come thither to hym to bzynge it: is not this pzoperly deuised?

Than stande they both styll there as thei fyrst meete, and that is in the strete by lykelyhode (foz there folke most comenly meete, that meete at aduenture as they doe) and there is all ß aunswere perused, the reading whereof standeth them at the least foure oz fyue howzes I trow. Howebeit there I was a lyttle ouersene. Foz they stande not there styl aboute the readyng, but there stande they still both twayne al the while that Bizance is as you se into theyr talking and cōmunicacion wziting it. And that is but if Bizace wzyte fast, I warrant the wozke of a weke.

Now than at the weekes ende whan all the .rri. chapters are wzytte: Bizāce in the .rrij. chapyter giueth Salē warning, that there is the aunswere of the pacister ended. And this was by the pacifier fole pzudently deuised. Foz elles woulde Salem weene that their owne talking togither in ß tother thzee chapters by mouth, had ben styl nothing els but onely Bizances wzitinge, and els woulde also Salem haue thought that hys own wozdes of exhoztaciō agaist the great Turke, and hys owne rehersing of that expoficion of the apocalips, had ben styl ß pacifiers wozdes against myne apology.

And finally in the very ende to shew that he could wzite, not in onely pzose: hee endeth all the whole booke in thys wyse with a glozïouse rime, ‡And thus ß glozyous trinitye, haue in his keping both thee and me, ‡and maketh Bizāce pzay foz no mo but foz them two, after the maner of the good man Gzyme, a musterde maker in Cambzidge, ß was wont to pzay foz hymselfe and his wise and

Gzime the musterde makers pzayer.

[✠₁]
Syr Thomas More knyght
to the chrysten reader.

After these fautes of the prenter escaped in this boke, I shall
not let good reders to geue you lyke warnynge of one faute of
myne own, escaped me in the begynnyng of this boke. In the   5
.xiii. lefe wherof, and in the fyrste syde, cancell and put oute one
of those ouersyghtes that I laye to the pacyfyer, in those .ix.
lynes, of whyche the fyrste is the .ix. lyne of the same syde, and
the laste is the .xviii. For of trouth not yᵉ pacifyer but my selfe
was ouersene in that place with a lytle haste, in mysse remem-   10
brynge one worde of hys. For where as he sayth in the person of
Byzance, in the thyrde lefe of Salem and byzance.

I wyl cause yt to be wryten into this dyaloge word for word as yt ys come to my
handes: I forgate whan I answered yt that he sayde, as yt is come /
and toke it as though he sayd as it cometh to myne handes. [✠₁v]   15

And therfore albe it that I haue knowen many that haue redde
it, of whiche I neuer founde ony yᵗ found it: yet syth it happed
me lately to loke theron & fynde myne ouersyght my selfe, I
wolde in no wyse leue it good reader vnreformed. Nor neuer
purpose whyle I lyue, where so euer I maye perceyue, eyther   20
myne aduersarye to say wel, or my self to haue sayd otherwyse, to
let for vs both indyfferently to declare and say the trewth.

And surely yf they wold vse yᵉ selfe same honest playne trewth
towarde me: you sholde sone se good readers all our conten-
cyons ended. For than shold you se, that lyke as I haue not letted   25
after myne apology, to declare that Tyndale had somewhat
amended and aswaged in one poynt, hys formare euyll asser-
cyons concernynge satysfaccyon: so shold he confesse the trouth

---

1 Syr] *1533 PB,* After that sir Thomas More hadde caused to be printed, this laste booke
(intitled, the answer to the first parte of the poysoned boke, which a nameless heretike
hath named the supper of the lord) he wrote and caused to bee printed in the ende
thereof (after certaine correccions of faultes escaped in the printyng thereof) this that
followeth. Sir *1557*   5 the begynnyng of this boke] *1533* my boke laste put forth of the
debellacyon of Salem and Bizance *PB 1557*   5–6 In the .xiii. . . . syde] *1533 PB,* In yᵉ
first capiter wherof (Numero .933. and in the seconde colume) *1557*   8 .ix.] *1533
PB,* .ii. *1557;* syde] *1533 PB,* colume *1557*   9 .xviii.] *1533 PB,* .19. (the first of which
.9. lines beginneth thus. Moreouer .&c.) *1557*   17 ony] *1533 PB,* any *1557*

that I hadde trewly touched hym / and that hym selfe had sore
erred, as well in the remanaunt therof [♃ 2] as in all his other
heresyes. And than also, lyke as I let not here for the pacyfyers
parte to declare my self ouersene wyth haste in thys one poynt:
5   so shold he not let well & honestly to say yᵉ trouth on the tother
syde, & confesse hym selfe very farre ouersene wyth longe
leysoure, in all yᵉ remanaunt by syde. I saye not in all that he
sayth, but in all yᵗ is debated betwene vs.
    I wote well the beste horse were he which were so sure of fote
10 that ronne he neuer so faste wolde neuer in hys lyfe neyther fall
nor stumble. But syth we can fynde none so sure: that horse is
not mych to be mysselyked, whych that wyth corage & pryckyng
forth in haste, happynge for all hys foure fete somtyme to cache
a fall, geteth vp agayne lyghtly by hym selfe, wythout touche of
15 spurre or any checke of the brydell. No nor yet that horse to be
caste awaye neyther, that getteth vp agayne apace with the cheke
of them bothe. Now lyke as wyth the best [♃ 2v] kynde can I not
compare: so of the thyrde sorte at the leste wyse wyll I neuer
fayle to be, that is to wyt ryse & reforme my self, whan any man
20 shew me my faut. And as nere as I can wil I serche them / & as
sone as I spye them, before any man controll them, aryse, and as
I now do myne owne selfe reforme theym. Whyche kynde ys you
wote well nexte vnto yᵉ beste. But yet on the tother syde, of all
myne aduersaryes could I neuer hytherto fynde any one, but
25 whan he catcheth ones a fall, as eche of theym hath caughte full
many, there lyeth he styll tumblynge & toltrynge in myre, and
neyther spurre nor brydyll can one ynche preuayle / but as
though they were not fallen in a puddle of dyrt, but rubbed &
layed in lytter vnder the manger at theyre ease, they whyne &
30 they byte, and they kycke, and they spurne at hym that wolde
helpe them vppe. And that is yet a fourth kynde, the wurste ye
wote well that can be.
                              Finis.

---

12 mych] *1533 PB*, much *1557*   22 Whyche] whyche *1533 PB*, Which *1557*
33 Finis.] *1533 PB, om. 1557*

APPENDIX B

Christopher St. German's
Salem and Bizance

APPENDIX B

Christopher St. German's
Salem and Bizance

THIS appendix reproduces the text of St. German's *Salem and Bizance* (London, Thomas Berthelet, 1533; *STC*² 21584) from a microfilm of the copy in the Bodleian Library, Oxford. The errata on sig. o₃ have been incorporated in this reprint, and obvious misprints not listed there have also been silently corrected. Pilcrows at the beginning of chapter headings have been omitted; at one point within the text a pilcrow has been replaced by indentation. The textura of the 1533 edition, as well as the occasional roman capitals used for proper names and dates, are here reproduced in roman typeface. Italic typeface in the copy-text has been retained. Except for &, all abbreviations, including Iohñ for Iohan, have been silently expanded. The printer occasionally lacked the uppercase "W" and "Y," and "w" and "y" have been capitalized when the sense requires it.

[A₂]
A dialogue betwixte two englyshe
men, wherof one was called Sa-
lem, and the other Bizance.
Thintroduction.

5 SALEM. There is a boke lately made by syr Thomas More, whiche he
calleth the Appologie of syr Tho. More knyght, wherin amonge dyuers
other thynges he layeth many obiections agaynste a booke, that he
calleth the booke of Diuisyon betwixte the spiritualtie and the temporaltie: haste thou my frende Bizance sene that boke of diuision?
10 BIZAN. I haue sene a lyttell boke, that in the begynnynge of the booke,
hath this name sette vppon hit, A treatise concernyng the diuision
betwixte the spiritualtie and temporaltie: and I suppose that hit is the
same booke, that thou menest of: For in dede sir Thomas More maketh
many obiections in the sayd Apologie ayenst the sayde [A₂v] treatise,
15 and recyteth in many places the very wordes of some parte of the
chapitres of the sayde treatise. Howe be it in some places he mysreherc-
eth it, and in some places he tourneth the sentence therof to an other
effect, than can be reasonably taken to folowe of it, as me semeth. SAL.
Than I see wel, it is the same boke, that I meane of: howe be it I
20 perceiue by thy wordes, that syr Thomas Moore somewhat varieth
from the very tru name of it. And verily if I were acqueynted with the
maker of the sayde treatise, I wolde moue hym to make an answere to
the sayde obiections. For me thynketh that in many places syr Thomas
Moore (as thou sayst) doth mystake his sayinges. And therfore I praye
25 the, if thou canste, make me acqueynted with hym: for if he wyll not
aunswere to it hym selfe, I trowe I knowe a frende of myne that wyll.
BIZ. To that purpose that thou spe[A₃]kest of, it shall not nede that ye
be acqueinted, for he hath made an answer to it hym selfe all redy, all
though he hath nat as yet set the name vpon it: And I knowe his mynde
30 so well, that I am sure he wyl be contented, that I shal shewe it to whom
so euer I wyll. SA. Than I pray the hartily let me se it. BIZ. I shall cause it
to be writen hereafter in this Dialoge worde for worde, as it is com to
my handes, and than thou shalte with good wyll haue it: And I praye
the let me than knowe thy further mynde, what thou thynkest in it.
35 And thou shalt vnderstonde, that his aunswere begynneth at the begynnynge of this next chapiter hereafter ensuynge, and contynueth
vnto the place, where I shal shew the that it endeth. And he hath
neither made as yet prologue, preface, nor introduction, but begynneth in this maner as foloweth. [A₃v]

Of the answere to the Apologie of
syr Tho. Moore knyghte.
The fyrste Chapiter.

WHAN I herde first that syr Thomas More had made a boke, towchyng a lyttell treatise that I had lately made, concernynge a Diuision that is betwixt the spiritualtie and temporaltie, I was ryght gladde: For I thoughte verily that he had diuised some more conuenient wayes for a good reformation in that behalfe, than I hadde done or coulde do: For I knewe ryght well, that he coude haue done it if he wold, and coulde yet doo, if he lyste. But whan his booke came to my handes, I perceyued well, that he hadde not done so, but that rather to the contrarye, he had taken many exceptions, and made many obiections ayenst it, wherof I meruayled greattely. And [A₄] whan I sawe that he had named his boke an Apologie, than I meruayled more than I dyd before. For *Apologia* in greke tongue, is as moche to say in latyn *responsio,* or *defentio,* that is to say an answere or a defence, wherby it semeth, that he shulde meane, that I had wrytten some thyng ageynst his workes, or mystaken som of his workes, that he had made in tyme paste, which he therfore purposed to maynteyne & defende. And verily I neuer wrote nor spake any thynge ageynst him. For I neuer red his Dialogue, his Confutations, ne yet none other of his workes: Howe be it that was not bycause I wold not rede his workes: but bycause I haue bene let by other occasion, and coulde not: and so I can not answere to his Apologie as an Apologie ayenst me, that nothyng haue done ayenst hym. But yet neuer theles that my silence shuld not make some other haply to thynke, that su[A₄v]che obiections as he hath made in his sayde Apologie ayenst the sayde treatise were good and reasonable, and also that he shulde not make the sayde treatise appere to be made to an other intent, than it was made for in dede: I haue made answere to some of his obiections, wherby (as I suppose) it shal appere euidently, that his obiections proceded of lyttell charitie, and that the sayde treatise is good and resonable, and that it was also made to a good intent, that is to say, to increce peace and quietnes thorough all the realme. Howe be it for the auoydyng of tediousnes to the reders, I intende not to answere to all his obieccions, but to some of them. And thoughe I do not make answere perticularly to all, yet I suppose it shal appere by the answeres, and by certayn considerations, and some declarations, that I shal make, concernyng the same, that his obiections are littel to be ponde[A₅]red, if the reders wyll diligently and auisedly serche the groundes and circumstances of the said obiections, and of the saide treatise to gether. And I wyll not make answere to his apologie

after the order of his chapiters, but as I shall thynke shall serue beste
for openinge of the treuth of the matier as nigh as I can.

The fyrste consideration,
the seconde Chap.

5   FIRST it is to consider, that sir Tho. More, fo. 89. of his Apologie
confesseth, that murmure and discencion ayenst the clergie is far gone
onward on his vnhappie iourney: And after fol. 106. he bryngeth in a
verye derke sentence, wherby it appereth, that he meaneth, that the
displesure & gruge betwyste them is in dede neyther so great as I make
10   it, and growen to so great as it is, but euen nowe of late, & so he
confesseth there also, that there [A₅v] is suche a grudge, but he sayeth
that that gruge hath not begonne but now of late. But verily if he wil
loke well and indifferently vpon the matier, he shall fynde, that it hath
bene in growyng of longer tyme than he speketh of there. And after, f.
15   241. he calleth it the late sprongen diuision: and so it apperith, that he
confesseth, that there is suche a diuision: and yet not withstandinge,
that he confesseth suche a diuision to be, yet for al that in al his Apologie, he deuiseth no remedy how to appese it, but only through the
execucion of streite lawes, and by harde correction of heresyes: and he
20   goeth very moche aboute also to perswade, that some of the thinges
that be aleid in the said treatise for part of tho causes of the said
diuison, be no causes of diuision. And somtyme he saith by general
wordes, that there is no sufficient cause of diuision aleyed, takynge that
as it were a good answere to the [A₆] said tretise. But surely it is not so,
25   for seinge that he hath confessed a diuision hym selfe, it foloweth that
al though he coude auoyde all the considerations that be aleyed for
causes of the sayde diuisyon, as he doeth not ne can not do: yet had he
littel done to helpe the diuision, that he confesseth to remayn betwene
them: but if he coulde haue proued them that I haue assigned for
30   causes of the sayde diuision, to be no causes of diuision: And than
wolde haue leyd som other cause therof hym selfe, and thervpon haue
diuised how the causes myght haue ben auoyded: then had it appered,
that he had some what endeuoyred hym selfe to haue made peace and
concorde: but as he hath now handled him selfe in the matier, it shulde
35   seme that he hath not so great a zele to haue the sayde diuision ap-
pesed, as he oughte to haue had. And surely considering not onely the
wisedome and lerning that is in him, [A₆v] but also the great auctoritie
and experience, that he hath had in this realme in tyme paste, wherby
he myght right well haue perceyued, and as I thinke verily doth per-
40   ceyue, that the gruges and murmures that hath ben and yet be betwixt

the spiritualtie & the temporaltie in this realme, haue begunne by other thinges more than by heresies, so that although heresies were clerely extincted: yet al thinges were not quiet betwixt them: it is to me a right great merueille, that he hath done no more to acquiete those other thynges, then he hath done. For surely many right good, trewe, and   5
catholyke men haue grudged & do yet grudge ayenst many spiritual men for them.

The seconde consideration.
The thyrde Chap.

Also it is to be considered, that sithe there are murmurs & gruges   10
in the people ayenste the spiritu[A7]altie, as is said before: it must nedes folow therupon, that though it were admitted, that all tho murmurs and grudges rose onely of a defaulte and vntrewe suspicion in the laye people, without any occasion gyuen to them by the spiritualtie, that yet hit were right highly necessary for al spiritual men to loke wel   15
vpon the matier, and with great diligence to put to al their study for helping of the people out of the offence, that they renne in by such wronge iugement and lyght suspicion: for surely the spiritualtie may not let the people lye styll in that wronge iugement, and thinke them selfe safe ynough, bicause they gyue no cause to it. For if the thing that   20
the lay people take occasion to offend by, may be left without offence, by whom so euer it be done: he is bounden in conscience to leue it tyll he haue opened the matier so playnely to them, that their offence shal therin cesse, oneles they be [A7v] fallen into the sclander of the Pharisies: how moche more then are spiritual men (that haue taken the   25
charge ouer the people) bounden to leaue all suche thinges, as the peple offende by their occasion, what so euer they be that may laufully be left, though they be indifferent, or percase good dedes of themselfe (verily moch more) & if thei be bound to leue such good dedes, or indifferent dedes, for the offence of the people, that myght folowe   30
therby: than ar they most specially bound to leaue all thynges, that be euylle, or haue apparance of euyl, to helpe the iudgement and suspicion of the people. And of this matter I haue somwhat spoken in the laste chapiter of the sayde tretise, but master Moore doth nat regard that poynt, but endeuoreth him selfe very moche to oppresse all them   35
that wyll shewe suche thynges of the spiritualtie, or speke of them, and diuiseth nothinge howe to haue the de[A8]fautes amended, ne prouideth not any maner of remedy therin, but after his minde proueth an intollerable defaut in the people, by suche iudgementes, where he thynketh they had no cause so to do, and yet they haue in dede, & there   40

he leauith them, as though the hole cause & principall defautes were
fully in them. And surely in that iugement he is right farre deceyued.
And yet though it were as he sayth therin, the spiritualte were not
therfore clerely discharged, for the causes before rehersed.

5   An aunswere to two obiections of
           the said Apologie, the .iiij. chap.

I HAVE in the saide treatyse shewed som defautis in spiritual men, and
also some in temporal men: And I haue said also, that spiritual men
somtyme haue spoken euil wordes of laie men, and haue sayde that
10 they loue no prestes: and that somtime laie men haue [A₈v] done like
wise of spiritual men, affirming that there is no good prest, and that
some lay men wyl cal them horeson priestes: And therfore I saye
ferther there, that if al these wordis were prohibited on bothe parties, it
wolde do gret good. And to proue that this maner of handling is not
15 conuenient for makinge of a peace, but rather to make more variance
betwyxte them, maister Moore bringeth in this example, that if there
were a variaunce betwixt a man and his wyfe, & one that intendeth to
pacifie them, wold shewe the one of them the defautes of the other:
that that shulde haplie displease them both, specially if it were shewed
20 before their neighbours: and than he thinketh it is so lykewyse in this
case, to shewe the defautes betwixt the spiritualtie and the temporaltie
openly. And verily I merueyle moche, that maister More wyll brynge
forth that example of a man and his wyfe, and [B₁] compare it to the
spiritualtie and the temporaltie: For there is moste comonly suche a
25 tendernesse of loue betwyxte a man and his wyfe, thoughe there appere somtyme some outward variance to be betwixte them, that if a
man wolde shewe the one of them the others defaute, & that specially
afore their neyghbours, he might haply displese them both & do but
lyttel good, as mayster More saith: but the more pitie is, there is no
30 suche tendernes of loue in this case nowe betwixt the spiritualtie and
temporalte: For as it is wel knowen, as the worlde goeth now the spiritualtie, as to the multitude, may bere it righte well in gree to here the
temporalte openly dispraised, and in lyke wyse some of the temporaltie
may bere it righte well in pacience, to here defautis leid in the spir-
35 itualte, in so moche that as it is oft times sene, if a priest be amonge lay
men, he can not better content them, as to mooste [B₁v] companies,
than to speke of the pride and couetice of priestes. And in lyke wyse a
lay man that is among prestis, can not better please them, as to many
priestes, than to say that laye men do not loue priestes, ne honour
40 them, as they shulde do. And therfore it appereth euidently, that

maister Mores similitude serueth not in this case: but what so euer it be
in this case of shewyng of the defautes of the one to the other, yet I wot
not what hurt coude come of it to prohibite, that neither partie shulde
speke vnsitting wordes of the other, and so it semeth that in these two
poyntes, mayster Moore wolde haue founde a defaute, where there   5
was none.

And then to an other obiection that he layeth, where it appereth that
he wold haue had the defautes of the spiritualtie, conteyned in the
second chap. of the said tretise more secretly shewid vnto them, than
they be in the sayd tre[B₂]tise, that is to say in latine tongue, as the   10
famous clerke Iohan Gerson reciteth them, & not in the englishe
tongue. To that it may be answered, that the said Iohan Gerson wrote
the sayd defautes to the general consaile, and to haue writen them
thither in his vulgare tongue, that is to say in the frenche tongue, it had
not ben conuenient: for there were mo at that general consaile, that   15
vnderstode not the frenche tongue, then that vnderstode it: but the
saide treatise was made onely for the peple of this realme, and therfore
the englishe tongue in this realme was moste conuenient. And ouer
that sith spirituall men haue had the sayde defautes, and diuers other,
whiche be omittid in the saide treatise, in latine euer sith the time of the   20
said Iohan Gerson, and yet appereth litell frute of amendement therby. And seinge also that it is not prohibitid, but that they might laufully
be translated into en[B₂v]glishe: therfore I haue brought som of them
into the englishe tongue, to the intent that some good man, that shal
rede them hereafter, shall haplie put them in remembrance in suche   25
maner that there shall folowe some good reformation: And I haue
spoken of defautes and abuses in the spiritualtie, more then of defautis
in the temporaltie, bicause the spiritualte ought to be the gyders &
gyuers of light by theyr doctrine and good examples to the temporaltie: & if their light be derkenes, where shal the temporalte then   30
fetche their light? truely I wote not where. And I doubt that then they
both shal walke styll in derkenes. And therfore it is that Ihoan
Chrysostom saith vppon Matthewe the .xxi. Chap. That if preesthode
be holle and sounde, all the churche flouryssheth: and if it be corrupte,
the feyth and vertue of the people fadeth also & vanisheth away. Let   35
this therfore as to this poynte be [B₃] the final conclusion for this tyme,
that who so euer proueth defautes to be in the temporaltie, he prouith
also defautes to reigne in the spiritualtie: and therfore the defautes in
the temporaltie wyll neuer be auoyded, tyl the defautes in the spiritualtie be fyrste reformed: and therfore haue I fyrst spoken of som   40
defautes that be in the spiritualtie. And though maister More can not
denie them, yet al the amendmentis that he aleith in his Apologie is

onely in punishment of heresies, as is said before: whervnto he specially moueth the ordinaries not to be slack nor the more remysse for
feare of euill wordes and sclaunder of the people. And if they be
therfore the more slack in calling, attaching, and examining, and far-
5   ther ordering of heretikes: he saith, god wyl not faile to make falle in
theyr neckes the double sclander of that, fro whens they fled. And in an
other place he moueth the temporalte [B₃v] to ioyn with the spiritualtie
eche with other louingly to represse & kepe vnder those vngratious
folke, by whom he meaneth heretikes. Vpon whiche mocion I shall
10 somewhat shewe my mynde, as here after foloweth in the nexte
chapitre.

An other consideration. The .v. chap.

IT is to be considered, that there ar in this realme, to that purpose
that I intend with goddis grace to speke of nowe in this chapitre, foure
15 sortis of people, wherof the first sort is of good men spiritual and
temporal, that liue wel and do good dedes, gyue good examples to the
people, do no wronge to their neighbours wittingly, and if they do any
ignorantly, they ar glad when they know it, to make amendes, and ouer
this they kepe the trewe catholical feith: how be it for a spiritual
20 weikenes that is in them, and for an inordinat loue that they haue to
their [B₄] owne bodily ease, they wylle take no peyne ne displeasure for
meintenance of the feithe, ne for the good ordre of the people, nor
care not for it: so that they lyue well them selfe.

The seconde sorte is noted to be of them that lyue wel, & do wel, &
25 beleue in euery thing, as the first sort do, and ouer that if they here of
any errours, heresies, or other defautis in any person, they will gladly
(to their power) helpe to reforme & remoue them from it. And al this
they do through special grace for the loue of god and of their neighbours. And these be of the beste sort of the people, our lorde sende vs
30 many of them. Amen.

The thirde sorte of peple is of them, that kepe the catholical feith, &
wolde gladly that al other shuld kepe it also as they do: howe be it their
feithe for lacke of good dedes, is but a naked feith: for they many times
greue their neighbours by their exactions, and [B₄v] shewe many euil
35 examples to the people, wherby many do offend almighti god: And yet
though they shewe such euil examples, and also vse and suffre to be
vsed many thinges ageinst charitie, and ageinst diuers thinges graciously ordeined by Christ, and by his churche for the welthe of his
christen people, and suche as they might also right wel amende, if they
40 wolde: yet they haue a feruent desire to punyshe heresies, and they

thinke it a greatte laude and preyse vnto them to do it, pretendinge
also, that euery man is bounde to helpe them forwarde in it.

The .iiii. sorte of people is of them that lyue as the thyrde sorte doo,
and wolde that heresies & other offenders were wel punisshed and
corrected, so that they might be suffred to lyue continually in the 5
honor, riches, & worldly plesures, as they do nowe: but yet they wyll not
put to their handes to helpe forwarde suche punishement or [B₅]
correction, ne take any peyne therin, though they sawe right great
nede in it: and these be of the worste sorte of people before all other:
excepte onely an other sort of peple, which sir Tho. Moore in his 10
Apologie calleth sometyme desperate wretches, sometyme sterke heretykes, and otherwhiles he calleth them the blessed brotherhode, or the
blessed bretherne, the newe broched bretherne, or the euangelical
bretherne: And those that he noteth for most principall doers amonge
them, he calleth them potheded postels, and sometyme the naughtie 15
bretherne, or the heretike bretherne. Thus he makith them a merueilous company: for sometyme he calleth them blessed bretherne,
and somtime the naughtie bretherne or heretike brethern, as before
appereth: and so he maketh them as in his wordes both good and
badde. These be strange names diuised after a merueilous railing fash- 20
ion, wherin [B₅v] I thinke verilye, he dothe not to this realme as he
wolde be done to: for it appereth in his apologie, that he loueth no
raylinge toward hym selfe. But what he shuld meane by that terme (the
newe brochid brethern) in good feith I can not tel: but when he calleth
them the euangelical bretherne, me thinketh it is a commendacion to 25
them, for it is good to folow the gospel, I prey god send vs mani that wil
do it. And now wyll I say somewhat ferther, concernyng this matier,
and that is this. I merueile moche, howe maister More durst for offence
of his conscience, & for drede of the kinges displeasure, and of the
holle realme, bring vp suche a sclanderous name in this realme, and 30
put it in print, that may lightly touch not only many of the comon
people, but also of the grettest of the realme, as well spirituall as temporall: if he and other of his affinitie lyste to calle any of theym one of
the blessed bre[B₆]therne, or of the good bretherne. And in this
poynte it semeth, that he forgate the honour of the realme, which he 35
semed moche to regarde, whan he said: he coulde not thinke it to the
honour of the realme, that other realmes shulde wene, that the hole
clergie of this realme shuld be so farre fallen into the grudge and
indignation of the hole temporaltie, as he saith it is spoken to be in the
sayd Tretise, whiche he calleth the boke of diuision: for certainly it is 40
more dishonour to the realme, to haue it noysed, that the realme is ful
of heretikes, than that the temporaltie grudgeth ageynst the spir-

itualte: and so he escheweth & fleeth the lesse sclander, though it were all true that he saith, and renneth heedling into the greatter.

And than ferthermore where sir Tho. Moore maketh this motion, that the hole corps of the spiritualtie and temporaltie bothe, with other
5 louingely [B₆v] shuld accord and agree to gether, and according to the good ancient lawes and commendable vses longe continued in this noble realme, either part shulde endeuoir them selfe diligently to oppresse and kepe vnder those euil & vngratious folke there remembred, wherbi he meaneth heretikes. I wold with his fauour witte, what he
10 wold say, if this mocion were made before that ioynynge together, that euerye man that intended that oppressing & kepyng vnder of those that he callith the euyll and vngracious folke, shuld firste auoyde all their owne abusions and euyl examples, that might be occasion to cause them, that they wolde so oppresse and kepe vnder, to murmure and
15 grudge, and to resiste the more al good corrections, and then louingly to ioyne together, and se them punished, that wold be obstinate, and not receyue the holsome monicions & good doctrines of theyr superiours. [B₇] And that therupon some other wolde saye agayne to them, that made that mocion thus: they nor ye nether haue nought to do with
20 our offences, ne euil examples: and thoughe we be offenders in som degree of offence, yet that offence is no cause to make them heretikes, ne to forsake the true catholic feithe: and therfore but ye ioyne with vs to helpe them punished, ye be worthye to be noted as fauorers of their heresies, and to be taken as men that care but lyttel for the true catholi
25 call feithe: I wolde suppose, that master More him selfe wold not thynke this to be a resonable and a charitable answere, nor certaynly no more it were: for they that wil correct other, ought after the due order of charitie to reforme them selfe firste, er they do that correction: howe be it I do not mene therbi, that it is not lauful for rulers, that be offend
30 ers, to do correction, ne that inferiours might therfore lauful[B₇v]ly resist it: but I meane, that it is not so conuenient for them, that be offenders, and that giue euill example to the people, to doo correction, as it is for them that lyue well and shewe good example to the people, ne that their correction shal not be so wel obeyed, as if they wolde
35 correcte them selfe fyrste. And therfore if they will yet nedely forthe with harde punysshmentes, and streit corrections, without remouing suche occasions, it is to fere, that litel profite shal grow therby, neither to them selfe, ne yet to them that they so punysshe, nor parauenture to other that shal here of it. And though master More speke moch of
40 suche a brotherhode, as is remembred before, whiche might be taken perauenture after his mynde, for the .v. sorte of people: yet I take it not so, for in good feith I knowe no suche brotherhode, and trust verily

also, that there is none suche in dede within this realme: wher[B₈]fore I counted them not for any of the sortes of people, that I intended to treate of in this chapitre.

That the sayde Apologie mystaketh
the letter of the sayd tretise in dyuers thinges. The .vi. Cha.

F IRSTE in the said treatise it is conteyned, that some men haue said, that as they thynke, it is laufull and also expedient, that the churche haue possessions, but they thinke that the great abundance, that is in the churche, doth great hurt, and enduceth in many of them a loue of worldly thinges, and letteth, & in maner strangleth the loue of god. And vpon these wordes maister Moore in his Apologie sayth, that the said reson renneth out ageynste euery kinde of men spiritual and temporall, that haue possessions: but he hathe not playnely declared, what he meaneth by tho wardes (renneth out) for if he meane therby, that [B₈v] the wordes of the said treatise shulde sounde to this effect, that it is neither lauful to spiritual men nor to temporal men to haue abundance of possessions, than he clerely mistaketh the lettre of the said treatise, for the said lettre is onely spoken of spirituall men, as it appereth euidently: And if his meaning be, that he wil compare the abundance of spirituall men, and temporal men to gether, and to be like to al intentes, so that it is as conuenient for spirituall men as for temporall men, to haue abundaunce of possessions: then me semeth, he erreth greatly: for though it be laufull to spirituall men to haue possessions, yet it standeth not so wel with the perfection of spiritual men, to haue abundance of possessions, as to temporal men: for it mai be that the orderinge and disposinge of that habundance shall many tymes let the feruour of charitie, the zele of soules, and the hyghnes of contemplacion, [C₁] that ought to be in spiritual men, moche more than in temporall men: so that the ordering and treatinge therof may be somtime a synne to spirituall men (at the leeste a veniall synne) that shulde be no synne to a temporal man. And there is no synne though it be onely veniall, but it letteth the feruour of charitie, though it clerely extincte hit not. And the wordes of the said tretise aboue rehersed be not, that habundance clerely strangleth the loue of god, but that in some of them, that is to say in som spiritual men, in maner it strangleth it, as who saythe, it minisheth in som of them the feruour of it. And so the sayd treatise renneth not out ageinst no temporal men, ne yet ageinst al spiritual men: for it mai stande therwith, that some spirituall men may haue abundaunce with the hyghnes of contemplation, but

that is a singuler gifte gyuen but to fewe. And therfore to thintent that
the pope [C₁v] Eugenius (which before that he was elected pope, was
monke vnder seint Bernarde) shuld the rather atteine to that gifte of
contemplacion, seynt Bernarde aduertised hym, that as to the order
5 and disposition of temporal thinges, he shuld commyt them to other
vnder hym, that he might the more frely take hede to heuenly thinges.
And for as moche as it semeth, that sir Tho. Moore, by these wordes
that he hath spoken afore, entendeth to fauour the possessions of the
churche: I somewhat merueile of his wordes, that he speaketh in the
10 later ende of the .xxij. chap. of his Apologie, where he saith thus: that
by his truth he meruaileth moche to se some folke nowe so moche and
so boldly to speake of takinge away any possessions of the clergie: for
he sayth, that ones in the tyme of the famous prince kynge Henry
the .iiij. about the time of a great rumble that the heretikes made, whan
15 they wolde [C₂] haue distroyed not the clergie onely, but the king also
and his nobilitie to, there was a folishe bil and a falce put into a parliament or twayn, and sped as they were worthy: yet hadde I neuer seith
he, founden in all my tyme, while I was conuersant in the court, of all
the nobilitie of this lande aboue the nombre of .vii. of whiche seuen
20 there ar nowe thre deed, that euer I perceyued to be of the mynde, that
it were either righte or reasonable, or coude be to the realm profitable,
without lauful cause, to take any possessions away from the clergie.
And sithe maister Moore seith, that he hath not knowen aboue seuen,
wherof he saith thre are deed, that were of the mynde, that it were
25 resonable without cause, to take possessions frome the clergie, In
whiche wordes it is includid, that he knewe seuen of that mynde, whose
opinions it liketh him to reherse and put in writinge and in printe also:
it [C₂v] semeth, that if they wolde haue sayde, that it had ben lauful
with a cause to take possessions from the churche, he wolde haue
30 allowed that saying moche better than the other: but what cause he
wolde thynke reasonable in that behalfe to take the possessions from
the clergie, and what not, I can not telle. But perauenture if he were
asked the question therin, by theym that had auctoritie to do it, he
wolde shewe what he mente therby: but in good feith taking his wordes
35 as they be, when they be leyd to gether, I can not perceyue whether his
meanynge be, that possessions maye be laufully taken from the clergie
or not, but he that list to rede his wordis aduisedly, shal perauenture
perceyue more in them than I do. And now by occasion of that that is
sayde before of the possessions of the churche I shal speke somwhat
40 ferther therin, than I thought to haue done, and that is this: that if it
were [C₃] ordeyned by parlyamente, that there shulde no possessions
come hereafter of new to the clergie, onles it were for any fundacion,

that the kingis grace wolde make of his owne mere mocion, that it were
a good ordenance. And ferthermore I wyl confesse also, that I haue
desired many tymes: that like charitie, mekenes, zele of sowles, zele of
the christen faith, the same spirite of counsayle, and the true doctrine,
that was in the apostelles and disciples of our lorde, may now be in our   5
bishops and pristes, which be their successors: for then certein it is, that
al these murmurs, gruges, and discentions shuld shortly haue an ende:
But to say, that euer I coueited or desired, that lyke pouertie, as was in
the apostels and disciples, shuld nowe be in bishops & pristes, I neuer
desired it: For I haue not sene ne yet can see, that like pouertie were   10
nowe expedient for the continuance of the faith, as was than ex-
pe[C₃v]diente for the begynnynge of the feithe: but yet I thinke that it
be right expedient, for them that haue aboundaunce of possessions, to
be welle ware, leste happely it be to them as a pricke or a thorne to
pricke them vp from the rest of prayour and contemplation that they   15
shulde haue to god: to the clamorous noyse of worldly busynes, and to
a loue of worldly thynges, and so hindre the cleane and pure loue and
affection, that they ought to haue to almighti god, & to their neighbours: for surely but they take good hede, it wyl be so.

An answere to two other obiec-   20
tions of the saide apologie.
The .vii. Chap.

I T is sayd in the begynninge of the said tretise, that it is to be lament-
id, that enuy, pride, diuision, and stryfe rayneth not onely betwene laye
men [C₄] and lay men, but also betwene religious and religious, and   25
betwene prestes & religious, And that is yet more to be lamented, also
betwene priestes and pristes. Vpon whiche wordes sir Tho. More in his
apologie taketh it that the saide treatise lamenteth more the variance
betwene pristes and pristes, then betwixt religious and religious, for
that as he taketh it, that I shuld accompt the state of priesthode more   30
perfit, then the state of religion, and so the offences of priesthode to be
greater than the offence of religious. And verilye that can not be taken
by the said wordes, and that for two causes, wherof the first is this: It
apperith, that al the said sentence of the said treatise, wherin the variance betwene spiritual persons is lamented, is one hole sentence, and   35
concerneth the variances that be and haue ben as well betwixt religious
and religious, and betwene priestes and religious, as al[C₄v]so betwixte
priestis and priestis. And bicause the variances, that be betwene them
al, ar more to be lamented, then if they had bene onely betwene parte
of them. Therfore when the variances betwixte religious and religious,   40

and betwixte priestes and religious, be fyrste recited in the said treatise, it foloweth after, And that is yet more to be lamented, that it is also betwene priestes and priestes: As who saithe, it is more to be lamented, when variances be betwene them all, in all the said thre degrees, then if
5 they were betwene them onely in the firste two degrees, that is to say betwixt religious and religious, and betwixt priestes & religious, and not betwene priestis & priestis. And therfore the said treatise sheweth, that variances be betwene spirituall men in all the said three degrees. Wherfore they be the more to be lamented, and not bicause the offence
10 of priestis is more than the offence of [C_5] religious. And surely by this exception it appereth, that maister More hath a right great & a high inuentiue wit, wherby he can lightly turn a sentence after his appetite. And therfore if he wil, to that high witte set a good wil, & a good intent in all his workes, he shall surely do moche good. And if he wil vse it to
15 derken a sentence, and to couert and kepe secrete the truthe: he may do great hurt, and that more than he shall thinke him selfe.

The seconde cause is this. Though it were admitted, that the said sentence shulde sounde to this effecte, that the variances betwixt priestis and priestis were more to be lamented, than the variances
20 betwixt religious & religious, or betwixte priestis and religious: yet in this case it coude not be reasonably taken to be so, bycause the state of priesthode is more perfite, then is the state of religion, but rather for this cause folowynge. It appereth, that [C_5v] al the intent of the said tretise is to lamente the diuision, that is nowe betwixt the spiritualtie
25 and the temporaltie in this realme, and therwith to moue howe and in what maner a vnitie might be had vpon the same: and therfore this name is sette vppon the said tretise, A treatise concerning the diuision betwixt the spiritualtie and temporaltie. And then immediatly folowing the name, in the declaration of the said treatise, whiche is in the begin-
30 nynge of the boke before the firste chapiter, it is said, That if they that may do most good towardes the said vnitie, wil take the articles of the said treatise, as lytell tytlinges to brynge som weightier thinges into their mindes concernynge the same: and then by their wisedomes wyll adde theym therunto, and as they shall seme necessarie to se them al
35 put in due execucion: that in short tyme they shal bring this matter to good effecte, to the ho[C_6]nour of god, and the common welthe & quietnes of al the kyngis subiectis. And so it appereth, that the said treatise hath a speciall respecte to a peace and vnitie to be had betwixt the spiritualtie and the temporalte, and to the common welthe and
40 quietnes of all the kingis subiectes. And for as moche as pristis be more vniuersally abrode in the realme in euery cite, towne, and many partic- ular houses & villages, more than religious men be, so that their good

example may do more good vniuersally amonge the people, then the
examples of religious men may, whiche be not so vniuersally conuersant among the people, as pristis be: And that the euyl examples of
pristis may by lyke reason do more hurte to the people, then the euil
examples of religious men maye do: Therfore it may be right conue-   5
niently saide, that the diuision betwixt priestis and pristes is more to be
lamented, then the [C₆v] diuision betwixt religious and religious, and
not for that, that the perfection of priestis is aboue the perfection of
religious. And if maister Moore wyll haply saye, that there is no suche
variance betwixt priestis and pristis, let hym loke vnto the variances   10
that be & haue ben in many places betwixt curates and chauntry priestis
vpon the statute prouincial, which appoynteth howe chauntrepriestis
and other priestis, beinge in the parisshe, shall ordre them selfe to the
curate. And let hym loke also to the variances, that somtyme haue risen
vpon presentmentes to benefices, in howe extreme and worldly maner   15
one prieste hath sued agaynst an other. And lyke wyse for tithes, and
other spirituall dueties. And though those variances and suites haue
not bene vniuersal in al places, god forbede they shulde, yet they haue
bene spoken of and knowen in right many places, to the great offence
[C₇] and euil example of a right gret multitude of the laie people. And   20
therfore it may be conueniently saide, that the diuision betwixte
priestis and pristis, is more to be lamented, then the diuision betwixt
religious and religious. And if maister Moore wold charitably, and to
the beste so haue taken it, he shulde not haue neded to haue taken so
moche peyn as he hath done in the making of the saide exception, ne   25
yet to haue caused men to haue taken so moch peyn in the answeryng.
How be it euery light exception wyl not be so sone answered, as it may
be taken. And than he goeth farther and takith yet a more light exception, than he dyd fyrste. For he sayth, f. 102. that some say, that some
religious be priestis, and that as many priestis be also religious, and   30
thervppon he maketh a doubte, what I shuld meane by these wordes
(betwixt priestis and pristes.) But howe lyttell morall lernynge or [C₇v]
gostely profite foloweth vpon that exception, it is apparant. For ywis
euerye man knoweth that some priestes be religious, and that as many
religious be pristes: But by that worde priestis I toke it, and yet do take   35
it to be vnderstande seculer priestes, and not religious priestis: for so it
hathe ben alway taken by a common acceptaunce and vse amonge the
people in tyme paste, that is to saye, that whan a man speketh of
priestes, it is to be vnderstande of seculer priestis, and not of religious
priestis. As if a man wil say, he sawe in suche a churche, or at suche a   40
sermon an .C. or .ij.C. pristes: All the herers wyl vnderstande, that he
meaneth it of seculer priestis, and not of religious: without he shew it

hym selfe that they were religious. And there is also in the lawe of the
realme (as maister Moore knoweth right well) some suche cases, that
the common opinion of the people hath [C₈] dryuen a certayntie of
meanynge in dyuers thynges, whiche the law hath amytted, so that no
5 man shall be receyued to say it was otherwise ment, but as the lawe
grounded vpon the common opinion of the peple hath acceptid it. As if
a man be bounde to pay an .C. li. at London it shal be vnderstand of the
citie of London, in so moche that thoughe there were an nother towne
called London, and that he that was bounde, thought that he shulde
10 haue payd it there: yet for the common amittaunce of al the people of
the realme in that case, that by this terme London hath vnderstonde
the citie of London, hit shall be vnderstande of the citie of London, and
there he shal be bounde to pay it. And so it is if a man be bound to
pay .xx. li. at Michaelmas in suche a yere, he shalbe bounde to paye it at
15 the feaste of sayncte Mighell, that is the .xxix. day of Septembre, and
yet there be other festes of seynt Michel, [C₈v] as *Michaelis in monte
tumba*, & also the apparition of saint Mighell, but these feastes are not
vnderstande amonge the people by that generall terme of Mighelmas,
but the other feest, wher at commonly rentes be payde, leases begyn,
20 seruantes be most commonly reteyned and depart, and suche other.
And therfore whanne it is spoken of Michaelmas, hit is vnderstande of
the said feest in the later ende of Septembre. And therfore though
maister Moore doo not vnderstonde by that worde priestis seculer
priestes, yet the common vse and acceptaunce of the people wyll take it
25 so. But nowe admitte it, that both the saide obiection of syr Tho. More
were good, & that it were graunted hym, that he shulde haue al his
mynd therin: yet if it were well considered, how lytel frute shulde
folowe of his exceptions, it might be meruayled, why he toke theym.
For surely no amendment ne reformation [D₁] coulde folowe vpon
30 them. And if his Apologie be well & throughely loked vpon, concernyng the said tretise: it is lyke wise of dyuers other of his obiections in
his apologie: And though I haue not said so at thende of euery such
obiection, that I haue answered to, and shal answere to: yet the reder
whan he hath redde any of my sayde answers, may consider to what
35 effect the obiection, that master More doth make in that behalfe, shuld
serue: Admytte it to be trewe all that he saide, & he shall fynde that in
many of them it serueth neither to make peace ne reformation, but
either to persuade, that som thing that I haue leide for cause of diuision, is no cause of diuision: or els to perswade streite punysshement
40 and correction for heresies: and that vnder suche maner, that if his
mynde were folowed in euery thing, it might happen that innocentes
might some tyme be therby punished, as well as [D₁v] the greattest
offenders.

Of worldly honour. The
viij. Chapitre.

I N the said treatise, in the fyrst chapitre, it is said thus: And some laie
men sey ferther, that though religious men haue varied with religious,
and that some priestis haue varyed also with religious in some poyntes,   5
concerning the preheminence of their perfection (as is said before)
that yet in suche thinges as perteyn to the maintenance of the worldely honour of the churche, and of spiritual men, whiche they cal the
honour of god, and in suche thinges as perteyn to the increase of the
ryches of spiritual men, religious or secular, they sey, they agree al in   10
one. And when maister More hath rehersed the saide wordes of the
saide treatise, he saith thus: As for calling the worldly honour of the
churche & of spiritual men the honour of god, I [D$_2$] wote nere
whether I perceyue well, what this man menith therbi. And therfore to
remoue the doubt, that maister Moore is in, in that behalfe, I shall   15
speke somwhat ferther of honour than I dydde in the said tretise, as I
haue fonde it writen by other, and that is: Fyrst I fynde written, that
honour is onely due for vertue. Also that no man may couet honour
withoute offence, except it be onely coueited to the honour of god.
And I fynde also, that an inordinate appetite of honour is deedly sinne   20
of hym that coueteth it: like as ambition is deedly synne. And therfore
it is sayde, *viij.q.i. in scripturis,* that to hym that desireth honour, it is to
be denied: and to hym that refuseth it, it is to be offered. And the
philosopher, *iij. Ethic.* sayth, that they be not sothfastly stronge, that for
honor do great thinges. Wherby it semeth, that his mening is, that   25
stronge thinges and thynges of great difficultie, [D$_2$v] ar to be done for
loue of vertu, rather then for loue of honour. Then I mene ferther,
that if any spiritual man wold accepte a worldly honour, by reason of
any spiritual dignitie, & god were therby dishonored, as it may be by
many circumstances, as if for suche worldly honour charitie be in any   30
maner broken or denied, iustice delaied, any of the .vij. sacramentes
not duly ministred: or the people not diligentely and plainly instructed: that then it is not to be called honour to god, but rather
dishonour, and that yet som laye men say, they cal it an honour to god.
And surely the truthe is, that many laie men sey, that for the meinte-   35
nance of such worldli honour, spiritual men both religious and seculer,
be negligent somtyme in suche thinges, as be before rehersed, and that
yet they call suche worldly honour the honour of god. And if it be not
so as they sey, then ar spiritual rulers bonden to help the [D$_3$] people
out of that iugement, and els they be not without offence them self.   40
And if it be as the people say, than ar spiritual men bounde to reforme
it. And whether there be such a iugement in many of the people or not,

that is to sey, that spiritual men agree in one to meynteyne the worldly
honour of the churche: let the common opinion of moche parte of the
people spirituall & temporal, be iuge, whether many lay men say so or
not.

5   And then maister Moore goeth ferther and sayth: that where I saye
(as before appereth) that some laie men saye, that in al suche thinges,
that is to say for the worldly honour and riches of the church, al the
clergie both seculer and religious agree to gether, he sayth: that I can
(if I wil) tel the same some laie men, that so tolde me, that some other
10   lay men say nay: for they sey that they se verie wel, that in al those
thingis there are nowe some [D₃v] suche of the clergie, such as it is pitie,
that euer they were therof, either secular priestes or religious persons.
And yet are there saith maister More some suche of bothe, whiche
nowe caste of their fauoure frome bothe twayne, and fro the christen
15   feithe also. This is a very derke sentence, so moche intriked with some
sayes, after the maner of a gestyng facion, that it is som what harde to
perceyue his mynde in it: but yet two thinges there be, that I note in tho
wordes, wherevnto I shall shewe my conceyte: One is, that he saith, that
I can tell, if I wyl, that some lay men say, that pristes and religious do
20   not agree in that poynt to meinteyn worldly honour and riches of
spiritual men: And in good faithe I do not remembre, that euer any lay
manne sayne nay therto. And ferther more it is but a smalle reason to
persuade that priestes and religious do not agree in that poynt, bicause
some [D₄] laie men shulde sey to me, that they se verie wel, that some of
25   the clergie be fallen from them bothe into heresies, that he there re-
membreth, that wyll not therfore as his menyng is, in tho poyntes, ne in
none other agree with them that be catholike. For though it were
admitted, that some be fallen into heresies: yet it is not like, that that
some is so great, ne maister Moore sayth not hym selfe, that it is so great
30   but that priestis and religious as to the multitude may yet beside them
agree in one to the meintenance of their worldly honoure.

The seconde is, that as I take it, he saith, that I can telle, if I will, that
some laie men sey, that they see verye wel, that there ar som such of the
clergie, suche as it is pitie that euer they were therof, either secular
35   priestes or religious persons. And verily if his wordes there shalbe
taken to be of that effecte, as I take them to be, that lay [D₄v] men say
so, then I shal answer to them thus, that in good feith there was neuer
any laie man, ne yet religious, to my remembrance, that hath tolde me,
that there were any suche in the clergie, suche as hit was pitie, that euer
40   they were therof. And I can not see how any man might sey so, & be
sure that he sayth truthe. For thoughe hit were so, that ther were som
such of the clergie, that were fallen into suche heresies, as he speketh
of: yet to sey, that it is pitie, that euer they were eyther secular priestes

or religious: I can not se howe that can be affirmed without offence. For none is so euil, but he may amende, and so may they, if any suche be, and shal than haue the accidentall rewarde for their estate of lyuynge, beside the common rewarde of charite, that euery good christen man shal haue, as wel as if they had neuer offended. And verily me thinketh tho wordes shulde be some what dange[D₅]rous for any man to sey, that it was pitie, that euer they were secular prestes or religious. For it shulde seme, that tho wordes shulde amount to as moche, as that repentance shulde not be of effecte hereafter to them: or that they wolde neuer repent. And that I can not thinke to be his meanynge. For many tymes he commendeth the sacrament of penance. And therfore his meanynge semeth to be, that tho lay men, that so reporte, shuld meane by thoo wordes, that there are nowe som of the clergie, both pristes & religious, that if they continue in the same mynde, as they be nowe of, withoute repentance: that they shulde not dye in the state of grace. But if he mente by his wordes so, it had ben wel done that he had plainly shewed his minde that he mente so: or elles peraduenture some other myghte mystake the intent of his writyng therin, as he him selfe might happen to do, if the same [D₅v] wordis were written by an other man. And though there were any men religious or pristis, whiche god forbede, that died finally without repentance: yet it is to me a great doubte, whether it might be saide & verified, that it was pitie that euer they were religious or pristis. For as me semeth, it may not be wel said, that it was pite, that euer the diuel was create. For he hath for his malice his iuste punicion, whiche commendeth hyghly in almighty god, his rightwise iugement.

Also me semeth, that som other wordes, that mayster Moore speaketh ageinst offenders, be somtime very sore and hardly standynge with charitie, as to cal any man desperate wretche, or to sey that he is perished in his obstinacie, or suche other. And I truste, that there is no suche desperate wretche lyuing in this world. And if there were, I think verily if maister More thought he coulde doo hym any com[D₆]forte, he wolde leaue honour, landis, & goodis, to se if he coude comfort hym, and so perauenture to saue hym in bodie and in soule, rather then to se him finally perishe. And surely so oughte euery christen man to do spirituall and temporal, but most specially spiritual men, by reson of the perfection of liuing, that they haue taken vpon them, more then any temporal man hath.

The .ix. Chapiter.

IN the said treatise, in the fyrst chapitre, it is recited among other thinges, that some men say, that all spiritual men, as to the multitude,

be more diligent to enduce the people to suche thinges as shall brynge
ryches to the church, as to giue money to trentals, and to funde chanteries and obites, and to obteyne pardons, and to go on pylgremages, and suche other, rather than they be to enduce them to the
5 pai[D_6v]ment of their debtis, to make restitucion for suche wronges as
they haue done, or to do the workes of mercy to their neighbours, that
be pore & nedi, and that somtyme be also in right extreme necessite.
And vpon these wordes mayster Moore in his Apologie persuadeth,
that it is to be considered, that littel profite cometh to the churche by all
10 these thinges, and specially of trentals, he sayth thus: Lo (sayth he) they
be the thinges ye wote wel, wherby the multitude of the clergie, and
specially the prelates, get euerye man amonge them an infinite tresure
in a yere, so that hit is no meruaylle, though the hole clergie secular and
religious, what variaunce so euer they haue amonge them selfe beside,
15 concerning the preheminence of their perfection, agree to gether. But
surely all·these wordes of maister More answere not to the effecte of
the sayde treatise. For the effecte of the saide treatise is, [D_7] that
debtes and restitutions ought after the due order of charitie, first to be
done before trentalles, foundynge of chantries and obites, or suche
20 other: but when debtis and restitutions be made, and poore men in
extreme necessitie somewhat prouyded for: then the said treatise
speaketh nothynge ageynst it, but that it is right good to haue obites,
trentals, chanteries, and suche other dedes of supererrogation done
for them & for their ancestours, after as their deuotion gyueth. And
25 surely seing that this matter is so necessarie a thinge for the good order
of charitie amonge a great parte of the people to be loked on, I meruaylle greatly, that maister Moore speketh no more to helpe it forwarde than he dothe. For the most that he doth therin is to make it
appere, that littel profite cometh therby to spiritual men, religious or
30 secular: so that there is no likelyhode, that al spirituall men, as [D_7v] to
the multitude, shulde be more diligent to induce the people to such
thinges, then to paiement of debtis, makinge of restitutions, or to do
good dedes for reliefe of their poore neighbours. But to what effecte
this persuasion serueth, verily I se not: For be the profite great or littel,
35 if spirituall men, for the profyte therof, suche as it is, be it more or lesse,
be more diligent to meinteine it, then the other before rehersed, that
be more charitable then that is: wolde it not be lokid on and refourmed,
and be broughte hens forward into a good charitable wey? Verily I
trowe no man wil sey the contrarie. And yet maister More doth no
40 more, but as it is said before, fyrste persuadeth the profites to be litell,
and after he thanketh god, he neuer harde of any one, that euer wolde
giue that conseile. But what helpeth that, though he neuer herde it, if it
be yet so in dede, as he denyeth not ex[D_8]presly, but that it is? But for a

likelihode, whether it be so or not, this may be considered, that certayne it is, that many wronges haue be done in tyme paste, bothe of
landes and goodes. Wherfore restitution ought to haue ben made er
that the sinne could haue be forgiuen. For saint Augustyn saith, *Non
dimittitur peccatum, nisi restituatur ablatum,* that is to saye, The synne is   5
not forgyuen, tyl the thing that is wrongfully taken away, be restored
ageyne. And if this be true, let it then be considered, what it shulde
meane, that so fewe restitutions haue ben made this .xx. or .xxx. yeres
passed, or perauenture more. And if it be said, that men be so loth to
haue their wronges knowen, that they wyl in no wise make restitution: 10
it may be answered, that though some percase be so harde harted, that
they wold be loth to haue their wronges knowen, yet it is not like that all
men wolde be so, if they had good cha[D₈v]ritable counsayle in that
behalfe: but if the spiritual counsayle wyl enclyne more to trentals,
obytes, makynge of chaunteries, and suche other, rather then to res-   15
titutions, the due examination that is requisite for making of restitutions, may lightly be forgoten, & so perauenture it hath bene in some
places in time past. Howe be it the right noble prince of blessed memory kyng HENRY the .VII. father of our souerayne lorde the kynge, that
nowe is, wylled restitutions to be made: but how his wyll was per-   20
fourmed, I can nat tel: how be it what so euer was done therin, I
suppose his good intente suffisith to him. And to the intent I wold haue
this matter the better loked on, I wolde here aduertise sir Thomas
Moore, not by way of argument but for the more clerenes of conscience, to consyder whether is the more charitable wey, first to make   25
restitutions, pay dettes, and releue extreme pouer[E₁]tie: and than
after to do the other, yf he haue wherwith to do both, and els to do the
firste and let the other passe? And if he thinke that this wey, that I haue
moued be the more charitable wey, that then he helpe hit forwarde,
rather than the other, and than not to blame any man that maketh that   30
mocion, as though he were ageynst trentals, obites, and suche other:
for he is not ageynst them directly, but onely intendeth to haue them
changed into a more charitable order. For though prayers be right
expedient and helthfull to the soule: yet they serue not in al cases, as to
discharge debtes or restitutions, where there is inough to paye them   35
with: no more then there can be founde any one salue, that can heale al
maner of soores.

The .x. Chapitre.

SIR Thomas More, in the .xxvii. chapitre of his apologie, fol. 162.
[E₁v] seyth thus: Verily for ought that I can se, a gret part of this   40
proude and pompose apparel, that many priestis in yeres not longe

paste ware by the pride and ouersight of som fewe, forced in a maner
ayenst theyr owne willes to weare, was before his goodly conseile, so by
this prety printed boke, priuely gyuen them in their ere (moch more I
trow then the one halfe spent and in maner well worne out) I wote wel it
5   is worne out with many, whiche intende hereafter to bye no more suche
ageyne. And for the residue of the countenaunce I dare be bolde to
warrant, that I canne fynde of those that moste may spende, whiche
were they sure, that it shulde in this matter do any good, wolde be well
content & withdrawe from al theyr other countenance the chiefe parte
10   of their mouables and of their yerely liuelode, & out of hande bestowe
the tone, & with their owne hande yerely bestowe the [E₂] other openly
amonge the poore. And I durst agayne be bolde to warrant, that if they
so dyd, euen the selfe same folke, that nowe gruge and call them
proude for theyr countenance, wolde then fynde as great a gruge, and
15   call them hypocrites for theyr almes, and sey that they spende vpon
naughtie beggers the good that was wonte to kepe good yomen. And
that therby they bothe infeble and also dishonour the realme. Thus far
go the wordes of sir Tho. More: wherby ye may perceyue the good
minde, that many pristes haue concernynge pompous apparel, whiche
20   they haue worne out, & neuer entende to bye no more, wherin they be
right moche to be commended. And ye may perceyue also by his said
wordes, the good mynde of some of those, that moste may spende,
whiche (as he sayth) he dare be bolde to warrant, that if they knewe it
wolde do good in this matier, wold well be con[E₂v]tented to withdrawe
25   from al theyr other countenance the chiefe parte of their mouables,
and of theyr yerely liuelode to: and out of hande bestowe the one, &
with their owne hande yerely bestowe the other upon the poore. And
verily by these wordes he hathe euidently declared, that there is a right
good, blessed, and charitable mynde in some spiritual men, that most
30   may despend, that is to say, to dispose their landes and goodis in
charitable maner, as before appereth. But then how the conclusion,
that he maketh thervpon, may stande with charitie, I can nat tell. For
he saythe after, that he durste be bolde agayne to warrante, that if they
so did, euen the same selfe folke, that nowe grudge and cal them
35   proude for their countenance, wolde then fynde as great a gruge, and
call them hypocritis for theyr almes, and say that they spende vppon
noughtie beggars the good that was wont to [E₃] kepe good yomen,
And that therby they both enfeble and also dishonour the realme. I can
not see, but that in this sayenge, he doth ageinst the gospell: For it is
40   said *Matt. viij. Nolite iudicare, & non iudicabimini,* that is, Iuge ye not, and
ye shal not be iuged. And yet maister More iudgeth in this case to the
worste a thing that is vncertayn. And he doth therin also ageynste the

doctrine of saint Paule, whiche seyth *Quis es tu, qui iudicas alienum seruum?* that is to say, who art thou that iugest an other mans seruant? And he sayth also, *Nolite iudicare ante tempus,* Iuge ye not before the time. And as me semith maister More by that iugement hath done ageinst all these doctrines. And me thynketh also, that he shuld rather   5
haue comforted them, that be of that good mynde, to folowe it, than any thynge to discourage them in it. And hit semeth rather to be a discourage than a comforte, to saye, that if they [E$_3$v] do it, som other wyl cal them hipocrites for their doing. Not withstanding for as moche as they that be of that good mynd, seme to be men of a good zele, and   10
that they wolde gladly doo good in this matier: it is to thinke, that they will nat deferre their good pourpose for no͛ suche suspicion that haply wil neuer com, ne yet for no such vncharitable wordes, though they were spoken in dede. And I prey god they do not, but that they procede in their good purpose. And if it were enacted by parliment, that diuers   15
good lawes, whiche be al redie made by the church, concerning the disposicion of goodis of spiritual men, shuld be duly put in execucion, with such articles added therto, as shall be thought necessarie by par-lyamente: I thynke it wold do moche good in this behalfe.

The leuenthe Cha-   20
pyter. [E$_4$]

I N the said treatise, fol. v. it is saide thus: Yet aboue all other thinges me thinketh that it is most to be lamented, that spiritual men knowing these gruges and murmurations amonge the peple, and knowing also that many laie men haue opinion, that a gret occasion therof riseth by   25
spiritual men, and that they do no more to appese them, ne to ordre them selfe in none other maner for the appesynge of them than they do: for al that they do therin moste commonly is this, they take it, that they that fynde defaute at suche abuses and disordre, loue not pristis. And therfore they esteme, that they do of malice al that they do to   30
distroy the churche, and to haue their goodis and possessions them selfe. And therfore they thinke it a good dede to see them punished, so that they shall not be able to bring their malice to effect. And therfore haue they punished many persons, which moch people haue [E$_4$v] iuged them to do vpon wil, and of no loue vnto the peple. This last   35
clause, that is to say, And therfore they haue punisshed many persons, whiche moche people haue iuged them to do vppon wyl and of no loue vnto the people, the said Apologie, in the .184. lefe reciteth truely. But in the .187. lefe maister Moore in his Apologie seith, that I mi selfe say pleinly, that the spiritualte haue punished many persons therfore, that   40

is to saye, bicause they take it, that they that fynde default at suche
abusions loue no priestis: And that therfore they esteme that they do of
malice all that they do to distroye the churche. And therfore they
thinke it is a good dede to se them punished. And in that he sayth there,
5 that I say playnely those wordes my selfe, he saith playnly ageinst the
letter of the said treatise, which is, that they haue punished many
persons, whiche moche people haue iuged them to do vpon [E₅] wyll
and of no loue vnto the people, and not that I saide so my selfe, but
what he meaneth so to varie in the rehersinge of the lettre I can not
10 redily tel, but it be that he wolde not haue it openly reported, that
moche people take it so. But if he wolde make ferther serche therin to
knowe the truth, he shall fynde, that moche people be of that opinion,
whiche as me semeth is right moche to be regarded by spiritual rulers,
whether it be true as they say or not. And vppon these matiers, thus
15 misreported, he bringeth in diuers thinges, that he takith exception to
rather vpon his own misreporting then vpon the said treatise.

Also in the said treatise, in the firste chapiter, it is said amonge other
thinges, that some men as of a policie to pull riches from the churche,
haue inuehid ageynste all suche thinges, as bringe riches to the
20 churche: and bicause great riches haue come to the [E₅v] churche for
preyeng for soules in purgatorie, haue by wordes affermed, that there
is no purgatorie, and that granting of perdons riseth of couetise of the
churche, and profitteth not the people: and that pylgremages be of no
effecte: And that the churche may make no lawes, and suche other
25 thinges, as foundinge of chanteries, making of bretherheedis, and
many mo: wherin they shewe outwardly to ryse ageinst al the thinges
before rehersid, & to despise them: and yet they know & beleue in their
hartis, that all these thinges be of them selfe righte good and profitable,
as they be in dede, if they were ordered as they shulde be.

30 Of these wordes master More gadereth, that I shulde say, that these
men be politike men, and therin he mistaketh the sentence of the saide
treatise greately: for the sentence is not, that they do it politikely, but
that they do it as of a policie. And therfore as a [E₆] man may sey by an
hypocrite, that he vseth hym selfe in this thinge or that, as he were a
35 vertuous man, and yet calle hym not vertuous: so may it be sayde, that
these men to pulle ryches from the churche seye this or that, as of a
policie, and yet call them not politike. And yf mayster Moore wolde
haue considered these wordes wel: he mighte haue perceyued, that I
calle them not politike in dede. And yet vpon that same acceptance of
40 hym selfe, and of his owne imaginacion, that I shulde do so, he taketh
many exceptions in dyuers places of his Apologi, and specially in one

place, that is to say, in the longe proces, that he maketh of the tynker,
he saith that if the tinker can not excuse hym selfe by simplicitie: that
then I haue taught him to say, that he dyd it of policie, to pull away
ryches from the churche, & that therfore it can be no heresie. But
surely I cal no man politike in that doing, [E₆v] and therfore maister   5
Mores inuention is but of smalle effect in this behalfe: howe be it if the
tynkar and the tylar that maister More so moche speketh of, can be any
reasonable and true allegiaunce so ordre them selfe, that it mai appere,
that they ought of iustice to be dismissed: god forbede but that they be
dismissed and go home ageine to their busines, as they did before.   10

The .xij. Chapitre.

Maister Moore in the .217. leffe of his Apologie, speakynge of
defautes, that as he thynkethe, shulde haue ben leide for causes of this
diuision, concludeth thus: If there be such a diuision: wherby hit appereth that he doubteth, whether there be any diuision or not: for this   15
coniunction, if, purporteth alwey a doubte. And after in the same
Apologie, fo. 241. he confesseth plainely, that there is a di[E₇]uision,
and maketh no doubte at it: and he callith it there the late spronge
diuision. And so in one place to make a dout, whether there be such a
diuision or not, & in an other place to agre, that there is suche a   20
diuision, semeth to be a variance and contradiction in it selfe: howe be
it surely I do not intende to lay that variance to hym as for any notable
defaute: For a lyke thing may soone happen in any man by a lighte
ouersighte. But the cause why I speke of it is this, to put hym in
remembrance, that he herafter ought the rather to beare suche light   25
defautes of other the more charitably, sith he him self hath likewise ben
ouersene. For we be al fraile, ignorant, and vnstable, though we be
estemed and taken as angels in our conuersation. And therfore is hit
saide in the firste boke of the folowynge of Christe the .xvi. Chapiter,
that no man is in this worlde without defaut, no man with [E₇v]out   30
burden, no man sufficient to hym selfe, ne no man wise inough of hym
selfe. Wherfore it behoueth ech one of vs to bere the burden of other,
to comfort other, to help other, to enforme other, & to instruct &
admonish other in al charitie. And if we wil note well the said wordes,
we shal the sooner lerne this lesson, to do in al thinges, as we wolde be   35
done to: and to do nothynge that we wolde not haue done to vs. And
that is as I take it one of the most souerayne doctrines that is, to instruct
a man howe he shall in euery thynge concernynge his neyghboure,
kepe hym selfe in a clere conscience, lerne it who so maye.

That the sayde treatise entendeth not
to bringe in amonge the people any
hatred ageinst the spiritualtie.
The .xiij. Chapytre.

5   I T is conteyned in the saide Apologie, fo. 239. that to make the
spiri[E₈]tualtie in more hatered, and to make the name of spiritual
men more odious amonge the people: I haue in diuers partes of the
saide tretise writen, that they wil make confederacies, to make and
meinteyn a part ageinst the temporaltie. And I meruaile that master
10 Moore dare of his conscience make that affirmaunce, and say that
myne intent was suche. For if I had intented to haue done so, and to
haue made the name of the clergie odious among the people: I wolde
not haue put into the sayde treatise dyuers articles, that be conteyned
therin: for fyrste in the later ende of the seconde chap. of the sayd
15 treatyse it is said thus: that nowe in these dayes our lorde hathe reserued many good men bothe spirituall men and temporall, that be not
in any maner partie, to the sayd diuision: whiche through helpe of
grace, & with the fauour of the superiours, shall be right well able to
brynge the [E₈v] other to a good accorde. And if I had intended to haue
20 made the name of spiritual men odious among the people, I wolde not
haue said, that many of them be good, and shall be able with helpe of
the superiours to bring the other to good accorde. Also in the fyfte
chapiter of the said treatise it is said thus: And I suppose verily, that this
diuision wyll neuer be perfitely & charitably refourmed and brought to
25 a good accorde, til the people come to this poynt, that they shall greatly
feare and drede to renne into the leste censure of the churche. And if I
hade thoughte to haue made the name of the spiritualtie odious
amonge the people: I wolde neuer haue moued the people to feare and
drede to renne in to the leest censure of the churche, whiche can not be
30 made but by spirituall men. Also in the .x. chapiter of the said treatise,
wherin dyuers abusions be leide in dyuers curates, it is [F₁] said thus:
And thoughe these abuses be not vsed vniuersally, God forbede they
shulde, for ther be many good curatis and other spirituall men, that
wold not vse them for the winning nor losyng of none erthly thinges.
35 And if I had thoughte to haue made the name of spiritual men odious
among the peple, I wold not haue seyd, that ther be many good curatis,
and other spiritual men: for it standeth not with reason, that they that
be good shulde be had in hatered.
        Also in the later ende of the last chapitre of the said tretise it is seyd
40 thus: And I beseche almightie god to sende these foure thinges habun-
dantly into the worlde, and that moste specially vnto the prelates and

spirituall reulers, that is to say zele of soules, pitie, good doctrine, and
deuoute prayer, & then I sey, that if it were so, that vndoubtedly a newe
light of grace and of tractabilitie shal shortlie shew and [F₁v] shyne
amonge the people. And if I had intended to haue made the name of
spiritual men odious, I wolde not haue seyde, that then a newe light of   5
grace and tractabilite shulde shortely shewe and shyne amonge the
people.

   Also I sey not in all the said treatise that the spiritualtie make confederacies to make a parte ageynst the temporaltie: but I seye thus in
the fyrste chapitre, that though spirituall men ought to faste and pray,   10
and do other good dedes .&c. crienge continually to our lorde, that this
diuision might cesse, that yet hit apperethe not, that they do so, but that
they rather continue still after the olde course, pretendynge by confederacies, worldly policie, and streite correction to rule the people.
And I sey there, that that is great pitie, and greatly to be lamented, and   15
that it wil be harde to bringe it so aboute. But if they wolde a litel meken
them selfe, and withdrawe su[F₂]che thinges as haue brought the people into this murmur & grudge: then I sey, that they shulde anone
bringe a newe lyght of grace into the world, and bringe the people to
perfite loue and obedience of their superiours: And that these wordes   20
doo not amount to the wordes of syr Thomas More aboue rehersed,
that is, that I shulde saye, that spirituall men make confederacies to
make & meinteyne a parte ageynst the temporaltie, it is euident to all
indifferente reders: And surely no more doth none other clause in all
that treatise: but that maister More liste for his pleasure to take it so.   25

Of them that fall into errours of sim-
plicitie or of an ignorance, & of wor-
des concerning heresie. The
.xiiii. Chapyter.

I SAIDE in the .viii. chapitre of the saide treatise, that it is a common   30
opinion amonge doctours, that none [F₂v] is an heritike, for that onely
that he erreth, but for that he defendeth opinatiuely his errour: and
therfore I seyd, that he that erreth by simplicite, may in no wise be
seyde an heretike. And I sey after in the same chapitre, that if that be
true, it were then great pitie, that there shulde be so greatte a desire in   35
some spirituall men to haue men abiured, or to haue the extreme
punysshement for heresie, as it is seid there is. For as som men haue
reported, if any man wil witnes, that an other hath spoken any thyng
that is heresie, though he speke it only of an ignorance, or of a passion,
or if he can by interrogatories and questions be driuen to confesse any   40

thinge, that is prohibite by the churche: Anone they wil driue hym to abiure, or holde hym atteynted, without examininge the intente or cause of his sayeng. And vpon these wordes sir Tho. More saithe in his Apologie, that I make men wene, [F₃] that the spirituall iudges in this

5 realme handled that thinge, that is to sey heresi, so cruelly, that al the world hath cause to wondre and gruge therat. And verilye I meruaylle moche, whervpon he groundeth his sayenge therin, for I neuer speke any wordis, that shulde sounde to that effect, that al the worlde had cause to wondre at the crueltie of spirituall men, concernynge heresie:

10 but I sayde as before appereth, that it were pitie, if it shuld be trewe, as it is reported, that there shuld be such a desire in spiritual men to haue men abiure, or to haue extreme punyshement for heresie, as it is seyd that there is. And those wordis proue not, that al the worlde hath cause to wondre and gruge at their demenure therin. How be it surely a great

15 noise hath gone abrode, that a right streite handlynge hath bene sene in that behalfe. And if master More wil serche and inquere for the truthe therin, he [F₃v] shal here more of that matier, then is spoken of in the saide treatise.

And where I sey ferther in the saide treatise, that if any wyl wytnes,

20 that a man hath spoken any thing, that is heresie though he speke it of an ignorance, or of a passion .&c. that he shall be driuen to abiure: master More denieth not those wordes, but anone he taketh those wordes, as thoughe I had spoken them of dampnable and obstinate deedly passions, where the lettre serueth plainely for passions of igno-

25 raunce and frailtie, and that be done for lacke of good aduysemente. For of them all the chapitre treateth moste proprely. And yet as it semeth, to blynd the reders, and to couert the truth the more, he goeth forth & saith, that men falle dayly into aduouterye through suche damnable passions, & that by the passion of ire and anger, men falle

30 into manslaughter: and so he shewethe dyuers other desperate [F₄] damnable passions that men offende by, and endeuoreth hym selfe as moche as he can, to make it appere, that the said tretise speketh of suche damnable passions, and wolde not that it shulde appere, that a man may haue a light passion of anger, and yet haue no wil to slee no

35 man, or of aduoutrie and yet do none in dede: and so maye a man speake lighte wordes of heresie, and yet fall not fro the true catholike feith.

And then ferther bicause master More seythe, that he can not gather of my wordes, what I wolde shuld be done with them that speke suche

40 euyl wordes, concerning heresie, and yet think wel in their mynd, wherby it semeth, that he wolde knowe my minde therin, I wolle saye to his mocion thus: that for as moche as he denyeth not the sayeng of

doctours therin, that is to sey, that a man is not an heretike, for that
onely that he speketh heresie, [F₄v] but for that he defendeth opinatiuely his heresie (as it is seyd before) therfore I wil desire him, that he
wil take the peine to aske that question of other great lerned men, as he
is: that can beste skille of that matier, & can beste folowe the mynde of   5
the auncient doctours, that haue spoken therof before their tyme. And
if he wil yet nedely desire, that I shuld shewe ferther of my mynde
therin, I wyll than firste assertein maister More, as far as in me is, that I
knowe not one heretike in al this realme, in worde nor dede. For howe
be it that I haue herd som tyme reported, that there be many heretykes,   10
yet I neuer harde so ferre profe therin, that I might with conscience
iuge or report, that this man or that manne is an heritike. And to euery
light worde a manne maye not gyue full credence in that behalfe, ne
reporte it lightly, that any man is an heretike by such light talis. And
sure[F₅]ly this poynt is moche to be noted of all men, but mooste   15
specially of them that daily ministre the sacramentes of the churche,
leste haply through suche reportes they ministre them somtime in
deedly syn, & yet wolde not thinke so them selfe. And nowe wyll I say a
lytell farther in this matter, concerning suche wordes, that is to sey, that
if any man now in this dangerous time, while this diuision continueth,   20
wylle shew vnto the ordinarie, that he herd any speke wordes, that as he
thought stode not with the catholical feithe, & the ordinarie myslyketh
the wordes also: I wolde then thinke, that if he, vpon whom the informacion is made, be suche a man, that he that complaineth of hym may
conueniently speke to hym withoute daunger, that then the ordinarie   25
shall aduise him to kepe the matter secrete, if it be yet secrete, and not
openly knowen: and that he shal than charitably aske of him, what
[F₅v] he mente by these wordes. And then when the question is asked
hym, if he make so reasonable an answere, that it soundeth to no
heresie, then is the matier answered. And if he auowe the wordis, and   30
yet they be in dede ayenst the catholicall feithe: then it semeth good,
that he that accused him, folow the gospell, & take wytnes with hym,
and efte charitably giue him monicion therof. And if he wyl yet stande
stil opinatiuely in his opinion, and not accept the good monicion of the
other: then I thinke it good, that he ageyne informe the ordinary   35
therof, and then it semeth to be conuenient that the ordinarie sende
for hym, not as for a man yet notoriously knowen or detected for an
heretike, but to knowe ferther, whether it be tru as the other hath
reported or not: and if he fynde it trewe by sufficient profe, or by his
owne confession, and he wyll not be reformed, then it semeth conue-   40
nient, [F₆] that he vpon the witnes of the other, be punished as he hath
deserued. And if he wil be by the ordinarie secretly reformed: then it

semeth good, that he departe without any open penance: but what were conueniente to be ferther done in that matter, I wyl commytte it to other. Ferther more if he be suche a man, that he that made the informacion vpon hym, dare not speke to hym, nor perauenture the

5   ordinarie neither dare procede accordinge to the lawe ageinste him: then it semeth conuenient, that the ordinarie shulde informe the kingis grace and his conseile of it: and then it is not to suppose but that they wold prouyde sufficient remedie, as wel for the witnes as for the ordinarie: and se also that the ordinarie shulde haue power with the

10 kingis fauour to se him punished, but as longe as there is an opinion amonge the people, that the ordinaryes and their officers will giue light credence [F₆v] vpon informacions made to them of heresie, and that they wil noyse them that be complayned on, as heretikes, before dewe examinacion in that behalfe: so longe wil the people gruge, and per-

15 auenture the kynge not gyue his assistence so redily to haue them attached, as he wolde do, if he herde that the ordinaries noysed no man to be an heretike without due examinacion, as is before rehersed. And surely I thinke, that great offences rise dayly in many persons by noysing of suche heresies before the tyme. For sith euerye heretike synneth

20 deedly, & that in the hyghest degree of deedly synne, what offence is it then to noise a man to be an heretike, & is not? or to noise it that he fauoreth heresies, and doth not? And though he be an heretike in dede, yet the noysinge that he is one, ought to be done in al charite, and after due forme and order of the lawe. And if it be other wise done, I

25 thinke [F₇] it is no smalle offence. And if this be true, then do many offende, that will sey they offende not: and that as wel they that dayly vse to ministre the sacramentes, as other, as it is saide before. And though they noise suche heresies somtyme of a good purpose, to make somme other aferde, that shall here of it: yet that can not excuse them.

30 For certayn it is, that no euil is to be done, that good shulde folowe. And I beseche almighty god, that all men mai take good hede to this point, and to suche other, as to reporte, that any man shulde not loue pristis. For they lightly offende deedly therin, and yet peraduenture wolde saye naye. For as he offended deedly, that loued no prieste, so they

35 offende deedly, that sey that a man loueth no pristes, that loueth them in dede, thoughe haply he fynde defaute at some abuses and disordre that ar in som priestes. Yea and if a man had such a malice to pristes, [F₇v] that in his herte he loued no prieste, but it were not openly knowen, I suppose that no man wyl sey, but that he that wold noyse it

40 openly, that he loueth no priestes, shuld offende righte hyghly therin. And I trowe there is no one poynte, that wolde doo more good to appease these variances and gruges, that be now amonge the people (if

it were wel obserued and kept) then the refreyninge of suche wordes
wold do. And ferthermore I suppose that this diuision wylle not perfitely be appeased, ne come to a charitable and ful agrement, til the
worlde come to this point, that if the ordinarie wil noyse any man to be
an heretyke, or wyl reporte, that there be many heretikes in the realme,   5
that not onely the kynges grace, but also all his lordes and al other, that
shal here of it, shall anon giue eare to the matier to assiste the ordinarie
therin, if nede shuld be, thinking verily that the ordinarie be[F₈]fore
he made that report, had so throughly serched the truthe of the matier,
that he was not therin deceyued, ne that els he wolde not haue made   10
that reporte, ne to his power haue suffred it to be made. And here I wyl
for this time make an ende of this chaptre vnder this maner, that it
might please almighty god, that there remayne not one heresie in
worde nor in dede in all this realme, neither concernynge pardons,
purgatorie, pilgremages, prayenge to seintes, settynge vp of ymages,   15
the seuen sacramentes, fre abitrement, feythe and good warkes,
makinge of lawes, what is the churche, ne any other: And that they that
most shew them selfe to maynteine the true catholicall feithe, therin
may take the very true sothfaste & charitable way, that they ought to
take for auoidyng of them, if any suche be. Amen.   20

T Of the sute *ex officio.* The .xv. Cha. [F₈v]

HEN to the conuentynge of men before spirituall iudges *ex officio,*
and wherupon maister More saythe in his Apologie, fo. 219. that if it
were left, the stretes were likely to swerme full of heritikes: Verily I
meruayle righte moche at his sayinge therein: and that for this cause: It   25
is certein, that no man may after the lawe be detected of heresie, but
that there is som manne that knoweth the cause before why he ought so
to be. For if it be secrete in his owne breste, none can be his iuge but god
only, that is the sercher of mans herte. And if any wylle aduowe, that he
knoweth the cause, & wil denounce him as an heretike therfore: than it   30
is reason, that he be taken as his accuser. And if he wyl not aduow to be
his accuser, it is to think that he doth it of some malice or craft rather
then for the truthe of the mattier. And if he say he dare not for fere of
his lyfe auowe it, I haue shewed a [G₁] meane in the .vij. chapiter of the
said treatise, howe the wytnes may be saued from daunger, as by shew-   35
ing the matter to the king and his counsaile, and that then it is not to
suppose nor to thynke, but that they wyll prouide sufficiently for the
indempnitie of the wytnesse in that behalfe. And this remedie maister
More denieth not to be conueniente for this realme. And yet he wil not
assent, that a lawe be made that it shall be so. And then if the witnes wil   40

not auow it, but an other wil gyue credence to hym and auowe it: then
hit semeth reasonable, that they that wyl gyue credence therto, & will
report it, be taken as accusers: taking those witnes for their warrante, if
it be denied. But to put the partie that is complayned on, to answere,
5 and to condempne hym, if he say contrary to that the witnes haue seyd,
not knowing who be the witnes, ne who be his accusers: it semeth not
reasonable to [G₁v] be accepted for a lawe. For as I haue seyd in the said
tretise, if he that is accused knewe their names, that accused hym, he
might percase allege and proue so great and so vehement cause of
10 rancour and malice in them, that accuse hym, or beare witnesse ageinst
hym, that their sayinges by no lawe ought to stande ageynste hym: as if
there were two men that had sworne the deth of an other: and bicause
they can not bringe it about, they imagine howe they may brynge hym
to all the shame and vexation that they can, and therupon they apeche
15 hym of heresie: if he in this case knewe theyr names, he might proue
their rancour and malyce, And bycause he knoweth theym not, he can
not proue it. And also the witnes may be such, as shal haue his landes by
eschete after his dethe. And if it be saide, that these cases fall so seldome, that it oughte lytell to be pondred: so may it be saide like wise,
20 [G₂] that it falleth but seldomme, that the witnesse in heresie stande in
any feare of them, that they accuse. And then to make a generall lawe
to prohibite all men, that they shulde not haue knowlege of the witnes
in no case, it is not reasonable.

Also sir Tho. More denieth not, but that by reason of the lawe, *Ex. de*
25 *haereticis ca. Ad abolendam,* whiche is recyted in the .vii. chapitre of the
said treatise that a man may be driuen to a purgation without any
offence in him, or be accursid, as if he be notabli suspectid, and yet not
giltie, as it may well be: & yet he wil not condescend, that that lawe
shulde be changed, but seithe in fortifienge therof, that verily he
30 thinketh, that he which can not be proued gilty in heresy, and yet vseth
suche maner of weyes, that al his honest neighburs wene he were one,
and therfore in their conscience dare not swere, that he is any other, is
well worthie to do [G₂v] some penance. Truely this is a merueilous
persuasion, that a man shuld be put to his pourgacion, bicause his
35 neighbours dare not swere that he is no heretyke. And verily the lawe
is, that their othe in that case shulde not be accepted: for the saide
chapitre *Ad abolendam,* is that if a man be notably suspected of heresi,
that he shal purge hym selfe after the wyl of thordinarie or be accursed: & so the purgacion of his neighbor will not serue: Let euery
40 man therfore consider, whether the said lawe be indifferent or not.
And if it be not, let them put to theyr hande to haue it broken. And I
thinke verily, they shal deserue gret thanke of god, if they tourne it to a

more indifferent weye, then it is at nowe: For vnder this maner the mooste innocent man that is, maye of malice be reported to be suspected of heresye, and be not so in dede, and so be driuen to his purgation or be accursed: and then there [G₃] is a nother lawe, that if he in that case of an indurate minde stande so accursed a yere, he shall be punisshed as an heretike, and that is by the lawe, *Extra de haereticis, ca. Excommunicamus.*

Then he goeth further for meyntenance of the said suite *Ex officio*, and resembleth it to arestinge for suspecion of felonie, and to the suretie of good aberynge, and to inditementes: wherupon men be put to answere at the common lawe. And howe farre these resemblances varie from the sute *Ex officio*, he in some place openeth it hym selfe. But yet for a more playne declaration therin, I shal sey a litel further in that matier. Fyrste as to the arrestynge for suspicion of felonie, it is in dede an olde lawe of this realme, that for suspicion of felonie, a man may be arrested, so that he that doth arreste hym vppon a reasonable cause, dothe suspecte him: but it is a general rule, that he shall neuer be put to answere [G₃v] vpon that arreste, but proclamation shalbe made, that if any man wil leye any thinge ageynst him, that is so suspected, that it shall be herde: and if none suche come he shall be delyuered without fine or any other punishment, with a good exhortation of the iudges, that he shal take good hede how he ordereth hym selfe in time to come. And then maister More lykeneth the penance of suche a man that hath ben in prison vppon suspicion of felony, and so deliuered by proclamation, to the bearinge of a fagotte for heresie. For he sayth, that the one of them shall come as openly to the barre as the other to the consistorie: And that somtyme his fetters shal wey a good pece of the fagot, besides that they lie lenger on the one mans legges, then the fagot on the other mans shulder: but he reherseth not howe they lye many tymes lenger in prison for heresi, then they do eyther for suspicion of felonie [G₄] or for good abering. And ouer that I dare say, that there are but fewe, but that they hadde well leauer abide the peyne to be thrise acquited by proclamation, and perauenture ofter, then ones to beare a fagot for heresie.

And then as to the arrestynge for good abearynge, trouthe it is, that a man by commandment of the Iustices may so be arrestid, but he shall neuer be putte to answere vpon that arrest, but onely be bounde, and sureties with hym of his good aberinge. And if he can no suche suretie fynde, & he haue lyen there longe in prison, then the iuges by their descrecion, may sende a writte to inquere of his fame, and of his behauour, whiche is called a writ *De gestu & fama*, wherof sir Tho. More maketh mention in his Apologie: & if it be founde for hym vpon that

writ, that he is of good fame & behauoure, then he shalbe delyuered. Wherby master More sayth, he is in a maner pur[G₄v]ged, and by that saying it semeth that his meanynge is, that that delyuerie shulde be resembled to his purgation vppon the suspicion of herisye, as is sayde
5   before. But howe ferre they be vnlyke, it appereth thus: when a man is deliuered vpon the said writte *De gestu & fama*, he is delyuered as a manne proued to be of good honestie, and to be clered bi his neighbours, of that he was suspected of. And when he is purged vpon the suite *Ex officio*, or for suspicion of herisie, he is put to penance by
10 thordinarie, as a man suspected, wherof he is not clered, and so shal he be taken amonge his neighbours, as a man worthye to do that penance for his offences, wherfore it appereth euidentely, that they be nothynge lyke.

And then master More seyth yet ferther, that vpon inditementes at
15 sessions, the inditers vse not to shewe the names of them that gaue them infor[G₅]macion. And he seythe ferther, that they may not shewe their names. For they may not disclose the kinges counsaile nor their owne. But as I take it, that prohibicion of openynge of the conseile in this case is onely to be vnderstande of their owne conseile amonge them
20 selfe, after that they be sworne, but for opening of the names of them, that gaue them information before they were sworne, I knowe no prohibition. And if they wil not shew their names, they be not bounde to do it: for they be not bounden to helpe the partie to his writte of Conspiracie, but as they liste to do in conscience. And then bicause he
25 can none otherwise do: but confesse a great diuersite betwixt them that be put to answer *Ex officio*, and them that be put to answere before the kynges Iustices vppon inditementes at the common lawe: for there the iudges haue sufficient & apparant matier to putte them to an[G₅v]swere vppon, and in the other there is none, but that the spir-
30 ituall iuge vpon a displeasure may do it *Ex officio*, if he wil. Therfore he goth yet ferther and saith, that the .xii. men may yet do the same, and make a man to be called, that is not giltie, if they were so disposed. And trouthe it is, they maye indite a man, that is absent, and that is also not giltie, and be vntrue, if they wil: but yet in suche case the .xii. men be
35 knowen that doo hit, and be also compelled to be vppon the inquirie: for they may not be vpon it, but they be therto assigned: and also the partie vpon their verdite shall not be put to answere before them, as it is vppon the suite *Ex officio*, but before the kingis iuges, before whom the inditement is no atteinder to the partie: but that he may be founde not
40 giltie, not withstanding that inditement. And though master More sey, that he neuer sawe the day yet, but that he durste as well [G₆] trust the truth of one Iuge as of two Iuries: I thinke the Iuges wil can hym but

littel thanke for that preise: for surely Iuries must nedely be beleued & trusted. And therfore it is not the maner of the iuges to ley vntruth vpon a iurie, ne yet to commende them that do it, but it be proued afore them of recorde after the order of the lawe.

And thus it appereth, that maister More can neyther proue the suite   5
Ex officio to be lyke to the aresting of men for suspicion of felony, for good abearinge, to puttinge of men to answere vpon inditementes, ne yet to them that may be accused by .xii. men, & knowe not of it, & that for the causes before remembred. Wherfore it semeth, that though it were clerely put away, the stretis shulde not swarme ful of heretikes   10
neuer a whit.

The syxtene Chapitre.

I SEYDE in the .vii. Chapitre of the said Treatise, concerning the diui[G$_6$v]sion betwene the spiritualtie and temporaltie, that there is a lawe made by the churche, *Libro sexto,* in the title *De haereticis,* in the   15
chapitre *Accusatus, Parag. Licet,* Wherby it appereth, that if a man be sworne to sey the truthe concernynge heresie, as well of hym selfe as of other, and he fyrste confessethe nothinge, and after contrarie to his fyrst sayenge, he appeleth bothe hym selfe and other: yet the saide lawe is, that if it appere by manifeste tokens, that he doeth hit not by   20
lyghtenes of mynde, ne of hatred, nor for corruption of money, that then his witnes in fauour of the feithe shall stande, as wel ageynst him self as ageinst other. And yet, as it is seyd in the said treatise, it appereth euidently in the same Courte, and in the same matier, that he is a periured person. And therfore it is saide in the sayd tretise, that this is a   25
daungerous lawe, and more like to cause vntrue and vnlauful men to [G$_7$] condempne innocentis, then to condempne offenders. And I sey there also, that it helpeth litel, that if there be tokens, that it is not done of lightnes of mynde, hatred, nor for corruption of money, that the witnes shuld stande. For I sey there, that somtime a wolfe may shewe   30
hym selfe in the apparel of a lambe, and that if the iuge be parcial, suche tokens may be sooner accepted then truely shewed.

And when master More hath rehersed these wordes, thanne he sayth ferther in this maner: This piece concerninge the testimonie of known-en euil persons, to be receyued and taken in heresi, I haue (seyth   35
master More) somwhat touched in the thirde chapitre of the third boke of my Dialoge: where sithe they may rede it that wil, I will here (seyth he) make no longe tale therof. But then he seyth, that I wote wel, that heresie, wherby a christen man becometh a false traitour to [G$_7$v] god, is in al lawes spiritual and temporal, both accompted as great a crime as   40

is treason committed ageynst any worldly man. And then seythe he,
why shulde we then fynde so great a faute, that suche witnes, shulde be
receiued in a cause of heresie, as are receyued not onely in a cause of
treason, but of murder also, and of other more single felonyes, not
5   onely in fauour of the prince and detestation of such odious crimes, but
also for the necessitie, whiche the nature of the matter worketh in the
profe. To those wordes of master More I wil sey thus: I wil agre with
hym, that heresie is as greate a crime, & as moch to be detested as treson
is. But yet I wil ferther sey this also, that as wel the makers of lawes for
10 punishment of heresie and treson, as for al other offences, are bound-
en in conscience as wel to for see, as moch as in them is, that innocentis
shalbe sauid harmles by their lawes, as that [G₈] offenders shulde be
punisshed. And as it is true, that an innocent may be taken and accused, and neuertheles be yet well worthie to be saued and deliuered:
15 right so it is tru, that an offender may be taken and accused, and be well
worthy to be punysshed: but yet that punysshement muste be by a due
and a reasonable order of tryall. And I can not se, what due or resonable order of trial it is, that he that vpon his oth hath first clered him selfe
and his neighbour also of all heresies, shulde after contrarie to his fyrst
20 othe be receiued ageyne as a wytnes to condemne hym that he clered
before, and that in the same courte, and also in the same mater. And
where master More seith, that suche wytnes shalbe receiued not onely
in treason, but in murther also, and in other more syngle felonyes.
Wherfore (he saith) he can not se why we shuld fynde so great defaulte,
25 that suche witnes shulde be receyued in a [G₈v] cause of heresi: verily I
am in a dout, howe maister Moore vnderstandeth there that worde
(witnes.) For if he vnderstande therby the wytnes at the common lawe,
that shall make an ende betwene the parties in treason, murder and
felonie, as witnes in the spirituall lawe doth concernynge heresie: then
30 it muste be vnderstande, that he meaneth by that worde, witnesse,
the .xij. men, that shal trie the issu betwixt the king and the partie, at
the comon lawe, and wherto bothe the kyng and the partie shall be
bounde to stonde. And if he meane soo, then I take the common lawe
of the realme to be this: that a lesse offence then an open periurie in the
35 same courte, shall be sufficient to disable a Iurour in treason, murdre,
and felony also. As if a man that is arraynid of treason, murder, or
felonie plede, Not giltie, and thervpon an issue is ioyned, and a panell
returned by the Sheriffe, and the par[H₁]tie challengeth one of the
Iurie, for that he hath bene atteynted of periurie, in an other iurie: this
40 is a good peremptorie challenge, though the periurie were done in an
other courte, if he haue the recorde in hande. And so it is, if he sey, that
he hath ben atteynted in a writte of forginge of fals dedes: for he shall

be iuged by that heynous falsehede to be vnable to passe vpon any
enquest in any of the kinges courtes: And than me thinketh, that if any
suche open periurie or falshode appered in any iurour there openly in
the same courte, as this case is: that then he moche more rather shulde
be iuged vnable therby: than for a lyke defaute in an other court. And   5
if master Moore by that terme, wytnesse, meane suche witnes, as be
sometyme broughte in to the kingis courtis, to giue euidencis to an
enquest, than is that witnesse no suche witnesse, as the witnes bene in
the spirituall courte, [H₁v] that shall acquite or condempne the parties:
for of tho witnes so brought into the kingis court to giue euidence to an   10
enquest at the common lawe, no mencion shalbe made in the recordes,
ne the iurie be not bounde alwey to folowe tho wytnes. For if the Iurie
of their owne knowledge or otherwyse knowe the truthe ageynst the
sayeng of suche wytnesse, they be bounde to fynde according to the
truthe, and let tho witnes goo. And yet if it hapned, that suche collat-   15
erall witnes firste testified vpon theyr oth, that the partie were not
giltie: and after it were informed the iudges, that they reuoked their
firste sayinge, and wold say that the partie were giltie, I can not thinke,
that the iudges wolde any more calle them to here their sayeng therin.
And though they wolde, yet as I sayd before, it were ferre vnlike to this   20
case. For their saying there, is but as an euidence, whiche the iurie
shuld not be [H₂] bounde to beleue, but as the truthe is. I can not see
therfore, howe maister More can proue his sayeng, that suche witnes,
that is to sey, suche as be periured in the same Courte, shulde be
afterwarde receyued as witnes in any of the kynges courtes.   25

And farthermore where I haue seyd in the said tretise, as before
appereth, that it helpeth littell, that if there be tokens, that it is not done
of lyghtnes of mynde, hatred, nor for corruption of money, that the
witnes shulde be taken. For I sey there, that some tyme a wolfe may
shewe hym selfe in a lambes skynne: and that if the iuge be parcial,   30
suche tokens may be soner accepted then truly shewed. And then seyth
maister More, that by that reason, that a iuge maye be parciall, not
onely suche wytnes shulde be reiectid in heresie, treson, murder, and
felony: but also by the other reson of a wolfe in a lambes skynne, al
maner of wit[H₂v]nes in euery matter. For in euery matier (seyth he)   35
may it happen, that he that cometh for a witnes, and semeth a lambe,
may be in dede a wolfe, & be nought, where he semeth good. And
therfore, he seithe, lyttell good wolde grow if folke wold folowe that
inuencion, & make of the lawes a chaunge. And nowe by reason of this
obiection I wyl speke somwhat farther in this matter, then I did in the   40
said tretise. And fyrst I wil sey thus, that it is to me a greatte meruayle,
to see maister More so farre ouerseen, orels if he be not ouersene

therin, that then he wold if he coulde, deceiue other, and make them so
farre ouersene, to beleue that it shulde be one lyke reson of a periured
wytnes, that wyl loke lyke a lambe, and then say contrarie to that he
hath deposed before, and of a witnes that comith to depose in a matter,
5   that he was neuer yet sworn vpon. For whan a witnes is brought in, that
was ne[H₃]uer sworne vppon the matter before, the iudge maye not by
the lawe refuse hym, nor iudge any defaulte in hym, onles he knowe a
sufficient cause him selfe in that behalfe, or that the parties do allege it:
but he muste beleue, that he is honest, good, and indifferent, tyll the
10   contrary be shewed, as euerye man is in charitie bounde to do of his
neighbour. But whan a witnes hath deposed in the courte, and than
wyll offre him selfe to depose to the contrary that he said before: the
iudge maye with good conscience mystruste and thinke, that he doth it
of lyghtnes of mynde, hatred, or for corruption of money: In so moche
15   that before that *Perag. Licet* was made, the iuge might none otherwise
haue done of Iustice, but to haue refused to haue taken any farther
examinacion of hym. And if he had, and the other had said contrarye
to that he had said before, his sayenge had ben voyde in the lawe. And
[H₃v] what the makers of the said *Parag. Licet* ment, to put it to the
20   discrecion of the iuge, that if he saw by euident tokens, that it is not
done of lyghtnes of mynde, of hatred, nor for corruption of money,
that his saying shal stande, as well ayenst hym selfe, as ayenst other, I
can not tell. For I can nat see howe there can be any euident token, in
any suche case, but that ther might be in suche a periured witnes,
25   somme inwarde hatered or corruption, that the iudge can not knowe:
so that he can not with conscience iudge of certayntie, that there is
none. And therfore me semeth, that the makers of the said *Perag.* leyde
ouer great a danger to the iuges, that they shuld haue libertie to accepte, if they wolde, the sayenge of hym that so offereth hym selfe
30   ageynste his fyrste othe: for so moche as the iudge can not be sure to
saue his conscience therin, but he clerly refuse to accept any thing, that
the [H₄] witnes wold sey contrarie to his fyrst othe. For if the iudge dyd
other wise, & thervpon the witnes testifie ayenst the partie, and yet the
partie not giltie in dede: I suppose verily that the iuge were partie to the
35   same offence.
     And where I sayde in the saide treatise, as before appereth, that
somtime a wolfe may shew hym selfe in the apparel of a lambe, & that if
the iuge be parcial, suche tokens may soner be accepted then truely
shewed: It is euident inough, that by those wordis I note no iuge to be
40   parcial, but I sey, that if the iuge be parcial, suche tokens may be sooner
accepted then truly shewed. As who seith, the iudge may accepte suche
a token to be true, though there appere some suspection of vntruthe in

the witnes. In whiche acceptance he shal more liberally and without offence of the law do wrong to the partie, that is accused, then he coude doo by accepting of any other witnesse a[H₄v]yenst the law, that were neuer sworne before. For if he accept any suche witnes contrarie to the rules of the law, it apperith to all them, that knowe the lawe, that he doth ayenst the law therin: and that wil sounde somewhat to his rebuke, and that will make hym the more loth to do it. But if the iuge accept suche a periured witnes, where there is no sufficient token to proue, that he dothe it not for lightenes of mynde, hatred, corruption, nor suche other: yet he breketh no lawe therin. For al is committed to his discretion. And that may haply giue a boldenes to some iuge, to accept suche a periured witnes, where he ought not to accept hym. And though the said *Peragr.* saye, that if there be suche tokens, as before apperethe, that then in fauour of the feithe his witnes shall be taken: yet I can not see, if the partie accused be gyltlesse in dede, as he may be for all that witnesse, howe it [H₅] can be taken in fauour of the feithe, to accepte the witnes. For it can not be seide in fauour of the feithe to condemne an innocent.

And farthermore it appereth also, that the wordes of the said tretise extende no ferther, but to such as be iuges, where there is before them suche a periured witnes, & not to all iuges. And in like wise those wordes, that a wolfe may shewe hym selfe in the apparel of a lambe, stretche only to such a periured witnes. For there is no other witnes spoken of in the said tretise in that place. And therby is ment, that suche a periured witnesse maye haply shewe him selfe to denie that he seyd before, of a compuncte harte and of a newe knowlege of the treuth, and of a very zele vnto the feith: and yet do it in dede of couetise, falshode, rancoure, and malice to the partie. And so as the gospell seyth, he may happe outwarde to appere in the apparell of [H₅v] a shepe, and within forthe be a raumpinge wolfe. And suche one may that periured witnes be, that is spoken of in the said treatise. And of suche a witnes in heresie the said treatise speketh only there, and of none other witnes, as to the reders wil appere. And therfore as me semeth, maister More findeth defaute in this behalfe, where he had no cause reasonable so to do.

And if any man wyll sey, that it is not conuenient, that any man shulde fynde defaute at lawes made by the churche: I wyll to that motion seye thus: That to fynde a defaute at lawes made by the churche vpon a reasonable consideration, for that they be not so purely made to the honour of god, ne to the welth of the people, as they shulde be, and he intendeth no other but to put the rulers in mynde to reforme them by authoritie of the lawe: I thinke it were not only a laufull dede, but

also a right good and a [H$_6$] meritorious dede, and no offence. But if
any man wolde take vppon him of his owne mynde and of his owne
auctoritie wylfully to breake any lawe made by the churche, oneles it
were directly ageynste the lawe of god: I thinke it were a great offence.
5   And I meane therby, not onely suche lawes as the churche had direct
power to make, but also suche lawes as the church had no direct power
to make, but that the people hathe assented to them, and by that assent
and by a custome risen vpon the same, hath confirmed them. And
therfore I thinke verily, it were none offence to sey, that hit were good
10   for the superiours to breke many particular excommunications, that
the churche hath made. For surely many of them stand right hardly
with conscience or charitie.

Of this terme (somesay) and of them
that be iuges in heresye. The
15   seuentene Chapytre. [H$_6$v]

Master More in his apologie speketh many times ageynst a certayn maner of spekinge, that I vsed in dyuers places of the saide treatise
whiche is this: when I recited what opinions I haue herde sey, there
were amonge the people, I seyd, that some seye, or they seye this or
20   that, or that many say so, and suche other lyke sayenges, withoute
affyrmynge that I knew it of myn owne knowlege, that it was so: for in
some thynges I dyd not in dede. At this maner of speking mayster
Moore findeth a defaute, in suche a straunge gesting maner, that I
merueile greatly at it. And I merueylle the more, bycause he vseth the
25   same termes hym selfe in dyuers places of his apologie, as appereth, fo.
77. and fo. 100. And I am well assured, that in his gestinge he speketh
of the saide termes of somesey, they sey, or such other, many tymes
more then I do in al the seid treatise. And surely [H$_7$] as he knoweth
right wel hym selfe, a man may somtime sey, that some men sey this or
30   that, and sey truely, where if he wolde sey, that he knewe it hym selfe,
or that al men seyd so, he shulde say vntruly. And then if the trouth be
so, that some seyd, thus it is in this matter or in that, and yet al men seyd
not soo, or if the truthe were soo, yet I knewe it not, I wotte not vnder
what maner master More wold haue had me spoken of the matter, but
35   onely vnder this maner, as I haue done that some saye soo: And then
that he fyndeth a defaut at that maner of spekinge, where I coude none
otherwise haue done, it is a meruayle to many persons. And I haue in
diuers places of the said treatise seyd, that some sey this or that, where
if I had seyd, that a great parte of al the laie people had seyd so, I had
40   sayde but truely. And one of the (som saies) that he fyndeth defaute at,

is this: I sey in the .viii. [H₇v] Chapitre of the saide treatyse thus: And
here some sey, that bicause there is so greatte a desyre in spiritualle
menne, to haue men abiured, or to be noted with herisie: And that
some as hit were of a policie doo noyse it, that the realme is fulle of
heritikes, more then it is in dede, that it is very perillous, that spirituall   5
men shulde haue auctorite to arest a man for euery lyght suspection or
complaynte of heresie, tyl that desire of punishement in spiritual men
be ceassed and gone, but that they shulde make processe ageyne them,
to bringe them in vppon peyne of cursynge: and then if they tarye .xl.
dayes, the kinges lawes to brynge them in, by a writte of *Excommunicato*   10
capiendo, and so to be brought forth out of the kinges gayole to answere.
And it folowith in the said .viii. Chap. thus: but surely as it is somwhat
touched before in the .vii. chapitre, it semeth, that the churche in [H₈]
tyme past haue done what they coude to bringe about, that they might
punishe heresi of them selfe, without callinge for any helpe therin of   15
the secular power, And therfore they haue made lawes, that heretikes
might be arested, and put in prison, and stockis, if nede were, as
appereth in *Clementinis de haereticis, Cap. Multorum quaerela.* And after at
the speciall callynge on of the spiritualtie, it was enacted by parliament,
that Ordinaries myght arest men, that preche, holde, teache, or en-   20
forme other in herisie, there prohibyte, or that therof holde any con-
uenticles or scholis. For somme men thynke, that the said Clementine
was not of effecte in the kynges lawes to arest any man for heresie. But
if a man were openly and notably suspected of herisie, & there were
sufficient recorde and witnes ageynst hym, and there were also a   25
doubte, that he wolde flee and not appere, wherby he mighte
in[H₈v]fecte other: it semeth conuenient, that he be arested by the
body, but not vpon euery light complaynt, that ful lightly may be
vntrue. And that it wyl be right expedient, that the kingis highnes and
his conseile loke specially vpon this matter, and not to cesse, tyll it be   30
brought to moore quietnes then it is yet: and to se with great diligence
that pride, couetise, nor worldly loue be not iuges, nor innocentis be
punished, ne yet that wilfull offenders go not without due correction.

And when maister More in his apologie hath recited the said wordes,
of the said treatise: then he endeuoyreth hym selfe very moche, to   35
make it appere, that the mocions, that be made in the said treatise, in
the place before rehersed, be vnresonable, and can nat be brought
aboute: orels that if they were brought aboute, they shulde do hurte
and no good. And to make his sayengis the more acceptable, he leith
[I₁] somtyme defaute in my sayengis, and seyth, that I therby defame   40
the iuges spiritual, where I defame them not, but sey onely, that it is
expedient, that the kingis highnes and his counseile see, that pride,

couetise, nor worldly loue be no iudges. And whether thoo wordes
amounte to that effecte, that master More seyth they do, that is to sey,
that I defame al spiritual iuges, it appereth euidently they do not: ne
yet they proue not, that I wold haue al spirituall iudges changed. For
5   the spiritual iuges that be nowe, may be iuges styl, and haue al the
propreties before rehersed, as well as other, for any thinge that I haue
seyd. And yet maister Moore taketh it other wyse, and seyth, I wolde
haue suche iuges, as haue noo spice of any of the sayde poyntis. And he
seyth, that tyll suche iuges may be founde, heretikes maye make mery
10   for a lyttell season, whyle men walke aboute and seche for suche [I₁v]
iuges, whiche he weneth wyll not be done in a wekis worke. And he
seyth, that it wil be the more harde to fynde suche iuges. For he seith,
that I haue putte that matter out of doubte, that where as men wolde
haue wende soneste to haue founde them, that there I sey, it wil be
15   meruaylous harde to fynd any one of them, either prelatis, secular
priestis, or religious persons. For he saithe, that I sey pleynly, that haue
they neuer so many vertues beside, that yet I sey, it wil be harde to
fynde any one spiritual man, but that he is so infected with desire and
affection to haue the worldely honour of priestis exalted, that he is
20   through suche pride farre fro suche indifferencie and equitie, as ought
and muste be in suche iudges, whiche as he saithe, I assigne to be such
that they must haue no spice of pride, couetise, nor loue towarde the
worlde.
     As to this laste rehersed sentence of [I₂] maister More, this is the
25   trouth therin, I say in an other place of the said treatise, other then
that, that maister Moore hath rehersed here, That is to say, in the .vii.
Chapitre of the said tretise, that though many spiritual men may be
founde, that haue many great vertues, and great gyftes of god, as
chastitie, liberalitie, pacience, sobrenes, temperance, cunnyng, & suche
30   other: yet it wyll be harde to fynde any one spiritual man that is not
infecte with the sayd desyre and affection, to haue the worldly honour
of pristis exalted. And there my sentence endeth, as to this purpose.
But then as it appereth before master More in his said apologie addeth
immediatly to those wordes of myn, wordes of his owne putting in,
35   which be these: That he is through suche pride ferre fro suche indifference and equitie, as ought and must be in tho iuges, whiche he saith
I assigne. And he combyneth tho wordes to myn, [I₂v] in suche maner
as thoughe I spake them my selfe. So that they that shal rede them, can
none otherwyse take them, but as my wordes: wherby he peruerteth
40   clerely my meanynge and my sentence therin. For my sentence, ne yet
my meanynge therin, is not but that iudges spirituall maye haue some
spice of pride, couetise, & worldly loue, and yet be mete iuges in herisy,
as the frayltie of man suffereth. For we be no angelles but synners, that

lightly maye falle and be deceyued. Ne I meane not, ne yet my wordes
amount not to it, but that a man may haue a desire and affection, to
haue the worldly honour of priestes exalted, and yet be a mete iudge in
herisie. For I suppose, that a man may haue that desire in some degree,
and to som intent, and not offende therin, specially deedly. How be it   5
he may also lightly offende therin, if he be not ryghte well ware. [I₃]

And farthermore, though it were as maister More taketh it to be, that
my wordes shulde sounde to that effecte, that the iudges that were
then, were through such pride far fro the indifferencie and equitie,
that I assigne: yet that proueth not, but that they be now indifferent &   10
rightwise. For they might sith the makynge of the sayde tretise, become
through grace, indifferent, rightwise, meke, lyberall, and louynge to
god and their neighbour, though they were not so then. And if they be
soo, then heretikes shall not make mery for lacke of iuges a weke ne yet
a day. For the same iuges may sit styll without chaunginge, to here and   15
examyn them, whan nede shalbe. Thus as me semeth, it appereth
euery way, that the exception that master Moore taketh of changinge
of spirituall iuges, is but of small effect.

Then saith maister Moore farther, that if somesay, be no sufficent
profe, [I₃v] then is my tale all loste. And to these wordes I wyll an-   20
swere thus. I wyl agree, that my sayeng, that some say this or this, is no
proofe, neither to proue that some sey so, ne yet to proue that it is so.
For in euery profe muste be two witnesse at the leest: but if two wyll
saye it is so: then is it a prouffe.

And surely if maister More wyll inquiere for the truth in this   25
matier, he shall fynde, that there be many moo then two, that sey so.
And verily if many men sey so, thoughe the truthe be not so, yet the
tale is not all lost to sey that some men sey so. For then it shall put the
byshops and rulers spirituall in mynde, that they are bounde in conscience to helpe them that seye soo, all that they can fro the danger   30
that they ronne in by that sayinge. And yf it be true, then may the
spiritual rulers order the matter as they shall see cause, and reforme it
in suche charitable maner, that none shall sey so hereafter: [I₄] but
they wyll of malyce do it, & renne into the sclander of the Phariseis:
and that wolde charitably be examyned, whether it be so or not.   35

Then seith maister Moore yet farther, that whiche is a lyght suspicion and whiche is an heuye, and whiche witnes be sufficient, and
whiche not, must be weyed by the spiritual iuges, and vpon their
weyinge of the matier for lyght or heuy, to folowe the arrest of the
partie, or the leuynge of the arreste. Nowe verily in this poynte me   40
thynketh that maister More maketh a righte good mocion, that is to
seye, that the matter shuld be examined before the arreste. For it hath
ben sayde in tymes paste, that in suche case the arreste hath many

tymes gone before the examination. Neuer the lesse vnder what maner the examination and the arest shulde be made in suche case, I wyll
make no diuise at this tyme: For haply maister More wolde anon [I₄v]
fynde a defaulte at it, and therfore I wyl leaue it to them that haue
5   auctoritie, to treate ferther of it, and to diuise how to auoyde the mase
that master More speketh of in his .xlvi. chapitre. And then maister
More concludeth thus: I lytel doubt (saith he) but that if the kinges
highnes do, as I doubte not but his highnes will do meynteine and
assiste the spiritualtie in executynge the lawes, euen those that are all
10 redye made ayenste heresies, and commande euery temporall officer
vnder hym to do the same for his part, though there were neuer no
newe lawes made therfore, yet shall bothe innocentes be saued
harmeles well inowghe, and offenders punysshed to.

Now verily to these wordes of maister More I dare sey thus, that
15 maister More, or he had spoken tho wordes, had occasion by reasonable coniectures to haue doubted more at the [I₅] matter thenne he
hathe done, and to haue thought it very lyke, that if the same lawes
shulde stonde as do nowe in euery poynte concernynge heresie, that
many innocentis, that be not giltie, might vpon suspection of heresie
20 be dryuen to pourge them selfe, after the wylle of the ordinarie, and
yet be not giltie. Ye and ouer that mayster Moore might haue resona-
bly doubted, and as I suppose in conscience he ought to haue doubted
more then he hath done, that sometyme innocentis might happen
vpon the sute *Ex officio,* or vpon lyght complayntis, by fauor of of-
25 ficers, or vpon malice or displesure, be arrested before examinacion,
and yet maister More him selfe assenteth, that the examination shulde
be before the arreste. And he might haue doubted also, that somme
innocentes myght by suche periured persons, as be aboue rehersed in
this chapytre be sometyme condemned. And therfore [I₅v] the saide
30 wordes of mayster Moore, wherby he taketh vpon hym to sey, as it
were in his owne auctoritie to performe it, that innocentis by the same
lawes, as be al redy made for heresie, shalbe saued harmeles well
inowgh, might happen to be of smal effecte to helpe an innocent man
or womanne, that shulde happen to be wrongfully troubled in tyme to
35 come ageynst his wordes before rehersed.

Of the prohibition to lay men,
to enquiere of heresye. The
eyghtene Chapitre.

I N the sayde treatyse, the .vii. chapiter, I recited a law made *Extra de*
40 *haereticis, li. vi. ca. Vt inquisitionis,* wherby it appereth, that al powers,

and al lordis temporal and rulers be prohibite, that they shall not in
any maner take knowlege or iuge vpon heresie, sith it is mere spirituall. And then it is seyd ferther there, in the said treatise, that [I₆] he
that inquereth of heresie, takethe knowlege of heresy, & that the
summe called Rosella so taketh it, *Titulo excommunicationis, peragr. iiij.*   5
And then hit is seyd ferther there, in the said treatise, that if this be
trewe, it semeth then, that al the iustices of peace in this realme be
excommunicate. For they by auctoritie of the kingis commissions, and
also by statute, enquere of heresi. And so be then also al stewardes of
letis, and the enqueste also, if they enquere of it: but whether they   10
may by auctoritie enquere of heresie in a lete or not, as maister Moore
seyth they may, I am in doubte, but if they do, though they haue no
auctoritie to do it, yet if the said lawe *Extra de haereticis, li. vi.* be of that
effect, that Summa Rosella seith it is, they be accursed: And to this
lawe master More answereth not, but passeth it ouer, as a thinge that   15
as it semeth he lyttell regardeth, but only that he seyth, that the lawes
[I₆v] of this realme, and of holy churche in heresies, may wel stand to
gether, for ought that he seeth: And yet it appereth, that vpon this
lawe they do not agree nor stonde to gether. And therfore me
thinketh it wolde not be soo lightly passed ouer as mayster More   20
dothe passe it ouer. For it is a dangerous thinge to fall into the leeste
censure of the churche. And if it be saide, that the saide lawe is voyde,
bycause the churche had no auctorite to make it: And that it is therfore not to be fered. And I wylle yet sey therto, that though it were
voyd, that yet as longe as it standeth so not repelled, it were good to   25
eschewe it, and not to fal wilfully into the daunger of it: and therfore
it were better to repelle it then to let it stonde styll, and rather do
hurte than good. For as longe as it standeth so vnrepelled, some
priestis that se it, wil sey, that they that do ageynst it, be accursed: and
so may lightly fal [I₇] therby into a wrongful and vntru iugement,   30
whiche though it be no great offence, oneles it be of pride, by dis-
pisynge of the temporall power in that behalfe, yet it wold be eschewed. And also if thei that be so noisid to be accursid, here of it,
they wil be discontentid. And so grudges and variances maye ryse and
encrease by occasion of it. And therfore it semeth right expedient that   35
the said lawe be repelled. And in like wise it were good to repelle al
suche lawes spirituall, as be made contrary to the kyngis lawes and the
custome of the realme. And if it be seyd, that it were good also, that
suche statutes and lawes, as be made and vsed bi the temporal power
to the grefe of the people were also reformed, and that if I were   40
indifferente, I wolde make some mocion so to haue it: And so it
semeth master More dothe partly moue, that I ought to haue done,

and to haue founde as well defaut in [I₇v] the temporal lawe, as in the
spiritual lawe: Howe be hit bicause he wolde beare no blame of the
temporal lawe in that mocion, it semeth that he some what mitigateth
his sentence therin, and saith, that if I doo soo, and that then I handle
5   them, that is to sey, the temporall lawes and fynde defautes at them,
as truely as I doo at these, that is to sey at the spirituall lawes: that then
I shulde make two lyes for one, and yet as I suppose, I haue assigned
some defautes in the spiritual lawe, whiche maister Moore can not tell
howe they shulde be excused.
10   And the cause why I haue not spoken of the defaultes in the temporall lawes, as I haue done of defautes in the spiritual lawes, is this.
This diuision hath risen specially throughe a gruge of the people
towarde the spiritualtie, for diuers vexations that haue come to them
by spirituall men, some by one meanes, somme by an other, [I₈]
15   wherby in theyr pouertie they haue many tymes bene made more
poore. Wherfore they haue gruged veri sore. And thervpon it hathe
folowed, that when spirituall men haue perceyued, that the people
haue gruged at many of them, they haue pretended, that it hath ben
without cause, and somtime haue punished som of them, that haue so
20   grudged at them, and haue borne the lesse fauor to other, that thei
haue not punished. But as for any wronge, that spirituall men haue
had by temporal men, or by the temporall lawe, as to the multitude,
hath ben but lyttell in comparison: for they haue commonly had great
frendes and money inough to defende them selfe with. And if percase
25   some of them haue ben somtyme wronged, they haue yet most commonly had inough beside for their sufficient liuinge, accordinge to
their charges, whiche is moste commonly as of necessite but for their
owne person. [I₈v] And therfore it greueth them but littell: but a
trouble and losse to a laye man, that is charged with wyfe children and
30   household, and hath not one peny of wages, but that he must pay his
rente, and kepe his house of his owne labour and prouision, pincheth
hym nerer, as whenne he is troubled vpon suites *Ex officio*, or for
tithes, or for suche other thynges, at the complaynt of the partie, and
that sommetyme without cause, or for suspicions of heresies, pro-
35   uinge or disprouinge of testamentes, halowynge of churches, for visitations, and before the statute of mortuaries, for mortuaries, or for
sequestracions of benefices, wherof they be fermours, and for suche
other: all whiche vexacions they haue aretted to spirituall menne, and
seyd that they haue great wronge by them. And therfore it is, that for
40   as moche as the defautes in spiritual lawis haue giuen more occasion
to this [K₁] diuision, then any defaute in the temporall lawe can do:

therfore I haue rather spoken of defautes in the spiritual lawe, then
in the temporal lawe. For I thinke no man wyll denie, but that though
it were granted, that spirituall men had as moche wronge as coude be
deuised in the kingis lawes: that yet that coude be no cause for the
spiritualtie to gruge ageinst the people. For their gruge in that case   5
shuld rather be ageynst the heedes and exequuters of the lawe. And
in like wise though pore men were wronged by the kingis lawes, yet
that were no cause to make the people gruge ageinst the spiritualte.
And therfore suche lawes as haue ben made and misvsed bi the spiritual auctoritie, I suppose verily haue ben the most cause of this gruge   10
amonge the people: and wolde therfore fyrste be reformed. And if
master More can shew any lawes, that haue ben made by parliament,
concernyng [K₁v] the spiritualtie, that the parliament had none auctoritie to make, or wher at the spiritualtie or the people haue iust
cause to complaine: it wyl be wel done that he shewe them. And verily   15
as me semeth, charitie shulde compell hym to do it, seinge that he is
lerned in the lawes of the realme, as he is.

Of confederacies. The
nyntene Chapitre.

WHERE I speke in diuers places of the said treatise of confederacies   20
of priestis, sir Tho. More seyth in his apologie, that he knoweth no
confederacies of pristis, but it shuld be the gathering to gether of the
clergie at Conuocations. And verily I finde no defaute at Conuocacions. For if they were wel kept, I thynke it wold do gret good. How be it
master More somewhat gesteth at suche Conuocations and seith: he   25
wolde not greatly [K₂] wishe to be confedred with them, and there
associate in any such confederacies. For he seyth, he coude neuer yet
wit them assemble for any gret winning: but that they come vp by the
kingis writte to their traueile, labour, coste, and peyne, and tary and
talke .&c. and so get them home ageyne. But yet I truste they haue   30
done more good in their Conuocacions then so, though maister More
hathe not knowen all. Howe be it the confederacies that I meane of, be
not the confederacies that he speketh of, of conuocacions, for they be
lauful: but the confederacies that I meane of, be the confederacies,
wherby spiritual men pretend to meyntene the lawes of the church,   35
where they be sometyme ageinste the kinges lawes, and the olde
customes of the realme, as it is of not puttinge of prestis to answere
afore the kingis Iustices, and to beare out the Constitution prouincial,
that is made ayenst [K₂v] the old custome of the realme, for tith of

wodde aboue .xx. yeres: whiche custome is confirmed by the statute
made in the .42. yere of kinge Edwarde the thirde, whiche is commonly
called the statute of *Silua sedua.* And so lykewise of dyuers other statutes concernyng the spiritualtie, as is the Statute of mortuaries, and
5   suche other: whiche statutes many priestes resist in many places to this
day, and other priestis agree with them in the same, and sey, they be
ayenst the libertie of the churche, & that they that obserue them be
accursed. And also of particular confederacies of priestes, as to meinteine obites, and the wages of priestis, and also to haue more at bur-
10 ialles in som places then they haue vsed to haue in tyme paste, or els to
shewe them selfe not contente, and that laie menne be righte lothe to
beare in many places. And also if a prieste haue a busines to do in some
contreys, other prestis (as [K₃] it is seyde) wil sometyme so confedre
with hym at arbitrementis and other metinges, or make them suche
15 frendes priuely, that thoughe the other partie be of right good substance, and also haue good ryghte: yet shall he sometyme haue moche a
do to obteine it. And these be some of the confederacies of priestis, that
I meane of, and not the gatherynge to gether of the clergie at Conuocations. And thoughe sir Tho. Moore seithe, that there is not any one
20 prouinciall constitution, that I speke of, that was made, or to any mans
grefe or gruge put in execution in the tyme of any of the prelates that
are nowe liuynge. And therfore he saith how coude then any of them
be called any suche confederacies, or be cause of this late sprongen
diuision? Nowe surely though none of them all had ben put in execu-
25 tion, yet they haue done great hurt, and that vnder this maner: Whan
[K₃v] Spirituall men haue seen those lawes, and seen also that they
haue not by reson of the temporal power, ben put in execution: som of
them haue thought that al they were accursed, that let the execucion of
them, and that the churche is greatly wronged and oppressed therby,
30 and that hathe engendred a gruge in theyr myndes, whiche hath ben so
longe continued, that some lay men haue herde of it, and haue denied
their sayinges, and spoken ageynste those constitutions: and so hath
part of this diuision spronge. And verily if maister More wolde haue
remembred hym selfe wel, howe ofte the seid constitution prouincial,
35 made for payenge of tithes of wodde aboue .xx. yeres, hath ben put in
execucion, nowe of late dayes, to the grefe of many lay men: he wolde
not haue sayde so generally, that there is not any one constitution
prouinciall, that I speke of, to any mans grefe or gruge put in
exe[K₄]cucion in the tyme of any of the prelatis that are nowe liuinge.
40 For surely that constitution hath of late dayes, and that in the tyme of
dyuers of the same selfe prelates that nowe be, ben put in execucion, to
the grefe & gruge of many persons within this realme.

The .xx. Chapitre.

I‌T is seyd in the fyrst chaptre of the saide treatise, that as longe as spiritual rulers wil either pretende, that their auctoritie is so highe and so immediatly deriued of god, that the people are bounde to obeye them, and to accept al that they do and teche, with out argument, resistence, or gruging ageynste them: or that they wyll pretende, that no defaute is in them, but in the people, and wyll yet continue styll in the same maner, and after the same worldly countenaunce, as they do now, and haue done late time past, [K₄v] the lighte of grace, that is spoken of before, wil not appere .&c. Al this lettre of the said treatise sir Tho. More, in the .xxvii. chapitre of his apologie, reciteth truly, except that he omitteth there, these wordes, but in the people, and also in the later ende of the saide sentence he putteth in for these wordes, will not appere, these wordes, be with you nowe and euer amen. But what he meneth therby I can not redily telle, but hit shulde be after his gestynge facion. And if it be so, it is of a smal effecte: and therfore I passe it ouer. But after, fo. 167. he turneth these wordes spiritual rulers into prelatis, and then therupon he seith, that prelatis neuer pretended to be obeyed in all thinges as wel badde as good, as if they preche heresie, he seyth they do not pretende, that they shuld be obeyed. And verily I neuer intended to ley to prelatis, that they preched heresie. And it was yet moche farther [K₅] from my purpose to ley it to al spiritual rulers. For there be many spiritual rulers, that be no prelatis, that I thinke verily wyll preache no heresie. But what maister More meaneth to chaunge these wordes, spirituall rulers, into prelatis, I can not tel. But nowe by occasion of the wordes, that maister More hath spoken in this behalfe, I wyll saye farther in the matter than I had thought to haue done, and that is this, that I thinke verely, that if so great an ouersight felle into prelates & spirituall rulers, that they wolde take vpon them to preche heresye, that they wolde that the people shuld beleue them therin, and to take it to be catholicall that they preched. For who wyll preache any thing, but suche as they wolde haue their audience to beleue? How be it the pretence that I meane of in prelatis and spiritual rulers is not that pretence, that they wolde be obeyed thoughe they [K₅v] preche heresie. But I mene that they pretende to be obeyed, when they declare what their auctoritie is, and to haue al suche lawes, as they make obeyed, without argument or resistence ageynst them. And then I meane ferther, that as longe as they do so, continuynge styll in the same maner, and after the same worldly countenance, as thei do now, that the light of grace wil not appere. And now shal I shew my mynde somewhat ferther then I dydde in the said treatise, why I seyd so, and shall shortely touche certayne pretences, that spirituall rulers haue made in tyme paste.

Fyrste they haue made pretence in tyme past, that the people be bounde to beleue, that al suche thinges be the libertie of the churche,
5 that the clergie calleth the libertie of the churche, as it is in this poynt, where it is seide in the lawe, that the will of god is, that thinges that are to be disposed of the [K₆] churche, perteyne to priestes to dispose, and not to worldly powers. Also that christen princis must subdu their executions to bysshops, & not to prefer them aboue them: And that no
10 charge shalbe set vpon clerkes by laie power. And there is also a pretence, that if a seculer iudge be negligent in doinge iustice, that a spirituall iudge may giue hym monicion to amend it: & if he wil not, that then the spiritual iuge may compell him to it, orels supplie his roume, and here the cause. And dyuers other thynges there be, whiche
15 were to longe to reherse now, wherof I haue recited part in the .xii. chapitre of the saide treatise: wherat vndoutedly many lay men haue gruged very sore. And neuertheles mayster More in the ende of the sayd chapitre, forgetinge all suche pretences, relyeth moste vpon this, that prelatis neuer intended to be beleued, if they preache heresie.
20 And therfore he [K₆v] concludeth thus, and seyth, that sithe prelates pretende not that, ne neuer did: that al my tale amounteth to no more, but that the lyght of grace wyl not appere, as longe as prelates doo the thynge that they do not ne neuer dyd. And then he seithe to the reders: Is not this good reders, by this good pacifiar broughte vnto a wyse
25 conclusion?

And nowe to this conclusion of master More I wyl sey thus, that I beseche almyghty god, that the ende of al these maters may come to this conclusion, that the very groundely causes of these diuisions, that nowe be not onely in this realme, but also in maner through all christen
30 realmes, may come to perfite knowledge. For surely I doo not take it, that they began eyther by heresies, or Apostasies, as master More in his apologie meaneth that they shulde do. And if maister More will nedely endeuour him [K₇] selfe to hyde the truth therin, as it semeth he hath done in this chapytre, & in dyuers other places of his Apologie, by
35 kepyng secrete suche abusions and pretences, as in my conscience haue bene mooste principall cause of this diuision, wherof part be recited in the saide Treatise, and part in this answer, but not al: I beseche almighty god, that he haue no power to doo it: but that the truthe may comme to knowledge therin, though he resist it al that he can. For if it
40 were knowen, and the defautis charitabli reformed, al these diuisions wolde shortly haue an ende, as I suppose. And then this were a better conclusion, then master Moore gothe aboute: for he gothe aboute

onely to proue, that all my tale is loste, bicause prelates pretende not to
be beleued, if they preache heresie, as he taketh it, that I shulde sey
they do, and yet I seid not so in dede. And if I did sey so, I seyd but
truely. For [K₇v] if they wolde preche heresie, it is certayne, they wolde
loke to be beleued, as I haue seid before: yea and if they wolde preche   5
and sey, that if they preched heresie, that they wolde the people shulde
not beleue them: yet if thei dyd after preche heresie in dede, they
wolde loke, that the people shulde beleue them. For they wolde seye,
they were no heresies that they preached: for who wyl confesse that he
precheth heresie? How be it in good feith I neuer intended to make it   10
appere, that prelates preched heresie: but maister Moore hathe gyuen
me occasyon to speake thus farre in the matter as I haue done: For he
wolde, if he coude, drounde all other pretences, that prelates and
spirituall rulers make, soo that they shulde neuer be spoken of: bycause as he thought, he had espied so great an ouersight in my wordes,   15
to sey that prelates shulde pretende to be beleued, if they preched
heresie. [K₈] And therfore I doubte me very sore, that maister More
gothe aboute rather to marre *al*, then to endeuoir him selfe to make al
wel.

And in this Chapitre maister More leith diuers other obiections to   20
proue the said lettre vnreasonable, whiche were very tedious to reherse
at length, and therfore I shal shortly as I can, touche some of them.

Fyrst he wolde that I shuld declare, whether I ment by these wordes,
the auctoritie of spirituall rulers, their hole auctoritie, as wel that they
haue immediatly of god, as that they haue of the graunte of princis.   25
And as to that mocion it appereth, that the letter is pleyne inough, that
it is only ment of suche auctorities, as they pretende to haue immediately of god. For the letter is, that as longe as spirituall rulers wil
pretende, that their auctoritie is so high and so immediatly diriued of
god, that the people ar bounde [K₈v] to obey them, withoute argu-   30
mente or resistence, that so longe the lighte of grace wil not appere.
And it is not to suppose, that spiritual rulers wyl pretende, that suche
auctoritie, as they haue of the graunte of princis, is immediately diriued of god. For they come to them by a meane, that is to sey, by the
meane of princis. And soo maister More myght haue satisfied hym   35
selfe in that question, & haue admitted, that it is only vnderstande of
such auctoritie, as they haue immediatly of god, as in the ministracion
of the sacramentes, & many other thyngis, without desiringe of any
ferther declaracion of me in that behalfe, yf he hadde lyste.

And then he goeth yet further, and seyth, that if I meane that the   40
lyghte of grace, that I speke of, wyl not appere as longe as the prelatis
pretende, that any parte of their auctoritie is so hyghe, that it is imme-

diately gyuen [L₁] them of god: then (saythe he) that I haue loste the lyghte of treuthe. By whiche wordes it apperith, that maister More mistaketh the lettre of the said treatise greatly. For he taketh it, that I shuld doute, whether any part of the auctoritie of prelates be imme-
5 diatly diriued of god. And surely let hym doubte therin if he liste, I doubt not of it, & that apperith by my wordis afore rehersed, wher I sey, that as longe as spiritual rulers wil pretend, that their auctoritie is so high, and so immediatly deriued of god, that the people are bounde to obey them withoute argumente or resistence. &c. By whiche wordes
10 I confesse, that they haue auctoritie immediatly diriued fro god. But as I seid before in the .7. chap. master More hath a right gret & a high inuentiue wit, wherbi he can lightly turne a sentence after his appetite, & so he doth here, and wolde haue it appere, that I shulde meane that [L₁v] the light of grace wyll not appere, as longe as prelates after his
15 inuencion or spirituall rulers after the letter of the seide treatise, pre-tende that their auctoritie is immediately diriued of god, and my mean-ynge is not so, nor my wordes amounte not therto: but be of suche effecte, as I haue seide before. And so I see not what charitie, nor what good affecte maister More sheweth in the takynge of that exception.
20 Then to shewe my mynde in somme thinges, that maister Moore hathe touched yet ferther in the sayde Chapitre: I wyl fyrst agree with master Moore, that in suche thynges as the hole clergi of christendom techeth and ordreth in spiritual thinges, and whiche of longe tyme haue bene by longe vsage and custome through the hole corps of christendome,
25 spiritualtie and temporaltie, ratified, agreed, and confirmed, ought with reuerence to be receiued: but yet if the same thin[L₂]ges through longe continuance, and through abusions that rise by occasion of them, proue hurtful and ouer greuous to the people to bere: then may the people gruge and compleyne laufully to their superiours, and desire
30 that they may be refourmed, as laufully as they may do to haue tem-porall lawes refourmed, whenne nede requyreth.

I wyll also agree, that in the congregation of the clergie, to goddes honour graciously gathered to gether: the good assistence of the spirite of god, accordynge to Christis promise, wyl be as verily present and
35 assistent with them, as it was with his blessed apostels, yf they ordre them selfe in mekenes and charitie and put al their truste in god, as the apostels dydde. But if they wyll truste in their owne wyt and in worldly policie: then may they lightely lese the spirite of god. And whether it were so at the making [L₂v] of the lawes, whiche maister Moore speketh
40 of concernyng heresie or not, I can not tel: but this I wil sey, that if they were not good and reasonable in them selfe at the first making, that they were neuer made by the assistence of the spirite of god. And surely I can not then se, how the vsage and longe continuance of them

can ratifie or confirme them. For as it is of an euil custome, that the lenger it is vsed, the greater is the offence: so is it of an euil lawe. And like as an euil custome is to be put awaye, so it is of an euyll lawe. And the lawes affirmed by vsage and agremente of the people be the lawes of fastynge and kepyng of holydays, and suche other as the people of 5 their free agrement accepte and agree vnto: but these lawes made for punysshement of heresies were neuer agreed by a commen assent of the people, but that some perticuler persons, wherof some haue bene giltie, & some [L₃] perauenture not giltie, haue ben punysshed therby right sore ayenst theyr wylles. And that can not be a confirmation of 10 them that so agree ageinst their wyl. But as to them that do the correction, it is a confirmation: for they do it with their good wylle. And though that correction were a sufficient confirmation, as anenst them that be so punyshed: yet it can nat be a confirmation to make the lawe approuid for all the residue of the people. 15

I can nat see therfore that any ratifienge, agreinge, or confirmynge of the peple can be proued in tho lawes, concernyng the correction for heresy. And then whether the lawes in them selfe be good and indifferent or not, I wyll remytte the iugement in that behalfe to them that haue auctoritie. But to shewe my conceyte therin, I shall with good wyl 20 euen as my conscience meueth me to, and that is, that I coulde neuer see, that it was reaso[L₃v]nable to be accepted as a lawe, that a man shulde be accused, and know not his accuser. And that it is yet more vnreasonable, that a man shulde be condempned, and knowe not the witnes that condemned him. Also that a man vppon suspection shulde 25 be driuen to make his purgacion at the wil of the ordinarie, or be accursed: Or that a periured witnesse shulde condempne hym, that he had clered afore: That a greate offender and a lesse offender shulde haue one lyke punishement, if they renunced: or be alike arested and put in prison: I neuer saw no indifferencie in it. And if any man wyl sey, 30 that these reasons wyll gyue a boldenes to heretikes: trewely I will not fully make answere therto: but this I wil sey, that I thynke verily, that they will giue a boldenes to trouthe, and to true men. And verilye I haue herde sey, that it were better to suffre an offender go vnpunysshed, than to [L₄] punyshe him vnrightwisely & ayenste due order 35 of iustyce.

The conclusion of this answere
The .xxi. Chapitre.

Fᴏʀ as moche as sir Tho. Moore in his Apologie saith vnder general wordes, that he coude if he wolde, make men see, that very fewe parties 40 of the sayde boke of diuision, wherby he vnderstandeth the sayd tre-

tise, had either such charitie or suche indifference therin, as not onely, the newe noughtie brotherhede bosteth, but also some good folke, as he saith, take it also as a superficial redynge. And bicause maister Moore by reason of the said general clause mai herafter note, what
5 article that he wylle in the saide tretise to lacke charitie and indifferencie, and sey that he ment so at the makynge of the sayde Apologie: Therfore to gyue him occasion to shew his [L₄v] mynde more pleinly in that behalfe, I shall make mencion of some suche articles, as many men thynke he shulde moste lykely meane it of, thoughe he haue no cause
10 soo to do. And I shall speke somewhat ferther of them, then I dyd in the said treatise, wherof one myght haply be this. In the .ij. Chapitre of the said tretise I rehersed the wordes of Iohan Gerson, where he seith, that clerkes shulde instruct euery man with their wordes, and to the intent that pore men shuld not be greued, that they shulde get their
15 liuinge with some handye crafte, as saincte Paule did. And whether master More think those wordis charitable & indifferent or not, I can not tell, & therfore I shall shewe somewhat my conceite, what as I thynke, mayster Gerson ment by them. And verily it shuld seme, that he ment not therby, that persons, vycars and parishe pristes, and suche
20 other as ministre to the people, shulde [L₅] gette their liuinge by handy craftes: for he seythe in dyuers places of his warkes, that the people be bounde by the lawe of god to fynde suche ministres theyr necessarie liuing. And therfore I thynke his meaninge was of clerkes, that haue no cure, that they shulde liue by somme honeste handye crafte, not con-
25 trary to their order as saincte Paule dyd, rather then to lyue of the people. And also peraduenture mayster Gerson might meane farther thus, that it were not inconuenient also for curates and spiritual ministres to the people, when their duetie and deuocion were fulfylled, & their feruour to prayer ouerpassed, for eschewynge of idelnes, to oc-
30 cupie them selfe with suche honeste handy crafte, not repugnant to the order of preesthoode, as sainct Paule did, that is to sey, with writinge, redynge, bynding of bokes, making of tentis, grauynge or caruinge of images, or suche other, and [L₅v] not to vse it as for their holle liuinge, but to be wel occupied, when feruour to preyer were ouerpassed. But if
35 any spirituall man had that grace, that he coulde in suche meane tymes occupie hym selfe with preyer and contemplacion, surely he were moste to be commended: but that is not gyuen but to a fewe: but that spiritual men shulde vse huntinge, hauking, and playeng, or any other outward labor or worldly studie, busines or recreation, as vniuersally as
40 lay men doo, or to kepe & continue ouer moche familiar companie with laie persons, wherby their deuocion mighte be slaked, and they made the more vnapte to preyer and contemplacion, when they shall returne

to it ageine, is not conueniente. For the people therby maye lightely take some euil example. Thus I suppose, that maister Gerson ment by the sayd wordes, and not that priestes oughte to go eyther to ploughe, carte, thres[L₆]shinge, mowinge, or any other suche great bodily labours. For they were not conuenient for their ministration. And trowe ye not that a man mighte saye here without offence, that it hath sometyme greatly diminished the honour that ought to be had and gyuen to the moste high and glorious sacrament of the alter, to see pristis in som placis immediatly after the receiuing of that glorious sacramente, dispose them selfe to worldly companye, and outwarde pleasures, as liberally, as if they had not that daye saide masse? Laye men be taught by priestis, as it is right conuenient that they shuld be: that they, the dai, that they be houseld on, shall haue a better await on them selfe, in eatinge, drinkinge, laboure, and all other demeanour, then they haue on any other dayes, so that nothinge shulde throughe their defaute happen, that might be to the dishonor of that glorious sacrament. But yet [L₆v] some prestis wil not do so them selfe: but as it were through a boldnes and a familiaritie of the ofte receiuyng of that glorious sacrament attempte to doo, and that in maner customablye, that they wolde saye them selfe were not conuenient for lay men to do, the day that they were houseled on: and surely they be bounde to take a more sure awayte of them selfe, as wel before they go to masse, as after than any lay man is the day that he is houseld. For they maye more lyghtly offende through negligence therin, then any laye man. And I suppose verily, that if due honoure were done by all the people as well spiritual as temporal, as there ought to be to this glorious sacrament, that is in verye truthe the verye bodye and bloode of our lorde Iesu Christe, whiche was borne of the virgin Mary, crucifyed, suffered dethe, rose agayne the thyrde day fro dethe to lyfe, ascended into heuen, sit[L₇]teth on the right hande of the father, and that shall comme to iudge this worlde, whiche is also the moste high and most soueraigne ioy and comfort to all good Christen men, that there shulde folowe thervpon greatte loue, charitie, peace, and quietnes amonge the people. Wherfore I beseche almighty god shortly to sende that due honour into the hartis of the people, as well spirituall as temporall. Amen.

And here I shal desire al them, that shal rede the wordis that I haue spoken before, of irreuerence done by som priestes to this glorious sacramente, that they thinke not, that I meane it of al priestis. For I know right wel, that there be many pristis, that ordre them selfe right wel, and with due reuerence, as well before the receiuyng of the sacrament as after. Howe be it I doubt yet very moche, that some of them, that doo soo, do not endeuour them selfe as they be bounde to do, to

[L₇v] reform them that do not so. And especially it is to be merueiled, that the fathers of the churche, that are bishops and ordinaries, haue done no more in tyme paste in their conuocations for reformyng of it, then they haue done: seinge that it perteyneth specially to them to do it.

5   And I thynke verily, that if such conuenient labours were appoynted by good auctorytie as is aforesaide, that there be righte many good, honest, and sadde priestes, that wolde be very gladde of it: and that wolde with good will vse them at tymes conuenient.

An other clause that maister More might perauenture take excep-
10   tion to hereafter, may be that, that is spoken in the .xii. Chap. of the said treatise, of lawes made by the churche, which lawes, as it is said there, the church had no power nor auctoritie to make, and that specially of that poynt, that priestes ought not to be putte to answere [L₈] before laie men. For vnder those general wordes, maister More may
15   sey herafter, if he will, that he founde defaute at that clause, and yet he dothe nat expressely speake ageynste it in no parte of his Apologie. But what he meaneth by reason of the said general wordes, to do therin herafter, I can. not tell. And if his meanyng be, that he will fynde defaute therat, and affirme, that it is ageynst the libertie of the
20   churche: the kinges Iustices can infourme hym beste, what the lawe of the realme is therin, and then that libertie & the said lawe, maye the better be accorded and agreed to gether.

He may also perauenture fynd a defaute bycause I sey in the seid tretise, that degradynge coulde not helpe in suche case, if priestis
25   ought not before degradinge by the lawe of god to be areyned: for not withstandynge the degradyng, I sey there, as the trouth is, that the carecter of preesthode, a[L₈v]bideth, so that they be priestis as they were before. And therfore I sey, that if they sey masse, they consecrate, and if they giue orders, they stand good: though they offend in the
30   doing. And they be also bound to sey their seruice as they were before, excepte that they may not sey *Dominus uobiscum,* nor suche other thyngis as perteyne to the dignitie of their ordre. And if they die repentant, they shall haue the aureole, as they that be not degrated. And if this be trewe, that they be yet pristis, and that it be true also, that
35   it is prohibitid by the law of god, that pristis shuld be put to answer before lay men: why then shuld a priest be put to answer before lay men, or be put in execution by lay men more after degrading then he might be before? Verily I can not se why. I suppose therfore that priestis may laufully be putte to answere before laie men, and also be
40   put in execution by lay men: excepte [M₁] suche poyntes, as they haue libertie to the contrary by the kynge, and by his lawes: wherof I haue recited som poyntes in the said .xii. chapitre. And here me thinketh I

mighte well sey, that all the spirituall men of this realme are specially
bounde in conscience to gether them selfe togyder, to se whether they
can proue it sufficiently by auctorite of scripture, that it is ageynste the
lawe of god, that priestis shulde be putte to answere before laie men or
not. And if they canne proue, that it is ageinste the lawe of god: I   5
doubte not but that the kingis grace, and all the realme wil gladdely
agree thervnto withoute ferther resistence. For who wolde worke directly ayenst the lawe of god? I truste no man. And if it can not be
proued, that their pretence therin is grounded vpon the law of god, but
vpon a singular loue and affection to them selfe, and that they haue   10
fortified & meynteyned the same [M₁v] by lawes and decrees of the
churche, whiche the churche had none auctoritie to make, ne that were
neuer accepted in this realme for lawes: then wil it be righte good and
expediente, that they charitably reuoke that pretence of their fre wil: &
that they be ouer that prohibited vpon greatte peynes, that thei shal not   15
any ferther make that pretence. And surely I thinke it wyll be harde to
brynge the spiritualtie and the temporaltie to a ful agrement, tyl that
article be brought to a good conclusion. And if spiritual men wil sey,
that if priestes shall vpon euerye light suspicion or light complaynt, be
put to answere in treasons, murders, and felonies, and suche other, as   20
generally as lay men shal: that then many priestis shulde be without
cause arrested, and vncharitablye handeled. For laie men be many
tymes cruell ageinst priestes. To that it may be answered, that it becometh not spiritual [M₂] men to sey, that laye men be cruell to them (if
it be welle consydered, howe moche good priestis be beloued and   25
cherisshed of laie men) and also what liuinge they haue by laie menne,
that nowe be, and by their auncesters. And surely if laie men be cruel to
prestis, it is through the defaute of priestis.

And ferthermore if priestis wold of their charitie, do that in them is,
to preuente and for se, that neither laie men nor priestis, as farre as   30
they coulde helpe it, shuld not be troubled in suche case vpon lighte
suspections and vntrue complayntes: then wold it somwhat appere,
that they pondred the welthe and quietnes of laie men, as they do of
priestis: and so are they bounde to do in dede: but as long as spiritualle
rulers care moore for the welthe & quietnes of pristis, then of laie men: 35
or that there be opinion amonge the people, that they doo soo, thoughe
it be not so in dede: so longe [M₂v] wil laie men, as to the multitude,
care but littel for priestes: and thus charitie wil waxe colde betwixt
them. And I trowe no Christen man wold haue it so, if he might let it.

And thus by occasion of the said generall wordes, in the saide Apolo-   40
gie, I haue spoken somwhat ferther of arreiginge of priestes afore laie
men, then I thoughte to haue done. And nowe shall I sey somwhat

ferther in a generalitie, as maister Moore hath done, and that is this: that all that I speke in the sayde treatise, was to appese this diuision, and not to begyn any ne to contynue it. And therfore howe they can saue their conscience, that sey I dyd rather entende a diuision then an agrement, I can not tel, their owne conscience shall be iudge. And I entended also sommewhat to moue that might be occasion to putte awey abusions, euyll examples, and heresies: and not to encrease them or [M₃] meinteine them I dare boldly sey.

And ferther as maister Moore knoweth better then I, *Mentire est contra mentem ire,* That is to seye, to lye is when a man seithe ageynste his owne mynde. And in good feithe in al that treatise I speke nothynge, but that I thought was true.

And farther I wyll ascertayne maister More as far as in me is, that I had neyther any subtil shrewes counsell, ne any euill counsel at the making of the said tretise, which he calleth the boke of diuision, as is said before.

And farthermore if maister Moore wol yet charitably shewe, what lacke of charite or of indifference he findeth in the residue of the said treatise, that he hath not touched, ne any thing spoken of in his Apologie, me thynketh he shulde do better, then vnder suche generall wordes to take exception to it, and shewe no cause why. For soo may a man lyghtly do to any thynge [M₃v] that is written, be it neuer soo good.

And to the intent that the Chapitres that maister More hath clerely omitted of the sayde Treatise, maye be the better knowen, I haue intitled them as herafter foloweth. That is to sey, the thirde chapitre, the fourth chapitre, the .v. chapitre, the .ix. chapitre, the .x. chapitre, the .xi. chapitre, the .xii. chapitre, the .xiii. chaptre, the .xiiii. chapitre, the .xv. chapitre, and the .xvi. chapitre, whiche is the laste chapitre of the said treatise. Of al these chapitres maister More toucheth nothing in his apologie, and the seconde chapitre he toucheth very lyttell, but he saith, that I fynde a fault, and wolde that priestis shulde eate no flesshe fro Quinquagesime tyl Easter, and that is aboute thre dayes lenger then laie men do. And verily if pristis that be able to do it, kept tho thre dais, to shew somme diuersitie therin betwixte laie men and them, it were no great mat[M₄]ter, ne no matter for maister More to tary so longe vpon as he doth, as me semeth. And yet I fynde not that defaute my selfe. For I do but onely recite the wordes of maister Gerson, concerninge that faste. And I am sure, if maister More had lyst, he could haue recited many other thynges, that be spoken by maister Gerson in the said .ij. chapitre, as well as that saienge: which had ben more necessary to haue ben spoken of, then that fastinge is. But what he meanith to speke of that thinge, that is lesse profitable, and

to leue other thynges that be in the said .ii. chap. vntouchid, that had
ben more profitable, & moche more charitable to haue spoken of, then
that is, and after to impugne them al by his said generall clause, in such
maner as he hath don: I can not tel, ne as I suppose no man els can tell,
tyll he hym selfe declare, what he mente therby. And here I make an   5
ende of my aunswere to the [M₄v] said Apologie, for this tyme.

The .xxij. Chapiter.

BYZANCE. It appereth in the later ende of the chap. next before this,
that the maker of the saide treatise there maketh an ende of his
aunswere to the saide Apologie, I preye the my frende Salem shewe me   10
thy mynde, how thou thinkest of it. SALEM. Verily I like it wel, howe be it
for as moche as it shulde seme, that he entended not at this tyme to
make a full answer to euery article of the said Apologie, I shall (if he
will) cause a frende of myn to make an answere to all the residue of the
saide Apologie. And I beseche our lorde that a good agreement may   15
shortly folowe accordynge to his desire. And I wolde not onely desyre
that, but also I wolde gladlie desyre, that all Christen princes mighte
also falle to a good peace [M₅] and amytie, and fynally to procede with
helpe of all the spiritualtie, the one with prayour, the other with power,
ayenst the most cruell ennemies of all Christen religion, that are the   20
Turkes, and all the cursed secte of Mahumete, whiche hath done more
hurt to the christen feithe, then any other sect hath done, sith Christis
feith began. And this were a better weye, then one christen man thus to
varye with an other, wherby no profite folowethe, nother for this
worlde, nor for the world to come. BYZAN. Verily it is as thou sayest, but   25
yet I can not see, what it wolde profite the and me, that can littel skille in
that mattier, and can do but littel good in that behalfe, to meddell
therin. And therfore it wyll be more expedient for vs, as I suppose, to
commytte that matter to other, that can & maye do good therin: and
that haue more occasion to speke therof then we haue: then to [M₅v]   30
treate any ferther of it. SALEM. As thou seyest we can do littel good
therin: but yet neuer the les a good wille no man may blame. And the
occasion that hath moued me to speke so far of that matier at this tyme,
as I haue done, is this, my name is Salem, & thy name is Bizance: and
Ierusalem was sometyme called Salem, as my name is: and by an other   35
name it was also somtyme called Iebus, and so of those two names it was
called Hiebussalem, and after by common speche and alteration of
letters it was called Hierusalem. And the citie of Constantinopole,
whiche had that name giuen vnto it by the great emperour Con-
stantyne, was sometyme called Bizance, as thy name is: whiche cities be   40

nowe in thraldome and captiuitie of the cursed Turkes. And soo the metinge of vs two nowe together by chaunce, whiche beare the names of those two cities, hath broughte the [M₆] remembrance of them into my mynd, whiche hathe moued me to consyder, howe greatte pitie it is,

5   to se so many people as be in the sayde cities and in the countreys theraboute, lye in the danger of the diuel, and daily perishe by their infidelitie, to their eternalle damnacion, as there dothe, and that yet christen men loke no more vpon it then they do. And I haue thought the more of the matier, bicause I suppose that the said secte is nygh at

10   an ende, and that it shall not longe contynue. BIZAN. But what maketh the to suppose, it shuld not longe continue? For as to mannes iudgement it was neuer in greatter power thenne it is nowe. And I thynke verilye, thou canste speake lyttell in that mattier of thy selfe. And if thou woldest, lytel credence wold be giuen to thy seying. SAL. It is true

15   as thou sayst: but I speke it by occasion of a texte, that is in the Apocalips, the .xiii. chapitre: [M₆v] whervpon I haue seen an exposition, that openeth the texte in suche maner, that me thinketh I can giue good credence to it. And if thou wilt, I shall recite the said exposition, as thoughe it hadde ben made this present yere, whiche is the yere of

20   our lorde god .MDXXXIII. but yet I wil kepe the same accompte of yeres, as is in the said exposition. And though I varye sometyme from the seid exposition in wordes, I wyll not varye from it in effect. And surely if the exposition be true, then that secte is nere at a point to be distroyed. BIZAN. I pray the lette me here that exposition. SAL. I shall shewe it to

25   the with good will in the nexte chapiter folowyng.

An exposition of a texte in the Apocalips, wherby it appereth, that of likelyhod the secte of Mahumete shal not longe endure. The .xxiii. Chapiter.

30   **I**N the said .XIII. chapitre of the Apocalips it is writen in this ma[M₇]ner: *Hic sapientia est, qui habet intellectum, computet numerum bestiae, numerus enim hominis est, & numerus eius sexcenti sexaginta sex,* That is to sey: Here is wisedome, he that hath vnderstandinge, lette hym counte the numbre of the beaste, it is forsoth the numbre of a man, and

35   his numbre is six hundred sixtie and sixe. And by this beaste, as it semeth, may conueniently be vnderstande Mahumete. For Mahumete ledde a voluptuous life: And that life after the philosopher *.i. Ethic.* is called a beastly life, And so it semeth that the numbre, wherof mencion is made before, concerneth Mahumete and his cursed sect, whiche for

40   his beastly lyfe is called a beaste, as is sayde before. And then hit is to be

noted, that sayncte Iohan in the saide texte makethe mencion of two numbres. For first he seith: It is forsoth the numbre of a man: and after he seith: and his numbre is .vj.C.lxvj. And firste I shal touche brefely, [M₇v] what me thinketh is to be vnderstande by the first numbre: And after I shall somewhat touche, what me thinketh he shulde meane by the seconde numbre: that is by the said nombre of sixe hundrede thre score and sixe. Neuer the les bycause I am not a prophete, nor the sonne of a prophete, I wil sey nothinge in this writinge, but as by way of protestation, trustinge not to say any thinge therin, that shal repugne ageynst scripture, nor ayenst the seyinges of holy sainctis or doctours of the churche. Then to touche somewhat of the firste numbre, where it is said, *Numerus enim hominis est,* it semeth, that that numbre maye conueniently be referred to the tyme of the continuance of the secte of Mahumete, that was begunne by that beastly man Mahumete. And it shulde seme also, that the numbre of the yeres, that the said secte shall contynue, is secretely conteyned & declared in the said wordes, [M₈] when it is said, *Numerus enim hominis est,* that is to sey, it is the numbre of a man. And that as me semeth appereth bi this reason. *Adam* in hebrewe is as moche to sey in latine as *homo,* that is to seye in englishe a man. And therfore saint Hieronyme seyth, that where so euer this worde *Homo* is in the latine translation, that there is in Ebrue, *Adam,* as in the .iiij. psalme, where it is seid: *Filij hominum usque quo graui corde .&c.* It is in Ebrue *Filij Adam. &c.* And then if *Adam* in hebrue be as moche to saye in latine as *homo,* whiche in englisshe is as moche to sey as a man: then as it semeth, by this worde *homo* in latine, maye in like wise as by an excellencie be vnderstande *Adam,* as most singuler man. For of al other men he was mooste excellent man, mooste perfite, moste wise, and moste counnynge before al other that was only man. For to hym that is god and man, is no comparison. And then lyke as yf a man [M₈v] speke of a prophete, not naming any prophete in certayne, it is commonly taken for the prophete Dauid, for his excellencie before other prophetes. And if a man speke of a boke, not naminge any boke in certayne, it is vnderstande by doctours to be mente of the Bible. For *Biblia* in hebrewe is in latin *liber,* that is to sey in englishe the boke: as who seith most singlar boke. And so by this terme, the virgine, is vnderstande our lady: so in like wise it may be saide by this worde man, is vnderstande *Adam,* as moste excellent man, as is afore saide. And thus me thynketh that the saide texte, that is to seye, *Numerus enim hominis est,* that is to sey, it is the numbre of a man, may be conueniently taken of this effecte, as if it had bene expressely saide, it is sothly the numbre of *Adam.* And then it is al one to sey, it is the noumbre of *Adam,* and to seye it is the noumbre of the yeres of the lyfe of *Adam.* And it

[N₁] appereth in the .v. chapiter of Genesis, that Adam lyued, ix.C. and .xxx. yeres. And nyghe about so many yeres it is sith the said Mahumete was borne, as it appereth by diuers wryters, that haue treated of that cursed man. For it is moste commonly agreed amonge al
5   wryters, that Mahumete was born about the yere of our lorde .fiue hundred. lxxxxvi. which was about the later ende of the great tirant Cosdroe king of Persie, that toke the holy crosse fro Ierusalem. And froo the sayde yere of our lorde fiue hundred. lxxxxvi. vnto this yere, whiche is the yere of oure lorde god .MDXXXIII, be ronne .ix.C.xxxv.
10   yeres or nigh aboute. And so that secte hath continued fyue yere lenger, then after this accompte is made mencion of in the sayd texte. And therfore after this accompte it may very wel be concluded, that it is like, that the said secte shulde shortly haue an ende. And though the [N₁v] saide secte cessed not the same yere, as the said accompt of the
15   said yeres serued to, by the said texte, it forceth littel. For it is not commenly seen, that scriptures, or reuelacions haue ben taken precisely to determin the very certeyntie of the yere, that suche thinge or suche shulde be done: but that hit shulde be done nigh about that tyme. And so it was taken, as it apperethe *Hieremie* .xxv. where our lorde
20   speketh of the destruction of the lande of Caldey, sayenge thus, *Cum impleti fuerint septuaginta anni, uisitabo super regem Babylonis, et super gentem illam, Dicit dominus, iniquitatem illorum, et super terram Chaldaeorum, et ponam illam in solitudines sempiternas.* And yet neuer the les when the saide. lxx. yeres were paste, the said distruction folowed not immedi-
25   ately after, but at conuenient tyme, nyghe folowynge thervpon. And so it may be of this secte, that it shal shortly hereafter be distroyed, accordinge to the effecte [N₂] of the saide wordes: thoughe it were not destroyed the same yere, that the saide texte, after the saide exposition, stretched to. And if it be said, that after this interpretation, the saide
30   secte shulde not of lykelihode yet ceasse of longe tyme: for Mahumete beganne not his secte tylle .xl. yere of his age, as most writers sey. And if the accompt of the tyme of the continuance of the said secte, shalbe taken from the said .xl. yeres of his age, as peraduenture some wyl sey it is moste reasonable to be, bycause his secte beganne then, and not
35   afore: and that then there is yet .xxxv. yeres to comme, or there about, ere that secte shulde come to an ende, as will appere to hym that wyl lay the yeres of Adam to the continuance of the said secte, begynninge at the said .xl. yeres. To that it maye be answered, that the said texte is as wel to be referred to the begynnynge of the lyfe of Mahumete, as to the
40   be[N₂v]ginninge of his secte. For the wordes of the said text be these: He that hath wisedome, may compte the noumbre of the beaste: and by that worde beest may be vnderstande as well the saide Mahumete, whiche may conueniently be called a beast for his beastly life, as is seyd

before, as his beastly secte. But if the said text hadde ben thus, He that
hath wisedom, may accompt the numbre of the secte of the beaste, then
their reason had bene somewhat to haue ben regarded. But as the
lettre is, it agreeth more with the lettre, that the accompte of the sayd
nombre shall be taken from the birth of Mahumete, to thende of his 5
secte, thenne fro the begynninge of his secte. For as the redemption of
man toke a gret special effecte at the birth of our lord, and at his
conception, though it was not fully accomplished vnto the passion: so it
may be seyd, that to al them, that folowe Mahumetis lawe, a spe[N₃]ciall
operacion to their dampnation was wrought by his byrthe. And so me 10
semeth, that it is most conuenient to begynne the saide accompte from
his byrth.

And as to the said numbre of six hundred sixtie and six yeres, after
Lyre on the said .xiii. chap. of the Apocalips, hit signifyeth the tyme
that was betwene the birthe of Christ and the dethe of the said Ma- 15
humete. For so many yeres were betwene them, as will appere to hym
that listeth to rede the accompte, that Lyre maketh therin and his
sayinges to gether. But for as moch as that last numbre seruith not to
the purpose, that I haue treated of before, that is to sei, to shew how
longe the said secte shall continue: therfore I entende not to speke any 20
ferther of it at this tyme. Thus farre gothe the said exposition.

And ferthermore lyke as I haue red in cronicles, that dyuers kynges
of [N₃v] this realme, and theyr people also haue in tyme paste hadde
great zeale and desyre to haue the holye lande brought ageyne in to
Christen mens handes: soo maye it be that nowe, throughe grace, a lyke 25
desyre maye comme amonge the people, to haue hit nowe recouered.
And if there come such a desire in the hertes of the people: it were not
vnlyke, but that they shulde haue the desyre of theyr herte fulfylled,
though other, whiche before them hadde lyke desire, had it not fulfill-
ed, for the tyme was not yet come. BYZAN. I praye the shewe me what 30
cronicles, or other thynges, hast thou harde, to proue that kinges of
this realme and their people haue had desire to recouer the holy land.
SALEM. I shall shewe the of somme with good wyll. [N₄]

Of diuers kinges, princis, and lordis
of this realme that haue hadde great 35
desire to recouer agein the holy lande
into christen mens handes, after
it was taken by Saladine fro
christen men. The .xxiiij. Cha.

SALEM. Thoughe this realme of Englande be one of the fertheste 40
christen realmes fro the holye lande, yet I supose, that it hathe done as

moche for to haue recouered the holy lande ageyn into christen mens handes, as any realme christened hathe done, that haue ben more nerer to the holy lande then this is. And therfore to thentent that it may the better appere, what great labours and peynes many princis and
5   noble men of this realme haue taken in that behalfe: I shal here after in this chapitre remembre certein cronicles, that trete of that matier, as hereafter appereth.

Fyrste in the yere of our lorde god .M.Clxxxx. kinge Richarde the fyrste, [N₄v] called Cure de lion, and Philip the french king, at Marsilia,
10   where saint Marie Magdalen lieth, in the vtas of the natiuite of seint Iohan Baptist, toke their iourneye towarde the holy lande, and there they wanne the citie of Acon, where by reason of a diuision, that fel betwixt them, the frenche kinge returned home agayne. And in that iourney Bauldwyn archebishop of Canturbury died in the holy lande.
15   Then king Richarde did there many notable actes, wherby the in- fidelles dred hym right sore. And amonge other thinges he subdued the lande of Cypres. And yet finally he retourned agayne into Eng- lande, without obteynynge that he desired: for the time was not yet come.

20   And in the yere of our lord god .M.CCxviii. wente out of Englande towarde the siege of Damiat Ranulphus the noble erle of Chester, William Arundell, and the noble barons [N₅] Robert the sonne of Walter, Iohan constable of Chestre, and William Harecourte, and Oliuere the kingis sonne of Englande, with great company: whiche
25   siege continued tylle the yere folowinge: and then it was taken into the handes of christen menne: but the thirde yere after, it was taken ageyne by the infidels.

And in the yere of our lord .M.CC. lx. the Erle Rychard, broder vnto the kinge Henry the thirde, whiche after was kinge of Almayne, accom-
30   panied with the kyng of Nauer, and the erle of Britayne, landed at Acon: & within two dayes after, the erle Richarde caused it to be proclaymed, that no souldiour, of what nacion so euer he was, shulde departe oute of the holye lande for lacke of wages: but that they shulde vnder hym haue wages to serue our lorde. And when the sarasins
35   harde that crye, thoughe the kinge of Nauerre and the erle of Bre[N₅v]tayne shortlie after withdrewe them selfe and fledde, yet the sarazins dred soore the wisedome and power of the erle Richarde, as welle bycause that name Richarde was yet moche dred to the infidels, as also for that he had great abundance of golde and syluer, as for that he
40   was the emperours systers sonne, and erle of Poicters and Cornewaile. And in this tyme dyed many pilgrimes of Englande, some goinge to- warde the holy lande, and some comynge from thens: that is to sey

Eudo, brother to the erle, Richard Hamo, Richarde Betune, Iohan fitz Iohan, stewarde to the saide erle, and Iohan Beauchampe a noble knighte.

And the yere folowynge the Erle of Salisbury came from the holy lande, and landed at Douer. 5

And in the yere of our lord god .M.CClxix. prince Edwarde, eldest sonne to kinge Henry the thirde, entending to fulfylle the aduowe, that he hadde [N₆] made into the holy lande, in May toke his iourney, with many nobles of the realme. And before him was gone towarde the same iourneye Lewes the frenche kinge with a stronge company. And prince 10 Edward went streight towarde Acon, and by the weye landed in the isle of Sardinia, and there he herde certaine tidynges of the deth of Lewes the frenche kinge, to whom Philip was heire. And thither came to hym Charles, brother to the sayde Lewes that was kinge of Cicyl. And though prince Edwarde entended only to distroy the ennemies of the 15 crosse of Christe, yet the saide Charles dyd not so: but toke of the sarazins, in tho parties, great sommes of money for a truce, whiche dyd great hurte. And after the saide Charles kynge of Cecile, and prince Edwarde, sailed towarde Cecile: and by the waye many of the shyppes of the sayde Charles were with great tempestes perisshed [N₆v] in the 20 see, with al the money that was taken of the sarazins: but the shyppes of prince Edwarde, that were in the myddes amonge the other, came saufely to lande, whiche was taken for a great miracle: whiche as many men toke it, was bycause prince Edwarde coueited not the money of the infidels, but to recouer the contreys, redemed with the bloudde of 25 Christe, into Christen mens handes ageyne.

Then Charles and Philippe returned into France, and prince Edward with a smal company went forwarde on his iourney towarde Acon: which ne hadde ben his comynge, was lyke within foure dayes, to haue ben delyuered into the handes of the sarazins. Then the citie 30 punysshed certayn fals christen men: and somme of Venice, that had ministred armoure and vitayle to the sarazins.

After prince Edwarde, with a greatte companye wente oute of Acon to Nazareth, and [N₇] by the castels of Cake and Caiphas, and slewe all the sarazins that he met with: but he retourned anon for fere of some 35 false christen men.

And in the yere of our lord .M.CC.lxxi. prince Edward was like to haue bene slayne in the citie of Acon by an Assyssyn, that camme to hym from a great prince of the Turkes, vnder colour that he wolde becomme a christen man, if he durste for feare of his people. And 40 when the false traitour, vnder that pretence was brought into the presence of the prince: sodainly with a venemed knyfe he strake the prince

vpon the breaste, intendinge to haue slayne him: whiche as god wold, had on a secrete cote of defence. And when the prince perceiued the treason, with his fote he strake downe the traitour, and starte sodeinly to hym to pull the knyfe out of his hande. And with the violence
5   happened to strike hym selfe, with the poynt of the poysoned knife, [N₇v] into his foreheed, wherby he was in great peril: but with the helpe of his phisicions and surgions, he escaped that dangere. And this yere dyuers noble men of Irelande, and also the noble manne Thomas de Clara, that broughte with hym foure sarazins, whiche he hadde
10 taken in captiuitie, cam from the holy lande into Englande. And the yere folowynge dyed kynge Henry the thyrde. And the same yere camme Edmonde, that was yonger brother to prince Edwarde, fro the holy lande into Englande. And after prince Edwarde, leauinge sufficiente numbre of souldiours in Acon, came into Cicell, and so into
15 Italy, and after into Burgondy, where many of the nobles of Englande mette hym. And than he went in to France, where he was honorably receyued of Philip the frenche king, for they were sisters children. And so he went into Gascoin. And when he had there set all thingis [N₈] in good order, he came into Englande. And so hit appereth, that this
20 noble prince obteyned not his desire, concernynge the recouery of the holy lande: for the tyme was not yet come.

Also I haue herde it many tymes reported, that kynge Henry the fyfthe had great desire to haue gone into the holy lande, and that after when he fel sicke, and that he sawe his syckenesse grewe sore vppon
25 hym, he seide this verse: *Benigne fac domine in bona uoluntate tua Sion, ut edificentur muri Hierusalem,* that is, lord do thou beningly in thy good will of Sion, that the walles of Iherusalem myght be reedified. And it is not to suppose, that by thoo wordes, the walles of Hierusalem, he vnderstode only the material walles of Hierusalem. For the buyldinge
30 of them was not so greattely to be regarded: but he ment the spiritual walles, that is the walles of the trewe catholicall feythe, whiche he desired might be re[N₈v]edified about Hierusalem, and al that countrey. And yet he had not his desire therin, for he died of the same sickenesse. And what shulde we thinke was the cause, that he had not
35 his desire graunted: but that the tyme, that our lorde hathe appoynted, that the christen feithe shulde be brought thider agayne, was not yet come?

And no more it was, whan the right noble prince of blessed memory kinge HENRY the .vij. father of our soueraigne lorde the kinge that
40 nowe is, wrote a lettre to the pope, puttynge hym in remembraunce, howe greatte pitie it was of the desolation of the holy lande, and of the citie of Constantinopole, and the countreyes there about, aduertising

him also to sturre al princis christened to the relefe therof: & he said
that he wold be redi with his power as nede shulde be. To whome the
pope wrote ageyne, giuynge him great thankes and commendacions,
[O_1] that he wolde put hym in mynde of so charitable a thinge, that he
hym selfe ought first before all other to haue remembred: How be it he 5
said two thinges caused him to doubt moche vpon that mocion: one
was, for that it had be sene in tyme paste, that when christen princis of a
good zeale, that they haue hadde to the christen feyth, haue gone
together into the holy land, they and theyr people haue varied: And
there as their purpose was to fyghte ageinst the infidels, they haue 10
fought amonges them selfe, and shedde christen mennes bloudde, and
fynallye haue returned ageyne with small encrese of the christen feith.
The seconde was this, that the power and ryches of the Turke was so
encreased, that it was more daunger nowe to warre ageynst him, than it
was before. 15

And as to the firste doubt, the king made answere ageine by an other
letter, and seide, that his pourpose was [O_1v] not that christen princis
shulde ioyne together in that iourney, but that euery prince, that wolde
goo, shulde be stronge inoughe of hym selfe, with helpe of god, to take
one quarter: & as for hym selfe, he saide he wolde go by water without 20
helpe of any other. And as to the seconde doubte: lyke a trewe catholicall prince he sayde, he lytell doubted the power or ryches of the
Turke: for the victorie of bataile standeth not in them, but in the hande
of god. And the briefes and copies of the saide letters were openly
redde in the sterre chaumbre before the archebysshop of Canturburye 25
Warrham, then being chancellour of Englande, where it was my
chaunce then to be, and with other to here them redde. And sithe that
tyme I haue herde but lyttell more speking of that pretence: for the
kinge anone after wexed sickely, and so continued in maner tyll he
dyed. But nowe if suche a desire felle [O_2] into the hertes of the people, 30
as hath done before: som trust might be had, that the time of the
conuersion of mani of the said infidels were nere at hande, with that
onely that christen menne wolde falle to a good peace and agremente
amonges them selfe. For tylle than, no good can growe ne encrease in
that matter. But yet I wolde not, that mayster Moore shulde take my 35
sayenges, concernyng that truste, as thoughe I shulde speake them as
prophecies, as he sometyme notethe the maker of the said treatise in
some thynges to do, whome he in his Apologie calleth many tymes the
pacifier: for I speake them not as prophecies, but as thynges, that as me
semethe by reason of the sayde exposition, and by dyuers reasonable 40
coniectures, are lykely to ensewe. BYZANCE. Verilye as thou sayest,
mayster Moore calleth the maker of the sayde treatyse many tymes in

his [O$_2$v] Appologie pacifier: And thoughe it appereth that he meaneth not soo, for he saithe sometyme, that the maker of the saide treatise
taketh away rather to the contrarye of a pacifier, then to make peace:
yet I dare seye, that if a good peace and agrement may ensue, by whose
5 meanes so euer it were, eyther as coulde be deuysed by mayster More
hym selfe, or by any other that coulde take a better waye therto then he
can: that he wolde be righte welle contented therwith. And thus the
glorious Trinitie haue in his keping bothe the and me. Amen.

Finis.

10   PSAL. CI.
Vt annunciant in Sion nomen domini:
Et laudem eius in Hierusalem,
In conueniendo populos in unum,
Et reges ut seruiant domino.

15   LONDINI IN AEDIBVS
THOMAE BERTHELETI.
M.D.XXXIII.
CVM PRIVILEGIO.

APPENDIX C

The Later Career
of Christopher St. German (1534–1541)

BY J. A. GUY

APPENDIX C

The Later Career
of Christopher St. German (1534–1541)

I
N THE YEARS between 1534 and his death in 1541, St. German investigated primarily the grounds and nature of royal supremacy over the church in England. Only in 1537, in his last and unpublished writings, did he turn his attention to doctrinal matters concerning the sacraments and the interpretation of scripture.

Henry VIII's break with Rome was accelerated by the Act of Supremacy, passed in November 1534.[1] The act was strictly declaratory: the king's power was to be restored to what it had allegedly been at an earlier point in history. The substantive novelty of the measure was its pronouncement that the revived royal control over the church in England was to be "taken, accepted and reputed," enabling Henry to govern the church and reform all its heresies, contempts, and abuses. The main point was that Henry VIII's headship sprang directly from God; its exercise was a return to historical truth following four centuries of papal usurpation. This theory had been adumbrated in the *Collectanea satis copiosa* as early as the autumn of 1530, and its promulgation in the act was perhaps not unexpected;[2] but for St. German, who had already refused to join the official circle of propagandists at Blackfriars in July 1534, the wording of the act was evidently a matter of crucial importance, obliging him to take stock of his ideas and goals. Before the act his principal targets had consistently been the shortcomings of the parochial clergy and the procedure of the church courts in heresy trials. What increasingly preyed on his mind in the wake of the Act of Supremacy was the ambiguity of a supremacy which had been declared but not defined by parliament. It is clear that after November 1534 St. German once again directed his study toward the questions of

---

[1]26 Henry VIII, c. 1. This appendix draws, by permission of the Selden Society, upon some material presented in Guy, *St. German*, pp. 38–55.

[2]Guy, *Public Career*, pp. 131–40, and "Henry VIII and the Praemunire Manoeuvres"; Lehmberg, pp. 202–03, 250.

parliamentary power and statutory competence that had previously absorbed him in *New Additions* and his parliamentary draft, and this shift of interest was immediately apparent in his *Treatise concerning the Power of the Clergy and the Laws of the Realm,* published near the end of 1534 or at the beginning of 1535.[1]

The Power of the Clergy apparently continued St. German's earlier assault on clerical immunity from secular jurisdiction, begun in the second dialogue of *Doctor and Student* and continued in *New Additions* and *A Treatise concerning the Division,* but it did so from a distinctly new angle. St. German now posited that the rights of the clergy and the question of the jurisdictional competence of statute and common law could be satisfactorily resolved only if the power of kings and princes within their territories was first accurately delineated.[2] The way to look at issues such as whether the judges in the church courts were bound to acknowledge the laws of the realm and obey statutes was to step back from the mêlée and investigate instead the status of England as a unitary sovereign state. St. German quickly decided that kings and princes had their authority directly from God and that the Jewish kings had regulated the affairs of their clergy. He went on to discuss early British and English history: Lucius I, who according to the ancient *Leges anglorum* had become the first Christian ruler of Britain in A.D. 187, and King Ethelbert, who was the first Christian king of "Englishmen." Did these kings suffer diminution of their power after they were christened? And if a pagan king received baptism and the articles of faith, would he and his subjects be bound to accept alien laws enacted outside the realm?[3] Since these questions touched the personal circumstances of those monarchs from whom the alleged historical truth of royal supremacy was derived, they immediately affected the definition of supreme headship in Henrician England. St. German's answers were firmly negative: the Christian faith was not bondage but liberty and freedom in God; the temporal power of kings owed nothing to the spiritual power of the clergy; and kings could never be constrained by their clergy. As Solomon had said, "Rex sapiens populi stabilimentum est" (Sap. 6:26):

> By which wordes it semeth that it must of necessyte folowe that kynges have also power and auctorite to stable their people. For wysdome withoute power can nat stable the people. But how can any kynge either by power or wysdome stable his people if the

---

[1] *STC*[2] 21588.
[2] *The Power of the Clergy,* chaps. 1–3, 17.
[3] *The Power of the Clergy,* chaps. 9–10.

clergy have power to make lawes to bynde him and his people, onles that he shuld be taken as iudge over those lawes? Wherfore we thinke that lyke as kinges and prynces before they were cristened had power to order their people after the lawe that they than were of, and had power to avoyde all suche thinges as might bringe any unquyetnesse among their people, that so the same princes after they were converted to the chrysten faythe hadde as full power to kepe their people in peace and quyetnes as they had before they were cristened.[1]

St. German argued that such "a prince as wolde be converted to the christen faythe maye refuce any of the ceremonyes and lawes made by the Clergye in tyme paste, and yet be receyved to the principall artycles of the cristen relygyon." The only spiritual laws binding on kings were those expressly pronounced by God, and proper distinction had to be made between law and mere ceremony. This had been common knowledge in former times, as St. German claimed, when the clergy had been pure and holy, but had been forgotten latterly as worldly priests extended their power, "where upon great grudges have rysen in manye places amonge the people." In order to restore the distinction and bring peace to the commonwealth, kings and princes thus "be bounden to knowe their own power."[2]

But St. German's sympathy with Henrician orthodoxy as proclaimed in the Act of Supremacy was not unbounded: his rhetoric on the subject of kingly power should not beguile us into classifying him as a wholehearted supporter of Henry VIII. St. German exalted kingly power as the means to regulate the clergy and subordinate canon law to English law, but he deviated from the official interpretation of the supreme headship when he articulated his opinion (shared by Thomas Cromwell)[3] that royal authority over church and clergy should be exercised in practice by the king in parliament, not by the king or his vicegerent alone.[4] *The Power of the Clergy* signals St. German's dissent from the official position. From the beginning he charted the ultimate boundaries of royal supremacy, repudiating the notion, not unequivocally abandoned when St. German was writing *The Power*, that Henry VIII had a right to the *potestas ordinis* as well as to the *potestas iurisdictionis*: the king "hath none auctorite to minister any of the sacramentes, ne to do any other thing spyrituall, wherof oure lorde gave power only

---

[1]*The Power of the Clergy*, sigs. D_5v–D_6.
[2]*The Power of the Clergy*, sig. E_1.
[3]Elton, *Studies*, 2, 215–35.
[4]*The Power of the Clergy*, sigs. G_1–I_8v.

to his apostles and discyples."[1] As it turned out, Henry VIII never claimed anything beyond the *potestas iurisdictionis* after the heady days of February 1531, and the point ceased to be controversial.[2] But other points remained so. St. German argued that princes were not learned enough to discover their power by themselves: they needed assistance lest they presume too much. He also thought that the most satisfactory check of all was that provided by existing English legal institutions, notably parliament.

St. German laid the groundwork for this part of his discussion by adopting the definition of *ecclesia* set forth in the *Defensor pacis* of Marsilius of Padua. "By that worde chyrche," explained St. German, "is nat understande only the clergye, for they undoutydly make nat the chyrche, for the hole congregation of Christen people maketh the chyrche."[3] But since for practical purposes the whole people of Christendom could never be gathered together, St. German was obliged to narrow the definition so as to make it feasible. How he did so was remarkable. First, he took the familiar text:

> If thy brother offend thee, correct him between him and thee only. And if he hear thee, thou hast won thy brother. And if he hear thee not, take with thee one or two witnesses, and if he hear thee not then, then show it to the church. And if he hear not the

---

[1] *The Power of the Clergy*, sig. G₂.

[2] Guy, "Henry VIII and the Praemunire Manoeuvres."

[3] *The Power of the Clergy*, sig. D₄. Admittedly, this definition is so general that it could include sharply differing views about authority, hierarchy, and jurisdiction. More himself would have been quite willing to accept it; see Brian Gogan, *The Common Corps of Christendom: Ecclesiological Themes in the Writings of Sir Thomas More* (Leiden, 1982). The influence of Marsilius on St. German has been questioned by Plucknett and Barton (*Doctor and Student*, p. xxi, n. 3) and by J. B. Trapp (*CW 9*, xlviii–xlix). But St. German's adoption of Marsilian ideas in his "Dyalogue shewinge what we be bounde to byleve as thinges necessary to Salvacion" encourages a return to Franklin L. Baumer's view that St. German had studied *Defensor pacis* ("Christopher St. German: The Political Philosophy of a Tudor Lawyer," *American Historical Review, 42* [1937], 637–38). St. German, like some of the reformers, would probably have read Marsilius in the Basel edition of 1522. He did not need to wait for the English translation by William Marshall, published in 1535 (*STC*² 17817). Nevertheless, since St. German and Marshall were both connected to Thomas Cromwell, there may have been an exchange of views between them. In particular, Marshall consistently glossed Marsilius's citizen legislative body in his edition of *Defensor pacis* as meaning parliament in a way resonant of St. German's developing opinions. He also focused attention on the questions of secularized charity and poor relief that interested St. German during the 1530s. The folios of Marshall's translation that raise these points are 27v, 28v, 35, 91v, 118, 119v, 128v, 138. Marshall asked Cromwell for a financial subvention for his translation of *Defensor pacis* (*LP 7*, nos. 422–23; *LP 11*, no. 1355).

church, let him be to thee like an heathen and a publican. (Matt. 18:15–17)[1]

St. German interpreted the word "church" in this text to mean the laws and customs of England. If a man would not make amends to his neighbor in a temporal matter, the neighbor was to show the offense to the "church" by reporting it to the royal justices or justices of the peace or "other offycers that after the lawe and custome of the realme may reforme it." In doing so, according to St. German, he had "right well fulfylled the gospell." If the matter was spiritual, it should rightfully be reported to the bishop or his officials—in the traditional way.[2] Now the wider significance of this passage was that in temporal matters St. German's supreme head was to be in charge of a church regulated by legal institutions. In spiritual matters things were already regulated by the clergy, and the supreme head had, in any case, only the *potestas iurisdictionis*. We thus conclude that St. German's theory preferred, when possible, to confine the prerogative of the supreme head to powers exercised through law and legal institutions.

St. German also analyzed the role of parliament in *The Power of the Clergy*. An obvious difficulty created by the Henrician Reformation was to know which measures to be provided for the government of the English church would be consistent with divine law and which would be against that law. Scripture, strictly interpreted in accordance with Augustinian principles, was the best yardstick, but many issues in debate between church and state were not precisely addressed by the Bible. St. German discussed a number of these in *The Power of the Clergy* and concluded that parliamentary statutes were a fail-safe test to be accepted by both clergy and laity in difficult cases, since statutes were the work of the king and the estates of the realm, who were themselves in another sense "the church." "For it is nat to presume that so many noble princes and their counseyle, ne the lordes and the nobles of the realme, ne yet the Comons gathered in the sayde parlyamente, wolde fro tyme to tyme renne in to so great offence of conscyence as is the breakynge of the lawe of God."[3] The idea that safety resided in numbers is curious, but St. German had opened a fascinating door with his statement on the efficacy of statute, because the clear implication is that the king in parliament would be less likely to break unintentionally the law of God than just one man, the supreme head Henry VIII.

In the course of his argument in *The Power of the Clergy*, St. German

---

[1] *The Power of the Clergy*, sig. D$_3$v.
[2] *The Power of the Clergy*, sig. D$_4$v.
[3] *The Power of the Clergy*, chap. 6.

also surveyed the canons made by past provincial assemblies in England to see how many were in derogation of English law and royal prerogative. He pursued this theme to its logical conclusion in *A Treatise concerning divers of the Constitutions Provincial and Legantines,* published in 1535.[1] Not surprisingly, several canons were ruled *ultra vires* and others were deemed vexatious to the people and uncharitable—but after the Submission of the Clergy this sort of enquiry had become secondary to St. German's main concern about royal supremacy.

In *An Answer to a Letter* (1535) St. German finally proffered his mature opinions on the question of the sovereignty of the king in parliament.[2] *An Answer* refined the ideas of *The Power of the Clergy,* which had been implicit rather than overt, and concluded St. German's writings on the subjects of parliamentary power and statutory competence. Couched in the form of a reply to a (fictitious) request for news which St. German pretended he had received from a friend in the provinces, *An Answer* began by reaffirming his views about the limitations on Henry VIII's power as supreme head of the English church.[3] Just as royal power had not been diminished when the early British kings were converted to Christianity, so also parliament's recognition of Henry VIII's supreme headship did not augment the authority of the kings of England. The Act of Supremacy professedly gave Henry VIII no more power than he had had before. The act had been strictly declaratory, nor could it have been otherwise. If parliament or convocation had tried to "make" the king supreme head, its grant would have been void: "for they have no auctorite to chaunge the lawe of God." Henry VIII was, and always had been, a lay bishop: he had no right to the *potestas ordinis* or to any authority "that our lorde gave only to his apostels or disciples in spirituall ministracyon to the people." The one novelty after November 1534 was that the power of the king was "more evydently knowen than it was before."[4] Yet problems unquestionably

---

[1] *STC*[2] 24236. The occasion for writing this treatise was plainly the first printing in 1534 of an English translation of William Lyndewode's *Provinciale* (*STC*[2] 17113) from which the canons attacked by St. German are drawn. Lyndewode's book (finished in 1430) was the most authoritative work available in England on canon law. Fifteen Latin editions had been printed since 1481. See J. H. Beale, *A Bibliography of Early English Law Books* (Cambridge, Mass., 1926), nos. T398–411, and R. B. Anderson, *A Supplement to Beale's Bibliography of Early English Law Books* (Cambridge, Mass., 1943), p. 22, no. T4086. See also *STC*[2] 17102–17112. Editions of 1483, 1501, 1505, and 1525 contained both Lyndewode's text and commentary (some other editions have only the text). These would have been available to More and St. German.

[2] *STC*[2] 21558.5.

[3] *An Answer,* chaps. 1–2.

[4] *An Answer,* sigs. A₃–B₃.

arose from the need to delineate precisely the boundaries between spiritual and temporal affairs. Some things were "mere spiritual," such as the sacrament of the altar, absolutions, orders, and religious ministry. Other matters had been falsely claimed as spiritual affairs by worldly and ambitious popes and prelates: for instance, provisions to benefices, visitations, clerical taxation, parochial enfranchisement, rights of sanctuary, dispensations, tithes, the proving of wills.[1] Such disputed matters had pertained to the church only "by a sufferaunce of princes" and might be resumed by the state without offending divine law, although St. German pointed out that the primary need was for the clergy to eliminate abuses and superstition, so that Henry VIII would not need to "nationalize" the church courts.

St. German next attacked the particular abuses and usurpations of popes and clergy in such matters as the celebration of mass and the sale of pardons, indulgences, and dispensations. Then he turned to a fascinating treatment of the conflict between English law and ecclesiastical law on the question of restitution.[2] But he soon returned to the kernel of both *The Power of the Clergy* and *An Answer*, which was to discover the best method by which semispiritual matters might be governed in a manner consistent with divine law and royal responsibility, when precise guidance on individual issues was not available in the Bible. As St. German presented his case, the first priority was to find an objective test against which reforming ideas could be judged to see whether or not they were consistent with the law of God, and *An Answer* proceeded to argue that this need would be satisfied if a valid method of "declaring" and "expounding" scripture could be found to answer these borderline questions.[3] In St. German's opinion, the clergy were automatically disqualified from interpreting scripture concerning issues disputed between church and state, because it was exactly those biblical texts concerning their power, jurisdiction, liberties, and possessions that were most controversial. Only a "singular and elect" priest who "through special grace" had cast aside worldly riches and ambition could furnish impartial guidance, but St. German appeared to doubt that any such person existed. *An Answer* thus proposed that in borderline cases kings and princes should oversee the interpretation of scripture, "For it appereth. Psalm ii. that it is said thus to kynges and princes, 'O ye kynges, understande ye: be ye lerned that iudge the worlde.' "[4] But the role of rulers was to be purely supervisory; their

---

[1] *An Answer*, sigs. A₆–A₇.
[2] *An Answer*, chaps. 4–6.
[3] *An Answer*, chaps. 7–8.
[4] *An Answer*, sig. G₃.

402   APPENDIX C

intervention is necessary to avoid "dyversyties of opinyons and unquyetnesse amonge the people" and to ensure that subjects did not
wilfully break divine law. St. German positively withheld from Henry
VIII as supreme head the right to construe the meaning of scripture,
for this was the preserve of the "catholyque churche." And St. German's church, in *An Answer* as in *The Power of the Clergy,* was not the
clergy alone, but "emperours, kynges and princes with their people as
well of the clergye as of the lay fee." However, since the universal
catholic church could not conveniently be assembled on each occasion
when scriptural exegesis was required, "therfore it semeth that kynges
and princes whom the people have chosen and agreed to be their rulers
and governours, and which have the whole voyces of the people, maye
with theire counsell spirytuall and temporall make exposycyon of such
scripture as is doutfull."[1]

At this point it might be thought that St. German had, after all,
ensnared himself into assigning to princes the right to decide disputed
points of scripture, but in fact the opposite was true. St. German's
allusion in *An Answer* to the elective element in kingship now became
the prelude to a vigorous reassertion of the representative theory of
law and government—the "constitutional" theory of Sir John Fortescue,[2] which St. German believed was visibly endangered by Henry
VIII's unhealthy attraction to the principles of theocratic kingship in
the aftermath of the break with Rome. Two other streams of medieval
thought were also brought into confluence with Fortescue's theory.
First, St. German's words "whom the people have chosen and agreed to
be their rulers and governours, and which have the whole voyces of the
people" encapsulated traditional populist denials of the theocratic dog-
ma that the people were "entrusted" to the sole authority of the king as
vicar of Christ and protector of the people.[3] Second, his adherence to
Marsilian theory of the church within the context of ideas of elective
kingship signaled overtones of the Paduan's controversial opinion that
governments were founded on the people's will as manifested through
the laws, to which all forms of government were accountable.[4] But the
primary inspiration of this section of the *Answer* was Fortescue, for St.
German proclaimed:

---

[1]*An Answer,* sig. G5.

[2]John Fortescue, *The Governance of England,* ed. Charles Plummer (Oxford, 1885);
cited hereafter as "Fortescue."

[3]Walter Ullmann, *Principles of Government and Politics in the Middle Ages* (London, 1966),
pp. 130–49, 269–79.

[4]Marsilius of Padua, *The Defender of Peace,* ed. Alan Gewirth, 2 vols. (New York, 1951–
56), *1,* 236–48; cited hereafter as *"The Defender of Peace."*

> There be two maner of powers that kynges and princes haue ouer theire subiectes: The one is called/*Jus regale*/that is to saye a kyngely gouernaunce: And he that hathe that power maye with his counsell make lawes to bynde his subiectes/and also make declaration of Scrypture for the good order of his subiectes/as nede shall requyre/for appeasyng of varyance. The other is called/*Jus regale politicum*/that is to saye a kynglye and a polytyke gouernaunce. And that is the most noble power that any prince hath ouer his subiectes/and he that ruleth by that power/maye make no Lawe to bynde his subiectes without their assent/but by their assent he maye so that the lawes that he maketh be nat agaynste the lawe of God/nor the lawe of reason: And this power hathe the kynges grace in this Realme: where he by assente of his lordes spirytuall and temperall: and of his commons gathered togyther by his commaundement in his parlyamente maye make lawes to bynde the people And of those lawes there nedeth no proclamation/bicause they be made by all the people/for the parliament so gathered togyther/~~the people~~ representeth the estate of al the people within this realme/that is to say of the whole catholyque churche therof.[1]

Of the "two maner of powers," England fell into the second category in Fortescue's theory. The English state was "*Dominium Politicum et Regale.*" In *An Answer* St. German meant to echo Fortescue's view in *The Governance of England* that England was less an empire than a constitutional monarchy.[2] Moreover, the representative character of parliament was even better appreciated in St. German's day than it had been in Fortescue's. Experienced common lawyers in the 1530s had started to grasp the idea of "making" law in the true sense of that term, so that the notion of imminent practical reform of the realm by parliamentary statute no longer caused much difficulty to most of them.[3] Of course, the touchstone was the consent given in parliament. And if this doctrine could be applied to reform of the common law, why then not also to that task of scriptural exegesis upon which St. German's system increasingly depended in the no-man's-land of semispiritual matters? "Why shuld nat the parlyament than whiche representeth the whole catholyke churche of Englande expounde scrypture?"[4] The combina-

---

[1]*An Answer*, sigs. G₅v–G₆.

[2]Fortescue, chaps. 1–3.

[3]Ullmann, *Principles of Government and Politics*, pp. 191–92; G. R. Elton, *English Law in the Sixteenth Century: Reform in an Age of Change*, Selden Society Lecture for 1978 (London, 1979), pp. 14–21; reprinted in Elton, *Studies, 3,* 274–88.

[4]*An Answer*, sig. G₆v.

tion of functions within England's principal representative body would not only liberate the community from clerical partiality and bias, but could also assure the smooth amalgamation of the Henrician Reformation into the bedrock of traditional law and custom without the reverberations that might otherwise derive from the "discovery" of royal supremacy. But the question of scriptural exegesis unfortunately did not admit an agreed solution during the remainder of St. German's lifetime, and *An Answer*, as it turned out, was his public valediction to legal and political theory.

The Power of the Clergy, the *Constitutions Provincial and Legantines*, and *An Answer* were all published by Thomas Godfray, a private printer who also produced William Marshall's edition of Valla's *Donation of Constantine* in 1534, but who had no connection whatsoever with Henry VIII's official propaganda.[1] Private publication was unquestionably a reflection of St. German's literary independence in the wake of the Act of Supremacy; it reinforced his earlier decision in July 1534 to stand apart from the activities of Cromwell's propagandists assembled at Blackfriars. The author of *Doctor and Student* did not cease completely to write in the final years of his life, as two extant manuscripts from the year 1537 prove, but he did not publish again after *An Answer*, and the reason seems plain enough—he had gone full circle. From an exploration of the foundations of law and legal theory in the first dialogue of his greatest work in 1528, he had returned seven years later in *An Answer*, and in very different circumstances, to the ultimate question of the mechanics by which the law of God, revealed for mankind and written in the Bible, might be declared in England. If that question could not be addressed beyond what had already been published in *An Answer*, St. German had nothing more to say.

Considering St. German's detachment, even isolation, from the official party after 1534, it was ironic that the leaders of the Pilgrimage of Grace should have singled him out at the end of 1536 as one of the principal heretics whose errors they wished to see corrected by Henry VIII, as they did in their first article:

> Copie of the articles to the Lordes of the King's Cownsell at our comyng to Pontefract
>
> The fyrst touching our faith to have the heericyes of luther Wyclif husse malangton Elicampadus [that is, Oecolampadius] bucerus

---

[1]Elton, *Policy and Police*, pp. 174 and 186, n. 2.

> Co[n]fessio germanie[1] Apolugia malancto[n]is[2] The workes of
> Tyndall of barnys of Marshall[3] Raskell [that is, Rastell][4] saynt
> germay[n]e and such oder herisies of Anibapt[i]st sherely [that is,
> completely] within this realm to be a[nn]ullid and distroyde[5]

Professor Elton has recently emphasized the factional background of
the Pilgrimage and reminded us that the opinions of London lawyers
of conservative tastes, notably Robert Aske, appear in various places in
the Pontefract Articles—"to some extent the Pilgrimage was bred at
the Inns of Court."[6] Certainly St. German would have been despised
by the leaders of the Pilgrimage: Lord Darcy, Lord Hussey and Sir
Robert Constable. These chiefs were, in effect, the remnant of the
party in England that had originally opposed Henry VIII's marriage to
Anne Boleyn; they would have especially detested St. German's *New
Additions* in the context of the divorce plans of 1530 and 1531.[7] Conservative lawyers would also have disliked St. German's anticlericalism
and attacks on ecclesiastical law and the church courts. The fact, however, remains that the list of heretics in the first Pontefract article was
probably drawn up from a selection of books which Richard Bowyer, a
burgess of York, had laid before the rebels' council at Pontefract priory
between December 2 and 4, 1536.[8] It may have been partly by accident
that St. German's books were among those offered by Bowyer; but it is
clear that his *New Additions* and *A Treatise concerning the Division*, both of
which had run through several editions, had reached as far north as
Yorkshire.

St. German's role as a purveyor of heterodox views, as opposed to
anticlericalism, did not, in any case, reach fruition until 1537, when he
prepared two treatises in the course of the debates that took place

---

[1]That is, the Augsburg Confession, which was drafted by Melanchthon.

[2]*The Apologie of Melanchthon for the Augsburg Confession* (London, 1536; STC 908) was
published by R. Redman together with the Confession, both translated by Richard
Taverner.

[3]William Marshall, translator of Marsilius of Padua.

[4]John Rastell wrote an unorthodox book on purgatory: *A new boke of purgatory . . .*
(London, 1530; STC[2] 20719).

[5]PRO, SP 1/112, fol. 119.

[6]*Reform and Reformation: England 1509–1558* (London, 1977), p. 264; see also his
article "Politics and the Pilgrimage of Grace," in *After the Reformation*, ed. Barbara C.
Malament (Philadelphia, 1980), pp. 25–56; reprinted in Elton, *Studies*, 3, 183–215.

[7]Guy, *Public Career*, chaps. 7–9.

[8]Madeline H. Dodds and Ruth Dodds, *The Pilgrimage of Grace, 1536–37, and the Exeter
Conspiracy, 1538*, 2 vols. (Cambridge, 1915), 1, 345–47.

throughout that year upon the nature and number of the sacraments.[1]
The focal point was the so-called *Bishops' Book,* the second Henrician
formulary of faith, commissioned by Henry VIII and published in
September 1537—but issued, thanks to Henry's immediate preoccupation with Prince Edward's birth, without the full personal approval of the supreme head.[2] The debates were running high in June
and July 1537 and crested during a two-day meeting of prelates con-
voked by Cromwell as vicegerent in spirituals at the House of Lords.[3]
Cromwell delivered an exhortation to the bishops at the opening of the
first session and identified two specific points of controversy about the
sacraments: the authority of learned doctors and church councils in
the matter of scriptural exegesis, and the status of "unwritten verities,"
or traditional doctrines and articles of belief, hitherto accepted by the
church but not actually based on the Bible.[4] It was exactly upon these
topics that St. German now prepared, and sent to Cromwell, two
manuscripts: the first was an essay of twenty pages entitled "A Discourse of the Sacramentes: howe many there are";[5] the second was a
weightier treatise of eighty pages entitled "A Dyalogue shewinge what
we be bounde to byleve as thinges necessary to Salvacion, and what
not."[6] St. German's manuscripts are undated, but their contents allude
so often to the arguments presented in the House of Lords by Archbishop Cranmer and the Scottish theologian Alexander Alesius, whom
Cromwell took with him to the earlier part of the meeting, that it is
impossible not to link the treatises, at least in part, to that occasion, and
to assume that St. German had gained information, at first or second
hand, about the points considered.

Alesius told the assembled bishops:

> Sacramentes be signes or ceremonys which make us certen and
> sure of the wil of God. But no man's hart can be certen and sure of
> the wil of God with out the word of God. Wherfor it foloweth that
> there be no sacramentes without the word of God, and such as can
> not be proved out of the holy scripture ought not to be called
> sacramentes.[7]

---

[1]St. German's "Dyalogue" may have been commissioned in 1536; see *LP 11,* no. 84.

[2]J. J. Scarisbrick, *Henry VIII* (London, 1968), pp. 400–15.

[3]The fullest account is by Alexander Alesius in his pamphlet *Of the auctorite of the word of God agaynst the bisshop of London* (n. p., n. d.), *STC* 292.

[4]Cromwell's address appears in Alesius's pamphlet (sigs. $A_5v–A_6v$). It is printed in full in Guy, *St. German,* p. 46, n. 140.

[5]PRO, SP 6/8, pp. 1–20.

[6]PRO, SP 6/2, pp. 89–168.

[7]*Of the auctorite of the word of God,* sig. B_5.

This was the kernel of the reformers' case, and St. German developed it in the "Discourse of the Sacramentes," a treatise which he couched in the form of a petition to Henry VIII and parliament.

The church had traditionally taught that there were seven sacraments, "and the people be so instructed that these vij must be beleved and accepted undre payne of heresie by that name of the vij sacramentes of the churche"—so St. German began (p. 1). But on what authority had the church adopted the sacraments, in particular those of matrimony and penance? Was it not on the authority of popes and clergy alone? If general councils were to be averred as the authority, was not that insufficient, too, because "none had voices in the generall counsailes but oonly the clergie"? (p. 3) In short, St. German now claimed, traditional sacramental theology did little beyond propping up the "usurped powers" of the clergy on the one hand and "ignorance" on the other. For instance, matrimony and penance (or contrition) had both existed before the birth of Christ and had been practiced by the Jews but were not then termed "sacraments." Why were they so termed after Christ's birth? (pp. 2–8) Second, baptism, which was undoubtedly a sacrament, was sufficient and valid, in St. German's opinion, without such rituals as the use of holy water, oils, creams, salt, and special prayers, however desirable such ceremonies might be when properly performed. In the past, the clergy had too often forced people "to observe and kepe the ceremonyes ordeyned by the bisshops of Rome and the clergie" in preference to what was expressly laid down by God (pp. 8–9).

Next, St. German scrutinized confirmation, asking whether or not "every preste might do it aswell as bisshops," and suggesting that the principal *raison d'être* of limiting this sacrament to bishops was in fact not the law of God, but rather "to sette the bisshops in an highe estimacion of the people over pristes." St. German thus proposed that Henry VIII and parliament should investigate all these matters in the light of a true appreciation of God's law, and should make it especially clear that the exclusive power of bishops to confirm henceforward "shall stande by the auctoritie and powere of your grace and of youre parliamente, and not by the ymmediate powere and gifte of God" (pp. 9–12).

St. German then turned to the sacraments of orders and of the altar, concerning which he overwhelmingly rejected Lutheran notions of the priesthood and Zwinglian beliefs about the eucharist (pp. 12–17). Despite the fact that the sacrament of the altar was, as he claimed, ordained for laymen as much as for priests, no layman can be a priest to minister to the people; neither were Christ's words on Maundy Thursday to be taken figuratively.

And then concernyng the grace of consecration of the bodie of oure lorde in forme of bred and wyne, we beseche youre grace that it may be prohibite to all men by auctoritie aforsaide, that no man undre greate payne to be appoynted by youre grace and your parliamente perswade any manner of person to thinke that these wordes of oure master Criste, when he toke bred, and blessed it, breke it, and gave it to his disciples and said, "Take and ete ye: this is my bodie that shalbe betraied for you," oughte to be understande figuratyvely and not litterally. For sithe he that speke those wordes was, and is, of power to performe theym litterally, thoughe no mannys reason may atteyne to knowe and serche howe that may be, yet they muste beleve it. And surelie they that beleve that God was of power to make all the worlde of noughte may lightly beleve that he was of powre to make of brede his very bodie. (pp 13–14)

St. German's conservatism was here in the ascendant, and this anti-protestant passage in his "Discourse of the Sacramentes" establishes that, whatever else he had thought and written on the clergy and church courts, royal supremacy, and the sacraments during his long life, he maintained until his death an orthodox belief about the priesthood and the eucharist.

In conclusion, St. German requested that extreme unction "may be used hereafter as it hathe ben in tyme paste," but with the proviso that anyone might be anointed "as ofte as necessitie of siknes shall requyre." As with baptism, the rituals surrounding unction had often undermined its true sacramental purpose: emphasis on the holiness of blessing oil, images, bells, fire, and water tends to make priests self-important and hypocritical. St. German added that unction should be administered as a duty of the priesthood, and not as a favor. Finally, he complained that the clergy were making a distinction between themselves and the laity in the manner of anointing: laymen were anointed on the navel "as an helpe to put away the rather the concupiscence and carnall desires that haplie hathe ben in the sik personne before." By contrast, the clergy were anointed on other parts of the body, for the alleged reason that "priestes be so preserved by the holynes of theire ordre, that they nede not to be anoynted in that behalf as laye men be; and howe nighe that opynyon goethe to veynglorie and to a full settyng of vertue in owtwarde thinges, it is apparaunte" (pp. 18–20). Upon that familiar anticlerical note, St. German wrote "Finis" beneath his essay.

Far more substantial was the "Dyalogue shewinge what we be

bounde to byleve as thinges necessary to Salvacion, and what not."
Hidden away for centuries among Cromwell's papers, this major treatise has been identified as St. German's on the persuasive evidence of
his autograph corrections in the manuscript, after the manner of his
parliamentary draft of 1531, combined with the fact that the work is
cast as another dialogue between doctor and student.[1] As St. German's
third dialogue, however, it was concerned not with legal questions but
with anatomizing the precise points of controversy raised at the vicegerent's assembly in 1537. And for this purpose, the roles of the pro-
tagonists were reversed from what appears to have been St. German's
previous method. It is to be suspected that hitherto the student of
common law had spoken frequently, though not exclusively, for the
author, especially in *New Additions*, but in the new "Dyalogue" the
doctor of divinity, the authority on theological matters, usually voiced
St. German's own views. The debate opened thus:

> STUDENTE) I pray thee, shewe me nowe what we be bounde to
> bileve as thowe thinkeste, as thinges necessary to salvacion, and
> what not.
> DOCTOURE) Scripture is fully to be beleved as a thing necessary to
> salvacion, thoughe the thing conteyned in scripture perteign not
> merelie to the faithe, as that Aaron had a berde and suche other.
> STUDENTE) And what be the sayinges of doctours, specially of
> theym that be canonised and be taken of all the people for holy
> and blessed, are not all men bounde to beleve theym?
> DOCTOURE) No verilie, oonles theire seyinges be grounded of
> Scripture and may be deryved owte therof in a probable conse-
> quence. (p. 89)

St. German argued that the authority of learned doctors in matters
of faith was unacceptable because "it cannot be assuredly knowen that
the doctours said it": the writings of the Fathers were subject to inter-
polations and posthumous additions, and there was never adequate
proof to establish that what was written was true (pp. 90–91). However,
the practical objections to an epistemology which rested exclusively
upon textual criticism were obvious, and the student of common law
raised the issue at once in terms of the histories, chronicles, and legal
records that were the daily routine of the Inns of Court. "By that
reason," he declared, "no man shulde be bounde to byleve nor to gyve

---

[1] The handwriting of the corrections corresponds exactly to that of St. German's holograph letter to Cromwell in 1539 (PRO, SP 1/152, fol. 249).

faithe to legendes, cronicles, stories, deedes, writinges or yet recordes, and that shulde be a greate confusion and disordre, and in maner a distruccion of all the politique ordre and Civile governaunce" (p. 91).

St. German continued by applying juristic formulae to the debate on textual exegesis. Within the limitations of human justice a pragmatic approach to belief of written documents is the precondition of conducting affairs, and methodology at this level is best addressed to the need to avoid inflicting wrongs on others as a consequence of men's assertions. Providing a man's statements did not hurt another, and providing he did not speak against the law of God (scripture) or that of Nature, he might seek to confute—whether correctly or incorrectly— the authority of learned doctors, chronicles, or histories, if he believed that what he said was well founded. Applying the idea of conscience in a juristic sense, St. German argued that the test of a man's morality in challenging incompletely documented beliefs rests upon an objective calculation of the hurt he would do to another, if he made his assertions without sufficient cause.

For a moment, indeed, it seems as though St. German was here tottering on the brink of a return to the themes of *Doctor and Student,* upon which, we may suspect, he had always intended to write more— but he soon retreated to the immediate concerns of the "Dyalogue." As the doctor of divinity blandly summed up this section of the work: "It is lawfull for all men to doubte at every thing that he dothe not knowe of his owne knowlege, excepte it be of scripture or that that is expreslie dirivied [*sic*] upon scripture" (pp. 92–94).

After this analysis, St. German turned to the contested status of "unwritten verities" as reviewed at Cromwell's vicegerential meeting. The doctor first attacked the term itself on grounds of inherent obfuscation: a "verity" was a "true thing," but if unwritten verities were taken as revealed truth, then "I shulde estop my self to speke any thing againste theym" (p. 95). Accordingly, the designation "opinions not written in scripture" was agreed between doctor and student as the basis for discussion, and several examples were selected for close scrutiny such as the perpetual virginity of Mary, whether the apostles devised the creed, the definition and constituency of the "universall churche," whether the pope could summon general councils "and that kinges be bounden to obey his summons," whether popes and doctors had authority to expound disputed passages of scripture, the extent of episcopal power, and the use of images. St. German accepts some of the opinions on some of these points and verities but rejects others because they have no scriptural basis. For example, Mary's virginity and the contents of the apostles' creed were matters sufficiently founded on scripture to be believed "of necessitie"; but to define the church as the clergy without the laity, to affirm the pope's right to summon general councils, and to invoke the personal authority of the apostles for the format of the creed, as opposed merely to its theological contents, and for existing levels of episcopal power and the use of images—these were doctrines devoid of scriptural backing, and thus invalid. The doctor of divinity even goes so far as to assert that traditional Roman ecclesiology and the alleged rights of papal monarchy as against church councils were so far divorced from the Bible and the primitive church as to be heretical (pp. 96–120).

Formerly unwritten verities had often been later promulgated in the decrees of general councils, so that St. German found it necessary to expatiate upon the errors of former councils. As previously in *An Answer to a Letter*, Marsilian definitions were sustained in the "Dyalogue," which embraced Marsilius's principles that general councils existed to preserve the unity of the faith and that a council "represented" the whole body of believers, laity as well as clergy.[1] In particular, St. German borrowed Marsilius's concept of the "faithful legislator," who summoned and assembled the council and enforced its decisions, although news of the abortive Council of Mantua, summoned by Paul III to meet in 1537, caused St. German to deviate from the strict populism of *Defensor pacis* by substituting Christian rulers for the "legislator."[2] St. German argued that the supremacy of the apostles and their successors over the universal church had ceased when kings were converted to Christianity. Thereafter Christian rulers had become the rightful governors of the church and the proper authority for the summoning of general councils. St. German observed that councils had not been correctly summoned since the First Council of Nicaea (A.D. 325) and claimed that even that body had been of dubious legitimacy because laymen had not participated in the making of decrees. Hence kings and princes were bound "under no lesse payne then dedlie synne" to institute the necessary reforms: as the doctor of divinity explained, "I wolde have a generall counsaile gathered and kepte by auctoritie of kinges and princes, and wherin notable men of the temporaltie, as they be callede, shulde have voices" (pp. 121–33). The council "in the name of the universall churche" should then "agre what bookes ar to be taken as bookes canonised for scripture, and what not, and that they shulde also expounde the doubtes of scripture and maynteyne oon catholique feithe thoroughe all cristen realmes." Mere

---

[1] *The Defender of Peace*, 2, 272–86.
[2] *The Defender of Peace*, 2, 287–98.

ceremonies were, however, to be ordered by "every king in his con-
treye" (pp. 122–23).

The decrees of former councils were to be accepted as valid only if
they were warranted by scripture, unless they had been subsequently
acknowledged as "lawful" customs of the church (pp. 133–34). Here
St. German was ambiguous about the means of verifying the "law-
fulness" of customs; it seems that his argument was actually directed
against the "unlawfulness" of attempts by the clergy to claim as justified by divine law what, in practice, they enjoyed solely on the basis of
human acceptance—"and that somtyme by lawes made by theymself,
and where they had no auctoritie to have made any lawe" (p. 135).

In conclusion, the "Dyalogue" proffered an immediate program of
reform: the doctor of divinity proposed that a properly constituted
general council should be summoned to review the entire Bible, particularly the apocrypha, in order to settle beyond any doubt which
were the books of canonical scripture. "I thinke that nothing perteynethe to the vniuersall churche more appropriatlie then that dothe,
and it perteynethe to the churche also to sette scripture in suche
order, that it may be surelie knowen what the people be boundon to
bileve, and what not, and to expounde the doubtis of scripture wherby diversitie of opynyons have risen in tyme paste in suche playne and
charitable manner that no diversitie be therin after" (pp. 136–61).[1]
As a result of this scholarly exercise, the true articles of faith would be
revealed with unprecedented clarity and purity: what every Christian
man was obliged to believe as matters necessary to his salvation would
be apparent and could be discerned by reason. In turn, the legitimate
powers of bishops and clergy by the law of God could be incontrovert-
ibly delineated. The church was authorized to act as St. German
hoped by the text, "Whatsoever ye shall bind on earth shall be bound
in heaven: and whatsoever ye shall loose on earth shall be loosed in
heaven" (Matt. 16:19)—so argued the doctor of divinity. For the
church "hathe nowe as highe power by the saide texte . . . as it had in
the tyme of the Apostles," and that power would remain until the end
of the world. St. German thus agreed with the Parisian conciliarist
Jean Gerson that while scripture was entirely sufficient for faith, authoritative interpretation came from the church. Yet what is striking
here is St. German's switch from proposing parliament in *An Answer to
a Letter* as the institution representative of the English Church, to ad-
vocating a general council as the appropriate organ for determining
the canonical scriptures in his "Dyalogue." The church could not

---

[1] Cf. *The Defender of Peace*, 2, 274–86.

make new articles of faith by exercising its authority as interpreter of scripture, but St. German quite distinctly visualized reform in a "universal" context in 1537:

> Trouthe it is that the church may not make newe articles of the faithe ne bynde the people to bileve any newe thing . . . but yet it may declare the doubtis of scripture, and what necessarilie followethe upon scripture, and what ministrac[i]ons and powers the bisshops and clergie have by the lawe of god, and what not. And if any doubte rise whether any booke that is in the bible be to be taken for a booke canonysed or not, it perteignith to the vniuersall churche gathered according to scripture to determyn that doubte . . . and therfore as it semythe a catholique generall councel shulde doo righte well if they made theym [the books of the Apocrypha] of like auctoritie as the scripture is, and yet therbie they shulde make no newe articles of the faithe, nor but oonly stablishe that that as many men thynke aughte to have ben stablisshed bifore. . . . (pp. 163–65)

St. German ended on a prophetic note reminiscent of *Salem and Bizance.* Just as "blessed times" had been chosen by God for Christ's revelation and for the first canonization of scripture by the church, so "there is evyn nowe a blissed tyme cummynge, and that is also partlie begonne" (p. 165). The time had come, he believed, in which false doctrines and abuses should be put away. Kings and princes, who if St. German's scheme came to fruition, would know their rightful power, should vanquish false doctrines and abuses, making it known, too, what power bishops and clergy had by the law of God. To do this was "more plesaunte to god . . . then it were to endevour theym self to dryve all turkes, sarysyns, and other infidels owte of all contreyes that they have wrongfully taken from Cristen men." To settle the faith and reduce the powers of the clergy to those laid down by God was, indeed, more important than converting infidels to the faith, "if they aftere theire convercion shulde see more pride, covetise, and evill example amonge cristen men, and in especiall in the clergie . . . then ever they sawe bifore in theire infidelitie" (p. 166). Only after the suppression of abuses at home would the work of conversion prosper. The pope and some other bishops lived lives "directlie againste the gospelles of Criste and his doctrynes" (pp. 167–68).

Even more than the "Discourse of the Sacramentes," St. German's "Dyalogue" purported to provide Cromwell with a blueprint for the means whereby scripture might be divested of the glosses, invalid opinions of doctors, and unwritten verities so abominated by the reformers in 1537.[1] Yet the sheer impracticalities of schemes which required a European solution by means of a general council in the context of the 1530s are painfully manifest. In particular, St. German's visionary idea that the essential unity of the faith could be preserved across western Europe despite events in Germany and England, and on the basis of a general council alone, showed that St. German had lost his grip on practical reality. Perhaps it was concern for the unity of the faith that had obliged St. German by 1537 to abandon his earlier position, as expressed in *The Power of the Clergy* and *An Answer to a Letter,* that scripture would be best expounded in England by the king and parliament. Perhaps by not publishing the "Dyalogue" St. German showed that he himself was aware that it made no realistic advance beyond *An Answer to a Letter.*

A final encounter between St. German and the government of Thomas Cromwell occurred in late 1537. The vicegerent's "remembrances" for that year included the note: "Item, to shew St. Jermyns opynyon upon the bisshopes boke."[2] The *Bishops' Book,* or more precisely *The Institucyon of a Christen Man,* had been issued in September 1537 but was published, for reasons of personal preoccupation, without the express approval of Henry VIII.[3] The formulary owed much to Lutheran advances in England between 1531 and 1536, and when Henry VIII at last gave it his full attention, he found over a hundred points of criticism and objection, which he immediately raised with Archbishop Cranmer.[4] The *Bishops' Book* had, however, been prepared under Cromwell's rather than Cranmer's aegis, and Cromwell constantly consulted bishops, theologians, and scholars in his vicegerential capacity. For two reasons, it is plain that Cromwell sought St. German's opinion during the controversy that succeeded, not preceded, publication of the *Bishops' Book.* First, Cromwell's memorandum was jotted down immediately after another concerning Jane Seymour's burial; but the queen, who died on October 24, was not buried until November 12, 1537, when the *Bishops' Book* had been in print for two months.[5] Second, St. German's comments, transcribed in "A boke of annotacions of certen defaultes founde in the bysshoppes boke," pertained to proposed corrections of passages actually contained in Berthelet's published quarto, citing a correct folio

[1]See, for example, Cromwell's address, identified on p. 406, n. 4, above.
[2]British Library, Cotton MS Titus B i, fol. 437 (*LP 12/2,* no. 1151 [2]).
[3]*LP 12/2,* nos. 402, 578, 618; Scarisbrick, *Henry VIII,* pp. 400–05.
[4]*Miscellaneous Writings and Letters of Thomas Cranmer,* ed. J. E. Cox, Parker Society (Cambridge, 1846), pp. 83–114.
[5]British Library, Cotton MS Titus B i, fol. 437.

reference to the printed edition.[1] It seems likely, then, that St. German gave his opinion of the *Bishops' Book* to Cromwell in December 1537 or thereabouts, at the same time that Henry VIII was himself working on his own intended revisions. The fact that Cromwell should have sought advice in this way, at the moment when the supreme head was conducting personal discussions with his archbishop, is an interesting reflection of the vicegerent's methods; Cromwell was constantly at work to impede the king's proclivities toward caesaropapism.

St. German's observations on the *Bishops' Book* addressed four points: Mary's virginity, the intercession of saints, penance, and orders. Where the *Bishops' Book* had referred to Mary's virginity, after Christ's birth, as pure and immaculate, and as clear without blot as when she was herself first born, St. German wrote concerning a proposed revision of this passage: "The perpetuall virgynyte of our lady is agreed in the correction, and yet no scripture is alleged to prove it. Wherfore it is like that it wilbe taken hereafter as an unwrytten veryte. And nevertheles the trouth is that it may be proved by scripture."[2] St. German had previously examined the doctrine of Mary's virginity in his "Dyalogue," where he deemed it to have been founded on scripture and thus to be believed "of necessitie."[3] St. German next turned to the statement in the *Bishops' Book* that Christ is our only mediator and intercessor, "yet thereby is not excluded the intercession of the holy saints." He commented about a proposed alteration of "intercession" to "mediation": "The bisshoppes boke maynteneth the intercession of sayntes by that worde intercession, and the correction calleth it the mediacion of sayntes, and that setteth the sayntes in more estymacion, as it semeth, then the other doth." Here St. German disagreed with Henry VIII, who in his own correspondence with Cranmer preferred "mediation and prayers" to "intercession."[4] Third, St. German examined penance. A draft revision of this sacrament as set out in papers laid before St.

---

[1]British Library, Royal MS 7 C xvi, fols. 199–210; see *CW 9*, Commentary at 18/10–11.

[2]British Library, Royal MS 7 C xvi, fol. 201; *Miscellaneous Writings . . . of Thomas Cranmer*, p. 88.

[3]See pp. 410–11, above. In the *Confutation*, impelled by Jerome's failure to use scripture to prove Mary's perpetual virginity, More asserted that it could not be proved by scripture—a position he reasserted in his *Apology* (*CW 8*, 481, 1005; *CW 9*, 18). In *A Dialogue concerning Heresies*, More again denied that it could be proved by scripture, though he attempted to show that Mary's reply to the angel at the Annunciation ("How can this be? For I know no man"—Luke 1:34) implied a vow of virginity (*CW 6*, 150–51). He repeated this same argument at greater length in *The Answer to a Poisoned Book* (*CW 11*, 58–61).

[4]Fol. 204; *Miscellaneous Writings . . . of Thomas Cranmer*, p. 93.

German had reinforced the original exhortation of the *Bishops' Book* that sinners should perform such penance "as Christ requireth of them," with the implication that penance began only after Christ's birth. St. German's "Discourse of the Sacramentes" had already emphasized that the Jews had practiced contrition before Christ's birth. Now he wrote, "In the sacrament of penaunce . . . though Christ commaunded all men to do penaunce, which is non other but sorowe for our synne, yet it may not be taken that penaunce began first in the tyme of the new law, for it alway put away actuell synne in the olde law, and non but that. And yet, as it semeth, the correction assentith that penaunce began in the new lawe."[1] Finally, concerning holy orders, our source informs us: "Also the saide sent Jermyn toucheth certen thinges in the sacrament of Orders as appereth in his papers or boke of annotacions."[2] That "boke of annotacions" is not extant, or still remains to be discovered (possibly among the collections of the British Library). But since the *Bishops' Book* had redefined the ministry in a strongly Lutheran way, it is possible that St. German here repeated one of the points he had made in his "Discourse of the Sacramentes": "But that any man shulde be of this opynyon that every man is a preste, so that he may exercise suche spirituall mynystracions as before appereth, surely we knowe none of that opynyon. . . ."[3]

How much influence did St. German have in the 1530s? A survey of St. German's writings during that decade indicates that he was an informal adviser to Henry VIII in 1531; four of his books were published by the king's printer in support of the Reformation between 1531 and 1534. In 1534 and 1537 he was an independent scholar in touch with, but not a pensioner of, the government of Thomas Cromwell. More himself was willing to admit that the "anonymous" author of *A Treatise concerning the Division* and *Salem and Bizance* was orthodox in his beliefs. But if "the Pacifier" was not himself a clever heretic, More thought he must be the instrument of certain wily, heretical "shrewes." St. German's later expressions on such points as the sacraments, *sola scriptura*, the value of images or pilgrimages, and the intercession of the saints, however much they might smack of heresy to someone of More's theological palate, might just barely be defended as orthodox in More's sense. In fact, St. German rarely considered such doctrines from a strictly theological point of view but rather as issues in his deeply felt campaign against clerical abuses and eccle-

---

[1]Fol. 205; *Miscellaneous Writings . . . of Thomas Cranmer*, p. 95.
[2]Fol. 205.
[3]*Miscellaneous Writings . . . of Thomas Cranmer*, pp. 96–100; PRO, SP 6/8, p. 12.

siastical encroachments. More was willing to trust the clergymen of his day, though he was aware of their faults; St. German was not. And he propounded drastic remedies and original theories that went far beyond the limited, practical issues of clerical jurisdiction and changes in the heresy laws which he and More disputed so stubbornly in their exchanges. More had no wish and (later) no opportunity to lock horns with St. German on the deeper issues of ecclesiology, caesaropapism, the nature of royal supremacy over the church, or the final authority to interpret scripture. There can be no doubt that More would have disagreed with him sharply on such matters. But St. German's last and unpublished work, his "Dyalogue," does show that he shared with More a deep concern for the unity of western Christendom. For both men it was a lost hope.

APPENDIX D

Table of Corresponding Pages

APPENDIX D

Table of Corresponding Pages

Signatures in 1533 Edition	Page numbers in 1557 Edition	Page numbers in Yale Edition
a_1	929	title page
a_1v	929	3
a_2	929	3
a_2v	929	3–4
a_3	929–30	4
a_3v	930	4
a_4	930	4–5
a_4v	930	5
a_5	930	5–6
a_5v	930	6
a_6	930–31	6–7
a_6v	931	7
a_7	931	7
a_7v	931	7–8
a_8	931	8
a_8v	931–32	8
b_1	932	8–9
b_1v	932	9
b_2	932	9
b_2v	932	9–10
b_3	932	10
b_3v	932–33	10–11
b_4	933	11
b_4v	933	11
b_5	933	11–12
b_5v	933	12
b_6	933–34	12–13
b_6v	934	13
b_7	934	13

Signatures in *1533 Edition*	Page numbers in *1557 Edition*	Page numbers in *Yale Edition*
b_7v	934	13–14
b_8	934	14
b_8v	934	14
c_1	934–35	14–15
c_1v	935	15
c_2	935	15–16
c_2v	935	16
c_3	935	16
c_3v	935–36	16–17
c_4	936	17
c_4v	936	17
c_5	936	17–18
c_5v	936	18
c_6	936	18–19
c_6v	936–37	19
c_7	937	19
c_7v	937	19–20
c_8	937	20
c_8v	937	20–21
d_1	937–38	21
d_1v	938	21–22
d_2	938	22
d_2v	938	22–23
d_3	938	23
d_3v	938–39	23
d_4	939	23–24
d_4v	939	24
d_5	939	24–25
d_5v	939	25
d_6	939	25
d_6v	939–40	25–26
d_7	940	26–27
d_7v	940	27
d_8	940	27
d_8v	940–41	27–28
e_1	941	28
e_1v	941	28–29
e_2	941	29
e_2v	941	29–30

Signatures in 1533 Edition	Page numbers in 1557 Edition	Page numbers in Yale Edition
e_3	941	30
e_3v	941–42	30
e_4	942	30–31
e_4v	942	31
e_5	942	31
e_5v	942	31–32
e_6	942	32
e_6v	942–43	32–33
e_7	943	33
e_7v	943	33–34
e_8	943	34
e_8v	943	34
f_1	943–44	34–35
f_1v	944	35
f_2	944	35
f_2v	944	35–36
f_3	944	36
f_3v	944	36–37
f_4	944	37
f_4v	944–45	37
f_5	945	37–38
f_5v	945	38
f_6	945	38–39
f_6v	945	39
f_7	945	39
f_7v	945–46	39–40
f_8	946	40
f_8v	946	40
g_1	946	40–41
g_1v	946	41
g_2	946	41–42
g_2v	946–47	42
g_3	947	42–43
g_3v	947	43
g_4	947	43
g_4v	947	43–44
g_5	947–48	44
g_5v	948	44
g_6	948	44–45

Signatures in 1533 Edition	Page numbers in 1557 Edition	Page numbers in Yale Edition
g_6v	948	45
g_7	948	45–46
g_7v	948	46
g_8	948–49	46
g_8v	949	46–47
h_1	949	47
h_1v	949	47–48
h_2	949	48
h_2v	949	48
h_3	949–50	48–49
h_3v	950	49
h_4	950	49
h_4v	950	49–50
h_5	950	50
h_5v	950–51	50–51
h_6	951	51
h_6v	951	51–52
h_7	951	52
h_7v	951	52
h_8	951–52	52–53
h_8v	952	53
i_1	952	53–54
i_1v	952	54
i_2	952	54
i_2v	952	54–55
i_3	952–53	55
i_3v	953	55–56
i_4	953	56
i_4v	953	56
i_5	953	56–57
i_5v	953	57
i_6	953–54	57–58
i_6v	954	58
i_7	954	58–59
i_7v	954	59
i_8	954	59
i_8v	954–55	59–60
k_1	955	60
k_1v	955	60–61

Signatures in 1533 Edition	Page numbers in 1557 Edition	Page numbers in Yale Edition
k₂	955	61
k₂v	955	61–62
k₃	955–56	62
k₃v	956	62–63
k₄	956	63
k₄v	956	63
k₅	956	63–64
k₅v	956	64
k₆	956–57	64
k₆v	957	64–65
k₇	957	65
k₇v	957	65
k₈	957	65–66
k₈v	957–58	66
l₁	958	66–67
l₁v	958	67
l₂	958	67–68
l₂v	958	68
l₃	958–59	68
l₃v	959	68–69
l₄	959	69
l₄v	959	69–70
l₅	959	70
l₅v	959	70
l₆	959–60	70–71
l₆v	960	71
l₇	960	71–72
l₇v	960	72
l₈	960–61	72–73
l₈v	961	73
m₁	961	73–74
m₁v	961	74
m₂	961	74
m₂v	961	74–75
m₃	961–62	75
m₃v	962	75–76
m₄	962	76
m₄v	962	76
m₅	962	76–77

Signatures in 1533 Edition	Page numbers in 1557 Edition	Page numbers in Yale Edition
m_5v	962–63	77
m_6	963	77–78
m_6v	963	78
m_7	963	78
m_7v	963	78–79
m_8	963	79
m_8v	963–64	79
n_1	964	79–80
n_1v	964	80
n_2	964	80–81
n_2v	964	81
n_3	964–65	81
n_3v	965	81–82
n_4	965	82
n_4v	965	82
n_5 [missigned o_5]	965	82–83
n_5v	965	83
n_6	965–66	83–84
n_6v	966	84
n_7	966	84
n_7v	966	84–85
n_8	966	85
n_8v	966	85–86
A_1	967	86
A_1v	967	86
A_2	967	86–87
A_2v	967	87
A_3	967	87–88
A_3v	967–68	88
A_4	968	88
A_4v	968	88–89
A_5	968	89–90
A_5v	968–69	90
A_6	969	90–91
A_6v	969	91
A_7	969	91
A_7v	969	91–92
A_8	969	92
A_8v	969	92–93

Signatures in 1533 Edition	Page numbers in 1557 Edition	Page numbers in Yale Edition
B_1	970	93
B_1v	970	93
B_2	970	93–94
B_2v	970	94
B_3	970–71	94–95
B_3v	971	95
B_4	971	95
B_4v	971	95–96
B_5	971	96
B_5v	971	96–97
B_6	971–72	97
B_6v	972	97
B_7	972	97–98
B_7v	972	98
B_8	972	98–99
B_8v	972–73	99
C_1	973	99
C_1v	973	99–100
C_2	973	100
C_2v	973	100–01
C_3	973–74	101
C_3v	974	101
C_4	974	101–02
C_4v	974	102
C_5	974	102–03
C_5v	974–75	103
C_6	975	103
C_6v	975	103–04
C_7	975	104
C_7v	975	104–05
C_8	975	105
C_8v	975-76	105–06
D_1	976	106
D_1v	976	106–07
D_2	976	107
D_2v	976–77	107
D_3	977	107–08
D_3v	977	108
D_4	977	108–09

Signatures in 1533 Edition	Page numbers in 1557 Edition	Page numbers in Yale Edition
D_4v	977	109
D_5	977–78	109–10
D_5v	978	110
D_6	978	110
D_6v	978	110–11
D_7	978	111
D_7v	978–79	111–12
D_8	979	112
D_8v	979	112–13
E_1	979	113
E_1v	979	113
E_2	979–80	114
E_2v	980	114
E_3	980	114–15
E_3v	980	115
E_4	980	115–16
E_4v	980–81	116
E_5	981	116
E_5v	981	116–17
E_6	981	117
E_6v	981	117–18
E_7	981–82	118
E_7v	982	118
E_8	982	118–19
E_8v	982	119
F_1	982	119–20
F_1v	982–83	120
F_2	983	120
F_2v	983	120–21
F_3	983	121
F_3v	983	121
F_4	983–84	121–22
F_4v	984	122–23
F_5	984	123
F_5v	984	123
F_6	984	123–24
F_6v	984–85	124
F_7	985	124
F_7v	985	124–25

Signatures in 1533 Edition	Page numbers in 1557 Edition	Page numbers in Yale Edition
F$_8$	985	125
F$_8$v	985	125–26
G$_1$	985–86	126
G$_1$v	986	126–27
G$_2$	986	127
G$_2$v	986	127–28
G$_3$	986	128
G$_3$v	986–87	128
G$_4$	987	128–29
G$_4$v	987	129
G$_5$	987	129–30
G$_5$v	987	130
G$_6$	987	130
G$_6$v	987–88	130–31
G$_7$	988	131
G$_7$v	988	131–32
G$_8$	988	132
G$_8$v	988	132–33
H$_1$	988–89	133
H$_1$v	989	133
H$_2$	989	133–34
H$_2$v	989	134
H$_3$	989	134–35
H$_3$v	989–90	135
H$_4$	990	135
H$_4$v	990	135–36
H$_5$	990	136
H$_5$v	990	136–37
H$_6$	990	137
H$_6$v	990–91	137
H$_7$	991	137–38
H$_7$v	991	138
H$_8$	991	138–39
H$_8$v	991	139
I$_1$	991–92	139
I$_1$v	992	139–40
I$_2$	992	140
I$_2$v	992	140–41
I$_3$	992	141

Signatures in 1533 Edition	Page numbers in 1557 Edition	Page numbers in Yale Edition
I$_3$v	992–93	141
I$_4$	993	141–42
I$_4$v	993	142
I$_5$	993	142–43
I$_5$v	993	143
I$_6$	993	143
I$_6$v	993–94	143–44
I$_7$	994	144
I$_7$v	994	144–45
I$_8$	994	145
I$_8$v	994	145
K$_1$	994	145–46
K$_1$v	994–95	146
K$_2$	995	146–47
K$_2$v	995	147
K$_3$	995	147
K$_3$v	995	147–48
K$_4$	995–96	148
K$_4$v	996	148–49
K$_5$	996	149
K$_5$v	996	149–50
K$_6$	996	150
K$_6$v	996–97	150–51
K$_7$	997	151
K$_7$v	997	151
K$_8$	997	151–52
K$_8$v	997	152
L$_1$	997–98	152–53
L$_1$v	998	153
L$_2$	998	153
L$_2$v	998	153–54
L$_3$	998	154
L$_3$v	998	154–55
L$_4$	998–99	155
L$_4$v	999	155–56
L$_5$	999	156
L$_5$v	999	156
L$_6$	999	156–57
L$_6$v	999–1000	157

Signatures in 1533 Edition	Page numbers in 1557 Edition	Page numbers in Yale Edition
L_7	1000	157–58
L_7v	1000	158
L_8	1000	158
L_8v	1000	158–59
M_1	1000–01	159
M_1v	1001	159–60
M_2	1001	160
M_2v	1001	160–61
M_3	1001	161
M_3v	1001–02	161–62
M_4	1002	162
M_4v	1002	162
M_5	1002	162–63
M_5v	1002	163
M_6	1002–03	163–64
M_6v	1003	164
M_7	1003	164
M_7v	1003	165
M_8	1003	165–66
M_8v	1003–04	166
N_1	1004	166
N_1v	1004	166–67
N_2	1004	167
N_2v	1004	167
N_3	1004–05	167–68
N_3v	1005	168–69
N_4	1005	169
N_4v	1005	169–70
N_5	1005–06	170
N_5v	1006	170
N_6	1006	170–71
N_6v	1006	171
N_7	1006	171–72
N_7v	1006–07	172
N_8	1007	172
N_8v	1007	172–73
O_1	1007	173
O_1v	1007	173–74
O_2	1007–08	174

Signatures in 1533 Edition	Page numbers in 1557 Edition	Page numbers in Yale Edition
O_2v	1008	174–75
O_3	1008	175
O_3v	1008	175–76
O_4	1008–09	176
O_4v	1009	176–77
O_5	1009	177
O_5v	1009	177–78
O_6	1009	178
O_6v	1009–10	178–79
O_7	1010	179
O_7v	1010	179–80
O_8	1010	180
O_8v	1010	180
P_1	1010–11	180–81
P_1v	1011	181
P_2	1011	181–82
P_2v	1011	182
P_3	1011–12	182
P_3v	1012	182–83
P_4	1012	183–84
P_4v	1012	184
P_5	1012	184
P_5v	1012–13	184–85
P_6	1013	185.
P_6v	1013	185–86
P_7	1013	186
P_7v	1013	186
P_8	1013–14	186–87
P_8v	1014	187
Q_1	1014	187–88
Q_1v	1014	188
Q_2	1014	188–89
Q_2v	1014–15	189
Q_3	1015	189–90
Q_3v	1015	190
Q_4	1015	190–91
Q_4v	1015	191
Q_5	1015–16	191
Q_5v	1016	191–92

Signatures in *1533 Edition*	Page numbers in *1557 Edition*	Page numbers in *Yale Edition*
Q_6	1016	192
Q_6v	1016	192–93
Q_7	1016	193
Q_7v	1016	193
Q_8	1016–17	193–94
Q_8v	1017	194
R_1	1017	194
R_1v	1017	194–95
R_2	1017	195
R_2v	1017–18	195–96
R_3	1018	196
R_3v	1018	196
R_4	1018	196–97
R_4v	1018	197
R_5	1018–19	197–98
R_5v	1019	198
R_6	1019	198
R_6v	1019	198–99
R_7	1019	199
R_7v	1019	199
R_8	1019–20	199–200
R_8v	1020	200
S_1	1020	200–01
S_1v	1020	201
S_2	1020	201–02
S_2v	1020–21	202
S_3	1021	202–03
S_3v	1021	203
S_4	1021	203–04
S_4v	1021	204
S_5	1021–22	204
S_5v	1022	204–05
S_6	1022	205
S_6v	1022	205
S_7	1022	205–06
S_7v	1022–23	206
S_8	1023	206–07
S_8v	1023	207
T_1	1023	207–08

Signatures in 1533 Edition	Page numbers in 1557 Edition	Page numbers in Yale Edition
T_1v	1023	208
T_2	1023–24	208–09
T_2v	1024	209
T_3	1024	209
T_3v	1024	209–10
T_4	1024	210
T_4v	1024–25	210–11
T_5	1025	211
T_5v	1025	211–12
T_6	1025	212
T_6v	1025	212
T_7	1025–26	212–13
T_7v	1026	213
T_8	1026	213–14
T_8v	1026	214
V_1	1026	214
V_1v	1026–27	214–15
V_2	1027	215
V_2v	1027	215–16
V_3	1027	216
V_3v	1027–28	216–17
V_4	1028	217
V_4v	1028	217–18
V_5	1028	218
V_5v	1028	218–19
V_6	1028–29	219
V_6v	1029	219–20
V_7	1029	220
V_7v	1029	220–21
V_8	1029	221
V_8v	1029–30	221
X_1	1030	221–22
X_1v	1030	222
X_2	1030	222
X_2v	1030	222–23
X_3	1030	223
X_3v	1030–31	223–24
X_4	1031	224
X_4v	1031	224

Signatures in 1533 Edition	*Page numbers in 1557 Edition*	*Page numbers in Yale Edition*
X₅	1031	224–25
X₅v	1031	225
X₆	1031–32	225–26
X₆v	1032	226
X₇	1032	226–27
X₇v	1032	227
X₈	1032	227
X₈v	1032–33	227–28
Y₁	1033	228
Y₁v	1033	228
Y₂	1033	229
Y₂v	1033	229
Y₃	1033	229–30
Y₃v	1033–34	230
Y₄	1034	230
Y₄v	1034	230–31
Y₅	1034	231
Y₅v	—	231

GLOSSARY

GLOSSARY

This glossary is intended to contain only words whose meanings or forms (not merely spellings) are obsolete or archaic according to *The Oxford English Dictionary*. It also includes a few words which might be puzzling because of their spelling or some other ambiguity. In general, if a word recurs more than twice, only the first instance, followed by "*etc.*," is given. Unusual spellings of proper names have also been included.

a *adj.* 36/12. *See n. to* 36/11–16
a *adv.* about 36/12
a *prep.* to 6/1; in 225/2
abashement *n.* confusion 154/8
abate *v.* end, mitigate 5/15
aberyng(e), abearynge *n.* conduct 121/17 *etc.*
abettement *n.* assistance 198/30
abiuracyon *n.* recantation 123/14 *etc. See n. to* 70/12–13
abiure *v.* recant 124/15 *etc. See n. to* 70/12–13; cause to recant 140/36 *etc.*
aboue *prep.* more than 32/19 *etc.*
aboundaunce *n. See* **hab(o)undaunce**
about(e) *adv.* around 17/8, 58/32; everywhere, to everyone 71/2, 71/7
about(e) *prep.* for the purpose of 3/29 *etc.*; go about(e). *See* **go**
abroche *adv. sette abroche. See* **set(te)**
abrode *adv.* in public 4/11 *etc.*
abusyons, abusions *n. pl.* offences, wrongs 65/16 *etc.*; heretical deceptions 225/20
abyde *v.* submit to, suffer 122/22
acceptaunce *n.* signification 37/5, 39/19
accompt(e) *n.* account, statement of expenditures 52/33; account of stewardship 176/1
accompted *v. pt.* considered 14/35, 147/2
accurse *v.* excommunicate 73/35; *pp.* **accursyd** 110/35
accusour *n.* accuser 128/4
accyon *n.* lawsuit 199/9
acertayne *v.* assure 226/28

acquyt(t)e *pp.* acquitted, set free 123/8, 130/12
actys *n. pl.* acts 55/34
adieccyon *n.* addition 44/5
admitte *v.* concede for the sake of argument 204/30 *etc.*
aduenture, auenture *n.* chance 130/16 *at aduenture (auenture)* by chance 12/7; at random 81/23, 133/31–32; *put . . . in thaduenture. See* **put(te)**
aduenture *v.* risk 94/29
aduertyse *v.* admonish 50/10
aduertysement *n.* admonition 50/15; advice 182/29
aduise *v.* consider 141/25, 222/21
aduisement *n.* deliberation 68/32 *etc.*
aduow(e) *v. See* **auow(e)**
aduowtry aduuotry *n.* adultery 68/26 *etc.*: desire to commit adultery 68/29
aferd(e), a ferde *adj.* afraid 56/18 *etc.*
affeccion, affeccyon *n.* bias 86/28, 176/14; emotion 99/25; inclination 174/15 *etc.*
affectyonate *adj.* inclined 19/24
afferme *v.* maintain, affirm 29/28, 57/7; confirm 220/17
affynyte, affinite, affinyte *n.* associates 26/12 *etc.*; kindred 28/25
afore *prep.* before 5/36 *etc.*
after *adv.* afterwards 8/9 *etc.*
after *prep.* according to 12/28 *etc.*; about 59/23; in proportion to 219/12
after hande *adv.* afterwards 86/22–23

439

after throwes *n. pl.* pains following childbirth 6/4
agayn(e) *adv.* in return 46/17 *etc.;* back
201/19
agayne *prep.* against 46/1, 168/18
agaynst(e) *prep.* in resistance to 6/4; with
regard to 188/2 *etc.*
aggreue *v.* harrass 191/12 *etc.*
aknowen *pp.* recognized 125/33
albe yt (it) (that, y^t) conj. *See* **all be (albe)
yt (it) (that, y^t)**
aleyth *v. pr. 3 s.* cites 22/10
algates *adv.* at any rate 91/8, 137/29–
30
Alkayre *n.* 34/6, 34/11. *See n. to* 34/6
al(l) *adv.* entirely 7/14 *etc.;* all *whole* entirely 10/5–6: *all one* one and the same
thing 20/33 *etc.; al(l) to gether. See* **al(l) to
gether;** *al(l) waye. See* **al(l) waye**
all *n. all to gether. See* **all to gether**
all be (albe) yt (it) (that, y^t) conj. although
6/24 *etc.*
allegeaunce *n.* citation of evidence 60/22
allegeth *v. pr. 3 s.* cites as authority 194/16
allow(e) *v.* approve 114/5 *etc.*
all to gether *adv. See* **al(l) to gether**
all to gether *n.* the whole thing 8/1
all waye *adv. See* **al(l) waye**
Almayne, Almain *n.* Germany 97/9,
210/24
almoyse *n.* alms-giving 53/30, 55/13
alowed *pp. See* **allow(e)**
al(l) to gether *adv.* entirely 198/34
al(l) waye, alway(e) *adv.* always 13/23 *etc.*
amende *v.* reform 23/24: correct 30/11,
209/23; improve 176/12
amendes *n.* compensation 196/15
amend(e)ment *n.* removal of faults 48/6,
143/31; correction 176/13
amonge *adv.* all the time 126/1
and *conj.* if 18/7 *etc.; and yf* if 3/20 *etc.*
angerly *adv.* angrily 197/15
anone *adv.* immediately 4/11
antiphrasys *n.* 24/26. *See n.*
any thyng(e) *adv.* in any respect 8/19 *etc.*
apayre *v.* weaken, damage 9/32 *etc.*
apeche *v.* accuse 105/34
Apology(e), apology(e), apologie *n.* defence, apologia 3/10 *etc. See n. to* 8/14–
15
apostatase *n. pl.* apostates 210/22

apparaunce, apparence *n.* appearance
23/10, 160/31–32
apparel *v.* adorn 156/8; *ppl. a.* **apparelled**
clad 156/6
apparell *n.* attire 156/6–7 *etc.*
apparence *n. See* **apparaunce**
appeace, appease *v.* settle 225/16, 225/28
appeyreth *v. pr. 3 s. See* **apayre**
approued *ppl. a.* established 9/17 *etc.;*
proved by experience 40/23
approuers *n. pl.* 107/15. *See n. to* 107/15–
17
arbitrement *n.* sentence 114/4, 114/31;
197/20, 197/28. *See n. to* 197/20–21
arreyghnynge *vbl. n.* arraignment 107/23
articles *n. pl.* charges of an indictment
112/36–113/1
assay(e) *v.* inquire 73/2; try 225/1
assenteth *v. pr. 3 s.* agrees 183/22
assigne, assynge, assygne *v.* specify
54/14 *etc.;* appoint 136/25 *etc.*
assoyled *ppl. a.* absolved from excommunication 186/8
assystente *adj.* attendant 215/12, 216/17
at *prep.* in 27/1, 40/5; before 86/19: with
167/2 *etc.*
attached *pp.* arrested 76/11; *vbl. n.* **attachynge, attaching** 22/14, 76/18
attaynt *n.* 154/33. *See n. to* 154/32–155/5
attaynted *v. pt.* 155/5. *See n. to* 154/32–
155/5
auaunced *pp.* promoted 200/13
auauntage *n.* advantage 7/28
auctoryte *n.* authority 168/16, 183/27
auenture *n. See* **aduenture**
aughte *adv.* at all 133/22
auncestours *n. pl.* ancestors 34/31
auow(e), aduow(e) *v.* maintain 72/13 *etc.;*
declare 89/12 *etc.*
auoyde *v.* refute 123/24, 143/2; render
void 171/21
Austayne *n.* Augustine 25/31
a warde, award *v.* judicially grant 121/13
etc.
awne *adj.* own 93/20
awter *n.* altar 208/1, 222/34

bable *n.* chatter 46/15
bable *v.* chatter 46/19, 46/20; speak fool-
ishly 190/25; *vbl. n.* **babelyng(e)** non-
sense 187/31, 187/32

bace *n.* 68/28. *See n. to* 68/27–28
band dogges, ban(d)dogges *n. pl.* 141/32 *etc. See n.*
bare *adj.* worthless 42/8 *etc.;* simple 144/15: mere 147/14 *etc.;* unelaborated 151/25
Barons *n. poss.* Barnes's 14/23. *See n. to* 14/22–23
barre *n.* barrier or rail at which prisoners stand in court and from which evidence is given 121/21 *etc.*
base court *n.* 170/35. *See n.*
bate makynge *adj.* strife-causing 78/20
be *v. pr. 3 pl.* are 3/12 *etc.; pp.* **ben(e), be** 12/19 *etc.*
before *adv. here before. See* **here byfore**
be gon(ne), by gonne, begonne *ppl. a.* begun 17/15 *etc.*
behalfe *n. in that (thys) behalfe* in reference to that (this) 23/5 *etc.*
behauour *n.* behavior 121/13, 126/29
belye, bylye *v.* tell lies about 18/34 *etc.*
ben(e) *pp. See* **be**
bendeth *v. pr. 3 s.* tends 86/9
bere *v. bere (. . . out)* support 55/21 *etc.; bere recorde* bear witness 164/35
beryalles *n. pl. See* **byryalles**
beshrew, beshrowe *v.* curse, invoke evil upon 46/19 *etc.*
beste *n.* beast, animal 12/1 *etc.; n. pl.* **bestes** cattle 142/9 *etc.; bestes of venory* game 142/5
besyde, by syde, bysyde *adv.* in addition (to) 10/23 *etc.*
besyde *prep.* wide of 204/8
besynesse, busynes(se), bysynes *n.* task, job 62/20, 197/19; tumult 119/21; trouble 125/27 *etc.;* fuss 221/26
betrapped *ppl. a.* trapped 45/12
betwyxte *prep.* between 132/27
Bizance, Bizans, Byzance *n.* Byzantium *title-page/2 etc.*
blew *adj. blew poynt* 209/11. *See n.*
blonte *adj.* stupid 48/37
bloweth *v. pr. 3 s. bloweth out* utters 16/17; *blowe . . . abrode* spread 76/29; *pp.* **blowen** 17/8; *blowen aboute* spread 17/8; *blowne forthe* spread 63/2
bode *v. pt. See* **byd**
body *n. by the body* bodily 169/1–2
boke *n.* book 4/4 *etc.*

boldyng *vbl. n.* emboldening 168/4
bounde *n.* bond 94/19
bounden, bound(e) *ppl. a., pp. See* **bynde**
boystuouse *adj.* bulky 142/26
brake *v. pt. See* **breke**
bred(e) *n.* bread 5/12 *etc.*
breke *v.* interrupt 28/24; fail to observe 43/15; abrogate 146/3; *pt.* **brake** 16/20, 16/22
bretherhed *n.* brotherhood 24/31, 29/2
brethern(e) *n.* 9/10 *etc. See n. to* 9/10
breyde *n.* short span of time 4/2
broched *ppl. a. See* **new broched**
brynge (...) forthe *v.* adduce 19/2, 29/6; make public 212/18–19, 212/21; *vbl. n.* **bryngyng(e) forth** 18/31
bulte out *v.* examine by sifting 91/20
busy *adj.* meddlesome 125/35
busynes(se) *n. See* **besynesse**
but *adv.* only 5/12 *etc.*
but *conj.* except 5/18 *etc.; but if (yf)* unless 10/7 *etc.; but that* except 17/34 *etc.; but euyn* only 153/37
by *prep.* about 24/9 *etc.; by and (&) by* at once 12/3 (variant) *etc.;* as a result 62/31
bycause (that), by cause *adv., conj.* because 11/4 *etc.*
byched *ppl a.* cursed 29/2
bycome *pp.* befit 32/5
byd *v.* command 54/8 *etc.;* entreat 118/36, 118/37; *pt.* **bode** 95/16
byelded *pp.* built 87/29; *pr. 3 s.* **byeldeth** 90/15; *byeldeth vp* builds 90/15; *vbl. n.* **byeldynge** 47/8
bye mater *n.* subsidiary concern 10/23
byfore *adv. here byfore. See* **here byfore**
byfore *prep.* in precedence over 206/14
by gonne *ppl. a. See* **be gon(ne)**
byhauour *n.* behavior 111/30
byll *n.* petition 68/5; indictment 144/4
bylye *v. See* **belye**
bynde *v.* oblige by legal authority 94/11 *etc.;* oblige to answer 98/6 *etc.;* agree 162/21, 162/22; *ppl. a., pp.* **bounden, bound(e)** restrained 32/12; obliged 45/19 *etc.*
byryalles, beryalles *n. pl.* funerals 197/12, 199/4
by syde, bysyde *adv. See* **besyde**
bysynes *v. See* **besynesse**

bytterly *adv.* grievously 65/36
by tyme *adv.* early 71/5
by tymes *adv.* forthwith 146/4
Byzance *n.* *See* **Bizance**

call *v.* summon 132/33 *etc.; vbl. n.* **callynge** 22/14, 168/29; *callynge on* appeal,
request 168/29
can *v.* know 33/24; *can . . . thanke* offer
thanks 19/18 *etc.; can . . . skyl(l)* have
knowledge 82/13 *etc.; pt.* **colde** 56/4
canker *n.* spreading malignancy, gan-
grene 71/15
cant *v.* apportion 35/4
carleshe *adj.* churlish 24/14
cast(e) *v.* throw (down) 62/8 *etc.; pp.* **caste**
convicted 107/16
catholikes, catholykes *n.* *pl.* orthodox
members of the Church 25/15 *etc.*
catholyque, catholike, catholyke *adj.*
orthodox 4/15 *etc.;* universal 15/29; belonging to the church universal 25/5
caudell *n.* 6/4. *See n.*
cause *n.* legal action, case 107/25 *etc.*
causeles(se) *adv.* without cause 14/7 *etc.*
cease *v.* appease 205/20; put a stop to
211/33; *cease of* discontinue 175/31
censure *n.* punishment by the ecclesiastical courts 188/22, 189/15
certayne *adj.* reliable 150/31, 151/2
chapyter, chapiter, chapeter, chapytre *n.*
chapter 5/4 *etc.*
charge *n.* responsibility 82/20
chauncery *n.* 37/35. *See n.*
chaunces *n.* *pl.* events 97/36
chaunteryes *n.* *pl.* chantries 49/26
chekke *v.* reproach 27/25, 136/33
choyse *n.* *put . . . in choyse.* *See* **put(te)**
chrysten, cristen *adj.* Christian 3/27 *etc.*
chrystened *ppl. a.* *See* **cristened**
Clementine *n.* canon from the Clementinae 168/33
clene *adj.* complete 43/30
clene *adv.* completely 50/6, 174/7
clere *adv.* entirely 50/6; distinctly 165/1,
165/16
clerely *adv.* entirely 142/35
clerenesse *n.* innocence 50/11
cleueth . . . on *v.* *pr. 3 s.* sticks to 26/33–
34

close *adj.* secret 97/34 *etc.*
close *n.* enclosed field 100/12, 100/15
clouted *ppl. a.* patched 60/26
cold(e) *adj.* ineffective 9/21 *etc.*
colde *v.* *pt.* *See* can
collacyon *n.* discourse 201/1
collaterall wytnes *n.* 150/2, 151/17. *See n.
to* 150/2
colour(e) *n.* pretence 15/8 *etc.;* appearance of truth 170/7
colour *v.* disguise 208/30; *ppl. a.*
colo(u)red 46/31, 170/31
colourable *adj.* specious 60/12
come *v.* *come out* be published 5/29; *cometh
vppon* attacks 43/31–32
comen *adj.* *comen entendement.* *See* **entendement**
comen *adv.* generally 30/5 *etc.*
comenly *adv.* publicly, generally 25/14
commodite, commodyte *n.* convenience
72/29, 86/31
**communycacyon, communicacion, com-
municacyon** *n.* conversation 10/22 *etc.;*
debate 195/9
commyssyon *n.* commission of the peace
129/7
complayned on *ppl. a.* complained of
76/9
compte *n.* account, statement of expenditures 35/3
compte *v.* consider 87/23, 186/27
compuncte *ppl. a.* contrite 165/18
compurgatours *n.* *pl.* witnesses who swear
to the credibility, orthodoxy or innocence of the accused 115/9 *etc.* *See notes
to* 47/14–16, 111/34–112/2
conce(y)lours *n.* *pl.* those who conceal
143/30 *etc.*
conceyte *n.* opinion 32/22–23 *etc.*
concurraunt *adj.* consistant 190/28
condempne *v.* condemn 105/24 *etc.; vbl. n.*
condempnynge 155/31
condescende *v.* agree 110/36
condycyon *n.* disposition, character
170/25; *pl.* **condycyons** moral nature,
character 177/8
confeder(e) *v.* unite 197/20, 197/28
confederacy(e) *n.* 65/23 *etc.* *See n. to*
198/7–11
conferre *v.* compare 6/18; *pp.* **conferred**
7/34

confesseth *v. pr. 3 s.* avows as an article of faith 223/2–3

confessyon *n.* profession 9/24

congregacyon *n.* assembly 216/14

coniecture *n.* ground, reason 183/12, 183/34

connynge *adj. See* **cunnyng(e)**

connynge *n.* wisdom 174/25, 175/26

conscience, conscyence *n.* (inward) knowledge 112/31 *etc.*

conseruacyon *n.* preservation 23/14, 113/10

conserue *v.* preserve 23/18

constitucion, constytucyon *n.* decree 195/2 *etc.*

constre *v.* interpret 56/32

construccions *n. pl.* interpretations 36/21

consystory(e) *n.* diocesan court 121/21, 124/5

co(u)ntenuance *n.* conduct 53/20 *etc.*

contrary *adj.* harmful 204/32

contreys *n. pl. See* **c(o)untrey**

controlled *v. pt.* verified 28/1

contumacy *n.* wilfull disobedience of a judicial order 117/16

contynua(u)nce *n.* retention 215/30 *etc.*

conuented *v. pt.* summoned 101/34 *etc.*; *vbl. n.* **conuentynge** 89/5 *etc.*

conuentycles *n. pl.* clandestine heretical meetings 168/32

conuenyent *adj.* suitable 9/2 *etc.*

conuersacyon *n.* behavior 61/23

conuersaunt *adj.* spending much time 32/18, 32/35

conuey *v.* manage 174/6

conuocacyons, conuocacions *n. pl.* 198/4 *etc. See* **n.**

copulatyues *n. pl.* conjunctions 33/23. *See n. to* 33/21–25

corage *n.* vigour 5/15

corps *n.* body 9/18 *etc.*

correccyon *n.* punishment 65/24 *etc.; do* (. . .) *correccyon. See* **do**

couetouse *n.* greed 173/11 *etc.*

counsayle *n.[1]* council 15/24 *etc.*

counsayle, counsaile *n.[2]* advice 17/29 *etc.*; adviser 192/19; *kepyng yt counsayle See* **kepe;** *made of counsayle* made privy 53/1 *etc.*

counsayle *v.* advise 51/29, 56/18

countenaunce *n. See* **co(u)ntenaunce**

countrepayse *v.* counterbalance 40/24–25, 151/35

countrey *n. See* **c(o)untrey**

course *n.* race 7/32; practice 146/28

craft(e) *n.* deceit, trick 6/26 *etc.*

craftye *adj.* deceitful 91/10

credence *n.* trustworthiness, credibility 27/35 *etc.*

cristen *adj. See* **chrysten**

cristened, chrystened *ppl. a.* converted to Christianity 21/29, 146/28

crymynouse, cryminouse *adj.* guilty 147/19, 164/17

cunnyng(e), connynge, cunning *adj.* learned 4/26 *etc.: superl.* **cunnyngest** 4/33

c(o)untrey *n.* county 121/14 *etc.; pl.* **contreys** 129/7

curiouse *adj.* painstaking 139/31

curse *n.* sentence of excommunication 118/16, 187/1

cursynge *n.* excommunication 168/19, 185/6

cyrcumsta(u)nce *n.* context 37/1–2

cytacyon *n.* summons 180/29, 182/16

dampnable, damnable *adj.* reprehensible 176/15, 176/17.

dampnacyon *n.* damnation 48/11

darke *adj.* obscure 14/18 *etc.; darke sentence. See* **sentence**

daynge(ou)r, daungeour *n.* jurisdiction 55/8, 55/27; liability 98/8

deale *n. neuer a deale* not at all 129/18–19

dealyng(e), delynge *n.* conduct 71/24, 118/5; action 74/2

debellacyon, Debellacyon, Debellacion *n.* conquest *title-page/1 etc.*

decaye *v.* cause to deteriorate 6/13

deceyued *pp.* disappointed 8/6

declaracyon *n.* explanation 3/1 *etc.*; exposition 25/13

declare *v.* explain (to) 31/24 *etc.*

decretalis *n. pl.* decretals 114/2

dede *n.* performance 129/6; *in very dede* indeed 47/18–19, 168/2; *n. pl.* **dedys** deeds 68/24

dedely *adv.* mortally 175/9, 177/5

defaced *pp.* discredited 27/29

defaute, defawt(e), defaulte *n.* fault,

failure, defect 18/17 *etc.; in defawt of* through want of 209/32

defference *n.* difference 144/7

deliueraunce *n.* judicial consideration of the release from prison 151/11

delycate *adj.* indolent 7/11

delynge *n. See* **dealyng(e)**

delyuered *pp.* released from prison 121/16 *etc.*

delyuerye *n.* release from prison 126/34; *sessyon of gaole delyuery. See* **sessyon**

deme(a)nure *n.* behavior, practice 125/31 *etc.*

demurred vppon *v. pt.* put in a demurrer 43/34. *See n. to* 38/13–15

demurrour *n.* 38/14. *See n. to* 38/13–15

denounce *v.* declare 186/8

depose *v.* testify 99/30 *etc.*

depraue *v.* disparage 222/15

derkenes *n.* darkness 20/17 *etc.*

descendeth *v. pr. 3 s.* proceeds 55/33–34

desperate *adj.* irreclaimable 29/25 etc.

desprayse *n.* censure, disparagement 60/2

desyrouse *adj.* eager 11/10

detecte *v.* accuse 72/20 *etc.;* give information (about) 99/11, 99/22; *ppl. a.* **detected** exposed 91/5

determinate *adj.* individual 54/10

determinately, determynately *adv.* definitely 34/4; conclusively 55/17

determynacyon *n.* discussion 198/8

deuyce, deuyse, deuise, diuise *n.* plan, scheme 35/7 *etc.;* notion, opinion 77/8 *etc.*

deuysed *v. pt.* recounted 5/11; *pr. 3 s.* **deuyseth** plots, schemes 15/25 *etc.*

deuysyon *n. See* **dyuysyon**

dignyte, dignite *n. See* **dygnyte**

dishonesty *n. See* **dyshonestye**

disposed *pp.* regulate 209/2

disposicyon *n.* regulation 209/1

disputed agaynst *v. pt.* argued against 146/8

dissembled *pp.* neglected 8/26 *etc.*

dissymuleth, dysssymuleth *v. pr. 3 s.* overlooks 151/11–12, 217/32

diuerse, dyuers(e) *adj.* various 4/25 *etc.*

diuise *n. See* **deuyce**

diuisyon, diuysyon *n. See* **dyuysyon**

do *v.* perform 30/20 *etc.;* confer 142/4;

act 187/24; *do (. . .) correccyon* inflict punishment 30/20, 217/16; *vbl. n.* **doyeng(e), doynge** doing, performing, action 23/15 *etc.*

doctryne *n.* instruction 65/10

double *adv.* twice 46/35, 190/13

dou(b)te *n. See* **dowt(e)**

doute, dowte *v.* fear 20/18 *etc.; doubted . . . at* doubted of 183/12; *I doute me* I am afraid 212/28

dowble *adj.* duplicitous 64/16

dowblenes *n.* ambiguity 66/31

dowch *adj.* German 167/31

dowt(e), dou(b)te *n.* fear 23/11, 168/36; *out of dowte* doubtless 15/27; *maketh no doute at yt. See* **make;** *make a doute. See* **make**

dowte *v. See* **doute**

doyeng(e), doynge *vbl. n. See* **do**

drawe *v.* drag 142/19; *pp.* **drawen** framed 229/17

dreamynge *ppl. a.* fanciful 192/29

driuen, dreuyn, dreuen *ppl. a., pp.* logically deduced 30/9; compelled 154/31, 155/6

drybbeth *v. pr. 3 s.* utters as in driblets 42/9

dull *adj.* foolish 6/21

dully *adv.* stupidly 220/1

durst(e) *v. pt.* dared 26/7 *etc.*

dyffamacion, dyffamacyon *n.* defamation 169/35 *etc.*

dyfferences *n. pl. verse dyfferences. See* **verse dyfferences**

dyfferre *v.* postpone 55/31

dygnyte, dygnite, dignyte, dignite *n.* rank, title 41/32 *etc.*

dylate *v.* spread abroad 222/28

dyner *n.* main meal (served at midday) 31/33

dyschargynge *vbl. n.* exoneration 67/1

dyscontent *adj.* displeased 137/13

dyscouered *pp.* revealed 27/28

dyshonestye, dishonesty *n.* disgrace 125/27 *etc.*

dysiunctyue *n.* disjunctive proposition 33/23, 33/25

dyspycyons *n. pl.* discussions 18/5, 124/25

dyssembleth *v. pr. 3 s. See* **dissembled**

dyssuade *v.* advise against 56/11

dyssymilitude *n.* dissimilarity 154/19
dyssymuleth *v. pr. 3 s. See* **dissymuleth**
dyuers(e) *adj. See* **diuerse**
dyuersyte *n.* difference 133/20 *etc.*
dyuynacyon *n.* foresight 58/5
dyuysyon, diuysyon, dyuysion, dyui-syon, deuysyon, diuisyon *n.* disagreement, discord 3/9–10 *etc. See n.*

effectual *adj.* valid 40/15, 212/21
efte *adv.* again 72/15
efte soon *adv.* soon afterwards 105/14
egall *adj.* equal 88/14
egally *adv.* equally 20/11
elles, ellys, el(l)s *adv.* otherwise 10/8 *etc.*
ellys, elles *adj.* else, other 17/33 *etc.*
embassyatours, embassiatours *n. pl.* ambassadors 144/27 *etc.*
embatayled *ppl. a.* fortified 3/18
embysye *v.* busy 222/12
enchaunted *pp.* endowed with magical properties 3/6
encorage *v.* embolden 23/15; *vbl. n.* **encoragynge** 9/19, 15/28
encrease, encreace *n.* growth 14/26 *etc.;* expansion 36/30
encrease, increase *v.* cause to grow 51/17 *etc.;* grow 88/5, 230/20
ende *n. vpon y*ᵉ *ende* ultimately 13/26
endeuour, endeuoyr *v.* exert 18/9–10, 212/29
enduce *v.* induce 49/25
endy(gh)tours, indyters *n. pl.* those who bring in an indictment against someone 130/1 *etc.*
enfecte *v.* corrupt with heretical opinions 182/2; *ppl. a.* **infecte, enfecte** tainted 174/27 *etc.*
enformacyon *n. See* **informacyon**
enforme, informe *v.* instruct 61/28; provide with accusatory information 72/18 *etc. See n. to* 73/9–12
englysh *n.* means of expression in English 167/31
enimyte *n.* enmity 106/24
enioy *v.* have the benefit of 206/12
enmye *n.* enemy 228/34
enormyties *n. pl.* breaches of morality 177/9
enquere *v. See* **inquere**

enquerours *n. pl.* investigators 109/19 *etc.*
enquest(e) *n.* 149/29 *etc. See n.*
enquyrable *adj.* subject to investigation 143/32
ensample, ensemple *n.* example 29/34 *etc.*
entende *v.* intend 15/7–8 *etc.*
entendement *n. comen entendement* rule of common law 37/35
entent(e) *n.* intention 52/24 *etc.;* meaning 63/35; *to thentent* in order (that) 25/25 *etc.*
ere, or *conj.* before 46/10 *etc.*
ere *prep.* before 115/11 *etc.*
ergo *adv.* therefore 97/16 *etc.*
eschete *n.* reversion 106/1, 108/22. *See n. to* 105/36–106/1
esheweth *v. pr. 3 s.* avoids 26/22
estymacyon, estimacyon *n.* reputation 23/17, 40/24
eth *adj.* easy 64/15
euangelicall *n.* 24/35, 25/7. *See n. to* 24/35–25/19
euangelicos *n. pseudo euangelicos* 25/19. *See n. to* 24/35–25/19
euangelycall *adj.* 25/8. *See n. to* 24/35–25/19
euen *adj. See* **euyn**
euen *adv. See* **euyn**
euer *adv.* always 164/11, 227/9
euerychone *pron.* each one 47/28, 231/4
eueryman *pron.* everyone 31/32
euydentely *adv.* clearly 169/20
euyl(l) *adv.* wickedly 54/12, 170/39
euyll *adj.* slanderous 24/2, 24/10; ill 76/15
euyn, euen *adj.* untroubled 4/5, 225/9
euyn, euen *adv.* quite 6/20, 61/6; just 12/3 *variant;* exactly 190/14, 199/24; *but euyn. See* **but**
except(e) *conj.* unless 24/13 *etc.*
excesse *n.* immoderation 143/23, 143/27
excludyng *vbl. n.* rejection 34/14
exclusyues *n. pl.* 33/13, 33/22. *See n. to* 33/13
excommunycate, excommunicate *ppl. a., pp.* excommunicated 117/16 *etc.*
excuse *n.* justification, reason 17/25–26 *etc.*
excuse *v.* defend, justify 17/28 *etc.;* extenuate 27/26

execucyon n. administrative action 209/8; *put . . . in execucyon.* See **put(te)**

extraduccyon n. conclusion 10/31

eyen n. pl. See **yien**

face n. 62/9. *See n. to* 62/8–13; *at the fyrste face* at first glance 13/26 *etc.*

facte n. crime 149/13

fade v. decay 21/12, 230/15

fag(g)ot(te), faggotte n. bundle of sticks for burning heretics or carried as punishment by renounced heretics 73/35 *etc. See n. to* 70/12–13

faith n. See **fayth**

fal(l) v. happen 15/30 *etc.;* become 46/14; *fall in hand . . . wyth* undertake 4/8; *fall vnto* proceed to 8/2; draw to 47/32; *fal(l) to* commit 16/12; begin 62/10 *etc.; fall (. . .) in* begin 16/15; enter upon 18/5; get into 122/31, 130/27: become liable to 187/8 *etc.; falleth in remembraunce* recalls 52/13–14; *fall fro . . . to* switch from . . . to 55/21–22; *fall vppon* light upon 164/25; *fal(l) into* become liable to 188/21–22, 188/35; befall 201/35; begin a discussion of 202/5; *was fallen into* began 200/33; *fall awaye* decay 230/15–16; *pt.* **fyll** 16/15

fall n. a throw onto one's back in wrestling 158/17

false adj. villainous 10/1 *etc.*

false adv. untruly 152/9 *etc.*

fals(h)ed, falshod n. villainy 92/17 *etc.:* lie 158/24

fame n. report 76/26, 76/30; reputation 121/13 *etc.*

fantasyes n. pl. inclinations 54/31–32

fantsyes n. pl. groundless suppositions 48/36

far(re), ferre, adv. very 4/22 *etc.;* by far 18/28 *etc.;* far 174/32; *comp.* **ferther, farther** further 5/23 *etc.*

fareth v. pr. 3 s. acts 139/4

farforth, far forth adv. See **ferforth**

farre adv. See **far(re)**

farre fet adj. far-fetched 205/30

farre fetchynge vbl. n. far-fetchedness 108/30

farre forthe adv. See **ferforth**

farther adj. comp. See **ferther**

farther adv. comp. See **far(re)**

farther forth adv. comp. See **ferforth**

farthermore adv. See **ferthermore**

fa(s)shyon n. style, manner 6/6 *etc.*

fasshyon adj. new *fasshyon* 140/26. *See n.*

faste adv. earnestly 182/26; firmly 228/4

fauoredly adv. See **well fauoredly**

fauour n. support 147/6

faute, fawt(e) n. error 8/10 *etc.;* blame 9/26; offence 124/10 *etc.;* wrong 126/9; responsibility 130/18; defect 136/27 *etc.*

fawte fyndynge n. fault-finding 136/25

fawtelesse, fauteless(e) adj. innocent 124/24 *etc.*

fawty(e) adj. blameworthy 39/30; guilty 123/8 *etc.*

faye n. *by my faye* indeed 43/3

fayle v. pr. 3 p. are wanting 182/22

fayn(e) adv. gladly, willingly 5/31 *etc.*

fayne adj. eager 38/7 *etc.;* obliged 143/34

fayne v. invent 27/30; lie 59/26 *etc.*

faynt(e) adj. weak 3/30, 179/12; feigned 118/3

fayre adj. honest 131/7

fayre adv. legibly, suitably 7/14; completely 27/33

fayth, faith n. *in good fayth (faith)* in truth 3/31 *etc.*

felesshyp n. group 39/30

felowe n. colleague 197/29

fere v. frighten 75/16; *I fere me* I am afraid 172/23–24; *ppl. a. ferd* frightened 94/29

forforth, farforth, far(re) forth(e) adv. far 4/28 *etc.; in as farforth* insofar 18/5; *comp.* **ferther (farther) forth** 50/22, 175/16

ferre adv. See **far(re)**

ferther, farther adj. comp. further 17/14 *etc.; superl.* **fertheste** 138/19–20

ferther adv. comp. See **far(re)**

ferther forth adv. comp. See **ferforth**

ferthermore, farthermore adv. moreover 149/22 *etc.*

fetely adv. deftly 68/17

fette v. fetch 12/3 *variant*

fewer adj. comp. smaller 51/32

fleryng n. engaging appearance 77/9

flex n. flax 27/32

flye n. *by . . . set a flye.* See **set(te)**

flyt v. depart 71/27

fole *n.* fool 54/21; *pl.* **folys** 54/22 *etc.*
folowynge *vbl. n.* imitation 61/24
fonde *adj.* foolish, mad 45/8 *etc.*
for *prep.* as 4/28 *etc.;* before 95/19; on account of 97/36, 103/10; about 178/27; in response to 197/4; *for to* in order to 5/18 *etc.; for all* despite 97/28, 154/24
forbede *v.* forbid 55/9 *etc.; pt.* **forbode** 54/18; *ppl. a.* **forboden** 143/21, 164/16
force *v.* care 24/8, 117/32
fore *adv. See* **far(re)**
forfaiture, forfaytoure *n.* fine 94/18 *etc.*
forgate *v. pt.* neglected 26/14
formar(e) *adj.* previous 9/10 *etc.*
forsoth(e) *adv.* in truth, indeed 28/11 *etc.*
forswere *v.* perjure 158/35; *ppl. a., pp.* **forsworen, forsworne** guilty of perjury 146/12 *etc.*
forth(e) *adv.* forward 176/5; *far(re) forth(e), ferther (farther) forth. See* **ferforth;** *helpe (. . .) forth(e). See* **helpe**
forther *v.* assist 17/25
fortifye *v.* corroborate 111/1, 111/9
fortune *v.* happen 7/20 *etc.*
founde, founden *ppl. a., pp. See* **fynde**
fourtyth *adj.* fortieth 88/24
frantike *adj.* insanely foolish 73/22
frere *n.* friar 14/22 *etc.*
fre(s)she *adj.* not salty 21/16; finely dressed 55/29
fro *prep.* from 9/26 *etc.*
fronte *n.* recto 10/18
frowarde *adj.* evil, refractory 215/20; adverse 215/21
frowardnesse *n.* perversity 176/15
fru(y)te, fruit *n.* benefit, advantage 38/9 *etc.*
frutelesse *adj.* unprofitable 38/10 *etc.*
ful(l) *adj.* universal 144/34; entire 173/34
ful(l) *adv.* very 36/19 *etc.;* fully, entirely 37/24 *etc.*
full *n. to the . . . full* completely 47/30
fygure *n.* figure of speech 24/25 *etc.*
fynde *v.* determine 123/13 *etc.;* declare (an offence) to have been committed 140/17; invent, contrive 67/26, 180/4; *ppl. a., pp.* **founden, founde** 7/1 *etc.; founde oute* invented 48/35; *vbl. n.* **fyndynge** provision 123/31
fyne *adj.* subtle 27/31

fyre *n.* fire of hell 54/21; penalty of death by burning 117/1; *pl.* **fyrys** 54/23

gadered *v. pt.* gathered 216/31
gamener *n.* gamester 197/3
gamynge *vbl. n.* gambling 55/21
gaole, gayole *n.* jail 168/21; *sessyon of gaole deliuery. See* **sessyon**
gappes *n. pl.* breaches 229/22
garded *ppl. a.* ornamentally turned up 55/19
garnyshynge *vbl. n.* adornment 47/8
gase *v.* look casually 124/5
gay(e) *adj.* specious, plausible 5/27 *etc.;* showy 55/19
gayly *adv.* speciously 125/15
gayole *n. See* **gaole**
generall *adj.* whole 43/6
generalytye *n.* general proposition 225/14; *pl.* **general(y)tyes** 225/12 *etc.*
gentle *adj.* well-bred 142/32; courteous 216/1
gently *adv.* courteously 216/2
gere *n.* business 103/31; nonsensical discourse 210/9
geue *v.* give 3/22 *etc.; geueth . . . warnynge of* calls to (his) attention 12/15–16, 23/22–23; *geue (. . .) ouer* give up, abandon 62/9 *etc.*
glose *v.* palliate, explain away 43/36
gloses *n. pl.* specious explanations 73/8
go *v. went in hande . . . wyth* proceeded with 4/1; *went there about* was occupied with it 6/36; *go about(e)* busy oneself, attempt 9/30 *etc.; go by* pass unnoticed 143/33; *go to* come on 207/12; *go to* get to work 225/2; *pr. 3 s.* **goth, gooth** 20/8, 67/1; *goth (goeth) . . . (vn)to* contributes to 67/1, 122/24–25
goddes, goddis *n. poss.* God's 10/7 *etc.*
good manne *n.* householder 12/28
gossepred *n.* relationship of a godparent 28/27
grace *n. the kynges (kinges) grace* the king 32/11 *etc.; his grace* the king 32/16, 138/14
graciouse, gracyouse *adj.* regenerate, pious 25/3, 201/2
graunte *n.* permission 206/3
great(e), gret *adj.* eminent 28/33, 75/28;

large 100/18; chief 144/31; widespread
176/21; *great turke. See* **turke;** *ouer great.*
See **ouer great;** *superl.* **gret(t)est** 29/14,
78/23

great *n.* eminent 29/1

grefe, gryefe *n.* grievance 110/11; suffering, injury 189/26 *etc.; pl.* **greues** 110/8

grene *adj.* youthful 6/3

gret *adj. See* **great(e)**

gret(t)est *adj. superl. See* **great(e)**

greue *v.* vex 4/21, 25/1

greues *n. pl. See* **grefe**

greuouse *adj.* severe 15/31; *ouer greuous.*
See **ouer greuous**

grote *n.* groat 34/32

groundely *adj.* well-founded 210/15

growen *pp.* grown 14/16, 192/23; *growynge*
to accruing to 13/12

grownd *n.* reason 184/10

grudge *n.* discontent, dissatisfaction 14/15
etc.; complaint 53/26 *etc.;* reluctance
214/11, 215/14

grudge *v. grudge (agaynste, at)* grumble (at),
complain (about) 26/21 *etc.; vbl. n.*
grudgynge complaint, reluctance
202/30

gryefe *n. See* **grefe**

guyded *v. pt.* conducted 48/15

gyders *n. pl.* guides 20/16

gylty to *adj.* liable to 54/21

haboundeth *v. pr. 3 s.* abounds 82/35

hab(o)undaunce, aboundaunce *n.* abundance, wealth 31/21 *etc.*

habundauntely *adv.* abundantly 65/9,
66/15

habylyte *n.* ability, aptitude 158/4

Halowentyde *n.* Halloween 3/11

halporth *adj.* of the value of a halfpenny,
tiny 227/33

hand(e) *n.* handwriting 4/31; *in hande wyth*
dealing with 10/17; *vppon myn hande* in
my responsibility 22/23–24; *out of hande*
immediately 56/6; *went in hande*
. . . wyth. See **go;** *fall in hand*
. . . wyth. See **fal(l);** *sette hande vppon. See*
sette; *stryken handes. See* **stryken**

hande whyle *n.* moment 5/30

hange (. . .) vppe *v. pr. 3 s.* hang 107/17,
218/34; *hangeth vppon (in, on)* depends
upon 33/35 *etc.*

hap(pe) *v.* befall 4/7 *etc.;* happen, chance
7/18 *etc.*

hap(p)ely, haply *adv.* perchance, perhaps
37/30 *etc.*

happes *n. pl.* mischances 130/29; *may hap-*
pys. See **may happys**

harde *v. pt., pp.* heard 84/32, 164/3

hardely *adv.* boldly 225/2

harlottes *n. pl.* rascals, villains 91/11

harmlesse, harme lesse *adj. saued harme-*
lesse (harme lesse). See **saue**

harte *n.* life 46/19

harty *adj.* sincere 118/11

hastely *adv. ouer hastely. See* **ouer hastely**

hasty *adj. ouer hasty. See* **ouer hasty**

hatered *n.* hatred 63/31 *etc.*

haue *v.* take 100/13 *etc; haue . . . for* consider as 23/6; *haue . . . in* regard with
193/38–194/1

hed *n.* head 12/3 *etc.; pl.* **hedys** 56/2

heedlynge *adv.* precipitately 26/23

helpe *v. helpe (. . .) forth(e)* assist 194/26,
197/29: *pp.* **holpen, holpe** 104/14 *etc.*

hempe *n.* rope used for hanging 55/22

here byfore (before) *adv.* beforehand
104/35, 151/5; herein before 220/29

heretyque *adj.* heretical 24/2

herkeneth *v. pr. 3 s.* listens 5/30

heuy *adj.* serious 181/11 *etc.*

heygth, heyght *adj.* highest point 208/20;
on heyght to an intense degree 119/7

heyg(h)nouse, hyghnouse *adj.* heinous
32/26 *etc.*

Hierome *n.* Jerome 24/26

Hierusalem *n.* Jerusalem 3/14, 48/17

high, hygh(e) *adj.* exalted, lofty 28/12 *etc.;*
supreme 67/31; serious 68/26 *etc.;*
strong 208/20; *hyghe mysseprisyon* 80/6.
See n.

hit *pron.* it 197/5

hode *n.* hood 46/16

holde *n.* substance 154/19; wrestling grip
158/19

holde *v.* keep inviolate 30/29, 168/30; stop
46/15; accord 47/7; side 47/23; *holde*
. . . scholys 168/32. *See n. to* 71/29; *hold-*

ynge ple 185/29–30. *See n.; pp.* **holden** 144/25; *pt.* **hylde** 82/4, 219/3

hol(l)e *adj.* healthy 20/21

holpe, holpen *pp. See* **helpe**

honest *adj.* upright, well-disposed 16/20, 28/34; respectable 35/1

honesty *n. othe . . . of honesty* 47/14. *See n. to* 47/14–16

hose *n. shypmans hose* loose-fitting trousers worn by sailors 115/21; *pl.* **hosyn** article of clothing for the leg, sometimes covering the foot as well 55/19

hoste *n.* innkeeper 139/5

houswyfe *n.* woman 46/16

how(e) be it (yt), howbeit *adv.* nevertheless 4/6 *etc.*

howe (. . .) so euer *adv.* however 24/11–12, 46/27

hurt(e) *n.* harme, injury 152/19 *etc.*

husband men *n. pl.* farmers 35/5; *poss. pl.* **husband mennes** householders' 142/8

hygh(e) *adj. See* **high**

hyghnouse *adj. See* **heyg(h)nouse**

hylde *v. pt. See* **holde**

hynderaunce *n.* harm 98/3

hyre *v.* bribe 108/27 *etc.*

hys *poss. pron.* its 14/12

ill *adv.* badly 141/34

illacyon *n.* conclusion 62/33

il fauored *adj.* ugly 142/22–23

imagynacyons *n. pl.* plots 16/10

imagyned *ppl. a.* invented 168/5

immediatly *adv. See* **immedyat(e)ly**

immedicable *adj.* incurable 73/36

immedyate, immediate *adj.* without any intervening agency 202/28 *etc.*

immedyat(e)ly, immediatly *adv.* without any intervening agency 203/14 *etc.*

importable *adj.* intolerable 87/11

importe *v.* imply 57/5; *pr. 3 s.* **inporteth** 62/25

importune *adj.* troublesome 10/7, 98/26

in *prep.* according to 4/12 *etc.*; on 6/33 *etc.*; into 25/18, 52/3; under 114/2, 114/8; of 121/6; concerning 146/24 *etc.*; by 178/31, 180/8

include *v.* imply 33/14; *vbl. n.* **includyng** 34/14

inclusyues *n. pl.* 33/13, 33/22. *See n. to* 33/13–14

inculketh *v. pr. 3 s.* urges persistently 23/1, 38/32

indempnyte *n.* protection 89/21

indifference *n. See* **indyfferency(e)**

indifferently *adv.* impartially 20/10

indurate *adj.* obstinate 113/34

indyfferency(e), indifference, indyferency *n.* impartiality, fairness 163/33 *etc.*

indyfferent(e) *adj.* impartial, fair, even-handed 177/34 *etc.;* morally neutral 54/11–12

indytementes *n. pl.* 121/35. *See n.*

indyters *n. pl. See* **endy(gh)tours**

infecte *ppl. a. See* **enfecte**

informacyon, informacion, enformacyon *n.* accusation, complaint 72/6 *etc. See n. to* 73/9–12

informe *v. See* **enforme**

Inne *n.* 37/35. *See n.*

innocent *adj.* unsuspecting 230/25

innocent *n.* guiltless person 147/30 *etc.*

inporteth *v. pr. 3 s. See* **importe**

inquere, enquere *v.* investigate 179/15, 180/2: ask 179/17: *inquere for* search into 178/27

inquiete *adj.* troublesome 74/36

inquisycyon *n.* judicial investigation 125/20

insoluble *adj.* irrefutable 37/21

interprysed *v. pt.* undertaken 209/32

intryke *v.* complicate 168/7

inuencyon *n.* plan 156/20, 178/18

inuolue *v.* entangle 168/7

inuyte *v.* present inducements 143/24

iolte hed *n.* 142/25. *See n.*

iubardye *n.* risk 116/32

iuberdouse *adj.* perilous 125/32

iury *n. See* **petyt iury**

I wysse, i wys *adv.* certainly, indeed 64/14–15 , *etc.*

kay *n.* key 41/5. *See n.*

kepe *v.* be on guard 22/25; observe 45/14; sustain 53/31; hold prisoner 124/18, 124/21; maintain 146/2, 193/35; *kepe vnder* suppress, keep under control 13/37 *etc.; kepyng yt counsayle* keeping it

secret 32/27–28; *kepe (. . .) sc(h)oles* engage in a disputation 36/32, 48/2; *kepe . . . scoles* 71/29. *See n.; kepynge no store of* not valuing 107/17; *vbl. n.* **kepyng(e)** retention 105/9 *etc.*
kepers *n. pl.* jail guards 24/14
knowen *ppl. a., pp.* known 40/21 *etc.*
knowledge *n.* judicial investigation 184/27 *etc.; take knowledge . . . vppon (of). See* **take**
knowledge *v.* acknowledge 200/8, 200/21
knytteth *v. pr. 3 s.* unite 192/20; *knytteth . . . vp* ends 198/1; *knytteth vppe* summarizes 219/24
kyll vp *v.* kill 141/32, 142/1

labour *n.* trouble 169/24
labour *v.* endeavor to persuade 49/36, 138/22
lacke *n.* defect 215/8
lapped, lapte *ppl. a.* wrapped 162/33, 230/31
larg(e) *adj.* generous 70/14; *at large* at liberty 71/27; *comp.* **larger** more inaccurate 169/30
largely *adv.* generously 209/20
late *adj.* recent; *of late dayes* recently 195/25
late *adv.* recently 24/32 *etc.*
lather *n.* steps to the gallows 107/15
laude *n.* praise 212/9
lay(e), ley *v.* transfer 9/26, 10/6; attribute 15/33; allege 17/3 *etc.;* charge 23/25 *etc.;* wager 62/12; put forward 129/5; present 179/22; *lay . . . in* attribute to 19/5–6; charge to 191/34, 192/1; *laye . . . vppon* charge to 133/10–11; *pr. 3 s.* **layth** 224/18
leasure *n. See* **leysour(e)**
left *pp. See* **leue**
lekelyhedes *n. pl. See* **lykelyhed**
lened *ppl a. lened vnto* relied upon 40/9
lenger *adj. comp. See* **longe**
lenger *adv. comp.* longer 19/5 *etc.*
length *n.* lengthiness 83/11
lese *v.* lose 4/8 *etc.; ppl. a.* **lesynge** 197/5
leser *n.* loser 197/6
lest(e) *adj. superl. at the lest(e) wyse* at least 13/15 *etc.*

lesynge *ppl. a. See* **lese**
lesynges *n. pl.* lies 68/15
let(te) *n.* impediment 8/11 *etc.; pl.* **lettis, lettes** 8/11
let(te . . . to) *v.¹* prevent from 13/20 *etc.*
let(te) *v.²* forbear 25/16 *etc.;* omit 52/18
lete *n.* type of manorial court 139/26, 185/3. *See n. to* 139/26–27; *n. pl.* **letys** 184/33, 184/34
letter *n.* literal meaning 30/32 *etc.*
leue, lyefe *adv. hadde I as leue (lyefe)* I would find it as desirable 131/31, 139/15; *comp.* **leuer** 48/36; *had(de . . .) leuer* would find it more desirable to 48/36 *etc.*
leue *v.¹* end 54/3; repeal 119/13; *leue of* end 8/2, 77/14; *left of* discontinued 143/12; *vbl. n.* **leuyng(e)** repeal 105/11 *etc.;* termination 181/14, 182/12
leue *v.²* allow 25/21
lewde *adj.* ill-mannered 28/29; foolish 68/23, 180/16; wicked 69/24 *etc.*
lewdely *adv.* wickedly 179/34
lewdenesse *n.* wickedness 68/22
ley *v. See* **lay(e)**
leysour(e), leasure *n.* opportunity 158/18, 225/4; *by leysoure* in course of time 17/13; *at a leysour* with opportunity for deliberation 29/33
light *adj. See* **lyght(e)**
lightnesse *n. See* **lyghtnes(se)**
like *adj. See* **lyke**
likelihed *n. See* **lykelyhed**
liken (to gether) *v. See* **lyken (to gether, . . . to gether)**
liste *v. pr. 3 s., pl. See* **lyst(e)**
lo *interj.* indeed, behold 24/19 *etc.*
lo *v.* moo 142/37
loke *v.* consider 158/15; appear 230/30; *loke (vppon)* examine 114/5, 226/11
longe *adj.* many 144/22; *comp.* **lenger** 56/21
loste *ppl. a.* vain 202/7
lurkys, lurkes *n. poss.* 88/17, 145/32. *See n. to* 88/17
lustely *adv.* vigorously 5/14
lusty(e) *adj.* vigorous 3/23, 45/22
lyberall *adj.* generous 178/2
lyberally *adv.* generously 209/20

lyberty *n.* freedom from the bondage of law 25/8; *n. pl.* **lybertyes** privileges 206/12, 206/17

lycens *n.* permission 32/13, 109/29

lyefe *adj.* precious 99/20

lyefe *adv. See* **leue**

lyght(e), light *adj.* venial 61/4; inconsequential 84/1 *etc.;* small 84/9; not respectable 84/20; ready 156/4; *ouer lyghte. See* **ouer**

lyght(e)ly(e) *adv.* nimbly 3/25; perhaps 26/10 *etc.;* slightly 67/34; for slight cause 84/2 *etc;* probably 169/2; readily, easily 175/4 *etc.*

lyghtnes(se), lightnesse *n.* thoughtlessness 68/19 *etc.:* unsteadiness 146/15 *etc.* credulousness 226/25

lyke, like *adj.* similar 19/13 *etc.; lyke maner* similar 24/26; *lyke wyse. See* **lyke wyse;** *in lyke wyse See* **wyse**

lyke *adv.* likely 146/17 *etc.;* in like manner 220/26; *lyke as* just as 16/11 *etc.*

lyke *n.* similar ones 155/30

lyke *v.* please 33/11 *etc; vbl. n.* **lykynge** enjoyment 48/36

lykelyhed, likelihed *n.* probability 57/13 *etc;* occurence 130/17; *by (of) lykelyhed (likelihed)* in all probability 12/6 *etc.; pl.* **lykelyhed(d)es, lekelyhedes** conjectures, surmises 160/24 *etc.*

lyken (together, . . . to gether), liken (to gether) *v.* compare 122/12 *etc.*

lyke wyse *adv.* just 10/28

lyke wyse *n. in lyke wyse. See* **wyse**

lykly *adj.* apt 3/24

lykynge *vbl. n. See* **lyke**

lymyte *v.* specify 32/14

lyst(e), liste *v. pr. 3 s., pl.* wish(es) 14/19 *etc.*

lyttel *adj.* trivial 56/12

lytter *n.* straw for animals to lie on 322/29

lyuynge *n.* landed property 99/18 *etc.*

maister *n. See* **mayster**

make *v.* write 3/29 *etc.;* act 12/2 *etc.; make yt straunge* refuse 35/18; *make serche* investigate 58/35, 59/4; *maketh no doute at yt* does not doubt it 61/13; *make a doute*

doubt 61/14; *make processe* initiate legal proceedings 168/18; *maketh for* asserts 189/10; *made of counsayle. See* **counsayle;** *vbl. n.* **makyng(e)** writing 14/32; framing 145/1; *a makyng* in preparation 4/25

maker *n.* author 9/24 *etc.*

mamerynge *n.* state of doubt 96/25

maner *n.* kind of 7/2 *etc.; in such (this, some) maner wyse (wise)* in such a (this, some) way 9/34 *etc.; in a maner* as it were 46/26; *his such maner of* such a way as he has of 191/28; *in maer* nearly 227/14

many say *n.* reported statement 68/9

may happys *n. pl.* possibilities 128/34

maynte(y)nyng(e) *vbl. n.* 43/24, 43/29–30. *See notes to* 43/23–25, 43/29–30

mayster, maister *n.* master 16/6 *etc;* director 34/35

maystryes *n. pl. worke . . . maystryes. See* **worke**

meane *adj.* tolerable 177/8: *meane season* meanwhile 71/19, 182/23

meane *n.* means 70/9 *etc.;* intermediary 206/15

meane whyle *n. in this meane whyle* meanwhile 59/6–7

meate *adj. See* **mete**

medle, medyll *v.* deal, concern oneself 6/7 *etc.*

mend(e) *v.* reform 4/17, *etc.;* correct 201/20

mene *v. mene of* speak of 55/35; *vbl. n.* **menyng(e)** intention 14/6 *etc.*

meruayle, meruaile *n.* wonder, astonishment 8/31 *etc.*

meruayle, meruaile *v.* be surprised 3/28 *etc.; meruaile of* be surprised at 101/36

meruaylouse *adv.* surprisingly 174/11

meruelous(e), merueylous *adj.* astonishing 3/6 *etc.;* marvelous 112/19

meruelousely *adv.* exceptionally 222/31, 223/1–2

mery *adj.* amusing, jesting 46/12 *etc.*

mete, meate *adj.* fit 14/35 *etc.*

metely *adj.* appropriate 84/31, 225/3
metely *adv.* tolerably, fairly 16/8 *etc.;* suitably 22/28 *etc.;* duly 149/24
meueth *v. pr. 3 s. See* **moue**
mindeth *v. pr. 3 s. See* **myndeth**
minisshement *n. See* **mynysshement**
ministracyon, minystracyon, mynystracyon *n.* administration 207/7 *etc.*
ministre, mynystre, mynyster *v.* administer, dispense 42/15 *etc.; vbl. n.* **mynystrynge** 45/15
minour *n.* minor premiss of a syllogism 185/23
minystracyon *n. See* **ministracyon**
misse happe *v. See* **mysse happe**
misse lyketh (in) *v. pr. 3 s. See* **mysse (misse) lyke (in)**
misseordre *v.* disturb 138/11–12
mo *adj.* more 5/28 *etc.*
moch(e) *adv. See* **mych(e)**
mocyon, mocion *n.* proposal 22/20 *etc.*
moder *n.* mother 6/2
modered *v. pt.* modified 160/16
monasyllable *n.* monosyllable 62/30
mone *n.* complaint 84/31
monycyon, monicyon, monicion *n.* instruction 70/23 *etc.;* warning 75/4 *etc.*
more *adj. comp. See* **mych(e)**
Mortuaryes, mortuaryes *n. pl.* 195/6, 199/2. *See n. to* 195/5–6
mortysed *pp.* alienated in mortmain 34/31; *vbl. n.* **mortysynge** 32/13 *See n. to* 32/9–10
mosel *n.* snout 142/25
most(e) *adj. superl. See* **mych(e)**
motable *adj.* 36/18. *See n. to* 36/18–19
mote *n. vacacyon mote* 37/34. *See n. to* 37/34–35
moue *v.* urge 22/12 *etc.;* propose 36/13 *etc.;* bring to trial 144/2; *pr. 3 s.* **meueth** 218/10
moulden *ppl. a.* moldy 5/13 *etc.*
mountayne *adj.* mountainous 4/27
mountenaunce *n.* value 179/31
multitude, multytude *n.* majority 49/34, 51/33
mum *n.* an inarticulate sound made with closed lips 140/12
mumbleth *v. pr. 3 s.* mutters 32/24; *vbl. n.* **mumblynge** babbling 202/33

mummery *n.* dumb show 103/32. *See n.*
murmure *n.* complaint 18/1 *etc.*
mych(e) *adj.* much 4/27 *etc.;* many 57/9 *etc.; mych(e) parte* a great deal 32/6, 44/25; *ouer mych. See* **ouer mych;** *comp.* **more** greater 15/12 *etc.; superl.* **most(e)** greatest 49/35 *etc.*
mych(e), moch(e) *adv.* greatly 3/21 *etc.*
myche *n.* much 5/31
myn(e) *poss. pron.* my, mine 4/11 *etc.*
myncyng *vbl. n.* minimizing 81/17
myndeth, mindeth *v. pr. 3 s.* intends 50/36 *etc.; ppl. a.* **mynded** inclined 3/21 *etc.; selfe mynded. See* **selfe mynded**
myne *poss. pron. See* **myn(e)**
mynistres *n. pl. See* **mynystres**
mynys(s)he *v.* weaken, lessen 31/26 *etc.*
mynysshement, minisshement *n.* lessening, weakening 15/29, 87/22
mynystracyon *n. See* **ministracyon**
mynystre, mynyster *v. See* **ministre**
mynystres, mynistres *n. pl.* judicial officers 163/28 *etc.*
mynystrynge *vbl. n. See* **ministre**
mysch(y)euous(e) *adj.* injurious, harmful 74/33 *etc.*
myschyefe, myschief(e) *n.* wickedness 71/2 *etc.;* harm 197/30
myschyefe *v.* injure 95/33
myschyeuous(e) *adj. See* **mysch(y)euous(e)**
mysprisyon, mysseprisyon *n.* 32/26–27, 80/6. *See n. to* 80/6
mysseconstre *v.* misconstrue 177/23
mysse gesseth *v. pr. 3 s.* guesses incorrectly 107/3
mysseguyded *ppl. a.* immoral 148/4–5
mysse happe, misse happe *v.* happen by misfortune 17/9 *etc.*
mysse (misse) lyke (in) *v.* be displeased (with) 24/1, 222/27
mysse order *n.* misconduct 65/16
mysseprisyon *n. See* **mysprisyon**
mysse reherse *v.* relate incorrectly 6/26, 6/28; misquote 177/23
mysse sayeth *v. pr. 3 s.* slanders 18/32–33
mysse vnderstondon *pp.* misunderstood 209/28
mysse vsed, myssevsed *v. pt., pp.* misconducted 48/12, 155/11–12

mytygateth *v. pr. 3 s.* renders less severe 189/31

namely *adv.* particularly, especially 8/13 *etc.*

namys *n. pl.* names 24/3

naturall *n.* born idiot 13/5

nay(e) *adv.* no 85/2 *etc.; say(e . . .) nay(e). See* **say(e)**

naye *n.* no 155/34

ne *conj.* nor 55/32 *etc.*

necke *n.* head from the neck up 16/20 *etc.; pl.* **neckes, neckys** 22/16 *etc.; in theyr (. . .) neckes (neckys)* on their shoulders 22/16 *etc.*

nede *n.* needful 4/2 *etc.*

nede *v.* be necessary 6/17 *etc.; me nedeth* it is necessary for me 209/30

nedely *adv.* necessarily 133/9

nedes, nedys *adv.* necessarily 21/23 *etc.*

nedyly *adv.* carefully 210/33

nere *adv.¹* not at all, never 32/28 *etc.*

nere *adv.²* closely 4/30 *etc.; comp.* **nere** 120/3; *neuer the nere* no nearer his end 120/2–3

new(e) *adv.* anew 7/4 *etc.;* recently 25/27, 34/34

new broched *ppl. a.* recently introduced 24/30 *etc.*

new fasshyon *adj.* 140/26. *See n.*

next *adv. next before* immediately before 58/10, 63/18

neyther nother *pron.* neither 99/37 *etc.*

no *adj. in no wise (wyse). See* **wyse**

nocentes *n. pl.* guilty people 121/28

nombred *pp.* given the number of 7/9

none *adj.* no 4/14 *etc.*

nonys *n. for the nonys* on purpose 126/15

notable *adj.* conspicuous 38/25; important 112/8 *etc.;* blameworthy 177/8

notably *adv.* commonly 110/35 *etc.*

note wyth (of) *v.* accuse of 168/13 *etc.*

nother *pron. See* **neyther nother**

nothynge, no thynge *adv.* in no way, not at all 8/28 *etc.*

nought(e) *adj.* wicked 4/18 *etc.;* bad 133/25 *etc.;* injurious 230/25

nought *adv.* wickedly 66/3, 225/27

nought(e) *n.* nothing 77/11, 123/10; *serue of noughte. See* **serue**

noughty(e) *adj.* wicked, immoral 8/24 *etc.*

no wise (wyse) *n. in no wise (wyse). See* **wyse**

noyse *n.* rumor 27/16, 84/35

noyse *v.* report, rumor 26/20 *etc.;* spread rumors about 76/8, 76/12

nuryshe *v.* nourish 19/23

obytes, obitis, obitys, obytys *n. pl.* 47/10 *etc. See n.*

occasyon *n.* cause 14/28 *etc.;* opportunity 193/11; circumstances 195/8; *by occasyon of* because of 179/14

odyouse *adj.* disagreeable 53/6

of *adv.* off, away 16/20 *etc.*

of *prep.* in 9/32 *etc.;* out of 59/3 *etc.;* for 28/32 *etc.;* by means of 29/34 *etc.;* to 36/4, 56/24: from 46/9 *etc.;* by 84/4 *etc.;* about 146/11 *etc.*

offendours *n. pl.* offenders 183/8

offyce, office *n.* function 164/7; post 164/13; *of offyce (office)* 60/29 *etc. See n. to* 60/28–29; *worde of offyce* 60/30 *See n.*

ofter *comp. adv.* more often 56/8 *etc.*

on *prep. See* **vn**

one *adj.* single 4/4

one *pron. all one. See* **all**

oneles *prep.* unless 156/36, 187/26

onely *adj.* mere 79/25; single 110/9

ones, onys *adv.* once 4/11 *etc;* at some future time, one day 5/15, 55/21

open *adj.* public 29/3 *etc.;* general 139/1

open *adv.* publicly 21/39, 124/3; clearly 27/20

openeth *v. pr. 3 s.* explains 122/1; *vbl. n.* **openynge** declaration 31/5 *etc.;* disclosure 130/35, 131/1

openly *adv.* generally 68/36, 175/30: publicly 139/19 *etc.*

opinatyuely *adj. See* **opynatyuely**

oppresse *v.* harass 18/10

oppressyon *n.* harassment 18/12

oppugneth *v. pr. 3 s.* assails 9/21, 220/26

opynatyuely, opinatyuely *adj.* obstinately 72/17 *etc.*

or *conj. See* **ere**

order *n.* established procedure 73/8 *etc.*

order *v.* conduct, behave 60/22, 122/11

orderynge *vbl. n.* punishment 22/15

ordinary *adj.* having regular jurisdiction 151/10

ordynary(e), ordinary(e) *n.* 6/10 *etc. See n.*
ordyned *pp.* decreed 146/9
othe *n. othe of . . . honesty* 47/14. *See n. to*
47/13–16
other *adv.* else 194/24
other wyse *n. none other wyse. See* **wyse**
ouer *adv.* too 27/21 *etc.*
ouer *prep.* in addition to 6/12 *etc.*
ouer borne wyth *pp.* overthrown by
152/16
ouer great *adj.* too great 161/2
ouer greuous *adj.* excessively oppressive
215/31
ouer hande *n.* victory 83/10
ouer hastely *adv.* precipitately 222/20
ouer hasty *adj.* precipitate 183/1
ouerloking *vbl. n.* inspection 5/28
ouer lyghte *adj.* credulous 226/19
ouer mych *n.* too much 222/14
ouersene, ouer sene, ouerseen *ppl. a., pp.*
mistaken 11/6 *etc.;* imprudent 79/32,
104/12; *pt.* **ouersaw** 181/27
ouer throwe, ouerthrow *n.* defeat 104/22,
141/9
outwarde *adv.* outwardly 165/21
owyng(e) *pr. p.* due to be paid 52/26, 52/33

panellys *n. pl.* juries 137/34
paragraffe, peragraph, Peragr. *n.* section
of a law 114/7 *etc.*
parcyally *adv.* with partiality 88/13
paral(l), perel(l) *n.* danger, risk 9/20 *etc.;*
put yt vppon the parell. See **put(te)**
parishon *n. See* **paryshen**
parte *n.¹* party 15/1 *etc.;* function 226/18
parte *n.² mych(e) parte. See* **mych(e);** *pl.* **par-**
tyes sections 7/16
parte *v. parte the stacke* share the stakes
62/11
partycularly *adv.* individually 13/18–19
partyes *n. pl. See* **parte**
paryshen, parishon *n.* parishioner 196/4–
5 *etc.*
passe *v.* surpass 81/14; render a verdict
155/4; *passe by* go unnoticed 135/35;
passe (. . .) ouer disregard, omit 186/11
etc.
passyon *n.* fit, frenzy 68/19 *etc.*
pauce *n.* shield, defense 132/11

payne *n.* penalty 122/22 *etc.;* trouble 225/4
peace *n. sessyon of peace. See* **sessyon**
pennys *n. pl.* pens 4/24
peny *n. of a peny* a bit 47/27
peraduenture *adv.* perhaps 9/4 *etc.*
peragraph, Peragr. *n. See* **paragraffe**
percase *adv.* perhaps, by chance 51/30 *etc.*
perdon *v.* pardon 52/14, 195/36
perdy(e) *interj.* indeed 30/3 *etc.*
perel(l) *n. See* **parel(l)**
perfeccyon *n.* fulfillment 25/13
perfyt, perfite *adj.* expert, complete,
135/12, 210/17
periured *ppl. a.* guilty of perjury 152/14
perleament *n.* parliament 15/23–24 *etc.*
person(e) *n.¹* identity 40/20; role 93/33; *to*
theyr persons to them individually 39/30–
31, 70/9–10
person *n.²* parson 195/21 *etc.; pl.* **personys**
196/19
persuasion *n.* belief 112/16
peruse *v.* deal with point by point, criticize
13/23 *etc.*
perylouse *adj.* harmful 230/19, 230/24
pestylent *adj.* pernicious 168/2 *etc.*
petyt iury *n.* trial jury 137/4 *etc.*
pewfelowe *n.* companion 46/14
pharysaycal *adj.* hypocritical 18/2
phylyppe *n.* fillip 120/25
place *n.* passage 5/8 *etc.*
plain *adv. See* **playn(e)**
plant in *v.* insert 11/28, 207/14
planynge *vbl. n.* levelling 100/13
plaster *n.* bandage 52/8
plate *n.* utensils and ornaments made
from precious metals 53/22
playeth *v. pr. 3 s.* behaves 103/32; gambols
about 223/27
playn *adj.* guileless 64/16
playn(e), plain *adv.* clearly 10/5 *etc.;* absolutely 27/7
ple *n. holdynge ple* 185/29–30. *See n.*
plumpe *n. on a plumpe* in a group 140/31
polycy(e) *n.* expediency 27/13; prudence
27/15 *etc.; as of polycy(e)* out of guile
27/9–10 *etc.; of (. . .) polycy(e)* as a prudent action 119/26; out of expediency
139/2; out of guile 168/14
polytyke, polytyque, polytike *adj.* prudent 27/13 *etc.;* shrewd 142/12

polytyques, polytykes *n. pl.* intriguers 59/30, 60/18

pore *adj.* poor 19/15 *etc.*

post *n.* 62/8. *See n. to* 62/8–13

Poule *n.* Paul 30/3 *etc.*

pourge *v. See* **p(o)urge**

powder *v.* spice, intersperse 64/10, 66/11

poynt *n. blew poynt* 209/11. *See n. to* 209/10–11

preace vppon *v.* urge importunately 53/7; press 85/2

preferre *v.* advance 175/29 *etc.*

prent(e) *n.* print 15/8 *etc.*

prent *v.* print 22/4 *etc.*

present *v.* make presentment of 139/32 *etc. See n. to* 126/12

presentement *n.* 126/12 *etc. See n.*

pretely *adv. See* **pretyly**

pretence *n.* assertion of a right 209/13 *etc.*

pretend(e) *v.* claim (as a right) 25/9 *etc.;* profess 41/8; attempt 65/23 *etc.; ppl. a.* **pretendyd** so-called 131/6

prety, pretie *adj.* cunning 6/26 *etc.*

pretyly, pretely *adv.* cunningly, cleverly 64/10, 220/20

preue *v. See* **proue**

preued *pp. See* **proue**

preuy(e), priuy *adj.* aware 125/34; secret 164/33; private 182/8

primer, prymer *n.* 7/12, 7/17. *See n. to* 7/11–12

princes *n. pl. See* **prynce**

priuy *adj. See* **preuy(e)**

processe *n.* argument 30/9, 70/25; discussion 60/6; *make processe. See* **make**

proclamacyon *n.* 122/7–8. *See n.*

procure *v.* persuade 39/1; contrive 230/11, 230/14–15

prof(f)e *n.* proof 64/30 *etc.; pl.* **proues** 39/35, 196/30

professyon *n.* promise 186/30

prohybyte *ppl. a.* forbidden 168/31

proper *adj.* individual 37/36; private 48/35; excellent 142/26

properly *adv.* admirably 12/4 *variant;* specifically 57/22

proue, preue *v.* test 222/21; prove 102/1; establish 195/39; *proue well* turn out well 20/30; *ppl. a.* **proued** 136/1, 184/17; *pp.* **preued** experienced 173/18

proues *n. pl. See* **prof(f)e**

prouincyall, prouincial(l), prouyncyall *adj.* of or pertaining to an ecclesiastical province 195/2–3 *etc.*

prouoketh *v. pr. 3 s.* calls upon 194/8, 194/10–11

prouyde *v.* ensure 147/30, 155/7

prouyncyall *adj. See* **prouincyall**

prudence *n.* widsom 76/22

prycke *v.* incite 221/20

prymer *n.* 7/17. *See n. to* 7/12

prynce *n.* ruler 28/4 *etc.*

pryuate *adj.* individual 21/1

pryuyly *adv.* secretly 197/21

psalmys *n. pl.* psalms 7/13, 7/14

pseudo euangelicos *n.* 25/19. *See n. to* 24/35–25/19

publyshynge *vbl. n.* public announcement 108/25

punyssed *pp.* punished 148/5

purgacyon, purgacion *n.* formal protestation of innocence 110/34 *etc.;* compurgation 113/26. *See notes to* 47/14–16, 70/12–13, 111/34–112/2

p(o)urge *v.* 111/36 *etc. See notes to* 70/12–13, 111/34–112/2; rid 158/30, 158/33

purpose *n. to the purpose* relevant 7/37; *of purpose* on purpose 14/30, 59/6; *to purpose* in the point at issue 49/9–10

purpose *v.* intend 6/9 *etc.*

pursued *pp.* prosecuted 143/35

put(te) *v.* displace 10/1, 59/21; propose 19/10 *etc.;* require 38/14; add 44/6; posit 45/24 *etc.;* assume 90/2; compel 121/36 *etc.;* set 127/17 *etc.;* dismiss 164/25; commit 219/14; *put . . . in thaduenture* hazard 3/19; *put(te) out(e)* publish 15/8 *etc.; putteth . . . in remembraunce* remind 16/3–4 *etc.; put (. . .) out(e) of* drive out from 23/21; expel from 129/7; *putteth for* assigns to 45/24; *put vp* lay it aside 68/33; *put(te . . .) away(e) (a way)* abolish 87/20 *etc.;* get rid of 141/18; put an end to 225/20; *put yt vppon the parell* take a chance 105/1; *put (. . . vn)to* subject to 111/18 *etc.; put in choyse* leave the choice to 128/25; *put(te) forth* publish 212/5; proposed 229/17; *put . . . in execucyon* arrest 217/31

pyece *n.* section 10/13; area 170/10

pystle *n.* epistle 48/31
pytuouse *adj.* compassionate 212/5
pytye *v.* be sorry 48/22

qualytees *n. pl.* accomplishments 40/8; social rank 154/26
querys *n. pl.* quires 4/34
quest(e) *n.* inquest 134/4 *etc. See n. to* 140/17
quinquagesime *n.* Quinquagesima Sunday, the Sunday before Lent 223/10
quod(e) *v. pt.* said 16/27 *etc.*
quyte *adj.* free 123/14
quyte *v.* exculpate 38/27; release 154/24, 155/9

raumpynge *ppl. a.* fierce 165/22
raylour *n.* railer 24/13
rebuke *n.* shame 163/9
reade *v.* lecture on law 79/21; *vbl. n.* **redyng(e)** lecture on law 38/1, 79/33
reasoned *v. pt.* argued 5/14, 31/9
receyue *v.* accept as a practice 37/11, 215/29; accept as true 145/11; admit as evidence 146/33 *etc.;* admit to testify 147/4 *etc.;* believe 215/14
receyuours *n. pl.* receivers of stolen goods 148/30
recorde *n.* witness 147/11 *etc.;* evidence 168/35, 181/35; *of recorde* on record 133/12, 134/28; *take recorde (of). See* **take;** *bere recorde. See* **bere**
recyteth *v. pr. 3 s.* quotes 110/33, 146/7; lists 221/28; *pt.* **recited** quoted 114/2
redargucyon *n.* refutation 193/33
rede *adj.* red 46/16
redy *adv.* readily 73/8
redynge *vbl. n. See* **reade**
regard *v.* value 155/3, 155/8
rehers(h)al(l) *n.* quotation 11/18 *etc.;* recitation 15/18
reherse *v.* recount, relate 5/11 *etc.;* quote 5/12 *etc.;* repeat 92/36; *vbl. n.* **rehersynge** 12/22 *etc.*
reken *v.* consider 16/31 *etc.;* calculate 139/6; *vbl. n.* **rekenynge** bill at an inn 139/4-5, 139/7
relapse *n.* return to heresy after recantation 116/32, 116/33
relygyon *n.* state of life bound by the vows of a religious order 36/25

relygyous(e) *adj.* bound by the vows of a religious order 38/18–19 *etc.*
relygyous(e) *n. pl.* persons bound by the vows of a religious order 38/23 *etc.*
remanaunt *n.* rest, remainder 5/9 *etc.*
remedelesse *adv.* beyond all remedy 48/23
remedylesse *adj.* beyond all remedy 131/13
remembraunce *n.* recollection 49/16 *etc.; putteth ... in remembraunce. See* **put(te);** *falleth in remembraunce. See* **fal(l)**
remembred *ppl. a.* mentioned 141/17, 142/33
remyt(te ... vn)to *v.* refer to 7/7–8; refer for consideration to 75/15, 218/8
renne *v.* run 26/23; *renne into* incur 179/2; *runneth out. See* **runne**
repell *v.[1]* debar 151/29 *etc.*
repell(e) *v.[2]* repeal 188/7 *etc.; vbl. n.* **repellyng(e)** 188/15 *etc.*
represse *v.* suppress 15/23 *etc.*
reprochynge of *vbl. n.* reproaching 63/20
reproued *ppl. a.* rejected 146/27
repryed *v. pt.* sent back to prison 124/17
requyre *v.* ask 23/6–7 *etc.*
rere *v.* wage 136/20, 213/7
rere warde *n.* 129/27. *See n. to* 129/27–28
resemble *v.* compare (together) 88/35 *etc.; resemble (. . .) vnto* compare to 19/12 *etc.; vbl. n.* **resemblyng** 128/22
resorte *v.* go 73/20, 227/6; refer 228/8
respecte vnto (of) *n.* regard for 94/32 *etc.*
resydue *n.* remainder 217/19
retourne *n.* sheriff's reply to a writ 121/14
ret(o)urned *pp.* reported by the sheriff in response to a writ 121/15, 121/16
reuen *ppl. a.* ornamentally slashed 55/20
riall *adj.* sumptuous 87/35
right, ryght(e) *adv.* very 40/26 *etc.;* at all 152/34
rome *n.* office 44/12 *etc.*
row *n. by row* one after another 223/24
rowne *v.* whisper 154/3
rufle *n.* contention 74/37
runne, ronne *v. runneth out* launch into bold speech 31/15, 31/19: *runne (ronne) in* incur 98/22; *renne. See* **renne**
ryally *adv.* splendidly 143/1
rychesse *n.* wealth 51/16
ryght *adj.* orthodox 223/2

ryght(e) *adv. See* **right**

ryghtwyse *adj.* just 178/1, 178/2

ryse *v.* arise 187/29; *ryse (. . .) vppon* be based upon 209/16, 209/30

rys(s)he *n.* rush 87/27; *not (. . .) worth(e) one (a) rys(s)he* of no value 87/27 etc.

sad(de) *adj.* grave 16/18 etc.; steadfast 35/1

sadnesse *n.* seriousness 16/11 etc.

sainge *vbl. n. See* **say(e)**

Salem *n.* Jerusalem 1/2 etc.

sample *n.* example 19/10 etc.

saufe *adj.* safe 73/26 etc.

saufe garde, sauf(e)gard(e), sauegarde *n.* protection 97/29 etc.

saue *prep.* except 36/27 etc.

saue *v.* preserve the credit of 214/32; *saued harmelesse (harme lesse)* kept free from punishment 131/12 etc.

sauegarde *n. See* **saufe garde**

sauyng(e) *conj.* except 53/19 etc.

say(e) *v.* deliver 38/5; *say(e . . .) nay(e)* deny 31/14 etc.; *vbl. n.* **sayeng(e), sayng, sainge** statement 26/32 etc.

scabbed *ppl. a.* having the scab or a similar skin disease 23/21

scant(e), skant *adv.* scarcely 10/20 etc.

scantely *adv.* scarcely 196/3

scape *v.* escape 40/26, 103/33

scla(u)nder *n. See* **slaunder**

sc(h)oles, scholys *n. pl. kepe (. . .) sch(h)oles. See* **kepe;** *holde . . . scholys. See n. to* 71/29

scoulke *v.* hide 145/31

scuse *n.* excuse 41/4 etc.

season *n.* time 28/18, 171/32; *meane season. See* **meane**

seche *v.* seek 171/32; *ppl. a.* **soughte** searched for 193/11

secret(e) *adj.* inmost 58/24 etc.; confidential 94/16

secret(e)ly *adv.* in concealment, 145/31; imperceptibly 162/19

secular(e), seculer *adj.* not belonging to a religious order 36/24 etc.

seculares *n. pl.* clerics not belonging to a religious order 43/1 etc.

seld(e) *adv.* seldom 109/36 etc.

seldome *adj.* rare 109/5 etc.

self(e) *adj.* same 40/11 etc.; *one self* one and the same 24/23–4

selfe mynded *ppl. a.* obstinate 30/5

selfe same *adj.* very same 6/8

sely *adj.* simple 78/9; pitiable 227/13

semeth *v. pr. 3 s. me semeth* it seems to me 31/4 etc.

sene *n.* ecclesiastical visitation 139/25; *pl.* **senys** 139/15

sentence *n.* meaning 35/10 etc; opinion 174/20 etc.; judgment 189/14, 218/5; *darke sentence* difficult problem 14/14

serche *n.* investigation of a question 17/14; *make serche. See* **make**

serche *v.* investigate 59/5

sermon(e) *n.* speech, discourse 5/1 etc.

serue *v.* be useful to 4/20; suffice 120/13, 163/28; *serue of nought* be useless 217/2

sessyon, sessyons *n.* court session 123/6 etc.: *sessyon of gaole delyuery* assizes at which prisoners in jail are brought to trial 139/26; *sessyon of peace* sitting of the justices of the peace 139/26

set(te), sett *v.* add 32/11; *setteth forth* declares as 15/3; promotes 15/35 etc.; *sette hande vppon* attacked 16/19; *sett on* placed on 16/26; *sette abroche* broached 24/32; *by . . . set a flye* regard as worthless 86/17. *See n.; set (. . .) vp(p)on* imposed upon 143/32–33 etc.; *setteth . . . by* values 151/31

seuerally *adv.* separately 154/7

sewynge *vbl. n.* following 60/13

sex *adj. vppon a sex leues* 36/12. *See n. to* 36/11–16

shamefaste *adj.* governed by virtuous restraint 109/7

sharpe *adj.* severe 218/32

shew *n.* example 221/35

shew(e) *v.* relate 4/10; profess 11/4, 11/10; present for legal examination 165/17; *shewe . . . forth* point out 18/35; *vbl. n.* **shewynge** demonstration 190/20

shold(e), shuld(e), sold *v. pt.* should 4/35 etc.

shortely *adv.* quickly 129/22

shrew(e)d(e) *adj.* wicked 6/8 etc; noughty 24/24; unsatisfactory 206/21

shrewe *n.* villain 9/27 etc.

shulde *v. pt. See* **shold(e)**

shyfte *n.* expedient 5/9 etc.

shypmans *n. poss. shypmans hose. See* **hose**

simple *adj. See* **symple**

simply *adv.* free from guile 230/30

sinnys *adv. See* **synnys**
sith *conj. See* **syth(e)**
sittynge vppon *pr. p.* deliberating upon 151/10
skant *adv. See* **scant(e)**
skused *ppl. a. See* **scuse**
skyl(l) *n. can . . . skyl(l)* See **can**
slaunder, scla(u)nder, slawnder *n.* slander 6/10 *etc.;* discredit 226/21
slaunder *v.* bring into disrepute 19/28 *etc.; vbl. n.* **slawnderynge, slaunderynge** slander 28/32, 64/23; disgrace 175/15
slaunderouse, slawnderous *adj.* slanderous 15/6 *etc.;* disgraceful 26/9 *etc.*
slawnder *n. See* **slaunder**
slawnderynge *vbl. n. See* **slaunder**
slenderly *adv.* ineffectively 125/10
sleuys *n. pl.* sleeves 55/20
sleyght *n.* trick 64/24, 86/26
smal *adj.* slender 142/27
small *n.* those of low social rank 28/35, 29/1
smarted *pp.* afflicted with suffering 103/25
sober *adj.* unhurried 70/31, 71/16
sodayne *adj.* rash 110/18
sodaynly *adv.* on the spur of the moment 4/1; speedily 30/18; immediately 46/17, 52/19
so euer *adv. howe (. . .) so euer. See* **howe (. . .) so euer;** *whyche . . . so euer. See* **whyche . . . so euer**
softe *adj.* leisurely 70/31
sold *v. pt. See* **shold(e)**
solem(p)ne *adj.* imposing 26/4; formal 35/28; serious 44/18–19
solempne *adv.* solemnly 30/9
solempn(e)ly *adv.* solemnly,formally 26/3 *etc.*
some *n. pl.* unspecified (group of) individuals 43/35 *etc.*
some parte *n.* some 192/23–24, 192/24
some say(e), Some saye, Som(me) say, Somsay *n.* reported statement 9/15 *etc. See n. to* 3/8
somewhat, some what *n. See* **som(e)what**
somtime, som(e)tyme, some tyme *adv.* formerly 3/3, 16/5; sometimes, occasionally 7/13 *etc.;* once 16/9
somwhat *adv.* to some extent, rather 10/14 *etc.*
som(e)what, som(e) what *n.* a certain

amount 7/10 *etc.;* something worth considering 134/32 *etc.*
sondry *adj.* several 28/18 *etc.*
sone *adv.* immediately 5/15 *etc; comp.* **soner** more quickly, more easily 7/3
soore *n. See* **so(o)re**
sope *n.* soup 71/5
sore *adj.* laborious 3/32, 6/1; severe, harsh 21/31 *etc.;* distressing 48/28; oppressive 83/3 *etc.;* strong 117/3, 118/4
sore *adv.* greatly 48/31 *etc.;* laboriously 59/21; with great distress 119/20, 163/34; deeply 137/13; grievously 162/31, 171/2
so(o)re *n.* pain, wound 50/32 *etc.*
sorte *n.* collection 192/23; *pl.* **sortys** 29/20
soth *n.* truth 47/18
sotle *adj. See* **subtyll**
sotylty *n.* subtlety 178/9
soughte *ppl. a. See* **seche**
sounde (. . .) to *v.* be suggestive of 72/12 *etc.*
sowle, soule *n.* person 6/3 *etc.*
soyleth *v. pr. 3 s.* refutes 62/21, 109/3
spake *v. pt.* spoke 5/12 *etc.*
speche *n.* rumor 4/27
specialtyes *n. pl.* particulars 196/34
specyall *adv.* especially 213/4
specyally, spycyally *adv.* especially 64/26, 84/4; in detail 169/4
spede *n.* success 5/33
speketh *v. pr. 3 s. speketh hym selfe* expresses himself 40/5
spende *v.* eat up 141/35; make use of 166/37; *spende oute* expend 173/19
spice *n. See* **spyce**
spiritual, spirytuall *adj. See* **spyrytual(l)**
sportynge *vbl. n.* sport 46/32
spoyle *v.* despoil 105/2
spronge, sprongen *ppl. a., pp.* arisen 61/13 *etc.*
spurrys *n. pl.* spurs 186/10
spyce, spice *n.* kind sort 171/30 *etc.*
spycyally *adv. See* **specyally**
spye *v.* observe 64/25, 223/29; discover 207/11, 229/22
spyghtful *adj.* disdainful 24/15
spyl *v.* waste 70/26; *ppl. a.* **spylt** corrupt 108/13
spyrytual(l), spiritual, spyrituall, spirytuall *adj.* clerical 26/11 *etc.;* canonical 189/23; *spyrytuall man* cleric 20/32 *etc.*

spyrytualty(e), spyritualty(e), spyritualtie, spyrytualt(i)e *n.* clergy 8/8 *etc.*

stacke *n. parte the stacke See* **parte**

stande *v. See* **stonde**

standen *pp. See* **stonde**

stark(e) *adj.* obdurate 29/25 *etc.*

start *v.* move suddenly 55/22; *pt.* **starte** rose suddenly 46/17

state *n.* class, profession 38/18 *etc.*

stay(e) *v.* defend 129/27; halt 145/27

stede *n.* place 91/33 *etc.; in the stead* instead 91/33 *etc.*

stewardes *n. pl.* heads of lords' households 184/33

sticke *v. See* **stycke**

stodyed *v. pt.* thought 100/21

stonde *v.* cost 12/8; consist 49/23 *etc.;* stand 183/14; *stande hym in none other stede* be of no other advantage to him 5/18; *stande vnto* accede to 47/13–14; *pp.* **standen** 117/12

stoppe *v.* repair 229/22

stoppe gappe *n.* argument in defence of an attacked point 128/14

store *n. keypynge no store of. See* **kepe**

stories *n. pl.* historical accounts 114/20

strageled *ppl. a.* strayed 31/31

straight *adj. See* **strayte**

stranglynge *ppl. a.* stifling 31/30–31

straunge *adj.* singular 12/1; unfamiliar 28/16; *make yt straunge. See* **make**

straungers *n. pl.* foreigners 39/33

strayt *adv.* directly, immediately 55/22

strayte, straight, streygth *adj.* severe 65/24 *etc.;* stringent 221/11, 229/35

strenger *adj. comp.* more convincing 159/10

streygth *adj. See* **strayte**

streyte *n.* difficulty 206/21

stryken *pp. stryken handes* shaken hands, come to agreement 30/28

stycke, sticke *v.* be reluctant 35/29; persist in arguing 53/4, 63/9; persist, adhere 227/34, 228/4; *stycke (. . .) vp(p)on* dwell upon in discourse 70/24, 147/25

subdue *v.* subject 209/7

substancyally *adv.* soundly 126/21

substaunce *n.* wealth 52/29, 197/22

subtyll, sotle *adj.* crafty, cunning 32/22 *etc.*

such *adj. his such maner of. See* **maner**

such(e) wyse (wise) *n. See* **wyse**

suerty(e), suertie, surety *n.* safety, security 94/36 *etc.*

sufferaunce *n.* toleration 70/12 *etc.*

suffre, suffer *v.* allow 93/11 *etc.; pp.* **suffered** tolerated 74/33

suffycyent *adj. suffycyent to hym selfe* self-sufficient 61/26

summe *n.* summa 194/16 *etc.*

supply *v.* discharge as a substitute 209/25

Supplycacyon *n.* petition 35/31

suppose *v.* intend 13/33; believe 14/18 *etc.*

sure *adv.* surely 18/22

surety *n. See* **suerty(e)**

surmysynge *pr. p.* alleging 27/11; *pr. 3 s.* **surmyseth** alleges 179/20; *ppl. a., pt.* **surmysed** feigned 46/30; charged 92/16–17

surmyttynge *pr. p.* alleging 27/9

suspect(e) *adj.* suspected 117/3 *etc.*

suspec(c)yon *n.* suspicion 121/34, 168/16

suyt *n.* litigation 44/34

sware *v. pt.* swore 152/12, 153/1; *ppl. a., pp.* **sworen** 99/13 *etc.; pp.* swore 160/23

swarue *v.* turn 88/15

swete *adj.* pleasant 61/3

swete *v.* suffer loss 162/21

swore *pp. See* **sware**

sworen *ppl. a., pp. See* **sware**

Swychis *n. pl.* Swiss 210/26

sybbe *adj.* similar 43/22

syde *n.* aspect 19/26

symple, simple *adj.* unadorned 24/25; foolish 28/11 *etc.;* honest 64/14 *etc.;* slight 204/26, 205/35; single 229/6

symplenesse *n.* innocence, ignorance 66/30

symply *adv.* 230/30. *See n. to* 230/30–31

syngle *adj.* 147/6. *See n.*

synnys, sinnys *adv.* subsequently 4/2, 43/36

synnys that *conj.* after 14/22

syth(e), sith *conj.* since, because 5/16 *etc.;* after 55/3; *syth that* because 209/29

take *v.* undertake 62/20; suffer 81/16 *etc.;* understand 111/32; catch 142/5; accept as true 146/33, 147/19; *take recorde (of)* call to witness 5/16 *etc.; takynge . . . to the worst* putting the worst construction upon 47/19–20; *take . . . in* include 61/5–6; *take (. . .) for* consider as 75/6, 110/30; *take knowledge . . . vppon (of)*

conduct a judicial investigation of
184/27 etc.; pt. **toke** 9/25 etc.
tale n. account 73/23 etc.; pl. **ta(y)lys**
46/30, 142/19
talkyng(e) n. conversation 10/24 etc.
taxed v. pt. assessed against 196/16
taye v. tie 142/18
temporalty(e), temporaltie n. laity, secular
power 8/8 etc.
tendable adj. attentive 35/2
than(ne) adv. then 4/24 etc.
thanke n. thanks 19/18 etc; can . . . thanke.
See **can**
that pron. who 3/16 etc.
the pron. you 11/16 etc.
then(ne) conj. than 7/4 etc.
there about adv. went there about. See **go**
there as conj. where 17/11
there at adv. there 144/27
therfore adv. 5/27 etc. See n. to 58/6–9
ther(e)on adv. therein 14/25; thereupon
46/18, 145/34; for it 48/17–18
therunto adv. thereto 13/20
theruppon adv. therefore 21/24
theym pron. them 7/15 etc.
they saye, They say n. reported statement
68/9, 78/7
thider, thyther adv. to there 3/22, 12/4
variant
thinketh, thynketh v. pr. 3 s. me thinketh
(thynketh) it seems to me 6/17 etc.; vbl. n.
thynkynge opinion 160/15
this adv thus 101/27. See n.
tho(o) demons. those 149/33 etc.
thorough, thorow(e) prep. throughout
40/1 etc.; by means of 139/36 etc.
thorow adv. from beginning to end 17/19
thorow oute prep. throughout 227/14
thou pron. you 11/13 etc.
thoughe that conj. although 136/21–22
thought v. pt. me thought. See **thinketh**
threfolde adv. See **thykke**
throwe n. after throwes. See **after throwes;**
ouer throwe. See **ouer throwe**
thryfte n. profitable occupation 136/8
thykke, thycke adv. densely 145/33; thykke
& threfolde in large numbers 4/24
thynketh v. pr. 3 s. me thynketh. See **thinketh**
thynkynge vbl. n. See **thinketh**
thyther adv. See **thider**
to prep. for 5/9 etc.; in regard to 5/10 etc.

to gyther, togyther, to geder adv. together
4/30–31 etc.
toke v. pt. See **take**
token n. piece of evidence 64/19 etc.
tolde ppl. a. recounted 42/34
toltrynge p. ppl. floundering 322/26
tone adj., pron. one 3/15 etc.
tother adj., pron. other 3/15 etc.
touche, towche v. mention 5/12; discuss
5/6 etc.; concern 23/31 etc.; vbl. n. **touch-
yng(e)** discussion 8/9; mention 8/22
tourne v. See **t(o)urne**
towarde, to . . . warde prep. concerning
15/5, 56/17; toward 134/17; aiming at
178/18, 178/19
towche v. See **touche**
townys n. pl. towns 3/13 etc.
tract(e) n. span (of time) 70/23 etc.
trauayled, trauailed v. pt. toiled, suffered
the pains of childbirth 5/34, 5/35
trayuayle, trauayle n. exertion, labor
5/32; childbirth 4/26, 5/30
treatye n. negotiation 62/10
trentalles, trentallys n. pl. 47/10 etc. See n.
trew(e) adv. truthfully 45/25 etc.
trewe adj. honest 136/28
trewell n. trowel 60/26
troubleouse adj. troublesome 125/35
trouth(e), trowth n. honesty 137/2 etc.; of
trouth(e) in fact 9/32 etc.; by my trowth indeed 220/8–9
trow(e) v. suppose 12/9 etc.
tryf(e)les, tryflys n. pl. false or idle tales
15/20, 49/37; trifles 63/9
tryflynge ppl. a. false 188/5
turke n. great turke Ottoman sultan 3/4
etc.
t(o)urne v. repent 118/10, 166/27; alter,
change 58/14 etc.; direct 227/28; turne
vppe overthrow 172/4
twayn(e), twanne pron. two 12/11 etc.
twayne adj. two 4/6 etc.
tyler, tylare n. one who covers roofs with
tiles 60/19, 60/29
tyme n. vppon a tyme one day 16/15
tynkar(e) n. one who mends kettles 60/19
etc.
tynked out pp. produced a sound by striking on metal 60/31
tytle n. heading of a section of a lawbook
114/3 etc.

vacacyon *n. vacacyon mote* 37/34. *See n. to* 37/34–35

varyaunce *n.* discord, disagreement 38/21 *etc.*

varye with *v.* quarrel 77/22

vehement *adj.* very strong 105/28 *etc.*

vehemently *adv.* very strongly 116/35

venory *n. See* **bestes**

verdyte *n.* verdict 133/3

verely, verily *adv. See* **veryly**

verse dyfferences *n. pl.* 138/16 *See note to* 133/31–32

vertue *n.* virtue 20/22 *etc.*

vertuouse *adj.* virtuous 9/22 *etc.*

very *adj.* true, real 10/24 *etc.*; mere 25/11

veryly, verily, verely *adv.* indeed, really 15/2 *etc.*

viage *n.* military expedition 223/25

vitayle, vytale *n.* food 141/35, 142/7

vn, on *prep.* on 44/7 *etc.*; in reference to 48/2; about 105/23

vncherytable *adj.* uncharitable 52/11, 55/32

vncherytably *adv.* uncharitably 39/2–3

vnderstondeth *v. pr. 3 s.* understands 194/20–21; *pp.* **vnderstand(e)** 54/9, 130/36

vngracyouse *adj.* reprobate 22/19 *etc.*

unknowen *ppl. a.* unknown 40/5 *etc.*

vnlyke *adj.* dissimilar 121/4 *etc.*; *vnlyke (vn)to* different from 127/33, 150/7

vnlykenes *n.* dissimilarity 154/20

vnmarked *ppl. a.* unnoticed 214/31

vnmayntened *ppl. a.* undefended 43/31

vnmete *adj.* unfit 178/17

vnproued *ppl. a.* untested 223/33

vnrepelled *ppl. a.* unrepealed 187/23

vnrestful *adj.* factious 74/37

vnsufficient *adj.* insufficient 98/35

vnswore, vnsworen *ppl. a.* not bound by oath 99/13 *etc.*

vnthryftes *n. pl* dissolute people 69/6, 136/6

vnto *prep.* in response to 4/29; to 7/8 *etc.*; on 46/3

vntouched, vntowched *ppl. a.* undiscussed 50/6 *etc.*

vntrew *adj.* unjust 155/20, 187/25

vntrew(e) *adv.* falsely 127/13 *etc.*

vnware *adv.* unawares 19/27 *etc.*

vnwyeldy *adj.* infirm 3/22

vouch(e)saufe *v.* be willing, agree 3/29, 56/27

vp(p)on *prep.* on the basis of 21/22 *etc.*; in reference to 36/13 *etc.*; to 76/7; about 114/13, 177/25; on the occasion of 123/29 *etc.*; at 124/14; on condition of 125/7 *etc.*; taking part as a member of 133/1, 133/2; against 138/2 *etc.*; on 185/30; by means of 210/22; *vppon a sex leues* 36/12. *See n. to* 36/11–16

vpryght *adj.* correct 177/31

vre *n.* effect 93/15

vse *v.* behave 29/18 *etc.*; are accustomed 121/17 *etc.*; observe 144/21, 144/22; utter 190/18, 190/21; *vbl. n.* **vsyng** custom 82/30

vtterly *adv.* straight out 64/22

vttermoste *n.* end 198/35

vttred *v. pt.* revealed 154/8

vye *n.* 62/8. *See n. to* 62/8–13

wageour of a lawe *n.* 113/1. *See n.*

walketh *v. pr. 3 s. walketh . . . wyde* misses the point 5/7; *ppl. a.* **walkynge** current 28/14; *pp.* **walked** gone 107/29

wan(ne) *v. pt. See* **wynne**

warde *n.* 129/28, 129/29. *See n. to* 129/27–28; *rere warde* 129/27. *See n. to* 129/27–28; *to . . . warde. See* **towarde**

ware *adj.* careful, wary 13/17 *etc.*; aware 41/21, 46/10

ware *n. wynter ware* 41/4. *See n.*

warnynge *vbl. n.* notification 53/1; *geueth . . . warnynge of. See* **geue**

warraunt *v. I (. . .) warraunt* I am sure, I assure, I promise 12/13 *etc.*

watche *v.* keep awake 142/14

wax(e) *v.* grow into 18/4; become 21/15 *etc.*; *pp.* **waxen** 16/8 *etc.*

way (at) *v.* value (as) 154/23, 154/30

weale *n.* welfare 143/22, 215/17

weigth *n. See* **weygth**

wel(l) *adv.* very 23/10; thoroughly 66/17; *as wel . . . as* both . . . and 7/33

well fauoredly *adv.* gracefully 36/19, 202/3–4

wene *v.* suppose 3/28 *etc.*; believe 6/29 *etc.*; *pp.* **went(e), wende** 47/11 *etc.*; *pt.* **went** 158/12

went *v. pt. See* **go**

wery *adj.* weary 38/2, 38/4

weryshe *adj.* tasteless 21/16

weygth, weyght(e), weigth *n.* seriousness 219/13; most important part 219/34; importance 220/2, 224/27

whan *adv.* when 4/2 *etc.*

what *adj.* whatever 25/23

where aboute *adv.* about which 49/4

where as *adv.* when 109/33–34

whereto *adv.* for what purpose 188/12

wherfore, wher fore *adv.* why 8/26 *etc.*

wherin, wher in *adv.* how 21/16

wherupon *conj.* wherefore 15/30; upon which 57/23

wherwith, wherwyth *adv.* with which, whereby 50/20 *etc.*

whit *n. See* **whyt(te)**

whole *adj.* integral 145/34

whole *adv.* entirely, completely 37/24 *etc.; all whole. See* **all**

who so *pron.* whoever 14/17 *etc.*

whyche . . . so euer *pron.* whichever 28/29

whyle *conj.* since 26/34

whyle *n. in whyche whyle* meanwhile 17/22–23; *in the whyle* meanwhile 118/2; *in this meane whyle. See* **meane whyle**

whyne *v.* whinny 322/29

whyt(te), whit *n. neuer a whyt* not at all 141/19, 205/12–13; *not one whyt* not at all 158/20; *euery whit (whytte)* entirely 203/26, 217/33

whyted *ppl. a. whyted wall* 24/15. *See n. to* 24/14–16

whyther *conj.* whether 19/32 *etc.*

whyther *pron.* which (of the two) 50/11, 152/15

whytte *n. See* **whyt(te)**

wise *n. See* **wyse**

withall, with all *adv. See* **wythall**

withinforth *adv.* within 165/22

witnessynge *vbl. n.* testifying 164/26

wittes *n. pl. See* **wyt**

wittyngly *adv. See* **wyttyngly**

wo *adj.* wretched 145/34

wold(e) *v. pt.* would 3/29 *etc.;* ordained 6/1; desired, wanted 17/34 *etc.;* required 18/23; should 187/27; *pr. p.* **wyllyng** desiring 4/16

woodcokkys *n. pl.* fools 67/25. *See n.*

word(e) *n.* Scripture 5/5; expression,

phrase 56/26 *etc.;* passage 134/32; *pl.* **wordis** 57/33, 175/21

worke *v. worke . . . maystryes* commit outrages 105/3–4

world *n.* marvel 180/3

worshyp(pe), wurshyppe *n.* renown, good name 137/10 *etc.; men of worshyp (wurshyppe)* people of repute and standing 104/1, 151/7

worshyp(pe)ful(l), wurs(s)hyp(e)full, wurshupfull *adj.* honorable, respectable 9/13 *etc.;* imposing 53/22

worshypfull *n.* honorable men 136/2

wote *v.* know 4/19 *etc.*

write *n.* writ 121/13

wrong(e) *adv.* incorrectly 5/12, 175/13

wroth(e) *adj.* angry 4/12 *etc.*

wrought *v. pt.* acted 154/16

wurshupfull, wurs(s)hyp(e)full *adj. See* **worshyp(pe)ful(l)**

wurshyppe *n. See* **worshyppe**

wyde *adv. See* **walketh**

wydos *n. pl.* widows 35/2

wyfe *n.* woman 46/13, 46/16

wyl *n. vp(p)on wyl* deliberately 58/1, 58/2

wylful(l) *adj.* voluntary 95/7; obstinate 182/25

wyllyng *pr. p. See* **wold(e)**

wylyly *adv.* deceitfully 57/24; cunningly 67/26, 168/6

wynked at *v. pt.* overlooked 172/5

wynne *v.* conquer 3/16; *pt.* **wan(ne)** won 120/5 *etc.; vbl. n.* **wynnyng** gain 195/38

wynter ware *n.* 41/4. *See n.*

wyse, wise *n.* way, manner 12/24; *in lyke wyse* in the same manner 7/28 *etc.; in no wise (wyse)* in no manner 8/21, 8/25; *in such(e) wyse (wise)* in such a way 36/20 *etc.; none other wyse* in no other way 127/25; *at the lest(e) wyse. See* **lest(e);** *in such (this, some) maner wyse (wise). See* **maner**

wyst(e) *v. pt. See* **wyt(te)**

wyste *pp. See* **wyt(te)**

wyt *n.* intellect 33/5 *etc.*

wyt(te) *v.* know 30/2 *etc.; to wyt(te)* namely 43/13 *etc.; pp.* **wyste** 136/2; *pt.* **wyst(e)** 6/17 *etc.*

wythall, withall, wyth (with) all *adv.* therewith 43/36 *etc.;* moreover 196/36 *etc.*

wythdrawen *pp.* withdrawn 199/26

wytnes(se) *n.* evidence 5/17, 5/18; testimony 156/13 *etc.; pl.* **wytnes(se)** 72/15 *etc. See* n.
wytte *v. See* **wyt(te)**
wyttyngly, wittyngly *adv.* deliberately 108/11 *etc.*

ye *adv.* yes 85/4 *etc.*
yᵉ *demons.* the 3/4 *etc.; pron.* thee 95/17
ye *interj.* indeed 6/27 *etc.*
ye *n.* affirmation 155/33

ye *pron.* you 19/3, 95/17
yeld(e) *v.* render 35/3, 154/31
yere *n.* years 18/27 *etc.*
yet *adv.* even 137/30 *etc.*
yien, eyen *n. pl.* eyes 7/25 *etc.*
yll *adj.* wicked 9/23
ymagyne *v.* plot 105/32
ypoc(h)rytes *n. pl.* hypocrites 53/30, 55/13
yᵗ *demons.* that 4/17 *etc.*

zuynglius *n.* Zwingli 210/26

INDEX

INDEX

Abell, Thomas, xxii and n.

Abjuration, xlix, liii, lv, lvi, lvii, lviii and n., lxi, lxii, lxv, lxx, lxxii, lxxix, lxxx, lxxxi, lxxxiii, 67, 70, 73, 83, 116, 123, 124, 127, 140, 166, 168, 170, 172, 179, 180, 181, 182, 219, 256, 266, 271, 273, 281, 284, 292, 351, 352, 365, 439; conditions of, lii, 266, 271; and "light proofs," liv, 284; as form of purgation, 283

Absolution, conditions of, xlviii, xlix, liii

Accusations: by heretics, l; by unnamed persons, l; secret, lxvi, 90–91, 99–100, 104, 161–62; open, 143–44, 145. *See also* Witnesses

Accusatus parag. Licet, 146, 154, 159, 161, 163, 294, 359–63. *See also* Witnesses: perjured

Acre, 388, 389

Actions *ad instantiam partium,* 274

Act of Appeals (1533), xxi, xxxiv, lxvii and n.

Act of Six Articles, lxvii

Act of Succession, First (1534), xxi, xxviii, xlvi and n., 270

Act of Supremacy (1534), 404; and St. German's *New Additions,* xxxix; as novel instrument of ecclesiastical reform, 395; as restoration of earlier royal power, 395; its legality, 395–97; and Henry VIII's power in parliament, 400

Acts, Book of, on heretics, 24, 30, 246, 249

Ad abolendam (canonical decree of Lucius III, 1184), 111, 113, 114; and conventicles, xlvii; and purgation, xlviii and notes, liii and n., 110, 356–57; and oath of innocence, lv

Adams, Norma, li notes, 239

Ad extirpanda (papal bull), permits torture, l

Adminicula probationis, 108, 279

Agricola, Rudolph, 289

Alberigo, Giuseppe, 282

Albigensians, li, 275

Alesius, Alexander, 406 and notes

Alexandria, patriarch of, 144, 294

Alnwick, William, 281

Ames, Joseph, xxxiii n.

Anabaptists, declared heretics by Pilgrims of Grace, 405

Anderson, R. B., 400 n.

Antioch, patriarch of, 293–94

Antwerp, xxv

Apocalypse, Book of, explicated by St. German, 384–87

Apocalypticism, in English thought and St. German's thought, xx n.

Approvers, 107, 279

Aquinas, St. Thomas, 246, 271

Argyropoulos, Johannes, 282

Articles Devised by the Whole Consent of the King's Most Honourable Council, and Henry VIII's propaganda campaign, xxvi and n., xxvii

Arundel, Thomas, archbishop of Canterbury, l, 278

Arundell, William, on crusade (1218), 388

Aske, Robert, 405

Astle, Thomas, 260

Attainder, acts of: against Fisher and More, xviii, 270; for heresy, liii, 256; for felony, liii, 279; and wrongful indictment at common law, lxxiii, lxxxiv; for treason, 290

Attaint, writs of, 154–55, 297, 360

Audley, Bishop, xc

Audley, Thomas, lix

Augsburg Confession, 405 and n.

Augustine, St., 25, 248, 272, 345, 440

Azais, Yvonne, xlvii n., 294

Babyla, St., 258–59

Baker, J. H., xxxii n., 239, 254, 297

DATE DUE
